Samuel Davies

Sermons on important Subjects

Vol. I

Samuel Davies

Sermons on important Subjects
Vol. I

ISBN/EAN: 9783337159610

Printed in Europe, USA, Canada, Australia, Japan

Cover: Foto ©ninafisch / pixelio.de

More available books at **www.hansebooks.com**

BY THE LATE REVEREND AND PIOUS

SAMUEL DAVIES, A. M.

Sometime President of the College in New-Jersey.

IN TWO VOLUMES.

THE SIXTH EDITION.

TO WHICH ARE NOW ADDED,

THREE OCCASIONAL SERMONS,

NOT INCLUDED IN THE ENGLISH EDITIONS;

MEMOIRS AND CHARACTER OF THE AUTHOR;

AND

TWO SERMONS ON OCCASION OF HIS DEATH,

By the Rev. Drs. Gibbons and Finley.

VOLUME I.

—Second American Edition—

PHILADELPHIA:

PRINTED FOR ROBERT CAMPBELL, BOOKSELLER.

THE following SERMONS by President DAVIES, have already been honoured with a high degree of public approbation. The sale of five impressions in the course of a few years, superadded to the present demand and known value of the Work, suggested to the Publisher that a *sixth Edition* might be printed with a probability of success. The contents of the former editions, in five and three, are here printed complete in two volumes, with the addition of *three Occasional Sermons;* which will doubtless be very acceptable to the admirers of this valuable Author. Thus, it may be truly said, the price is reduced, and the value of the Work considerably enhanced.

A few Biographical Anecdotes of the Author are prefixed to the present volumes, from which we may collect that his principles and practices

CONTENTS

OF

VOLUME I.

Funeral Sermon on the Death of Mr. Davies, 7—24
Appendix, — — — 25—29
A Sermon, preached at Haberdasher's-Hall, occasioned by Mr. Davies's Death, 31—51
Character of the Author, — 52—56

SERMON I.

The Divine Authority and Sufficiency of the Christian Religion.

Luke xvi. 27—31. *Then he said, I pray thee therefore, father, that thou wouldest send him to my father's house: for I have five brethren: that he may testify unto them, lest they also come into this place of torment. Abraham said unto him, they have Moses and the prophets; let them hear them. And he said, Nay, father Abraham; but if one went unto them from the dead, they will repent. And he said unto him, If they hear not Moses and the prophets, neither will they be persuaded though one rose from the dead.* — — 57—81

SERMON II.

The Nature of Salvation through Jesus Christ explained and recommended.

John iii. 16. *For God so loved the world, that he gave his only begotten Son, that whosoever believeth in him should not perish, but have everlasting life.* 81—99

SERMON III.

Sinners intreated to be reconciled to God.

2 Cor. v. 20. *Now then we are ambassadors for Christ, as though God did beseech you by us: we pray you in Christ's stead, Be ye reconciled to God.* 99—114

CONTENTS.

SERMON IV.

The Nature and Universality of Spiritual death.

Ephef. ii. 1 and 5. *Who were dead in trespasses and sins.—Even when we were dead in sins.* Page 115—131

SERMON V.

The Nature and Process of Spiritual Life.

Ephef. ii. 4, 5. *But God who is rich in mercy, for his great love wherewith he loved us, even when we were dead in sins, hath quickened us together with Christ.*
139—146

SERMON VI.

Poor and Contrite Spirits the Objects of the Divine Favour.

Isaiah lxvi. 2. *To this man will I look; even to him that is poor, and of a contrite spirit, and trembleth at my word.* 146—158

SERMON VII.

The Nature and Danger of making light of Christ and Salvation.

Matt. xxii. 5. *But they made light of it.* 159—170

SERMON VIII.

The Compassion of Christ to weak Believers.

Matt. xii. 20. *A bruised reed shall he not break, and smoking flax shall he not quench.* 170—183

SERMON IX.

The Connection between Present Holiness and future Felicity.

Heb. xii. 14. *Follow——Holiness, without which no man shall see the Lord.*
183—194

SERMON X.

The Mediatorial Kingdom and Glories of Jesus Christ.

John xviii. 37. *Pilate therefore said unto him, Art thou a king then? Jesus answered, thou sayest that I am a king. To this end was I born, and for this cause came I into the world, that I should bear witness unto the truth.* 194—215

CONTENTS.

SERMON XI.

Things unseen to be preferred to Things seen.

2 Cor. iv. 18. *While we look not at the things which are seen, but at the things which are not seen; for the things which are seen are temporal; but the things which are not seen are eternal.* Page 215—225

SERMON XII.

The sacred Import of the Christian Name.

Acts xi. 26. *The disciples were called Christians first at Antioch.* 226—238

SERMON XIII.

The Divine Mercy to Mourning Penitents.

Jer. xxxi. 18, 19, 20. *I have surely heard Ephraim bemoaning himself thus, Thou hast chastised me, and I was chastised as a bullock unaccustomed to the yoke: turn thou me, and I shall be turned; for thou art the Lord my God. Surely after that I was turned, I repented; and after that I was instructed I smote upon my thigh: I was ashamed, yea, even confounded, because I did bear the reproach of my youth. Is Ephraim my dear son? is he a pleasant child? for since I spake against him, I do earnestly remember him still: therefore my bowels are troubled for him; I will surely have mercy upon him, saith the Lord.* 238—254

SERMON XIV.

Christ precious to all true Believers.

1 Pet. ii. 7. *Unto you therefore which believe, he is precious.* 254—270

SERMON XV.

The Danger of Lukewarmness in Religion.

Rev. iii. 15,16. *I know thy works, that thou art neither cold nor hot: I would thou wert cold or hot. So then, because thou art lukewarm, and neither cold nor hot, I will spue thee out of my mouth.* 270—282

SERMON XVI.

The Divine Government the Joy of our World.

Psalm xcvii. 1. *The Lord reigneth, let the earth rejoice: let the multitude of the isles be glad thereof.* 282—294

CONTENTS.

SERMON XVII.

The Name of God proclaimed by himself.

Exod. xxxiii. 18, 19. *And he said, I beseech thee shew me thy glory. And he said, I will make all my goodness pass before thee, and I will proclaim the name of the Lord before thee---*

With chap. xxxiv. 6, 7.

And the Lord passed by before him, and proclaimed, The Lord, the Lord God, merciful and gracious, long-suffering, and abundant in goodness and truth; keeping mercy for thousands; forgiving iniquity, and transgression, and sin, and that will by no means clear the guilty. Page 294—308

SERMON XVIII.

God is Love.

1 John iv. *God is Love.* 309---326

SERMON XIX.

The General Resurrection.

John v. 28, 29. *The hour is coming in the which all that are in the graves shall hear his voice, and shall come forth; they that have done good, unto the resurrection of life; and they that have done evil, unto the resurrection of damnation.* 327--342

SERMON XX.

The Universal Judgment.

Acts xvii. 30, 31. *And the times of this ignorance God winked at; but now commandeth all men every where to repent, because he hath appointed a day in the which he will judge the world in righteousness by that man whom he hath ordained; whereof he hath given assurance unto all men, in that he hath raised him from the dead.* 342--364

SERMON XXI.

The one Thing needful.

Luke x. 41, 42. *And Jesus answered and said unto her, Martha, Martha, thou art careful and troubled about many things; but one thing is needful: and Mary hath chosen that good part, which shall not be taken away from her.* 365---381

CONTENTS.

SERMON XXII.

Saints saved with Difficulty, and the certain perdition of Sinners.

1 Pet. iv. 18. *And if the righteous scarcely be saved, where shall the ungodly and the sinner appear?* 382—394

SERMON XXIII.

Indifference to Life urged from its Shortness and Vanity.

1 Cor. vii. 29, 30, 31. *But this I say, brethren, that the time is short: it remaineth that they that have wives, be as though they had none; and they that weep as though they wept not; and they that rejoice, as though they rejoiced not; and they that buy, as though they possessed not; and they that use this world, as not abusing it: for the fashion of this world passeth away.* Page 395—410

SERMON XXIV.

The Preaching of Christ crucified the Mean of Salvation.

1 Cor. i. 22, 23, 24. *For the Jews require a sign, and the Greeks seek after wisdom: but we preach Christ crucified, unto the Jews a stumbling block, and unto the Greeks foolishness; but unto them which are called, both Jews and Greeks, Christ the power of God and the wisdom of God.* 410-430

Preface to the first Edition.

AN epistolary correspondence commenced between the Rev. Mr. *Samuel Davies* and myself, in the year 1752, and was continued till the time of his decease.

When I began the intercourse with him, I could not entertain any very probable hopes that we should ever have an interview in our world, but Mr. *Davies*'s visit to *Great-Britain*, in the year 1753, with that venerable man the Rev. Mr. *Gilbert Tennent*, of *Philadelphia*, to solicit benefactions for the college of *New-Jersey*, gave me a pleasure beyond all reasonable expectation; and the friendship which was kindled at the distance of several thousand miles from each other, was increased by free and frequent converses during the time, almost a year, of Mr. *Davies*'s residence on this side the *Atlantic*.

After his departure from our country to *America*, I received several letters from Mr. *Davies*, and had the honour of being numbered among his particular friends, to whom he communicated the very secrets of his bosom.

In a letter, dated *September* 12, 1757, Mr. *Davies* (at that juncture scarce recovered from a violent and dangerous fever) thus writes to me: "I want to live "after I am dead, not in name, but in public useful-"ness: I was therefore about to order in my will that "all my notes, which are tolerably full, might be sent "to you, to correct and publish such of them as you "might judge conducive to the public good. Pray, "what do you think of the project, if the like occasi-"on should return while you are among mortals?"

What answer I gave to my friend's proposal I cannot exactly recollect, but I am persuaded that my affection to him would not permit me to put a negative upon his requeft.

On the 4th of *February*, 1761, this excellent man was by a violent fever removed from our world: and, though he died univerfally lamented, yet, as he had an uncommon intereft in my affection while living, fo his deceafe opened the fprings of the moft afflicting forrow in my breaft, and perhaps I may truly apply, with a little variation, the words of the *Poet*,

Multis ille flebilis occidit,
Nulli flebilior quam mihi.—
HORAT. Od. Lib. I. Od. 24.

But, though the prophet is afcended, his mantle is left behind. A very confiderable number of his SERMONS has been tranfmitted to me, and thence I have felected what were fufficient to compofe the enfuing volumes.

As the Sermons which I now lay before the public were Mr. *Davies*'s ufual popular difcourfes, it may naturally be fuppofed that they required patient and accurate revifal in order to their publication; and that the *Editor*, if he would difcharge his duty as he ought, muft find himfelf under the neceflity of making fome occafional alterations and amendments as to the language, and efpecially of adjufting the pointing. Thefe liberties I have taken, and have endeavoured to execute my truft in the fame manner which I have reafon to think Mr. *Davies*, if he had been living, would have approved and commended; and in which I fhould wifh my own Sermons, fhould I leave any behind me worthy of the public view, might be corrected and fent into the world.

They who knew and heard Mr. *Davies* will need no further proof than the perufal of the difcourfes themfelves that they are the real productions of the author to whom they are afcribed. The fun fhews himfelf to be the fun by the very beams with which he irradiates and enlivens mankind, and is eafily diftinguifhed from other luminaries by his furpaffing luftre.

PREFACE.

The *Sermons* I have chosen for publication strictly answer the *Advertisement* in the PROPOSALS for printing them; namely, *Sermons on the most* USEFUL *and* IMPORTANT *Subjects, adapted to the* FAMILY *and* CLOSET. The reader will meet with no discourses in these volumes but what are calculated for general use, or such as relate to the common conditions, duties, and interests of mankind in one form or another; and in how many of them has both the Saint and the Sinner a *portion of meat* provided for him? May it prove a portion in due season! and may both the one and the other rise from the sacred feast divinely strengthened and blessed!

Amidst an attention to the very numerous and important duties of my several departments in life, the additional weight of a due preparation of Three Volumes of posthumous discourses for the eye of the public, and of the careful reviews of the proof-sheets as they came from the press, has taken up no small portion of my time, and been no inconsiderable accession to my constant labours; but I have most cheerfully devoted both my hours and my toils to the very valuable purposes—of fulfilling the desires of my dear friend Mr. *Davies*, which I own have a kind of irresistible power over me;—of contributing, as I would hope, to the spiritual benefit of my fellow-heirs of immortality, by putting into their hands a collection of very pious and useful Sermons;—and, of assisting and comforting the mournful widow and orphans of a friend who was as dear to me as a brother.

I take the liberty of returning thanks, in the name of Mrs. *Davies*, (for to her *only* the profits of the publication shall be applied) to the numerous SUBSCRIBERS to the work; and I hope they will find themselves amply recompensed for their benevolence to the widow and fatherless, by the sacred advantage and pleasure they and their families will receive in the perusal of these discourses; in which piety and genius seem to have vied with each other which should excel, and triumph in the superior glory.

PREFACE.

Notwithstanding all the time and pains the present work has cost me, and the strong sense I have that a like proportion of both would be required in the execution of a like undertaking, yet I beg leave to assure the public, that, as I have a large number of Mr. *Davies*'s manuscript Sermons still in my hands, I shall be ready (health being continued to me) to revise and publish the Author's remaining discourses, whenever there shall be an encouraging prospect of benefit to Mrs. *Davies*, or her orphans, by a fresh publication. *As to visit*, or relieve, *the fatherless and the widow in their affliction** is an essential branch of christian duty, so it is a duty I trust will never be wanting, whenever an opportunity offers for exemplifying it, from my first regards and practice.

Mr. *Davies* annexed to some of his Sermons HYMNS of his own composition. Had this been uniformly the case they might have accompanied his Discourses to the press, but as it is not, I have omitted them; but, if death or incapacity prevent not my design, I intend hereafter to collect what HYMNS of his have fallen into my hands, and publish them together with some of my own on the like occasions.

I have prefixed to these Volumes a SERMON upon the death of our Author by that excellent man the Rev. Dr. *Samuel Finley*, Mr. *Davies*'s successor to the presidency of *New-Jersey* College: I have also re-published the Discourse I preached to my people the next LORD's day after I received the distressing news of Mr. *Davies*'s decease; and have ventured to add an Elegiac Poem to the memory of my dear friend; in which if the reader finds not a vein of poesy worthy of the subject, yet he will not, I presume, be displeased at the efforts, however languid and inadequate, of bereaved mourning friendship to do honour to the character of a person so amiable and deserving.

The idea I have given of our Author in my Sermon, and particularly in my Poem, and above all, the just and lively, the strong and elegant picture which

* Jam. i. 27.

Dr. *Finley* has exhibited of him in his difcourfe upon his death, render it unneceffary to enlarge this preface with an account of Mr. *Davies*'s merit and accomplifhments; I fhall therefore only add, that I moft fincerely wifh that young minifters more efpecially would perufe thefe Volumes with the deepeft attention and ferioufnefs, and endeavour, in conjunction with earneft prayer for divine illumination and affiftance, to form their difcourfes according to the model of our Author; in which if I miftake not, a critical Scrutiny into the facred Texts which he choofes for his fubjects, a natural Eduction and clear Reprefentation of their genuine meaning, an elaborate and fatisfactory Proof of the various heads of doctrine, a fteady profecution of his point, together with an eafy and plain, but yet ftrong and pertinent Enlargement, and a free, animated, and powerful Application and improvement, wonderfully adapted to awaken the confciences, and ftrike the hearts of both faints and finners, mingle the various excellencies of learning, judgment, eloquence, piety, and feraphic zeal, in one uncommon glory; not unlike the beams of the fun collected by a burning glafs, that at once fhine with a moft dazzling brightnefs, and fet fire wherever the blaze is directed, to objects fufceptive of their celeftial influence, and a transformation into their own nature.

THOMAS GIBBONS.

Hoxton-Square, Nov. 14, 1765.

THE

DISINTERESTED AND DEVOTED CHRISTIAN:

A

SERMON,

PREACHED AT

NASSAU-HALL, PRINCETON,

MAY 28, 1761.

OCCASIONED BY THE DEATH OF THE

Rev. SAMUEL DAVIES, A. M.

Late Prefident of the College of New-Jerfey.

BY SAMUEL FINLEY, D. D.

PRESIDENT OF THE SAID COLLEGE.

TO WHICH ARE ADDED,

SOME MEMOIRS OF MR. DAVIES.

BY ANOTHER HAND.

Qui confiderat qualis erit in Morte, femberque pavidus erit in operatione, atque inde in Oculis fui Conditoris vivet, nil quod tranfeat, appetit : cunctis vitæ prefentis defideriis contradicit, et pene mortumm fe confiderat, qui moriturum fe minime ignorat. GREGOR. L. 12. Moral.

TO

Mrs. MARTHA DAVIES, the Mother,

AND

Mrs. JEAN DAVIES, the Widow,

OF THE LATE

Rev. PRESIDENT DAVIES, deceased,

The following Sermon,

Preached on Occasion of his lamented Death,

IS

With the tenderest Respect

PRESENTED BY

Their sincere and affectionate Friend,

and humble Servant,

SAMUEL FINLEY.

ROMANS, xiv. 7, 8.

For none of us liveth to himself, and no man dieth to himself. For whether we live, we live unto the LORD; *or whether we die we die unto the* LORD; *whether we live, therefore or die, we are the* LORD's.

AS the very dear and reverend man, whose premature and unexpected death, we, amongst thousands, this day lament, expressed his desire, that, upon this mournful event, a Sermon should be preached from these words, he plainly intimated his expectation, that the audience should be entertained, not with an Ornamented funeral Oration, but with such an instructive discourse as the text itself naturally suggests. The subject being his own choice, I cannot doubt but this friendly audience will the more closely and seriously attend, as conceiving him *though dead, yet speaking,* to them the solemn truths it contains. For having been admitted into the full knowledge of his religious principles, I may presume on speaking many of the sentiments he intended from this text, though not in his more sublime and oratorial manner.

When I reflect on the truly christian, generous, yet *strict Catholicism* that distinguishes this whole chapter, and how deeply it was imprinted on Mr. *Davies*'s own spirit, and influenced the course of his life, I am ready to conclude, that perhaps no text could be more aptly chosen on the occasion. It expresses the very temper that should be predominant in all, and which actually is so in every pious breast.

That we may apprehend the scope and genuine sense of the words, it is necessary to observe, that warm debates at that time arose between the *Jewish* and *Gentile* converts, about the difference of *meats* and *days,* established by the *Mosaic* law; and, so sharp was the contention, that they were mutually disposed to exclude each other from christian communion. The *Gentile,* being under no bias from the powerful prejudices of education and custom, was sooner and easier convinced of his freedom from that *yoke of bondage,* and despised the *Jew* as weak to admiration, and scrupulous to a fault.

The *Jew,* on the other hand, persuaded that these ancient divine institutions were still obligatory, censured and condemned the *Gentile* as inconscientious, and profanely regardless of GOD's awful authority.

The Apostle, in order to quell the growing strife, maturely determines that, though the *Gentile* held the right side of the question, yet both parties were wrong as to their temper of mind, and the manner in which they managed the controversy; and that they laid an undue stress on the matters of difference, and carried their censures higher than the merits of the cause would at all justify. He therefore recommends moderation to both, and sets before them sufficient reasons why they should judge of each other more charitably, since they agreed in all those principal points that would justly denominate them " the servants of the LORD." For if they would reckon it a bold intrusion to call before their tribunal, condemn, and punish *another man's servant*, over whom they had no legal authority; how much more arrogant and presumptuous must it be so to treat *a servant of the* LORD ?" ver. 4.

Again, let them be so candid as to persuade themselves, that, unless the contrary be evident, they who differ from them, mistaken or not, are influenced by a conscientious regard to the divine glory, ver. 6. *This* admitted, their personal censures will necessarily be milder, even though their judgment of the points in debate continue unaltered; and this must be admitted, if they can charitably judge, that their respective opponents are real christians : for in *all such* the governing principle is, " not to live to themselves, but to the LORD. For none of us liveth to " himself, and no man dieth to himself. For whether we live, " we live unto the LORD ; or whether we die we die unto the " LORD : whether we live therefore, or die, we are the " LORD's." Now, if no pious person lives merely to please himself, we ought not to judge that his aversion from, or attachment to certain meats and days, arises *only* from a selfish humour : but, on the contrary, since his whole life is governed by an honest regard to the will of GOD, it is altogether credible that, in his different conduct respecting meats and days, he acts from the same principle; for whatever is true of the general, is also true of all the particulars contained under it. Suppose a man to be a real Christian, you then suppose him to be of an upright heart, of a tender conscience, and one who dares not to neglect, nor live in contradiction to known duty. He makes it his main business to please GOD, and shall we be implacably disgusted because he does not rather endeavour to please us ? GOD forbid.

Thus, while our text affords a convincing argument for moderation in judging of other Christians, who differ from us in circumstantials, it teaches us what should be the *principle* and *end* of our life, and that both *negatively* and *positively*. We may not live nor die to ourselves, but to the LORD.

I. " We may not live to ourselves."

This proposition supposes, what is a demonstrable truth, that we are not the absolute proprietors, and therefore have not the rightful difpofal of our lives. For fince we could exert no kind of efficiency in bringing ourfelves from nothing into exiftence, we could not poffibly defign ourfelves for any end or purpofe of our own. Hence it is evident, that, whofe property foever we are, we belong not to ourfelves; confequently, it is the higheft indecency to behave as though we were accountable to none other. As rationally may we claim 'felf-exiftence and independence. It will, therefore, be an eternal folecifm in action to aim chiefly at our own glory, feek only our *own things*, or purfue moft eagerly our own pleafures. Right reafon itfelf peremptorily denies that the dictates of our own minds are our fupreme rule of conduct, or that our own will is our law; much lefs may we fubject ourfelves to the government of blind paffions, or indulge to irregular appetites.

We are not at liberty, nor have we any authority to employ either the members of our bodies, or powers of our foul, at pleafure, as if we had originally defigned their ufe. Hence it will appear criminal, on the one hand, to wafte our time, or expend our ftrength in ufelefs exercifes; and, on the other, to allow an idle negligence of neceffary bufinefs. Our *tongues* themfelves, thofe *unruly members*, muft be patient of reftraint, for it is the language only of haughty rebels to fay, " Our lips are our own, who is Lord over us?" *(a)* Our very thoughts are to be confined within prefcribed limits, and all our rational powers *ftatedly* exercifed, not in merely curious and amufing refearches, but in matters the moft ufeful and important.

It alfo follows, that the product of our activity, whatever is acquired by the exertion of thefe powers, ought not to terminate in ourfelves. Are we in purfuit of learning, that ornament of human minds, it fhould not be with a view only to fhine more confpicuous, but that we may ferve our generation to better advantage. Has GOD bleffed " the hand of the dili-" gent" with abundant riches,? We are not to confider them as the means of gratifying vanity, or " fulfilling the de-" fires of the flefh, and of the mind;" for we muft " honour the LORD with our fubftance,"*(b)* Has GOD clothed any of us with power? This is not a difcharge from his fervice, nor a freedom from fubjection to his laws, but a ftronger obligation to duty, as it gives us an opportunity of more extenfive ufefulnefs.

Finally, fince we were not the authors of our lives, we can have no right to take them away. We have no power to determine, either the time or kind of death, any more than we

(a) Pfalm xii. 4.   *(b)* Prov. iii. 9.

can ward off, or suspend its blow when commissioned to destroy. Therefore, amidst all the miseries that can make life an insupportable burden, and all the glorious prospects that can make us impatiently pant for dissolution, it must be our determinate purpose, that " all the days of our appointed time, we will wait till our change come."*(c)*

As these particulars, examined by the strictest reason, will all appear to be immediate consequences from self-evident principles, and must all be confessed by him, who acknowledges that " he is not his own lord and master;" it will follow as an evi-
" dent truth, that the evangelical duty of self-denial is found-
" ed on the everlasting reason of things."

Reflecting farther on the preceding observations, they force upon us the disagreeable conviction, that our whole race has revolted from the race of GOD, and risen up in rebellion against him. " The world evidently lies in wickedness;" for the allowed practice of men supposes principles, which, they themselves being judges, must confess to be palpably false and absurd. They act as if they believe they were made for themselves, and had no other business in life but the gratification of their respective humours. One exerts all his powers, and spends all his time in nothing else but endeavouring to amass heaps of wordly treasure: another, by riotous living, disperses what had been collected with anxious care and assiduous labour. Some live in malice and envy, whose favourite employ is calumny and wrathful contentions, as if they had been created for no other end but to be the pests of society : others blaspheme the name of GOD, despise his authority, mock at religion, and ridicule. serious persons and things. One has no other purpose in life but sport and merriment: another eats to gluttony, and drinks to besottedness. Yet all these, and nameless ranks of other daring offenders, would be ashamed in a christian country to possess it as their serious belief, that they were made by a most wise, holy, and righteous GOD, preserved, blessed, and loaded with benefits every day, on purpose that they " might work all
" these abominations," or, in order to live just as they do.

If, then, it is confessedly impious and unreasonable to live to *ourselves*, it necessarily follows that we are the property of another, for it will ever be " lawful for one " to do what he will with his own." And whose can we be but *his* who gave us existence? Or, if ties of gratitude can more powerfully influence ingenious minds than even those of nature, who can so justly claim us as He, " who, as we hope, loved us, and washed us " from our sins in his own blood?"*(d)* This leads me to observe,

(c) Job, xiv. 14.

II. That we should "live and die to the LORD." This can admit of no debate; for if our Maker and Redeemer be our rightful owner, then whatever we are, or have, or can do, must be for him. Being his servants, we must "shew all good fidelity" in his business. The talents with which he has entrusted us, more or fewer, or of whatever kind, may not be returned without improvement; for, as is fit and proper, he "requires his own with usury."*(e)* He is our King, whose prerogative it is to direct our course of action, and propose the end at which we are to aim; to "mete "out the bounds of our habitation," and carve our portion; and it becomes us to give the most ready and chearful obedience to his commands, and submit to all his disposals.

Our living thus to the LORD plainly supposes our being sensible of our entire dependence on him, and that we devote ourselves to his service. We must "present" our bodies a living sacrifice,"*(f)* without reserve or hesitation; and "avouch the LORD to be our GOD, to "walk in his ways, and to keep his "statutes, and judgments, and commandments, and to hearken to his voice."*(g)* We bind ourselves to him in a firm covenant, not for a limited term of months and years, but for ever and ever, and acquiesce in *Him* as our chief good.

The solemnity of such an infinitely important transaction between the glorious majesty of heaven, and such mean creatures as we, who are "but dust and ashes," cannot but strike us with reverential awe. And what will make it yet more humbling is the consideration of our guilt. We not only *as Creatures* take upon us to speak unto the LORD our Maker, but *as Criminals* approach to the seat of our offended and most righteous Judge. Dare we then trifle, and not rather be most serious and deliberate? Reflecting that we are in the presence of the heart-searching GOD will naturally make us watchful over every thought and motion of our spirits, and engage us to the greatest sincerity in surrendering to him our all. We will give him our hearts themselves; keep nothing back; nor except against any terms he shall please to propose, but yield at discretion.

On this occasion a consciousness of our having revolted from him, neglected his service, purloined his goods, and, in every respect, behaved most ungratefully and undutifully, will effect us with the most genuine sorrow. Therefore, when repentant we return to him, we shall, covered with shame, approach with the *Prodigal's* self abasing confession, "Father! I have sinned against heaven, and in thy sight, and am no

(d) Rev. i. 6.   (e) Matt. xxv. 27.
(f) Rom. xii. 1.   (g) Deut. xxvi. 17.

"more worthy to be called thy son."*(h)* He will "surely hear us bemoaning ourselves, like *Ephraim*," that we have too long wrought the will of the flesh, and suffered " other usurping lords to have dominion over us ;" but now we humbly beg forgiveness, his gracious acceptance of our persons, and admission into his family, should it be only on trial, " as hired servants."

But though our sins have made us vile, and the view of their odious nature makes us " loathe ourselves in " our own sight," yet a conviction of the free grace and mercy of God in Christ will comfort and encourage our dejected and diffident hearts. The cords of love will draw us nearer and nearer, until we shall assume an humble " boldness, to enter into the holiest of " all by the blood of Jesus."*(i)* Sacred love, and a grateful sense of the unmerited favours of our God will now dispose us to, and animate us in the performance of every duty. Religion will be our chosen course, and the commandments of God will be so far from being burdensome to us, that we shall rejoice in them, and delight in " doing the things that please him." Our whole time will be consecrated to his service: no part of it can be spared for fleshly indulgencies, or sinful pleasures, but will be employed either in some positive duty, or in preparation for it in the proper season.

This religious bent of mind will manifest itself in all our conduct, and give even common actions a different direction. If we attend our ordinary callings, we shall be active and diligent, not in order to gratify an earthly temper, but from an obediental regard to supreme authority. When our spirits flag through intense application to business, and recreation becomes necessary, our very diversions will be considered as our duty, and so as a branch of our religion: and as they will always be innocent in their nature, so they will be no otherwise regarded than as means to fit us for the repetition of our work. If our friends or country demand our service, we shall not give place to selfishness and indolence, but, as lovers of God and men, generously exert ourselves for the common good. Thus will our whole life be religion, upon such a sincere, entire, and affectionate dedication of ourselves to the Lord. And such as is our course so will be its end. When the date of time is concluded we shall also " die to the Lord." This in general imports, our living under the rational, affecting impression of our desolation, and appearing before God, and our constant endeavours after actual preparation to enjoy him for ever. Then, upon the approach of death, we shall confidently " commit our spi-

(h) Luke, xv. 19.   *(i)* Heb. x. 19.

rits into, " his hands," recommend his ways to survivors, and glorify him with our dying breath.

But, on the other hand, if our lives are not thus consecrated to our GOD, we cannot be supposed to perform any duty in an acceptable manner, as the requisite principle and end are wanting. He, to whom the secret springs of action are all obvious, will not, cannot accept pretended services; nor be pleased with the " blind and the lame for sacrifice," when the best are esteemed too good for him. To compliment him with our lips, when we refuse to give him our hearts, will be judged similar to the conduct of those, who " bowed the knee in de-" rision," and in derision said, " Hail! King of the Jews!" " He, " with whom we have to do," cannot be deceived, nor " will be mocked. He requires " Truth in the inward parts," which cannot subsist without an honest and upright *design* to serve him all the days of our lives.

Now to live wholly to the LORD, will appear to be our *reasonable service*, if we consider, 1. That " such a life is most " worthy of rational and immortal creatures." From the " powers and faculties given us it may naturally be concluded that we are created for some very important purpose; but what can be so important, or bear so just a correspondence to our capacities, as to live to the glory of our great Creator? This being our ultimate end, to which we refer all our actions, and perform each of them in such a manner as may best answer it, will influence our hearts, and frame our whole conversation agreeable to the divine approving will. And what can so ennoble the soul as conformity to the pattern of perfection? But to neglect this, and chiefly regard our temporal affairs, would be infinitely unworthy of beings capable of the highest pursuits, and formed for immortality. Why should we have been " wiser than the beasts of the field, or the fowls " of heaven," if we are to have no sublimer aims than they? In a word, we could never vindicate the wisdom of GOD in our formation, if he intended us for meaner things than those for which we are qualified. Therefore,

2. " Such a life is most worthy of GOD our Maker." Nothing can appear more condecent and proper, than that he who is *the beginning*, should also be the *end*; that as all are *of him*, all should be *to him*. And if his glory be the most excellent thing, and He the most perfect Being, it will necessarily follow, that he *cannot* ultimately design what is less excellent. Therefore the scripture speaks agreeable to ever lasting truth, when it asserts, that " he made all things for himself;" and, that ⁎ for his pleasure they are, and were created."*(k)* And can it

be rationally supposed, that he allows us, whom he made for his own glory, to act for a different or opposite end? It cannot. We must therefore peremptorily affirm, that he cannot, in consistency with his perfections, require less, than that " whether, we " eat or drink, or whatever we do, we should do all " to his glory."(*l*) And this he does require, not because he needs our service, or can be happier, or more glorious in himself by our praises, but because it is fit and right, and results as our duty from the eternal reason of things.

3. " Such a life is our own happiness:" for, acting as prescribed, we move in our proper sphere, and tend to our native centre. We live as near the fountain of blessedness as our present state can admit, and nothing can be so animating as the glorious and blissful prospects our course affords. Our hearts, being fixed on *the chief good*, are at rest, and no more tortured with anxious hesitation, and uneasy suspence, as to what we shall chuse for our portion, nor do our desires wander in quest of a more suitable object. We can wish for no more but the full enjoyment of GOD, whom we " serve "with our spirits ;" whose " peace, that passeth all " understanding, rules in our hearts ;" and for whose glory we hope, secure from confounding disappointment in the day of the LORD.

Now me thinks every attentive hearer prevents my improvement of the subject, being ready, of his own accord to make such reflections as these.—How serene and placid is the life, and how triumphant must be the death, of a true Christian!—How reasonable a service do we perform, when we consecrate ourselves to the LORD, and receive him, freely offering himself to be our portion, our father, and our friend ! None can plausibly urge, that some things unfit, or detrimental, are required. None can pretend a conscientious scruple about complying with the proposal, nor dare any, however secretly reluctant, openly avow their dissent. Every mouth is stopped, and all acknowledge their obligation to this plain duty. What then should hinder the unanimous agreement of this whole assembly to so advantageous an overture ? Why may we not join ourselves, this day, to the LORD in an everlasting covenant ? Would it not seem uncharitable to suppose, that any one in this christian audience rejects a proposal so infinitely just and kind ? How pleasing is the very imagination of an universal concurrence ! Not only would each of our hearts who are here present exult, but unnumbered hosts of angels, and all " the spirits of just " men made perfect" would rejoice.

(*k*) Rev. iv. 11.   (*l*) 1 Cor. x. 31.

Since therefore all things that pertain to our present or future happiness, conspire to urge this point, let us with one accord, in the most affectionate and reverent manner, approach the throne of our august Sovereign, and cheerfully resign ourselves to him for ever; spend our lives in his service, and expect his compensating approbation at our end.

In some such train, but more diffusive and sublime, would our reverend and dear deceased Friend have addressed us on such a subject. We may imagine how fervent his desire was of "living to the LORD" himself, and persuading others to the same course, when he fixed on this for the subject of his Funeral Sermon. Now, as it is generally agreed that example has the most powerful influence, perhaps a few sketches of his own Life and Character may best recommend the preceding discourse, as they will prove the life described to be practicable. And though he on whom this task is devolved owns himself inferior to it, yet he is encouraged to undertake it from a persuasion, that a simple and unornamented narrative of what he knows, either personally or by certain information, concerning President *Davies*, will set him in a very agreeable point of light. He is now disinterested in all the praises and censures of mortals, and can neither receive benefit, or suffer detriment by them; but his example may profit the living, as it tends to excite a laudable emulation; and some brief hints of the dispensations of divine providence towards him may not be without very useful instruction.

He was an only son, and, which is more, was a son of prayers and vows; was given in answer to fervent supplications, and, in gratitude, wholly devoted to GOD from the womb by his eminently pious mother, and named *Samuel*, on the like occasion as the ancient Prophet. The event proved, that GOD accepted the consecrated Boy, took him under his special care, furnished him for, and employed him in the service of his church, prospered his labours with remarkable success, and not only blessed him, but made himself a blessing.

The first twelve years of his life were wasted in the most entire negligence of GOD and Religion, which he often afterwards bitterly lamented, as having too "long" wrought the will of the flesh." But about that time the GOD to whom he was dedicated by his Word and Spirit awakened him to solemn thoughtfulness, and anxious concern about his eternal state. He then saw sufficient reason to dread all the direful effects of divine displeasure against sin. And so deeply imprinted was the rational sense of his danger, as to make him habitually mieasy and restless, until he might obtain satisfying scriptural evidence of his interest in the forgiving love of GOD.

While thus exercised he clearly saw the absolute necessity, and certain reality of the gospel-plan of salvation, and what abundant and suitable provision it makes for all the wants of a sinner. No other solid ground of hope, or unfailing source of comfort could he find, besides the merits and righteousness of him, " whom " GOD set forth to be a propitiation for sin, through faith " in his blood"(m) On this righteousness he was enabled confidently to depend; by this blood his conscience was purged from guilt; and " believing, he rejoiced ", with joy unspeakable, and full of glory."(n) Yet he was afterwards exercised with many perplexing doubts for a long season, but at length, after years of impartial repeated self-examination, he attained to a settled confidence of his interest in redeeming Grace, which he retained to the end.

A diary, which he kept in the first years of his religious life and continued to keep as long as his leisure would permit, clearly shews how intensely his mind was set on heavenly things; how observant he was of the temper of his heart; and how watchful over all his thoughts, words, and actions. Did any censure his foibles, or juvenile indiscretions? They would have done it compassionately, had they known how severely he censured them himself. The tribunal daily erected in his own bosom was more critical in scrutinizing, and more impartial and severe in passing sentence, than either his friends or enemies could be.

His love to GOD, and tender concern for perishing sinners, excited his eager desire of being in a situation to serve mankind to the best advantage. With this view he engaged in the pursuit of learning, in which, amidst many obvious inconveniencies, he made surprising progress, and, sooner than could have been expected, was found competently qualified for the ministerial office. He passed the usual previous trials with uncommon approbation; having exceeded the raised expectations of his most intimate friends and admirers.

When he was licensed to preach the gospel, he zealously declared the counsel of GOD, the truth and importance of which he knew by happy experience; and did it in such a manner as excited the earnest desires of every vacant congregation, where he was known, to obtain the happiness of his stated ministrations. But, far from gratifying his natural inclination to the society of his friends, or consulting his ease, moved by conscience of duty,

(m) Rom. iii. 25.   (n) 1 Pet. i. 8.

he undertook the self-denying charge of a diffenting congregation in *Virginia*, separated from all his brethren, and exposed to the censure and resentment of many. But the more he was known in those parts, the more were prejudices removed; contempt was gradually turned into reverence; and the number of his enemies daily diminished, and his friends increased.

Nor did he there labour in vain, or " spend his strength for " nought." The " LORD, who counted him faithful, put- " ting him into the ministry," succeeded his faithful endeavours, so that a great number both of *whites* and *blacks*, were hopefully converted to the living GOD: for the proof of this, I must refer you to his own narrative, sent to the Rev. Mr. *Beliamy*, and by him published, and to his letters to some gentlemen of *the Society in* London *for propagating Religion among the Poor*.

As to his natural genius, it was strong and masculine. His understanding was clear; his memory retentive; his invention quick; his imagination lively and florid; his thoughts sublime; and his language elegant, strong, and expressive. And I cannot but presume that true and candid critics will readily discern a great degree of true poetic fire, stile, and imagery in his poetical compositions; and will grant that he was capable to have shone in that way, had his leisure permitted the due cultivation of his natural talent.

His appearance in company was manly and graceful his behaviour genteel, not ceremonious; grave, yet pleasant; and solid, but sprightly too. In a word he was an open, conversable, and entertaining Companion, a polite Gentleman, and devout Christian, at once.

In the sacred Desk, zeal for GOD, and love to men animated his addresses, and made them tender, solemn, pungent, and persuasive; while at the same time they were ingenious, accurate, and oratorial. A certain dignity of sentiment and stile, a venerable presence, a commanding voice, and emphatical delivery, concurred both to charm his audience, and overawe them into silence and attention.

Nor was his usefulness confined to the Pulpit. His comprehensive mind could take under view the grand interests of his Country and of Religion at once; and these interests, as well as those of his Friends, he was ever ready zealiously to serve. It is known what an active instrument he was in stirring up a patriot spirit, a spirit of courage and resolution in *Virginia*, where he resided during the late barbarous *French* and *Indian* ravages.

His natural temper was remarkably sweet and dispassionate *; and his heart was one of the tenderest towards the distressed. His sympathetic soul could say, " Who is weak, and I am not weak?" Accordingly his charitable disposition made him liberal to the poor, and that often beyond his ability. He was eminently obliging to all, and very sensible of favours confered; which he could receive without servility, and manifest his grateful sense of them with proper dignity.

To his friend he was voluntarily transparent, and fully acted up to the *Poet*'s advice :

> Thy friend put in thy bosom : wear his eyes
> Still in thy heart, that he may see what's there.

And perhaps none better understood the ingenuities and delicacies of friendship, or had an higher relish for it, or was truer or more constant in it than he. He was not easily disgusted : his knowledge of human nature in its present state, his candid heart, and enlarged soul both disposing and enabling him to make allowances for indiscretions, which narrower and more selfish minds could not make. He readily and easily forgave offences against himself, whilst none could be more careful to avoid offending others ; which, if he at any time inadvertently did, he was forward and desirous to make the most ample satisfaction.

He was amongst the first and brightest examples of filial piety, a very indulgent parent, and humane master. As an husband he was kind, tender, cordial, and respectful, with a fondness that was manly and genuine. In a word, think what might rationally be expected, in the present imperfect state, in a mature Man, a Christian in minority, a Minister of JESUS of like passions with others, in a Gentleman, Companion, and cordial Friend, and you conceive of President *Davies*.

It would hardly be expected, that one so rigid with respect to his own faith and practice, could be so generous and catholic in his sentiments of those who differed from him in both, as he was. He was strict, not bigoted ; conscientious, not squeamishly scrupulous. His clear and extensive knowledge of religion enabled him to discern where the main stress should be laid, and to proportion his zeal to the importance of things, too generous to be confined to the interests of a party as such. He

---

* The Rev. Mr. *John Rodgers*, one of his most intimate friends, in a letter to me since his death, says, " I never saw him angry during several years
" of unbounded intimacy, though I have repeatedly known him to be ungene-
" rously treated."

considered the visible kingdom of CHRIST as extended beyond the bounderies of *this* or *that* particular denomination, and never supposed that his declarative glory was wholly dependent on the religious community which he most approved. Hence he gloried more in being a Christian, than in being a *Presbiterian*, though he was the latter from principle. His truly catholic address to the established Clergy of *Virginia* is a demonstration of the sincere pleasure it would have given him, to have heard that " CHRIST was preached," and substantial religion, common Christianity, promoted by those who " walked not with him," and whom he judged in other points to be mistaken. His benevolent heart could not be so soured, nor his enlarged soul so contracted, as to value men from circumstantial distinctions, but acccording to their personal worth.

He sought truth for its own sake, and would profess his sentiments with the undisguised openness of an honest Christian, and the inoffensive boldness of a manly spirit; yet, without the least apparant difficulty or hesitation, he would retract an opinion on full conviction of its being a mistake. I have never known one, who appeared to lay himself more fully open to the reception of truth, from whatever quarter it came, than he; for he judged the knowledge of truth only to be real learning, and that endeavouring to defend an error was but labouring to be more ignorant. But, until fully convinced, he was becommingly tenacious of his opinion.

The unavoidable consciousness of native power made him bold and enterprizing. Yet the event proved that his boldness arose not from a partial, groundless self-conceit, but from true self-knowledge. Upon fair and candid trial, faithful and just to himself, he judged what he could do; and what he could, when called to it, he attempted; and what he attempted he accomplished.

It may here be properly observed, that he was chosen by the Synod of *New-York*, at the instance of the Trustees of *New-Jersey*, College, as a fit person to accompany the Rev. Mr. *Gilbert Tennent* to *Great-Britain* and *Ireland*, in order to solicit benefactions for the said college. As this manifested the high opinion which both the Synod and Corporation entertained of his popular talents and superior abilites, so his ready compliance to undertake that service, hazardous and difficult in itself, and precarious in its consequences, which required him to overlook his domestic connections, however tender and endearing, manifested his resolution and self-denial. How well he was qualified as a solicitor, is witnessed by the numerous and large benefactions he received. His services, as was meet, were gratefully accepted by his conſtituents; and to the pious, generous, and public-ſpirited charity of the friends of Religion and Learning in *Great-Britain*, received on that occaſion, does the college of *New-Jerſey*, in a great degree, owe its preſent flouriſhing condition.

As his light ſhone, his abilites to fill the Preſident's chair in this College, then vacant, was not doubted by the honourable board of Truſtees. He was accordingly choſen, and earneſtly invited to accept the charge of the Society. Yet he once and again excuſed himſelf, not being convinced that he was called in duty to leave his then important province. But repeated application at length prevailed to make him apprehend that it was the will of God he ſhould accept the call; yet, left he ſhould miſtake in ſo important a caſe, he withheld his expreſs conſent, until the Reverend Synod of *New-York* and *Philadelphia* gave their opinion in favour of the College. This determined his dubious mind. He came, and undertook the weighty charge.

And what were the conſequences? had his inceſſant labours in travelling and preaching the goſpel, his diſadvantageous ſituation, and want of opportunity for improvement made ſome of his beſt friends diffident of his capacity and acquirements for moving with honour in this unaccuſtomed ſphere; He agreeably diſappointed their friendly fears, and convinced them that ſtrength of genius, joined to induſtrious application, had ſurmounted all other diſadvantages. Had any ſuch raiſed expectations as ſeemed hard to anſwer? they were fully ſatisfied: ſo that from being highly approved he came to be admired.

His manner of conducting the College did honour to himſelf, and promoted its intereſts. Whatever alterations in the plans of education he introduced were confeſſedly improvements on thoſe of his predeceſſors. Had I never had other means of intelligence, ſave only my knowledge of the man, I ſhould naturally have expected that all his public appearances would have been conducted with ſpirit, elegance, and decorum; that his government would be mild and gentle, tempered with wiſdom and authority, and calculated to command reverence while it attracted love, and that his manner of teaching would be agreeable and ſtriking.

But I propoſe not theſe as mere conjectures. The learned Tutors of the College, the partners of his counſels and deliberations for its good, and theſe young Gentlemen, once his care and charge, who judged themſelves happy under his tuition, all know more than I ſhall ſpeak.

You know the tenderneſs and condeſcenſion with which he treated you; the paternal care with which he watched over *on the Death of Mr.* DAVIES.

you; the reluctance with which he at any time inflicted the prescribed punishment on a delinquent; and how pleased he was to succeed in reforming any abuse by private and easy methods. You felt yourselves voluntarily confined by the restraints of love, and obliged to subjection, not from slavish fear, but from principle and inclination. You have yet fresh in memory his instructive Lectures, and can tell with what ease he communicated his sentiments, and impressed his ideas on your minds, and the entertaining manner in which he would represent even a common thought.

But his persuasive voice you will hear no more. He is removed far from mortals, has taken his aerial flight, and left us to lament, that " a great man has fallen in Israel!" He lived " much in a little time ; " he finished his course," performed " sooner than many others his assigned task, and, in that view, might be said to have died mature. He shone like a light set in a high place, that burns out and expires.

He went through every stage of honour and usefulness, compatible to his character as a dissenting Clergy-man: and while we flattered our fond hopes of eminent services from him for many years to come, the fatal blow was struck: our pleasing prospects are all at an end, and he is cut down like a tree that had yielded much fruit, and was loaden with blossoms even in its fall.

This dispensation, how misteriously! how astonishing! nay, how discouraging does it seem! Why was he raised, by Divine Providence, in the prime of life, to so important a station, and, amidst useful labours, whilst he was fast encreasing in strength adapted to his business, quickly snatched away? This is a perplexing case ; and the more so that it so soon succeeded the yet shorter continunnce of the venerable *Edwards*. Were they set in so conspicuous a point of view, only that their imitable excellencies might be more observable? or, was *Nassau-Hall* erected by Divine Providence for this, among other important purposes, that it might serve to adorn the latter end of some eminent servants of the living GOD, itself being adorned by them? In this view, the short Presidency of a *Dickinson*, a *Burr*, an *Edwards*, and a *Davies*, instead of arguing the displeasure of the Almighty, will evidence His peculiar favour to this institution; which I know was planned, and has been carried on with the most pious, benevolent, and generous designs. These designs GOD's goodness has hitherto amazingly prospered, amidst apparent frowns; and, if we may infer any thing from what he has already done, it is an encouraging expectation that he will continue to bless this Society, and make

VOL. I. E

it an honour and happiness to this venerable Board to have been engaged in so noble and successful an undertaking.

Now one more shining orb is set on our world. *Davies* is departed, and with him all that love, zeal, activity benevolence, for which he was remarkable. This the Church, and this the bereaved College mourns. For this we hang our once cheerful harps, and indulge the plaintive strains. Yet we are not to lament as those who are hopeless, but rather with humble confidence to " pray the LORD of the harvest," with whom is " the residue of the Spirit," that he would send forth another *Davies* to assist our labour and forward his work.

Nor should the decease of useful labourers, the extinction of burning and shining lights, only send us to the throne of grace for supplies, but excite us to greater diligence and activity in our business, as we have for the present the more to do. And, instead of being dispirited by the loss of such eminent assistants, we should be animated by their example, and hope for the same divine aids that carried them through all the duties and dangers of life with safety, success, and honour.

Finally, this dispensation should lessen our esteem of this trantory disappointing world, and raise our affections to Heaven, that place and state of permanent blessedness. Thither ascends, as to its native home, all the goodness that departs from earth; and the more of our pious friends that go to glory; so many more secondary motives have we to excite our desires of " departing and being with CHRIST ; which is far better" than any state under the sun : for there, in addition to superior felicity, " we shall come to the general assembly, and church of " the first-born who are written in Heaven,—and to the spirits of just men made perfect."(*o*) *Amen.*

(*o*) Heb. xiii. 23.

AN APPENDIX.

THE following facts, drawn up by a gentleman, who was Mr. *Davies*'s intimate Friend, and lived in the same town with him, while he was President of the College, were collected partly from Mr. *Davies*'s private papers, and partly from the gentleman's personal knowledge, and, as they illustrate several things just hinted in the preceding discourse, and contain some anecdotes not before mentioned, may be properly subjoined to the narrative already given.

The Rev. Mr. *Samuel Davies*, late President of the College of *New-Jersey*, was born on the 3d day of *November*, A. D. 1724, in the county of *Newcastle*, on *Delaware*. His father was a planter, who lived with great plainness and simplicity, and supported the character of a honest and pious man to his death; which happened about two years ago. His mother, who is still living*, and greatly distinguished for her eminent piety, some time before the conception of this favourite only son, earnestly desired such a blessing; and as she then had only borne a daughter, who was near five years old, she had special occasion for the exercise of her faith, in waiting for the divine answer to her petition. In this situation she took example from the mother of the prophet *Samuel*, and " Vowed a vow unto " the LORD; that if he would indeed give her a man-child, she " would devote him to his service all the days of his life."*(p)*

It may well be supposed that the parents received this child as from GOD, and that the mother especially, who had reason to look upon him as a token of the divine favour, and an express answer to her prayers, would, with the greatest tenderness, begin the rearing of this beloved plant. As there was no school in the neighbourhood, she herself taught him to read: and, although he was then very young, he is said to have made such proficiency as surprised every person who heard it.

---

* The reader is desired to observe that the following account was drawn up some years ago, since which time I find it has pleased Providence to remove from our world the Mother of Mr. *Davies*, who is mentioned as living by the writer of the *Appendix*.

(p) 1 Sam. i. 11.

He continued at home with his parents till he was about ten years old; during which time he appeared to have no remarkable impreffions of a religious kind; but behaving himfelf as is common for a fprightly towardly child, under the influence of pious example and inftruction. He was then fent to an Englifh fchool, at fome diftance from his father's, where he continued two years, and made great progrefs in his learning; but, for want of the pious inftruction with which he was favoured at home, he grew fomewhat more carelefs of the things of religion.

It appears, that about this time of life, carelefs as he was, he made a practice of fecret prayer, efpecially in the evening. The reafons (as he tells it in his diary) why he was fo punctual in the evening was, that " he feared left he fhould perhaps die before " morning." What is farther obfervable in his prayers at this time is, that " he was more ardent in his fupplications for be- " ing introduced into the Gofpel-Miniftry, than for any other " thing."

[It is here prefumed that Dr. *Finley*'s Sermon, preached on occafion of his Death, by defire of the Truftees, contains fufficient Memorials of his Life, from the time in which it pleafed GOD more deeply to imprefs his mind with the important realities of another world, until he was elected Prefident of the College.]

It may perhaps not be amifs to mention that when he returned home from his voyage to *Great-Britain*, he entered again on his laborious and beloved tafk of preaching the Gofpel to his feveral Congregations; and continued in this work until the year 1759, when he was elected Prefident of the College of *New-Jerfey*, in the room of the Rev. Mr. *Jonathan Edwards*. The College, before he came, had been in an unhappy fituation; partly owing to the length of that melancholy period between the death of Prefident *Burr* and his acceffion, and partly to the evil difpofitions and practices of a few members of the Society. Prefident *Burr* died in *September*, 1757: and although Mr. *Edwards* was elected a few days after, he did not take upon himfelf the government of the College till *February*, 1758; and about a fortnight after took the fmall-pox, of which he died in *March* following. Mr. *Davies* was not initiated in his office till the latter end of *July*, 1759. So that the College lay under the obvious difadvantages of a bereaved condition for almoft two years. But the prudent meafures taken by Prefident *Davies* foon furmounted thefe difadvantages; fo that in a few months a fpirit of emulation in Learning and Morality, as had been ufual, evidently characterized the Students of *Naffau-Hall.*

APPENDIX. xxvii

While he continued President his labours were great, and his application to study was necessarily more intense than that of his predecessors. For he came to this seat of the Muses, when its learning, by the eminent abilities of President *Burr*, was advanced to a very considerable degree; and he had just emerged from a sea of ministerial labour in various places, wherein a common Genius would have been able to have made but little improvement in academical learning. Besides, the speedy passage he made through the course of his studies, previous to his entering into the ministry, made his after application the more necessary for so important and elevated a situation. He was determined not to degrade his office, but be in reality what his station supposed him, and accordingly exerted himself to the utmost. The labours of the day seemed to him rather an incentive to study than to rest in the night; for he commonly sat up till twelve o'clock, and often later, although he rose by break of day. The success was proportionable; for by the mighty efforts of his great genius, and by dint of industry, he left the College of *New-Jersey*, at his death, in as high a state of literary merit as it ever had been in since its first institution.

It is a piece of justice due to his memory to remark, that the few innovations he made in the academical exercises, were certainly improvements upon the plans of his predecessors. Among other things the monthly Orations he instituted deserve particular notice. In order to give his Pupils a taste for composition, and to form them for public speaking, he directed the members of the senior class each to choose his subject, and compose a popular harangue to be delivered publicly in the College-Hall before the Masters and Students, and as many of the inhabitants of the town as chose to attend. When each had written his discourse, he brought it to the President, who made such observations and corrections as he judged proper; and, after their discourses were spoken, they severally attended him again for his remarks on their delivery. About six of the young Gentlemen usually delivered their Orations in the afternoon of the first *Wednesday* in every Month, to crowded audiences; and it is hard to say, whether the entertainment of the hearers, or the improvement of the students, was the greater.

There is reason to believe, that the intense application with which Mr. *Davies* attended to the duties of his office was one great cause of his death. The habit of his body was plethoric: and it is not to be doubted but that his health for some years had very much depended upon the exercise of riding, to which he was necessarily obliged while he lived in *Virginia*, though even then he had several severe fevers, supposed to arise principally from his application to study in the intervals of riding abroad. When he came to the College he scarcely used any bodily exercise save what was required in going from his own house to *Nassau-Hall*, which is a space about ten rods, five or six times a day.

In the latter end of *January*, A. D. 1761, a bad cold seized him, and for his relief he was bled. The same day he transcribed for the press the Sermon, which was soon after published, on the death of the late King, and the day after preached twice in the College-Hall; by all which the arm, in which he was bled, became much inflamed, and increased his former indisposition. On the *Monday* morning after, at breakfast, he was seized with a violent chilly fit, which was succeeded by an inflammatory fever, and in ten days brought on the period of his important life.

Although premonitions of Death in the present state of the world are seldom, if ever, given to mankind; and they who are disposed to interpret ordinary occurrences into such premonitions, when, by something similar in the event those occurrences would seem as if predictive, generally discover their weakness; yet the circumstances of the death of an eminent person are commonly very acceptable to the public, and for this reason it may not be amiss to mention an anecdote which Mr. *Davies* more than once took notice of in his last sickness.

An intimate friend of his, a few days before the beginning of the year in which he died, in conversation told him, that a Sermon would be expected from him on the new-year's day; and, among other things, happened to mention that the late President *Burr*, on the first day of the year wherein he died, preached a Sermon on *Jer.* xxviii. 16. *Thus saith the* LORD, *This year thou shalt die;* and after his death, the people took occasion to say it was premonitory; upon which Mr. *Davies* observed, that " although it ought not to be viewed in that light, yet it was very remarkable." When new year's day came he preached; when the congregation were not a little surprized at his taking the same text of scripture. Upon his being taken with his last sickness, about three weeks after, he soon adverted to this circumstance, and mentioned it as remakable that he had been undesignedly led to preach, as it were, his own Funeral Sermon.

It is much to be lamented that the violence of the disorder, of which this excellent man died, deprived him of the regular exercise of his reason the greater part of the time of his sickness, otherwise the public would undoubtedly have been gratified with his remarks on the views of an approaching eternity, and would have received another evidence of the superior excellency and power of that Religion, which alone can support the soul, and make the, otherwise gloomy, prospect of death cheerful. For the issues of this decisive period his life had been eminently calculated from his youth. It abundantly appears, that from twelve or fourteen years of age, he had continually maintained the strictest watch over his thoughts and actions, and daily lived under a deep sense of his own unworthiness, of the transcendent excellency of the Christian Religion, of the great importance of a public spirit, and the necessity of exerting it in promoting the general good. Even in his delirium his mind discovered the favourite objects of his concern, the prosperity of CHRIST's Church and the good of mankind. His bewildered brain was continually imagining, and his faultering tongue expressing some expedient for these important purposes. Alas! for us that so great a light could no longer continue in this dark world!

DIVINE CONDUCT Vindicated;

OR, THE

OPERATIONS of GOD

SHOWN TO BE THE

OPERATIONS of WISDOM:

IN THE SUBSTANCE OF

TWO DISCOURSES,

PREACHED AT

HABERDASHERS-HALL,

LONDON, MARCH 29, 1761.

OCCASIONED BY THE DECEASE OF THE

Rev. SAMUEL DAVIES, A. M.

And President of the College of *Nassau-Hall*, in *New-Jersey*.

By THOMAS GIBBONS, *D. D.*

Sive tribulemur & augustemur, sive lætemur, & exultemus, Deus laudandus est, qui & in Tribulationibus erudit, & in Lætitia consolatur. Laus enim Dei a Corde & Ore Christiani recedere non debet, non ut laudet in prosperis & maledicat in adversis: sed quemadmodum Psalmus ille scribit, semper Laus ejus in Ore meo. Gaudes, agnosce Patrem blandientem: tribularis agnosce Patrem emendantem: sive blandiatur, sive emendet, eum erudit, cui parat Hæreditatem.

Augustin. in Psal. liv.

EPHES. i. 11.

—Who works all things after the counsel of his own will.

THE laſt week gave me the awful aſſurance, of the ſudden and unexpected death of that moſt excellent and amiable man and miniſter of JESUS CHRIST, the Rev. Mr. *Samuel Davies*, Preſident of the college of *Naſſau-Hall*, in *New-Jerſey*, by a moſt moving and melting letter from a gentleman of *Philadelphia*, an acquaintance of Mr. *Davies*, and who well knew his worth, to a correſpondent of the gentleman's here in *London*.

A greater loſs, all things conſidered, could not perhaps befal the church of GOD in the death of a ſingle perſon. The GOD of nature had endowed Mr. *Davies* with extraordinary talents. Perhaps in ſublimity and ſtrength of genius there were very few, if any, who ſurpaſſed him. To the brighteſt and richeſt intellects Mr. *Davies* had ſuperadded the improvements of ſcience, and a large acquaintance with books, and poſſibly, had he lived, there would have been ſcarcely a man in our world a more accompliſhed Divine, or a more eminent Scholar. His character in life was wonderfully accommodated both to his natural and acquired abilities. He was Preſident of *New-Jerſey* college, in the diſcharge of which office there would have been a demand for the exertion of his amazing talents, and the exhibition of all his treaſures of literature and knowledge. Thus, as he was a ſtar of the firſt magnitude, ſo he was placed in a ſituation where he might have ſhone without any waſte of his diſtinguiſhed and ſupereminent glories.

But what crowned all or advanced his diſtinction as a man and a ſcholar into the higheſt value and luſtre, was, that his pious character appeared not at all inferior to his great intellects, and acquired accompliſhments. Nay, (let me not be thought, for I intimately knew him, to exceed the limits of truth in the ardor of my friendſhip) his pious character as much ſurpaſſed all elſe that was remarkable in him, as the ſparkling eye in the countenance of a great genius does all the other features of the face. If Mr. *Davies*'s good ſenſe and learning were *the pictures of ſilver*, his graces and virtues were *the apples of gold. (a)*

Here let me ſtay awhile; and, though I ſhall only give you a few outlines of his piety and amiable diſpoſition, yet let me be allowed to preſent you with ſuch a view of him as ſhall not only be ſufficient to demonſtrate him to be the beſt of men and mini-

(a) Prov. xxv. 11.

sters, but as shall leave room for you to conclude that great additions might be made to his character by persons who had a longer acquaintance with him than myself, and the collected testimonies of the friends who were favoured with his intimate correspondence.

He informed me in one of his letters, for I was honoured with a close intimacy with him several years, " That he was blessed " with a mother whom he might account, without filial vanity " or partiality, one of the most eminent saints he ever knew " upon earth. And here, says he, I cannot but mention to " my friend an anecdote known but to few, that is, that I am " a son of prayer, like my name-sake *Samuel* the prophet; and " my mother called me *Samuel* because, she said, I have asked " him of the LORD, 1 Sam. i. 20. This early dedication to " GOD has always been a strong inducement to me to devote " myself to Him by my own personal act; and the most impor- " tant blessings of my life I have looked upon as immediate an- " swers to the prayers of a pious mother. But, alas! what a " degenerate plant am I! How unworthy of such a parent, and " such a birth!"

From the accounts Mr. *Davies* gave of himself in the conversation that passed between us when he was here in *England*, I learnt, as the inference from related fact, that he must have been very assiduous in his studies. When he was about entering the ministry, or had not long entered upon it, if I remember right, he was judged to be in a deep and irrecoverable consumption. Finding himself upon the borders of the grave, and without any hopes of recovery, he determined to spend the little remains of an almost exhausted life, as he apprehended it, in endeavouring to advance his master's glory in the good of souls. Accordingly he removed from the place where he was to another about an hundred miles distance, that was then in want of a minister. Here he laboured in season and out of season; and, as he told me, preached in the day, and had his hectic fever by night, and that to such a degree as to be sometimes delirious, and to stand in need of persons to sit up with him. Here GOD gave him some glorious first-fruits of his ministry, for two instances of the conversion of two gentlemen he related to me were very remarkable, and he had the satisfaction, as he informed me, to find in the after-accounts of them, that there was good reason to believe that they were saints indeed: their goodness being by no means " like the grass upon the house tops, " which withers afore it grows up, and with which the mower " filleth not his hand," Psal. cxxix. 6, 7, but yielding the fruits meet for repentance in an holy and well-ordered conversation.

Afterwards he settled in *Virginia*, a colony where profaneness and immorality called aloud for his sacred labours. His patience and perseverance, his magnanimity and piety, together with his powerful and evangelical ministrations, were not without success. The wilderness and the solitary places in the course of his stay there, bloomed and blossomed before him. His tract of preaching, if I remember right, for some time was not less than sixty miles, and by what I have learnt, though not from himself, he had but little of this world's goods to repay his zealous and indefatigable labours; but his reward, as he well knew, was in Heaven; and he felt, I doubt not, the animated joy that every Negro slave, which under his ministrations became the LORD's freemen, would furnish an additional jewel to his eternal crown.

Upon the decease of that excellent man the Rev. Mr. *Jonathan Edwards*, President of the college of *Nassau-Hall*, in *New-Jersey*, Mr. *Davies* writes me word, that Mr. *Lockwood* in *New-England*, a gentleman of worthy character, was chosen to fill up the vacancy. " I have not heard, says Mr. *Davies*, whe-
" ther he has accepted the place. The Trustees were divided
" between him, another gentleman, and myself, but I happily
escaped." But so it was ordered, by Mr. *Lockwood's* not accepting the invitation, that Mr. *Davies* was afterwards elected President of the college; and what concern, and indeed what consternation this choice gave him, his letters to me amply testify; and I could particularly relate to you what views he had of things, and what steps he took to determine what was his duty. At last he accepted the call to his important office of presiding in the college; and tells me in a letter, dated *June* 6, 1759,
" That the evidence of his duty was so plan, that even his
" sceptical mind was satisfied; and that his people saw the hand
" of providence in it, and dared not to oppose."

Here he was settled for about eighteen months; and as he could exercise his ministry as well as preside over the college, great things might have been expected from that rare and remarkable union there was in him of what was great and good; and with pleasure I have received the information from his friends how well he supported and adorned his character, and what high expectations were formed as to the benefit and blessing he was likely to prove to that seminary of religion and learning.
" His whole soul (says the letter that gives the news of his
" death) was engaged for the good of the youth under his care."
" And again, "*Nassau-Hall* in tears, disconsolate, and refusing
" to be comforted."

But, alas! in the midst of his days, (little more than thirty-six years of age) he was called away from this but opening scene of large and extraordinary ufefulnefs to the invifible world, the world of glory and bleffednefs, never to fojourn in mortal clay, or to irradiate and blefs the church militant more. He is dead, he is departed—*America* in groans proclaims her inexpreffible lofs, and we in *Great-Britain* fhare the diftrefs, and echo groan for groan.

Thus ended the days on earth of this truly great and good man; having in his little circle of life fhed more beams, and done more fervice than many a languid and lefs illuminated foul, even in a public fphere, in the revolution of fixty or fourfcore years.

Truly great and good I may ftile him without the fufpicion of flattery, and without the flight of hyperbole. Let me call to your remembrance, as proofs of what I fay, the excellent difcourfes he has delivered in this pulpit, and the feveral Sermons of his which have been publifhed, ftrong in manly fenfe, loaden with full ideas, rich with evangelical truth, and animated with the moft facred fervor for the good of fouls. And to thefe evidences of the admirable fpirit that dwelt in him, let me add a few paragraphs from the many letters with which, in the courfe of about nine years correfpondence, he has favoured me.

Speaking in one of his letters concerning his children, he fays, " I am folicitous for them when I confider what a contagious " world they have entered into, and the innate infection of " their natures. There is nothing that can wound a parent's " heart fo deep, as the thought that he fhould bring up chil- " dren to difhonour his God here, and be miferable hereafter. " I beg your prayers for mine, and you may expect a retalia- " tion in the fame kind."

In another letter he fays, " We have now three fons and two " daughters; whofe young minds as they open I am endea- " vouring to cultivate with my own hand, unwilling to truft " them to a ftranger; and I find the bufinefs of education much " more difficult than I expected.—My dear little creatures fob " and drop a tear now and then under my inftructions, but I " am not fo happy as to fee them under deep and lafting im- " preffions of religion; and this is the greateft grief they afford " me. Grace cannot be communicated by natural defcent, " and, if it could, they would receive but little from me. I " earneftly beg your prayers for them."

In another letter, " I defire ferioufly to devote to God and " my dear country, all the labours of my head, my heart, my hand, " and pen; and if he pleafes to blefs any of them I hope I fhall be " thankful, and wonder at his condefcending grace.—Oh! my " dear brother, could we fpend and be fpent all our lives in " painful, difinterefted, indefatigable fervice for God and the

to be the Operations of *Wisdom*. xxxvii

" world, how serene and bright would it render the swift ap-
" proaching eve of life! I am labouring to do a little to save
" my country, and, which is of much more consequence, to
" save souls—from death—from that tremendous kind of death,
" which a *soul* can die. I have but little success of late, but
" blessed be GOD, it surpasses my expectation, and much more
" my desert. Some of my bretheren labour to better purpose.
" The pleasure of the LORD prospers in their hands."

Another epistle tells me, " As for myself, I am just striving
" not to live in vain. I entered the ministry with such a sense
" of my unfitness for it, that I had no sanguine expectations of
" success, And a condescending GOD (O, how condescend-
" ing!) has made me much more serviceable than I could hope.
" But, alas! my brother, I have but little, very little true re-
" ligion. My advancements in holiness are extremely small:
" I feel what I confess, and am sure it is true, and not the rant
" of excessive or affected humility. It is an easy thing to make
" a noise in the world, to flourish and harangue, *to dazzle the*
" *crowd, and set them all agape,* but deeply to imbibe the spirit
" of christianity, to maintain a secret walk with GOD, to be
" holy as he is holy, this is the labour, this the work. I beg
" the assistance of your prayers in so grand and important an en-
" terprize.—The difficulty of the ministerial work seems to
" grow upon my hands. Perhaps once in three or four months
" I preach in some measure as I could wish; that is, I preach as
" in the sight of GOD, and as if I were to step from the pulpit
" to the supreme tribunal. I *feel* my subject. I melt into tears,
" or I shudder with horror, when I denounce the terrors of the
" LORD. I glow, I soar in sacred extasies, when the love of
" JESUS is my theme, and, as Mr. *Baxter* was wont to express
" it, in lines more striking to me than all the fine poetry in the
" world,

" I preach as if I ne'er should preach again;
" And as a dying man to dying men.

" But, alas! my spirits soon flag, my devotions languish, and
" my zeal cools. It is really an afflictive thought, that I serve
" so good a Master with so much inconstancy; but so it is, and
" and my soul mourns upon that account."

In another letter he says, " I am labouring to do a little
" good in the world. But, alas! I find I am of little use or im-
" portance. I have many defects, but none gives me so much
" pain and mortification as my slow progress in personal holiness.
" This is the grand qualification of the office we sustain, as well
" as for that heaven we hope for, and I am shocked at myself
" when I see how little I have of it."

In another of his letters, he acquaints me, "That he indeed
"feels an union of hearts which cannot bear without pain the
"intervention of the huge *Atlantic*, nor even the abfence of a
"week. But our condefcending LORD, adds he, calls his mi-
"nifters *Stars*, and he knows beft in what part of the firmament
"of the church to fix them: and (O the delightful thought!)
"they can never be out of the reach of his beams, though they
"fhine in different hemifpheres with regard to each other. This
"leads me, undefignedly, to a criticifm on *Jude* 13, on which
"perhaps an aftronomer would be the beft commentator, *Wan-*
"*dering ftars, to whom is referved the blacknefs of darknefs for*
"*ever*. Perhaps an aftronomical critic would obferve that falfe
"teachers are reprefented as *planetary* or *wandering* ftars, that
"in their eccentricities run out into an eternal *Aphelion* from
"the fun of righteoufnefs, beyond the fyftem which he warms,
"illuminates, and beatifies, and are conftantly receding from
"the fountain of light, life, and blifs, and therefore muft wan-
"der through the blacknefs of darknefs for ever; a darknefs
"unpierced by one ray from the great fun and center of the
"moral world—*blacknefs of darknefs*, an abftract predicated of
"an abftract. How gloomy and ftrong the expreffion!"

Let me give you another quotation from his letters. "I am
"very much pleafed and affected, fays he, with the fubject of
"this week's ftudy, and next LORD's day's entertainment,
"namely, *A bruifed reed fhall he not break, and the fmoking flax*
"*fhall he not quench*. Such a *bruifed reed* at beft am I: a
"weak, oppreffed, ufelefs thing: a *ftridens ftipula* that can
"make no agreeable melody to entertain my great Shepherd.
"Yet this *bruifed reed* I have reafon to hope he will not break,
"but bind up and fupport. This fhattered pipe of ftraw he
"will not caft away, but repair and tune to join in the angelic
"concert on high. I am at beft but *fmoking flax*; a dying
"fnuff in the candleftick of his church; a wick juft put out in
"the lamp of his fanctuary. The flame of divine love, funk
"deep into the focket of a corrupt heart, quivers, and breaks,
"and catches, and feems juft expiring at times. The devil and
"the world raife many ftorms to blow upon it. And yet this
"*fmoking flax*, where the leaft fpark of that facred paffion ftill
"remains which renders it more fufceptive of his love, as a can-
"dle juft put out but ftill fmoking, is eafily rekindled.—This
"*fmoking flax* he will not quench, but blow it to a flame, which
"fhall fhine brighter and brighter till it mingle with its kindred
"flames in the pure element of love."

I fhall conclude my extracts from his epiftolary correfpondence with a part of a letter, dated *Hanover, September* 12,
1757.

" My ever dear Friend,

" I am juft beginning to creep back from the valley of the
" fhadow of death, to which I made a veay near approach a
" few days ago. I was feized with a moft violent fever, which
" came to a crifis in a week, and now it is much abated, though
" I am ftill confined to my chamber. In this fhattered ftate my
" trembling hand can write but little to you, and what I write
" will be languid and confufed, like its author. But as the *Vir-*
" *ginia* fleet is about to fail, and I know not when I fhall have
" another opportunity, I cannot avoid writing fomething. I
" would fit down on the grave's mouth, and talk awhile with
" my favorite friend; and from my fituation you may forefee
" what fubjects my converfation will turn upon—Death—Eter-
" nity—the fupreme Tribunal.

" Bleffed be my Mafter's name, this diforder found me em-
" ployed in his fervice. It feized me in the pulpit, like a foldier
" wounded in the field. This has been a bufy fummer with me.
" In about two months I rode about five hundred miles,
" preached about forty fermons. This affords me fome pleafure
" in the review. But, alas! the mixture of fin and of many
" namelefs imperfections that run through and corrupt all my
" fervices, give me fhame, forrow, and mortification. My fe-
" ver made unufual ravages upon my underftanding, and ren-
" dered me frequently delirious, and always ftupid. But, when
" I had any little fenfe of things, I generally felt pretty calm
" and ferene, and death, that mighty terror, was difarmed.
" Indeed the thought of leaving my dear family deftitute, and
" my flock fhepherdlefs, made me often ftart back and cling to
" life; but in other refpects death appeared a kind of indiffe-
" rency to me. Formerly I have wifhed to live longer that I
" might be better prepared for Heaven, but this confideration
" had but very little weight with me, and that for a very unu-
" fual reafon, which was this—After long trial I found this
" world is a place fo unfriendly to the growth of every thing
" Divine and Heavenly, that I was afraid, if I fhould live longer,
" I fhould be no better fitted for Heaven than I am. Indeed I
" have hardly any hopes of ever making any great attainments
" in holinefs while in this world, though I fhould be doomed to
" ftay in it as long as *Methufelah*. I fee other chriftians indeed
" around me make fome progrefs, though they go on with but a
" fnail-like motion: but when I confider that I fet out about
" twelve years old, and what fanguine hopes I then had of my
" future progrefs, and yet that I have been almoft at a ftand
" ever fince, I am quite difcouraged.—O my good Mafter, if I
" may dare to call thee fo, I am afraid I fhall never ferve thee

"much better on this side the region of perfection. The thought grieves me: it breaks my heart, but I can hardly hope better. But if I have the least spark of true piety in my breast I shall not always labour under this complaint. No, my LORD, I shall yet serve thee—serve thee through an immortal duration—with the activity, the fervor, the perfection of *the rapt seraph that adores and burns.* I very much suspect this desponding view of the matter is wrong, and I do not mention it with approbation, but only relate it as an unusual reason for my willingness to die, which I never felt before, and which I could not suppress.

"In my sickness I found the unspeakable importance of a Mediator in a religion for sinners. O! I could have given you the word of a dying man for it, that that JESUS whom you preach is indeed a necessary, and an all-sufficient Saviour. Indeed he is the only support for a departing soul. *None but* CHRIST, *none but* CHRIST. Had I as many good works as *Abraham* or *Paul*, I would not have dared to build my hopes upon such a quicksand, but only on this firm eternal rock.

"I am rising up, my brother, with a desire to recommend him better to my fellow-sinners, than I have done. But, alas! I hardly hope to accomplish it. He has done a great deal more by me already than I ever expected, and infinitely more than I deserved. But he never intended me for great things. He has beings both of my own, and of superior orders, that can perform him more worthy service.—O! if I might but untie the latchet of his shoes, or draw water for the service of his sanctuary, it is enough for me. I am no angel, nor would I murmur because I am not——

"My strength fails me, and I must give over—pray for me—write to me—love me living and dying, on earth and in heaven."—

Judge you from these passages, written in the freedom of friendship, and to one to whom he scrupled not to lay open the secrets of his bosom, what a loss the church has sustained, and how much our world is impoverished by the death of Mr. *Davies*, in the vigour of his days, and in the meridian of his usefulness!

Such a blow, such an uncommon and distressing blow has been given in the death of Mr. *Davies*. And now what shall we do? to what shall we recur, or to what quarter shall we look for help under such an awful Providence? My advice is, that we should seriously and attentively turn our minds to the passage of sacred writ which I mentioned at the beginning of my discourse:

Who (that is, GOD) *works all things after the counsel of his own will.*

Without enquiring into the context, the words may be regarded as a diſtinct propoſition. He, (that is, GOD) works. He works, or he works with energy and irreſiſtible power, in ſuch a manner as none beſides him either has ability or right to work. He works like himſelf, he works with the omnipotence that belongs to him, and which is his eſſential and diſtinguiſhed attribute*. Farther, not only does GOD work, but he works all things, all things done by him in heaven and earth, in all the provinces of his vaſt empire, all things in Nature, Providence, and Grace, all things in time, and all things in eternity. And he works all things after the counſel of his own will; that is, as he pleaſes. His will is the ſource of his action. He gives an account of his matters to none. None in the army of heaven, or among the inhabitants of the earth, have any authority to ſay unto him, What doſt thou? He depends upon none, but all, all worlds and beings depend upon him; and therefore none are to preſume to dictate to him, or direct him what is or what is not to be done by him. But obſerve, that though he works, and works all things, and all this as he pleaſes, yet it is after the counſel of his own will. We are to conſider GOD indeed as a great ſovereign, as LORD of all, higher than the higheſt, ſupreme and unrivalled in perfection and glory, who is not to be called to the tribunal of his creatures, or to be queſtioned by them, as to what he pleaſes to perform. We are not to ſnatch the ſceptre or the balance from his hands. But yet this we may be aſſured of, that whatever the ALMIGHTY GOD does is done not from a kind of blind though omnipotent neceſſity, neither is it by an unguided or unmeaning exertion of power; but that he works all things after the counſel, the deſign, or wiſdom of his own will.† Survey the great JEHOVAH as he is indeed in his own nature, and in the revelation he has made of himſelf to us. If he is ſovereign, and not in the leaſt accountable to any one, yet he is wiſe, and infinitely wiſe.

* That the word ('Ενεργοῦντ@-) here tranſlated *who works*, contains in it that forcible meaning which I have here aſcribed to it, we may learn from what the critics have ſaid upon it :—" Hac voce ſignificatur actio conjuncta " cum efficacia, & quidem ſumma, quæ prohiberi nullo modo poſſit. Iſaiah " xli, 4."—LEIGHTIUS in verb. " At Græca vox magis ſonat, ejus cujus vi & " virtute fiunt omnia, h. e. omnia agentis ac moderantis."—ERASMUS in loc. Could we admit of ſuch an Engliſh word, the original might be rendered who *energizes* all things, &c.

† The word (βουλη) he tranſlated *counſel*, may, according to the learned Stephens in the *Theſaurus Græcæ Linguæ*, be rendered a *decree* or *reſolution*, a *counſel* or *advice*, whether good or bad, or a *conſultation* or *deliberation*. If we underſtand the word here of *decree* or *reſolution* as applied to God, we are certain that ſuch a decree or reſolution in Deity had its birth in wiſdom, or in no way derogatory to it. If we interpret the word of *counſel* or *advice*, who ſees not that wiſdom is taken into the account? it is the counſel, it is the advice of the God of unerring wiſdom. But if we take the word, and what forbids that

We are not to view GOD partially, but as far as we can completely, as the fountain of all perfection; as containing in his nature an harmony of all that is excellent and glorious. He has a right to do, and he can do whatever he pleases in all his wide-extended dominions; yet what he pleases is always worthy of himself. He is the aggregate, the system of excellence; and one attribute never displays itself to the diminution or eclipse of another. As he is greatest, so he is the best of beings. Wisdom dwells eternally and essentially in the divine will; and it must be obvious, that though none can limit GOD, yet he, with reverence be it spoken, limits himself by the rule which infinite wisdom prescribes to infinite power. Hear the account scripture gives of him—*He is the rock, his works are perfect, for all his ways are judgment; a GOD of truth, and without iniquity, just and right is he.* Deut. xxxii, 4. *He is wise in heart, as well as mighty in strength.* Job ix, 4. *His judgments are a great deep.* Psal. xxxvi, 6,—but they are judgments, the children of wisdom and counsel still. *If clouds and darkness are round about him, yet righteousness and judgment are the habitation of his throne.* Psal. xcvii. 2. *His works are truth, and his ways judgment.* Dan. iv. 37. *The* ALMIGHTY *will not pervert judgment.* Job xxxiv. 12. *His ways are equal.* Ezek. xviii. 25, directed by the straight unerring line of infinite wisdom. Be this then an established truth with us, that, whatever perplexity and darkness may encompass the divine proceedings, there is nothing which GOD does, that GOD *who works all things after the counsel of his own will,* but what is just, and right, and good; and that his every action is no other than the birth of consummate counsel, or that the plan of wisdom is laid as the foundation of all his government. And particularly in such an event as we are now considering, the removal of such an excellent and worthy person as Mr. *Davies* from our world, in the prime of life, and at such a juncture as this, when there are so few surviving persons of such ability and character, we are to believe and own that, as the blow was unquestionably given by GOD, it was perfectly right, and that not the least shadow or suspicion of

we should not so translate it? as denoting consultation or deliberation, then we are led in the strongest manner to conclude that the will of God proceeds upon wisdom. Not that there is properly or strictly any such thing as consultation or deliberation in the divine mind: but we may hereby conceive, speaking of God after the manner of men, that God when he wills, wills in such a wise manner, and upon such worthy reasons, as if he had first consulted and deliberated with himself what was proper to be done. " Libere quidem, quia " ex voluntate, sed tamen etiam sapienter et juste quia ex consilio voluntatis." ZANCH. " But because (says the great Howe) he orders all things according " to the counsel of his will, we must conceive some weighty reason did induce " hereto."—Howe's *Redeemer's Dominion over the Invisible World*, p. 72. Folio Edition, Vol. II.

blame or wrong is to be afcribed to the moft high, moft holy, moft wife, moft faithful, and moft merciful God. And even though we could not difcern fo much as one reafon, one end of wifdom or goodnefs anfwered by fuch an awful Providence, yet neverthelefs we are not to doubt but that the All-wife as well as the Almighty God has proceeded upon motives, though abfolutely impenetrable by us, worthy of himfelf; that he dwells in the thickeft darknefs, and that the glories of his perfections are inthroned at the centre, though not a ray of them penetrates and breaks through the external veil. But perhaps, upon a careful and fteady furvey of this moft afflictive Providence, we may attain to fome difcovery of the purpofes or counfels of Deity in the deceafe of fuch an excellent perfon as Mr. *Davies* in the prime of his days, and in the very height of his ufefulnefs. And, though we are not to call the Lord of all to our tribunal, yet perhaps we may not venture beyond our line, or deviate from the path of duty; nay, we may, on the other hand, be glorifying God as well as compofing and comforting ourfelves, if, with profound humility and reverence, we make the enquiry, Wherefore it is that God, *who works all things after the counfel of his own will,* is pleafed to call away by death the excellent of the earth in the vigour of life, and in the meredian of their fervices for the glory of God, and the good of his church? Thefe hard myfteries may not upon a diligent refearch be altogether inexplicable; and thefe dark paffages of Providence upon a clofe furvey may appear illuminated with evident and illuftrious beams of wifdom and love. Accordingly I fhall endeavour, I truft with a decency becoming a poor imperfect creature examining into the ways of the moft high and glorious God, to refolve this problem of Providence, "Why the excellent of the earth fhould be taken away in the flower or prime of their age, and from the moft enlarged fpheres of ufefulnefs, or what inftructions and improvements we may gather from fuch feemingly unkind and undefirable difpenfations?"

(1.) In the removal of the excellent of the earth in the flower or prime of their days, and in the height of their ufefulnefs, we may be taught the wonderful Majefty and independent glories of the great God over all bleffed for ever more. "God will have it known, fays the venerable Mr. *Howe*, on an occafion not unlike that which has given rife to our difcourfe*, that though he ufes inftruments, he needs them not. It is a piece of divine royalty and magnificence, that when he hath prepared and polifhed fuch an utenfil, fo as to be capable of great fervice, he can

---

* Howe's Redeemer's Dominion over the Invifible World, on the death of John Houghton, Efq.

lay it by without lofs."—GOD can maintain and carry on his own caufe, and anfwer his counfels, without the interpofition of his creatures, or, if he pleafes, he may employ only meaner inftruments, and call home from the vineyard the ableft and beft of his fervants, to fhew his church he can accomplifh his pleafure without them.

(2.) GOD may cut off the excellent of the earth in the flower or prime of their days, and in the height of their ufefulnefs, to endear and magnify his power and grace in unexpectedly raifing up others amidft the defponding fears and forrows of his people. When GOD takes away the excellent of the earth, fuch as were moft eminently formed for fervice, in the midft of their days, the Church of GOD, the friends of Zion, are apt to fink into great anxiety and diftrefs, and to fay with Zion of old, *The* LORD *has forfaken me, and my* GOD *hath forgotten me;* Ifa. xlix. 14. or with Jacob, *All thefe things are againft me.* Gen. xlii. 36.—Now at the very juncture when the people of GOD are thus dejected, when their hearts are trembling for the ark of the LORD, for GOD then to arife and to make the time of his church's extremity the time of his mercy in raifing up others, and pouring out his fpirit upon them in a plentiful effufion of gifts and graces, how does he hereby moft wonderfully illuftrate his power and love! His light, his favour towards Zion appears as it were with a double brightnefs, thus breaking out from amidft a night of thick darknefs; and the people of GOD, with a moft lively and powerful fenfe of the divine goodnefs, acknowledge that GOD has done great things for them, which they looked not for; and that nothing but his own arm and his own love could have helped them in fuch a diftreffing feafon. Hereby GOD is more eminently feen and glorified, and the work appears to be the LORD's, and is wonderful in his people's eyes.

(3.) GOD may take away the excellent of the earth in the flower or prime of their days, and in the meridian of their ufefulnefs, to fhew us more powerfully and affectingly the vanity of the prefent ftate. GOD fhows us the vanity of the prefent ftate when he takes away perfons in old age, when they have reached their threefcore years and ten, to fourfcore years; for by fuch inftances we are taught what a mere hand's breadth of being this life is, even in its utmoft extent, and how foon our exiftence in this world will be terminated, even though it is protracted to its fartheft limit. But when death, ufurping, as it were, by violence the fickle from the delaying hands of time, cuts off perfons in the bloom or in the prime of life, then is the vanity of the prefent ftate preached to us in the moft ftriking, affecting manner. And if with the bloom of youth or prime of manhood, great intellectual abilities, and fuperior acquired accompliſhments, diſtinguiſhed piety, and moſt enlarged uſefulneſs are cut off, then, in the moſt ſolemn awful accents, is the vanity of the preſent ſtate proclaimed to us, and our ears receive the leſſon not in ſoft whiſpers, not in a common voice, but in peals of thunder. Then we hear the cry ſounding, as it were, in an overwhelming and irreſiſtible energy, *All fleſh is graſs, and all the goodlineſs thereof is as the flower of the field: the graſs withers, the flower fades, becauſe the ſpirit of the* LORD *blows upon it.* Iſai. xl. 6, 7.—I ſee a man in the vigour and ſtrength of conſtitution, a man ennobled beyond the common multitude by a bright and lively imagination, by a clear and piercing judgment, by a ſuperior, manly, and commanding eloquence : I ſee a man ſuperior to his fellow-chriſtians and his fellow-miniſters, by a moſt ſublime, ſteady, rational, and uniform piety, and by an unextinguiſhable zeal, and unwearied labour for the glory of GOD, and the good of ſouls; this man, thus richly furniſhed and qualified, is taken away by a ſudden ſtroke, or after but a few days illneſs, and an end is put to all his luſtre and benefit in our world. What inference reſults from all this, but that all is vanity here below ? If the beſt we meet with on earth is thus fugitive and uncertain ; if it may ſo ſoon be gone, for ever gone from us, then *verily every man at his beſt eſtate*, and the beſt of men too, are *altogether vanity.* Pſal. xxxix. 5.—The pearls and jewels of our world may be as ſoon taken from it as the dirt and droſs. There is mortality, there is death in my choiceſt enjoyments. I ſee that the tall cedar may be cut down as well as the humble plant.—Stars of the firſt magnitude, as well as the leſſer orbs, may quit the ſkies, and vaniſh from my ſight. Death makes no diſtinction between good and bad, between the greateſt and the meaneſt, the beſt and worſt. Now he ſtrikes his dart at the poor peaſant, and now he launches it at the monarch on his throne. Now his ſhaft ſmites the chriſtian in his private walks of life, and now his unerring ſtroke lays the eminent genius, ſcholar, and miniſter in the duſt.—*All things,* in this ſenſe, *come alike to all*. Eccl. ix. 2. And is this the caſe, do the floods of death alike overwhelm the ſtately and richly freighted ſhip as the ſmall bark or boat, then why ſhould I doat upon the creature?—If I build my fond expectations of peace and comfort upon the beſt of men, I build upon the ſand. My deareſt friendſhips, and richeſt joys on earth may be daſhed in pieces in an hour, in a moment. All on earth is ſhadow, and when I look even to the very beſt it can afford, I ſee the ſame vanity and frailty there, which are common to lower and meaner things.

(4.) GOD may cut off the excellent of the earth in the flower or prime of their days, and in the height of their uſefulneſs, to bring our hearts into a nearer and more intimate dependence upon himself. How pleased are we apt to be with our enjoyments here below, and especially with our pious friendships and connexions? And it may be that we are in such cases the less aware of danger, and the less upon our guard as to excess, as we are certain that it is no way sinful, but on the other hand acceptable in the sight of God, to value the excellent of the earth, and to be delighted with their conversation and company. But even here we may exceed, and by an inordinate regard to only creatures and instruments, we may be led astray from God; or may not so much consider, adore, and enjoy him in them as we ought. God has a right to our entire hearts; and, unless we look to him, and own him in all our best enjoyments, we may provoke him to remove them from us; and this he may do, that he may bring us into more intimate union with himself, and dependence upon him, that the creature may be shewn to be nothing better than a creature, and that he may be honoured and acknowledged as all in all. Peter, upon the mount of transfiguration, says, that it *was good for them to be there,* " and was for making three tabernacles, one for his Lord, one for Moses, and one for Elias; but it is told us he knew not what he said," Luke ix. 33, and the bright vision was soon concluded. God may righteously, and indeed graciously remove creatures, the best creatures from us, if they draw off too much of the current of our affections from himself. The cistern breaking may endear us to the living fountain. The reed sinking may recommend us to the rock of ages. God may take away this and the other created excellency that our weakness has set up a veil between him and our souls, that we may lie the more open to his immediate communications, and that we may better remember and practise our duty, *to love the* Lord God *with all* our *heart, with all* our *soul, with all* our *mind, and with all* our *strength.* Mark xii. 30.

(5.) As by the death of the excellent of the earth in the flower or prime of their days, we are taught that no strength of constitution, or eminency, or usefulness are securities from death, so we may hereby be excited the more diligently to attend to our work, and prepare for our dismission. If we see others taken away younger and stronger than ourselves, then what is the inference, but that we may be cut off as well as they, and indeed more easily than they? If we observe others more eminent and more serviceable than ourselves called away from life, if their brighter splendors and more extensive benefit to mankind were no protection from the arrest of death, then what may we their inferiors expect? We have no exemption from sickness, pain, or sudden death, or death in the midst of our days, any more than others. If we had the wifdom of Solomon, or the zeal and ufefulnefs of St. Paul, ftill, like them, we fhould be no better than mortal. Hear then the voice of GOD to you, fpeaking from the afhes of the young, the ftrong, the learned, the eminently pious and ufeful:—*Stand with your loins girded, and your lamps burning. Give diligence, to make your calling and election fure. Work while it is day; the night comes when no man can work. Whatfoever thine hand finds to do, do it with thy might.* Do not think that becaufe you are a tree, even a palm, or a vine, *whofe fruit cheers both* GOD *and man,* Judges ix. 13, that therefore the order will not be iffued out, " Hew down the tree, cut off its branches, and even pluck up its roots."— Flatter not yourfelf becaufe you are a faint and fervant of GOD, or a minifter of fome confiderable influence and importance in the church, that death can have no power over you; dream not of an abiding-place here; you dwell in a tabernacle that may be foon taken down, even though it is a tabernacle which is holinefs to the LORD. Attend then to your work; every day look out for death, and view yourfelf as at the brink of the grave and at the door of eternity.

(6.) By the death of the excellent of the earth in the flower or prime of their days, and in the midft of their fervices to GOD and his church, we may be led to inquire, whether there is no anger expreffed againft us by their fudden, and in refpect of the common age of man, untimely removal.

As (1.) We may do well to confider whether there may not be fome judgments impending over us. If ambaffadors are called home, it may become the nation, where they were, to confider whether a rupture is not likely to enfue. Every good man that is taken away from our world is a lofs to it, a deduction from its worth, in proportion to his goodnefs. There is a lofs of his inftructions, his example, and his prayers. And if the beft of men are cut off, the lofs grows fo much the greater, and our apprehenfions of the divine refentment may very juftly be fo much the more awakened. Doves fly home to their windows at the coming ftorm. *The righteous perifhes, and no man lays it to heart; and merciful men are taken away, none confidering that the righteous is taken away from the evil to come.* Ifaiah lvii. 1. Lot leaves Sodom; and when he is gone the floodgates of vengeance are fet open, and the city is turned into deftruction Do not let us think lightly of the matter, that we fee the beft. of men, men that were holy wreftlers with GOD, and ftood in the breach to plead with him to turn away his wrath, removed from our world in the midft of their days, efpecially when fo

H

few servants and saints of God remained behind, and the world is so generally filled with impiety, and all manner of wickedness. Good Hezekiah, and after him good Josiah, must go to their graves before the destruction comes upon Judah and Jerusalem.

(2.) And as we know not but the deaths of the excellent of the earth in the midst of their days, and in the midst of their usefulness, may portend some judgments from God coming upon us, so let us hence be excited the more earnestly to deprecate them, and pray for his merciful regards to us. If the excellent of the earth are taken away, and taken away in the midst of their usefulness, and if, in such dispensations of Providence we may hear, as it were, the first alarms of the Almighty anger from his secret place of thunder, let us be the more fervent in our supplications that he would turn away his anger, and not deal with us after our sins, nor reward us according to our iniquities. The more gloomy apprehension, the more apparent danger, the more should we be excited to prayer, lively and importunate prayer. Let us beg of God, and beg the more earnestly, that he would have compassion upon us, and that the tokens of his judgments may proceed no farther, and not continue upon us in a storm of resistless and overwhelming vengeance. And,

(3.) As we know not but the deaths of the excellent of the earth, in the midst of their days and usefulness, may be the forerunners of some judgments from God at the door, let us prepare to meet our God if he should come out against us in the way of his judgments. Do we hear the sound of his anger, and are there some awful flashes, though at present at a distance, that seem to signify an approaching tempest, then let us prepare to meet our God. *Prepare to meet thy* God, *O Israel.* Amos iv. 12. Let us gird our christian armour close about us. Let us strengthen ourselves in our God, and abound in the exercises of a dependence upon him, whose *grace only is sufficient for us, and whose strength alone can be perfected in our weakness.* 2 Cor. xii. 9. Let us be in readiness to follow our God at his call, either through the waters or fires of affliction, being as willing magnanimously to suffer for him as we are cheerfully to serve him, and not being at all shaken in mind or spirit by the most grievous calamities and trials of life; having an inviolable connexion with and a sure interest in him " who will make all things work together for our good," Rom. viii. 28, and who has promised us a better life and a better world, after we have suffered a while, *even an inheritance incorruptible, undefiled, and that fades not away,* 1 Peter i. 4, and an admission into his palace and presence, where *there is fulness of joy, and a place at his right hand, where are pleasures for evermore.* Psal. xvi. 11.

(7.) By the deaths of the excellent of the earth in the flower or prime of their days, and in the midst of their usefulness, let us be excited to exert ourselves more vigorously and constantly to glorify GOD, and serve our generation, than hitherto we have done. Their removal shews us that we may be removed, and so quickens us to our duty; and their loss likewise, their loss to the world, should also excite us to duty; since though there is as much work as ever, yet there are fewer labourers to perform it. The more the world is impoverished, the more let us endeavour to enrich it. If an army is reduced of its number, let the officers, the folders that remain, not be unwilling to go through double service, and to exert themselves with a double activity and vigour.

(8.) By the removal of the excellent of the earth in the flower or prime of their days, and in the height of their usefulness, we are sure that we have lost by their departure from our world one tie to earth, and gained one attachment more to heaven. The excellent of the earth are taken away; our friends, our companions with whom we took sweet counsel. In every such instance one or more bond to earth and time is consequently broken. We are in one more degree detached from the charms of the creature, and hereby may come nearer, if we rightly improve the providence, to a deliverance from this world, that may have had too fast an hold of our hopes and affections. Had our pious and excellent friends stayed behind us, the thought of parting from them, though but for a time, might have thrown a gloom upon our expiring moments, and sharpened the sting of death. But they are gone, and life has lost by the departure of each of them one of its strongest engagements. And as we have dropt one tie to earth by their removal, so we have gained one more argument for heaven. Heaven lets down one more attractive, and a most sweet and powerful attractive it is, to draw up our hearts and hopes to it; heaven, where our immortal treasure lies, and whether our pious friends are gone. Let us feel the attachment; and the more heaven enlarges its glorious and blessed company of saints made perfect, the more let us look by faith within the veil, and the more ready let us be to follow our brethren that have died in CHRIST to the world of glory, that we may share with them in their eternal blessedness, and in the joys of an intimate, perfect, and indissoluble friendship.

(9.) And lastly, Let the removal of the excellent of the earth, in the flower or prime of their days, and in the meridian of their usefulness, quicken us to importunate and incessant prayer that

GOD would pour out his spirit upon such of his servants as remain, and upon our rising ministry, and rising generation. The residue of the spirit is with GOD, and it is a residue copious enough to qualify and consecrate such as survive, or such as are entering into life, and service, with as eminent gifts and as eminent graces as those who are gone before us. O for the spirit of the ascending Elijahs, to rest upon our young Elishas! *The harvest truly is great, but the labourers are few;* let us earnestly and incessantly beseech *the* LORD *of the harvest that he would send forth labourers into his harvest.* Matt. ix. 37, 38. O that GOD would kindle by his Almighty breath, and a rich unction from himself, bright and burning lamps, to fill up the places of those which are removed from his sanctuary below, to shine in his temple above! Let the death of such an eminent servant of CHRIST as Mr. *Davies,* in the prime of his age, and in the height of his usefulness, excite us to importunate and abundant prayer that GOD would be pleased, in compassion to our world, to raise up like instruments of his glory, both in our land and wherever his name is known, or there are any opportunities to preach his gospel! O for the descent of a double portion of the spirit upon surviving ministers, and upon all other nurseries of religion and learning at home and abroad! " Where is the LORD GOD of Elijah?" He lives, he is still with us, though Elijah is gone. To him therefore let us look, to him let us pray with holy importunity and zeal, that the time, even the set time to favour his Zion, may come. Let but the LORD " give the word, and pour out of his spirit, and great shall be the number of those that publish it." Psal. lxviii. 11. " Let him but *clothe his priests with salvation, and his people shall shout aloud for joy."* Psal. cxxxii. 16.

And thus have I endeavoured, from various considerations, to resolve this problem in providence, " Why the excellent of the earth should be taken away in the flower or prime of their age, and from the most enlarged spheres of usefulness, or what instruction and improvement we may gather from such seemingly unkind and undesirable dispensations." I pretend not to assign all the reasons of such a conduct in Deity, in that " GOD, who works all things after the counsel of his own will," but yet possibly I may have assigned some, and some such as may convince us that even these afflictive, and perhaps frequently supposed impenetrable proceedings, are not without evident traces of the divine wisdom, righteousness, and mercy upon them to a duly observing eye, so that we may not only as the voice of faith, but as the confession of experience say, *I know, O* LORD, *that thy judgments are right, and that thou in faithfulness hast afflicted me.* Psal. cxix. 75.

to be the Operations of Wisdom.

I shall only add, that whether we can or cannot investigate the motives in the counsels of a holy, wise, and merciful GOD, why such providences should take place as the removal of the excellent of the earth in the flower or prime of their days, and in the height of their usefulness; yet two things methinks are indispensible duties upon us in such dispensations, congratulation and submission, congratulation that our pious friends are gone to a better world; for as one says, " Was not self-love too predominant, and our faith of invisible realities too weak, we should rejoice at a pious relative (or friend's) admission into the society of the blessed. We congratulate them on some petty advantage, gained in this low state of being, and we mourn their advancement to the highest degree of honour and felicity, because out of our ken!—Such aukward and preposterous creatures are we."

The other duty is submission—submission to the high and holy, though awful will of Heaven. Patience has its hour of exertion and effulgence in the darkness of providence, and the season of our greatest trials. " Father, not my will, but thine be done," how glorious, how pleasant to hear from a soul under the pressures of the sorest afflictions! I have often thought of the noble speech of the Archbishop of Cambray, who, when he heard the news of the Duke of Burgundy's death, to whom he had been preceptor, and for whom he had the most tender affection, burst into tears, but yet presently said, " If I knew that by the turn of a straw I could recover him to life, and yet at the same time was assured that it was contrary to the will of GOD, I would not do it."—O for a complacent acquiescence in the divine disposals! O for the meek and cheerful surrender of our wills to the will of our GOD! May this be our experience till faith is turned into sight, and hope and patience shall be swallowed up in boundless and everlasting fruition and joy.

CHARACTER

OF THE

AUTHOR.

By the Rev. DAVID BOSTWICK, M. A.
OF NEW-YORK.

"IT will doubtless be acknowledged on all hands, that a decent respect, and a proportionable tribute of honour are due to the memory of those deceased, whom the God of Nature and Grace had furnished with every valuable endowment, and in his providence had advanced to an extensive sphere of usefulness while they lived: And that this was eminently the case of my reverened friend and brother, no one, who had the happiness of his personal acquaintance, or could rely on the testimony of universal fame, will pretend to dispute.

"I am, however, truly sensible that to exhibit a just portraiture of President Davies, and draw the lineament of his amiable character, is a task too arduous for me, and would require a genius not inferior to his own; but however, the friendship with which he was pleased to honour me, the esteem and veneration I had for him while he lived, with the just sense I still entertain of his uncommon worth, unitedly demand the present exertion of my feeble attempts, especially as his death has taken place in the intervening time between the preaching of the following Discourse, and its publication, which was committed to my care.

"Mr. Davies was a man of such uncommon furniture, both of gifts and grace, and adorned with such an assemblage of amiable and useful qualities, and each shining with such distinguished lustre, that it is truly hard to say in which he most excelled, and equally hard to mention one valuable or useful accomplishment in which he did not excel. A large and capacious understanding—a solid, unbiassed, and well-regulated judgment—a quick apprehension—a genius truly penetrating—a fruitful invention—an elegant taste,—were all happily united in him, and constituted a real greatness of mind, which never failed to strike every observer with an agreeable surprise.

" To this extraordinary natural capacity were added the improvements of a learned and polite education, which, though in the early years of his study it was embarrassed with many peculiar disadvantages, yet by the strength of his genius, and dint of indefatigable application, was cultivated to such a degree of elegance and refinement, that attracted the notice and admiration of all the friends of science wherever he was known.

" And as the powers of his mind were enriched with every valuable human accomplishment, so they were eminently improved by the influence and efficacy of sanctifying grace; in consequence of which they were all sincerely devoted to the service of God, and the good of mankind. In the early stages of his life, it pleased a Sovereign God to call him effectually from his natural alienation to the knowledge and love of himself, to take a powerful possession of his heart, and seize all the faculties of his active and capacious soul for his service. Upon finishing therefore the course of his preparatory studies, he entered into the sacred employment of the gospel-ministry, and solemnly dedicated himself with all his superior talents to the work of the sanctuary.

" In the exercise of this sacred office, his fervant zeal and undissembled piety, his popular talents and engaging methods of address, soon acquired him a distinguished character, and general admiration. Scarce was he known as a public preacher but he was sent, on the earnest application of the people, to some of the distant settlements of Virginia, where many of the inhabitants, in respect of religion, were but a small remove from the darkness and ignorance of uncultivated heathenism, and where the religion of Jesus, which he endeavoured to propagate, had to encounter with all the blindness, prejudice, and enmity, that are natural to the heart of the most depraved sinner. Yet under all apparent disadvantages, his labours were attended with such remarkable success, that all opposition quitted the unequal combat, and gave way to the powerful energy of the divine spirit, which was graciously pleased by his ministry to add many new subjects to the spiritual kingdom of our glorious Immanuel.

" The work of the ministry was Mr. Davies's great delight; and for it he was admirably furnished with every valuable qualification of nature and grace. Divinity was a favourite study, in which he made a proficiency uncommon for his years, and yet he generally preferred the most necessary and practical branches of it to the dark mazes of endless controversy and intricate disputes; aiming chiefly at the conversion of sinners, and to change the hearts and lives of men by an affecting representation of the plain, but moſt important, intereſting truths of the law and the goſpel. His talent at compoſition, eſpecially for the pulpit, was equalled by few, and perhaps exceeded by none. His taſte was judicious, elegant, and polite, and yet his diſcourſes were plain and pungent, peculiarly adapted to pierce the conſcience and affect the heart. His diction was ſurpaſſingly beautiful and comprehenſive, tending to make the moſt ſtupid hearer ſenſibly feel, as well as clearly underſtand. Sublimity and elegance, plainneſs and perſpicuity, and all the force and energy that the language of mortals could convey, were the ingredients of al‑moſt every compoſition. His manner of delivery, as to pro‑nunciation, geſture, and modulation of voice, ſeemed to be a perfect model of the moſt moving and ſtriking oratory.

"Whenever he aſcended the ſacred deſk, he ſeemed to have not only the attention, but all the various paſſions of his auditory entirely at his command. And as his perſonal appearance was auguſt and venerable, yet benevolent and mild, ſo he could ſpeak with the moſt commanding authority, or melting tenderneſs, according to the variation of his ſubject. With what majeſty and grandeur, with what energy and ſtriking ſolemnity, with what powerful and almoſt irreſiſtible eloquence would he il‑luſtrate the truths, and inculcate the duties of chriſtianity! Mount Sinai ſeemed to thunder from his lips, when he de‑nounced the tremendous curſes of the law, and ſounded the dreadful alarm to guilty, ſecure impenitent ſinners. The ſo‑lemn ſcenes of the laſt judgment ſeemed to riſe in view, when he arraigned, tried, and convicted ſelf‑deceivers, and formal hypocrites. And how did the balm of Gilead diſtil from his lips, when he exhibited a bleeding dying Saviour to ſinful mortals, as a ſovereign remedy for the wounded heart, and anguiſhed conſcience! In a word, whatever ſubject he undertook, per‑ſuaſive eloquence dwelt upon his tongue; and his audience was all attention. He ſpoke as on the borders of eternity, and as viewing the glories and terrors of an unſeen world, and con‑veyed the moſt grand and affecting ideas of theſe important realities; realities which he then firmly believed, and which he now ſees in the cleareſt light of intuitive demonſtration.

"The unuſual luſtre with which he ſhone could not long be confined to that remote corner of the world, but ſoon attracted the notice and pleaſing admiration of men of genius, or piety, far and near; and therefore, on a vacancy at the college of New‑Jerſey, occaſioned by the deceaſe of two former Preſidents*, in

---

* The Rev. Mr. Aaron Burr, in 1757, and the Rev. Mr. Jonathan Edwards, who ſucceeded him, and died the winter following.

a close and awful succeffion, he was elected to that important office in the year 1759.

"Diftreffing as it was both to him and his people, united in the ftrongeft bonds of mutual affection, to think of a feparation, yet a conviction of abfolute duty, refulting from the importance of the ftation, from the various concurring providences, and laftly, from the unanimous advice of his reverend brethren convened in fynod, determined him to accept the propofal. Great and pleafing were the expectations with which we beheld him enter into that exalted fphere of fervice, yet I may boldly fay that they were vaftly exceeded in every refpect by the reputable manner in which he difcharged the arduous truft. The progrefs he made in all the branches of fcience, with his capacity and diligence to acquire new improvements, enabled him to conduct the youth with great advantage through the feveral ftages of ufeful and polite literature. And, while he endeavoured to improve the minds, he was not lefs folicitous to reform the hearts and lives of his pupils, to make them good as well as great, and fit them for both worlds. He knew that religion was the brighteft ornament of the human, and the faireft image of the divine nature, that all true benevolence to men muft have its foundation laid in a fupreme love to God, and that undiffembled piety in the heart was the beft fecurity for ufefulnefs in every character of life. It was therefore his conftant endeavour to promote the eternal as well as the temporal good of the youth intrufted to his tuition, not only by his fervent preaching and exemplary life, but by inculcating at the proper feafons the worth of their fouls, and the vaft, the inexpreffible importance of their everlafting interefts.

"In the government of the college, he had the peculiar art of mingling authority and lenity in fuch a due proportion, as feldom or never failed of the defired fuccefs. Hence he was revered and loved by every member of that collected family over which he prefided. His performances at public anniverfary commencements, as they never failed to do honour to the inftitution, fo they always furprifed his friends themfelves by exceeding, far exceeding their moft fanguine expectations. His poetical compofitions, and his elegant tafte for cultivating the Mufes, gave additional embellifhments to thofe performances, and greatly heightened the pleafure of his crowded auditors.

"His acquaintance with mankind, his eafy and polite behaviour, his affability and condefcenfion, his modefty and candor, his engaging manner of addrefs, with his fprightly and entertaining converfation, all the genuine fruits of the moft benevolent heart, rendered him greatly beloved through the large circle of his acquaintance, and as greatly admired even by ftrangers, whose occasional excursions gave them only the opportunity of a transient interview.

"His natural temper, amiable in itself, and sweetened with all the charms of divine grace, rendered him peculiarly dear in all the relative characters of social life, whether as an husband, a father, a tutor, or a friend.

"With this excellent man at the head of the college, what pleasing prospects did we form of the extensive usefulness of that infant seminary, both to the church and to the commonwealth! He was, in short, all we could wish or desire in a man, to promote the valuable interests of learning and piety, and render the college reputable and useful.

"But, alas! all his ample furniture of gifts and graces, all the amiable qualities of the mind, with the advantages of the happiest constitution of body, could not secure him from the fate of mortals. He is gone; he has quitted this inferior world amidst the unfeigned sorrows of his family, his friends, the college, and our country: he has taken his flight to his native skies, and joined with kindred spirits in the regions of a glorious immortality, while his remains are gathered to those of his predecessors, in the dark and dreary repository of the grave.

"O the unutterable and extensive loss to a distressed family, to a bereaved college, to the ministry, to the church, to the community, to the republic of letters, and in short to all the valuable interests of mankind!"

SERMON I.

The divine Authority and Sufficiency of the Christian Religion.

LUKE xvi. 27—31. *Then he said, I pray thee therefore, father, that thou wouldest send him to my father's house, for I have five brethren, that he may testify unto them, left they alfo come into this place of torment. Abraham faith unto him, They have Mofes and the prophets; let them hear them. And he said, Nay, father Abraham, but if one went unto them from the dead, they would repent. And he said unto him, If they hear not Mofes and the prophets, neither will they be perfuaded, though one rofe from the dead.*

WHAT Micah said fuperftitioufly, when he was robbed of his idols, *ye have taken away my gods ; and what have I more?* (Judg. xviii. 24.) may be truly fpoken with regard to the religion of Jefus, If that be taken from us, what have we more? *If the foundations be deftroyed, what fhall the righteous do?* Pfal. xi. 3. The generality of you owe all your hopes of a glorious immortality to this heaven-born religion, and you make it the rule of your faith and practice ; confident that in fo doing you pleafe God.

But what if after all you fhould be miftaken? What if the religion of Jefus fhould be an impofture?—I know you are ftruck with horror at the thought, and perhaps alarmed at my making fo fhocking a fuppofition. But this fufpicion, horrid as it is, has probably been fuggefted to you at times by infernal agency ; this fufpicion may at times have rifen in your minds in their wanton and licentious excurfions, or from the falfe alarms of a melancholy and timorous imagination : and if this fufpicion has never been raifed in you by the fophiftical converfation of loofe wits and affected rationalifts, it has been owing to your happy retirement from the polite world, where infidelity makes extenfive conquefts, under the fpecious name of Deifm. Since therefore you are fubject to an affault from fuch a fufpicion, when you may not be armed ready to repel it, let me this day ftart it from its ambufh, that I may try the force of a few arguments upon it, and furnifh you with weapons to conquer it.

Let me also tell you, that *that* faith in the christian religion which proceeds from insufficient or bad principles, is but little better than infidelity.. If you believe the christian religion to be divine, because you hardly care whether it be true or false, being utterly unconcerned about religion in any shape, and therefore never examining the matter;—If you believe it true, because you have been educated in it; because your parents or ministers have told you so; or because it is the religion of your country; if these are the only grounds of your faith, it is not such a faith as constitutes you true christians; for upon the very same grounds you would have been Mahometans in Turkey, disciples of Confucius in China, or worshippers of the devil among the Indians, if it had been your unhappy lot to be born in those countries: for a Mahometan, or a Chinese, or an Indian, can assign these grounds for his faith. Surely, I need not tell you, that the grounds of a mistaken belief in an imposture, are not a sufficient foundation for a saving faith in a divine revelation. I am afraid there are many such implicit believers among us, who are in the right only by chance: and these lie a prey to every temptation, and may be turned out of the way of truth by every wind of doctrine. It is therefore necessary to teach them the grounds of the christian religion, both to prevent their seduction, and to give them a rational and well-grounded faith, instead of that which is only blind and accidental.

Nay, such of us as have the clearest conviction of this important truth, had need to have it inculcated upon us, that we may be more and more impressed with it; for the influence of christianity upon our hearts and lives will be proportioned to the realizing, affecting persuasion of its truth and certainty in our understandings.

If I can prove that christianity answers all the ends of a religion from God;—if I can prove that it is attended with sufficient attestations;—if I can prove that no sufficient objections can be offered against it;—and that men have no reason at all to desire another; but that if this proves ineffectual for their reformation and salvation, there is no ground to hope that any other would prove successful:—I say, if I can prove these things, then the point in debate is carried, and we must all embrace the religion of Jesus as certainly true.—These things are asserted or implied in my text, with respect to the scriptures then extant, *Moses and the prophets.*

My text is a parabolical dialogue between *Abraham* and one of his wretched posterity, once rioting in the luxuries of high life, but now tormented in infernal flames.

We read of his brethren in his father's house. Among these probably his estate was divided upon his decease; from whence we may infer that he had no children; for had he had any, it would have been more natural to reprefent him as folicitous for their reformation by a meffenger from the dead, than for that of his brothers. He feems therefore, like fome of our unhappy modern rakes, juft to have come to his eftate, and to have abandoned himfelf to fuch a courfe of debaucheries as foon fhattered his conftitution, and brought him down to the grave, and alas! to hell, in the bloom of life, when they were far from his thoughts. May this be a warning to all of his age and circumftances!

Whether, from fome remaining affection to his brethren, or (which is more likely) from a fear that they who had fhared with him in fin would increafe his torment, fhould they defcend to him in the infernal prifon, he is folicitous that Lazarus might be fent as an apoftle from the dead to warn them. His petition is to this purpofe: " Since no requeft in my own favour can be granted; fince I cannot obtain the poor favour of a drop of water to cool my flaming tongue, let me at leaft make one requeft in behalf of thofe that are as yet in the land of hope, and not beyond the reach of mercy. In my father's houfe I have five brethren, gay, thoughtlefs, young creatures, who are now rioting in thofe riches I was forced to leave, who interred my mouldering corpfe in ftate, little apprehenfive of the doom of my immortal part; who are now treading the fame enchanting paths of pleafure I walked in; and will, unlefs reclaimed, foon defcend, like me, thoughtlefs and unprepared, into thefe doleful regions: I therefore pray, that thou wouldeft fend Lazarus to alarm them in their wild career, with an account of my dreadful doom, and inform them of the reality and importance of everlafting happinefs and mifery, that they may reform, and fo avoid this place of torment, whence I can never efcape."

Abraham's anfwer may be thus paraphrafed: " If thy brothers perifh, it will not be for want of means; they enjoy the facred fcriptures of the Old Teftament, written by *Mofes and the prophets;* and thefe are fufficient to inform them of the neceffary truths to regulate their practice, and particularly to warn them of everlafting punifhment! Let them therefore hear and regard, ftudy and obey, thofe writings; for they need no further means for their falvation."

To this the wretched creature replies, "Nay, father Abraham, thefe means will not avail; I enjoyed them all; and yet here I am, a loft foul; and I am afraid they will have as little effect upon them as they had upon me. Thefe means are common and familiar, and therefore difregarded. But if one arofe from the dead; if an apoftle from the invifible world was fent to them, to declare as an eye-witnefs the great things he has feen, surely they would repent. The novelty and terror of the apparition would alarm them. Their senses would be struck with so unusual a messenger, and they would be convinced of the reality of eternal things; therefore I must renew my request; send Lazarus to them in all the pomp of heavenly splendor; Lazarus whom they once knew in so abject a condition, and whom they will therefore the more regard, when they see him appear in all his present glory."

Thus the miserable creature pleads (and it is natural for us to wish for other means, when those we have enjoyed are ineffectual, though it should be through our own neglect); but, alas! he pleads in vain.

Abraham continues inexorable, and gives a very good reason for his denial: "If they pay no regard to the writings of *Moses and the prophets*, the standing revelation God has left in his church, it would be to no purpose to give them another: they would not be persuaded though one rose from the dead; the same disposition that renders them deaf to such messengers as *Moses and the prophets*, would also render them impersuasible by a messenger from the dead. Such a one might strike them with a panic, but it would soon be over, and then they would return to their usual round of pleasures; they would presently think the apparition was but the creature of their own imagination, or some unaccountable illusion of their senses. If one arose from the dead, he could but declare the same things substantially with *Moses and the prophets;* and he could not speak with greater authority, or give better credentials than they; and therefore they who are not benefited by these standing means, must be given up as desperate; and God, for very good reasons, will not multiply new revelations to them."

This answer of Abraham was exemplified when another Lazarus was raised from the dead in the very sight of the Jews, and Christ burst the bands of death, and gave them incontestible evidences of his resurrection; and yet after all they were not persuaded, but persisted in invincible infidelity.

This parable was spoken before any part of the New Testament was written, and added to the sacred canon; and if it might be then asserted, that the standing revelation of God's will was sufficient, and that it was needless to demand farther, then much more may it be asserted now, when the canon of the scriptures is completed, and we have received so much additional light from the New Testament. We have not only *Moses and the prophets*, but we have also Christ, who is a messenger from the dead, and his apostles; and therefore, surely "if we do not hear them, neither would we be persuaded, though one arose from the dead." The gospel is the last effort of the grace of God with a guilty world; and if this has no effect upon us, our difeafe is incurable that refufes to be healed.

I cannot infift upon all the important truths contained in this copious text, but only defign,

I. To fhew the fufficiency of the ftanding revelation of God's will in the fcriptures, to bring men to repentance; and,

II. To expofe the vanity and unreafonablenefs of the objections againft this revelation, and of demanding another.

I. I am to fhew the fufficiency of the ftanding revelation in the fcriptures to bring men to repentance.

If the fcriptures give us fufficient inftructions in matters of faith, and fufficient directions in matters of practice,—if they are attended with fufficient evidences for our faith,—and produce fufficient excitements to influence our practice, then they contain a fufficient revelation; for it is for thefe purpofes we need a revelation, and a revelation that anfwers thefe purpofes has the directeft tendency to make us truly religious, and bring us to an happy immortality. But that the revelation in the fcriptures (particularly in the New Teftament, which I fhall more immediately confider as being the immediate foundation of Chriftianity) is fufficient for all thefe purpofes, will be evident from an induction of particulars.

1. The fcriptures give us fufficient inftructions what we fhould believe, or are a fufficient rule of faith.

Religion cannot fubfift without right notions of God and divine things; and entire ignorance or miftakes in its fundamental articles, muft be deftructive of its nature; and therefore a divine revelation muft be a collection of rays of light, a fyftem of divine knowledge;—and fuch we find the chriftian revelation to be, as contained in the facred writings.

In the fcriptures we find the faint difcoveries of natural reafon illuftrated, its uncertain conjectures determined, and its miftakes corrected; fo that chriftianity includes natural religion in the greateft perfection. But it does not reft here; it brings to light things which *eye hath not feen, nor ear heard, neither the heart of man conceived*, 1 Corin. ii. 9,—things, which our feeble reafon could never have difcovered without the help of a fupernatural revelation; and which yet are of the utmoft importance for us to know.

In the fcriptures we have the cleareft and moft majeftic account of the nature and perfections of the Deity, and of his being the Creator, Ruler, and Benefactor of the univerfe; to whom therefore all reafonable beings are under infinite obligations.

In the fcriptures we have an account of the prefent ftate of human nature, as degenerate, and a more rational and eafy account of its apoſtacy, than could ever be given by the light of nature.

In the ſcriptures too (which wound but to cure) we have the welcome account of a method of recovery from the ruins of our apoſtacy, through the mediation of the Son of God; there we have the aſſurance which we could find no where elſe, that God is reconcileable, and willing to pardon penitens upon the account of the obedience and ſufferings of Chriſt. There all our anxious enquiries, *Wherewith ſhall I come before the Lord? or bow myſelf before the moſt high God? ſhall I come before him with burnt-offerings?* &c. Micah vi. 6, 7, are ſatisfactorily anſwered; and there the agonizing conſcience can obtain relief, which might have ſought it in vain among all the other religions in the world.

In the ſcriptures alſo, eternity and the inviſible worlds are laid open to our view; and " life and immortality are brought to light by the goſpel;" about which the heathen ſages, after all their enquiries, laboured under uneaſy ſuſpicions. There we are aſſured of the ſtate of future rewards and puniſhments, according to our conduct in this ſtate of probation; and the nature, perfection, and duration of the happineſs and miſery, are deſcribed with as much accuracy as are neceſſary to engage us to ſeek the one and ſhun the other.

I particularize theſe doctrines of Chriſtianity as a ſpecimen, or as ſo many general heads, to which many others may be reduced; not intending a complete enumeration, which would lead me far beyond the bounds of one ſermon; and for which my whole life is not ſufficient. I therefore proceed to add,

2. The holy ſcriptures give us complete directions in matters of practice, or are a ſufficient rule of life.

A divine revelation muſt not be calculated merely to amuſe us, and gratify our curioſity with ſublime and refined notions and ſpeculations, but adapted to direct and regulate our practice, and render us better as well as wiſer.

Accordingly, the ſacred writings give us a complete ſyſtem of practical religion and morality. There, not only all the duties of natural religion are inculcated, but ſeveral important duties; as love to our enemies, humility, &c. are clearly diſcovered; which the feeble light of reaſon in the heathen moraliſts did either not perceive at all, or but very faintly. In ſhort, there we are informed of our duties towards God, towards our neighbours, and towards ourſelves. The ſcriptures are full of particular injunctions and directions to particular duties, left we ſhould not be ſagacious enough to infer them from general rules; and ſometimes all theſe duties are ſummed up in ſome ſhort maxim, or general rule; which we may eaſily remember, and always carry about with us. Such a noble summary is that which Christ has given us of the whole moral law ; " Thou shalt love the Lord thy God with all thy heart, &c. and thy neighbour as thyself." Or that all-comprehending rule of our conduct towards one another, " Whatsoever ye would that men should do unto you, do ye the same unto them."

What recommends these doctrinal instructions and practical directions is, that they are plain and obvious to common sense. It is as much the concern of the illiterate and vulgar to be religious, as of the few endowed with an exalted and philosophic genius ; and consequently, whatever difficulties may be in a revelation to exercise the latter, yet all necessary matters of faith and practice must be delivered in a plain manner, level to the capacities of the former ; otherwise it would be no revelation at all to them who stand in most need of it. Accordingly the religion of Jesus, though it has mysteries equal and infinitely superior to the largest capacity, yet in its necessary articles is intelligible to all ranks who apply themselves with proper diligence to the perusal of them : and I dare affirm, that a man of common sense, with the assistance of the sacred scriptures, can form a better system of religion and morality than the wisest philosopher, with all his abilities and learning, can form without this help. This I dare affirm, because it has been put to trial, and attested by mater of fact ; for whoever is acquainted with the writings of the ancient heathen philosophers, cannot but be convinced, that, amidst all their learning and study, amidst all their shining thoughts and refined speculations, they had not such just notions of God and his perfections, of the most acceptable way of worshipping him, of the duties of morality, and of a future state, as any common christian among us has learned from the scriptures, without any uncommon natural parts, without extensive learning, and without such painful study and close application as the heathen moralists were forced to use to make their less perfect discoveries. In this sense the least in the kingdom of heaven, *i. e.* any common christian, is greater than all the Socrateses, the Platos, the Ciceros, and the Senecas of antiquity ; as one that is of a weak sight can see more clearly by the help of day-light, than the clearest eye can without it.

And by whom was this vast treasure of knowledge laid up to enrich the world ? by whom were these matchless writings composed, which furnish us with a system of religion and morality so much more plain, so much more perfect, than all the famous sages of antiquity could frame ? Why, to our astonishment, they were composed by a company of fishermen, or persons not much superior ; by persons generally without any liberal education ; persons who had not devoted their lives to intellectual improvement ; persons of no extraordinary natural parts, and who had not travelled, like the ancient philofophers, to gather up fragments of knowledge in different countries, but who lived in Judea, a country where learning was but little cultivated, in comparifon of Greece and Rome. Thefe were the moſt accompliſhed teachers of mankind that ever appeared in the world. And can this be accounted for, without acknowledging their infpiration from heaven? If human reafon could have made fuch difcoveries, furely it would have made them by thofe in whom it was improved to the greateſt perfection, and not by a company of ignorant mechanics.

The perfons themfelves declare that they had not made thefe difcoveries, but were taught them immediately from heaven (which indeed we muſt have believed, though they had not told us fo.)—Now we muſt believe their declaration, and own them infpired, or fall into this abfurdity, That a company of illiterate, wicked, and daring impoſtors, who were hardy enough to pretend themfelves commiſſioned and infpired from God, have furniſhed us with an incomparable more excellent fyſtem of religion and virtue, than could be furniſhed by all the wifeſt and beſt of the fons of men befide; and he that can believe this may believe any thing; and fhould never more pretend that he cannot believe the chriſtian religion upon the account of the difficulties that attend it.

I have touched but fuperficially upon the fufficiency of the fcriptures as a rule of faith and practice; for to dwell long upon this, would be to fight without an antagoniſt. Our infidels reject the chriſtian religion, becaufe they fuppofe it requires them to believe and practife too much, rather than too little. Hence they are for lopping off a great part of its doctrines and precepts, as fuperfluities, or incumbrances, and forming a meagre fkeleton of natural religion. Their intellectual pride will not ſtoop to believe doctrines which they cannot comprehend; and they cannot bear fuch narrow bounds as the precepts of chriſtianity fixes for them in their purfuits of pleafure, and therefore they would break thefe bands afunder. That which they affect moſt to complain of, is the want of evidence to convince them of the truth of this ungrateful religion; it will therefore be neceſſary to prove more largely, that,

3. The fcriptures are attended with fufficient evidences of their truth and divinity.

It is certain that as God can accept no other worſhip than rational from reafonable creatures, he cannot require us to believe a revelation to be divine without fufficient reafon; and therefore, when he gives us a revelation, he will atteſt it with fuch evidences as will be a fufficient foundation of our belief.

Accordingly, the fcriptures are atteſted with all the evidences, intrinfic and extrinfic, which we can reafonably defire, and with all the evidences the nature of the thing will admit.

As for intrinſic evidences, many might be mentioned; but I muſt at preſent confine myſelf in proper limits. I ſhall reſume the one I have already hinted at, namely, that the religion of the Bible has the directeſt tendency to promote true piety and ſolid virtue in the world; it is ſuch a religion as becomes a God to reveal; ſuch a religion as we might expect from him, in caſe he inſtituted any; a religion intended and adapted to regulate ſelf-love, and, to diffuſe the love of God and man through the world, the only generous principles and vigorous ſprings of a ſuitable conduct towards God, towards one another, and towards ourſelves; a religion productive of every humane, ſocial, and divine virtue, and directly calculated to baniſh all ſin out of the world; to tranſform impiety into devotion; injuſtice and oppreſſion into equity and univerſal benevolence; and ſenſuality into ſobriety: a religion infinitely preferable to any that has been contrived by the wiſeſt and beſt of mortals. And whence do ye think could this godlike religion proceed? does not its nature prove its origin divine? does it not evidently bear the lineaments of its heavenly parent? can you once imagine that ſuch a pure, ſuch a holy, ſuch a perfect ſyſtem, could be the contrivance of wicked infernal ſpirits, of ſelfiſh, artful prieſts, or politicians, or of a parcel of daring impoſtors, or wild enthuſiaſts? Could theſe contrive a religion ſo contrary to their inclination, ſo deſtructive of their intereſt, and ſo directly conducing to promote the cauſe they abhor? If you can believe this, you may alſo believe that light is the product of darkneſs, virtue of vice, good of evil, &c.—If ſuch beings as theſe had contrived a religion, it would have borne the ſame appearance in the Bible as it does in Italy or Spain, where it is degenerated into a mere trade, for the benefit of tyrannical and voracious prieſts; or it would have been ſuch a religion as that of Mahomet, allowing its ſubjects to propagate it with the ſword, that they might enrich themſelves with the plunder of conquered nations; and indulging them in the gratification of their luſts, particularly in polygamy, or the unbounded enjoyment of women. This religion, I fear, would ſuit the taſte of our licentious free-thinkers much better than the holy religion of Jeſus. Or if we ſhould ſuppoſe chriſtianity to be the contrivance of viſionary enthuſiaſts, then it would not be that rational ſyſtem which it is, but a huddle of fanatical reveries and ridiculous whims. If, then, it could not be the contrivance of ſuch authors as theſe, to whom ſhall we aſcribe it? it muſt have had ſome author: for it could not come into being without a cauſe, no more than the ſyſtem of the univerſe. Will you then aſcribe it to good men? But theſe men were either inſpired from heaven, or they were not; if they were not, then they could not be good men, but moſt audacious liars; for they plainly declared, they were divinely infpired, and ftood in it to the laft; which no good man would do, if fuch a declaration was falfe. If they were infpired from heaven, then the point is gained; then chriftianity is a religion from God; for to receive a religion from perfons divinely infpired, and to receive it from God, is the fame thing.

Another intrinfic evidence is that of prophecy.

Thofe future events which are contingent, or which fhall be accomplifhed by caufes that do not now exift or appear, cannot be certainly foreknown or foretold by man, as we find by our own experience. Such objects fall within the compafs of omnifcience only; and therefore when fhort-fighted mortals are enabled to predict fuch events many years, and even ages before they happen, it is a certain evidence that they are let into the fecrets of heaven, and that God communicates to them a knowledge which cannot be acquired by the moft fagacious human mind; and this is an evidence that the perfons thus divinely taught are the meffengers of God, to declare his will to the world.

Now there are numberlefs inftances of fuch prophecies in the facred writings. Thus a prophet foretold the deftruction of Jeroboam's alter by the good Jofiah, many ages before 1 *Kings* xiii. 2. Cyrus was foretold by name as the reftorer of the Jews from Babylon, to re-build their temple and city, about an hundred years before he was born. *Ifaiah* xlv. 1, &c.—Several of the prophets foretold the deftruction of various kingdoms in a very punctual manner, as of Jerufalem, Babylon, Egypt, Nineveh, &c. which prediction was exactly fulfilled. But the moft remarkable prophecies of the Old Teftament are thofe relating to the Meffiah; which are fo numerous and full, that they might ferve for materials of his hiftory; they fix the time of his coming, *viz.* while the fceptre continued in Judah, *Gen.* xlix. 10, while the fecond temple was yet ftanding, *Hag.* ii. 7, *Mal.* iii. 2, and towards the clofe of Daniel's feventy weeks of years, *i. e.* four hundred and ninety years from the re-building of Jerufalem. *Dan.* ix. 24, &c.—Thefe prophecies alfo defcribe the lineage of the Meffiah, the manner of his conception, his life and miracles, his death, and the various circumftances of it; his burial, refurrection, afcenfion, and advancement to univerfal empire, and the fpread of the gofpel through the world. In the New Teftament alfo we meet with fundry remarkable prophecies. There Chrift foretels his own death, and the manner of it, and his triumphant refurrection; there, with furprifing accuracy, he predicts the deftruction of Jerufalem by the Romans. We find various prophecies alfo in the apoftolic epiftles, particularly that of St. Paul, *Rom.* xi. concerning the converfion of the Jews; which, though it be not yet accomplifhed, yet we fee a remarkable providence making way for it, in keeping the Jews, who are fcattered over all the earth, distinct from all other nations for about one thousand seven hundred years, though they are hated of all nations, and consequently under the strongest temptation to coalesce with, and lose themselves among them; and though all other nations have in a much shorter time mixed in such a manner, that none of them can now trace their own original; *e. g.* Who can now distinguish the posterity of the ancient Romans from the Goths and Vandals, and others that broke in upon their empire and settled among them; or of the ancient Angli from the Danes, &c. that mingled with them?

These and many other plain predictions are interspersed through the scriptures, and prove their original to be from the Father of lights, who alone knows all his works from the beginning, and who declares such distant contingent futurities from ancient times. *Isaiah* xlv. 21.

I might, as another intrinsic evidence of the truth of christianity, mention its glorious energy on the minds of men, in convincing them of sin, easing their consciences, inspiring them with unspeakable joy, subduing their lusts, and transforming them into its own likeness; which is attested by the daily experience of every true Christian. Every one that believeth hath this witness in himself: and this is an evidence level to the meanest capacity, which may be soon lost in a course of sublime reasoning. But as the Deists declare, alas! with too much truth, that the gospel hath no such power upon them, it is not to my purpose to insist upon it. I therefore proceed to mention some of

The *extrinsic* evidences of the religion of Jesus, particularly the miracles with which it was confirmed, and its early propagation through the world.

Miracles of this case are events above or contrary to the established law of nature, done with a professed design to attest a revelation; and as they are obvious and striking to the senses of the most ignorant and unthinking, they are the most popular and convictive evidences, adapted to the capacities of the generality of mankind, who are incapable of a long train of argumentation, or of perceiving the origin of a religion from its nature and tendency.

Now the religion of Jesus is abundantly attested with this kind of evidence. The history of the life of Jesus, and his apostles, is one continued series of miracles. Sight was restored to the blind, the deaf were enabled to hear, the lame to walk, the maimed furnished with new-created limbs, the sick healed, the rage of winds and seas controled, yea, the dead were raised; and all this with an air of sovereignty, such as became a God; the apostles were also endowed with miraculous powers, enabled to speak with tongues, and communicate the Holy Spirit to others. These miracles were done not in a corner, but in the most public places, before numerous spectators, friends and foes; and the persons that wrought them appealed to them as the evidences of their divine mission; and the account of them is conveyed down to us by the best medium, written tradition, in a history that bears all the evidences of credibility, of which any composure of that kind is capable.

Another extrinsic evidence of the truth of christianity is its extensive propagation through the world in the most unpromising circumstances.

The only religion, besides the Christian, which has had any very considerable spread in the world; is that of Mahomet; but we may easily account for this, without supposing it divine, from its nature, as indulging the lusts of men; and especially from the manner of its propagation, not by the force of evidence, but by the force of arms. But the circumstances of the propagation of christianity were quite otherwise, whether we consider its contrariety to the corruptions, prejudices, and interests of men;—the easiness of detecting it, had it been false;—the violent opposition it met with from all the powers of the earth;—the instruments of its propagation;—or the measures they took for that purpose.

Christianity was directly contrary to the corruptions, prejudices, and interests of mankind. It grants no indulgence to the corrupt propensions of a degenerate world: but requires that universal holiness of heart and life which, as we find by daily observation, is so ungrateful to them; and which is the principal reason that the religion of Jesus meets with so much contempt and opposition in every age.

When christianity was first propagated, all nations had been educated in some other religion; the Jews were attached to Moses, and the Gentiles to their various systems of heathenism; and were all of them very zealous for their own religion: but christianity proposed a new scheme, and could not take place without antiquating or exploding all other religions; and therefore it was contrary to the inveterate prejudices of all mankind; and could never have been so generally received, if it had not brought with it the most evident credentials; especially considering that some of its doctrines were such as seemed to the Jews a stumbling block, and to the Greeks foolishness; particularly that one of obscure birth and low life, who was publicly executed as a slave and malefactor, should be worshipped and honoured as God, upon pain of everlasting damnation! that there should be a resurrection of the dead: the last of which was an object of ridicule to all the wits and philosophers of the heathen world.—Again, as some religion or other was established in all nations, there were many, like Demetrius and his craftsmen, whose temporal livings and interest depended upon the continuance of their religion; and if that was changed, they fell into poverty and disgrace. There was a powerful party in every nation, and they would exert themselves to prevent the spread of an innovation so dangerous to their interest, which we find by all histories of those times they actually did.—And yet the despised religion of Jesus triumphed over all their opposition, and maintained its credit in spite of all their endeavours to detect it as an imposture; and this proves it was not an imposture; for,

In the next place, it was easy to have detected christianity as an imposture, nay, it was impossible it should not have been detected, if it had been such; for the great facts upon which the evidence of it rested, were said to be obvious and public, done before thousands, and in all countries; for wherever the apostles travelled, they carried their miraculous powers along with them. Thousands must know whether Christ had fed many thousands with provisions only sufficient for a few; whether Lazarus was raised from the dead before the admiring multitude; whether the apostles spoke with tongues to those various nations among whom they endeavoured to propagate their religion (as indeed they must have done, otherwise they would not have been understood.) These things, and many others, upon which the evidence of christianity depends, were public in their own nature; and therefore, if they had not been matters of fact, the cheat must have been unavoidably detected, especially when so many were concerned to detect it.

Farther: christianity met with the most strenuous opposition from all the powers of the earth. The Jewish rulers and most of the populace were implacable enemies; and as they lived on the spot where its miraculous attestations were said to be given, it was in their power to crush it in its birth, and never have suffered it to spread farther, had it not been attended with invincible evidence. All the power of the Roman empire was also exerted for its extirpation; and its propagators and disciples could expect no profit or pleasure by it, but were assured from the posture of affairs, from daily experience, and from the predictions of their master, that they should meet with shame, persecution, and death itself in its most tremendous shapes; and in the next world they could expect nothing, even according to their own doctrine, but everlasting damnation, if they were wilful impostors: and yet, in spite of all these discouragements, they courageously persisted in their testimony to the last, though they might have secured their lives, and helped their fortunes (as Judas did) by retracting it; nay, their testimony prevailed in defiance of all opposition; multitudes in all nations then known embraced the faith; though they expected tortures and death for it; and in a few centuries, the vast and mighty Roman empire submitted to the religion of a crucified Jesus. And who were those mighty heroes that thus triumphed over the world? Why, to our surprise,

The instruments of the propagation of Christianity were a company of poor mechanics, publicans, tent-makers, and fishermen, from the despised nation of the Jews! And by what strange powers or arts did they make these extensive conquests?

The measures they took were a plain declaration of their religion; and they wrought miracles for its confirmation. They did not use the power of the sword, no secular terrors, or bribery; they were without learning, without the arts of reasoning and persuasion; and without all the usual artifice of seducers to gain credit to their imposture.

Here I cannot but take particular notice of that matchless simplicity that appears in the history of Christ and his apostles. The evangelists write in that artless, calm, and unguarded manner, which is natural to persons confident of the undeniable truth of what they assert; they do not write with that scrupulous caution which would argue any fear that they might be confuted. They simply relate the naked facts, and leave them to stand upon their own evidence. They relate the most amazing, the most moving things, with the most cool serenity, without any passionate exclamations and warm reflections. For example, they relate the most astonishing miracles, as the resurrection of Lazarus, in the most simple, and, as it were, careless manner, without breaking out and celebrating the divine power of Christ. In the same manner they relate the most tragical circumstances of his condemnation and death, calmly mentioning matter of fact, without any invectives against the Jews, without any high eulogies upon Christ's innocence, without any rapturous celebrations of his grace in suffering all these things for sinners, and without any tender lamentations over their deceased master. It is impossible for a heart so deeply impressed with such things, as theirs undoubtedly were, to retain this dispassionate serenity, unless laid under supernatural restraints; and there appears very good reasons for this restraint upon them, viz. that the gospel history might carry intrinsic evidences of its simplicity and artless impartiality; and that it might appear adapted to convince the judgments of men, and not merely to raise their passions. In this respect, the gospel-history is distinguished from all histories in the world: and can we think so plain, so undisguised, so artless a composure, the contrivance of designing impostors?—Would not a consciousness that they might be detected keep them more upon their guard, and make them more ready to anticipate and confine objections, and take every artifice to recommend their cause, and prepossess the reader in its favour?

It only remains under this head, that I should

(4.) Shew that the religion of Jesus proposes sufficient excitements to influence our faith and practice.

To enforce a system of doctrines and precepts, two things are especially necessary,—that they should be made duty by competent authority,—and matters of interest by a sanction of rewards and punishments. To which I may add, that the excitements are still stronger, when we are laid under the gentle obligations of gratitude. In all these respects the christian religion has the most powerful enforcements.

The authority upon which we are required to receive the doctrines, and observe the precepts of christianity, is no less than the authority of GOD, the supreme Lawgiver and infallible Teacher; whose wisdom to prescribe and right to command, are indisputable; and we may safely submit our understandings to his instructions, however mysterious, and our wills to his injunctions, however difficult they may seem to us. This gives the religion of Jesus a binding authority upon the consciences of men; which is absolutely necessary to bring piety and virtue into practice in the world; for if men are left at liberty, they will follow their own inclinations, however wicked and pernicious. And in this respect christianity bears a glorious preference to all the systems of morality composed by the heathen philosophers; for though there were many good things in them, yet who gave authority to Socrates, Plato, or Seneca, to assume the province of lawgivers and dictators to mankind, and prescribe to their consciences?—All they could do was to teach, to advise, to persuade, to reason: but mankind were at liberty, after all, whether to take their advice or not. And this shews the necessity of supernatural revelation, not merely to make known things beyond human apprehension, but to enforce with proper authority such duties as might be discovered by man; since without it they would not have the binding force of a law.

As to the sanction of rewards and punishments in christianity, they are such as became a God to annex to his majestic law, such as are agreeable to creatures formed for immortality, and such as would have the most effectual tendency to encourage obedience, and prevent sin; they are no less than the most perfect happiness and misery which human nature is capable of, and that through an endless duration. If these are not sufficient to allure rational creatures to obedience, then no considerations that can be proposed can have any effect. These tend to alarm our hopes and our fears, the most vigorous springs of human activity; and if these have no effect upon us, nothing that God can reveal, or our minds conceive, will have any effect. God, by adding the greatest sanctions possible to his law, has taken the best possible precautions to prevent disobedience; and since even these do not restrain men from it, we are sure that less would not suffice.—If men will go on in sin, though they believe the punishment due to it will be eternal, then much more would they persist in it, if it were not eternal; or, if they say they will indulge themselves in sin, because they believe it not eternal, then this proves from their own mouth, that it should be eternal in order to restrain them. The prevalence of sin in the world tends to render it miserable; and therefore, to prevent it, as well as to display God's eternal regard to moral goodness, it is fit that he should annex the highest degree of punishment to disobedience in every individual; for the indulgence of sin in one individual would be a temptation to the whole rational creation; and, on the other hand, the threatenings of everlasting punishment to all sinners indefinitely, is necessary to deter the whole rational world, and every particular person from disobedience. Thus in civil government, it is necessary that robbery should be threatened indefinitely with death, because, though one robber may take from a man but what he can very well spare; yet, if every man might rob and plunder his neighbour, the consequence would be universal robbery and confusion. It is therefore necessary that the greatest punishment should be threatened to disobedience, both to prevent it and to testify the divine displeasure against it; which is the primary design of the threatening; and since the penalty was annexed with this view, it follows, that it was primarily enacted with a view to the happiness of mankind, by preventing what would naturally make them miserable, and but secondarily with a view to be executed; for it is to be executed only upon condition of disobedience; which disobedience it was intended to prevent, and consequently it was not immediately intended to be executed, or enacted for the sake of the execution, as though God took a malignant pleasure in the misery of his creatures. But when the penalty has failed of its primary end, restraining from sin, then it is fit it should answer its secondary end, and be executed upon the offender, to keep the rest of reasonable creatures in their obedience, to illustrate the veracity and holiness of the lawgiver, and prevent his government from falling into contempt. There are the same reasons that threatenings should be executed when denounced, as for their being denounced at first; for threatenings never executed, are the same with no threatenings at all.

Let me add, that the gospel lays us under the strongest obligations from gratitude. It not only clearly informs us of our obligations to God, as the author of our being and all our temporal blessings, which natural religion more faintly discovers, but superadds those more endearing ones derived from the scheme of man's redemption through the death of the eternal Son of God. Though the blessings of creation and Providence are great in themselves, they are swallowed up, as it were, and lost in the love of God;

which is commended to us by this matchless circumstance, "that while we were yet sinners, Christ died for us;" and while under the constraints of this love, we cannot but devote ourselves entirely to God, 2 *Corinth.* v. 14, 15.

Thus I have hinted at a few things among the many that might be mentioned to prove the divinity of the religion of Jesus, and its sufficiency to bring men to repentance and salvation. And if it be so, why should it be rejected, or another sought?—This reminds me that I promised,

II. To expose the vanity and unreasonableness of the objections against the Christian Religion, or of demanding another, &c.

What can our ingenious infidels offer against what has been said? It must be something very weighty indeed to preponderate all this evidence. A laugh, or a sneer, a pert witticism, declaiming against priestcraft and the prejudices of education, artful evasions, and shallow sophisms, the usual arguments of our pretended free-thinkers, these will not suffice to banter us out of our joyful confidence of the divinity of the religion of Jesus; and I may add, these will not suffice to indemnify them. Nothing will be sufficient for this but demonstration: it lies upon them to prove the Christian religion to be certainly false; otherwise, unless they are hardened to a prodigy, they must be racked with anxious fears lest they should find it true to their cost; and lest that dismal threatening should stand firm against them :—" *He that believeth not, shall be damned.*" What mighty objections, then, have they to offer? Will they say that the Christian religion contains mysterious doctrines, which they cannot comprehend, which seem to them unaccountable? As that of the Trinity, the Incarnation, and Satisfaction of Christ, &c. But will they advance their understanding to be the universal standard of truth? Will they pretend to comprehend the infinite God in their finite minds? then let them go, and measure the heavens with a span, and comprehend the ocean in the hollow of their hand. Will they pretend to understand the divine nature, when they cannot understand their own? when they cannot account for or explain the union betwixt their own souls and bodies? Will they reject mysteries in christianity, when they must own them in every thing else? Let them first solve all the phænomena in nature; let them give us a rational theory of the infinite divisibility of a piece of finite matter; let them account for the seemingly magical operation of the loadstone; the circulation of the blood upwards as well as downwards, contrary to all the laws of motion; let them inform us of the causes of the cohesion of the particles of matter; let them tell us, how spirits can receive ideas from material organs; how they hear and see, &c. let them give us intelligible theories of these things, and then they may, with something of a better grace, set up for critics upon God and his ways; but, while they are mysteries to themselves, while every particle of matter baffles their understandings, it is the most impious intellectual pride to reject christianity upon the account of its mysteries, and to set up themselves as the supreme judges of truth.

Or will they object that there are a great many difficult and strange passages in scripture, the meaning and propriety of which they do not see? And are there not many strange things in the book of nature, and the administration of Providence, the design and use of which they cannot see, many things that to them seem wrong and ill-contrived? Yet they own the world was created by God, and that his providence rules it: and why will they not allow that the scriptures may be from God, notwithstanding these difficulties and seeming incongruities? When a learned man can easily raise his discourse above the capacity of common people, will they not condescend to grant that an infinite God can easily overshoot their little souls? Indeed a revelation which we could fully comprehend, would not appear the production of an infinite mind; it would bear no resemblance to its Heavenly Father; and therefore we should have reason to suspect it spurious. It is necessary we should meet with difficulties in the scriptures to mortify our pride. But farther, will they make no allowance for the different customs and practices of different ages? It is certain, that may be proper and graceful in one age which would be ridiculous and absurd in another; and since the scriptures were written so many years ago, we may safely make this allowance for them, which will remove many seeming absurdities. There should also allowance be made for the scriptures being rendered literally out of dead difficult languages; for we know that many expressions may be beautiful and significant in one language, which would be ridiculous and nonsensical if literally translated into another. Were Homer or Virgil thus translated into English, without regard to the idiom of the language, instead of admiring their beauties, we should be apt to think (as Cowley expresses it) " that one madman had translated another madman."

Will they object the wicked lives of its professors against the holiness and good tendency of christianity itself? But is it christianity, as practised in the world, or christianity as taught by Christ and his apostles, and continued in the Bible, that I am proving to be divine? You know it is the latter, and consequently the poor appearance it makes in the former sense, is no argument against its purity and divinity in this. Again, are the bad lives of professors taught and enjoined by genuine christianity, and agreeable to it? No; they are quite contrary to it, and subversive of it; and it is so far from encouraging such professors, that it pronounces them miserable hypocrites; and their doom will be more severe than that of heathens. Again, are there not hypocritical profeſſors of morality and natural religion, as well as of revealed? Are there not many who cry up morality and religion of nature, and yet boldly violate its plaineſt precepts? If therefore this be a ſufficient objection againſt chriſtianity, it muſt be ſo too againſt all religion. Further: do men grow better by renouncing the religion of Jeſus? Obſervation aſſures us quite the contrary. Finally, are there not ſome of the profeſſors of chriſtianity, who live habitually according to it? who give us the beſt patterns of piety and virtue that ever were exhibited to the world? This is ſufficient to vindicate the religion they profeſs, and it is highly injurious to involve ſuch promiſcuouſly in the odium and contempt due to barefaced hypocrites. How would this reaſoning pleaſe the Deiſts themſelves in parallel caſes? " Some that have no regard to chriſtianity have been murderers, thieves, &c. therefore all that diſregard it are ſuch." Or " ſome that pretended to be honeſt, have been found villains; therefore all that pretend to it are ſuch; or therefore honeſty is no virtue."

Or will they change the note, and inſtead of pleading that chriſtianity leads to licentiouſneſs, object that it bears too hard upon the pleaſures of mankind, and lays them under too ſevere reſtraints?. Or that its penalties are exceſſive and cruel? But does it rob mankind of any pleaſures worthy the rational nature, worthy the purſuit of creatures formed for immortality, and conſiſtent with the good of the whole? It reſtrains them indeed; but it is only as a phyſician reſtrains his patient from poiſon or an improper regimen; it reſtrains men from living like beaſts; it reſtrains them from thoſe pleaſures which will ruin their ſouls and bodies in the event; it reſtrains them from gratifying a private paſſion at the expence of the public; in ſhort, it reſtrains them from making themſelves and others miſerable. Hard reſtraints indeed! and the Deiſts, to be ſure, are generous patrons of human liberty, who would free us from ſuch grievances as theſe! However, this objection lets us into the ſecret, and informs us of the reaſon why our pretended free-thinkers are ſuch enemies to chriſtianity; it is becauſe it checks their luſts, and will not permit them to act, as well as to think freely, i. e. as they pleaſe. If they would content themſelves with manly and rational pleaſures, they would not count the reſtraints of chriſtianity intolerable; nay, they would find in it a ſet of peculiarly noble and refined pleaſures, which they might ſeek in vain elſewhere; for it is ſo far from being an enemy to the happineſs of man, that it was deſigned to promote it; and then we make ourſelves miſerable when we reject it, or it becomes our intereſt that it ſhould be falſe. As to the penalty of everlaſting puniſhment annexed to ſin, which is but a temporal evil, I would aſk them whether they are competent judges in a matter in which they are parties? Are they capable to determine what degree of punishment should be inflicted upon disobedience to the infinite Majesty of heaven, when they are not only shortsighted creatures, but also concerned in the affair, and their judgments may be perverted by self-interest? Whether is it most fit that the Judge of all the earth should determine this point, or a company of malefactors, as they are? Is it allowed to criminals in civil courts to determine their own doom, nor pronounce their own sentence? If it were, few of them would be punished at all, and government would fall into contempt. Again, let me remind them, that the penalty was annexed to prevent disobedience, and so to render the execution needless; and consequently it was primarily intended for their good. Why then will they frustrate this design, and, when they have rendered the execution necessary, complain of its severity? If they think the penalty so terrible, let them watch against sin, let them accept the salvation the gospel offers, and so avoid it instead of quarrelling with its severity, and yet rushing upon it. Or, if they say they will persist in sin because they do not believe the punishment is eternal; this gives me room to appeal to themselves whether a less penalty than everlasting misery would be sufficient to restrain them from sin; and whether God would have taken all proper precautions to prevent sin, if he had annexed a less punishment to his law, since, by their own confession, nothing less could deter them from it. I shall only add, that as the human soul must always exist, and as by indulgence in sin in the present state it contracts such habits as render it incapable of happiness in the holy enjoyment of the heavenly world, it must by a natural necessity be forever miserable, though God should not exert any positive act for its punishment. And if the devil say, that punishment for some time would reclaim offenders from sin and bring them to repentance, the difficulty is not removed, unless they can prove that misery will bring men to love that Gd who inflicts it, which they can never do;— and it is evident, that *that* repentance which proceeds merely from self-love, without any regard to God at all, can never be pleasing to him, nor prepare them for happiness in the enjoyment of him. Punishment would produce a repentance like that of a sick-bed, forced, servile, and transitory.

Will they object, that miracles are not a sufficient evidence of the truth and divinity of a revelation, because infernal spirits may also work miracles, as in the case of the magicians of Egypt, to confirm an imposture? But it is known that our free-thinkers explode and laugh at the existence and power of evil spirits in other cases, and therefore must not be allowed to admit them here to serve a turn. However, we grant there are infernal spirits, and that they can perform many things above human power, which may appear to us miraculous, and yet the evidence in favour of christianity taken from miracles stands unshaken ; for (1) Can we suppose that these malignant and wicked spirits, whose business it is to seduce men to sin and ruin, would be willing to exert their power to work miracles to confirm so holy a religion, a religion so contrary to their design, and so subversive of their kingdom and interest? This would be wretched policy indeed. Or if we should suppose them willing, yet, (2) Can we think that God, who has them all at his control, would suffer them to counterfeit the great seal of heaven, and annex it to an imposture? that is, to work such miracles as could not be distinguished from those wrought by him to attest an imposture? Would he permit them to impose upon mankind in a manner that could not be detected? This would be to deliver the world to their management, and suffer them to lead them blindfold to hell in unavoidable delusion: for miracles are such dazzling and pompous evidences, that the general run of mankind could not resist them, even though they were wrought to attest a religion that might be demonstrated by a long train of sublime reasoning to be false. God may indeed suffer the devil to mimic the miracles wrought by his immediate hand, as in the case of Jannes and Jambres; but then, as in that case too, he will take care to excel them, and give some distinguishing marks of his almighty agency, which all mankind may easily discriminate from the utmost exertion of infernal power. But though Satan should be willing, and God should permit him to work miracles, yet, (3) Can we suppose that all the united powers of hell united, are able to work such astonishing miracles as were wrought for the confirmation of the Christian religion? Can we suppose that they can control the laws of nature at pleasure, and that with an air of sovereignty, and professing themselves the lords of the universe, as we know Christ did? If we can believe this, then we deny them, and may as well ascribe the creation and preservation of the world to them. If they could exert a creating power to form new limbs for the maimed, or to multiply five loves and two fishes into a sufficient quantity of food for five thousand, and leave a greater quantity of fragments when that were done than the whole provision at first, then they might create the world, and support all the creatures in it. If they could animate the dead and remand the seperate soul back to its former habitation, and reunite it with the body, then I see not why they might not have given us life at first. But to suppose this, would be to dethrone the King of Heaven, and renounce his providence entirely. We therefore rest assured that the miracles related in the scriptures were wrought by the finger of God.

But our free-thinkers will urge, How do we at this distance know that such miracles were actually wrought? they are only related in scripture-history; but to prove the truth of scripture from arguments that suppose the scripture true, is a ridiculous method of reasoning, and only a begging of the question. But, (1.) the reality of those miracles were granted by the enemies of christianity in their writings against it; and they had no answer to make, but this sorry one, that they were wrought by the power of magic. They never durst deny that they were wrought; for they knew all the world could prove it. Indeed, an honourable testimony concerning them could not be expected from infidels; for it would be utterly inconsistent that they should own these miracles sufficient attestations of christianity, and yet continue infidels. And this may answer an unreasonable demand of the Deists, that we should produce some honourable testimony concerning these attestations from Jews and Heathens, as well as from Christians, who were parties. We should have much more reason to suspect the testimony of the former as not convictive when it did not convince the persons themselves. But,

(2.) As these miracles were of so public a nature, and as so many were concerned to detect them, that they would unavoidably have been detected when related in words if they had not been done; so, for the same reasons, they could not but have been detected when related in writing; and this we know they never were. If these miracles had not been matters of undoubted fact, they could not have been inserted at first in the gospel-history; for then many thousands in various countries were alive to confute them; and they could not have been introduced into it afterwards, for all the world would see that it was then too late, and that if there had been such things, they should have heard of them before: for they were much more necessary for the first propagation of christianity than for its support when received.

But it may be objected, How can we at this distance know that these histories are genuine? May they not have been corrupted, and many additions made to them by designing men in ages since? And why is it not also asked, how do we know that there were such men as Alexander, Julius Cæsar, or King William the Third? How do we know but their histories are all romance and fable? How do we know that there were any generations of mankind before ourselves? How do we know but all the acts of parliament of former reigns are corrupted, and we are ruled by impositions? In short, How can we know any thing, but what we have seen with our eyes? We may as well make difficulties of all these things, and so destroy all human testimony, as scruple the genuineness of the sacred writings; for never were any writings conveyed down with so good evidence of their being genuine and uncorrupted as these. Upon their first publication they were put into all hands, they were scattered into all nations, translated into various languages, and all perused them; either to be taught by them, or to cavil at them. And ever since, they have been quoted by thousands of authors, appealed to by all parties of christians, as the supreme judge of controversies; and not only the enemies of christianity have carefully watched them to detect any alterations which pious fraud might attempt to make, but one sect of christians has kept a watchful eye over the other, lest they should alter any thing in favour of their own cause. And it is matter of astonishment as well as conviction, that all the various copies and translations of the scriptures in different nations and libraries are substantially the same, and differ only in matters of small moment; so that from the worst copy of translation in the world, one might easily learn the substance of christianity.

Or will our infidels insist to be eye-witnesses of these facts? Must one arise from the dead, or new miracles be wrought to convince them by occular demonstration? This is a most unreasonable demand, for (1) The continuance of miracles in every age would be attended with numerous inconveniences. For example, Multitudes must be born blind, deaf, or dumb; multitudes must be afflicted with incurable diseases, and possessed by evil spirits; multitudes must be disturbed in the sleep of death; and all the laws of nature must be made precarious and fickle, in order to leave room for miraculous operations; and all this to humour a company of obstinate infidels, who would not believe upon less striking though entirely sufficient evidence. (2.) The continuance of miracles from age to age would destroy their very nature, to which it is essential, that they be rare and extraordinary; for what is ordinary and frequent, we are apt to ascribe to the established laws of nature, however wonderful it be in itself. For example, if we saw dead bodies rise from their graves, as often as we see vegetables spring from seed rotton in the earth, we should be no more surprised at the one phænomenon than we are at the other, and our *virtuosi* would be equally busy to assign some natural cause for both.

And had we never seen the sun rise until this morning, we should justly have accounted it as great a miracle as any recorded in the scriptures; but because it is common, we neglect it as a thing of course. Indeed, it is not any thing in the event itself, or in the degree of power necessary for its accomplishment, that renders it miraculous, but its being uncommon, and out of the ordinary course of things; for example, the generation of the human body is not in itself less astonishing; nor does it require less power, than its resurrection: the revolution of the sun in its regular course, is as wonderful, and as much requires a divine power, as its standing still in the days of Joshua. But we acknowledge a miracle in the one case, but not in the other, because the one is extraordinary, while the other frequently occurs. Hence it follows, that the frequent repetition of miracles, as often as men are pleased to plead the want of evidence to excuse their infidelity, would destroy their very nature; and consequently, to demand their continuance is to demand an impossibility. But (3) Suppose that men should be indulged in this request, it would not probably bring them to believe. If they are unbelievers now, it is not for want of evidence, but through wilful blindness and obstinacy; and as they that will shut their eyes can see no more in meridian light than in the twilight, so they that reject a sufficiency of evidence would also resist a superfluity of it. Thus the Jews, who were eye-witnesses of the miracles recorded in the scriptures, continued invincible infidels still. They had always some trifling caval ready to object against the brightest evidence. And thus our modern infidels would no doubt evade the force of the most miraculous attestation by some wretched hypothesis or other: they would look upon miracles either as magical productions, or illusions of their senses; or rather, as natural and necessary events, which they would indeed have some reason to conclude, if they were frequently performed before their eyes. Some have pretended to doubt of the existence and perfections of God, notwithstanding the evidences thereof upon this magnificent structure of the universe; and must God be always creating new worlds before these obstinate creatures for their conviction? Such persons have as much reason to demand it in this case, as our Deists have to insist for new miracles in the other. I might add, that such glaring evidence, as, like the light of the sun, would force itself irresistibly upon the minds of the most reluctant, would not leave room for us to show our regard to God in believing, for we should then believe from extrinsic necessity, and not from choice. It is therefore most correspondent to our present state of probation, that there should be something in the evidence of a divine revelation to try us; something that might fully convince the teachable and yet not remove all umbrages for cavilling from the obstinate,

Thus I have answered as many objections as the bounds of a sermon would admit; and I think they are the principal ones which lie against my subject in the view I have considered it. And as I have not designedly selected the weakest, in order to an easy triumph, you may look upon the answers that have been given as a ground of rational presumption, that all other objections may be answered with equal ease. Indeed, if they could not, it would not invalidate the positive arguments in favour of christianity; for when we have sufficient positive evidence for a thing, we do not reject it because it is attended with some difficulties which we cannot solve.

My time will allow me to make but two or three short reflections upon the whole.

1. If the religion of Jesus be attested with such full evidence, and be sufficient to conduct men to everlasting felicity, then how helpless are they that have enjoyed it all their life without profit: who either reject it as false, or have not felt its power to reform their hearts and lives? It is the last remedy provided for a guilty world; and if this fails, their disease is incurable, and they are not to expect better means.

2. If the religion of Jesus be true, then wo unto the wicked of all sorts: wo to infidels both practical and speculative, for all the curses of it are in full force against them, and I need not tell you how dreadful they are.

3. If the religion of Jesus be true, then I congratulate such of you, whose hearts and lives are habitually conformed to it, and who have ventured your everlasting All upon it. You build upon a sure foundation, and your hope shall never make you ashamed.

Finally, Let us all strive to become rational and practical believers of this heaven-born religion. Let our understandings be more rationally and thoroughly convinced of its truth; and our hearts and lives be more and more conformed to its purity; and ere long we shall receive those glorious rewards it ensures to all its sincere disciples; which may God grant to us all for Jesus' sake. Amen!

SERMON II.

The Method of Salvation through Jesus Christ.

JOHN iii. 16. *For God so loved the world, that he gave his only begotten Son, that whosoever believeth in him should not perish, but have everlasting life.*

I HAVE been solicitously thinking in what way my life, redeemed from the grave, may be of most service to my dear people. And I would collect all the feeble remains of my strength into one vigorous effort this day to promote this benevolent end. If I knew what subject has the most direct tendency to save your souls, that is the subject to which my heart would cling with peculiar endearment, and which I would make the matter of the present discourse.

And when I consider I am speaking to an assembly of sinners, guilty, depraved, helpless creatures, and that, if ever you be saved, it will be only through Jesus Christ, in that way which the gospel reveals; when I consider that your everlasting life and happiness turn upon this hinge, namely, the reception you give to this Saviour, and this way of salvation; I say, when I consider these things, I can think of no subject I can more properly choose than to recommend the Lord Jesus to your acceptance, and to explain and inculcate the method of salvation through his mediation; or, in other words, to preach the pure gospel to you; for the gospel, in the most proper sense, is nothing else but a revelation of a way of salvation for sinners of Adam's race.

My text furnishes me with proper materials for my purpose. Let heaven and earth hear it wth wonder, joy, and raptures of praise! *God so loved the world, that he gave his only begotten Son, that whosoever*, or that every one that *believeth in him should not perish, but have everlasting life.*

This is a part of the most important evening conversation that ever was held; I mean, that between Christ and Nicodemus, a Pharisee and ruler of the Jews. Our Lord first instructs him in the doctrine of regeneration, that grand constituent of a christian, and pre-requisite to our admission into the kingdom of heaven; and then he proceeds to inform him of the gospel-method of salvation, which contains these two grand articles, the death of Christ, as the great foundation of blessedness; and faith in him, as the great qualification upon the part of the sinner.—He presents this important doctrine to us in various forms, with a very significant repetition. *As Moses lifted up the serpent in the wilderness, even so shall the Son of man be lifted up;* that is, hung on high on a cross, *that whosoever believeth in him should not perish, but have everlasting life.* Then follows my text, which expresses the same doctrine with great force:—*God so loved the world, that he gave his only begotten Son,* gave him up to death, *that whosoever believeth in him should not perish, but have everlasting life.* He goes on to mention a wonder. This earth is a rebellious province of Jehovah's dominions, and therefore if his Son should ever visit it, one would think it would be as an angry judge, or as the executioner of his Father's vengeance. But, O astonishing! *God sent not his Son into the world to condemn the world, but that the world through him might be saved.* Hence the terms of life and death are thus fixed, *He that believeth in him is not condemned: but he that believeth not is condemned already, because he hath not believed in the name of the only begotten Son of God.* Sure the heavenly rivers of pleasure flow in these verses! Never, methinks, was there so much gospel expressed in so few words! Here take the gospel in miniature, and bind it to your hearts for ever. These verses alone, methinks, are a sufficient remedy for a dying world.

The truths I would infer from the text for prefent improvement are thefe :—that without Chrift you are all in a perifhing condition ;—that through Jefus Chrift a way is opened for your falvation ; that the grand pre-requifite to your being faved in this way, is faith in Jefus Chrift ; that every one, without exception, whatever his former character has been, that is enabled to comply with this pre-requifite, fhall certainly be faved ;—and that the conftitution of this method of falvation, or the miffion of Chrift into our world, as the Saviour of finners, is a moft ftriking and aftonifhing inftance and difplay of the love of God.

I. My text implies, that without Chrift you are all in a perifhing condition. This holds true of you in particular, becaufe it holds true of the world univerfally : for the world was undoubtedly in a perifhing condition without Chrift, and none but he could relieve it, otherwife God would never have given his only begotten Son to fave it. God is not oftentatious or prodigal of his gifts, efpecially of fo ineftimable a gift as his Son, whom he loves infinitely more than the whole creation. So great, fo dear a perfon would not have been fent upon a miffion which could have been difcharged by any other being. Thoufands of rams muft bleed in facrifice, or ten thoufands of rivers of oil muft flow ; our firft-born muft die for our tranfgreffions, and the fruit of our body for the fin of our fouls ; or Gabriel, or fome of the upper ranks of angels, muft leave their thrones, and hang upon a crofs, if fuch methods of falvation had been fufficient. All this would have been nothing in comparifon of the only begotten Son of God leaving his native heaven, and all its glories, affuming our degraded nature, fpending thirty-three long and tedious years in poverty, difgrace, and perfecution, dying as a malefactor and a flave in the midft of ignominy and torture, and lying a mangled breathlefs corpfe in the grave. We may be fure there was the higheft degree of neceffity for it, otherwife God would not have given up his dear Son to fuch an horrid fcene of fufferings.

This, then, was the true ftate of the world, and confequently yours without Chrift ; it was hopelefs and defperate in every view. In that fituation there would not have been fo much goodnefs in the world as to try the efficacy of facrifices, prayers, tears, reformation, and repentance, or they would have been tried in vain. It would have been inconfiftent with the honour of the divine perfections and government, to admit facrifices, prayers, tears, repentance, and reformation, as a fufficient atonement.

What a melancholy view of the world have we now before us ! We know the ftate of mankind only under the gracious government of a Mediator ; and we but feldom realize what our miferable condition would have been, had this gracious adminiftration never been fet up. But exclude a Saviour in your thoughts for a moment, and then take a view of the world—helpless!—hopeless!—under the righteous displeasure of God; and despairing of relief!—the very suburbs of hell!—the range of malignant devils!—the region of guilt, misery, and despair!—the mouth of the infernal pit!—the gate of hell!—This would have been the condition of our world had it not been for that Jesus who redeemed it; and yet in this very world he is neglected and despised.

But you will ask me, "How comes it that the world was in such an undone, helpless, hopeless condition without Christ; or what are the reasons of all this?"

The true account of this will appear from these two considerations, that all mankind are sinners; and that no other method but the mediation of Christ could render the salvation of sinners consistent with the honour of the divine perfections and government, with the public good, and even with the nature of things.

All mankind are sinners. This is too evident to need proof. They are sinners, rebels against the greatest and best of beings, against their Maker, their liberal Benefactor, and their rightful Sovereign, to whom they are under stronger and more endearing obligations than they can be under to any creature, or even to the entire system of creatures; sinners, rebels in every part of our guilty globe; none righteous, no, not one; all sinners, without exception: sinners from age to age for thousands of years: thousands, millions, innumerable multitudes of sinners. What an obnoxious race is this! There appears no difficulty in the way of justice to punish such creatures. But what seeming insuperable difficulties appear in the way of their salvation! Let me mention a few of them to recommend that blessed Saviour who has removed them all.

If such sinners be saved, how shall the holiness and justice of God be displayed? How shall he give an honourable view of himself to all worlds, as a Being of perfect purity, and an enemy to all moral evil?

If such sinners be saved, how shall the honour of the divine government and law be secured? How will the dignity of the law appear, if a race of rebels may trifle with it with impunity? What a sorry law must that be that has no sanctions, or whose sanctions may be dispensed with at pleasure? What a contemptible government, that may be insulted and rejected, and the offender admitted into favour without exemplary punishment! No government can subsist upon such principles of excessive indulgence.

How can such sinners be saved, and yet the good of the public secured, which is always the end of every wise and good ruler? By the public good I do not mean the happiness of mankind alone, but I mean the happiness of all worlds of reasonable creatures collectively, in comparison of which the happiness of mankind alone may be only a private interest, which should always give way to the public good. Now sin has a direct tendency, not only according to law, but according to the nature of things, to scatter misery and ruin wherever its infection reaches. Therefore the public good cannot be properly consulted without giving a loud and effectual warning against all sin, and dealing with offenders in such a manner as to deter others from offending. But how can this be done? how can the sinner be saved, and yet the evil of sin be displayed, and all other beings be deterred from it for ever? How can sin be discouraged by pardoning it? its evil displayed by letting the criminal escape punishment? These are such difficulties, that nothing but divine wisdom could ever surmount them.

These difficulties lie in the way of a mere pardon and exemption from punishment: but salvation includes more than this. When sinners are saved, they are not only pardoned, but received into high favour, made the children, the friends, the courtiers of the King of Heaven. They are not only delivered from punishment, but also advanced to a state of perfect positive happiness, and nothing short of this can render such creatures as we happy. Now, in this view, the difficulties rise still higher, and it is the more worthy of observation, as this is not generally the case in human governments; and as men are apt to form their notions of the divine government by human, they are less sensible of these difficulties.—But this is indeed the true state of the case here; how can the sinner be not only delivered from punishment, but also advanced to a state of perfect happiness? not only escape the displeasure of his offended Sovereign, but be received into full favour, and advanced to the highest honour and dignity? how can this be done without casting a cloud over the purity and justice of the Lord of all; without sinking his law and government into contempt; without diminishing the evil of sin, and emboldening others to venture upon it, and so at once injuring the character of the supreme Ruler, and the public good? How can sinners, I say, be saved without the salvation being attended with these bad consequences?

And here you must remember, that these consequences must be provided against. To save men at random, without considering the consequences, to distribute happiness to private persons with an undistinguishing hand, this would be at once inconsistent with the character of the supreme Magistrate of the universe, and with the public good. Private persons are at liberty to forgive private offences; nay, it is their duty to forgive; and they can hardly offend by way of excess in the generous virtues of mercy and compassion. But the case is otherwise with a magistrate; he is obliged to consult the dignity of his government and the interest of the public; and he may easily carry his lenity to a very dangerous extreme, and by his tenderness to criminals do an extensive injury to the ſtate. This is particularly the caſe with regard to the great God, the univerſal ſupreme Magiſtrate of all worlds. And this ought to be ſeriouſly conſidered by thoſe men of looſe principles among us, who look upon God only under the fond character of a father, or a being of infinite mercy; and thence conclude, they have little to fear from him for all their audacious iniquities.— There is no abſolute neceſſity that ſinners ſhould be ſaved: juſtice may be ſuffered to take place upon them.—But there is the moſt abſolute neceſſity that the Ruler of the world ſhould both be, and appear to be, holy and juſt. There is the moſt abſolute neceſſity that he ſhould ſupport the dignity of his government, and guard it from contempt, that he ſhould ſtrike all worlds with a proper horror of ſin, and repreſent it in its genuine infernal colours, and ſo conſult the good of the whole, rather than a part. There is, I ſay, the higheſt and moſt abſolute neceſſity for theſe things; and they cannot be diſpenſed with as matters of arbitrary pleaſure.— And unleſs theſe ends can be anſwered in the ſalvation of men, they cannot be ſaved at all. No, they muſt all periſh, rather than God ſhould act out of character, as the ſupreme Magiſtrate, of the univerſe, or beſtow private favours to criminals, to the detriment of the public.

And in this lay the difficulty. Call a council of all the ſages and wiſe men of the world, and they can never get over this difficulty, without borrowing aſſiſtance from the goſpel. Nay, this, no doubt puzzled all the angelic intelligences, who pry ſo deep into the myſteries of heaven, before the goſpel was fully revealed.— Methinks the angels, when they ſaw the fall of man, gave him up as deſperate. "Alas! (they cried) the poor creature is gone! he and all his numerous race are loſt for ever." This, they knew, had been the doom of their fellow angels that ſinned; and could they hope better for man? Then they had not ſeen any of the wonders of pardoning love and mercy and could they have once thought that *that* glorious perſon, who filled the middle throne, and was their Creator and Lord, would ever become a man, and die, like a criminal, to redeem an inferior rank of creatures? No, this thought they would probably have ſhuddered at as blaſphemy.

And muſt we then give up ourſelves and all our race as loſt beyond recovery? There are huge and ſeemingly inſuperable difficulties in the way; and we have ſeen that neither men nor angels can preſcribe any relief. But *ſing, O ye heavens, for the Lord hath done it: ſhout ye lower parts of the earth: break forth into ſinging, ye mountains, O foreſt, and every tree therein: for the Lord hath redeemed Jacob, and glorified himſelf in Iſrael.* Iſaiah xliv. 23. Which leads me to add,

II. My text implies, that through Jeſus Chriſt a way is opened for your ſalvation. He, and he only was found equal to the undertaking; and before him all these mountains became a plain; all these difficulties vanish; and now God can be just, can secure the dignity of his character, as the Ruler of the world, and answer all the ends of government, and yet justify and save the sinner that believeth in Jesus.

This is plainly implied in this glorious epitome of the gospel: *God so loved the world, that he gave his only begotten Son, that whosoever believeth in him should not perish, but have everlasting life.* Without this gift all was lost: but now, whosoever believeth in him may be saved; saved in a most honourable way. This will appear more particularly if we consider the tendency the mediation of Christ had to remove the difficulties mentioned. But I would promise two general remarks.

The first is, That God being considered in this affair in his public character, as supreme Magistrate, or Governor of the world, all the punishment which he is concerned to see inflicted upon sin is only such as answers the ends of government. Private revenge must vent itself on the very person of the offender, or be disappointed. But to a ruler, as such, it may in some cases be indifferent, whether the punishment be sustained by the very person that offended, or by a substitute suffering in his stead. It may also be indifferent whether the very same punishment, as to kind and degree, threatened in the law, be inflicted, or a punishment equivalent to it. If the honour of the ruler and his government be maintained, if all disobedience be properly discountenanced; if, in short, all the ends of government can be answered, such things as these are indifferences. Consequently, if these ends should be answered by Christ's suffering in the stead of sinners, there would be no objection against it. This remark introduces another, namely, (2) That Jesus Christ was such a person that his suffering as the substitute or surety of sinners, answered all the ends of government which could be answered by the execution of the punishment upon the sinners themselves. To impose suffering upon the innocent, when unwilling, is unjust; but Jesus was willing to undertake the dreadful task. And besides, he was a person *(sui juris)* at his own disposal, his own property, and therefore he had a right to dispose of his life as he pleased; and there was a merit in his consenting to that which he was not obliged to previous to his consent. He was also a person of infinite dignity, and infinitely beloved by his Father; and these considerations rendered the merit of his sufferings for a short time, and another kind of punishment than that of hell, equal, more than equal to the everlasting sufferings of sinners themselves. Jesus Christ was also above law; that is, not obliged to be subject to that law which he had made for his creatures, and consequently his obedience to the law, not being necessary for himself, might be imputed to others; whereas creatures are incapable of works of supererogation, or of doing more than they are bound to do, being obliged to obey their divine lawgiver for themselves to the utmost extent of their abilities, and consequently their obedience, however perfect, can be sufficient only for themselves, but cannot be imputed to others. Thus it appears, in general, that the ends of government are as effectually answered by the sufferings of Christ in the room of sinners, as they could be by the everlasting punishment of the sinners themselves; nay, we shall presently find they are answered in a more striking and illustrious manner. To mention particulars:

Was it necessary that the holiness and justice of God should be displayed in the salvation of sinners? See how bright they shine in a suffering Saviour! Now it appears that such is the holiness and justice of God, that he will not let even his own Son escape unpunished, when he stands in the law-place of sinners, though guilty only by the slight stain (may I so speak) of imputation. Could the execution of everlasting punishment upon the hateful criminals themselves ever give so bright a display of these attributes? It were impossible. Again,

Was it a difficulty to save sinners, and yet maintain the rights of the divine government, and the honour of the law? See how this difficulty is removed by the obedience and death of Christ! Now it appears, that the rights of the divine government are so sacred and inviolable, that they must be maintained, though the darling Son of God should fall a sacrifice to justice; and that not one offence against this government can be pardoned, without his making a full atonement. Now it appears, that the supreme Ruler is not to be trifled with, but that his injured honour must be repaired, though at the expence of his Son's blood and life. Now, the precept of the law is perfectly obeyed in every part, and a full equivalent to its penalty endured, by a person of infinite dignity; and it is only upon this footing, that is, of complete satisfaction to all the demands of the law, that any of the rebellious sons of men can be restored into favour. This is a satisfaction which Christ alone could give: to sinners it is utterly impossible, either by doing or suffering. They cannot do all the things that are written in the law; nor can they *endure* its penalty, without being for ever miserable: and therefore the law has received a more complete satisfaction in Christ than it would ever receive from the offenders themselves. Further,

Was it a difficulty how sinners might be saved, and yet the evil of sin be displayed in all its horrors? Go to the cross of Christ; there, ye fools that make a mock of sin, there learn its malignity, and its hatefulness to the great God. There you may see it is so great an evil, that when it is but imputed to the man that is God's fellow, as the surety of sinners, it cannot escape punishment. No, when that dreadful ftain lay upon him, immediately the commiffion was given to divine juftice, *Awake O fword, againft my fhepherd, againft the man that is my fellow, faith the Lord of hofts; fmite the fhepherd.* Zech. xiii. 7.—When Chrift ftood in the room of finners, even the Father fpared not his own Son, but gave him up to death. That the criminals themfelves, who are an inferior race of creatures, fhould not efcape would not be ftrange: but what an enormous evil muft that be, which cannot be connived at even in the favourite of heaven, the only begotten Son of God! Surely nothing befides could give fo ftriking a difplay of its malignity!

Was it a difficulty how to reconcile the falvation of finners, and the public good? that is, how to forgive fin, and yet give an effectual warning againft it? How to receive the finner into favour, and advance him to the higheft honour and happinefs, and in the mean time deter all other beings from offending? All this is provided for in the fufferings of Chrift as a furety. Let all worlds look to his crofs, and receive the warning which his wounds, and groans, and blood, and dying agonies proclaim aloud; and fure they can never dare to offend after the example of man. Now they may fee that the only inftance of pardon to be found in the univerfe was not brought about but by fuch means as are not likely to be repeated; by the incarnation and death of the Lord of Glory. And can they flatter themfelves that he will leave his throne and hang upon a crofs, as often as any of his creatures wantonly dare to offend him? No; fuch a miracle as this, the utmoft effort of divine grace, is not often to be renewed; and therefore, if they dare to fin, it is at their peril. They have no reafon to flatter themfelves they fhall be favoured like fallen man; but rather to expect they fhall fhare in the doom of the fallen angels.

Or if they fhould think fin may efcape with but a flight punifhment, here they may be convinced of the contrary. If the Darling of Heaven, the Lord of Glory, though perfonally innocent, fuffers fo much when fin is but imputed to him, what fhall the finners themfelves feel, who can claim no favour upon the footing of their own importance, or perfonal innocence? "If thefe things be done " in the green tree, what fhall be done in the dry?"

Thus, my brethren, you may fee how a way is opened through Jefus Chrift for our falvation. All the ends of government may be anfwered, and yet you pardoned, and made happy. Thofe attributes of the divine nature, fuch as mercy and juftice, which feemed to clafh, are now reconciled; now they mingle their beams, and both fhine with a brighter glory in the falvation of finners, than either of them could apart. And muft you not acknowledge this divine God-like fcheme? Can you look round you over the works of the creation, and fee the divine wifdom in every object, and can you not perceive the divine agency in this ftill more glorious work of redemption? Redemption, which gives a full view of the Deity, not as the fun in eclipfe, half dark, half bright, but as

A God all o'er, confummate, abfolute,
Full orb'd, in his whole round of rays complete.   YOUNG.

And fhall not men and angels join in wonder and praife at the furvey of this amazing fcheme? Angels are wrapt in wonder and praife, and will be fo to all eternity. See! how they pry into this myftery! hark, how they fing! " Glory to God in the higheft;" and celebrate the Lamb that was flain! and fhall not men, who are perfonally interefted in the affair, join with them? O! are there none to join with them in this affembly? Surely, none can refufe!

Now, fince all obftructions are removed on God's part, that lay in the way of our falvation, why fhould we not all be faved together? What is there to hinder our crowding into heaven promifcuoufly? Or what is there requifite on our part, in order to make us partakers of this falvation? Here it is proper to pafs on to the next truth inferred from the text, namely,

III. That the grand pre-requifite to your being faved in this way, is faith in Jefus Chrift. Though the obftructions on God's part are removed by the death of Chrift, yet there is one remaining in the finner, which cannot be removed without his confent; and which, while it remains, renders his falvation impoffible in the nature of things; that is, the depravity and corruption of his nature. Till this is cured, he cannot relifh thofe fruitions and employments in which the happinefs of heaven confifts, and confequently he cannot be happy there. Therefore there is a neceffity, in the very nature of things, that he fhould be made holy, in order to be faved; nay, his falvation itfelf confifts in holinefs. Now, faith is the root of all holinefs in a finner. Without a firm realizing belief of the great truth of the gofpel, it is impoffible a finner fhould be fanctified by their influence: and without a particular faith in Jefus Chrift, he cannot drive from him thofe fanctifying influences by which alone he can be made holy, and which are conveyed through Jefus Chrift, and through him alone.

Further: It would be highly incongruous, and indeed impoffible, to fave a finner againft his will, or in a way he diflikes. Now faith, as you fhall fee prefently, principally confifts in a hearty confent to and approbation of the way of falvation through Jefus Chrift, the only way in which a finner can be faved confiftently with the divine honour; fo that the conftitution of the gofpel is not only juft, but as merciful as it can be, when it ordains, that only *he that believeth fhall be faved; but that he that believeth not, fhall be damned.*

Again: We cannot be saved through Jesus Christ, till his righteousness be so far made ours as that it will answer the demands of the law for us, and procure the favour of God to us; but his righteousness cannot be thus imputed to us, or accounted ours in law, till we are so united to him as to be one in law, or one legal person with him. Now faith is the bond of union; faith is that which interests us in Christ; and therefore without faith we cannot receive any benefit from his righteousness.

Here then a most interesting inquiry presents itself: "What is it to believe in Jesus Christ? or what is that faith which is the grand pre-requisite to salvation?" If you are capable of attention to the most interesting affair in all the world, attend to this with the utmost seriousness and solemnity.

Faith in Christ includes something speculative in it; that is, it includes a speculative rational belief, upon the testimony of God, that Jesus Christ is the only Saviour of men. But yet it is not entirely a speculation, like the faith of multitudes among us: it is a more practical experimental thing; and that you may understand its nature, you must take notice of the following particulars.

(1.) Faith pre-supposes a deep sense of our undone, helpless condition. I told you before, this is the condition of the world without Christ; and you must be sensible at heart that this is your condition in particular, before you can believe in him as your Saviour. He came to be a Saviour in a desperate case, when no relief could possibly be had from any other quarter, and you cannot receive him under that character till you feel yourselves in such a case; therefore, in order to your believing, all your pleas and excuses for your sins must be silenced, all your high conceit of your own goodness must be mortified, all your dependence upon your own righteousness, upon the merit of your prayers, your repentance, and good works, must be cast down, and you must feel that indeed you lie at mercy, that God may justly reject you for ever, and that all you can do can bring him under no obligation to save you. These things you must be deeply sensible of, otherwise you can never receive the Lord Jesus in that view in which he is proposed to you, namely, as a Saviour in a desperate case.

I wish and pray you may this day see yourselves in this true, though mortifying light. It is the want of this sense of things that keeps such crowds of persons unbelievers among us. It is the want of this that causes the Lord Jesus to be so little esteemed, so little sought for, so little desired among us. In short, it is the want of this that is the great occasion of so many perishing from under the gospel, and, as it were, from between the hands of a Saviour. It is this, alas! that causes them to perish, like the impenitent thief on the cross, with a Saviour by their side. O that you once rightly knew yourselves, you would then soon know Jesus Christ, and receive salvation from his hand.

(2.) Faith implies the enlightening of the understanding to discover the suitableness of Jesus Christ as a Saviour, and the excellency of the way of salvation through him. While the sinner lies undone and helpless in himself, and looking about in vain for some relief, it pleases a gracious God to shine into his heart, and enable him to see his glory in the face of Jesus Christ. Now this once neglected Saviour appears not only absolutely necessary, but also all-glorious and lovely, and the sinner's heart is rapt away, and for ever captivated with his beauty: now the neglected gospel appears in a new light, as different from all his former apprehensions as if it were quite another thing. I have not time at present to enlarge upon this discovery of Christ and the gospel which faith includes; and indeed should I dwell upon it ever so long, I could not convey just ideas of it to such of you as have never had the happy experience of it. In short, the Lord Jesus, and the way of salvation through him, appear perfectly suitable, all-sufficient, and all-glorious; and in consequence of this,

(3.) The sinner is enabled to embrace this Saviour with all his heart, and to give a voluntary cheerful consent to this glorious scheme of salvation. Now all his former unwillingness and reluctance are subdued, and his heart no more draws back from the terms of the gospel, but he complies with them, and that not merely out of constraint and necessity, but out of free choice, and with the greatest pleasure and delight. How does his heart now cling to the blessed Jesus with the most affectionate endearment! How is he lost in wonder, joy, and gratitude at the survey of the divine perfections, as displayed in this method of redemption! How does he rejoice in it, as not only bringing happiness to him, but glory to God; as making his salvation not only consistent with, but a bright illustration of, the divine perfections, and the dignity of his government! While he had no other but the low and selfish principles of corrupt nature he had no concern about the honour of God; if he might be but saved it was all he was solicitous about: but now he has a noble generous heart; now he is concerned that God should be honoured in his salvation, and this method of salvation is recommended and endeared to him by the thought that it secures to God the supremacy, and makes his salvation subservient to the divine glory.

(4.) Faith in Jesus Christ implies a humble trust or dependence upon him alone for the pardon of sin, acceptance with God, and every blessing. As I told you before, the sinner's self-confidence is mortified; he gives up all hopes of acceptance upon the footing of his own righteousness: he is filled with self-despair, and yet he does not despair absolutely; he does not give up himself as lost, but has cheerful hopes of becoming a child of God, and being for ever happy, guilty and unworthy as he is; and what are these hopes founded upon? Why, upon the mere free grace and mercy of God, through the righteousness of Jesus Christ. On this he ventures a guilty, unworthy, helpless soul, and finds it a firm, immoveable foundation, while every other ground of dependence proves but a quicksand. There are many that flatter themselves they put their trust in God; but their trust wants sundry qualifications essential to a true faith. It is not the trust of a humble helpless soul that draws all its encouragement from the mere mercy of God, and the free indefinite offer of the gospel; but it is the presumptuous trust of a proud self-confident sinner, who draws his encouragement in part at least from his own imaginary goodness and importance. It is not a trust in the mercy of God through Jesus Christ, as the only medium through which it can be honourably conveyed; but either in the absolute mercy of God, which, without a proper reference to a Mediator, or in his mercy, as in some measure deserved or moved by something in the sinner.— Examine whether your trust in God will stand this test.

I have now given you a brief answer to that grand question, What is it to believe in Jesus Christ? and I hope you understand it, though I have not enlarged so much upon it as I willingly would. I shall only add, that this faith may also be known by its inseparable effects; which are such as follow. Faith purifies the heart, and is a lively principle of inward holiness. Faith is always productive of good works, and leads us to universal obedience: faith overcomes the world and all its temptations: faith realizes eternal things, and brings them near; and hence it is defined by the apostle, *The substance of things hoped for, and the evidence of things not seen.* Heb. xi. 1. Here I have a very important question to propose to you: Who among you can say, " Well, notwithstanding all my imperfections, and all my doubts and fears, I cannot but humbly hope, after the best examination I can make, that such a faith has been produced in this heart of mine?" And can you say so indeed? Then I bring you glad tidings of great joy; you shall be saved: yes, saved you shall be, in spite of earth and hell; saved, however great your past sins have been. Which thought introduces the glorious truth that comes next in order, namely,

IV. My text implies, that every one, without exception, whatever his former character has been, that is enabled to believe in Jesus Christ, shall certainly be saved.

The number or aggravations of sin do not alter the case; and the reason is, the sinner is not received into favour, in whole or in part, upon the account of any thing personal, but solely and entirely upon the account of the righteousness of Jesus Christ. Now, this righteousness is perfectly equal to all the demands of the law:

and therefore, when this righteousness is made over to the sinner as his by imputation, the law has no more demands upon him for great sins than for small, for many than for few; because all demands are fully satisfied by the obedience of Jesus Christ to the law. You see that sinners of all characters who believe in him are put upon an equality in this respect: they are all admitted upon one common footing, the righteousness of Christ; and that is as sufficient for one as another.

This encouraging truth has the most abundant support from the holy scriptures. Observe the agreeable indefinite *whosoever* so often repeated. " Whosoever believeth in him, shall not perish, but have everlasting life." Whosoever he be, however vile, however guilty, however unworthy, if he does but believe, he shall not perish, but have everlasting life. What an agreeable assurance is this from the lips of him who has the final states of men at his disposal! The same blessed lips have also declared, *Him that cometh unto me, I will in no wise cast out.* John vi. 37. And *Whosoever will, let him take the water of life freely.* Rev. xxii. 17. He has given you more than bare words to establish you in the belief of this truth: upon this principle he has acted, choosing some of the most abandoned sinners to make them examples, not of his justice, as we might expect, but of his mercy, for the encouragement of others. In the days of his flesh he was reproached by his enemies for his friendship to publicans and sinners; but sure it is, instead of reproaching, we must love him on this account. When he rose from the dead, he did not rise with angry resentment against his murderers; no, but he singles them out from a world of sinners, to make them the first offers of pardon through the blood which they had just shed. He orders *that repentance and remission of sins should be preached in his name to all nations, beginning at Jerusalem.* Luke xxiv. 47. At Jerusalem, where he had been crucified a few days before, there he orders the first publication of pardon and life to be made. You may see what monsters of sin he chose to make the monuments of his grace in Corinth. *Neither fornicators, nor idolaters, nor adulterers, nor effeminate, nor abusers of themselves with mankind, nor thieves, nor covetous, nor drunkards, nor revilers, nor extortioners, shall inherit the kingdom of God.* What a dismal catalogue is this! It is no wonder such a crew should not inherit the kingdom of heaven; they are fit only for the infernal prison; and yet, astonishing! it follows, *such were some of you; but ye are washed, but ye are sanctified, but ye are justified in the name of the Lord Jesus, and by the spirit of our God.* 1 Cor. vi. 9—11. What sinner after this can despair of mercy upon his believing in Jesus! St. Paul was another instance of the same kind: " This," says he, " is a faithful saying;" a saying that may be depended on as true, " and worthy of all acceptation," from a guilty world, *that Christ*

Jesus came into the world to save sinners, of whom I am chief: howbeit, for this cause I obtained mercy, that in me the chief, Jesus Christ might shew forth all long-suffering, for a pattern to them which should hereafter believe in him to life everlasting. 1 Tim. i. 15, 16. A sinner of less size would not have answered this end so well; but if Saul the persecutor obtains mercy upon his believing, who can despair?

You see upon the whole, my brethren, you are not excluded from Christ and life by the greatness of your sins; but if you perish it must be from another cause; it must be on account of your wilful unbelief in not accepting of Jesus Christ as your Saviour. If you reject him, then indeed you must perish, however small your sins have been; for it is only his death that can make atonement for the slightest guilt; and if you have no interest in that, the guilt of the smallest sin will sink you into ruin.

Here is a door wide enough for you all, if you will but enter in by faith. Come then, enter in, you that have hitherto claimed an horrid precedence in sin, that have been ringleaders in vice, come now take the lead, and shew others the way to Jesus Christ; harlots, publicans, thieves, and murderers, if such be among you, there is salvation even for you, if you will but believe. O! how astonishing is the love of God discovered in this way: a consideration which introduces the last inference from my text, namely,

V. That the constitution of this method of salvation, or the mission of a Saviour into our world, is a most striking and astonishing display of the love of God:—*God so loved the world as to give his only begotten Son,* &c.

View the scheme all through, and you will discover love, infinite love, in every part of it. Consider the great God as self-happy and independent upon all his creatures, and what but love, self-moved love, could excite him to make such provision for an inferior part of them! Consider the world sunk in sin, not only without merit, but most deserving of everlasting punishment, and what but love could move him to have mercy upon such a world? Consider the Saviour provided, not an angel, not the highest creature, but his Son, his only begotten Son; and what but love could move him to appoint such a Saviour? Consider the manner in which he was sent, as a gift, a free unmerited gift; " God gave his only begotten Son:" And what but infinite love could give such an unspeakable gift? Consider the blessings conferred through this Saviour, deliverance from perdition and the enjoyment of everlasting life, and what but the love of God could confer such blessings? Consider the condition upon which these blessings are offered, faith, that humble, self-emptied grace, so suitable to the circumstances of a poor sinner, that brings nothing but receives all, and what but divine love could make such a gracious appointment?

It is by faith, that it may be of grace. Rom. iv. 16. Confider the indefinite extent, or the univerfality of the offer, which takes in finners of the vileft characters, and excepts againſt none: *Whofoever believeth shall not perish,* &c. O what love is this! But I muſt leave it as the theme of your meditations; not only in the houſe of your pilgrimage, but through all eternity: eternity will be ſhort enough to pry into this myſtery, and it will employ the underſtandings of men and angels through the revolutions of eternal ages.

And now, my brethren, to draw towards a concluſion, I would hold a treaty with you this day about the reconciliation to God through Jeſus Chriſt. I have this day ſet life and death before you: I have opened to you the method of ſalvation through Jeſus Chriſt: the only method in which you can be ſaved; the only method that could afford a gleam of hope to ſuch a ſinner as I in my late approach to the eternal world*. And now I would bring the matter home, and propoſe it to you all to conſent to be ſaved in this method, or, in other words, to believe in the only begotten Son of God; this propoſal I ſeriouſly make to you; and let heaven and earth, and your own conſciences, witneſs that it is made to you; I alſo inſiſt for a determinate anſwer this day; the matter will not admit of a delay, and the duty is ſo plain, that there is no need of time to deliberate. A Roman ambaſſador, treating about peace with the ambaſſador of a neighbouring ſtate, if I remember rightly, and finding him deſirous to gain time by ſhuffling and tedious negociations, drew a circle about him, and ſaid, "I demand an anſwer before you go out of this circle."—Such a circle let the walls of this houſe, or the extent of my voice, be to you: before you leave this houſe, or go out of hearing, I inſiſt on a full deciſive anſwer to this propoſal, Whether you will believe in Jeſus Chriſt this day or not?

But before I proceed any farther, I would remove one ſtumbling-block out of your way. You are apt to object, "You teach us that faith is the gift of God, and that we cannot believe of ourſelves; why then do you exhort us to it? or how can we be concerned to endeavour that which it is impoſſible for us to do?"

In anſwer to this, I grant the premiſes are true; and God forbid I ſhould ſo much as intimate that faith is the ſpontaneous growth of corrupt nature, or that you can come to Chriſt without the Father's drawing you: but the concluſions you draw from theſe premiſes are very erroneous. I exhort and perſuade you to believe in Jeſus Chriſt, becauſe it is while ſuch means are uſed with ſinners, and by the uſe of them, that it pleaſes God to enable them to comply; or to work faith in them. I would therefore uſe thoſe means

---

* This ſermon was preached a little after recovery from a ſevere fit of ſickneſs, and it is dated Hanover, Oct. 2, 1757.

which God is pleased to bless for this end. I exhort you to believe, in order to set you upon the trial; for it is putting it to trial, and that only, which can fully convince you of your own inability to believe; and till you are convinced of this, you can never expect strength from God. I exhort you to believe, because, sinful and enfeebled as you are, you are capable of using various preparatives to faith. You may attend upon prayer, hearing, and all the outward means of grace with natural seriousness; you may endeavour to get acquainted with your own helpless condition, and, as it were, put yourselves in the way of divine mercy; and though all these means cannot of themselves produce faith in you, yet it is only in the use of these means you are to expect divine grace to work it in you: never was it yet produced in one soul, while lying supine, lazy, and inactive.

I hope you now see good reasons why I should exhort you to believe, and also perceive my design in it; I therefore renew the proposal to you, that you should this day, as guilty, unworthy, self-despairing sinners, accept of the only begotten Son of God as your Saviour, and fall in with the gospel-method of salvation; and I once more demand your answer. I would by no means, if possible, leave the pulpit this day till I have effectually recommended the blessed Jesus, my Lord and Master, to your acceptance. I am strongly bound by the vows and resolutions of a sick bed to recommend him to you; and now I would endeavour to perform my vows. I would have us all this day, before we part, consent to God's covenant, that we may go away justified to our houses.

To this I persuade and exhort you, in the name and by the authority of the great God, by the death of Jesus Christ for sinners, by your own most urgent and absolute necessity, by the immense blessings proposed in the gospel, and by the heavy curse denounced against unbelievers.

All the blessings of the gospel, pardon of sin, sanctifying grace, eternal life, and whatever you can want, shall become yours this day, if you but believe in the Son of God: then let desolation over-run our land, let public and private calamities crowd upon you, and make you so many Jobs for poverty and affliction, still your main interest is secure; the storms and waves of trouble can only bear you to heaven, and hasten your passage to the harbour of eternal rest. Let devils accuse you before God, let conscience indict you and bring you in guilty, let the fiery law make its demands upon you, you have a righteousness in Jesus Christ that is sufficient to answer all demands, and, having received it by faith, you may plead it as your own in law. Happy souls! rejoice in hope of the glory of God, for your hope will never make you ashamed!

But I expect, as usual, some of you will refuse to comply with this proposal. This, alas! has been the usual fate of the blessed gospel in all ages and in all countries; as some have received it, so some have rejected it. That old complaint of Isaiah has been justly repeated thousands of times; *Who hath believed our report? and to whom is the arm of the Lord revealed?* Isai. liii. 1. And is there no reason to pour it out from a broken heart over some of you, my dear people! Are you all this day determined to believe? If so, I pronounce you blessed in the name of the Lord; but if not, I must denounce your doom.

Be it known to you then from the living God, that if you thus continue in unbelief, you shut the door of mercy against yourselves, and exclude yourselves from eternal life. Whatever splendid appearances of virtue, whatever amiable qualities, whatever seeming good works you have, the express sentence of the gospel lies in full force against you, *He that believeth not shall be damned.* Mark xvi. 16. *He that believeth not is condemned already, because he hath not believed on the only begotten Son of God.* John iii. 18. *He that believeth not shall not see life; but the wrath of God abideth upon him.* John iii. 36. This is your doom repeatedly pronounced by him whom you must own to be the best friend of human nature; and if he condemn, who can justify you?

Be it also known to you, that you will not only perish, but you will perish with peculiar aggravations; you will fall with no common ruin; you will envy the lot of heathens who perished without the law: for O! you incur the peculiarly enormous guilt of rejecting the gospel, and putting contempt upon the Son of God. This is an horrid exploit of wickedness, and this God resents above all the other crimes of which human nature is capable. Hence Christ is come for judgment as well as for mercy into this world, and he is set for the fall as well as the rising again of many in Israel. You now enjoy the light of the gospel, which has conducted many through this dark world to eternal day; but remember also, *this is the condemnation;* that is, it is the occasion of the most aggravated condemnation, *that light is come into the world, and men love darkness rather than light.* On this principle Jesus pronounced the doom of Chorazin and Bethsaida more intolerable than that of Sodom and Gomorrah. Matth. xi. 21, 22. And would it not be hard to find a place in Virginia where the doom of unbelievers is likely to be so terrible as among us?

And now does not all this move you? Are you not alarmed at the thought of perishing; of perishing by the hand of a Saviour rejected and despised; perishing under the stain of his profaned blood; perishing not only under the curse of the law, but under that of the gospel, which is vastly heavier? O! are you hardy enough to venture upon such a doom? This doom is unavoidable if you refuse to comply with the proposal now made to you.

I must now conclude the treaty; but for my own acquittance, I must take witness that I have endeavoured to discharge my commission, whatever reception you give it. I call heaven and earth, and your own consciences to witness, that life and salvation, through Jesus Christ, have been offered to you on this day; and if you reject it, remember it; remember it whenever you see this place; remember it whenever you see my face, or one another; remember it, that you may witness for me at the supreme tribunal, that I am clear of your blood. Alas! you will remember it among a thousand painful reflections millions of ages hence, when the remembrance of it will rend your hearts like a vulture. Many sermons forgotten upon earth are remembered in hell, and haunt the guilty mind for ever. O that you would believe, and so prevent this dreadful effect from the present sermon!

SERMON III.

Sinners intreated to be reconciled to God.

2 COR. v. 20. *We then are ambassadors for Christ, as though God did beseech you by us: we pray you in Christ's stead, be ye reconciled to God.*

TO preside in the solemnities of public worship, to direct your thoughts, and choose for you the subjects of your meditation on those sacred hours which you spend in the house of God, and upon the right improvement of which your everlasting happiness so much depends, this is a province of the most tremendous importance that can be devolved upon a mortal; and every man of the sacred character, who knows what he is about, must tremble at the thought, and be often anxiously perplexed what subject he shall choose, what he shall say upon it, and in what manner he shall deliver his message. His success in a great measure depends upon his choice; for, though the blessed Spirit is the proper agent, and though the best means, without his efficacious concurrence, are altogether fruitless, yet he is wont to bless those means that are best adapted to do good; and after a long course of languid and fruitless efforts, which seem to have been unusually disowned by my divine Master, what text shall I choose out of the inexhaustible treasure of God's word? In what new method shall I speak upon it? What new untried experiments shall I make? Blessed Jesus! my heavenly Master! direct thy poor perplexed servant who is at a loss, and knows not what to do; direct him that has tried, and tried again, all the expedients he could think of, but almost in vain;

and now scarcely knows what it is to hope for succefs! Divine direction, my brethren, has been fought; and may I hope it is that which has turned my mind to addrefs you this day on the important fubject of your reconciliation to God, and to become an humble imitator of the great St. Paul, whofe affecting words I have read to you. *We then are ambaffadors for Chrift; as though God did befeech you by us: we pray you in Chrift's ftead, be ye reconciled to God.*

The introduction to this paffage you find in the foregoing verfes, *God hath given to us* (the apoftles) *the miniftry of reconciliation;* the fum and fubftance of which is, namely, "That God was in Chrift reconciling the world unto himfelf, not imputing their trefpaffes unto them." As if he had faid, "The great Soveregin of the univerfe, though highly provoked, and juftly difpleafed with our rebellious world, has been fo gracious as to contrive a plan of reconciliation whereby they may not only efcape the punifhment they deferve, but alfo be reftored to the favour of God, and all the privileges of his favourite fubjects. This plan was laid in Chrift; that is, it was he who was appointed, and undertook to remove all obftacles out of the way of their reconciliation, fo that it might be confiftent with the honour and dignity of God and his government. This he performed by a life of perfect obedience; and an atoning death, inftead of rebellious man. Though "he knew no fin" of his own; yet "he made fin," that is, a fin-offering, or a finner by imputation "for us," that we might "be made the righteoufnefs of God in him." Thus all hindrances are removed on God's part. The plan of a treaty of reconciliation is formed, approved, and ratified in the court of heaven; but then it muft be publifhed, all the terms made known, and the confent of the rebels folicited and gained. It is not enough that all impediments to peace are removed on God's part; they muft alfo be removed on the part of man; the reconciliation muft be mutual; both the parties muft agree. Hence arifes the neceffity of the miniftry of reconciliation which was committed to the apoftles, thofe prime minifters of the kingdom of Chrift, and in a lower fphere to the ordinary minifters of the gofpel in every age. The great bufinefs of their office is to publifh the treaty of peace; that is, the articles of reconciliation, and to ufe every motive to gain the confent of mankind to thefe articles. It is this office St. Paul is difcharging, when he fays, *We are ambaffadors for Chrift, as though God did befeech you by us: we pray you in Chrift's ftead, be ye reconciled to God.*

We are ambaffadors for Chrift. The proper notion of an ambaffador, is that of a perfon fent by a king to tranfact affairs in his name, and according to his inftructions, with foreign ftates, or part of his fubjects, to whom he does not think proper to go himself and treat with them in his own person. Thus a peace is generally concluded between contending nations, not by their kings in person, but by their plenipotentiaries acting in their name, and by their authority; and, while they keep to their instructions, their negociations and agreements are as valid and authentic as if they were carried on and concluded by their masters in person. Thus the Lord Jesus Christ is not personally present in our world to manage the treaty of peace himself, but he has appointed first his apostles, and then the ministers of the gospel through every age, to carry it on in his name. This is their proper character; they are ambassadors for Christ, his plenipotentiaries, furnished with a commission and instructions to make overtures of reconciliation to a rebel world, and treat with them to gain their consent.

Indeed, aspiring ecclesiastics have assumed highsounding titles merely to produce extravagant honours to themselves. They have called themselves ambassadors of Christ, messengers from God, the plenipotentiaries and viceroys of heaven, and I know not what, not with a design to do honour to their Master, but to keep the world in a superstitious awe of themselves. This priestly pride and insolence I utterly abhor; and yet I humbly adventure to assume the title of an ambassador of the great King of heaven, and require you to regard me in this high character : but then you must know, that while I am making this claim, I own myself obliged inviolably to adhere to the instructions of my divine Master contained in the Bible. I have no power over your faith; no power to dictate or prescribe; but my work is only just to publish the articles of peace as my Master has established and revealed them in his word, without the least addition, diminution, or alteration. I pretend to no higher power than this, and this power I must claim, unless I would renounce my office; for who can consistently profess himself a minister of Christ without asserting his right and power to publish what his Lord has taught, and communicate his royal instructions?

Therefore without usurping an equality with St. Paul, or his fellow apostles, I must tell you in his language, I appear among you this day as the ambassador of the most high God; I am discharging an embassy for Christ*; and I tell you this with no other design than to procure your most serious regard to what I say. If you consider it only as my declaration, whatever regard you pay to it, the end of my ministry will not be answered upon you. The end of my office is not to make myself the object of your love and veneration, but to reconcile you to God; but you cannot be reconciled to God while you consider the proposal as made to you only by your fellow mortal. You must regard it as made to you by

---

* This is the most literal translation of ἀπρεσβεύομεν ὑπὲρ χριστοῦ.

the Lord Jesus Christ, the great Mediator between God and man. I not only allow, but even invite and charge you to enquire and judge whether what I say be agreeable to my divine instructions, which are as open to your inspection as mine, and to regard it no farther than it is so: but if I follow these instructions, and propose the treaty of peace to you just as it is concluded in heaven, then I charge you to regard it as proposed by the Lord of heaven and earth, the King of kings, and Lord of lords, though through my unworthy lips. Consider yourselves this day as the hearers not of a preacher formed out of the clay like yourselves, but of the Lord Jesus Christ. Suppose him here in person treating with you about your reconciliation to God, and what regard you would pay to a proposal made by him in person, with all his divine royalties about him, that you should now shew to the treaty I am to negociate with you in his name and stead.

The next sentence in my text binds you still more strongly to this; *as though God did beseech you by us.* As if he had said, "God the Father also concurs in this treaty of peace, as well as Christ the great peacemaker; and as we discharge an embassy for Christ, so we do also for God; and you are to regard our beseeching and exhorting*, as though the great God did in person beseech and exhort you by us." What astonishing condescension is here intimated! not that the ministers of Christ should beseech you; this would be no mighty condescension: but that the supreme Jehovah should beseech you; that he should not only command you with a stern air of authority as your Sovereign, but as a friend, nay, as a petitioner should affectionately beseech you, you despicable, guilty worms, obnoxious rebels! How astonishing, how God-like, how unprecedented and inimitable is this condescension! Let heaven and earth admire and adore! It is by us, indeed, by us your poor fellow mortals, that he beseeches; but O! let not this tempt you to disregard him or his intreaty : though he employs such mean ambassadors, yet consider his dignity who sends us, and then you cannot disregard his message even from our mouth.

The apostle, having thus prepared the way, proceeds to the actual exercise of his office as an ambassador for Christ: *We pray you*, says he, *in Christ's stead, be reconciled to God*. As if he had said, "If Christ were now present in person among you, this is what he would propose to you, and urge upon you, that you would be reconciled to God; but him the heavens must receive till the time of the restitution of all things; but he has left us his poor servants to officiate in his place as well as we can, and we would prosecute the same design, we would urge upon you what he would urge, were he to speak; therefore we pray you, in his stead, be ye reconciled to God: we earnestly pray you to be reconciled: that is the utmost which such feeble worms as we can do : we can only

---

* παρακαλέω signifies *exhorting*, as well as *beseeching*.

pray and beg, but your compliance is not within the command of our power;. the compliance belongs to you; and remember, if you refuse, you must take it upon yourselves, and answer the consequence."

Having thus explained the text, I proceed in my poor manner to exemplify it by negociating the treaty with you for your reconciliation to God; and you see my business lies directly with such of you as are as yet enemies to God: you are the only persons that stand in need of reconciliation. As for such of you (and I doubt not but there are such among you) whose innate enmity has been subdued, and who are become the friends and subjects of the King of heaven after your guilty revolt, I must desire you as it were to stand by yourselves for the present hour, and help me by your prayers, while I am speaking to your poor brethren, who still continue in that state of hostility and rebellion against God, in which you once were, and the miseries of which you well know, and still lament and deplore.

But by this proposal I am afraid I have deprived myself of hearers on this subject; for have you not all already placed yourselves among the lovers of God, who consequently do not need to be reconciled to him? Is not every one of you ready to say to me, "If your business only lies with the enemies of God, you have no concern with me in this discourse? for, God forbid that I should be an enemy to him. I have indeed been guilty of a great many sins, but I had no bad design in them, and never had the least enmity against my Maker; so far from it, that I shudder at the very thought!" This is the first obstacle that I meet with in discharging my embassy: the embassy itself is looked upon as needless by the persons concerned, like an attempt to reconcile those that are good friends already. This obstacle must be removed before we can proceed any farther.

I am far from charging any of you with so horrid a crime as enmity and rebellion against God, who can produce satisfactory evidences to your own conscience that you are his friends. I only desire that you would not flatter yourselves, nor draw a rash and groundless conclusion in an affair of such infinite moment, but that you would put the matter to a fair trial, according to evidence, and then let your conscience pass an impartial sentence as your judge, under the supreme Judge of the world.

You plead "Not guilty" to the charge, and alledge that you have always loved God; but if this be the case, whence is it that you have afforded him so few of your affectionate and warm thoughts? Do not your tenderest thoughts dwell upon the objects of your love? But has not your mind been shy of him who gave you your power of thinking? Have not you lived stupidly thoughtless of him for days and weeks together? Nay, have not serious thoughts of him been unwelcome, and made you uneafy? and have you not turned every way to avoid them? Have you not often prayed to him, and concurred in other acts of religious worfhip, and yet had but very few or no devout thoughts of him, even at the very time? And is that mind well affected towards him that is fo averfe to him, and turns every way to fhun a glance of him? Alas! is this your friendfhip for the God that made you, whofe you are, and whom you ought to ferve!

Would you not have indulged the fool's wifh, that there were no God, had not the horror and impoffibility of the thing reftrained you? But, notwithftanding this reftraint, has not this blafphemy fhed its malignant poifon at times in your hearts? If there was no God, then you would fin without controul, and without dread of punifhment; and how fweet was this! Then you would have nothing to do with that melancholy thing, religion; and what an agreeable exemption would this be! But is this your love for him, to wifh the Parent of all being out of being! Alas! can the rankeft enmity rife higher!

Again, if you are reconciled to God, whence is it that you are fecretly, or perhaps openly difaffected to his image, I mean the purity and ftrictnefs of his law, and the lineaments of holinefs that appear upon the unfafhionable religious few? If you loved God, you would of courfe love every thing that bears any refemblance to him. But are you not confcious that it is otherwife with you; that you murmur and cavil at the reftraints of God's law, and would much rather abjure it, be free from it, and live as you lift? Are you not confcious that nothing expofes a man more to your fecret difguft and contempt, and perhaps to your public mockery and ridicule, than a ftrict and holy walk, and a confcientious obfervance of the duties of devotion? And if you catch your neighbour in any of thefe offences, do not your hearts rife againft him? and what is this but the effect of your enmity againft God? Do you thus difguft a man for wearing the genuine image and refemblance of your friend? No; the effect of love is quite the reverfe.

Again, If you do but reflect upon the daily fenfations of your own minds, muft you not be confcious that you love other perfons and things more than God? that you love pleafure, honour, riches, your relations and friends, more than the glorious and everblefled God? Look into your own hearts, and you will find it fo: you will find that this, and that, and a thoufand things in this world, engrofs more of your thoughts, your cares, defires, joys, forrows, hopes, and fears, than God, or any of his concerns.— Now it is effential to the love of God that it be fupreme. You do not love him truly at all, in the leaft degree, if you do not love him above all; above all perfons and things in the whole univerfe. He is a jealous God, and will not fuffer a rival. A lower degree of love for supreme excellence is an affront and indignity. Is it not therefore evident, even to your own conviction, that you do not love God at all; and what is this but to be his enemy? To be indifferent towards him, as though he were an infignificant being, neither good nor evil, a mere cypher; to feel neither love nor hatred towards him, but to neglect him, as if you had no concern with him one way or other; what an horrible difpofition it this towards him, who is fupremely and infinitely glorious and amiable, your Creator, your Sovereign, and Benefactor; who therefore deferves and demands your higheft love; or, in the words of his own law, *that you should love him with all your heart, with all your soul, with all your mind, and with all your strength.* Mark xii. 30. From what can fuch indifferency towards him proceed but from difaffection and enmity? It is in this way that the enmity of men towards God moft generally difcovers itfelf. They feel, perhaps, no pofitive workings of hatred towards him, unlefs when their innate corruption, like an exafperated ferpent, is irritated by conviction from his law; but they feel an apathy, a littleffnefs, an indifferency towards him; and becaufe they feel no more, they flatter themfelves they are far from hating him; efpecially as they may have very honourable fpeculative thoughts of him floating on the furface of their minds. But alas! this very thing, this indifferency, or liftlefs neutrality, is the very core of their enmity; and if they are thus indifferent to him now, while enjoying fo many bleffings from his hand, and while he delays their punifhment, how will their enmity fwell and rife to all the rage of a devil againft him, when he puts forth his vindictive hand and touches them, and fo gives occafion to it to difcover its venom! My foul fhudders to think what horrid infurrections and direct rebellion this temper will produce when once irritated, and all reftraints are taken off; which will be the doom of finners in the eternal world; and then they will have no more of the love of God in them than the moft malignant devil in hell! If therefore you generally feel fuch an indifferency towards God, be affured you are not reconciled to him, but are his enemies in your hearts.

Again, All moral evil, or fin, is contrary to God; it is the only thing upon earth, or in hell, that is moft oppofite to his holy nature; and the object of his implacable and eternal indignation. He is of purer eyes than to behold it or endure it. It is his hatred to fin that has turned his heart againft any of his creatures; and is the caufe of all the vengeance that he has inflicted upon the guilty inhabitants of our world, or the fpirits of hell. There is no object in the whole compafs of the univerfe fo odious to you as every fin is to a pure and all-holy God : now it is impoffible you fhould at once love two things fo oppofite, fo eternally irreconcileable. As much love as you have for any unlawful pleafure, juft fo much enmity there is in your hearts towards God. Hence, says St. Paul, *you were enemies in your minds by wicked works*. Col. i. 21. Intimating, that the love and practice of our wicked works is a plain evidence of inward enmity of mind towards God. The works of the flesh are sinful: hence, says the same apostle, *the carnal mind, or the minding of the flesh*, φρόνημα σαρκός, Rom. viii. 7. *is enmity against God; it is not subject to the law of God, neither indeed can it be: so then they that are in the flesh*, or under the power of a carnal mind, *cannot please God*. Rom. viii. 8. Because, whatever seeming acts of obedience they perform, and whatever appearances of friendship they put on, they are at heart enemies to God, and therefore cannot please him, who searches their heart, and sees the secret principle of their actions. Hence also St. James tells us, *that if any man would be a friend to the world, he is the enemy of God, because the friendship of the world is enmity against God*. Jam. iv. 4. For the world enflames the lusts of men, and occasions much sin; and if we love the tempter, we love the sin to which it would allure us; and if we love the sin, we are the enemies of God; and therefore the friendship of the world is enmity against God. This then is an established maxim, without straining the matter too far, that as far as you love any sin, so far are you enemies to God. The love, as well as the service of such opposite masters, is utterly inconsistent. Now, do not your own consciences witness against you, that you have indulged, and still do habitually indulge the love of some sin or other? Whether it be covetousness or sensual pleasure, or ambition, or some angry passion, or whatever sin it be, as far as you love it, so far you are enemies to God; and if you take a view of your temper and practice, must you not unavoidably be convicted of this dreadful guilt? Horrible as the crime is is, it not an undeniable matter of fact, that you do really love some sin, and consequently hate the infinitely amiable and ever blessed God? and therefore you are the persons I have to deal with, as needing reconciliation with God.

Farther, Take a view of your general manner of serving God in the duties of religion: your manner of praying, meditation, hearing the word of God, and other acts of devotion, and then inquire, Do you perform this service as the willing servants of a master you love? Do you not enter upon such service with reluctance or listlessness, and perform it with langour and indifferency, as a business to which you have no heart? But is this your manner of performing a labour of love to a friend? Will your own reason suffer you to think you would be so luke-warm and heartless in the worship of God if you sincerely loved him? No; love is an active principle, a vigorous spring of action; and if this were the principle of your religious services, you would infuse more spirit and life into them, you would exert all your powers, and be *fervent in spirit, serving the Lord*. Rom. xii. 11.

But when you have performed offices of devotion with some degree of earnestness, which no doubt you have sometimes done, what was the principle or spring of your exertion? Was it the love of God? or was it purely the low principle of self-love? Why did you pray with such eager importunity, and attend upon the other means of grace with so much seriousness, but because you apprehended your dear selves were in danger, and you were not willing to be miserable for ever? This servile, mercenary kind of religious earnestness will not prove that you love God, but only that you love yourselves; and this you may do, and yet have no more true goodness, or genuine love to God, than an infernal spirit; for there is not a spirit in hell but what loves himself. Indeed self-love is so far from being an evidence of the love of God, that the extravagant excess of it is the source of that wickedness that abounds among men and devils. I do not mean by this utterly to exclude self-love out of genuine religion; it must have its place in the most excellent and best beings, but then it must be kept in a proper subordination, and not advance the creature above the Creator, and dethrone the supreme King of the universe. —His love must be uppermost in the heart, and when that has the highest place, the indulgence of self-love in pursuing our own happiness is lawful, and an important duty. Now, do you not find from this view of the case, that you are not reconciled to God, even in your most devout and zealous hours, much less in the languid inactive tenour of your lives? If so, place yourselves among those that I have to do with to-day; that is, the enemies of God-

So also, when you perform good offices to mankind; when you are harmless, obliging neighbours; when you are charitable to the poor, or strictly just in trade; is the love of God, and a regard to his authority, the reason and principle of your actions? That is, do you do these things because God commands them, and because you delight to do what he commands? or rather, do you not do them merely because it is your nature to perform humane and honourable actions in such instances; or because you may acquire honour, or some selfish advantage by them? Alas! that God should be neglected, forgotten, and left out of the question, as of no importance, even in those actions that are materially good! that even what he commands should be done, not because he commands it, but for some other sordid selfish reason! O! if you did really love God, would you thus disregard him, and do nothing for his sake; not only when you are doing what he forbids, but even when you are performing what he has made your duty! Would he be such a cypher, a mere nothing in your practical esteem, if your hearts were reconciled to him as your God? No; such of you must look upon yourselves as the very persons whom I am to pray, in Christ's stead, to be reconciled to God.

I might thus, from obvious facts, lay before you many more evidences of your disaffection to the great God ; but I must leave some room for the other part of my addrefs to you, in which I am to perfuade you to accept of the propofal of reconciliation ; and therefore I shall add only one more teft of your pretended friendfhip, a teft which is eftablifhed by the great Founder of our religion, as infallibly decifive in this cafe ; and that is, obedience, or the keeping of the commandments of God. This, I fay, is eftablifhed in the ftrongeft terms by Jefus Chrift himfelf, as a decifive teft of love, *If you love me, keep my commandments.* John xiv. 15. *Then are ye my friends if ye do whatfoever I command you.* John xv. 14. *If any man love me, he will keep my words. He that loveth me not, keepeth not my faying.* John xiv. 23, 24. *This is the love of God,* fays St. John, *that we keep his commandments ; and his commandments are not grievous.* 1 John v. 3 ; that is, they are not grievous when love is the principle of obedience. The fervice of love is always willing and pleafing. Now, my brethren, bring your hearts and lives to this ftandard, and let confcience declare, Are there not fome demands and reftraints of the divine law fo difagreeable to you that you labour to keep yourfelves ignorant of them, and turn every way to avoid the painful light of conviction? Are there not feveral duties which you know in your confciences to be fuch, which you do not fo much as honeftly endeavour to perform, but knowingly and wilfully neglect? And are there not fome favourite fins which your confciences tell you God has forbidden, which yet are fo pleafing to you, that you knowingly and allowedly indulge and practife them ? If this be your cafe, you need not pretend to plead any thing in your own defence, or hefitate any longer ; the cafe is plain, you are, beyond all doubt, enemies to God ; you are undeniably convicted of it this day by irrefiftible evidence. You perhaps glory in the profeffion of Chriftians, but you are, notwithftanding, enemies to God. You attend on public worfhip, you pray, you read, you communicate, you are perhaps a zealous churchman or diffenter, but you are enemies of God. You have perhaps had many fits of religious affection, and ferious concern about your everlafting happinefs, but notwithftanding you are enemies of God. You may have reformed in many things, but you are ftill enemies of God. Men may efteem you Chriftians, but the God of Heaven accounts you his enemies. In vain do you infift upon it, that you have never hated your Maker all your life, but even tremble at the thought, for undeniable facts are againft you ; and the reafon why you have not feen your enmity was, becaufe you were blind, and judged upon wrong principles : but if you this day feel the force of conviction from the law, and have your eyes opened, you will fee and be fhocked at your horrid enmity againft God, before yonder fun fets.

And now, when I have fingled out from the reft thofe I am now to befeech to reconciliation with God, have I not got the majority of you to treat with? Where are the fincere lovers of God? Alas! how few are they! and how imperfect even in their love, fo that they hardly dare call themfelves lovers of God, but tremble left they fhould ftill belong to the wretched crowd that are ftill unreconciled to him!

Ye rebels againft the King of Heaven! ye enemies againft my Lord and Mafter Jefus Chrift! (I cannot flatter you with a fofter name) hear me; attend to the propofal I make to you, not in my own name, but in the name and ftead of your rightful Sovereign; and that is, that you will this day be reconciled to God. " I pray you in his ftead (that is all I can do) " be ye reconciled to God." That you may know what I mean, I will more particularly explain this overture to you.

If you would be reconciled to God, you muft be deeply fenfible of the guilt, the wickednefs, the bafenefs, the inexpreffible malignity of your enmity and rebellion againft him. You muft return to your rightful fovereign as convicted, felf-condemned, penitent, broken-hearted rebels, confounded and afhamed of your conduct, loathing yourfelves becaufe you have loathed the fupreme Excellence, mourning over your unnatural difaffection, your bafe ingratitude, your horrid rebellion againft fo good a King. And what do you fay to this article of the treaty of peace? Is it an hard thing for fuch caufelefs enemies to fall upon the knee, and to mourn and weep as proftrate penitents at the feet of their injured Maker? Is it an hard thing for one that has all his life been guilty of the blackeft crime upon earth, or even in hell, I mean enmity againft God, to confefs " I have finned," and to feel his own confeffion? to feel it, I fay; for if he does not feel it, his confeffion is but an empty compliment, that increafes his guilt.

Again, If you would be reconciled to God, you muft heartily confent to be reconciled to him in Chrift; that is, you muft come in upon the footing of that act of grace which is publifhed in the gofpel through Chrift, and expecting no favour at all upon the footing of your own goodnefs. The merit of what you call your good actions, of your repentance, your prayers, your acts of charity and juftice, muft all pafs for nothing in this refpect : you muft depend only and entirely upon the merit of Chrift's obedience and fufferings as the ground of your acceptance with God; and hope for forgivenefs and favour from his mere mercy beftowed upon you, only for the fake of Chrift, or on account of what he has done and fuffered in the ftead of finners. The context informs you, that it is only in Chrift that God is reconciling the world to himfelf; and confequently it is only in Chrift that the world muft accept of reconciliation and pardon. It does not confift with the dignity and perfections of the King of Heaven to receive rebels into favour upon any other footing. I would have you confent to every article of the overture as I go along; and therefore here again I make a paufe to afk you, what do you think of this article? Are you willing to comply with it, willing to come into favour with God, as convicted, felf-condemned rebels, upon an act of grace procured by the righteoufnefs of Chrift alone? Is it a mortification to creatures that never have done one action truly good in all their lives, because they have never loved God in one moment of their lives; creatures that have always, even in what they accounted their beft difpofitions, and beft actions, been hateful to God, becaufe even in their beft difpofitions and beft actions they were utterly deftitute of his love? Is it a mortification to fuch creatures to renounce all their own merit, and confent to be faved only through grace, on account of the righteoufnefs of another, even of Jefus Chrift the great peace-maker? Can it be a mortification to you to renounce what you have not, and to own yourfelves guilty, and utterly unworthy, when you are really fuch? O! may I not expect your compliance with this term of reconciliation?

Again, If you would be reconciled to God, you muft engage yourfelves in his fervice for the future, and devote yourfelves to do his will. His law muft be the rule of your temper and practice: whatever he commands, you muft honeftly endeavour to perform, without exception of any one duty as difagreeable and laborious; and whatever he forbids, you muft, for that reafon, abftain from, however pleafing, advantageous, or fafhionable. You muft no longer look upon yourfelves as your own, but as bought with a price, and therefore bound to glorify God with your fouls and your bodies, which are his. And can you make any difficulty of complying with this term; of obeying Him, whom the happy angels in heaven obey; of obferving that law which always unites your duty and your happinefs, and forbids nothing but what is itfelf injurious to you in the nature of things; of doing the will of the wifeft and beft of beings rather than your own, who are ignorant and depraved creatures? O! can you make any difficulty of this? If not, you will return home this day reconciled to God; an happinefs you have never yet enjoyed for one moment.

Finally, If you would be reconciled to God, you muft break off all friendfhip with his enemies; your friendfhip with the world, I mean your attachment to its wicked fafhions and cuftoms, and your fondnefs for its rebellious inhabitants, who continue enemies to God; your love of guilty pleafures, and every form of fin, however pleafing or gainful you might imagine it to be; your old habits and practices, while enemies to God; all thefe you muft break off for ever; for your friendfhip with thefe is utterly inconsistent with the love of God. As long as you are resolved to love the world, to keep up your society with your old companions in sin, to retain your old pleasures and evil practices; as long, I say, as you are resolved upon this course, farewell all hope of your reconciliation to God: it is absolutely impossible. And do any of you hesitate at this article? Is sin so noble a thing in itself, and so happy in its consequences, as that you should be so loth to part with it? Is it so sweet a thing to you to sin against God, that you know not how to forbear? Alas! will you rather be an implacable enemy to the God that made you, than break your league with his enemies and your own? Do you love your sins so well, and are you so obliged to them, that you will lay down your life, your eternal life, for their sake?

I might multiply particulars, but these are the principal articles of that treaty of peace I am negociating with you; and a consent to these includes a compliance with all the rest. And are you determined to comply? Does the heaven-born purpose now rise in your minds, "I am determined I will be an enemy of God no longer; but this very day I will be reconciled to God upon his own terms!" Is this your fixed purpose? or is there any occasion to pray and persuade you?

I well know, and it is fit you should know, that you are not able of yourselves to consent to these terms, but that it is the work of the power of God alone to reconcile you to himself; and that all my persuasions and intreaties will never make you either able or willing. You will then ask me, perhaps, "Why do I propose the terms to you, or use any persuasives or intreaties with you?" I answer, Because you never will be sensible of your inability till you make an honest trial, and because you never will look and pray for the aid of the blessed spirit till you are deeply sensible of your own insufficiency: and further, because, if the blessed spirit should ever effectually work upon you, it will be by enlightening your understandings to see the reasonableness of the terms, and the force of the persuasives; and in this way, agreeably to your reasonable natures, sweetly constraining your obstinate wills to yield yourselves to God: therefore the terms must be proposed to you, and persuasives used, if I would be subservient to this divine agent, and furnish him with materials with which to work: and I have some little hope that he will, as it were, catch my feeble words from my lips before they vanish into air, and bear them home to your hearts with a power which you will not be able to resist. Finally, a conviction of the true state of your case may constrain you from self-love and the low principles of nature to use the means of reconciliation with zeal and earnestness: this you are capable of, even with the mere strength of degenerate nature: and it is only in this way of earnest endeavours that you have any encouragement to hope for divine aid: therefore, notwithstanding your utter impotence, I must pray, intreat, and perfuade you to be reconciled to God.

I pray you, in the name of the great God your heavenly Father, and of Jefus Chrift your Redeemer. If God fhould once more renew the thunder and lightning, and darkness and tempeft of Sinai, and fpeak to you as he once did to the trembling Ifraelites; or if he fhould appear to you in all the amiable and alluring glories of a fin-pardoning reconcileable God, and pray you to be reconciled to him, would you not then regard the propofal? or if Jefus, who once prayed for you from the crofs, fhould now pray to you from his throne in heaven, and beg you with his own precious voice to be reconciled, O! could you difregard the intreaty? Surely no. Now the overture of peace is as really made to you by the bleffed God and Son Jefus Chrift, as if it were exprefsly propofed to you by an immediate voice from heaven. For I befeech you, *as though God did befeech you* by me, and it is *in Chrift's ftead*, that I pray you *be reconciled to God*. Therefore, however lightly you may make of a mere propofal of mine, can you difregard an overture from the God that made you, and the Saviour that bought you with his blood; in which I am but the faint echo of their voice from heaven.

In the name of God I pray you; the name of the greateft and beft of beings; that name which angles love and adore, and which ftrikes terror through the hardieft devil in the infernal regions; the name of your Father, the immediate Father of your fpirits, and the Author of your mortal frames; the name of your Preferver and Benefactor, in whom you live, and move, and have your being; and who gives you life, and breath, and all things; the name of your rightful Sovereign and Lawgiver, who has a right to demand your love and obedience; the name of your fupreme Judge, who will afcend the tribunal, and acquit or condemn you, as he finds you friends or foes; the name of that God, rich in goodnefs, who has replenifhed heaven with an infinite plenitude of happinefs, in which he will allow you to fhare, after all your hoftility and rebellion, if you confent to the overture of reconciliation; in the name of that God of terrible majefty and juftice, who has prepared the dungeon of hell as a prifon for his enemies, where he holds in chains the mighty powers of darknefs, and thoufands of your own race, who perfifted in that enmity to him of which you are now guilty, and with whom you muft have your everlafting portion, if, like them, you continue hardened and incorrigible in your rebellion; in the name of that compaffionate God, who fent his dear Son (O the tranfporting thought!) to fatisfy divine juftice for you by his death, and the precepts of the law by his life, and thus to remove all obftructions out of the way of your reconciliation on the part of God; in this great, this endearing and tremendous name, I pray you be reconciled to God. I pray you for his sake; and has this name no weight with you? Will you do nothing for his sake? what, not so reasonable and advantageous a thing as dropping your unnatural rebellion, and being reconciled to him? Is your contempt of God risen to that pitch that you will not do the most reasonable and profitable thing in the world, if he intreat you to do it? Be astonished, O ye heavens! at this.

I pray you both in the name and for the sake of Jesus Christ, the true friend of publicans and sinners, in his name, and for his sake, who assumed your degraded nature, that he might dignify and save it; who lived a life of labour, poverty, and persecution upon earth, that you might enjoy a life of everlasting happiness and glory in heaven; who died upon a torturing cross, that you might sit upon heavenly thrones; who was imprisoned in the gloomy grave, that you might enjoy a glorious resurrection; who fell a victim to divine justice, that you might be set free from its dreadful arrest; who felt trouble and agony of soul, that you might enjoy the smiles, the pleasures of divine love; who, in short, has discovered more ardent and extensive love for you than all the friends in the world can do; in his name, and for his sake, I pray you to be reconciled to God. And is his dear name a trifle in your esteem? Will you not do any thing so reasonable and so necessary, and conducive to your happiness for his sake; for his sake who has done and suffered so much for you? Alas! has the name of Jesus no more influence among the creatures he bought with his blood! It is hard indeed if I beg in vain, when I beg for the sake of Christ, the Friend, the Saviour of perishing souls.

But if you have no regard for him, you certainly have for yourselves; therefore, for your own sakes, for the sake of your precious immortal souls, for the sake of your own everlasting happiness, I pray you to be reconciled to God. If you refuse, you degrade the honour of your nature, and commence incarnate devils. For what is the grand constituent of a devil but enmity against God? You become the refuse of the creation, fit for no apartment of the universe but the prison of hell. While you are unreconciled to God you can do nothing at all to please him. He that searches the heart knows that even your good actions do not proceed from love to him, and therefore he abhors them. Ten thousand prayers and acts of devotion and morality, as you have no principles of real holiness, are so many provocations to a righteous God. While you refuse to be reconciled, you are accessary to, and patronize all the rebellion of men and devils; for if you have a right to continue in your rebellion, why may not others? why may not every man upon earth? why may not every miserable ghost in the infernal regions? And are you for raising an universal mutiny and rebellion against the throne of the most High! O the inexpressible horror of the thought! If you refuse to be reconciled, you will soon weary out the mercy and patience of God towards you, and he will come forth against you in all the terrors of an almighty enemy. He will give death a commission to seize you, and drag you to his flaming tribunal. He will break off the treaty, and never make you one offer of reconciliation more : he will strip you of all the enjoyments he was pleased to lead you, while you were under a reprieve, and the treaty was not come to a final issue ; and will leave you nothing but bare being, and an extensive capacity of misery, which will be filled up to the uttermost from the vials of his indignation. He will treat you as his implacable enemy, and you shall be to him as *Amalek*, Exod. xvii. 16. with whom he will make war for ever and ever. He will reprove you, and set your sins in order before you, and tear you in pieces, and there shall be none to deliver. He will meet you as a lion, " and as a bear bereaved of her whelps, and will rend the caul of your hearts." Hos. xiii. 8. He hath for a long time held his peace, and endured your rebellion; but ere long he will go forth as a mighty man ; he shall stir up jealousy like a man of war ; he shall cry, yea roar ; he shall prevail against his enemies. Ah! he will ease him of his adversaries, and avenge him of his enemies. He will give orders to the executioners of his justice : *These mine enemies, that would not that I should reign over them, bring them hither, and slay them before me.* Luke xix. 27. And now, if you will not submit to peace, prepare to meet your God, O sinners ; gird up your loins like men ; put on all the terror of your rage, and go forth to meet your almighty adversary, who will soon meet you in the field, and try your strength. Call the legions of hell to your aid, and strengthen the confederacy with all your fellow-sinners upon earth ; put briars and thorns around you to inclose from his reach. Prepare the dry stubble to oppose devouring flame. Associate yourselves, but ye shall be broken in pieces; gird yourselves ; but, alas ! ye shall be broken to pieces.

But O ! I must drop this ironical challenge, and seriously pray you to make peace with him whom you cannot resist: then all your past rebellion will be forgiven ; you shall be the favourites of your sovereign, and happy for ever ; and earth and heaven will rejoice at the conclusion of this blessed peace ; and my now sad heart will share in the joy. Therefore, for your own sakes, I pray you to be reconciled to God."

SERMON IV.

The Nature and Universality of Spiritual Death.

EPHES. ii. 1. and 5. *Who were dead in trespasses and sins.—Even when we were dead in sins.*

THERE is a kind of death which we all expect to feel that carries terror in the very sound, and all its circumstances are shocking to nature. The ghastly countenance, the convulsive agonies, the expiring groan, the coffin, the grave, the devouring worm, the stupor, the insensibility, the universal inactivity, these strike a damp to the spirit, and we turn pale at the thought. With such objects as these in view, courage fails, levity looks serious, presumption is dashed, the cheerfully passion sink, and all is solemn, all is melancholy. The most stupid and hardy sinner cannot but be moved to see these things exemplified in others; and when he cannot avoid the prospect, he is shocked to think that he himself must feel them.

But there is another kind of death little regarded indeed, little feared, little lamented, which is infinitely more terrible—the death, not of the body, but of the soul: a death which does not stupify the limbs, but the faculties of the mind: a death which does not separate the soul and body, and consign the latter to the grave, but that separates the soul from God, excludes it from all the joys of his presence, and delivers it over to everlasting misery: a tremendous death indeed! "A death unto death." The expression of St. Paul is prodigiously strong and striking:  Death unto death, death after death, in all dreadful succession, and the last more terrible than the first, 2. Cor. ii. 16. and this is the death meant in my text, *dead in trespasses and sins.*

To explain the context and shew you the connection, I shall make two short remarks.

The one is, That the apostle had observed in the nineteenth and twentieth verses of the foregoing chapter, that the same almighty power of God, which raised Christ from the dead, is exerted to enable a sinner to believe—*We believe,* says he, *according to the working* or energy Ενέργειαν *of his mighty power which he wrought in Christ, when he raised him from the dead.* The one, as well as the other, is an exploit of omnipotence. The exceeding greatness of his mighty power is exerted towards us that believe, as well as it was upon the dead body of Christ to restore it to life, after it had been torn and mangled upon the crofs, and lain three days and three nights in the grave. What ftrong language is this! what a forcible illuftration! Methinks this paffage alone is fufficient to confound all the vanity and felf-fufficiency of mortals, and entirely deftroy the proud fiction of a felf-fprung faith produced by the efforts of degenerate nature. In my text the apoftle affigns the reafon of this. The fame exertion of the fame power is neceffary in the one cafe and the other; becaufe, as the body of Chrift was dead, and had no principle of life in it, fo, fays he, *ye were dead in trefpaffes and fins;* and therefore could no more quicken yourfelves than a dead body can reftore itfelf to life. But God, verfe 4th, *who is rich in mercy, for his great love wherewith he loved us;* that God, who raifed the entombed Redeemer to life again, that fame almighty God, by a like exertion of the fame power, *hath quickened us,* verfe 5th, *even when we were dead in fins;* dead, fenfelefs, inactive, and incapable of animating ourfelves. Let any man carefully read thefe verfes, and confider their moft natural meaning, and I cannot but think common fenfe will direct him thus to underftand them. The fcriptures were written with a defign to be underftood; and therefore that fenfe which is the moft natural to a plain unprejudiced underftanding is moft likely to be true.

The other remark is, That the apoftle having pronounced the Ephefians dead in fin, while unconverted, in the firft verfe, paffes the fame fentence upon himfelf and the whole body of the Jews, notwithftanding their high privileges, in the fifth verfe. The fenfe and connection may be difcovered in the following paraphrafe: "You Ephefians were very lately Heathens, and, while you were in that ftate, you were fpiritually dead, and all your actions were dead works. In time paft ye walked in trefpaffes and fins, nor were you fingular in your courfe: though it be infinitely pernicious, yet it is the common courfe of this world, and it is alfo agreeable to the temper and inftigation of that gloomy prince, who has a peculiar power in the region of the air; that malignant fpirit who works with dreadful efficacy in the numerous children of difobedience; but this was not the cafe of you Heathens alone: we alfo who are Jews, notwithftanding our many religious advantages, and even I myfelf, notwithftanding my high privileges and unblemifhable life as a Pharifee, we alfo, I fay, had our converfation in times paft among the children of difobedience; we all, as well as they, walked in the lufts of the flefh, fulfilling the defires and inclinations (Θελ'ηματα) of our fenfual flefh, and of our depraved minds; for thefe were tainted with fpiritual wickednefs, independent upon our animal paffions and appetites; and we were all, even by nature, children of wrath, even as others: in this refpect we Jews were juft like the reft of mankind, corrupt from our very birth, transgressors from the womb, and liable to the wrath of God. Our external relation and privileges as the peculiar people of God, distinguished with a religion from heaven, makes no distinction between us and others in this matter. As we are all children of disobedience by our lives, so we are all, without exception, children of wrath by nature: but when we are all dead in sins, when Jews and Gentiles were equally dead to God, then, even then, God, who is rich in mercy, had pity upon us; *he quickened us;* " he inspired us with a new and spiritual life by his own almighty power, which raised the dead body of Christ from the grave." *He quickened us together with Christ :* "We received our life by virtue of our union with him as our vital head, who was raised to an immortal life, that he might quicken dead souls by those influences of his spirit, which he purchased by his death ; and therefore by grace are ye saved. It is the purest, richest, freest grace, that ever such dead souls as we were made alive to God, and not suffered to remain dead for ever.

This is the obvious meaning and connection of these verses; and we now proceed to consider the text, Dead *in trespasses and sins;* you dead, we dead, Jews and Gentiles, all *dead* together *in trespasses and sins.* A dismal, mortifying character! " This one place," says Beza, " like a thunder-bolt, dashes all mankind down to the dust, great and proud as they are ; for it pronounces their nature not only hurt but dead by sin, and therefore liable to wrath."*

Death is a state of insensibility and inactivity, and a dead man is incapable of restoring himself to life ; therefore the condition of an unconverted sinner must have some resemblance to such a state, in order to support the bold metaphor here used by the apostle. To understand it aright we must take care, on the one hand, that we do not explain it away in flattery to ourselves, or in compliment to the pride of human nature : and, on the other hand, that we do not carry the similitude too far, so as to lead into absurdities, and contradict matter of fact.

The metaphor must be understood with several limitations or exceptions; for it is certain there is a wide difference between the spiritual death of the soul, and the natural death of the body, particularly in this respect, that death puts an entire end to all the powers, actions, and sensations of our animal nature universally, with regard to all objects of every kind : but a soul dead in sin is only partially dead ; that is, it is dead only with regard to a certain kind of sensations and exercises, but in the mean time it may be all life and activity about other things. It is alive, sensible, and vi-

* " Hoc uno loco, quasi fulmine, totus homo, quantus quantus est prosternitur. Neque enim naturam dicit læsam, sed mortuam, per peccatum; ideoque iræ obnoxiam."

gorous about earthly objects and purſuits; theſe raiſe its paſſions and engage its thoughts. It has alſo a dreadful power and faculty of ſinning, though this is not its life but its diſeaſe, its death, like the tendency of a dead body to corruption. It can likewiſe exerciſe its intellectual powers, and make conſiderable improvements in ſcience. A ſinner dead in treſpaſſes and ſins may be a living treaſury of knowledge, an univerſal ſcholar, a profound philoſopher, and even a great divine, as far as mere ſpeculative knowledge can render him ſuch; nay, he is capable of many ſenſations and impreſſions from religious objects, and of performing all the external duties of religion. He is able to read, to hear, to pray, to meditate upon divine things; nay, he may be an inſtructor of others, and preach perhaps with extenſive popularity: he may have a form of godlineſs, and obtain a name to live among men: he is in ſome meaſure able, and it is his duty to attend upon the means God has inſtituted for quickening him with ſpiritual life, and God deals with him as with a rational creature, by laws, ſanctions, promiſes, expoſtulations, and invitations: theſe conceſſions I make, not only to give you the ſenſe of the text, but alſo to prevent the abuſe of the doctrine, and anticipate ſome objections againſt it, as though it were an encouragement to continue idle, and uſe no means to obtain ſpiritual life: or as though it rendered all the means of grace needleſs and abſurd, like arguments to the dead, to reſtore themſelves to life. But, notwithſtanding all theſe conceſſions, it is a melancholy truth that an unregenerate ſinner is dead. Though he can commit ſin with greedineſs, though he is capable of animal actions and ſecular purſuits, nay, though he can employ his mind even about intellectual and ſpiritual things, and is capable of performing the external duties of religion, yet there is ſomething in religion with regard to which he is entirely dead: there is a kind of ſpiritual life of which he is entirely deſtitute: he is habitually inſenſible with regard to things divine and eternal: he has no activity, no vigour in the pure, ſpiritual, and vital exerciſes of religion: he has no prevailing bent of mind towards them: he has not thoſe views and apprehenſions of things which a ſoul ſpiritually alive would neceſſarily receive and entertain: he is deſtitute of thoſe ſacred affections, that joy, that love, that deſire, that hope, that fear, that ſorrow, which are, as it were, the innate paſſions of the new man. In ſhort, he is ſo inactive, ſo liſtleſs, ſo inſenſible in theſe reſpects, that death, which puts an end to all action and ſenſation, is a proper emblem of his ſtate; and this is the meaning of the apoſtle in my text. He is alſo utterly unable to quicken himſelf. He may indeed uſe means in ſome ſort; but to implant a vital principle in his ſoul, but to give himſelf vivid ſenſations of divine things, and make himſelf alive towards God, this is entirely beyond his utmoſt ability: this is as peculiarly the work of almighty power as the reſurrection of a dead body from the grave. As to this death it is brought upon him by and confifts in *trefpaffes and fins*. The innate depravity and corruption of the heart, and the habits of fin contracted and confirmed by repeated indulgences of inbred corruption, thefe are the poifonous, deadly things that have flain the foul; thefe have entirely indifpofed and difabled it for living religion. *Trefpaffes and fins* are the grave, the corrupt effluvia, the malignant damps, the rottennefs of a dead foul: it lies dead, fenfelefs, inactive, buried *in trefpaffes and fins*. *Trefpaffes and fins* render it ghaftly, odious, abominable, a noifome putrefaction before an holy God, like a rotten carcafs, or a mere mafs of corruption: the vileft lufts, like worms, riot upon and devour it, but it feels them not, nor can it lift a hand to drive the venom off. Such mortifying ideas as thefe may be contained in the ftriking metaphor, *dead in trefpaffes and fins;* and I hope you now underftand its general meaning.

If you would know what has turned my thoughts to this fubject, I will candidly tell you, though with a forrowful heart. I am fure, if any objects within the compafs of human knowledge have a tendency to make the deepeft impreffions upon our minds, they are thofe things which chriftianity teaches us concerning God, concerning ourfelves, and a future ftate; and if there be any exercifes which fhould call forth all the life and powers of our fouls into action, they are thofe of a religious nature: but, alas! I often find a ftrange, aftonifhing ftupor and liftleffnefs about thefe things. In this I am not fingular; the beft among us complain of the fame thing; the moft lively Chriftians feel this unaccountable langour and infenfibility; and the generality are evidently deftitute of all habitual concern about them: they are all alive in the purfuit of pleafure, riches, or honours; their thoughts are eafily engaged, and their affections raifed by fuch things as thefe: but the concerns of religion, which, above all other things are adapted to make impreffions upon them, and ftir up all the life within them, feem to have little or no effect. When I have made this obfervation with refpect to others, and felt the melancholy confirmation of it in my own breaft, I have really been ftruck with amazement, and ready to cry out, " Lord, what is this that has befallen me, and the reft of my fellow mortals? what can be the caufe of fuch a conduct in rational nature, to be active and eager about trifles, and ftupid and carelefs about matters of infinite importance? O whence is this ftrange infatuation!" Thus I have been fhocked at this aftonifhing fact, and I could account for it in no other way but by reflecting that we have all been *dead in trefpaffes and fins.*—In fuch a folemn hour the apoftle's expreffion does not feem at all too ftrong. I have no fcruple at all to pronounce, not only from the authority of an apoftle, but from the evidence of the thing, that I, and all around me, yea, and all the fons of men have been dead; in the spiritual sense, utterly dead. Multitudes among us, yea, the generality are dead still; hence the stillness about religion among us; hence the stupor, the carelessness about eternal things, the thoughtless neglect of God, the insensibility under his providential dispensations, the impenitence, the presumption that so much prevail. God has indeed, out of the great love wherewith he loved us, quickened some of us, even when we were dead in sins; and we have a little life, some vital sensations and impressions at times, but O! how little, how superficial, how much of a deadly stupor yet remains! how little life in prayer, in hearing, or in the nearest approach to the living God! The reflection is shocking, but, alas! it is too true; consult your own hearts and you will find it even so. Animal life seems to be a gradual thing; it gradually grows in an infant, it is perfect in mature age, and in old age it gradually decays, till all is gone; but how small is the degree of life when the fœtus is just animated, or the infant born into the world! but little superior to that of a plant or an oyster. What faint sensations, what obscure and languid perceptions, what feeble motions! Such are the children of grace in the present state. Spiritual life is gradual; it is infused in regeneration; but O! how far from perfection while on this side heaven! Alas! the best of us are like the poor traveller that fell among thieves, and was left half dead: however, it is an unspeakable mercy to have the least principle of spiritual life; and we should prize it more than crowns and empires.

If you would know my design in choosing this subject, it is partly, for the conviction of sinners, that they may be alarmed with their deplorable condition, which is the first step towards their being quickened; partly to rouse the children of grace to seek more life from their vital head; and partly to display the rich grace of God in quickening such dead sinners, and bestowing upon them a spiritual and immortal life; and surely nothing can inflame our gratitude and raise our wonder more than the consideration that we were dead in trespasses and sins! If I may but answer these ends, it will be an unspeakable blessing to us all. And O that divine grace may honour this humble attempt of a poor creature, at best but half alive, with success! I hope, my brethren, you will hear seriously, for it is really a most serious subject.

You have seen that the metaphorical expression in my text is intended to represent the stupidity, inactivity, and impotence of unregenerate sinners about divine things. This truth I might confirm by argument and scripture-authority; but I think it may be a better method for popular conviction to prove and illustrate it from plain instances of the temper and conduct of sinners about the concerns of religion, as this may force the conviction upon them from undoubted matters of fact and their own experience.

This, therefore, is the method I intend to purfue; and my time will allow me to particularize only the following inftances.

I. Confider the excellency of the divine Being, the fum total, the great original of all perfections. How infinitely worthy is he of the adoration of all his creatures! how deferving of their moft intenfe thoughts and moft ardent affections! If majefty and glory can ftrike us with awe and veneration, does not Jehovah demand them, who is clothed with majefty and glory as with a garment, and before whom all the inhabitants of the earth are as grafs-hoppers, as nothing, as lefs than nothing, and vanity? If wifdom excites our pleafing wonder, here is an unfathomable depth. O the depth of the riches of the wifdom and knowledge of God! If goodnefs, grace, and mercy attract our love and gratitude, here thefe amiable perfections fhine in their moft alluring glories. If juftice ftrikes a damp to the guilty, here is juftice in all its tremendous majefty. If veracity, if candour, if any, or all of the moral virtues engage our efteem, here they all center in their highest perfection. If the prefence of a king ftrikes a reverence; if the eye of his judge awes the criminal, and reftrains him from offending, certainly we fhould fear before the Lord all the day, for we are furrounded with his omniprefence, and he is the Infpector and Judge of all our thoughts and actions. If riches excite defire, here are unfearchable riches: if happinefs has charms that draw all the world after it, here is an unbounded ocean of happinefs; here is the only complete portion for an immortal mind. Men are affected with thefe things in one another, though found in a very imperfect degree. Power awes and commands; virtue and goodnefs pleafe; beauty charms; juftice ftrikes with folemnity and terror; a bright genius is admired; a benevolent merciful temper is loved: thus men are affected with created excellencies. Whence is it then they are fo ftupidly unaffected with the fupreme original excellencies of Jehovah? Here, my brethren, turn your eyes inward upon yourfelves, and enquire, are not feveral of you confcious that, though you have paffions for fuch objects as thefe, and you are eafily moved by them, yet, with regard to the perfections of the fupreme and beft of beings, your hearts are habitually fenfelefs and unaffected. It is not an eafy thing to make impreffions upon you by them; and what increafes the wonder, and aggravates your guilt, is, that you are thus fenfelefs and unaffected, when you believe and profefs that thefe perfections are really in God, and that in the higheft degree poffible. In other cafes you can love what appears amiable, you revere what is great and majeftic, you eagerly defire and purfue what is valuable, and tends to your happinefs; and all this you do freely, fpontaneoufly, vigoroufly, by the innate inclination and tendency of your nature, without reluctance, without compulfion, nay, without perfuafion; but as to God and all his perfections, you are ftrangely infenfible, backward, and averfe. Where is there one being that has any confeſſed excellency in the compaſs of human knowledge, that does not engage more of the thoughts and affections of mankind than the glorious and ever bleſſed God? The ſun, moon, and ſtars, have had more worſhippers than the uncreated fountain of light from which they derive their luſtre. Kings, and miniſters of ſtate, have more punctual homage and frequent applications made to them than the King of kings, and Lord of lords. Created enjoyments are more eagerly purſued than the ſupreme Good. Search all the world over, and you will find but very little motions of heart towards God; little love, little deſire, little ſearching after him. You will often, indeed, ſee him honoured with the compliment of a bended knee, and a few heartleſs words, under the name of a prayer; but where is the heart, or where are the thoughts, where the affections? Theſe run wild through the world, and are ſcattered among a thouſand other objects. The heart has no prevailing tendency toward God, the thoughts are ſhy of him, the affections have no innate propenſity to him. In ſhort, in this reſpect the whole man is out of order: here he does not at all act like himſelf; here are no affectionate thoughts, no delightful meditations, no ardent deſires, no eager purſuits and vigorous endeavours, but all is liſtleſs, ſtupid, indiſpoſed, inactive, and averſe; and what is the matter?—" Lord! what is this that has ſeized the ſouls of thine own offspring, that they are thus utterly diſordered towards thee!" The reaſon is, they are dead, *dead in treſpaſſes and ſins.* It is impoſſible a living ſoul ſhould be ſo ſtupid and unaffected with ſuch an object: it muſt be a dead ſoul that has no feeling. Yes, ſinners, this is the melancholy reaſon why you are ſo thoughtleſs, ſo unconcerned, ſo ſenſeleſs about the God that made you; you are dead. And what is the reaſon that you who have been begotten again to a ſpiritual life, and who are united to Chriſt as your vital head, what is the reaſon that you ſo often feel ſuch languiſhments; that the pulſe of ſpiritual life beats ſo faint and irregular, and that its motions are ſo feeble and ſlow? All this you feel and lament, but how comes it to paſs? what can be the cauſe that you who have indeed taſted that the Lord is gracious, and are ſenſible that he is all-glorious and lovely, and your only happineſs? O! what can be the cauſe, that you, of all men in the world, ſhould be ſo little engaged to him? Alas! the cauſe is, you have been dead, and the deadly ſtupor has not yet left you: you have (bleſſed be the quickening ſpirit of Chriſt!) you have received a little life; but, alas! it is a feeble ſpark; it finds the principles of death ſtill ſtrong in your conſtitution; theſe it muſt ſtruggle with, and by them it is often borne down, ſuppreſſed, and juſt expiring. Walk humbly, then, and remember your ſhame, that you were once dead, and children of wrath, even as others. The carelessness and indisposition of the soul towards the supreme excellence will appear yet more evident and astonishing, if we consider.

II. The august and endearing relations the great and blessed God sustains to us, and the many ways he has taken to make dutiful and grateful impressions upon our hearts. What tender endearments are there contained in the relation of a Father! This he bears to us : *he made us, and not we ourselves.* Our bodies indeed are produced in a succession from Adam by generation, but who was it that began the series ? It was the Almighty, who formed the first man of the dust : it was he who first put the succession of causes in motion; and therefore he is the grand original cause, and the whole chain depends upon him. Who was it that first established the laws of generation, and still continues them in force ? It is the all-creating Parent of nature; and without him men would have been no more able to produce one another than stones or clods of earth. As to our souls, the principal part of our persons, God is their immediate author, without the least concurrence of secondary causes. Hence he is called the Father of your spirits in a peculiar sense *Heb.* xii. 9. and he assumes the endearing name of " the God of the spirits of all flesh." *Numb.* xvi. 22. Now the name of a father is wont to carry some endearment and authority. Children, especially in their young and helpless years, are fond of their father; their little hearts beat with a thousand grateful passions towards him; they love to be dandled on his knees, and fondled in his arms : and they fly to him upon every appearance of danger; but if God be a father, where is his honour ? here, alas ! the filial passions are senseless and immoveable. It is but a little time since we came from his creating hand, and yet we have forgotten him. It seems unnatural for his own offspring to enquire " where is God my Maker ?" They shew no fondness for him, no affectionate veneration, and no humble confidence ; their hearts are dead towards him, as though there were no such being, or no such near relation subsisting between them. In childhood a rattle, or a straw, or any trifle, is more thought of than their heavenly Father : in riper years their vain pleasures and secular pursuits command more of their affections than their divine original and only happiness.

Compare your natural temper towards your heavenly Father, and towards your earthly parents, and how wide is the difference ! Nature works strong in your hearts towards them, but towards him all the filial passions are dull and dead; and why? alas! the reason is, you *are dead in trespasses and sins.* But this relation of a Father is not the only relation our God sustains to you; he is your supreme King, to whom you owe allegiance; your Lawgiver, whose will is the rule of your conduct; and your Judge, who will call you to an account, and reward or punish you according to your works; but how unnatural is it to men to revere the most high God under thefe auguft characters! Where is there a king upon earth, however weak or tyrannical, but is more regarded by his fubjects than the King of heaven by the generality of men? Were ever fuch excellent laws contemned and violated? Did ever criminals treat their judge with fo much neglect and contempt? And are thefe fouls alive to God who thus treat him? No. Alas! "they are dead in trefpaffes and fins;" however lively they are towards other things, yet in this refpect they are feized with a deadly ftupor. God is alfo our Guardian and Deliverer; and from how many dangers has he preferved us! from how many calamities has he delivered us! Dangers, diftreffes, and deaths crowd upon us, and furround us in every age and every place; the air, the earth, the fea, and every element are pregnant with numberlefs principles of pain and death ready to feize and deftroy us; ficknefs and death fwarm around us: nay, they lie in ambufh in our own conftitution, and are perpetually undermining our lives, and yet our divine Guardian preferves us for months and years unhurt, untouched; or, if he fuffers the calamity to fall, or death to threaten, he flies to our deliverance; and how many falvations of this kind has he wrought for us; falvations from accidents, from ficknefses, from pain, from forrows, from death; falvations for our perfons and our poffeffions, for ourfelves, and for our friends and relations; falvations from dangers feen and unfeen; falvations in infancy, in youth, and in maturer years! Thefe things we cannot deny without the moft ftupid ignorance, and an atheiftical difbelief of divine Providence. Now, fuch repeated, fuch long-continued, fuch unmerited favours as thefe would not pafs for nothing between man and man. We have hearts to feel fuch obligations; nay, the ten thoufandth, the millionth part of fuch gracious care and goodnefs would be gratefully refented, and thankfully acknowledged. Indeed it is impoffible we fhould receive even this fmall, this very fmall proportion of favours from men in comparifon of what we receive from God; and even when they are the inftruments of our deliverance, he is the original Author. But, after all, is there a natural aptitude in the hearts of men to think of their gracious Guardian and Saviour? Does the principle of gratitude naturally lead them to love him, and to make thankful acknowledgments to him? Alas! no. They may indeed feel fome tranfient, fuperficial workings of gratitude when under the frefh fenfe of fome remarkable deliverance; but thefe impreffions foon wear off, and they become as thoughtlefs and ftupid as ever. But let a man, like yourfelves, fave you from fome great diftrefs, you will always gratefully remember him, think of him often with pleafure, and take all opportunities of returning his kindnefs, efpecially if your deliverer was much your superior, and independent upon you, if you had forfeited his favour, provoked him, and incurred his displeasure: great favours from such an one would make impressions upon the most obdurate heart.

But though God be infinitely superior to us, and it is nothing to him what becomes of us, though we have rebelled against him, and deserve his vengeance, yet ten thousand deliverances from his hands have little or no effect upon the hearts of men: all these cannot bring them to think of him, or love him as much as they do a friend, or a common benefactor of their own species: and does such stupid ingratitude discover any spiritual life in them? No: they are dead in this respect, though they are all alive to those passions that terminate upon created objects. Farther, God is the *Benefactor* of mankind, not only in delivering them from dangers and calamities, but in bestowing unnumbered positive blessings upon them. Here I cannot pretend to be particular, for the list of blessings is endless; and it will be the happy employment of an eternity to recollect and enumerate them. What an extensive and well furnished world has our God formed for our accommodation! For us he has enriched the sun with light and heat, and the earth with fruitfulness. The numerous inhabitants of every element, the plants, minerals, and beasts of the earth, the fishes of the sea, the fowls of the air, are all rendering their service to man; some afford him food, and others work for him: the winds and seas, fire and water, stones and trees, all conspire to be useful to him. Our divine Benefactor crowns us with the blessings of liberty, of society, of friendship, and the most endearing relations: he preserves our health, gives us " rain from heaven, and fruitful seasons, and fills our hearts with food and gladness." In short, he gives us life, and breath, and all things; every day, every hour, every moment has arrived to us richly freighted with blessings; blessings have resided with us at home, and attended us abroad; blessings presented themselves ready for our enjoyment as soon as we entered into the world; then God provided hands to receive us, knees to support us, breasts to suckle us, and parents to guard and cherish us; blessings have grown up with us, and given such constant attendance, that they are become familiar to us, and are the inseparable companions of our lives. It is no new or useful thing to us to see an illustrious sun rising to give us the day, to enjoy repose in the night, to rise refreshed and vigorous in the morning, to see our tables spread with plenty, the trees covered with fruit, the fields with grain, and various forms of animals growing up for our support or service. These are such familiar blessings to us, that they too often seem things of course, or necessary appendages of our being. What a crowd of blessings have crowned the present morning!

You and yours are alive and well, you have not come hither ghaſtly and pining with hunger, or agonizing with pain. How many refreſhing draughts of air have you drawn this morning! how many ſprightly and regular pulſes have beat through your frame! how many eaſy motions have you performed with hands, feet, eyes, tongue, and other members of your body! and are not all theſe favours from God? Yes, undoubtedly; and thus has he gone on bleſſing you all your days, without any interruption at all in many of theſe particulars of kindneſs, and with but very little in the reſt. Sinful and miſerable as this world is, it is a treaſury rich in bleſſings, a ſtore-houſe full of proviſions, a dwelling well furniſhed for the accommodation of mortals, and all by the care, and at the expence of that gracious God who firſt made and ſtill preſerves it what it is. " Lord, whence is it then that the inhabitants forget and neglect thee, as though they were not at all obliged to thee? O! whence is it that they love thy gifts, and yet diſregard the Giver? that they think leſs of thee than of an earthly father or friend, or an human benefactor; that there ſhould be ſo little gratitude towards thee, that of all benefactors thou ſhouldeſt be the leaſt acknowledged; that the benefactors of nations, and even of private perſons, in inſtances unworthy to be mentioned with thoſe of thy goodneſs, ſhould be celebrated, and even adored, while thou art neglected, thine agency overlooked, and thy goodneſs forgotten? O! whence is this ſtrange phænomenon, this unaccountable, unprecedented ſtupidity and ingratitude in reaſonable creatures? Surely, if they had any life, any ſenſation in this reſpect, they would not be capable of ſuch a conduct; but they are dead, dead to all the generous ſenſations of gratitude to God: and as a dead corpſe feels no gratitude to thoſe that perform the laſt friendly office, and cover it with earth, ſo a dead ſoul ſtands unmoved under all the profuſion of bleſſings which Heaven pours upon it.

The bleſſings I have mentioned, which are confined to the preſent ſtate, are great, and deſerve our wonder and thankſgiving, eſpecially conſidering that they are beſtowed upon a race of rebellious, ungrateful creatures, who deſerve the ſevereſt vengeance; but there is a ſet of bleſſings yet unmentioned, of infinitely greater importance, in which all others are ſwallowed up, by the glory of which they are obſcured, like the ſtars of night by the riſing ſun. To ſome of our race God has given crowns and kingdoms. For Iſrael Jehovah wrought the moſt aſtoniſhing miracles; ſeas and rivers opened to make way for them; rocks burſt into ſprings of water to quench their thirſt; the clouds poured down manna, and fed them with bread from heaven: their God delivered Daniel from the jaws of hungry lions, and his three companions from the burning fiery furnace. He has reſtored health to the ſick, ſight to

Serm. 4. *of spiritual Death.* 127

the blind, and life to the dead. These blessings and deliverances have something majestic and striking in them; and had we been the subjects of them, we could not but have regarded them as great and singular; but what are these in comparison of God's gift of his Son, and the blessings he has purchased! his Son, who is of greater value, and dearer to him than ten thousand worlds; his beloved Son, in whom he is well pleased; him has he given for us, given up to three and thirty years of the most mortifying abasement, and an incessant conflict with the severest trials; given up to death, and all the ignominy and agonies of crucifixion. Thus has God loved our world! and never was there such a display of love in heaven or on earth. You can no more find love equal to this among creatures, than you can find among them the infinite power that formed the universe out of nothing. This will stand upon record to all eternity, as the unprecedented, unparalleled, inimitable love of God. And it appears the more illustrious when we consider that this unspeakable gift was given to sinners, to rebels, to enemies, that were so far from deserving it, that, on the other hand, it is a miracle of mercy that they are not all groaning for ever under the tremendous weight of his justice. O! that I could say something becoming this love; something that might do honour to it! but, alas! the language of mortals was formed for lower subjects. This love passes all description and all knowledge. Consider also what rich blessings Christ has purchased for us: purchased not with such corruptible things as silver and gold, but with his own precious blood: the price recommends and endears the blessings, though they are so great in themselves as to need no such recommendation. What can be greater or more suitable blessings to persons in our circumstances, than pardon for the guilty, redemptions for slaves, righteousness and justification for the condemned, sanctification for the unholy, rest for the weary, comfort for mourners, the favour of God for rebels and exiles, strength for the impotent, protection for the helpless, everlasting happiness for the heirs of hell, and, to sum up all, grace and glory, and every good thing, and all the unsearchable riches of Christ for the wretched and miserable, the poor, the blind, and naked! These are blessings indeed, and, in comparison of them, all the riches of the world are impoverished, and vanish to nothing; and all these blessings are published, offered freely, indefinitely offered to you, to me, to the greatest sinner on earth, in the gospel; and we are allowed,—allowed did I say? we are invited with the utmost importunity, intreated with the most compassionate tenderness and condescension, and commanded by the highest authority, upon pain of eternal damnation, to accept the blessings presented to us! And what reception does all this love meet with in our world! I tremble to think of it. It is plain, these things are proposed to a world dead

S

in sin; for they are all still, all unmoved, all senseless under such a revelation of infinite grace; mankind know not what it is to be moved, melted, transported with the love of a crucified Saviour, till divine grace visits their hearts, and forms them into new creatures: they feel no eager solicitude, nay, not so much as a willingness to receive these blessings, till they become willing by almighty power: and judge ye, my brethren, whether they are not dead souls that are proof even against the love of God in Christ, that are not moved and melted by the agonies of his cross, that are careless about such inestimable blessings as these? Has that soul any spiritual life in it that can sit senseless under the cross of Jesus, that can forget him, neglect him, dishonour him, afterall his love and all his sufferings; that feels a prevailing indifferency and langour towards him; that loves him less than an earthly friend, and seeks him with less eagerness than gold and silver? Is not every generous passion, every principle of gratitude quite extinct in such a spirit? It may be alive to other objects, but towards this it is dead, and alas! is not this the common case! O look round the world, and what do you see but a general neglect of the blessed Jesus, and all the blessings of his gospel? How cold, how untoward, how reluctant, how averse are the hearts of men towards him? how hard to persuade them to think of him and love him? Try to persuade men to give over their sins which grieve him dishonour him, and were the cause of his death; try to engage them to devote themselves entirely to him, and live to his glory, alas! you try in vain; their hearts still continue cold and hard as a stone; try to persuade them to murder or robbery, and you are more likely to prevail. Suffer me, in my astonishment, to repeat this most melancholy truth again; the generality of mankind are habitually careless about the blessed Jesus; they will not seek him, nor give their hearts and affections, though they must perish for ever by their neglect of him! Astonishing, and most lamentable, that ever such perverseness and stupidity should seize the soul of man! Methinks I could here take up a lamentation over human nature, and fall on my knees with this prayer for my fellow-men, "Father of Spirits, and Lord of life, quicken, O quicken these dead souls!" O, Sirs, while we see death all around us, and feel it benumbing our own souls, who can help the most bitter wailing and lamentation! who can restrain himself from crying to the great Author of life for a happy resurrection! While the valley of dry bones lies before me, while the carnage, the charnel-house of immortal souls strikes my sight all around me far and wide, how can I forbear crying, *Come from the four winds, O breath; breathe upon these slain, that they may live?* But to turn from this digression, into which I was unavoidably hurried by the horror of the subject, I would observe farther, that kind usage and pleasing treatment may not be always best for such creatures as we are: fatherly severities and chastisements, though not agreeable to us, yet may be necessary and conducive to our greatest good. Accordingly, God has tried the force of chastisements to make impressions on our hearts: these indeed have been but few in comparison of his more agreeable dispensations; yet recollect whether you have not frequently felt his rod. Have you not languished under sickness and pain, and been brought within a near view of the king of terrors? Have you not suffered the bereavement of friends and relations, and met with losses, adversity, and disappointments! Others have felt still greater calamities in a closer succession, and with fewer mercies intermixed. These things, one would think, would immediately bring men to regard the hand that smites them, and make them sensible of their undutiful conduct, which has procured the correction; these are like the application of fire to one in a lethargy, to awaken him to life; but alas! under all these afflictions, the stupor and insensibility still remain. Sinners groan by reason of oppression, but it is not natural for them to inquire, *Where is God my Maker, that giveth songs in the night?* It is not natural for them to repent of their undutiful conduct and amend; or if they are awakened to some little sense, while the painful rod of the Almighty is yet upon them, as soon as it is removed they become as hardened and senseless as ever. And is not a state of death a very proper representation of such sullen, incorrigible stupidity? Living souls have very tender sensations; one touch of their heavenly Father's hand makes deep impressions upon them; they tremble at his frown, they fall and weep at his feet, they confess their offences, and mourn over them; they fly to the arms of mercy to escape the impending blow; and thus would all do were they not quite destitute of spiritual life.

I have materials sufficient for a discourse of some hours; but at present I must abruptly drop the subject: however, I cannot dismiss you without making a few reflections. And,

1. What a strange affecting view does this subject give us of this assembly! I doubt not but I may accommodate the text to some of you with this agreeable addition, "You hath he quickened, though you were once dead in trespasses and sins." Though the vital pulse beats faint and irregular, and your spiritual life is but very low, yet, blessed be God, you are not entirely dead: you have some living sensations, some lively and vigorous exercises in religion. On the other hand, I doubt not but some of you not only were, but still are *dead in trespasses and sins.* It is not to be expected in our world, at least not before the millennium, that we shall see such a mixed company together, and all living souls.— Here then is the difference between you; some of you are spiritually alive, and some of you are spiritually dead: here the living

and the dead are blended together in the same assembly, on the same seat, and united in the nearest relations: here sits a dead soul, there another, and there another, and a few living souls are scattered here and there among them: here is a dead parent and a living child, or a dead child and a living parent; here life and death (O shocking!) are united in the bonds of conjugal love, and dwell under the same roof: here is a dead servant and a living master; and there a dead master (O terrible!) commands a living servant. Should I trace the distinction beyond this assembly into the world, we shall find a family here and there that have a little life; perhaps one, perhaps two, discover some vital symptoms; but O what crowds of dead families! all dead together, and no endeavours used to bring one another to life; a death-like silence about eternal things; a deadly stupor and insensibility reign among them; they breathe out no desires and prayers after God, nor does the vital pulse of love beat in their hearts towards him; but, on the contrary, their souls are putrifying in sin, which is very emphatically called *corruption* by the sacred writers; they are overrun and devoured by their lusts, as worms insult and destroy the dead body. Call to them, they will not awake; thunder the terrors of the Lord in their ears, they will not hear; offer them all the blessings of the gospel, they will not stretch out the hand of faith to receive them; lay the word of God, the bread of life, before them, they have no appetite for it. In short, the plain symptoms of death are upon them: the animal is alive, but alas! the spirit is dead towards God. And what an affecting, melancholy view does this give of this assembly, and of the world in general! *O that my head were waters, and mine eyes fountains of tears, that I might weep day and night for the slain of the daughter of my people!* Weep not for the afflicted, weep not over ghastly corpses dissolving into their original dust, but O! weep for dead souls. Should God now strike all those persons dead in this assembly whose souls are *dead in trespasses and sins*, should he lay them all in pale corpses before us, like Ananias and Sapphira at the apostle's feet, what numbers of you would never return from this house more, and what lamentations would there be among the surviving few! One would lose a husband or a wife, another a son or a daughter, another a father or a mother; alas! would not some whole families be swept off together, all blended in one promiscuous death! Such a sight as this would strike terror into the hardiest heart among you. But what is this to a company of rational spirits slain and dead in trespasses and sins? How deplorable and inexpressibly melancholy a sight this! Therefore,

2. *Awake thou that sleepest, and arise from the dead, that Christ may give thee light.* This call is directed to you dead sinners; which is a sufficient warrant for me to exhort and persuade you,

The principle of reason is still alive in you; you are also sensible of your own interest, and feel the workings of self-love. It is God alone that can quicken you, but he effects this by a power that does not exclude, but attends rational instructions and persuasions to your understanding. Therefore, though I am sure you will continue dead still if left to yourselves, yet with some trembling hopes that his power may accompany my feeble words, and impregnate them with life, I call upon, I intreat, I charge you sinners to rouse yourselves out of your dead sleep, and seek to obtain spiritual life. Now, while my voice sounds in your ears, now, this moment, waft up this prayer, "Lord, pity a dead soul, a soul that has been dead for ten, twenty, thirty, forty years, or more, and lain corrupting in sin, and say unto me, "Live: from this moment let me live unto thee." Let this prayer be still upon your hearts: keep your souls always in a supplicating posture, and who knows but that he, who raised Lazarus from the grave, may give you a spiritual resurrection to a more important life? But if you wilfully continue your security, expect in a little time to suffer the second death; the mortification will become incurable; and then, though you will be still dead to God, yet you will be " tremblingly alive all over" to the sensations of pain and torture. O that I could gain but this one request of you, which your own interest so strongly enforces! but alas! it has been so often refused, that to expect to prevail is to hope against hope.

3. Let the children of God be sensible of their great happiness in being made spiritually alive. Life is a principle, a capacity necessary for enjoyments of any kind. Without animal life you would be as incapable of animal pleasures as a stone or a clod; and without spiritual life you can no more enjoy the happiness of heaven than a beast or a devil. This therefore is a preparative, a previous qualification, and a sure pledge and earnest of everlasting life. How highly then are you distinguished, and what cause have you for gratitude and praise!

4. Let us all be sensible of this important truth, that it is entirely by grace we are saved. This is the inference the apostle expresly makes from this doctrine; and he is so full of it, that he throws it into a parenthesis (verse the 5th) though it breaks the connection of his discourse; and as soon as he has room he resumes it again (verse 8th) and repeats it over and over, in various forms, in the compass of a few verses. *By grace ye are saved.—By grace are you saved through faith.—It is the gift of God;—not of yourselves,—not of works* (verse 9th.) This, you see, is an inference that seemed of great importance to the apostle; and what can more naturally follow from the premises? If we were once dead in sin, certainly it is owing to the freest grace that we have been quickened; therefore, when we survey the change, let us cry, " Grace, grace unto it."

SERMON V.

The Nature and Process of Spiritual Life.

EPHES. ii. 4, 5. *But God, who is rich in mercy, for his great love wherewith he loved us, even when we were dead in sins, hath quickened us together with Christ.*

IT is not my usual method to weary your attention by a long confinement to one subject; and our religion furnishes us with such a boundless variety of important topics, that a minister who makes them his study will find no temptation to cloy you with repetitions, but rather finds it difficult to speak so concisely on one subject, as to leave room for others of equal importance; however the subject of my last discourse was so copious and interesting, that I cannot dismiss it without a supplement. I there shewed you some of the symptoms of spiritual death; but I would not leave you dead as I found you; and therefore I intend now to consider the counterpart of that subject, and shew you the nature and symptoms of spiritual life.

I doubt not but a number of you have been made alive to God by his quickening spirit; but many, I fear, still continue *dead in trespasses and sins;* and, while such are around me, I cannot help imagining my situation something like that of the prophet Ezekiel (ch. xxxvii.) in the midst of the valley full of dry bones, spread far and wide around him: and should I be asked, *Can these dry bones,* can these dead souls *live?* I must answer with him,— *O Lord God, thou knowest.* " Lord, I see no symptoms of life in them, no tendency towards it. I know nothing is impossible to thee: I firmly believe thou canst inspire them with life, dry and dead as they are: and what thy designs are towards them, whether thou intendest to exert thy all-quickening power upon them, thou only knowest, and I would not presume to determine; but this I know that, if they are left to themselves, they will continue dead to all eternity; for, O Lord, the experiment has been repeatedly tried; thy servant has over and over made those quickening applications to them which thy Word, that sacred dispensary, prescribes; but all in vain; they still continue dead towards thee, and lie putrifying more and more in trespasses and sins: however, at thy command, I would attempt the most unpromising undertaking; I would proclaim even unto dry bones and dead souls, *O ye dry bones, O ye dead souls, hear the word of the Lord.* Ezek. xxxvii. 4. I would also cry aloud for the animating breath of the holy Spirit, *Come from the four winds and breathe; breathe upon these slain, that they may live.* v. 9.

Ye dead sinners, I would make one attempt more in the name of the Lord to bring you to life; and if I have the least hope of success, it is entirely owing to the encouraging peradventure that the quickening spirit of Christ may work upon your hearts while I am addressing myself to your ears. And, O Sirs, let us all keep our souls in a praying posture, throughout this discourse. If one of you should fall into a swoon or an apoplexy, how would all about you bestir themselves to bring you to life again! And alas! shall dead souls lie so thick among us, in every assembly, in every family; and shall no means be used for their recovery? Did Martha and Mary apply to Jesus with all the arts of importunity in behalf of their sick and deceased brother, and are there not some of you that have dead relations, dead friends and neighbours, I mean dead in the worst sense, " dead in trespasses and sins?" and will you not apply to Jesus, the Lord of life, and follow him with your importunate cries, till he come and call them to life? Now let parents turn intercessors for their children, children for their parents, friend for friend, neighbour for neighbour, yea enemy for enemy. O! should we all take this method, we might soon expect to see the valley of dry bones full of living souls, *an exceeding great army.* Ezek. xxxvii. 10.

In praying for this great and glorious event, you do not pray for an impossibility. Thousands, as dead as they, have obtained a joyful resurrection by the power of God. Here in my text you have an instance of a promiscuous crowd of Jews and Gentiles that had lain dead in sin together, and even St. Paul among them, who were recovered to life, and are now enjoying an immortal life in the heavenly regions; and, blessed by God, this spiritual life is not entirely extinct among us. Among the multitudes of dead souls that we every where meet with, we find here and there a soul that has very different symptoms: once indeed it was like the rest; but now, while they are quite senseless of divine things, and have no vital aspirations after God, this soul cannot be content with the richest affluence of created enjoyments; it pants and breathes after God; it feeds upon his word, it feels an almighty energy in eternal things, and receives vital sensations from them. It discovers life and vigour in devotion, and serves the living God with pleasure, though it is also subject to fits of languishment, and at times seems just expiring, and to lose all sensation. And whence is this vast difference? Why is this soul so different from what it once was, and what thousands around still are? Why can it not, like them, and like itself formerly, lie dead and senseless in sin, without any vital impressions or experiences from God or divine things? The reason is, the happy reason, my brethren, is, this is a living soul: " God, out of the great love wherewith he loved it, hath quickened it together with Christ," and hence it is alive to him.

My present design is to explain the nature and properties of this divine life, and to shew you the manner in which it is usually begun in the soul: I shall open with the consideration of the last particular.

Here you must observe, that, though spiritual life is instantaneously infused, yet God prepares the soul for its reception by a course of previous operations. He spent six days in the creation of the world, though he might have spoken it into being in an instant.—Thus he usually creates the soul anew after a gradual process of preparatory actions. In forming the first man, he first created chaos out of nothing, then he digested it into earth; on the sixth day he formed and organized the earth into a body, with all its endless variety of members, juices, muscles, fibres, veins, and arteries; and then, after this process, he inspired it with a living soul; and what was but a lump of clay, sprung up a perfect man. Thus also the fœtus in the womb is for some months in formation before the soul or the principle of life is infused. In like manner the Almighty proceeds in quickening us with spiritual life; we all pass through a course of preparation, though some through a longer, and some shorter. And as one reason why the great Creator took up so much time in the creation of the world probably was, that he might allow the angels time for leisurely surveys of the astonishing process, so he may advance thus gradually in the new creation, that we may observe the various steps of the operation, and make proper reflections upon it in future life. My present design is to trace these steps to their grand result, that you may know whether ever divine grace has carried you through this gracious process.

And that you may not fall into needless perplexities, it may be necessary for me to premise farther, that there is a great variety in these preparatory operations, and in the degrees of spiritual life. Indeed the difference is only circumstantial, for the work is substantially the same, and spiritual life is substantially the same in all; but then, in such circumstances as the length of time, the particular external means, the degree of previous terror, and of subsequent joy and vitality, &c. God exercises a sovereign freedom, and shews that he has a variety of ways by which to accomplish his end; and it is no matter how we obtain it, if we have but spiritual life. I shall therefore endeavour to confine myself to the substance of this work, without its peculiarities, in different subjects; and, when I cannot avoid descending to particulars, I shall endeavour so to diversify them, as that they may be easily adapted to the various cases of different Christians. To draw their common lineaments, whereby they may be distinguished from all others, is sufficient to my present purpose; whereas, to draw the particular lineaments, or peculiar features, whereby they may be distinguished from one another, is a very difficult task, and cannot be of any great service to what I have now in design.

I have only one thing more to premise, and that is, that the way by which divine grace prepares a sinner for spiritual life, is by working upon all the principles of the rational life, and exciting him to exert them to the utmost to obtain it. Here it is proper for you to recollect what I observed in my last discourse, that even a sinner dead in trespasses and sins is alive, and capable of action in other respects: he can not only perform the actions, and feel the sensations of animal life, but he can also exercise his intellectual powers about intellectual objects, and even about divine things: he is capable of thinking of these, and of receiving some impressions from them: he is also capable of attending upon the ordinances of the gospel, and performing the external duties of religion. These things a sinner may do, and yet be dead in sin. Indeed he will not exercise his natural powers about these things while left to himself: he has the power, but then he has no disposition to employ it: he is indeed capable of meditating upon spiritual things, but what does this avail when he will not turn his mind to such objects? Or if he does, he considers them as mere speculations, and not as the most interesting and important realities. How few, or how superficial and unaffecting are a sinner's thoughts of them! Heaven and hell are objects that may strike the passions, and raise the joys and fears of a natural man, but in general he is little or nothing impressed with them. He is capable of prayer, hearing, and using the means of grace; but I believe, if you make observations upon the conduct of mankind, that you will find they are but seldom employed in these duties, or that they perform them in such a careless manner, that they have no tendency to answer the end of their institution. In short, the more I know of mankind, I have the lower opinion of what they will do in religion when left to themselves. They have a natural power, and we have seen all possible means used with them to excite them to put it forth; but alas! all is in vain, and nothing will be done to propose till God stir them up to exert their natural abilities: and this he performs as a preparative for spiritual life. He brings the sinner to exert all his active powers in seeking this divine principle: nature does her utmost, and all outward means are tried before a supernatural principle is implanted.

The evangelist John has given us the history of the resurrection of the dead body of Lazarus after it had been four days in the grave; and I would now give you the hiftory of a more glorious refurrection, the refurrection of a foul that had lain dead for months and years, and yet is at laft quickened by the fame almighty power with a divine and immortal life.

Should I exemplify it by a particular inftance, I might fix upon this or that perfon in this affembly, and remind you, and inform others, of the procefs of this work in your fouls. And O! how happy are fuch of you, that you may be produced as inftances in this cafe!

You lay for ten, twenty, thirty years, or more, dead in trefpaffes and fins; you did not breathe and pant like a living foul after God and holinefs; you had little more fenfe of the burden of fin than a corpfe of the preffure of a mountain; you had no appetite for the living bread that came down from heaven; the vital pulfe of facred paffions did not beat in your hearts towards God and divine things, but you lay putrifying in fin; filthy lufts preyed upon you like worms on the bodies of the dead; you fpread the contagion of fin around you by your converfation and example, like the ftench and corrupt effluvia of a rotten carcafs; you were odious and abominable to God, fit to be fhut up in the infernal pit out of his fight; and you were objects of horror and lamentation to all that knew and daily confidered your cafe, your deplorable cafe. During this time many quickening applications were made to you; you had friends that ufed all means to bring you to life again; but alas! all in vain; confcience proved your friend, and pierced and chafed you, to bring you to fome feeling, but you remained ftill fenfelefs, or the fymptoms of life foon vanifhed.—God did not caft you away as irrecoverably dead, but ftirred and agitated you within, and ftruggled long with the principles of death to fubdue them: and if it was your happy lot to live under a faithful miniftry, the living oracles that contain the feeds of the divine life were applied to you with care and folicitude. The terrors of the Lord were thundered in your ears to awaken you. The experiment of a Saviour's dying love, and the rich grace of the gofpel, were repeatedly tried upon you: now you were carried within hearing of the heavenly mufic, and within fight of the glories of Paradife, to try if thefe would charm you; now you were, as it were, held over the flames of hell, that they might by their pungent pains fcorch and ftartle you into life. Providence alfo concurred with thefe applications, and tried to recover you by mercies and judgments, ficknefs and health, loffes and poffeffions, difappointments and fucceffes, threatenings and deliverances. If it was your unhappy lot to lie among dead fouls like yourfelf, you had indeed but little pity from them, nay, they and Satan were plying you with their opiates and poifon to confirm the deadly fleep. And O! how aftonifhing is it that you fhould be quickened in a charnel-house, in the mansions of the dead, with dead souls lying all round you! But if it was your happiness to be in the society of the living, they pitied you, they stirred and agitated you with their warnings and persuasions, they, like Martha and Mary in behalf of their deceased brother, went to Jesus with their cries and importunities, "Lord, my child, my parent, my servant, my neighbour is dead, O come and restore him to life! Lord, if thou hadst been here, he would not have died; but even now I know it is not too late for thee to raise him." Thus, when one is dead in our heavenly Father's family, the whole house should be alarmed, and all the domestics be busy in trying to bring him to life again. But O! reflect with shame and sorrow how long all these quickening applications were in vain; you still lay in a dead sleep, or, if at times you seemed to move, and gave us hopes you were coming to life again, you soon relapsed, and grew as senseless as ever. And alas! are there not some of you in this condition to this very moment? O deplorable sight! May the hour come, and O that this may be the hour, in which such dead souls *shall hear the voice of the Son of God and live.* John v. 25.

But as to such of you in whom I would exemplify this history of a spiritual resurrection when your case was thus deplorable, and seemingly helpless, the happy hour, the time of love came, when you must live. When all these applications had been unsuccessful, the all-quickening spirit of God determined to exert more of his energy, and work more effectually upon you. Perhaps a verse in your Bible, a sentence in a sermon, an alarming Providence, the conversation of a pious friend, or something that unexpectedly occurred to your own thoughts, first struck your minds with unusual force; you found you could not harden yourselves against it as you were wont to do; it was attended with a power you never before had felt, and which you could not resist: this made you thoughtful and pensive, and turned your minds to objects that you were wont to neglect; this made you stand and pause, and think of the state of your neglected souls: you began to fear matters were wrong with you; "What will become of me when I leave this world? Where shall I reside for ever? Am I prepared for the eternal world? How have I spent my life?" These, and the like inquiries put you to a stand, and you could not pass over them so superficially as you were wont to do; your sins now appeared to you in a new light; you were shocked and surprised at their malignant nature, their number, their aggravations, and their dreadful consequences. The great God, whom you were wont to neglect, appeared to you as a Being that demanded your regard; you saw he was indeed a venerable, awful, majestic Being, with whom you had the most important concern: in short, you saw that such a life as you had led would never bring you to heaven : you saw you must make religion more your business than you had ever done, and hereupon you altered your former course ; you broke off from several of your vices, you deserted your extravagant company, and you began to frequent the throne of grace, to study religion, and to attend upon its institutions ; and this you did with some degree of earnestness and solicitude.

When you were thus reformed, you began to flatter yourselves that you had escaped out of your dangerous condition, and secured the divine favour ; now you began to view yourselves with secret self-applause as true Christians ; but all this time the reformation was only outward, and there was no new principle of a divine supernatural life implanted in your hearts : you had not the generous passions and sensations of living souls towards God, but acted entirely from natural, selfish principles : you had no clear heart-affecting views of the intrinsic evil, and odious nature of sin, considered in itself, nor of the entire universal corruption of your nature, and the necessity not only of adorning your outer man by an external reformation, but of an inward change of heart by the almighty power of God : you were not deeply sensible of the extent and spirituality of the divine law, nor of the infinite purity and inexorable justice of the Deity : you had no love for religion and virtue for their own sakes, but only on account of their happy consequences. Indeed your love of novelty and a regard to your own happiness might so work upon you, for a time, that you might have very raised and delightful passions in religious duties ; but all your religion at that time was a mere system of selfishness, and you had no generous disinterested delight in holiness for its own excellency, nor did you heartily relish the strictness of pure, living religion : you were also under the government of a self-righteous spirit : your own good works were the ground of your hopes, and you had no relish for the mortifying doctrine of salvation through the mere mercy of God and the righteousness of Jesus Christ : though your education taught you to acknowledge Christ as the only Saviour, and ascribe all your hopes to his death, yet in reality he was of very little importance in your religion ; he had but little place in your heart and affections, even when you urged his name as your only plea at the throne of grace : in short, you had not the spirit of the gospel, nor any spiritual life within you. And this is all the religion with which multitudes are contented : with this they obtain a name that they live ; but in the sight of God, and in reality, they are dead ; and had you been suffered to rest here, according to your own desire, you would have been dead still.

But God, who is rich (O how inconceivably rich !) in mercy, for the great love wherewith he loved you, resolved to carry on his

Serm. 5.   *of spiritual Life.*   139

work in you; and therefore, while you were flattering yourselves, and elated with a proud conceit of a happy change in your condition, he surprized you with a very different view of your case; he opened your eyes farther, and then you saw, you felt those things of which till then you had little sense or apprehension; such as the corruption of your hearts, the awful strictness of the divine law, your utter inability to yield perfect obedience, and the necessity of an inward change of the inclinations and relishes of your soul. These, and a great many other things of a like nature, broke in upon your minds with striking evidence, and a kind of almighty energy; and now you saw you were still " dead in sin," weak, indisposed, averse towards spiritual things, and " dead in law," condemned to everlasting death and misery by its righteous sentence: now you set about the duties of religion with more earnestness than ever; now you prayed, you heard, and used the other means of grace as for your life, for you saw that your eternal life was indeed at stake; and now, when you put the matter to a thorough trial, you were more sensible than ever of your own weakness, and the difficulties in your way. " O! who would have thought my heart had been so depraved that it should thus fly off from God, and struggle and reluctate against returning to him?" such was then your language. Alas! you found yourselves quite helpless, and all your efforts feeble and ineffectual; then you perceived yourselves really dead in sin, and that you must continue so to all eternity, unless quickened by a power infinitely superior to your own: not that you lay slothful and inactive at this time; no, never did you exert yourselves so vigorously in all your life, never did you besiege the throne of grace with such earnest importunity, never did you hear and read with such eager attention, or make such a vigorous resistance against sin and temptation: all your natural powers were exerted to the highest pitch, for now you saw your case required it: but you found all your most vigorous endeavours insufficient, and you were sensible that, without the assistance of a superior power, the work of religion could never be effected.

Now you were reduced very low indeed. While you imagined you could render yourselves safe by a reformation in your own power, you were not much alarmed at your condition, though you saw it bad. But O! to feel yourselves dead in sin, and that you cannot help yourselves; to see yourselves in a state of condemnation, liable to execution every moment, and yet to find all your own endeavours utterly insufficient to relieve you; to be obliged, after all you had done, to lie at mercy, and confess that you were as deserving of everlasting punishment as ever the most notorious criminal was of the stroke of public justice: this was a state of extreme dejection, terror, and anxiety indeed. The proud, self-confident creature was never thoroughly mortified and humbled till now, when he is slain by the law, and entirely cut off from all hopes from himself.

And now, finding you could not save yourselves, you began to cast about you, and look out for another to save you: now you were more sensible than ever of the absolute need of Jesus; and you cried and reached after him, and stirred up yourselves to take hold of him. The gospel brought the free offer of him to your ears, and you would fain have accepted of him; but here new difficulties arose. Alas! you did not think yourselves good enough to accept of him, and hence you took a great deal of fruitless pains to make yourselves better: you also found your hearts strangely averse to the gospel-method of salvation, and, though a sense of your necessity made you try to work up yourselves to an approbation of it, yet you could not affectionately acquiesce in it, and cordially relish it.

And now, how melancholy was your situation! you were "shut up to the faith," Gal. iii. 23. there was no other possible way of escape, and yet, alas! you could not take this way: now you were ready to cry, "I am cut off: my strength and my hope are perished from the Lord;" but, blessed be God, he did not leave you in this condition. Man's extremity of distress is God's opportunity for relief and salvation; and so you found it.

Now the process of preparatory operations is just come to a result. Now it is time for God to work, for nature has done her utmost, and has been found utterly insufficient; now it is proper a divine supernatural principle should be infused, for all the principles of nature have failed, and the proud sinner is obliged to own it, and stand still, and see the salvation of God. In this situation you wanted nothing but such a divine principle to make you living christians indeed. These preparatives were like the taking away the stone from the sepulchre of Lazarus, which was a prelude of that almighty voice which called him from the dead. Now you appear to me like the dry bones in Ezekiel's vision, in one stage of the operation. After there had been a noise, and a shaking among them, and the bones had come together, bone to his bone; *I beheld,* says he, *and lo, the sinews and the flesh came up upon them, and the skin covered them above; but there was no breath in them;* Ezek. xxxvii. 8. this was all that was wanting to make them living men. In like manner you at this time had the external appearance of christians, but you had no divine supernatural life in you; you were but the fair carcases of christians; your religion had a body completely formed, but it had no soul in it; and, had the holy spirit now given over his work, you would have continued dead still.

But now the important crisis is come, when he who stood over the grave of Lazarus, and pronounced the life-restoring mandate, *Lazarus, come forth;* when he who breathed into Adam the breath of life, and made him a living foul ; I fay, now the crifis is come, when he will implant the principles of life in your fouls ; fuddenly you feel the amazing change, and find you are acting from principles entirely new to you ; for now your hearts that were wont to reluctate, and ftart back from God, rife to him with the ftrongeft afpirations : now the way of falvation through Chrift, which you could never relifh before, appears all amiable and glorious, and captivates your whole fouls. Holinefs has lovely and powerful charms, which captivate you to the moft willing obedience, notwithftanding your former difguft to it ; and, though once you were enamoured with fin, or difliked it only becaufe you could not indulge it with impunity, it now appears to you a mere mafs of corruption and deformity, an abominable thing, which you hate above all other things on earth or in hell. At this juncture you were animated with a new life in every faculty of your fouls, and hereupon you felt the inftincts, the appetites, the fympathies and antipathies of a new life, a divine life, juftly ftiled by the apoftle *the life of God;* the life of God in the foul of man. The pulfe of facred paffions began to beat towards fpiritual objects ; the vital warmth of love fpread itfelf through your whole frame ; you breathed out your defires and prayers before God ; like a new-born infant you began to cry after him, and at times you have learned to lifp his name with filial endearment, and cry *Abba, Father ;* you hungered and thirfted after righteoufnefs, and as every kind of life muft have its proper nourifhment, fo your fpiritual life fed upon Chrift, the living bread, and the fincere milk of his word. You alfo felt a new fet of fenfations ; divine things now made deep and tender impreffions upon you ; the great realities of religion and eternity now affected you in a manner unknown before ; you likewife found your fouls actuated with life and vigour in the fervice of God, and in the duties you owed to mankind. This ftrange alteration, no doubt, filled you with furprife and amazement, fomething like that of Adam when he found himfelf ftart into life out of his eternal non-exiftence. With thefe new fenfations every thing appeared to you in a quite different light, and you could not but wonder that you had never perceived them in that manner before.

Thus, my dear brethren, when you were even dead in fin, God quickened you together with Chrift, It is true, the principle of life might be very weak at firft, like the life of a new-born infant, or a fœtus juft animated in the womb ; nay, it may be but very weak ftill, and at times may languifh, and feem juft expiring in the agonies of death ; but, bleffed be the quickening fpirit of Chrift, fince the happy hour of your refurrection you have never been, and you never will be to all eternity, what you once were, "dead in trespasses and sins." Should I give you your own history since that time, it would be to this purpose, and you will discern many symptoms of life in it. You have often known what sickness of soul is, as well as of body; and sometimes it has risen to such a height as to endanger your spiritual life. The seeds of sin, that still lurk in your constitution, like the principles of death, or a deadly poison circulating through your veins, have often struggled for the mastery, and cast you into languishing or violent disorders; then was the divine life oppressed, and you could not freely draw the breath of prayer and pious desires; you lost the appetite for the word of God, and what you received did not digest well and turn to kindly nourishment; the pulse of sacred passions beat faint and irregular, the vital heat decayed, and you felt a death-like cold creeping upon you and benumbing you. Sometimes you have been afflicted, perhaps, with convulsions of violent and outrageous passions, with the dropsy of insatiable desires after things below, with the lethargy of carnal security, or the fever of lust: at other times you have felt an universal disorder through your whole frame, and you hardly knew what ailed you, only you were sure your souls were not well; but perhaps your most common disorder that seizes you is a kind of consumption, a lowness of spirits, a langour and weakness, the want of appetite for your spiritual food, or perhaps a nausea and disgust towards it; you also live in a country very unwholesome to living souls; you dwell among the dead, and catch contagion from the conversation of those around you, and this heightens the disorder: add further, that old serpent the devil labours to infect you with his deadly poison, and increase the peccant humours by his temptations: at such times you can hardly feel any workings of spiritual life in you, and you fear you are entirely dead; but examine strictly, and you will discover some vital symptoms even in this bad habit of soul; for does not your new nature exert itself to work off the disorder? Are not your spirits in a ferment, and do you not feel yourselves in exquisite pain, or at least greatly uneasy? Give all the world to a sick man, and he despises it all: "O give me my health," says he, " or you give me nothing." So it is with you; nothing can content you while your souls are thus out of order. Do you not long for their recovery, that you may go about your business again; I mean that you may engage in the service of God with all the vigour of health? and do you not apply to Christ as your only physician in this condition? And O! what an healing balm is his blood! what a reviving cordial is his love! and how kindly does his spirit purge off the corrupt humours, and subdue the principles of sin and death! Has not experience taught you the meaning of the apostle, when he says, *Christ is our life:* and *I live, yet not I, but Christ liveth in me,* Gal. ii. 20. Do you not perceive that Christ is your vital head, and that you revive or languish just as he communicates or withholds his influence? And have you not been taught in the same way what is the meaning of that expression so often repeated, *The just shall live by his faith?* Hab. ii. 4. Do you not find that faith is, as it were, the grand artery by which you derive life from Christ, and by which it is circulated through your whole frame; and that when faith languishes, then you weaken, pine away, and perhaps fall into a swoon, as though you were quite dead? Are you not careful of the health of your souls? You endeavour to keep them warm with the love of God; you shun those sickly regions as far as you can, where the example and conversation of the wicked spread their deadly infection, and you love to dwell among living souls, and breathe in their wholesome air. Upon the whole, it is evident, notwithstanding your frequent indispositions, you have some life within you: life takes occasion to shew itself, even from your disorders. It is a plain symptom of it, that you have something within you that makes such a vigorous resistance against the principles of sin and death, and throws your whole frame into a ferment, till it has wrought off the distemper. In short, you have the sensations, the sympathies and antipathies, the pleasures and pains of living souls.

And is it so indeed? Then from this moment begin to rejoice and bless the Lord, who raised you to spiritual life. O let the hearts he has quickened beat with his love; let the lips he has opened, when quivering in death, speak his praise, and devote that life to him which he has given you, and which he still supports!

Consider what a divine and noble kind of life he has given you. It is a capacity and aptitude for the most exalted and divine services and enjoyments. Now you have a relish for the Supreme Good as your happiness, the only proper food for your immortal souls, and he will not suffer you to hunger and thirst in vain, but will satisfy the appetites he has implanted in your nature. You have some spirit and life in his service, and are not like the dead souls around you, that are all alive towards other objects, but absolutely dead towards him: you have also noble and exalted sensations; you are capable of a set of pleasures of a more refined and sublime nature than what are relished by groveling sinners. From your inmost souls you detest and nauseate whatever is mean, base, and abominable, and you can feast on what is pure, amiable, excellent, and worthy of your love. Your vitiated taste for trash and poison is cured, and you feed upon heavenly bread, upon food agreeable to the constitution of your spiritual nature; and hence you may infer your meetness for the heavenly world, that region of perfect vitality. You have a disposition for its enjoyments and services, and this is the grand preparative. God will not encumber the heaven of his glory with dead souls, nor infect the pure salubrious air of Paradise with the poison of their corruption; but the everlasting doors are always open for living souls, and not one of them shall ever be excluded; nay, the life of heaven is already within you; the life that reigns with immortal health and vigour above, is the very same with that which works in your breasts; only there it is arrived to maturity and perfection, and here it is in its rudiments and weakness. Your animal life, which was hardly perceivable in the womb, was the very same with that which now possesses you, only now it is come to perfection. Thus you are now angels in embryo, the fœtus (might I be allowed the expression) of glorified immortals; and when you are born out of the womb of time into the eternal world, this feeble spark of spiritual life will kindle and blaze, and render you as active and vigorous as " the rapt seraph that adores and burns. Then you will feel no more weakness, no more langours, no more qualms of indisposition; the poison of temptation and the contagion of bad example cannot reach you there; and the inward seeds of sickness and death will be purged entirely out of your souls: you will be got quite out of the sickly country, and breathe a pure reviving air, the natural element of your souls. There you will find the fountain, yea, whole rivers of the waters of life, of which you will drink in large draughts for ever and ever, and which will inspire you with immortal life and vigour. O how happy are you in this single gift of spiritual life! this is a life that cannot perish, even in the ruins of the world. What though you must ere long yield your mortal bodies and animal life to death and rottenness? your most important life is immortal, and subject to no such dissolution; and therefore be courageous in the name of the Lord, and bid defiance to all the calamities of life, and all the terrors of death: for *your life is hid with Christ in God; and when Christ, who is your life, shall appear, then shall you also appear with him in glory.* Col. iii. 3, 4.

I would willingly go on in this strain, and leave the pulpit with a relish of these delightful truths upon my spirit; but, alas! I must turn my address to another set of persons in this assembly; but " where is the Lord God of Elijah," who restored the Shunamite's son to life by means of that prophet? I am going to call to the dead, and I know they will not hear, unless he attend my feeble voice with his almighty power. I would pray over you like Elijah over the dead child, *O Lord God, let this sinner's life come into him again.* 1 Kings xvii. 21. Are not the living and the dead promiscuously blended in this assembly? Here is a dead soul, there another, and there another all over the house; and here and there a few living souls thinly scattered among them. Have you ever been carried through such a preparatory process as I have described? or if you are uncertain about this, as some may be who are animated with spiritual life, inquire, have you the feelings, the appetites and aversions, the pleasing and the painful sensations of living souls? Methinks conscience breaks its silence in some of you, whether you will or not, and cries, " O no; there is not a spark of life in this breast."

Well, my poor deceased friends (for so I may call you) I hope you will seriously attend to what I am going seriously to say to you. I have no bad design upon you, but only to restore you to life. And though your case is really discouraging, yet I hope it is not quite desperate. The principles of nature, reason, self-love, joy, and fear are still alive in you and you are capable of some application to divine things. And, as I told you, it is upon the principles of nature that God is wont to work, to prepare the soul for the infusion of a supernatural life. And these I would now work upon, in hopes you are not proof against considerations of the greatest weight and energy, I earnestly beg you would lay to heart such things as these.

Can you content yourselves with an animal life, the life of beasts, with that superfluity, reason, just to render you a more ingenious and self-tormenting kind of brutes; more artful in gratifying your sordid appetites, and yet still uneasy for want of an unknown something; a care that the brutal world, being destitute of reason, are unmolested with? O! have you no ambition to be animated with a divine immortal life, the life of God?

Can you be contented with a mere temporal life, when your souls must exist for ever? That infinite world beyond the grave is replenished with nothing but the terrors of death to you, if you are destitute of spiritual life. And O can you bear the thought of residing among its grim and ghastly terrors for ever?

Are you contented to be cut off from God, as a mortified member from the body, and to be banished for ever from all the joys of his presence? You cannot be admitted to heaven without spiritual life. Hell is the sepulchre for dead souls, and thither you must be sent, if you still continue dead. And does not this thought affect you?

Consider also, now is the only time in which you can be restored to life. And O! will you let it pass by without improvement?

Shall all the means that have been used for your revival be in vain? Or the strivings of the spirit, the alarms of your own consciences, the blessings and chastisements of Providence, the persuasions, tears, and lamentations of your living friends, O! shall all these be in vain? Can you bear the thought? Surely, no. Therefore, O heave and struggle to burst the chains of death. Cry mightily to God to quicken you. Use all the means of vivification, and avoid every deadly and contagious thing.

I know not, my brethren, how this thought will affect us at parting to-day, that we have left behind us many a dead soul. But suppose we should leave as many bodies here behind us as there are of dead souls among us; suppose every sinner destitute of spiritual life should now be struck dead before us, O how would this floor be overlaid with dead corpses! How few of us would escape! What bitter lamentations and tears would be among us! One would lose a husband or a wife, another a child or a parent, another a friend or a neighbour. And have we hearts to mourn and tears to shed over such an event as this, and have we no compassion for dead souls? Is there none to mourn over them? Sinners, if you will still continue dead, there are some here to-day who part with you with this wish, *O that my head were waters, and mine eyes fountains of tears, that I might weep day and night for the slain of the daughter of my people.* And O that our mournings may reach the ears of the Lord of life, and that you might be quickened from your death in trespasses and sins! Amen and Amen.

SERMON VI.

Poor and contrite Spirits the Objects of the Divine Favour.

Isaiah lxvi. 2. *To this man will I look; even to him that is poor and of a contrite Spirit, and trembleth at my word.*

AS we consist of animal bodies as well as immortal souls, and are endowed with corporeal senses as well as rational powers, God, who has wisely adapted our religion to our make, requires bodily as well as spiritual worship; and commands us not only to exercise the inward powers of our minds in proper acts of devotion, but also to express our inward devotion in suitable external actions, and to attend upon him in the sensible outward ordinances which he has appointed. Thus it is under the gospel; but it was more remarkably so under the law, which, compared with the pure and spiritual worship of the gospel, was a system of carnal ordinances, and required a great deal of external pomp and grandeur, and bodily services. Thus a costly and magnificent structure was erected, by divine direction, in the wilderness, called the tabernacle, because built in the form of a tent, and moveable from place to place; and afterwards a moſt ſtately temple was built by Solomon with immenſe coſt, where the divine worſhip ſhonld be ſtatedly celebrated, and where all the males of Iſrael ſhould ſolemnly meet for that purpoſe three times in the year.

Theſe externals were not intended to exclude the internal worſhip of the Spirit, but to expreſs and aſſiſt it. And theſe ceremonials were not to be put into the place of morals, but obſerved as helps to the practice of them, and to prefigure the great Meſſiah. Even under the Moſaic diſpenſation, God had the greateſt regard to holineſs of heart and a good life; and the ſtricteſt obſerver of ceremonies could not be accepted without them.

But it is natural to degenerate mankind to invert the order of things, to place apart the eaſieſt and meaneſt part of religion, for the whole of it, to reſt in the externals of religion as ſufficient, without regarding the heart, and to depend upon a phariſaical ſtrictneſs in ceremonial obſervances, as an excuſe or atonement for neglecting the weightier matters of the law, judgment, mercy, and faith.

This was the unhappy error of the Jews in Iſaiah's time; and this the Lord would correct in the firſt verſes of this chapter.

The Jews gloried in their having the houſe of God among them, and were ever truſting in vain words, ſaying, *The temple of the Lord, the temple of the Lord, the temple of the Lord are theſe.* Jer. vii. 4. They filled his alters with coſtly ſacrifices; and in theſe they truſted to make atonement for ſin, and ſecure the divine favour.

As to their ſacrifices God lets them know, that while they had no regard to their morals, but choſe their own ways, and their ſouls delighted in their abominations, while they preſented them in a formal manner, without the fire of divine love, their ſacrifices were ſo far from procuring his acceptance, that they were odious to him. He abhors their moſt expenſive offerings as abominable and profane. He *that killeth an ox for ſacrifice* is as far from being accepted, *as if he unjuſtly ſlew a man; he that ſacrificeth a lamb, as if he cut off a dog's neck,* &c. Iſaiah lxvi. 3.

To remove this ſuperſtitious confidence in the temple, the Lord informs them that he had no need of it; that, large and magnificent as it was, it was not fit to contain him; and that, in conſecrating it to him, they ſhould not proudly think that they had given him any thing to which he had no prior right. " Thus ſaith the Lord, the heaven is my throne, where I reign conſpicuous in the viſible majeſty and grandeur of a God; and though the earth is not adorned with ſuch illuſtrious diſplays of my immediate preſence, though it does not ſhine in all the glory of my royal palace on high, yet it is a little province in my immenſe empire, and ſubject to my authority; it is my footſtool. If, then, heaven is my throne, and earth is my footstool; if the whole creation is my kingdom, where is the house that ye build unto me? where is your temple which appears so stately in your eyes? it is vanished, it is sunk into nothing. Is it able to contain that infinite Being to whom the whole earth is but a humble footstool, and the vast heaven but a throne? Can you vainly imagine that my presence can be confined to you in the narrow bounds of a temple, when the heaven and the heaven of heavens cannot contain me? Where is the place of my rest? can you provide a place for my repose, as though I were weary? or can my presence be restrained to one place, incapable of acting beyond the prescribed limits? No: infinite space only can equal my being and perfections; infinite space only is a sufficient sphere for my operations.

"Can you imagine you can bribe my favour, and give me something I had no right to before, by all the stately building you can rear to my name? Is not universal nature mine? For all these things hath mine hand made out of nothing, and all these things have been, or still subsist by the support of my all-preserving hand; and what right can be more valid and inalienable than that founded upon creation? Your silver and gold are mine, and mine the cattle upon a thousand hills; and therefore of mine own do you give me, faith the Lord."

These are such majestic strains of language as are worthy a God. Thus it becomes him to advance himself above the whole creation, and to assert his absolute property in and independency upon the universe.

Had he only turned to us the bright side of his throne, that dazzles us with insufferable splendor; had he only displayed his Majesty unallayed with grace and condescension in such language as this, it would have overwhelmed us, and cast us into the most abject despondency, as the outcasts of his providence beneath his notice. We might fear he would overlook us with majestic disdain, or careless neglect, like the little things that are called great by mortals, or as the busy emmets of our species are apt to do. In the hurry of business they are liable to neglect, and in the power of pride and grandeur to overlook or disdain their dependents. We should be ready in hopeless anxiety to say, " Is all this earth which to us appears so vast, and which is parcelled into a thousand mighty kingdoms, as we call them, is it all but the humble footstool of God? hardly worthy to bear his feet? What then am I? an atom of an atom-world, a trifling individual of a trifling race. Can I expect he will take any notice of such an insignificant thing as I? The vast affairs of heaven and earth lie upon his hand, and he is employed in the concerns of the wide universe, and can he find leisure to concern himself with me, and my little interests? Will a king, deliberating upon the concerns of nations, interest

Serm. 6. *the Objects of Divine Favour.*

himself in favour of the worm that crawls at his footstool? If the magnificent temple of Solomon was unworthy of the divine inhabitant, will he admit me into his presence, and give me audience? how can I expect it? It seems daring and presumptuous to hope for such condescension. And shall I then despair of the gracious regard of my Maker?"

No, desponding creature! mean and unworthy as thou art, hear the voice of divine condescension, as well as of Majesty: *To this man will I look, even to him that is poor, and of a contrite spirit, and that trembleth at my word.* Though God dwelleth not in temples made with hands, though he pours contempt upon princes, and scorns them in all their haughty glory and affected majesty, yet there are persons whom his gracious eye will regard. The high and lofty One that inhabiteth eternity, and dwelleth in the high and holy place, he will look down through all the shining ranks of angels upon—whom? Not on the proud, the haughty and presumptuous, but upon him *that is poor, and of a contrite spirit, and trembleth at* his *word.* To this man will he look from the throne of his majesty, however low, however mean he may be. This man is an object that can, as it were, attract his eyes from all the glories of the heavenly world, so as to regard a humble self-abasing worm. This man can never be lost or overlooked among the multitude of creatures, but the eyes of the Lord will discover him in the greatest crowd, his eyes will graciously fix upon this man, this particular man, though there were but one such in the compass of the creation, or though he were banished into the remotest corner of the universe, like a diamond in a heap of rubbish, or at the bottom of the ocean.

Do you hear this, you that are poor and contrite in spirit, and that tremble at his word? ye that, above all others, are most apt to fear you shall be disregarded by him, because you, of all others, are most deeply sensible how unworthy you are of his gracious notice: God, the great, the glorious, the terrible God, looks down upon you with eyes of love, and by so much the more affectionately, by how much the lower you are in your own esteem. Does not your heart spring within you at the sound? Are you not lost in pleasing wonder and gratitude, and crying out, "Can it be? can it be? is it indeed possible? is it true?" Yes, you have his own word for it, and do not think it too good news to be true, but believe, and rejoice, and give glory to his name; and fear not what men or devils can do unto you.

This, my brethren, is a matter of universal concern. It is the interest of each of us to know whether we are thus graciously regarded by that God on whom our very being and all our happiness entirely depend. And how shall we know this? In no other way than by discovering whether we have the characters of that happy man to whom he condefcends to look. Thefe are not pompous and high characters, they are not formed by earthly riches, learning, glory, and power: But *to this man will I look*, faith the Lord, *even to him that is poor, and of a contrite fpirit, and* that *trembleth at my word.* Let us inquire into the import of each of the characters.

I. It is the poor man to whom the Majefty of heaven condefcends to look.

This does not principally refer to thofe that are poor in this world; for, though it be very common that "the poor of this world are chofen to be rich in faith, and heirs of the kingdom," *James* ii. 5. yet this is not an univerfal rule; for many, alas! that are poor in this world are not rich towards God, nor rich in good works, and therefore fhall famifh through eternity in remedilefs want and wretchednefs. But the poor here fignifies fuch as Chrift characterizes more fully by the *poor in fpirit*. Matt. v. 3. And this character implies the following ingredients:

(1.) The poor man to whom Jehovah looks is deeply fenfible of his own infufficiency, and that nothing but the enjoyment of God can make him happy.

The poor man feels that he is not formed felf-fufficient, but a dependent upon God. He is fenfible of the weaknefs and poverty of his nature, and that he was not endowed with a fufficient ftock of riches in his creation to fupport him through the endlefs duration for which he was formed, or even for a fingle day. The feeble vine does not more clofely adhere to the elm than he does to his God. He is not more fenfible of the infufficiency of his body to fubfift without air, or the productions of the earth, than of that of his foul without his God, and the enjoyment of his love. In fhort, he is reduced into his proper place in the fyftem of the univerfe, low and mean in comparifon with fuperior beings of the angelic order, and efpecially in comparifon with the great Parent and fupport of nature. He feels himfelf to be, what he really is, a poor impotent dependent creature, that can neither live, nor move, nor exift without God. He is fenfible that his *fufficiency is of God*, 2 Cor. iii. 5. " and that all the fprings of his happinefs are in him."

This fenfe of his dependence upon God is attended with a fenfe of the inability of all earthly enjoyments to make him happy, and fill the vaft capacities of his foul, which were formed for the enjoyment of an infinite good. He has a relifh for the bleffings of this life, but it is attended with a fenfe of their infufficiency, and does not exclude a ftronger relifh for the fuperior pleafures of religion. He is not a precife hermit, or a four afcetic, on the one hand; and, on the other, he is not *a lover of pleafure more than a lover of God*.

If he enjoys no great share of the comforts of this life, he does not labour, nor so much as wish for them as his supreme happiness: he is well assured they can never answer this end in their greatest affluence. It is for God, it is for the living God, that his soul most eagerly thirsts. In the greatest extremity he is sensible that the enjoyment of his love is more necessary to his felicity than the possession of earthly blessings; nay, he is sensible, that if he is miserable in the absence of these, the principal cause is the absence of his God. O! if he were blest with the perfect enjoyment of God, he could say with Habakkuk, *Though the fig-tree should not blossom, and there should be no fruit in the vine; though the labour of the olive should fail, and the fields yield no meat; though the flock should be cut off from the fold, and there be no herd in the stall;* though universal famine should strip me of all my earthly blessings, *yet I will rejoice in the Lord,* as my complete happiness; *I will joy in the God of my salvation.* Hab. iii. 17, 18.

If he enjoys an affluence of earthly blessings, he still retains a sense of his need of the enjoyment of God. To be discontent and dissatisfied is the common fate of the rich as well as the poor; they are still craving, craving an unknown something to complete their bliss. The soul, being formed for the fruition of the Supreme Good, secretly languishes and pines away in the midst of other enjoyments, without knowing its cure. It is the enjoyment of God only that can satisfy its unbounded desires; but, alas! it has no relish for him, no thirst after him; it is still crying, "More, more of the delights of the world;" like a man in a burning fever, that calls for cold water, that will but inflame his disease, and occasion a more painful return of thirst. But the poor in spirit know where their cure lies. They do not ask with uncertainty, *Who will shew us* any sort of *good?* but their petitions centre in this, as the grand constituent of their happiness, *Lord, lift thou up the light of thy countenance upon us;* and this puts more gladness into their hearts *than the abundance of corn and wine.* Psalm iv. 6, 7. This was the language of the Psalmist, *There is none upon earth that I desire besides thee. My flesh and my heart faileth; but thou art the strength of my heart, and my portion for ever.* Psalm lxxiii. 25, 26. And as this disposition extends to all earthly things, so it does to all created enjoyments whatsoever, even to those of the heavenly world; the poor man is sensible that he could not be happy even there without the enjoyment of God. His language is, *whom have I in heaven but thee?* It is *beholding thy face in righteousness, and awaking in thy likeness, that alone can satisfy me.* Psalm xvii. 15.

(2.) This spiritual poverty implies deep humility and self-abasement.

The poor man on whom the God of heaven condescends to look, is mean in his own apprehensions; he accounts himself not a being of mighty importance. He has no high esteem of his own good qualities, but is little in his own eyes. He is not apt to give himself the preference to others, but is ready to give way to them as his superiors. He has a generous sagacity to behold their good qualities, and a commendable blindness towards their imperfections: but he is not quick to discern his own excellencies, nor sparing to his own frailties.

Instead of being dazzled with the splendor of his own endowments or acquisitions, he is apt to overlook them with a noble neglect, and is sensible of the weakness and defects of his nature.

And as to his gracious qualities, they appear small, exceeding small to him: when he considers how much they fall short of what they should be, they as it were vanish and shrink into nothing. How cold does his love appear to him in its greatest fervour! How feeble his faith in its greatest confidence! How superficial his repentance in its greatest depth! How proud his lowest humility! And as for the good actions he has performed, alas! how few, how poorly done, how short of his duty do they appear! After he has done all, he counts himself an unprofitable servant. After he has done all, he is more apt to adopt the language of the publican than the pharisee, *God be merciful to me a sinner*. In his highest attainments he is not apt to admire himself; so far is he from it, that it is much more natural to him to fall into the opposite extreme, and to account himself the least, yea, less than the least of all other saints upon the face of the earth: and if he contends for any preference, it is for the lowest place in the list of christians. This disposition was remarkably exemplified in St. Paul, who probably had made greater advancements in holiness than any saint that was ever received to heaven from this guilty world.

He that is poor in spirit has also a humbling sense of his own sinfulness. His memory is quick to recollect his past sins, and he is very sharp-sighted to discover the remaining corruptions of his heart, and the imperfections of his best duties. He is not ingenious to excuse them, but views them impartially in all their deformity and aggravations. He sincerely doubts whether there be a saint upon earth so exceeding corrupt; and, though he may be convinced that the Lord has begun a work of grace in him, and consequently, that he is in a better state than such as are under the prevailing dominion of sin, yet he really questions whether there be such a depraved creature in the world as he sees he has been. He is apt to count himself the chief of sinners, and more indebted to free grace than any of the sons of men. He is intimately acquainted with himself; but he sees only the out-side of others, and hence he concludes himself so much worse than others;

Serm. 6.   *the Objects of Divine Favour.*   153

hence he loaths himfelf in his own ,fight for all his abominations. *Ezek.* xxxvi. 31. Self-abafement is pleafing to him; his humility is not forced; he does not think it a great thing for him to fink thus low. He plainly fees himfelf to be a mean, finful, exceeding finful creature, and therefore is fure that it is no condefcenfion, but the moft reafonable thing in the world for him to think meanly of himfelf, and to humble and abafe himfelf. It is unnatural for one that efteems himfelf a being of great importance to ftoop: but it is eafy, and appears no felf-denial for a poor mean creature to do fo, who looks upon himfelf, and feels himfelf, to be fuch.

Finally, the poor man is deeply fenfible of his own unworthinefs. He fees that in himfelf he deferves no favour from God for all the good he has ever done, but that he may after all juftly reject him. He makes no proud boafts of his good heart, or good life, but falls in the duft before God, and cafts all his dependence upon his free grace :—which leads me to obferve,

(3.) That he who is poor in fpirit is fenfible of his need of the influences of divine grace to fanctify him, and enrich him with the graces of the fpirit.

He is fenfible of the want of holinefs ; this nece ffarily flows from his fenfe of his corruption, and the imperfection of all his graces. Holinefs is the one thing needful with him, which he defires and longs for above all others ; and he is deeply fenfible that he cannot work it in his own heart by his own ftrength; he feels that without Chrift he can do nothing, and that it is God who muft work in him both to will and to do. Hence, like a poor man that cannot fubfift upon his ftock, he depends entirely upon the grace of God to work all his works in him, and to enable him to work out his falvation with fear and trembling.

(4.) He is deeply fenfible of the abfolute neceffity of the righteoufnefs of Chrift for his juftification.

He does not think himfelf rich in good works to bribe his judge, and procure acquittance, but, like a poor criminal that, having nothing to purchafe a pardon, nothing to plead in his own defence, cafts himfelf upon the mercy of the court, he places his whole dependence upon the free grace of God through Jefus Chrift. He pleads his righteoufnefs only, and trufts in it alone. The rich fcorn to be obliged; but the poor, that cannot fubfift of themfelves, will cheerfully receive. So the felf-righteous will not fubmit to the righteoufnefs of God, but the poor in fpirit will cheerfully receive it.

(5.) And laftly, the man that is poor in fpirit is an importunate beggar at the throne of grace.

He lives upon charity ; he lives upon the bounties of heaven; and, as thefe are not to be obtained without begging, he is frequently lifting up his cries to the Father of all his mercies for them. He attends upon the ordinances of God, as Bartimeus by the way side, to ask the charity of passengers. Prayer is the natural language of spiritual poverty; *The poor*, saith Solomon, *useth intreaties*: Prov. xviii. 23. whereas they that are rich in their own conceit can live without prayer, or content themselves with the careless formal performance of it.

This is the habitual character of that poor man to whom the Majesty of heaven vouchsafes the looks of his love. At times indeed he has but little sense of these things; but then he is uneasy, and he labours to re-obtain it, and sometimes is actually blessed with it.

And is there no such poor man or woman in this assembly? I hope there is. Where are ye poor creatures? stand forth, and receive the blessings of your Redeemer, *Blessed are the poor in spirit*, &c. He who has his throne in the height of heaven, and to whom this vast earth is but a footstool, looks upon you with eyes of love. This spiritual poverty is greater riches than the treasures of the universe. Be not ashamed therefore to own yourselves poor men, if such you are. May God thus impoverish us all! may he strip us of all our imaginary grandeur and riches, and reduce us to poor beggars at his door!

But it is time to consider the other character of the happy man upon whom the Lord of heaven will graciously look: and that is,

II. Contrition of spirit. *To this man will I look, that is of a contrite spirit.*

The word *contrite* signifies one that is beaten or bruised with hard blows, or an heavy burden. And it belongs to the mourning penitent whose heart is broken and wounded for sin. Sin is an intolerable burden that crushes and bruises him, and he feels himself pained and sore under it. His stoney heart, which could not be impressed, but rather repelled the blow, is taken away; and now he has an heart of flesh, easily bruised and wounded. His heart is not always hard and senseless, light and trifling; but it has tender sensations; he is easily susceptive of sorrow for sin, is humbled under a sense of his imperfections, and is really pained and distressed because he can serve his God no better, but daily sins against him. This character may also agree to the poor anxious soul that is broken with cruel fears of its state. The stout-hearted can venture their eternal all upon uncertainty, and indulge pleasing hopes without anxiously examining their foundation; but he that is of a contrite spirit is tenderly sensible of the importance of the matter, and cannot be easy without some good evidence of safety. Such shocking suppositions as these frequently startle him, and pierce his very heart: " What if I should be deceived at last? What if after all I should be banished from that God in whom lies all my happiness," &c. These are suppositions full of insupportable terror, when they appear but barely possible; and much more when there seems to be reason for them. Such an habitual pious jealoufy as this, is a good fymptom; and to your pleafing furprize, ye doubtful chriftians, I may tell you that *that* Majefty, who you are afraid difregards you, looks down upon you with pity. Therefore lift up your eyes to him in wonder and joyful confidence. You are not fuch neglected things as you think. The Majefty of heaven thinks it beneath him to look down through all the glorious orders of angels, and through interpofing worlds, down, down even upon you in the depth of your felf-abhorrence. Let us,

III. Confider the remaining character of the happy man to whom the Lord will look : *Him that trembleth at my word.*

This character implies a tender fenfe of the great things of the word, and an heart eafily impreffed with them as the moft important realities. This was remarkably exemplified in tender-hearted Jofiah. 2. Chron. xxxiv. 19, 20, 27. To one that trembles at the divine word, the threatenings of it do not appear vain terrors, nor great fwelling words of vanity, but the moft tremendous realities. Such an one cannot bear up under them, but would tremble, and fall, and die away, if not relieved by fome happy promife of deliverance. He that trembles at the word of God is not a ftupid hearer or reader of it. It reaches and pierces his heart as a fharp two-edged fword; it carries power along with it, and he feels that it is the word of God, and not of men, even when it is fpoken by feeble mortals. Thus he not only trembles at the terror, but at the authority of the word;—which leads me to obferve farther, that he trembles with filial veneration of the majefty of God fpeaking in his word. He confiders it as his voice who fpake all things into being, and whofe glory is fuch, that a deep folemnity muft feize thofe that are admitted to hear him fpeak.

How oppofite is this to the temper of multitudes who regard the word of God no more than (with horror I exprefs it) the word of a child or a fool. They will have their own way, let him fay what he will. They perfift in fin, in defiance of his threatenings. They fit as carelefs and ftupid under his word, as though it were fome old, dull, trifling ftory, It feldom makes any impreffions upon their ftony hearts. Thefe are the brave, undaunted men of the world, who harden themfelves againft the fear of futurity, But, unhappy creatures! the God of heaven difdains to give them a gracious look, while he fixes his eyes upon the man that " is contrite, and that trembles at his word."

And where is that happy man? Where in this affembly, where is the contrite fpirit? Where the man that trembleth at the word? You are all ready to catch at the character, but be not prefumptuous on the one hand, nor exceffively timorous on the other. Inquire whether this be your prevailing character. If fo, then claim it, and rejoice in it, though you have it not in perfection.

But if you have it not prevailingly, do not seize it as your own. Though you have been at times distressed with a sense of sin and danger, and the word strikes a terror to your hearts, yet, unless you are habitually of a tender and contrite spirit, you are not to claim the character.

But let such of you as are poor and contrite in spirit, and that tremble at the word of the Lord, enter deeply into the meaning of this expression, that the Lord looks to you. He does not look on you as a careless spectator, not concerning himself with you, or caring what will become of you, but he looks upon you as a father, a friend, a benefactor: his looks are efficacious for your good.

He looks upon you with acceptance. He is pleased with the sight. He loves to see you labouring towards him. He looks upon you as the objects of his everlasting love, and purchased by the blood of his Son, and he is well pleased with you for his righteousness sake. Hence his looking upon him that is poor, &c. is opposed to his hating the wicked and their sacrifices, ver. 3. And is he whom you have so grievously offended, he whose wrath you fear above all other things, is he indeed reconciled to you, and does he delight in you? what cause of joy, and praise, and wonder is here?

Again, he looks to you so as to take particular notice of you. He sees all the workings of your hearts towards him. He sees and pities you in your honest, though feeble conflicts with indwelling sin. He observes all your faithful though weak endeavours to serve him. His eyes pierce your very hearts, and the least motion there cannot escape his notice. This indeed might make you tremble, if he looked upon you with the eyes of a judge, for O how many abominations must he see in you! But be of good cheer, he looks upon you with the eyes of a friend, and with that love which covers a multitude of sins. He looks upon you with the eyes of compassion in all your calamities. He looks upon you to see that you be not overborne and crushed. David, who passed through as many hardships and afflictions as any of you, could say from happy experience, *the eyes of the Lord are upon the righteous, and his ears are open to their cry.* Psal. xxxiv. 15.

Finally, he looks to you so as to look after you, as we do after the sick and weak. He looks to you so as to provide for you: and he will give you grace and glory, and *no good thing will be held from you.* Psal. lxxxiv. 11.

And are you not safe and happy under the inspection of a father and a friend? Let a little humble courage then animate you amid your many dejections, and confide in that care of which you feel yourself to be so unworthy.

Here it may not be amiss to observe, what must give you no

small pleasure, that those very persons who according to the estimate of men are the most likely to be overlooked, are those whom God graciously regards. The persons themselves are apt to cry "Happy I, could I believe that the God of heaven thus graciously regards me; but, alas! I feel myself a poor unworthy creature; I am a trembling broken-hearted thing, beneath the notice of so great a Majesty." And art thou so indeed? then I may convert thy objection into an encouragement. Thou art the very person upon whom God looks. His eyes are running to and fro through the earth in quest of such as thou art; and he will find thee out among the innumerable multitudes of mankind. Wert thou surrounded with crowds of kings and nobles, his eyes would pass by hem all to fix upon thee. What a glorious artifice, if I may so speak, is this to catch at and convert the person's discouragement as a ground of courage! to make that the character of the favourites of heaven, which they themselves look upon as marks of his neglect of them! "Alas!" says the poor man, "if I was the object of divine notice, he would not suffer me to continue thus poor and broken-hearted." But you may reason directly the reverse, he makes you thus poor in spirit, sensible of your sinfulness and imperfections, because that he graciously regards you. He will not suffer you to be puffed up with your imaginary goodness, like the rest of the world, because he loves you more than he loves them.

However unaccountable this procedure seems, there is very good reason for it. The poor are the only persons that would relish the enjoyment of God, and prize his love: they alone are capable of the happiness of heaven, which consists in the perfection of holiness.

To conclude, Let us view the perfection and condescension of God as illustrated by this subject. Consider, ye poor in spirit, who He is that stoops to look upon such little things as you. It is He whose throne is in the highest heaven, surrounded with myriads of angels and archangels; it is he whose footstool is the earth, who supports every creature upon it; it is he who is exalted above the blessing and praise of all the celestial armies, and who cannot without condescension behold the things that are done in heaven; it is He that looks down upon such poor worms as you. And what a stoop is this?

It is he that looks upon you in particular, who looks after all the worlds he has made. He manages all the affairs of the universe; he takes care of every individual in his vast family; he provides for all his creatures, and yet he is at leisure to regard you. He takes as particular notice of you as if you were his only creatures. What perfection is this! what an infinite grasp of thought! what unbounded power! and what condescension too!—Do but consider what a small figure you make in the universe of beings. You are not so much in comparison with the infinite multitude of creatures in the compass of nature, as a grain of sand to all the sands upon the sea-shore, or as a mote to the vast globe of earth? and yet he, that has the care of the whole universe, takes particular notice of you—you who are but trifles, compared with your fellow-creatures; and who, if you were annihilated, would hardly leave a blank in the creation. Consider this and wonder at the condescension of God; consider this, and acknowledge your own meanness; you are but nothing not only compared with God, but you are as nothing in the system of creation.

I shall add but this one natural reflection: If it be so great a happiness to have the great God for our patron, then what is it to be out of his favour? to be disregarded by him? methinks an universal tremour may seize this assembly at the very supposition. And is there a creature in the universe in this wretched condition? methinks all the creation besides must pity him. Where is the wretched being to be found? must we descend to hell to find him? No, alas! there are many such on this earth? nay, I must come nearer you still, there are many such probably in this assembly: all among you are such who are not poor and contrite in spirit, and do not tremble at the word of the Lord. And art thou not one of the miserable number, O man? What! disregarded by the God that made thee! not favoured with one look of love by the Author of all happiness! He looks on thee indeed, but it is with eyes of indignation, marking thee out for vengeance; and canst thou be easy in such a case? wilt thou not labour to impoverish thyself, and have thy heart broken, that thou mayest become the object of his gracious regard?

SERMON VII.

The Nature and Danger of making light of Chriſt and Salvation.

—>○◇○◇○◇○◇<—

MATT. xxii. 5. *But they made light of it.*

THERE is not one of us in this aſſembly that has heard any thing, but what has heard of Chriſt and ſalvation: there is not one of us but has had the rich bleſſings of the goſpel freely and repeatedly offered to us: there is not one of us but ſtands in the moſt abſolute need of theſe bleſſings, and muſt periſh for ever without them; I wiſh I could add, there is not one of us but has cheerfully accepted them according to the offer of the goſpel. But, alas! ſuch an aſſembly is not to be expected on earth! Multitudes will make light of Chriſt and the invitations of the goſpel, as the Jews did.

This parable repreſents the great God under the majeſtic idea of a king.

He is repreſented as making a marriage-feaſt for his Son; that is, God in the goſpel offers his Son Jeſus Chriſt as a Saviour to the guilty ſons of men, and, upon their acceptance of him, the moſt intimate, endearing union, and the tendereſt mutual affection take place between Chriſt and them; which may very properly be repreſented by the marriage relation. And God has provided for them a rich variety of bleſſings, pardon, holineſs, and everlaſting felicity, which may be ſignified by a royal nuptial feaſt, verſe 2.

Theſe bleſſings were firſt offered to the Jews, who were bidden to the wedding by Moſes and the prophets, whoſe great buſineſs it was to prepare them to receive the Meſſiah, verſe 3.

The ſervants that were ſent to call them that were thus bidden, were the apoſtles and ſeventy diſciples, whom Chriſt ſent out to preach that the goſpel kingdom was juſt at hand, verſe 3.

When the Jews rejected this call, he ſent forth other ſervants, namely, the apoſtles after his aſcenſion, who were to be more urgent in their invitations, and to tell them that, in confequence of Chriſt's death, all things were now ready, verſe 4.

It is ſeldom that invitations to a royal feaſt are rejected; but, alas! the Jews rejected the invitation of the goſpel, and would

Y

not accept of its important bleſſings. They made light of Chriſt and his bleſſings; they were careleſs to them, and turned their attention to other things.

Theſe things were not peculiar to the Jews, but belong to us ſinners of the Gentiles in theſe ends of the earth. Chriſt is ſtill propoſed to us; to the ſame bleſſings we are invited; and I have the honour, my dear brethren, of appearing among you as a ſervant of the Heavenly King, ſent out to urge you to embrace the offer.

I doubt not but ſundry of you have complied; and you are enriched and made for ever.

But, alas! muſt I not entertain a godly jealouſy over ſome of you? have you not made light of Chriſt and ſalvation, to which you have been invited for ſo many years ſucceſſively?

Your caſe is really lamentable, as I hope you will ſee before I have done; and I moſt ſincerely compaſſionate you from my heart. I now riſe up in this ſolemn place with the deſign to addreſs you with the moſt awful ſeriouſneſs, and the moſt compaſſionate concern; and did you know how much your happineſs may depend upon it, and how anxious I am leaſt I ſhould fail in the attempt, I am ſure you could not but pray for me, and pity me. If ever you regarded a man in the moſt ſerious temper and addreſs, I beg you would now regard what I am going to ſay to you.

You cannot receive any benefit from this, or indeed any other ſubject, till you apply it to yourſelves. And therefore, in order to reform you of the ſin of making light of Chriſt and the goſpel, I muſt firſt inquire who are guilty of it. For this purpoſe let us conſider,

What it is to make light of Chriſt and the invitations of the goſpel.

I can think of no plainer way to diſcover this, than to inquire how we treat thoſe things that we highly eſteem; and alſo by way of contraſt, how we treat thoſe things which we make light of; and hence we may diſcover whether Chriſt and the goſpel may be ranked among the things we eſteem, or thoſe we diſregard.

I. Men are apt to remember and affectionately think of the things that they highly eſteem; but as for thoſe which they diſregard, they can eaſily forget them, and live from day to day without a ſingle thought about them.

Now do you often affectionately remember the Lord Jeſus, and do your thoughts affectionately go after him? do they pay him early viſits in the morning? do they make frequent excurſions to him through the day? and do you lie down with him in your hearts at night? Is not the contrary evident as to many of you? Can you not live from day to day thoughtlefs of Jefus, and your everlafting falvation? Recollect now, how many affectionate thoughts have you had of thefe things through the week paſt, or in this facred morning. And can you indeed highly efteem thofe things which you hardly ever think of? Follow your own hearts, Sirs; obferve which way they moſt naturally and freely run, and then judge whether you make light of the gofpel or not. Alas! we cannot perfuade men to one hour's ferious confideration what they fhould do for an intereſt in Chriſt; we cannot perfuade them fo much as to afford him only their thoughts, which are fuch cheap things; and yet they will not be convinced that they make light of Chrift. And here lies the infatuation of fin; it blinds and befools men, fo that they do not know what they think of, what they love, or what they intend, much lefs do they know the habitual bent of their fouls. They often imagine themfelves free from thofe fins to which they are moft enflaved, and particularly they think themfelves innocent of the crime of making light of the gofpel, when this is the very crime that is likely to deftroy them for ever.

II. The things that men value, if of fuch a nature as to admit of publication, will be the frequent fubjects of their difcourfe: the thoughts will command the tongue, and furnifh materials for converfation. But thofe things that they forget and difregard they will not talk of.

Do not they therefore make light of Chriſt and falvation, who have no delight in converfing about them, and hardly ever mention the name of Chriſt but in a trifling or prophane manner? They do not like the company where divine things are difcourfed of, but think it precife and troublefome. They had much rather be entertained with humourous tales and idle ftories, or talk about the affairs of the world. *They are of the world*, fays St. John, *therefore fpeak they of the world, and the world heareth them.* 1 John iv. 5. They are in their element in fuch converfation. Or others may talk about religion; but it is only about the circumftances of it, as, "How fuch a man preached; it was a very good or a bad fermon," &c. but they care not to enter into the fpirit and fubftance of divine things; and if they fpeak of Chriſt and experimental religion, it is in an heartlefs and infipid manner. And do not fuch make light of the gofpel? and is not this the character of many of you?

III. Men make light of thofe things, if they are of a practical nature which they only talk about, but do not reduce into practice.

Chriftianity was intended not to furnifh matter for empty talkers, but to govern the heart and practice. But are there not some that only employ their tongues about it, especially when their spirits are raised with liquor, and then a torrent of noisy religion breaks from them. Watch their lives, and you will see little appearance of christianity there. And do not these evidently make light of Christ, who make him the theme of their drunken conversation, or who seem to think that God sent his Son from heaven just to set the world a talking about him? There is nothing in nature that seems to me more abominable than this.

IV. We take the utmost pains and labour to secure the things we value, and cannot be easy while our property in them is uncertain; but those things that we think lightly of we care but little whether they be ours or not.

Therefore, have not such of you made light of Christ and salvation, who have lived twenty or thirty years uncertain whether you have interest in them, and yet have been easy and contented, and take no method to be resolved? Are all that hear me this day determined in this important question, " What shall become of me when I die?" Are you all certain upon good grounds, and after a thorough trial, that you shall be saved? O that you were! but, alas! you are not. And do you think you would bear this uncertainty about it, if you did not make light of salvation? No; you would carefully examine yourselves; you would diligently peruse the scriptures to find out the marks of those that shall be saved; you would anxiously consult those that could direct you, and particularly pious ministers, who would think it the greatest favour you could do them to devolve such an office upon them. But now ministers may sit in their studies for a whole year, and not ten persons perhaps in five hundred agreeably intrude upon them on this important business.

O, Sirs, if the gospel should pierce your hearts indeed, you could but cry out with the convicted Jews, *Men and brethren, what shall we do to be saved?* Acts ii. 37. Paul, when awakened, cries out, in a trembling consternation, *Lord! what wilt thou have me to do?* But when shall we hear such questions now-a-days?

V. The things that men highly esteem, deeply and tenderly affect them, and excite some motions in their hearts; but what they make light of, makes no impression upon them.

And if you did not make light of the gospel, what workings would there be in your hearts about it? what solemn, tender, and vigorous passions would it raise in you to hear such things about the world to come! what sorrows would burst from your hearts at the discovery of your sins! what fear and astonishment would seize you at the consideration of your misery! what transports of joy and gratitude would you feel at the glad tidings of salvation by the blood of Christ! what strong efficacious purposes would be raised in you at the discovery of your duty! O what hearers should we have, were it not for this one sin, the making light of the gospel! whereas now we are in danger of wearying them, or preaching them asleep with our most solemn discourses about this momentous affair. We talk to them of Christ and salvation till they grow quite tired of this dull old tale, and this foolishness of preaching. Alas! little would one think, from the air of carelessness, levity, and inattention that appears among them, that they were hearing such weighty truths, or have any concern in them.

VI. Our estimate of things may be discovered by the diligence and earnestness of our endeavours about them. Those things which we highly value, we think no pains too great to obtain; but what we think lightly of we use no endeavours about, or we use them in a languid careless manner.

And do not they make light of Christ and salvation, who do not exert themselves in earnest to obtain them, and think a great deal of every little thing they do in religion? they are still ready to cry out, "What need of so much pains? we hope to be saved without so much trouble." And, though these may not be so honest as to speak it out, it is plain from their temper and practice, they grudge all the service they do for Christ, as done to a master they do not love. They love and esteem the world, and therefore for the world they will labour and toil all day, and seem never to think they can do too much: but for the God that made them, for the Lord that bought them, and for their everlasting salvation, they seem afraid of taking too much pains. Let us preach to them as long as we will, we cannot bring them in earnest to desire and pursue after holiness. Follow them to their houses, and you will hardly ever find them reading a chapter in their Bibles, or calling upon God with their families, so much as once a day. Follow them into their retirements, and you will hear no penitent confessions of sin, no earnest cries for mercy. They will not allow to God that one day in seven which he has appropriated to his own immediate service, but they will steal and prostitute some even of those sacred hours for idleness, or worldly conversation, or business. And many of them are so malignant in wickedness, that they will reproach and ridicule others that are not so made as themselves in these respects. And is not Christ worth seeking? Is not eternal salvation worth so much trouble? does not that man make light of these things that think his ease or carnal pleasure of greater importance? Let common sense judge.

VII. That which we highly value we think we cannot buy too dear; and we are ready to part with every thing that comes in competition with it. The merchant that found one pearl of great price, sold all that he had to purchase it, *Matt.* xiii. 46. but those things that we make light of, we will not part with things of value for them.

Now, when Christ and the blessings of the gospel come in competition with the world and sinful pleasures, you may know which you most highly esteem, by considering which you are most ready to part with. You are called to part with every thing that is inconsistent with an interest in Christ, and yet many of you will not do it. You are called but to give God his own, to resign all to his will, to let go all those profits and pleasures which you must either part with, or part with Christ, and yet your hearts cling to these things, you grasp them eagerly, and nothing can tear them from you. You must have your pleasures, you must keep your credit in the world, you must look to your estates, whatever becomes of Christ and salvation; as if you could live and die better without Christ than without these things; or as if Christ could not make you happy without them. And does not this bring the matter to an issue, and plainly shew that you make light of Christ in comparison with these things? Christ himself has assured you, over and over, that unless you are willing to part with all for his sake, you cannot be his disciples; and yet, while you have the quite contrary disposition, you will pretend to be his disciples; as if you knew better what it is that constituted his disciples than he.

VIII. Those things which we highly value, we shall be for helping our friends to obtain.

Do not those, then, make light of Christ who do not take half so much pains to help their children to an interest in him, as to set them up in credit in the world, and leave them large fortunes? They supply the outward wants of their families, but they take little or no care about their everlasting salvation.—Alas! Sirs, the neglected, ignorant, and vicious children and servants of such of you can witness against you, that you make very light of Christ and salvation, and their immortal souls.

IX. That which men highly esteem they will so diligently pursue, that you may see their regard for it in their endeavours after it, if it be a matter within their reach.

You may therefore see that many make light of the gospel by the little knowledge they have of it, after all the means of instruction with which they have been favoured. Alas! where is their improvement in holiness! how little do they know of their own hearts, of God and Christ, and the world to come, and what they must do to be saved! Ask them about these things, and you will find them stupidly ignorant: and yet they have so much conceited knowledge that they will not acknowledge it; or if they do, they have no better excuse than to say they are no scholars, or they have a poor memory; as if it required extensive learning, or a great genius to know the things that are necessary to salvation.

O! if they had not made light of these things; if they had bestowed but half the pains upon them which they have taken to understand matters of trade and worldly business, they would not be so grossly ignorant as they are? When men that can learn the hardest trade in a few years, when men of bright parts, and perhaps considerable learning, after living so many years, are still mere novices in matters of religion, and do not so much as know the terms of life according to the gospel, is it not plain that they care but little about these things, and that they make light of the Son of God, and all his inestimable immortal blessings?

Thus I have offered you sufficient matter of conviction in this affair. And what is the result? does not conscience smite some of you by this time, and say, "I am the man that have made light of Christ and his gospel?" If not, upon what evidence are you acquitted? Some of you, I doubt not, can say, in the integrity of your hearts, "Alas! I am too careless about this important affair, but God knows I am often deeply concerned about it; God knows that if ever I was in earnest about any thing in all my life, it has been about my everlasting state; and there is nothing in all the world that habitually lies so near my heart." But are there not some of you whom conscience does not accuse of this crime of too much carelessness about the gospel, not because you are innocent, but because you make so very light of it, that you will make no thorough search into it? and does not this alone prove you guilty? I beseech such to consider the folly of your conduct. Do you then think to excuse your crime, by being careless whether you are guilty of it or not? Can you avoid the precipice by shutting your eyes? If you discover your sin now, it may be of unspeakable service, but if you now shut your eyes you must see it hereafter, when it will be too late; when your conviction will be your punishment. I beseech you also to consider the dreadful evil of your conduct in making light of a Saviour. And here I shall offer such arguments to expose its aggravations as I am sure cannot fail to convince and astonish you, if you act like men of reason and understanding.

I. Consider you make light of him who did not make light of you, when you deserved his final neglect of you. You were worthy of nothing but contempt and abhorrence from him. As a man you are but a worm to God, and as a sinner you are viler than a toad or a serpent. Yet Christ was so far from making light of you, that he left his native heaven, became a man of sorrows, and died in the most exquisite agonies, that a way might be opened for the salvation of your miserable soul: and can you make light of him after all his regard to you? What miracles of love and mercy has he shewn towards you, and can you neglect him after all? Angels, who are less concerned in these things than we, can not but pry into them with delightful wonder, 1 *Peter* i. 12. and shall sinners, who have the most intimate personal concern in them, make light of them? This is a crime more than devilish; for the devils never had a Saviour offered to them, and consequently never could despise him. And can you live in a carelessness of Christ all your days, and yet feel no remorse?

II. Consider you make light of matters of the greatest excellency and importance in all the world. O, Sirs, you know not what it is that you slight; had you known these things you would not have ventured to make light of them for ten thousand worlds. As Christ said to the woman of Samaria, *If thou hadst known the gift of God, and who it is that speaketh to thee, thou wouldest have asked of him living water.* John iv. 13. Had the Jews known, they would not have crucified the Lord of Glory. 1 Cor. ii. 8. So had you known what Jesus is, you would not have made light of him; he would have been to you the most important being in the universe. O had you been but one day in heaven, and seen and felt the happiness there! or had you been one hour under the agonies of hell, you could never more have trifled with salvation.

Here I find my thoughts run so naturally into the same channel with those of the excellent Mr. Baxter, about an hundred years ago, that you will allow me to give a long quotation from him, that you may see in what light this great and good man viewed the neglected things which the gospel brings to your ears. His words are these; and I am sure to me they have been very weighty:—" O, Sirs, they are no trifles or jesting matters that the gospel speaks of. I must needs profess to you that when I have the most serious thoughts of these things, I am ready to wonder that such amazing matters do not overwhelm the souls of men: that the greatness of the subject doth not so overmatch our understandings and affections, as even to drive men beside themselves, but that God hath always somewhat allayed it by distance; much more do I wonder that men should be so blockish as to make light of such things. O Lord, that men did but know what everlasting glory and everlasting torments are! would they then hear us as they do? would they read and think of these things as they do? I profess I have been ready to wonder when I have heard such weighty things delivered, how people can forbear crying out in the congregation, and much more do I wonder how they can rest, till they have gone to their ministers and learned what they shall do to be saved, that this great business should be put out of doubt. O that heaven and hell should work no more upon men! O that eternity should work no more! O how can you forbear when you are alone to think with yourselves what it is to be everlastingly in joy or torment! I wonder that such thoughts do not break your sleep, and that they do not crowd into your minds when you are about your labour! I wonder how you can almost do any thing else! How can you have any quietness in your minds? how can you eat or drink, or rest, till you have got some ground of everlasting consolations? Is that a man or a corpse that is not affected with matters of this moment? that can be readier to sleep than to tremble, when he hears how he must stand at the bar of God? Is that a man or a clod of clay that can rise up and lie down without being deeply affected with his everlasting state? that can follow his worldly business, and make nothing of the great business of salvation or damnation, and that when he knows it is so hard at hand? Truly, Sirs, when I think of the weight of the matter, I wonder at the best saints upon earth, that they are no better, and do no more in so weighty a case. I wonder at those whom the world accounts more holy than needs, and scorns for making too much ado, that they can put off Christ and their souls with so little; that they do not pour out their souls in every prayer; that they are not more taken up with God; that their thoughts are not more serious in preparation for their last account. I wonder that they are not a thousand times more strict in their lives, and more laborious and unwearied for the crown than they are. And for myself (says that zealous, flaming, and indefatigable preacher) as I am ashamed of my dull and careless heart, and of my slow and unprofitable course of life, so the Lord knows I am ashamed of every sermon that I preach: when I think what I am, and who sent me, and how much the salvation and damnation of men is concerned in it, I am ready to tremble, lest God should judge me as a slighter of his truth and the souls of men, and lest in my best sermon I should be guilty of their blood. Methinks we should not speak a word to men in matters of such consequence without tears, or the greatest earnestness that possibly we can. Where we not too much guilty of the sin which we reprove, it would be so. Whether we are alone or in company, methinks our end, and such an end, should still be in our mind, and as before our eyes; and we should sooner forget any thing, or set light by any thing, or by all things, than by this."

And now, my brethren, if such a man as this viewed these things in this light, O what shall we, we languishing careless creatures, what shall we think of ourselves? Into what a dead sleep are we fallen! O let the most active and zealous among us awake, and be a thousand times more earnest: and ye frozen-hearted, careless sinners, for God's sake awake, and exert yourselves to good purpose in the pursuit of salvation, or you are lost to all eternity.

III. Consider whose salvation it is you make light of. It is your own. And do you not care what becomes of your own selves? Is it nothing to you whether you be saved or damned for ever?

Is the natural principle of self-love extinct in you? Have you no concern for your own preservation? Are you commenced your own enemies? If you slight Christ and love sin, you virtually love death. Prov. viii. 36. You may as well say, "I will live, and yet neither eat nor drink," as say, "I will go to heaven, and yet make light of Christ." And you may as well say this in words as by your practice.

IV. Consider your sin is aggravated by professing to believe that gospel which you make light of. For a professed infidel, that does not believe the scripture-revelation concerning Christ, and a future state of rewards and punishments, for such a one to be careless about these things, would not be so strange; but for you that make these things your creed, and a part of your religion, for you that call yourselves christians, and have been baptized into this faith; for you, I say, to make light of them, how astonishing! how utterly inexcusable! What! believe that you shall live for ever in the most perfect happiness or exquisite misery, and yet take no more pains to obtain the one, and escape the other? What! believe that the great and dreadful God will shortly be your judge, and yet make no more preparation for it? Either say plainly, " I am no christian, I do not believe these things;" or else let your hearts be affected with your belief, and let it influence and govern your lives.

V. Consider what those things are which engross your affections, and which tempt you to neglect Christ and your salvation. Have you found out a better friend, or a more substantial, and lasting happiness than his salvation? O! what trifles and vanities, what dreams and shadows are men pursuing, while they neglect the important realities of the eternal world! If crowns and kingdoms, if all the riches, glories, and pleasures of the world were insured to you as a reward for making light of Christ, you would even then make the most foolish bargain possible; for what are these in the scale to eternal joy or eternal tempest? and *what shall it profit a man if he gain even the whole world, and lose his own soul?* Matt. xvi. 26. But you cannot hope for the ten thousandth part; and will you cast away your souls for this? You that think it such a great thing to live in riches, pleasures, and honours, consider, is it such a mighty happiness to die rich? to die after a life of pleasure and honour? Will it be such a great happiness to give an account for the life of a rich sensualist, rather than of a poor mortified creature? Will Dives then be so much happier than Lazarus? Alas! what does the richest, the highest, the most voluptuous sinner, what does he do, but lay up treasures of wrath against the day of wrath? O how will the unhappy creatures torture themselves for ever with the most cutting reflections for selling their Saviour and their souls for such trifles! Let your sins and earthly enjoyments save you then, if they can; let them then do that for you which Christ would have done for you if you had chosen him. Then go and cry to the gods you have chosen: let them deliver you in the day of your tribulation.

VI. Your making light of Christ and salvation is a certain evidence that you have no interest in them.—Christ will not throw himself and his blessings away upon those that do not value them. "Those that honour him he will honour; but they that despise him shall be lightly esteemed." 1 Sam. ii. 30. There is a day coming, when you will feel you cannot do without him; when you will feel yourselves perishing for want of a Saviour; and then you may go and look for a Saviour where you will; then you may shift for yourselves as you can; he will have nothing to do with you; the Saviour of Sinners will cast you off for ever. I tell you, Sirs, whatever estimate you form of all these things, God thinks very highly of the blood of his Son, and the blessings of his purchase; and if ever you obtain them, he will have you think highly of them too. If you continue to make light of them, all the world cannot save you. And can you find fault with God for denying you that which was so little in your account.

VII. And lastly, the time is hastening when you will not think so slightly of Christ and salvation. O, Sirs, when God shall commission death to tear your guilty souls out of your bodies, when devils shall drag you away to the place of torment, when you find yourselves condemned to everlasting fire by that Saviour whom you now neglect, what would you then give for a Saviour? When divine justice brings in its heavy charges against you, and you have nothing to answer, how will you then cry, "O if I had chosen Jesus for my Saviour, he would have answered all!" When you see that the world has deserted you, that your companions in sin have deceived themselves and you, and all your merry days are over for ever, would you not then give ten thousand worlds for Christ? And will you not now think him worthy of your esteem and earnest pursuit? Why will ye judge of things now quite the reverse of what you will do then, when you will be more capable of judging rightly!

And now dear immortal souls! I have discovered the nature and danger of this common but unsuspected and unlamented sin, making light of Christ. I have delivered my message, and now I must leave it with you, imploring the blessing of God upon it. I cannot follow you home to your houses to see what effect it has upon you, or to make application of it to each of you in particular; but, O may your consciences undertake this office! Whenever you spend another prayerless, thoughtless day, whenever you give yourselves up to sinful pleasures, or an over-eager pursuit of the world, may your conscience become your preacher, and sting you with this expostulation: " Alas! is this the effect of all I have heard? Do I still make light of Christ and the concerns of religion? O what will be the end of such a conduct!"

I cannot but fear after all, that some of you, as usual, will continue careless and impenitent. Well, when you are suffering the punishment of this sin in hell, remember that you were warned, and acquit me from being accessary to your ruin. And when we all appear before the supreme Judge, and I am called to give an account of my ministry; when I am asked, " Did you warn these creatures of their danger? Did you lay before them their guilt in making light of these things?" you will allow me to answer, " Yes, Lord, I warned them in the best manner I could but they would not believe me; they would not regard what I said, though enforced by the authority of thy awful name, and confirmed by thine own word." O Sirs! must I give in this accusation against any of you? No, rather have mercy upon yourselves, and have mercy upon me, that I may give an account of you with joy, and not with grief.

SERMON VIII.

The Compassion of Christ to weak Believers.

MATTH. xii. 20. *A bruised reed shall he not break, and smoking flax shall he not quench.*

THE Lord Jesus possesses all those virtues in the highest perfection, which render him infinitely amiable, and qualify him for the administration of a just and gracious government over the world. The virtues of mortals, when carried to a high degree, very often run into those vices which have a kind of affinity to them. " Right, too rigid, hardens into wrong." Strict justice steels itself into excessive severity; and the man is lost in the judge. Goodness and mercy sometimes degenerate into softness and an irrational compassion inconsistent with government. But in Jesus Christ these seemingly opposite virtues center and harmonize in the highest perfection, without running into extremes. Hence he is at once characterized as a Lamb, and as the Lion of the tribe of Judah: a Lamb for gentleness towards humble penitents, and a Lion to tear his enemies in pieces. Christ is said to *judge and make war*, Rev. xix. 11. and yet he is called *The Prince of Peace*. Isa. ix. 6. He will at length shew himself terrible to the workers of iniquity; and the terrors of the Lord are a very proper topic whence to persuade men; but now he is patient towards all men, and he is all love and tenderness towards the meanest penitent. The meekness and gentleness of Christ is to be the pleasing entertainment of this day; and I enter upon it with a particular view to those mourning desponding souls among us, whose weakness renders them in great need of strong consolation. To such in particular I address the words of my text, *A bruised reed shall he not break, and smoking flax shall he not quench.*

This is a part of the Redeemer's character, as delineated near three thousand years ago by the evangelical prophet Isaiah, Isa. xlii. 1—4. and it is expressly applied to him by St. Matthew: *Behold*, says the Father, *my servant whom I have chosen* for the important undertaking of saving the guilty sons of men; "*my beloved, in whom my soul is well pleased;*" my very soul is well pleased with his faithful discharge of the important office he has undertaken. *I will put my spirit upon him;* that is, I will completely furnish him by the gifts of my spirit for his high character; and *he shall shew judgment to the Gentiles:* to the poor benighted Gentiles he shall shew the light of salvation; by revealing the gospel to them; which, in the style of the Old Testament, may be called his judgments. Or he will shew and execute the judgment of this world by casting out its infernal prince, who had so long exercised an extensive cruel tyranny over it. *He shall not strive nor cry, neither shall any man hear his voice in the streets;* that is, though he enters the world as a mighty prince and conqueror to establish a kingdom of righteousness, and overthrow the kingdom of darkness, yet he will not introduce it with the noisy terrors and thunders of war, but shall shew himself mild and gentle as the prince of peace. Or the connection may lead us to understand these words in a different sense, namely, He shall do nothing with clamorous ostentation, nor proclaim his wonderful works, when it shall answer no valuable end. Accordingly the verse of our text stands thus connected: *Great multitudes followed him; and he healed them all, and charged them that they should not make him known. That it might be fulfilled which was spoken by Isaiah the prophet, saying,—He shall not cry, neither shall any man hear his voice in the streets;* that is, he shall not publish his miracles with noisy triumph in the streets, and other public places. And when it is said, *He shall not strive,* it may refer to his inoffensive passive behaviour towards his enemies that were plotting his death. For thus we may connect this quotation from Isaiah with the preceding history in the chapter of our text: *Then the Pharisees went out, and held a council against him, how they might destroy him. But when Jesus knew it*, instead of praying to his Father for a guard of angels, or employing his own miraculous power to destroy them, *he withdrew himself from thence;—that it might be fulfilled which was spoken by the prophet Isaiah, saying,— He shall not strive.*

The general meaning of my text seems to be contained in this observation: "That the Lord Jesus has the tenderest and most compassionate regard to the feeblest penitent, however oppressed and desponding; and that he will approve and cherish the least spark of true love towards himself.

The bruised reed seems naturally to represent a soul at once feeble in itself, and crushed with a burden; a soul both weak and oppressed. The reed is a slender frail vegetable in itself, and therefore a very proper image to represent a soul that is feeble and weak. A bruised reed is still more frail, hangs its head, and is unable to stand without some prop. And what can be a more lively emblem of a poor soul, not only weak in itself, but bowed down and broken under a load of sin and sorrow, that droops and sinks, and is unable to stand without divine support? Strength may bear up under a burden, or struggle with it, till it has thrown it off; but oppressed weakness, frailty under a burden, what can be more pitiable? and yet this is the case of many a poor penitent. He is weak in himself, and in the mean time crushed under an heavy weight of guilt and distress.

And what would become of such a frail oppressed creature, if, instead of raising him up and supporting him, Jesus should tread and crush him under the foot of his indignation? But though a reed, especially a bruised reed, is an insignificant thing, of little or no use, yet, " a bruised reed he will not break," but he raises it up with a gentle hand, and enables it to stand, though weak in itself, and easily crushed in ruin.

Perhaps the imagery, when drawn at length, may be this: " The Lord Jesus is an almighty conqueror, marches in state through our world; and here and there a bruised reed lies in his way. But instead of disregarding it, or trampling it under foot, he takes care not to break it: he raises up the drooping straw, trifling as it is, and supports it with his gentle hand," Thus, poor broken-hearted penitents, thus he takes care of you, and supports you, worthless and trifling as you are. Though you seem to lie in the way of his justice, and it might tread you with its heavy foot, yet he not only does not crush you, but takes you up, and inspires you with strength to bear your burden, and flourish again.

Or perhaps the imagery may be derived from the practice of the ancient shepherds, who were wont to amuse themselves with the music of a pipe of reed or straw; and when it was bruised they broke it, or threw it away as ufelefs. But the bruifed reed fhall not be broken by this divine Shepherd of fouls. The mufic of broken fighs and groans is indeed all that the broken reed can afford him: the notes are but low, melancholy, and jarring: and yet he will not break the inftrument, but he will repair and tune it, till it is fit to join in the concert of angels on high; and even now its humble ftrains are pleafing to his ears. Surely every broken heart among us muft revive, while contemplating this tender and moving imagery!

The other emblem is equally fignificant and affecting. *The fmoking flax shall he not quench.* It feems to be an allufion to the wick of a candle or lamp, the flame of which is put out, but it ftill fmokes, and retains a little fire, which may again be blown into a flame, or rekindled by the application of more fire. Many fuch dying fnuffs or fmoking wicks are to be found in the candle-fticks of the churches, and in the lamps of the fanctuary. The flame of divine love is juft expiring, it is funk into the focket of a corrupt heart, and produces no clear fteady blaze, but only a fmoke that is difagreeable, although it fhews that a fpark of the facred fire ftill remains; or it produces a faint quivering flame that dies away, then catches and revives, and feems unwilling to be quenched entirely. The devil and the world raife many ftorms of temptation to blow it out; and a corrupt heart, like a fountain, pours out water to quench it. But even this fmoking flax, this dying fnuff, Jefus will not quench, but he blows it up into a flame, and pours in the oil of his grace to recruit and nourifh it. He walks among the golden candlefticks, and trims the lamps of his fanctuary. Where he finds empty veffels without oil or a fpark of heavenly fire, like thofe of the foolifh virgins, he breaks the veffels, or throws them out of his houfe. But where he finds the leaft fpark of true grace, where he difcovers but the glimpfe of fincere love to him, where he fees the principle of true piety, which, though juft expiring, yet renders the heart fufceptive of divine love, as a candle juft put out is eafily rekindled, there he will ftrengthen the things which remain, and are ready to die: he will blow up the dying fnuff to a lively flame, and caufe it to fhine brighter and brighter to the perfect day. Where there is the leaft principle of true holinefs he will cherifh it. He will furnifh the expiring lamp with frefh fupplies of the oil of grace, and of heavenly fire; and all the ftorms that beat upon it fhall not be able to put it out, becaufe fheltered by his hand.

I hope my dear brethren, fome of you begin already to feel the pleafing energy of this text. Are you not ready to fay, " Bleffed Jefus! is this thy true character? Then thou art juft fuch a Saviour as I want, and I moft willingly give up myfelf to thee." You are fenfible you are at beft but a bruifed reed, a feeble, fhattered, ufelefs thing; an untuneable, broken pipe of ftraw, that can make no proper mufic for the entertainment of your divine fhepherd. Your heart is at beft but fmoking flax; where the love of God often appears like a dying fnuff; or an expiring flame that quivers and catches, and hovers over the lamp, juft ready to go out. Such fome of you probably feel yourfelves to be. Well, and what think ye of Chrift? "He will not break the bruifed reed, nor quench the fmoking flax;" and therefore, may not even your guilty eyes look to this gentle Saviour with encouraging hope? May you not fay to him, with the fweet finger of Ifrael, in his laft moments, *He is all my Salvation, and all my defire.* 2. Sam. xxiii. 5.

In profecuting this fubject I intend to illuftrate the character of a weak believer, as reprefented in my text, and then to illuftrate the care and compaffion of Jefus Chrift even for fuch a poor weakling.

I. I am to illuftrate the character of a weak believer as reprefented in my text by " a bruifed reed, and fmoking flax."

The metaphor of a bruifed reed, as I obferved, feems moft naturally to convey the idea of a ftate of weaknefs and oppreffion. And therefore in illuftrating it I am naturally led to defcribe the various weakneffes which a believer fometimes painfully feels, and to point out the heavy burdens which he fometimes groans under; I fay, fometimes, for at other times even the weak believer finds himfelf ftrong, *ftrong in the Lord, and in the power of his might, and ftrengthened with might by the Spirit in the inner man.* The joy of the Lord is his ftrength; and he " can do all things through Chrift ftrengthening him." Even the oppreffed believer at times feels himfelf delivered from his burden, and he can lift up his drooping head, and walk upright. But, alas! the burden returns, and crufhes him again. And under fome burden or other many honeft-hearted believers groan out the moft part of their lives.

Let us now fee what are thofe weakneffes which a believer feels and laments. He finds himfelf weak in knowledge; a fimple child in the knowledge of God and divine things. He is weak in love; the facred flame does not rife with a perpetual fervor, and diffufe itfelf through all his devotions, but at times it languifhes and dies away into a fmoking fnuff. He is weak in faith; he cannot keep a ftrong hold of the Almighty, cannot fufpend his all upon his promifes with cheerful confidence, nor build a firm immoveable fabric of hope upon the rock Jefus Chrift. He is weak in hope; his hope is dafhed with rifing billows of fears and jealoufies, and fometimes juft overfet. He is weak in joy; he cannot extract the fweets of chriftianity, nor tafte the comforts of his religion. He is weak in zeal for God and the interests of his kingdom; he would wish himself always a flaming seraph, always glowing with zeal, always unwearied in serving his God, and promoting the designs of redeeming love in the world; but, alas! at times his zeal with his love, languishes and dies away into a smoking snuff. He is weak in repentance; troubled with that plague of plagues, an hard heart. He is weak in the conflict with indwelling sin, that is perpetually making insurrections within him. He is weak in resisting temptations; which crowd upon him from without, and are often likely to overwhelm him. He is weak in courage to encounter the king of terrors, and venture through the valley of the shadow of death. He is weak in prayer, in importunity, in filial boldness in approaching the mercy-seat. He is weak in abilities to endeavour the conversion of sinners, and save souls from death. In short, he is weak in every thing in which he should be strong. He has indeed, like the church of Philadelphia, a little strength; Rev. iii. 8. and at times he feels it; but O! it seems to him much too little for the work he has to do. These weaknesses or defects the believer feels, painfully and tenderly feels, and bitterly laments. A sense of them keeps him upon his guard against temptations: he is not venturesome in rushing into the combat. He would not parley with temptation, but would keep out of its way; nor would he run the risk of a defeat by an ostentatious experiment of his strength. This sense of weakness also keeps him dependent upon divine strength. He clings to that support given to St. Paul in an hour of hard conflict, *My grace is sufficient for thee; for my strength is made perfect in weakness;* and when a sense of his weakness has this happy effect upon him, then with St. Paul he has reason to say, *When I am weak, I am then strong.* 2 Cor. xii. 9. 10.

I say the believer feels and laments these weaknesses; and this is the grand distinction in this case between him and the rest of the world. They are weak too; much weaker than he, nay, they have, properly, no spiritual strength at all; but, alas! they do not feel their weakness, but the poor vain creatures boast of their strength, and think they can do great things when they are disposed for them. Or if their repeated falls and defeats by temptation extort them to a confession of their weakness, they plead it rather as an excuse, than lament it as at once a crime and a calamity. But the poor believer tries no such artifice to extenuate his guilt. He is sensible that even his weakness itself has guilt in it, and therefore he laments it with ingenuous sorrows among his other sins.

Now, have I not delineated the very character of some of you? such weaklings, such frail reeds you feel yourselves to be. Well, hear this kind assurance, "Jesus will not break such a feeble reed, but he will support and strengthen it."

But you perhaps not only feel you are weak, but you are oppreſſed with ſome heavy burden or other. You are not only a reed for weakneſs, but you are a bruiſed reed, trodden under foot, cruſhed under a load. Even this is no unuſual or diſcouraging caſe; for,

The weak believer often feels himſelf cruſhed under ſome heavy burden. The frail reed is often bruiſed; bruiſed under a due ſenſe of guilt. Guilt lies heavy at times upon his conſcience, and he cannot throw it off. Bruiſed with a ſenſe of remaining ſin, which he finds ſtill ſtrong within him, and which at times prevails, and treads him under foot. Bruiſed under a burden of wants, the want of tenderneſs of heart, of ardent love to God and mankind, the want of heavenly-mindedneſs and victory over the world; the want of conduct and reſolution to direct his behaviour in a paſſage ſo intricate and difficult, and the want of nearer intercourſe with the Father and his ſpirit: in ſhort, a thouſand preſſing wants cruſh and bruiſe him, He alſo feels his ſhare of the calamities of life in common with other men. But theſe burdens I ſhall take no farther notice of, becauſe they are not peculiar to him as a believer, nor do they lie heavieſt upon his heart. He could eaſily bear up under all the calamities of life if his ſpiritual wants were ſupplied, and the burden of guilt and ſin were removed. Under theſe laſt he groans and ſinks. Indeed theſe burdens lie with all their full weight upon the world around him; but they are dead in treſpaſſes and ſins, and feel them not: they do not groan under them, nor labour for deliverance from them. They lie contented under them, with more ſtupidity than beaſts of burden, till they ſink under the intolerable load into the depth of miſery. But the poor believer is not ſo ſtupid, and his tender heart feels the burden and groans under it. *We that are in this tabernacle*, ſays St. Paul, *do groan, being burdened.* 2. Cor, v. 4, The believer underſtands feelingly that pathetic exclamation, *O wretched man that I am! who ſhall deliver me from the body of this death?* Rom. vii. 24. He cannot be eaſy till his conſcience is appeaſed by a well-atteſted pardon through the blood of Chriſt; and the ſins he feels working within him are a real burden and uneaſineſs to him, though they ſhould never break out into action, and publicly diſhonour his holy profeſſion.

And is not this the very character of ſome poor oppreſſed creatures among you? I hope it is. You may look upon your caſe to be very diſcouraging, but Jeſus looks upon it in a more favourable light; he looks upon you as proper objects of his compaſſionate care. Bruiſed as you are, he will bind you up, and ſupport you.

II. But I proceed to take a view of the character of a weak chriſtian, as repreſented in the other metaphor in my text, namely, *ſmoking flax*, The idea moſt naturally conveyed by this metaphor is, that of grace true and sincere, but languishing and just expiring, like a candle just blown out, which still smokes and retains a feeble spark of fire. It signifies a susceptibility of a farther grace, or a readiness to catch that sacred fire, as a candle just put out is easily re-kindled. This metaphor therefore leads me to describe the reality of religion in a low degree, or to delineate the true christian in his most languishing hours. And in so doing I shall mention those dispositions and exercises which the weakest christian feels, even in these melancholy seasons; for even in these he widely differs still from the most polished hypocrite in his highest improvements. On this subject let me solicit your most serious attention; for, if you have the least spark of real religion within you, you are now likely to discover it, as I am not going to rise to the high attainments of christians of the first rank, but to stoop to the character of the meanest. Now the peculiar dispositions and exercises of heart which such in some measure feel, you may discover from the following short history of their case.

The weak christian in such languishing hours does indeed sometimes fall into such a state of carelessness and insensibility, that he has vey few and but superficial exercises of mind about divine things. But generally he feels an uneasiness, an emptiness, an anxiety within, under which he droops and pines away, and all the world cannot heal the disease. He has chosen the blessed God as his supreme happiness; and, when he cannot derive happiness from that source, all the sweets of created enjoyments become insipid to him, and cannot fill up the prodigious void which the absence of the Supreme Good leaves in his craving soul. Sometimes his anxiety is indistinct and confused, and he hardly knows what ails him; but at other times he feels it is for God, the living God, that his soul pants. The evaporations of this smoking flax naturally ascend towards heaven. He knows that he never can be happy till he can enjoy the communications of divine love. Let him turn which way he will, he can find no solid ease, no rest, till he comes to this center again.

Even at such times he cannot be thoroughly reconciled to his sins. He may be parleying with some of them in an unguarded hour, and seem to be negociating a peace; but the truce is soon ended, and they are at variance again. The enmity of a renewed heart soon rises against this old enemy. And there is this circumstance remarkable in the believer's hatred and opposition to sin, that they do not proceed principally, much less entirely, from a fear of punishment, but from a generous sense of its intrinsic baseness and ingratitude, and its contrariety to the holy nature of God. This is the ground of his hatred to sin, and sorrow for it; and this shews that there is at least a spark of true grace in his heart, and that he does not act altogether from the low, interested, and mercenary principles of nature.

At such times he is very jealous of the sincerity of his religion, afraid that all his past experiences were delusive, and afraid that, if he should die in his present state, he would be for ever miserable. A very anxious state is this! The stupid world can lie secure while this grand concern lies in the most dreadful suspence. But the tender-hearted believer is not capable of such fool-hardiness: he shudders at the thought of everlasting separation from that God and Saviour whom he loves. He loves him, and therefore the fear of separation from him, fills him with all the anxiety of bereaved love. This to him is the most painful ingredient of the punishment of hell. Hell would be a sevenfold hell to a lover of God, because it is a state of banishment from him whom he loves. He could for ever languish and pine away under the consuming distresses of widowed love, which those that love him not cannot feel. And has God kindled the sacred flame in his heart in order to render him capable of the more exquisite pain? Will he exclude from his presence the poor creature that clings to him, and languishes for him? No, the flax that does but smoke with his love was never intended to be fuel for hell; but he will blow it up into a flame, and nourish it till it mingles with the seraphic ardors in the region of perfect love.

The weak believer seems sometimes driven by the tempests of lust and temptation from off the rock of Jesus Christ. But he makes towards it on the stormy billows, and labours to lay hold upon it, and recover his station there; for he is sensible there is no other foundation of safety, but that without Christ he must perish for ever It is the habitual disposition of the believer's soul to depend upon Jesus Christ alone. He retains a kind of direction or tendency towards him, like the needle touched with the load-stone towards the pole; and, if his heart is turned from its course, it trembles and quivers till it gains its favourite point again, and fixes there. Sometimes indeed a consciousness of guilt renders him shy of his God and Saviour; and after such base ingratitude he is ashamed to go to him: but at length necessity as well as inclination constrains him, and he is obliged to cry out, *Lord, to whom shall I go? thou hast the words of eternal life.* John vi. 68. " In thee alone I find rest to my soul; and therefore to thee I must fly, though I am ashamed and confounded to appear in thy presence."

In short, the weakest christian upon earth sensibly feels that his comfort rises and falls, as he lives nearer to or farther from his God. The love of God has such an habitual predominancy even in his heart, that nothing in the world, nor even all the world together can fill up his place. No, when he is gone, heaven and earth cannot replenish the mighty void. Even the weakest christian upon earth longs to be delivered from sin, from all sin without exception; and a body of death hanging about him is the burden of his life. Even the poor jealous languishing christian has his hope, all the little hope that he has, built upon Jesus Christ. Even this smoking flax sends up some exhalations of love towards heaven. Even the poor creature that often fears he is altogether a slave to sin, honestly, though feebly, labours to be holy, to be holy as an angel, yea, to be holy as God is holy. He has an heart that feels the attractive charms of holiness, and he is so captivated by it, that sin can never recover its former place in his heart: no, the tyrant is for ever dethroned, and the believer would rather die than yield himself a tame slave to the usurped tyranny again.

Thus I have delineated to you in the plainest manner I could, the character of a weak christian. Some of you I am afraid cannot lay claim even to this low character. If so, you may be sure you are not true christians, even of the lowest rank. You may be sure you have not the least spark of true religion in your hearts, but are utterly destitute of it.

But some of you, I hope, can say, "Well, after all my doubts and fears, if this be the character of a true, though weak christian, then I may humbly hope that I am one. I am indeed confirmed in it that I am less than the least of all other saints upon the face of the earth, but yet I see that I am a saint; for thus has my heart been exercised, even in my dark and languishing hours. This secret uneasiness and pining anxiety, this thirst for God, for the living God, this tendency of soul towards Jesus Christ, this implacable enmity to sin, this panting and struggling after holiness; these things have I often felt." And have you indeed? then away with your doubts and jealousies! away with your fears and despondencies! There is at least an immortal spark kindled in your hearts, which the united power of men and devils, of sin and temptation, shall never be able to quench. No, it shall yet rise into a flame, and burn with seraphic ardors for ever.

For your farther encouragement I proceed,

II. To illustrate the care and compassion of Jesus Christ for such poor weaklings as you.

This may appear a needless task to some; for who is there that does not believe it? But to such would I say, it is no easy thing to establish a trembling soul in the full belief of this truth. It is easy for one that does not see his danger, and does not feel his extreme need of salvation, and the difficulty of the work, to believe that Christ is willing and able to save him. But O! to a poor soul, deeply sensible of its condition, this is no easy matter. Besides, the heart may need to be more deeply affected with this truth, though the understanding should need no farther arguments of the speculative kind for its conviction; and to impress this truth is my present design.

For this purpofe I need but read and paraphrafe to you a few of the many kind declarations and affurances which Jefus has given us in his word, and relate the happy experiences of fome of his faints there recorded, who found him true and faithful to his word.

The Lord Jefus feems to have a peculiar tendernefs for the poor, the mourners, the broken-hearted; and thefe are peculiarly the objects of his mediatorial office. *The Lord hath anointed me,* fays he, *to preach good tidings to the meek; he hath fent me* all the way from my native heaven down to earth, upon this compaffionate errand, *to bind up the broken-hearted, to appoint unto them that mourn in Zion, to give unto them beauty for afhes, the oil of joy for mourning, the garment of praife for the fpirit of heavinefs.* Ifa. lxi. 1—3. *Thus faith the Lord,* in ftrains of majefty that become him, *the heaven is my throne, and the earth is my footftool: where is the houfe that ye build unto me? and where is the place of my reft? For all thefe things hath my hand made, faith the Lord.* Had he fpoken uniformly in this majeftic language to us guilty worms, the declaration might have overwhelmed us with awe, but could not have infpired us with hope. But he advances himfelf thus high, on purpofe to let us fee how low he can ftoop. Hear the encouraging fequel of this his majeftic fpeech: *To this man will I look, even to him that is poor, and of a contrite fpirit, and trembleth at my word.* Let heaven and earth wonder that he will look down through all the fhining ranks of angels, and look by princes and nobles, to fix his eye upon this man, this poor man, this contrite, broken-hearted, trembling creature. *Ifa.* lxvi. 1, 2. He loves to dwell upon this fubject, and therefore you hear it again in the fame prophecy: " Thus faith the high and lofty One that inhabiteth eternity, whofe name is holy,—" what does he fay?—*I dwell in the high and holy place.* Ifa. lvii. 15. This is faid in character. This is a dwelling in fome meafure worthy the inhabitant. But O! will he ftoop to dwell in a lower manfion, or pitch his tent among mortals? yes, he dwells not only in his *high and holy place,* but alfo *with him that is of a contrite and humble fpirit, to revive the fpirit of the humble, and to revive the heart of the contrite ones.* He charges Peter to *feed his lambs* as well as his fheep; that is, to take the tendereft care even of the weakeft in his flock. *John* xxi. 15. And he feverely rebukes the fhepherds of Ifrael, *Becaufe,* fays he, *ye have not ftrengthened the difeafed, neither have ye healed that which was fick, neither have ye bound up that which was broken.* Ezek. xxxiv. 4. But what an amiable reverfe is the character of the great Shepherd and Bifhop of fouls! *Behold,* fays Ifaiah, *the Lord will come with a ftrong hand, and his arm shall rule for him: behold his reward is with him, and his work before him.* How juftly may we tremble at this proclamation of the approaching God! for who can ftand when he appeareth? But how agreeably are our fears difappointed in what follows! If he comes to take vengeance on his enemies, he also comes to shew mercy to the meanest of his people. *He shall feed his flock like a shepherd? he shall gather the lambs with his arms, and carry them in his bosom, and shall gently lead those that are with young;* Isa. xl. 10, 11. that is, he shall exercise the tenderest and most compassionate care towards the meanest and weakest of his flock. *He looked down,* says the Psalmist, *from the height of his sanctuary; from heaven did the Lord behold the earth;* not to view the grandeur and pride of courts and kings, nor the heroic exploits of conquerors, but *to hear the groaning of the prisoner, to loose those that are appointed to die. He will regard the prayer of the destitute, and not despise their prayer. This shall be written for the generation to come.* Psalm. cii. 17—20. It was written for your encouragement, my brethren. Above three thousand years ago this encouraging passage was entered into the sacred records for the support of poor desponding souls in Virginia, in the ends of the earth. O what an early provident care does God shew for his people! There are none of the seven churches of Asia so highly commended by Christ as that of Philadelphia; and yet in commending her, all he can say is, "Thou hast a little strength." *I know thy works; behold I have set before thee an open door, and no man can shut it, for thou hast a little strength.* Rev. iii. 8. O how acceptable is a little strength to Jesus Christ, and how ready is he to improve it! *He giveth power to the faint,* says Isaiah, *and to them that have no might he increaseth strength.* Isa. xl. 29. Hear farther what words of grace and truth flowed from the lips of Jesus: *Come unto me all ye that labour and are heavy laden, and I will give you rest; for I am meek and lowly in heart.* Matt. xi. 28, 29. *Him that cometh unto me, I will in no wise cast out.* John vi. 57. *If any man thirst, let him come unto me and drink.* John vii. 37. *Let him that is athirst come; and whosoever will, let him come and take of the water of life freely.* Rev. xxii. 17. O what strong consolation is here! what exceeding great and precious promises are these! I might easily add to the catalogue, but these may suffice.

Let us now see how his people in every age have ever found these promises made good. Here David may be consulted, *instar omnium*, and he will tell you, pointing to himself, *This poor man cried, and the Lord heard and delivered him out of all his troubles.* Psalm xxxiv. 6. St. Paul, in the midst of affliction, calls God the Father of mercies, and God of all comfort, who comforteth us in all our tribulation. 2 Cor. i. 3, 4. God, says he, *that comforteth those that are cast down, comforteth us.* 2 Cor. vii. 6. What a sweetly emphatical declaration is this! "God the comforter of the humble, comforted us*." He is not only the Lord of hosts, the

---

* This is the most literal translation of—ὁ παρακαλῶν τοὺς ταπεινοὺς παρεκάλεσεν ἡμᾶς, ὁ Θεός.

King of kings, the Creator of the world, but among his more august characters he assumes this title, "The Comforter of the humble." Such Saint Paul found him in an hour of temptation, when he had this supporting answer to his repeated prayer for deliverance, *My grace is sufficient for thee; for my strength is made perfect in weakness.* 2 Cor. xii. 9. Since this was the case, since his weakness was more than supplied by the strength of Christ, and was a foil to set it off, St. Paul seems quite regardless what infirmities he laboured under. Nay, *most gladly,* says he, *will I rather glory in my infirmities, that the power of Christ may rest upon me. Therefore I take pleasure in infirmities—for when I am weak, then am I strong.* He could take no pleasure in feeling himself weak; but the mortification was made up by the pleasure he found in leaning upon this almighty support. His wounds were painful to him; but, O! the pleasure he found in feeling this divine physician dressing his wounds, in some measure swallowed up the pain. It was probably experience, as well as inspiration, that dictated to the apostle that amiable character of Christ, that he is *a merciful and faithful high-priest, who being himself tempted, knows how to succour them that are tempted.* Heb. ii. 17, 18. And *we have not an high-priest which cannot be touched with the feeling of our infirmities, but was in all points tempted like as we are, yet without sin.* Heb. iv. 15.

But why need I multiply arguments? Go to his cross, and there learn his love and compassion, from his groans and wounds, and blood, and death. Would he hang there in such agony for sinners if he were not willing to save them, and cherish every good principle in them? There you may have much the same evidence of his compassion as Thomas had of his resurrection; you may look into his hands, and see the print of the nails; and into his side, and see the scar of the spear; which loudly proclaim his readiness to pity and help you.

And now, poor trembling doubting souls, what hinders but you should rise up your drooping head, and take courage? May you not venture your souls into such compassionate and faithful hands? Why should the bruised reed shrink from him, when he comes not to tread it down, but raise it up?

As I am really solicitous that impenitent hearts among us should be pierced with the medicinal anguish and sorrow of conviction and repentance, and the most friendly heart cannot form a kinder wish for them, so I am truly solicitous that every honest soul, in which there is the least spark of true piety, should enjoy the pleasure of it. It is indeed to be lamented that they who have a title to so much happiness should enjoy so little of it; it is very incongruous that they should go bowing the head in their way towards heaven, as if they were hastening to the place of execution, and that they should serve so good a Master with such heavy hearts. O lift up the hands that hang down, and strengthen the feeble knees. *Comfort ye, comfort ye my people, saith your God. Be strong in the Lord, and in the power of his might.* Trust in your all-sufficient Redeemer, trust in him though he should slay you.

And do not indulge causeless doubts and fears concerning your sincerity. When they arise in your minds examine them, and search whether there be any sufficient reason for them; and if you discover there is not, then reject them and set them at defiance, and entertain your hopes in spite of them, and say with the Psalmist, *Why art thou cast down, O my soul, and why art thou disquieted within me? Hope thou in God, for I shall yet praise him, the health of my countenance, and my God.* Psalm xliii. 11.

SERMON IX.

The Connexion between Present Holiness and Future Felicity.

HEB. xii. 14. *Follow—holiness; without which no man shall see the Lord.*

AS the human soul was originally designed for the enjoyment of no less a portion than the ever-blessed God, it was formed with a strong innate tendency towards happiness. It has not only an eager fondness for existence, but for some good to render its existence happy. And the privation of being itself is not more terrible than the privation of all its blessings. It is true, in the present degeneracy of human nature, this vehement desire is miserably perverted and misplaced: man seeks his supreme happiness in sinful, or at best in created enjoyments, forgetful of the uncreated fountain of bliss; but yet still he seeks happiness; still this innate *impetus* is predominant, and though he mistakes the means, yet he still retains a general aim at the end. Hence he ransacks this lower world in quest of felicity; climbs in search of it the slippery ascent of honour; hunts for it in the treasures of gold and silver; or plunges for it in the foul streams of sensual pleasures. But since all the sordid satisfaction resulting from these things are not adequate to the unbounded cravings of the mind, and since the satisfaction is transitory and perishing, or we may be wretched from it by the inexorable hand of death, the mind breaks through the limits of the present enjoyments, and even of the lower creation, and ranges through the unknown scenes of futurity in quest of some untried good. Hope makes excursions into the dark duration between the present *now* and the grave, and forms to itself pleasing images of approaching blessings, which often vanish in the embrace, like delusive phantoms. Nay, it launches into the vast unknown world that lies beyond the grave, and roves through the regions of immensity after some complete felicity to supply the defects of sublunary enjoyments. Hence, though men, till their spirits are refined by regenerating grace, have no relish for celestial joys, but pant for the poor pleasures of time and sense, yet, as they cannot avoid the unwelcome consciousness that death will ere long rend them from these sordid and momentary enjoyments, are constrained to indulge the hope of bliss in a future state: and they promise themselves happiness in another world when they can no longer enjoy any in this. And as reason and revelation unitedly allure them that this felicity cannot then consist in sensual indulgences, they generally expect it will be of a more refined and spiritual nature, and flow more immediately from the great Father of spirits.

He must indeed be miserable that abandons all hope of this blessedness. The christian religion affords him no other prospect but that of eternal, intolerable misery in the regions of darkness and despair; and if he flies to infidelity as a refuge, it can afford him no comfort but the shocking prospect of annihilation.

Now, if men were pressed into heaven by an unavoidable fatality, if happiness was promiscuously promised to them all without distinction of characters, then they might indulge a blind unexamined hope, and never perplex themselves with anxious enquiries about it. And he might justly be deemed a malignant disturber of the repose of mankind that would attempt to shock their hope, and frighten them with causeless scruples.

But if the light of nature intimates, and the voice of scripture proclaims aloud, that this eternal felicity is reserved only for persons of particular characters, and that multitudes, multitudes who entertained pleasing hopes of it, are confounded with an eternal disappointment, and shall suffer an endless duration in the most terrible miseries, we ought each of us to take the alarm, and examine the grounds of our hope, that, if they appear sufficient, we may allow ourselves a rational satisfaction in them; and, if they are found delusive, we may abandon them and seek for a hope which will bear the test now while it may be obtained. And however disagreeable the task be to give our fellow-creatures even profitable uneasiness, yet he must appear to the impartial a friend to the best interests of mankind, who points out the evidences and foundation of a rational and scriptural hope, and exposes the various mistakes to which we are subject in so important a case.

And if, when we look around us, we find perfons full of the hopes of heaven, who can give no fcriptural evidences of them to themfelves or others; if we find many indulging this pleafing delufion, whofe practices are mentioned by God himfelf as the certain marks of perifhing finners; and if perfons are fo tenacious of thefe hopes, that they will retain them to their everlafting ruin, unlefs the moft convictive methods are taken to undeceive them; then it is high time for thofe to whom the care of fouls (a weightier charge than that of kingdoms) is intrufted, to ufe the greateft plainnefs for this purpofe.

This is my chief defign at prefent, and to this my text naturally leads me. It contains thefe doctrines:

Firft, That without holinefs here it is impoffible for us to enjoy heavenly happinefs in the future world. To fee the Lord, is here put for enjoying him; fee Rom. viii. 24. and the metaphor fignifies the happinefs of the future ftate in general; and more particularly intimates that the knowledge of God will be a fpecial ingredient therein. See a parallel expreffion in Matt. v. 8.

Secondly, That this confideration fhould induce us to ufe the moft earneft endeavours to obtain the heavenly happinefs. Purfue holinefs, becaufe *without it no man can fee the Lord.*

Hence I am naturally led,

I. To explain the nature of that *holinefs, without which no man fhall fee the Lord.*

II. To fhew what endeavours fhould be ufed to obtain it. And,

III. To urge you to ufe them by the confideration of the abfolute neceffity of holinefs.

I. I am to explain the nature of holinefs. And I fhall give you a brief definition of it, and then mention fome of thofe difpofitions and practices which naturally flow from it.

The moft intelligible defcription of holinefs, as it is inherent in us, may be this, " It is a conformity in heart and practice to the revealed will of God." As the Supreme Being is the ftandard of all perfection, his holinefs in particular is the ftandard of ours. Then we are holy when his image is ftamped upon our hearts and reflected in our lives; fo the apoftle defines it, *And that ye put on the new man, which after God is created in righteoufnefs and true holinefs.* Eph. iv. 24. *Whom he did predeftinate to be conformed to the image of his Son.* Rom. viii. 29. Hence holinefs may be defined, " A conformity to God in his moral perfections." But as we cannot have a diftinct knowledge of thefe perfections but as they are manifefted by the revealed will of God, I choofe to define holinefs, as above, " A conformity to his revealed will." Now his revealed will comprizes both the law and the gofpel: the law informs us of the duty which we as creatures owe to God as a being of supreme excellency, as our Creator and Benefactor, and to men as our fellow-creatures; and the gospel informs us of the duty which as sinners we owe to God as reconcileable through a Mediator. Our obedience to the former implies the whole of morality, and to the latter the whole of evangelical graces, as faith in a Mediator, repentance, &c.

From this definition of holiness it appears, on the one hand, that it is absolutely necessary to see the Lord; for unless our dispositions are conformed to him, we cannot be happy in the enjoyment of him: and, on the other hand, that they who are made thus holy, are prepared for the vision and fruition of his face, as they can relish the divinest pleasure.

But as a concise definition of holiness may give an auditory but very imperfect ideas of it, I shall expatiate upon the dispositions and practices in which it consists, or which naturally result from it; and they are such as follow:

1. A delight in God for his holiness. Self-love may prompt us to love him for his goodness to us; and so many unregenerate men may have a selfish love to God on this account. But to love God because he is infinitely holy, because he bears an infinite detestation to all sin, and will not indulge his creatures in the neglect of the least instance of holiness, but commands them to be holy as he is holy, this is a disposition connatural to a renewed soul only, and argues a conformity to his image. Every nature is most agreeable to itself, and a holy nature is most agreeable to an holy nature.

Here I would make a remark, which may God deeply impress on your hearts, and which for that purpose I shall subjoin to each particular, that holiness in fallen man is supernatural; I mean, we are not born with it, we give no discoveries of it, till we have experienced a great change. Thus we find it in the present case; we have no natural love to God because of his infinite purity and hatred to all sin; nay, we would love him more did he give us greater indulgences; and I am afraid the love of some persons is founded upon a mistake; they love him because they imagine he does not hate sin, nor them for it, so much as he really does; because they think he will bring them to heaven at last, let them live as they list; and because they do not expect he is so inexorably just in his dealings with the sinner. It is no wonder they love such a soft, easy, passive being as this imaginary deity; but did they see the lustre of that holiness of God which dazzles the celestial armies; did they but know the terrors of his justice, and his implacable indignation against sin, their innate enmity would shew its poison, and their hearts would rise against God in all those horrible blasphemies with which awakened sinners are so frequently shocked. Such love as this is so far from being acceptable, that it is the greatest affront to the Supreme Being, as, if a profligate loved you, on the mistaken supposition that you were such a libertine as himself, it would rather inflame your indignation than procure your respect.

But to a regenerate mind how strong, how transporting are the charms of holiness! Such a mind joins the anthem of seraphs with the divinest complacency, Rev. iv. 8. and anticipates the song of glorified saints, *Who would not fear thee, O Lord, and glorify thy name, for thou only art holy?* Rev. xv. 4. The perfections of God lose their lustre, or sink into objects of terror or contempt, if this glorious attribute be abstracted. Without holiness power becomes tyranny, omniscience craft, justice revenge and cruelty, and even the amiable attribute of goodness loses its charms, and degenerates into a blind promiscuous prodigality, or foolish undiscerning fondness: but when these perfections are clothed in the beauties of holiness, how Godlike, how majestic, how lovely and attractive do they appear! and with what complacence does a mind fashioned after the divine image acquiesce in them! It may appear amiable even to an unholy sinner that the exertions of almighty power should be regulated by the most consummate wisdom; that justice should not without distinction punish the guilty and the innocent; but an holy soul only can rejoice that divine goodness will not communicate happiness to the disgrace of holiness; and that, rather than it should overflow in a blind promiscuous manner, the whole human race should be miserable. A selfish sinner has nothing in view but his own happiness; and if this be obtained, he has no anxiety about the illustration of the divine purity; but it recommends happiness itself to a sanctified soul, that it cannot be communicated in a way inconsistent with the beauty of holiness.

2. Holiness consists in an hearty complacence in the law of God, because of its purity. The law is the transcript of the moral perfections of God; and if we love the original we shall love the copy. Accordingly it is natural to a renewed mind to love the divine law, because it is perfectly holy; because it makes no allowance for the least sin, and requires every duty that it becomes us to perform towards God. Psalm cxix. 140. and vix. 7—10. Romans vii. 12, compared with 22.

But is this our natural disposition? Is this the disposition of the generality? Do they not, on the contrary, secretly find fault with the law, because it is so strict? And their common objection against that holiness of life which it enjoins is, that they connot bear to be so precise. Hence they are always for abating the rigour of the law, for bringing it down to some imaginary standard of their own, to their present ability, to sins of practice without regard to the sinful dispositions of the heart; or to the prevailing dispositions of the heart without regard to the first workings of concupiscence, those embryos of iniquity; and if they love the law at all, as they profess to do, it is upon supposition that it is not so strict as it really is, but grants them greater indulgences. Rom. vii. 7.

Hence it appears that, if we are made holy at all, it must be by a supernatural change; and when that is effected, what a strange and happy alteration does the sinner perceive? with what pleasure does he resign himself a willing subject to that law to which he was once so averse? And when he fails (as, alas! he does in many things) how is he humbled! he does not lay the fault upon the law as requiring impossibilities, but lays the whole fault upon himself as a corrupt sinner.

3. Holiness consists in an hearty complacence in the gospel-method of salvation, because it tends to illustrate the moral perfections of the Deity, and to discover the beauties of holiness.

The gospel informs us of two grand pre-requisites to the salvation of the fallen sons of men, namely, The satisfaction of divine justice by the obedience and passion of Christ, that God might be reconciled to them consistently with his perfections; and the sanctification of sinners by the efficacy of the Holy Ghost, that they might be capable of enjoying God, and that he might maintain intimate communion with them without any stain to his holiness. These two grand articles contain the substance of the gospel; and our acquiescence in them is the substance of that avangelical obedience which it requires of us, and which is essential to holiness in a fallen creature.

Now, it is evident, that without either of these the moral perfections of the Deity, particularly his holiness, could not be illustrated, or even secured in the salvation of a sinner. Had he received an apostate race into favour, who had conspired in the most unnatural rebellion against him, without any satisfaction, his holiness would have been eclipsed; it would not have appeared that he had so invincible an abhorrence of sin, so zealous a regard for the vindication of his own holy law; or to his veracity, which had threatened condign punishment to offenders. But by the satisfaction of Christ, his holiness is illustrated in the most conspicuous manner; now it appears, that God would upon no terms save a sinner but that of adequate satisfaction, and that no other was sufficient but the suffering of his co-equal Son, otherwise he would not have appointed him to sustain the character of Mediator; and now it appears that his hatred of sin is such that he would not let it pass unpunished even in his own Son, when only imputed to him. In like manner, if sinners, while unholy, were admitted into communion with God in heaven, it would obscure the glory of his holiness, and it would not then appear that such was the purity of his nature that he could have no fellowship with sin. But now it is evident, that even the blood of Immanuel cannot purchase heaven to be enjoyed by a sinner while unholy, but that every one that arrives at heaven must first be sanctified. An unholy sinner can be no more saved, while such, by the gospel than by the law; but here lies the difference, that the gospel makes provision for his sanctification, which is gradually carried on here, and perfected at death, before his admission into the heavenly glory.

Now it is the genius of true holiness to acquiesce in both these articles. A sanctified soul places all its dependence on the righteousness of Christ for acceptance. It would be disagreeable to it to have the least concurrence in its own justification. It is not only willing, but delights to renounce all its own righteousness, and to glory in Christ alone. Phil. iii. 3. Free grace to such souls is a charming theme, and salvation is more acceptable, because conveyed in this way. It would render heaven itself disagreeable, and wither all its joys, were they brought thither in a way that degrades or does not illustrate the glory of God's holiness; but O how agreeable the thought, that he that glorieth must glory in the Lord, and that the pride of all flesh shall be abased!

So an holy person rejoices that the way of holiness is the appointed way to heaven. He is not forced to be holy merely by the servile consideration that he must be so or perish, and so unwillingly submits to the necessity which he cannot avoid, when in the mean time, were it put to his choice, he would choose to reserve some sins, and neglect some painful duties. So far from this, that he delights in the gospel-constitution, because it requires universal holiness, and heaven would be less agreeable, were he to carry even the least sin thither. He thinks it no hardship that he must deny himself in his sinful pleasures, and habituate himself to so much strictness in religion; no, but he blesses the Lord for obliging him to it, and where he fails he charges himself with it, and is self-abased upon the account.

This is solid rational religion, fit to be depended upon, in opposition to the antinomian licentiousness, the freaks of enthusiasm, and the irrational flights of passion and imagination on the one hand; and in opposition to formality, mere formality, and the self-sprung religion of nature on the other. And is it not evident we are destitute of this by nature? Men naturally are averse to this gospel-method of salvation; they will not submit to the righteousness of God, but fix their dependence, in part at least, upon their own merit. Their proud hearts cannot bear the thought that all their performances must go for just nothing in their justification. They are also averse to the way of holiness; hence they will either abandon the expectation of heaven, and, since they cannot obtain it in their sinful ways, desperately conclude to go on in sin come what will; or, with all the little fophiftry they are capable of, they will endeavour to widen the way to heaven, and perfuade themfelves they fhall attain it, notwithftanding their continuance in fome known iniquity, and though their hearts have never been thoroughly fanctified. Alas! how evident is this all around us! How many either give up their hopes of heaven rather than part with fin, or vainly hold them, while their difpofitions and practices prove them groundlefs? And muft not fuch degenerate creatures be renewed ere they can be holy, or fee the Lord?

4. Holinefs confifts in an habitual delight in all the duties of holinefs towards God and man, and an earneft defire for communion with God in them. This is the natural refult of all the foregoing particulars. If we love God for his holinefs, we fhall delight in that fervice in which our conformity to him confifts; if we love his law, we fhall delight in that obedience which it enjoins; and if we take complacence in the evangelical method of falvation, we fhall take delight in that holinefs, without which we cannot enjoy it. The fervice of God is the element, the pleafure of an holy foul; while others delight in the riches, the honours, or the pleafures of this world, the holy foul defires one thing of the Lord, that it may behold his beauty while enquiring in his temple. Pfal. xxvii. 4. Such a perfon delights in retired converfe with heaven, in meditation and prayer. Pfal. cxxxix. 17. and lxiii. 5, 6. and lxxiii. 28. He alfo takes pleafure in juftice, benevolence, and charity towards men, Pfal. cxii. 5, 9. and in the ftricteft temperance and fobriety. 1 Cor. ix. 27.

Moreover, the mere formality of performing religious duties does not fatisfy the true faint, unlefs he enjoys a divine freedom therein, receives communications of grace from heaven, and finds his graces quickened. Pfalm xlii. 1, 2.

This confideration alfo fhews us that holinefs in us muft be fupernatural; for do we naturally thus delight in the fervice of God? or do you all now thus delight in it? is it not rather a wearinefs to you, and do you not find more pleafures in other things? Surely you muft be changed, or you can have no relifh for the enjoyment of heavenly happinefs.

5. To conftitute us faints indeed there muft be univerfal holinefs in practice. This naturally follows from the laft, for as the body obeys the ftronger volitions of the will, fo when the heart is prevailingly difpofed to the fervice of God, the man will habitually practife it. This is generally mentioned in fcripture as the grand characteriftic of real religion, without which all our pretenfions are vain. 1 John iii. 3—10. and v. 3. John xv. 14. True chriftians are far from being perfect in practice, yet they are prevailingly holy in all manner of converfation; they do not live habitually in any one known fin, or wilfully neglect any one known duty. Pfalm cxix. 6.

Without this practical holiness no man shall see the Lord; and if so, how great a change must be wrought on most before they can see him, for how few are thus adorned with a life of universal holiness? Many profess the name of Christ, but how few of them depart from iniquity? But to what purpose do they call him Master and Lord, while they do not the things which he commands them?

Thus I have, as plainly as I could, described the nature and properties of that holiness, without which no man shall see the Lord; and they who are possessed of it may lift of their heads with joy, assured that God has begun a good work in them, and that he will carry it on; and on the other hand, they that are destitute of it may be assured, that, unless they are made new creatures, they cannot see the Lord. I come,

II. To shew you the endeavours we should use to obtain this holiness. And they are such as these:

1. Endeavour to know whether you are holy or not by close examination. It is hard indeed for some to know positively that they are holy, as they are perplexed with the appearances of realities, and the fears of counterfeits; but it is then easy for many to conclude negatively that they are not holy, as they have not the likeness of it. To determine this point is of great use to our successful seeking after holiness. That an unregenerate sinner should attend on the means of grace with other aims than one that has reason to believe himself sanctified. The anxieties, sorrows, desires, and endeavours of the one should run in a very different channel from those of the other: The one should look upon himself as a guilty and condemned sinner; the other should allow himself the pleasure of a justified state: the one should pursue after the implantation; the other after the increase of holiness: the one should indulge a seasonable concern about his lost condition; the other repose an humble confidence in God as reconciled to him: the one should look upon the threatenings of God as his doom; the other embrace the promises as his portion. Hence it follows that, while we are mistaken about our state, we cannot use endeavours after holiness in a proper manner. We act like a physician that applies medicines at random, without knowing the disease. It is a certain conclusion that the most generous charity, under scriptural limitations, cannot avoid, that multitudes are destitute of holiness, and ought not we to enquire with proper anxiety whether we belong to that number? Let us be impartial, and proceed according to evidence. If we find those marks of holiness in heart and life which have been mentioned, let not an excessive scrupulosity frighten us from drawing the happy conclusion: and, if we find them not, let us exercise so much wholesome severity against ourselves, as honestly to conclude we are unholy

sinners, and must be renewed before we can see the Lord. The conclusion no doubt will give you painful anxiety; but if you was my dearest friend, I could not form a kinder wish for you than that you might be incessantly distressed with it till you are born again. This conclusion will not be always avoidable; the light of eternity will force you upon it; and whether it is better to give way to it now, when it may be to your advantage, or be forced to admit it then, when it will be only a torment?

2. Awake, arise, and betake yourself in earnest to all the means of grace. Your life, your eternal life is concerned, and therefore it calls for all the ardor and earnestness you are capable of exerting. Accustom yourself to meditation, converse with yourselves in retirement, and live no longer strangers at home. Read the word of God and other good books, with diligence, attention, and self-application. Attend on the public ministrations of the gospel, not as a trifler, but as one that sees his eternal All concerned. Shun the tents of sin, the rendezvous of sinners, and associate with those that have experienced the change you want, and can give you proper directions. Prostrate yourself before the God of heaven, confess your sin, implore his mercy, cry to him night and day, and give him no rest, till the importunity prevail, and you take the kingdom of heaven by violence.

But after all, acknowledge that it is God that must work in you both to will and to do, and that when you have done all these things you are but unprofitable servants. I do not prescribe these directions as though these means could effect holiness in you; no, they can no more do it than a pen can write without a hand. It is the holy Spirit's province alone to sanctify a degenerate sinner, but he is wont to do it while we are waiting upon him in the use of these means, though our best endeavours give us no title to his grace! but he may justly leave us after all in that state of condemnation and corruption into which we have voluntarily brought ourselves. I go on,

III. And lastly, to urge you to the use of these means from the consideration mentioned in the text, the absolute necessity of holiness to the enjoyment of heavenly happiness.

Here I would shew that holiness is absolutely necessary, and that the consideration of its necessity may strongly enforce the pursuit of it.

The necessity of holiness appears from the unchangeable appointment of heaven, and the nature of things.

1. The unchangeable appointment of God excludes all the unholy from the kingdom of heaven; see 1 Cor. ix. 6. Rev. xxi. 27. Psalm v. 4, 5. 2 Cor. v. 17. Gal. vi. 15. It is most astonishing that many who profess to believe the divine authority of the scriptures, will yet indulge vain hopes of heaven in opposition to

the plaineſt declarations of eternal truth. But though there were no poſitive conſtitution excluding the unholy from heaven, yet,

2. The very nature of things excludes ſinners from heaven; that is, it is impoſſible in the nature of things, that while they are unholy, they could receive happineſs from the employments and entertainments of the heavenly world. If theſe conſiſted in the affluence of thoſe things which ſinners delight in here; if its enjoyments were earthly riches, pleaſures and honours; if its employments were the amuſements of the preſent life, then they might be happy there, as far as their ſordid natures are capable of happineſs. But theſe trifles have no place in heaven. The felicity of that ſtate conſiſts in the contemplation of the divine perfections, and there diſplays in the works of creation, providence, and redemption; hence it is deſcribed by ſeeing the Lord, Matt. v. 8. and as a ſtate of knowledge, 1 Cor. xiii. 10—12. in the ſatisfaction reſulting thence, Pſalm xvii. 15. and a complacency in God as a portion, Pſalm lxxiii. 25, 26. and in perpetual ſerving and praiſing the Lord; and hence adoration is generally mentioned as the employ of all the hoſts of heaven. Theſe are the entertainments of heaven, and they that cannot find ſupreme happineſs in theſe, cannot find it in heaven. But it is evident theſe things could afford no ſatisfaction to an unholy perſon. He would pine away at the heavenly feaſt, for want of appetite for the entertainment; an holy God would be an object of horror rather than delight to him, and his ſervice would be a wearineſs, as it is now. Hence it appears, that if we do not place our ſupreme delight in theſe things here, we cannot be happy hereafter; for there will be no change of diſpoſitions in a future ſtate, but only the perfection of thoſe predominant in us here, whether good or evil. Either heaven muſt be changed, or the ſinner, before he can be happy there. Hence alſo it appears, that God's excluding ſuch from heaven is no more an act of cruelty than our not admitting a ſick man to a feaſt, who has no reliſh for the entertainments; or not bringing a blind man into the light of the ſun, or to view a beautiful proſpect.

We ſee then that holineſs is abſolutely neceſſary; and what a great inducement ſhould this conſideration be to purſue it? If we do not ſee the Lord, we ſhall never ſee good. We are cut off at death from all earthly enjoyments, and can no longer make experiments to ſatisfy our unbounded deſires with them; and we have no God to ſupply their room. We are baniſhed from all the joys of heaven, and how vaſt, how inconceivably vaſt is the loſs! We are doomed to the regions of darkneſs for ever, to bear the vengeance of eternal fire, to feel the laſhes of a guilty conſcience, and to ſpend an eternal in an horrid intimacy with infernal ghoſts! and will we not then rather follow holineſs, than incur ſo dreadful a doom? By the terrors of the Lord, then be perſuaded to break off your ſins by righteouſneſs, and follow holineſs; *without which no man ſhall ſee the Lord.*

SERMON X.

The Mediatorial Kingdom and Glories of Jeſus Chriſt.

JOHN xviii. 37. *Pilate therefore ſaid unto him, Art thou a King then? Jeſus anſwered, Thou ſayeſt that I am a King. To this end was I born, and for this cauſe came I into the world, that I ſhould bear witneſs unto the truth.*

KINGS and kingdoms are the moſt majeſtic ſounds in the language of mortals, and have filled the world with noiſe, confuſions, and blood, ſince mankind firſt left the ſtate of nature, and formed themſelves into ſocieties. The diſputes of kingdoms for ſuperiority have ſet the world in arms from age to age, and deſtroyed or enſlaved a conſiderable part of the human race; and the conteſt is not yet decided. Our country has been a region of peace and tranquility for a long time, but it has not been becauſe the luſt of power and riches is extinct in the world, but becauſe we had no near neighbours, whoſe intereſt might claſh with ours, or who were able to diſturb us. The abſence of an enemy was our ſole defence. But now, when the colonies of the ſundry European nations on this continent begin to enlarge, and approach towards each other, the ſcene is changed: now encroachments, depredations, barbarities, and all the terrors of war begin to ſurround and alarm us. Now our country is invaded and ravaged, and bleeds in a thouſand veins. We have already,* ſo early in the year, received alarm upon alarm: and we may expect the alarms to grow louder and louder as the ſeaſon advances.

Theſe commotions and perturbations have had one good effect upon me, and that is, they have carried away my thoughts of late into a ſerene and peaceful region, a region beyond the reach of confuſion and violence; I mean the kingdom of the Prince of Peace. And thither, my brethren, I would alſo tranſport your minds this day, as the beſt refuge from this boiſterous world, and the moſt agreeable manſion for the lovers of peace and tranquility.

---

* This ſermon was preached in Hanover, Virginia, May 9, 1756.

Glories of Jesus Christ.

I find it advantageous both to you and myself, to entertain you with those subjects that have made the deepest impression upon my own mind: and this is the reason why I choose the present subject. In my text you hear one entering a claim to a kingdom, whom you would conclude, if you regarded only his outward appearance, to be the meanest and vilest of mankind. To hear a powerful prince, at the head of a victorious army, attended with all the royalties of his character, to hear such an one claim the kingdom he had acquired by force of arms, would not be strange. But here the despised Nazarene, rejected by his nation, forsaken by his followers, accused as the worst of criminals, standing defenceless at Pilate's bar, just about to be condemned and hung on a cross, like a malefactor and a slave, here he speaks in a royal style, even to his judge, *I am a King:* for this purpose *was I born; and for this cause came I into the world.* Strange language indeed to proceed from his lips in these circumstances! But the truth is, a great, a divine personage is concealed under this disguise? and his kingdom is of such a nature, that his abasement and crucifixion were so far from being a hindrance to it, that they were the only way to acquire it. These sufferings were meritorious; and by these he purchased his subjects, and a right to rule them.

The occasion of these words was this: the unbelieving Jews were determined to put Jesus to death as an imposter. The true reason of their opposition to him was, that he had severely exposed their hypocrisy, claimed the character of the Messiah, without answering their expectations as a temporal prince and a mighty conqueror; and introduced a new religion, which superseded the law of Moses, in which they had been educated. But this reason they knew would have but little weight with Pilate the Roman governor, who was an heathen, and had no regard to their religion. They therefore bring a charge of another kind, which they knew would touch the governor very sensibly, and that was, that Christ had set himself up as the King of the Jews; which was treason against Cæsar the Roman emperor, under whose yoke they then were. This was all pretence and artifice. They would now seem to be very loyal to the emperor, and unable to bear with any claims inconsistent with his authority; whereas, in truth, they were impatient of a foreign government, and were watching for any opportunity to shake it off. And had Christ been really guilty of the charge they alledged against him, he would have been the more acceptable to them. Had he set himself up as a King of the Jews, in opposition to Cæsar, and employed his miraculous powers to make good his claim, the whole nation would have welcomed him as their deliverer, and flocked round his standard. But Jesus came not to work a deliverance of this kind, nor to erect such a kingdom as they desired, and therefore they rejected him as an impostor. This charge, however, they bring against him, in order to carry their point with the heathen governor. They knew he was zealous for the honour and interest of Cæsar his master; and Tiberius, the then Roman emperor, was so jealous a prince, and kept so many spies over his governors in all the provinces, that they were obliged to be very circumspect, and shew the strictest regard for his rights, in order to escape degradation, or a severer punishment. It was this that determined Pilate, in the struggle with his conscience, to condemn the innocent Jesus. He was afraid the Jews would inform against him, as dismissing one that set up as the rival of Cæsar; and the consequence of this he well knew. The Jews were sensible of this, and therefore they insist upon this charge, and at length plainly tell him, *If thou let this man go, thou art not Cæsar's friend.* Pilate therefore, who cared but little what innovations Christ should introduce into the Jewish religion, thought proper to inquire into this matter, and asks him. " Art thou the King of the Jews?" dost thou indeed claim such a character, which may interfere with Cæsar's government? Jesus replies, *My kingdom is not of this world;* as much as to say, " I do not deny that I claim a kingdom, but it is of such a nature, that it need give no alarm to the kings of the earth. Their kingdoms are of this world, but mine is spiritual and divine,* and therefore cannot interfere with theirs. If my kingdom were of this world, like theirs, I would take the same methods, with them to obtain and secure it; my servants would fight for me, that I should not be delivered to the Jews; but now, you see, I use no such means for my defence, or to raise me to my kingdom: and therefore you may be assured, my kingdom is not from hence, and can give the Roman emperor no umbrage for suspicion or uneasiness." Pilate answers to this purpose: Thou dost, however, speak of a kingdom; and *art thou a king then?* dost thou in any sense claim that character? The poor prisoner boldly replies, *Thou sayest that I am a king;* that is, " Thou hast struck upon the truth: I am indeed a king in a certain sense, and nothing shall constrain me to renounce the title." *To this end was I born, and for this cause came I into the world, that I should bear witness to the truth;* " particularly to this truth, which now looks so unlikely, namely, that I am really a king. I was born to a kingdom and a crown, and came into the world to take possession of my right." This is that great confession which St. Paul tells us, 2 Tim. vi. 13.

---

* The Domitian, the Roman emperor, being apprehensive that Christ's earthly relations might claim a kingdom in his right, inquired of them concerning the nature of his kingdom, and when and where it should be set up. They replied, " It was not earthly, but heavenly and angelical, and to be set up at the end of the world."—Ου κοσμικη μεν ουδε επιγει@, δι οι αγγελικη ουρανει επι συντελεια τε αιωνι@ συνηγμενη.

our Lord witnessed before Pontius Pilate. Neither the hopes of deliverance, nor the terrors of death, could cause him to retract it, or renounce his claim.

In prosecuting this subject I intend only to inquire into the nature and properties of the kingdom of Christ. And in order to render my discourse the more familiar, and to adapt it to the present state of our country, I shall consider this kingdom in contrast with the kingdoms of the earth, with which we are better acquainted.

The scriptures represent the Lord Jesus under a great variety of characters, which, though sufficient fully to represent him, yet in conjunction assist us to form such exalted ideas of this great personage, as mortals can reach. He is a Surety, that undertook and paid the dreadful debt of obedience and suffering, which sinners owed to the divine justice and law: He is a Priest, a great High Priest, that once offered himself as a sacrifice for sin; and now dwells in his native heaven, at his Father's right hand, as the advocate and intercessor of his people: He is a Prophet, who teaches his church in all ages by his word and spirit: He is the supreme and universal Judge, to whom men and angels are accountable; and his name is Jesus, a Saviour, because he saves his people from their sins. Under these august and endearing characters he is often represented. But there is one character under which he is uniformly represented, both in the Old and New Testament, and that is, that of a King, a great King, invested with universal authority. And upon his appearance in the flesh, all nature, and especially the gospel-church, is represented as placed under him, as his kingdom. Under this idea the Jews were taught by their prophets to look for him; and it was their understanding these predictions of some illustrious king that should rise from the house of David, in a literal and carnal sense, that occasioned their unhappy prejudices concerning the Messiah as a secular prince and conqueror. Under this idea the Lord Jesus represented himself while upon earth, and under this idea he was published to the world by his apostles. The greatest kings of the Jewish nation, particularly David and Solomon, were types of him; and many things are primarily applied to them, which have their complete and final accomplishment in him alone. It is to him ultimately we are to apply the second psalm: *I have set my king*, says Jehovah, *upon my holy hill of Zion. Ask of me, and I will give thee the heathen for thy inheritance, and the utmost parts of the earth for thy possession.* Psalm ii. 6, 8. If we read the seventy-second psalm we shall easily perceive that one greater than Solomon is there. *In his days shall the righteous flourish; and abundance of peace so long as the moon endureth. All kings shall fall down before him; all nations shall serve him. His name shall continue for ever; his name *shall endure as long as the sun: and men shall be blessed in him; and all nations shall call him blessed.* Psalm lxxii. 7, 11, 17. The hundred and tenth psalm is throughout a celebration of the kingly and priestly office of Christ united. *The Lord*, says David, *said unto my Lord*, unto that divine person who is my Lord, and will also be my Son, *sit thou at my right hand*, in the highest honour and authority, *until I make thine enemies thy footstool.*—Rule thou in the midst of thine enemies. *Thy people shall be willing in the day of thy power*, and submit to thee in crowds as numerous as the drops of morning dew. Psalm cx. 1—3. The evangelical prophet Isaiah is often transported with the foresight of his illustrious king, and the glorious kingdom of his grace:—*Unto us a child is born unto us a son is given; and the government shall be upon his shoulder; and he shall be called—the Prince of Peace. Of the increase of his government and peace there shall be no end, upon the throne of David and upon his kingdom, to order and to establish it with judgment and with justice, from henceforth even for ever.* Isa. ix. 6, 7. This is he who is described as another David in Ezekiel's prophecy, *Thus saith the Lord, I will take the children of Israel from among the heathen. And I will make them one nation—and one king shall be king to them all even David my servant shall be king over them.* Ezek. xxxvii. 21, 22, 24. This is the kingdom represented to Nebuchadnezzar in his dream, as *a stone cut out without hands, which became a great mountain, and filled the whole earth.* And Daniel, in expounding the dream, having described the Babylonian, the Persian, the Grecian, and Roman empires, subjoins, *In the days of these kings*, that is, of the Roman emperors, *shall the God of heaven set up a kingdom, which shall never be destroyed: and the kingdom shall not, like the former, be left to other people; but it shall break in pieces and consume all these kingdoms, and it shall stand for ever.* Dan. ii. 34, 35, 44. There is no character which our Lord so often assumed in the days of his flesh as that of the Son of Man; and he no doubt alludes to a majestic vision in Daniel, the only place where this character is given him in the Old Testament: *I saw in the night visions*, says Daniel, *and behold, one like the Son of Man came to the Ancient of Days, and there was given to him dominion, and glory, and a kingdom, that all people, nations and languages, should serve him: his dominion is an everlasting dominion, which shall not pass away, and his kingdom that which shall not be destroyed,* Dan. vii. 13, 14. like the tottering kingdoms of the earth, which are perpetually rising and falling. This is the king that Zechariah refers to when, in prospect of his triumphant entrance into Jerusalem, he calls the inhabitants to give a proper reception to so great a Prince. *Rejoice greatly, O daughter of Zion; shout, O daughter of Jerusalem: behold thy King coming unto thee,* &c. Zech. ix. 9. Thus the prophets conspire to ascribe royal titles and a glorious kingdom to the Meſſiah. And theſe early and plain notices of him raiſed a general expectation of him under this royal character. It was from theſe prophecies concerning him as a king, that the Jews took occaſion, as I obſerved, to look for the Meſſiah as a temporal prince; and it was a long time before the apoſtles themſelves were delivered from theſe carnal prejudices. They were ſolicitous about poſts of honour in that temporal kingdom which they expected he would ſet up; and even after his reſurrection they cannot forbear aſking him, *Lord, wilt thou at this time reſtore again the kingdom to Iſrael?* Acts i. 6. that is, "Wilt thou now reſtore the Jews to their former liberty and independency, and deliver them from their preſent ſubjection to the Romans?" It was under this view that Herod was alarmed at his birth, and ſhed the blood of ſo many innocents, that he might not eſcape. He was afraid of him as the heir of David's family and crown, who might diſpoſſeſs him of the government; nay, he was expected by other nations under the character of a mighty king; and they no doubt learned this notion of him from the Jewiſh prophecies, as well as their converſation with that people. Hence the Magi, or eaſtern wiſemen, when they came to pay homage to him upon his birth, inquired after him in this language,— "Where is he that is born King of the Jews?" Matt. ii. 2. And what is ſtill more remarkable, we are told by two heathen hiſtorians, that about the time of his appearance a general expectation of him under this character prevailed through the world. "Many," ſays Tacitus, "had a perſuaſion that it was contained in the ancient writings of the prieſts, that at that very time the eaſt ſhould prevail, and that ſome deſcendant from Judah ſhould obtain the univerſal government."* Suetonius ſpeaks to the ſame purpoſe: "An old and conſtant opinion," ſays he, "commonly prevailed through all the eaſt, that it was in the fates, that ſome ſhould riſe out of Judea who ſhould obtain the government of the world."* This royal character Chriſt himſelf aſſumed, even when he converſed among mortals in the humble form of a ſervant. *"The Father,"* ſays he, *has given me power over all fleſh.* John. xvii. 2. Yea, *all power in heaven and earth is given to me.* Matt. xxviii. 13. The goſpel-church which he erected is moſt commonly called

---

* Fluribus perſuaſio inerat, antiquis ſacerdotum literis contineri, eo ipſo tempore fore, ut valeſcerat oriens, profectique Judea rerum potirentur. Tacit. Hiſt. l. 5. p. 621.

* Percrebuerat oriente toto vetus & conſtans opinio, eſſe in fatis, ut eo tempore Judea profecti rerum potirentur. Suet. in Veſp. c. 4.

The ſameneſs of the expectation is remarkably evident, from the ſameneſs of the words in which theſe two hiſtorians expreſs it. *Judea profecti rerum potirentur.* It was not only a common expectation, but it was commonly expreſſed in the ſame language.

the kingdom of heaven or of God, in the evangelists: and when he was about to introduce it, this was the proclamation: *The kingdom of heaven is at hand.* Under this character also his servants and disciples celebrated and preached him. Gabriel led the song in foretelling his birth to his mother. *He shall be great, and the Lord shall give unto him the throne of his father David; and he shall reign over the house of Jacob for ever: and of his kingdom there shall be no end.* Luke i. 32, 33. St. Peter boldly tells the murderers of Christ, *God hath made that same Jesus whom you crucified, both Lord and Christ,* Acts ii. 36. *and exalted him, with his own right hand, to be a Prince and a Saviour.* Acts v. 31. And St. Paul repeatedly represents him as advanced *far above principality, and power and might, and dominion, and every name that is named, not only in this world, but also in that which is to come: and that God hath put all things under his feet, and given him to be head over all things to his church.* Eph. i. 21, 22. Phil. ii. 9—11. Yea, to him all the hosts of heaven, and even the whole creation in concert, ascribe *power and strength, and honour and glory.* Rev. v. 12. Pilate the heathen was over-ruled to give a kind of accidental testimony to this truth, and to publish it to different nations, by the inscription upon the cross in the three languages then most in use, the Latin, Greek, and Hebrew: *This is Jesus of Nazareth, King of the Jews;* and all the remonstrances of the Jews could not prevail upon him to alter it. Finally, it is he that wears *upon his vesture, and upon his thigh, this name writen, King of kings, and Lord of lords,* Rev. xix. 16. and as his name is, so is he.

Thus you see, my brethren, by these instances, selected out of many, that the kingly character and dominion of our Lord Jesus runs through the whole Bible. That of a king is his favourite character in which he glories, and which is the most expressive of his office. And this consideration alone may convince you that this character is of the greatest importance, and worthy of your most attentive regard.

It is the mediatorial kingdom of Christ that is here intended not that which as God he exercises over all the works of his hands: it is that kingdom which is an empire of grace, an administration of mercy over our guilty world. It is the dispensation intended for the salvation of fallen sinners of our race by the gospel; and on this account the gospel is often called the kingdom of heaven; because its happy consequences are not confined to this earth, but appear in heaven in the highest perfection, and last through all eternity. Hence, not only the church of Christ on earth, and the dispensation of the gospel, but all the saints in heaven, and that more finished œconomy under which they are placed, are all included in the kingdom of Christ. Here his kingdom is in its infancy, but in heaven is arrived to perfection; but it is substantially the same. Though the immediate design of this kingdom is the salvation of believers of the guilty race of man, and such are its subjects in a peculiar sense; yet it extends to all worlds, to heaven, and earth, and hell. The whole universe is put under a mediatorial head; but then, as the apostle observes, *he is made head over all things to his church*, Eph. i. 22. that is, for the benefit and salvation of his church. As Mediator he is carrying on a glorious scheme for the recovery of man, and all parts of the universe are interested or concern themselves in this grand event; and therefore they are all subjected to him, that he may so manage them as to promote this end, and baffle and overwhelm all opposition. The elect angels rejoice in so benevolent a design for peopling their mansions, left vacant by the fall of so many of their fellow-angels with colonies transplanted from our world, from a race of creatures that they had given up for lost. And therefore Christ, as a Mediator, is made the head of all the heavenly armies, and he employs them as *his ministering spirits, to minister to them that are heirs of salvation*. Heb. i. 14. These glorious creatures are always on the wing ready to discharge his orders in any part of his vast empire, and delight to be employed in the services of his mediatorial kingdom. This is also an event in which the fallen angels deeply interest themselves; they have united all their force and art for near six thousand years to disturb and subvert his kingdom, and blast the designs of redeeming love; they therefore are all subjected to the controul of Christ, and he shortens and lengthens their chains as he pleases, and they cannot go an hair's breadth beyond his permission. The scriptures represent our world in its state of guilt and misery as the kingdom of Satan; sinners, while slaves to sin, are his subjects; and every act of disobedience against God is an act of homage to this infernal prince. Hence Satan is called *the God of this world*, 2 Cor. iv. 4. *the prince of this world*, John xii. 31. *the power of darkness*, Luke xxii. 53. *the prince of the power of the air, the Spirit that now worketh in the children of disobedience.* Eph. ii. 3. And sinners are said to be *taken captive by him at his will.* 2. Tim. ii. 26. Hence also the ministers of Christ, who are employed to recover sinners to a state of holiness and happiness, are represented as soldiers armed for war; not indeed with carnal weapons, but with those which are spiritual, plain truth arguments, and miracles; and *these are made mighty through God to the pulling down of strong holds, casting down imaginations, and every high thing that exalteth itself against the knowledge of God, and bringing into captivity every thought to the obedience of Christ.* 2 Cor. x. 3, 4, 5. And christians in general are represented as *wrestling, not with flesh and blood, but against principalities, against powers, against the rulers of the darkness of this world, against spiritual wickednesses in high places.* Eph. vi. 12. Hence also in particular it is that the death of Christ is represented not as a defeat, but as an illustrious conquest gained over the powers of hell; because, by this means a way was opened for the deliverance of sinners from under their power, and restoring them into liberty and the favour of God. By that strange contemptible weapon, the cross, and by the glorious resurrection of Jesus, he *spoiled principalities and powers, and made a shew of them openly, triumphing over them.* Col. ii. 15. *Through death,* says the apostle, *he destroyed him that had the power of death; that is, the devil.* Heb. ii. 14. Had not Christ by his death offered a propitiatory sacrifice for the sins of men, they would have continued for ever under the tyranny of Satan; but he has purchased liberty, life, and salvation for them; and thus he hath destroyed the kingdom of darkness, and translated multitudes from it into his own gracious and glorious kingdom.

Hence, upon the right of redemption, his mediatorial authority extends to the infernal regions, and he controuls and restrains those malignant, mighty, and turbulent potentates, according to his pleasure. Farther, the inanimate world is connected with our Lord's design to save sinners, and therefore is subjected to him as Mediator. He causes the sun to rise, the rain to fall, and the earth to yield her increase, to furnish provision for the subjects of his grace, and to raise, support and accommodate heirs for his heavenly kingdom. As for the sons of men, who are more immediately concerned in this kingdom, and for whose sake it was erected, they are all its subjects; but then they are of different sorts, according to their characters. Multitudes are rebels against his government; that is, they do not voluntarily submit to his authority, nor chuse they to do his service: they will not obey his laws. But they are his subjects notwithstanding; that is, he rules and manages them as he pleases, whether they will or not. This power is necessary to carry on successfully his gracious design towards his people; for unless he had the management of his enemies, they might baffle his undertaking, and successfully counteract the purposes of his love. The kings of the earth, as well as vulgar rebels of a private character, have often set themselves against his kingdom, and sometimes they have flattered themselves they had entirely demolished it.* But Jesus reigns absolute and supreme over the kings of the earth, and over-rules and controuls them as he thinks proper; and he disposes all the revolutions, the rises and falls of kingdoms and empires, so as to be subservient to the great designs

---

* In the 10th and last Roman persecution, *Dioclesian* had a medal struck with this inscription, " The christian name demolished, and the worship of the gods restored."

of his mediation; and their united policies and powers cannot fruſtrate the work which he has undertaken. But beſides theſe rebellious involuntary ſubjects, he has (bleſſed be his name!) gained the conſent of thouſands, and they have become his willing ſubjects by their own choice. They regard his authority, they love his government, they make it their ſtudy to pleaſe him, and to do his will. Over theſe he exerciſes a government of ſpecial grace here, and he will make them the happy ſubjects of the kingdom of his glory hereafter. And it is his government over theſe that I intend more particularly to conſider. Once more, the kingdom of Jeſus is not confined to this world, but all the millions of mankind in the inviſible world are under his dominion, and will continue ſo to everlaſting ages. *He is the Lord of the dead and the living*, Rom. xiv. 9. and has the keys of Hades, the vaſt inviſible world (including heaven as well as hell) and of death. Rev. i. 18. It is he that turns the key, and opens the door of death for mortals to paſs from world to world: it is he that opens the gates of heaven, and welcomes and admits the nations that keep the commandments of God: and it is he that opens the priſon of hell, and locks it faſt upon the priſoners of divine juſtice. He will for ever exerciſe authority over the vaſt regions of the unſeen world, and the unnumbered multitudes of ſpirits with which they are peopled. You hence ſee, my brethren, the univerſal extent of the Redeemer's kingdom; and in this reſpect how much does it differ from all the kingdoms of the earth? The kingdoms of Great-Britain, France, China, Perſia, are but little ſpots of the globe. Our world has indeed been oppreſſed in former times with what mortals call univerſal monarchies; ſuch were the Babylonian, the Perſian, the Grecian, and eſpecially the Roman. But in truth, theſe were ſo far from being ſtrictly univerſal, that a conſiderable part of the habitable earth was not ſo much as known to them. But this is an empire ſtrictly univerſal. It extends over land and ſea; it reaches beyond the planetary worlds, and all the luminaries of heaven; nay, beyond the throne of the moſt exalted archangels, and downward to the loweſt abyſs in hell. An univerſal empire in the hands of a mortal is an huge, unwieldy thing; an heap of confuſion; a burthen to mankind; and it has always ruſhed headlong from its glory, and fallen to pieces by its own weight. But Jeſus is equal to the immenſe province of an empire ſtrictly univerſal: his hand is able to hold the reins; and it is the bleſſing of our world to be under his adminiſtration. He will turn what appears to us ſcenes of confuſion into perfect order, and convince all worlds that he has not taken one wrong ſtep in the whole plan of his infinite government.

The kingdoms of the world have their laws and ordinances,

and so has the kingdom of Christ. Look into your Bibles, and there you will find the laws of this kingdom, from its first foundation immediately upon the fall of man. The laws of human governments are often defective or unrighteous; but these are perfect, holy, just, and good. Human laws are enforced with sanctions; but the rewards and punishments can only effect our mortal bodies, and cannot reach beyond the present life: but the sanctions of these divine laws are eternal, and there never shall be an end to their execution. Everlasting happiness and everlasting misery, of the most exquisite kind and the highest degree, are the rewards and punishments which the immortal King distributes among his immortal subjects; and they become his character, and are adapted to their nature.

Human laws extend only to outward actions, but these laws reach the heart, and the principle of action within. Not a secret thought, not a motion of the soul, is exempted from them. If the subjects of earthly kings observe a decorum in their outward conduct, and give no visible evidence of disloyalty, they are treated as good subjects, though they should be enemies in their hearts. "But Jesus is the Lord of souls;" he makes his subjects bow their hearts as well as the knee to him. He sweetly commands their thoughts and affections as well as their external practice, and makes himself inwardly beloved as well as outwardly obeyed. His subjects are such on whom he may depend: they are all ready to lay down their lives for him. Love, cordial, unfeigned, ardent love, is the principle of all their obedience; and hence it is that his commandments are not grievous, but delightful to them.

Other kings have their ministers and officers of state. In like manner Jesus employs the armies of heaven as ministering spirits in his mediatorial kingdom: besides these he has ministers, of an humbler form, who negociate more immediately in his name with mankind. These are intrusted with the ministry of reconciliation, to beseech men, in his stead, to be reconciled to God. These are appointed to preach his word, to administer his ordinances, and to manage the affairs of his kingdom. This view gives a peculiar dignity and importance to this office. These should be adorned, not like the ministers of earthly courts, with the trappings of gold and silver, but with the beauties of holiness, the ornament of a meek and quiet, zealous and faithful spirit, and a life becoming the gospel of Christ.

Other kings have their soldiers: so all the legions of the elect angels, the armies of heaven, are the soldiers of Jesus Christ, and under his command. This he asserted when he was in such defenceless circumstances, that he seemed to be abandoned by heaven and earth. " I could pray to my Father, says he, and he would *send me more than twelve legions of angels.* Matt. xxvi. 53. I cannot forbear reading to you one of the most majestic descriptions of this all-conquering hero and his army, which the language of mortality is capable of. Rev. xix. 11. 16. *I saw heaven open,* says St. John, *and behold a white horse,* an emblem of victory and triumph, *and he that sat upon him was called Faithful and True.* How different a character from that of mortal conquerors! "And in righteousness he doth judge and make war." War is generally a scene of injustice and lawless violence; and those plagues of mankind we call heroes and warriors, use their arms to gratify their own avarice or ambition, and make encroachments upon others. Jesus, the Prince of peace, makes war too, but it is in righteousness; it is in the cause of righteousness he takes up arms. The divine description proceeds: *His eyes were as a flame of fire; and on his head were many crowns,* emblems of his manifold authority over the various kingdoms of the world, and the various regions of the universe. *And he was clothed with a vesture dipt in blood,* in the blood of his enemies; *and his name was called, The Word of God: and the armies which were in heaven, followed him upon white horses, clothed in fine linen, white and clean:* the whitest innocence and purity, and the beauties of holiness are, as it were, the uniform, the regimentals of these celestial armies. *And out of his mouth goeth a sharp sword, that with it he should smite the nations: and he shall rule them with a rod of iron; and he treadeth the wine press of the fierceness and wrath of Almighty God; and he hath on his vesture and on his thigh a name written, King of kings, and Lord of lords.* In what manner the war is carried on between the armies of heaven and the powers of hell, we know not; but that there is really something of this kind, we may infer from *Rev.* xii. 7, 9. *There was war in heaven: Michael and his angels fought against the dragon; and the dragon fought and his angels, and prevailed not, neither was there place found any more in heaven. And the great dragon was cast out, that old serpent called the Devil and Satan.*

Thus you see all the host of heaven are volunteers under the Captain of our salvation. Nay, he marshals the stars, and calls them by their names. *The stars in their courses,* says the sublime Deborah, *fought against Sisera,* the enemy of God's people. *Judges* v. 20. Every part of the creation serves under him, and he can commission a gnat, or a fly, or the meanest insect, to be the executioner of his enemies. Fire and water, hurricanes and earthquakes; earthquakes which have so lately shattered so great a part of our globe, now tottering with age, and ready to fall to pieces, and bury the guilty inhabitants in its ruins, all these fight under him, and conspire to avenge his quarrel with the guilty sons of men. The subjects of his grace in particular are all so many soldiers; their life is a constant warfare; and they are incessantly engaged in hard conflict with temptations from without, and the insurrections of sin from within. Sometimes, alas! they fall; but their General lifts them up again, and inspires them with strength to renew the fight. They fight most successfully upon their knees. This is the most advantageous posture for the soldiers of Jesus Christ; for prayer brings down recruits from heaven in the hour of difficulty. They are indeed but poor weaklings and invalids; and yet they overcome, through the blood of the Lamb; and he makes them conquerors, yea more than conquerors. It is the military character of christians that gives the apostle occasion to address them in the military stile, like a general at the head of his army. *Eph.* vi. 10—18. *Be strong in the Lord, and in the power of his might. Put on the whole armour of God, that ye may be able to stand against the wiles of the devil. Stand therefore, having your loins girt about with truth, and having on the breast plate of righteousness, and your feet shod with the preparation of the gospel of peace; above all, taking the shield of faith, wherewith ye shall be able to quench all the fiery darts of the wicked. And take the helmet of salvation, and the sword of the spirit, which is the word of God, praying always with all prayer and supplication.* The ministers of the gospel in particular, and especially the apostles, are soldiers, or officers, in this spiritual army. Hence St. Paul speaks of his office, in the military stile; *I have,* says he, *fought the good fight.* 2 Tim. iv. 7. *We war,* says he, *though it be not after the flesh.* The humble doctrines of the cross are our weapons, and these *are mighty* through God, *to demolish the strong holds of the prince of darkness,* and to *bring every thought into* a joyful *captivity to the obedience of faith.* 2 Cor. x. 3—5. *Fight the good fight* says he to Timothy. 1 *Tim.* vi. 12. And again, *thou therefore endure hardness, as a good soldier of Jesus Christ.* 2 Tim. ii. 3. The great design of the gospel-ministry is to rescue enslaved souls from the tyranny of sin and Satan, and to recover them into a state of liberty and loyalty to Jesus Christ; or, in the words of the apostle, *to turn them from darkness to light, and from the power of Satan unto God.* Acts xxvi. 18. Mortals indeed are very unequal for the conflict; but their success more conspicuously shews that the *excellency of the power is of God:* and many have they subdued, through his strength, to the obedience of faith, and made the willing captives of the cross of our divine Immanuel. Other kingdoms are often founded in blood, and many lives are lost on both sides in acquiring them. The kingdom of Christ, too, was founded in blood; but it was the blood of his own heart: life was lost in the conflict; but it was his own; his own life lost, to purchase life for his people. Others have waded to empire through the blood of mankind, and even of their own subjects, but Christ shed only his own blood to spare that of his soldiers. The general devotes his life as a sacrifice to save his army. The Fabii and Decii of Rome, who devoted themselves for their country, were but faint shadows of this divine bravery. O! the generous patriotism, the ardent love of the Captain of our salvation! How amiable does his character appear, in contrast with that of the kings of the earth! They often sacrifice the lives of their subjects, while they keep themselves out of danger, or perhaps are rioting at ease in the pleasures and luxuries of a court; but Jesus engaged in the conflict with death and hell alone. He stood a single champion in a field of blood. He conquered for his people by falling himself: he subdued his and their enemies by resigning himself to the power. Worthy is such a general to be Commander in Chief of the hosts of God, and to lead the armies of heaven and earth! Indeed much blood has been shed in carrying on this kingdom. The earth has been soaked with the blood of the saints; and millions have resisted even unto blood, striving against sin, and nobly laid down their lives for the sake of Christ and a good conscience. Rome has been remarkably the seat of persecution; both formerly under the Heathen Emperors, and in latter times, under a succession of Popes, still more bloody and tyrannical. There were no less than ten general persecutions under the Heathen Emperors, through the vast Roman empire, in a little more than two hundred years which followed one another in a close succession; in which innumerable multitudes of christians lost their lives by an endless variety of tortures. And since the church of Rome has usurped her authority, the blood of the saints has hardly ever ceased running in some country or other; though, blessed be God, many kingdoms shook off the yoke at the ever-memorable period of the Reformation, above two hundred years ago: which has greatly weakened that persecuting power. This is that mystical Babylon which was represented to St. John as *drunken with the blood of the saints, and with the blood of the martyrs of Jesus*. Rev. xvii. 6. In her was found the blood of the prophets, and of the saints, and of all that were slain upon the earth. *ch.* xviii. 24. And these scenes of blood are still perpetrated in France, that plague of Europe, that has of late stretched her murderous arm across the wide ocean to disturb us in these regions of peace. There the Protestants are still plundered, chained to the gallies, broken alive upon the torturing wheel, denied the poor favour of abandoning their country and their all, and flying naked to beg their bread in other nations. Thus the harmless subjects of the Prince of Peace have ever been slaughtered from age to age, and yet they are represented as triumphant conquerors. Hear a poor persecuted Paul on this head: *In tribulation, in distress, in persecution, in nakedness, in peril and sword, we are conquerors, we are more than conquerors, through him that loved us.* Rom. viii. 36, 37.

Thanks be to God who always causeth us to triumph in Christ. 2 Cor. ii. 14. *Whatsoever is born of God,* says the evangelist, *overcometh the world.* 1 John v. 4. Whence came that glorious army which we so often see in the Revelation? We are told, *they came out of great tribulation*.. ch. vii. 14. *And they overcame by the blood of the Lamb, and by the word of their testimony; and they loved not their lives unto the death.* ch. xii. 11. They that suffered tortures and death under the beast, are said *to have gotten the victory over him.* ch. xv. 2. Victory and triumph sound strange when thus ascribed;—but the gospel helps us to understand this mystery. By these sufferings they obtained the illustrious crown of martyrdom, and peculiar degrees of glory and happiness through an endless duration. Their death was but a short transition from the lowest and more remote regions of their Redeemer's kingdom into his immediate presence and glorious court in heaven. A temporal death is rewarded with an immortal life; and *their light afflictions, which were but for a moment, wrought out for them a far more exceeding and eternal weight of glory.* 2 Cor. iv. 17. Even in the agonies of torture their souls were often filled with such delightful sensations of the love of God, as swallowed up the sensations of bodily pain; and a bed of flames was sweeter to them than a bed of roses. Their souls were beyond the reach of all the instruments of torment; and as to their bodies they shall yet have a glorious resurrection to a blessed immortality. And now I leave you to judge, whether they or their enemies got the victory in this conflict; and which had most cause to triumph. Like their Master, they rose by falling; they triumphed over their enemies by submitting, like lambs, to their power. If the soldiers of other generals die in the field, it is not in the power of their commanders to reward them. But the soldiers of Jesus Christ, by dying, are, as it were, carried in triumph from the field of blood into the presence of their Master, to receive his approbation, and a glorious crown. Death puts them into a capacity of receiving and enjoying greater rewards than they are capable of in the present state. And thus it appears, that his soldiers always win the day; or, as the apostle expresses it, he *causes them always to triumph;* and not one of them has ever been or ever shall be defeated, however weak and helpless in himself, and however terrible the power of his enemies.—And O! when all these warriors meet at length from every corner of the earth, and, as it were, pass in review before their General in the fields of heaven, with their robes washed in his blood, with palms of victory in their hands, and crowns of glory on their heads, all dressed in uniform with garments of salvation, what a glorious army will they make! and how will they cause heaven to ring with shouts of joy and triumph!

The founders of earthly kingdoms are famous for their heroic actions. They have braved the dangers of sea and land, routed powerful armies, and subjected nations to their will. They have shed rivers of blood, laid cities in ruins, and countries in desolation. These are the exploits which have rendered the Alexanders, the Cæsars, and other conquerors of this world, famous through all nations and ages. Jesus had his exploits too; but they were all of the gracious and beneficent kind. His conquests were so many deliverances, and his victories salvations. He subdued, in order to set free; and made captives to deliver them from slavery. He conquered the legions of hell, that seemed let loose at that time, that he might have opportunity of displaying his power over them, and that mankind might be sensible how much they needed a deliverer from their tyranny.—He triumphed over the temptations of Satan in the wilderness, by a quotation from his own word. He rescued wretched creatures from his power by an almighty command. He conquered the most inveterate and stubborn diseases, and restored health and vigour with a word of his mouth. He vanquished stubborn souls with the power of his love, and made them his willing people. He triumphed over death, the king of terrors, and delivered Lazarus from the prison of the grave, as an earnest and first-fruits of a general resurrection. Nay, by his own inherent powers he broke the bonds of death, and forced his way to his native heaven. He destroyed him that had the power of death, *i. e.* the devil, by his own death, and laid the foundation in his own blood for destroying his usurped kingdom, and forming a glorious kingdom of willing subjects redeemed from his tyranny.

The death of some great conquerors, particularly of Julius Cæsar, is said to be prognosticated or attended with prodigies: but none equal to those which solemnized the death of Jesus. The earth trembled, the rocks were burst to pieces, the vail of the temple was rent, the heavens were clothed in mourning, and the dead started into life. And no wonder, when the Lord of nature was expiring upon a cross. He subdued and calmed the stormy wind, and the boisterous waves of the sea. In short, he shewed an absolute sovereignty over universal nature, and managed the most unruly elements with a single word. Other conquerors have gone from country to country, carrying desolation along with them; Jesus went about doing good. His miraculous powers were but powers of miraculous mercy and beneficence. He could easily have advanced himself to a temporal kingdom, and routed all the forces of the earth; but he had no ambition of this kind. He that raised Lazarus from the grave could easily restore his soldiers to vigour and life, after they had been wounded or killed. He that fed five thousand with five loaves and two fishes, could have supported his army with plenty of provision in the greatest scarcity. He that walked upon the boisterous ocean, and enabled Peter to do the same, could easily have transported his forces from country to country, without the conveyance of ships. Nay, he was capable by his own single power to have gained universal conquest. What could all the armies of the earth have done against him, who struck an armed company down to the earth with only a word of his mouth? But these were not the victories he affected: Victories of grace, deliverances for the oppressed, salvation for the lost; these were his heroic actions. He glories in his being mighty to save. Isaiah lxiii. 1. When his warm disciples made a motion that he should employ his miraculous powers to punish the Samaritans who ungratefully refused him entertainment, he rebuked them, and answered like the Prince of Peace, *The Son of man is not come to destroy mens lives, but to save.* Luke ix. 56. *He came to seek and to save that which was lost.* Luke xix. 10. O how amiable a character this! How much more lovely the Saviour of sinners, the Deliverer of souls, than the enslavers and destroyers of mankind; which is the general character of the renowned heroes of our world? Who has ever performed such truly heroic and brave actions as this almighty conqueror? He has pardoned the most aggravated crimes, in a consistency with the honours of the divine government: he has delivered an innumerable multitude of immortal souls from the tyranny of sin and the powers of hell, set the prisoners free, and brought them into the liberty of the Son of God; he has peopled heaven with redeemed slaves, and advanced them to royal dignity. *All his subjects are kings.* Rev. i. 6. *To him that overcometh,* says he, *will I grant to sit with me in my throne, even as I also overcame, and am set down with my father in his throne.* Rev. iii. 21. They shall all be adorned with royal robes and crowns of unfading glory. They are advanced to empire over their lusts and passions, and all their enemies. Who ever gave such encouragement to his soldiers as this, *If we suffer with him, we know we shall also reign with him?* 2 Tim. ii. 12. What mortal general could bestow immortality and perfect happiness upon his favourites? But these boundless blessings Jesus has to bestow. In human governments merit is often neglected, and those who serve their country best are often rewarded with degradation. But none have ever served the King of kings in vain. The least good action, even the giving a cup of water to one of his necessitous saints, shall not pass unrewarded in his government.

Other kings have their arms, their swords, their cannon, and other instruments of destruction; and with these they acquire and defend their dominions. Jesus, our king, has his arms too, but O! of how different a kind! The force of evidence and conviction in his doctrine, attested with miracles, the energy of his dying love, the gentle, and yet efficacious influence of his holy spirit; these are the weapons with which he conquered the world. His gospel is the great magazine from whence his apostles, the first founders of his kingdom, drew their arms; and with these they subdued the nations to the obedience of faith. *The gospel*, says St. Paul, *is the power of God unto salvation*. Rom. i. 16. The humble doctrines of the cross became almighty, and bore down all before them, and after a time subdued the vast Roman empire which had subdued the world. The holy spirit gave edge and force to these weapons; and, blessed be God, though they are quite impotent without his assistance, yet when he concurs they are still successful. Many stubborn sinners have been unable to resist the preaching of Christ crucified: they have found him indeed the power of God. And is it not astonishing that any one should be able to stand it out against his dying love, and continue the enemy of his cross? *I*, says he, *if I be lifted up from the earth*, i e, if I be suspended on the cross, *will draw all men unto me.* John xii. 32. You see he expected his cross would be an irresistible weapon. And O! blessed Jesus, who can see thee expiring there in agonies of torture and love; who can see thy blood gushing in streams from every vein, who can hear thee there, and not melt into submission at thy feet! Is there one heart in this assembly proof against the energy of this bleeding, agonizing, dying love? Methinks such a sight must kindle a correspondent affection in your hearts towards him; and it is an exploit of wickedness, it is the last desperate effort of an impenetrable heart, to be able to resist.

Other conquerors march at the head of their troops, with all the ensigns of power and grandeur, and their forces numerous, inured to war, and well armed; and from such appearances and preparations who is there but what expects victory? But see the despised Nazarene, without riches, without arms, without forces, conflicting with the united powers of earth and hell; or see a company of poor fishermen and a tent-maker, with no other powers but those of doing good, with no other arms but those of reason, and the strange unpopular doctrines of a crucified Christ! see the professed followers of a master that was hung like a malefactor and a slave, see these men marching out to encounter the powers of darkness, the whole strength of the Roman empire, the lusts, prejudices, and interests of all nations, and travelling from country to country, without guards, without friends, exposed to insult and contempt, to the rage of persecution, to all manner of tormented deaths which earth or hell could invent: see this little army marching into the wide world, in these circumstances, and can you expect they will have any success? Does this appear a promising expedition? No; human reason would forebode they will soon be cut in pieces, and the christian cause buried with them. But these unpromising champions, with the aid of the Holy Spirit, conquered the world, and spread the religion of the crucified Jesus among all nations. It is true they lost their lives in the cause, like brave soldiers; but the cause did not die with them. Their blood proved the seed of the church. Their cause is immortal and invincible. Let devils in hell, let Heathens, Jews, and Mahometans, let Atheists, Free-thinkers, Papists, and persecutors of every character, do their worst; still this cause will live in spite of them. All the enemies of Christ will be obliged to confess at last, with Julian the apostate Roman emperor, who exerted all his art to abolish christianity; but, when mortally wounded in battle, outrageously sprinkled his blood towards heaven, and cried out, *Vicisti, O Galilæe!* " Thou has conquered, O Galilean !" Yes, my brethren, Jesus, the Prophet of Galilee, will push his conquest, from country to country, until all nations submit to him. And, blessed be his name, his victorious arm has reached to us in these ends of the earth: here he has subdued some obstinate rebels, and made their reluctant souls willingly bow in affectionate homage to him. And may I not produce some of you as the trophies of his victory? Has he not rooted out the enmity of your carnal minds, and sweetly constrained you to the most affectionate obedience? Thus, blessed Jesus! thus go on conquering, and to conquer. *Gird thy sword upon thy thigh, O most mighty!* and in thy glory and majesty ride prosperously through our land, and make this country a dutiful province of the dominion of thy grace. My brethren, should we all become his willing subjects, he would no longer suffer the perfidious slaves of France, and their savage allies, to chastise and punish us for our rebellion against him; but *peace should again run down like a river, and righteousness like a mighty stream.*

The kingdoms of the world have their rise, their progress, perfection, declension, and ruin. And in these things, the kingdom of Christ bears some resemblance to them, excepting that it shall never have an end.

Its rise was small at first, and it has passed through many revolutions in various ages. It was first founded in the family of Adam, but in about 1600 years, the space between the creation and the flood, it was almost demolished by the wickedness of the world; and at length confined to the little family of Noah. After the flood, the world soon fell into idolatry, but, that this kingdom of Christ might not be destroyed quite, it was erected in the family of Abraham; and among the Jews it continued until the coming of Christ in the flesh. This was indeed but the infancy of his kingdom, and indeed is seldom called by that name. It is the gospel constitution that is represented as the kingdom of Christ, in a special sense. This was but very small and unpromising at first. When its Founder was dying upon Calvary, and all his followers had forsaken him and fled, who would have thought it would ever have come to any thing, ever have recovered? But it revived with him; and, when he furnished his apostles with gifts and graces for their mission, and sent them forth to increase his kingdom, it made its progress through the world with amazing rapidity, notwithstanding it met with very early and powerful opposition. The Jews set themselves against it, and raised persecutions against its ministers, wherever they went. And presently the tyrant Nero employed all the power of the Roman empire to crush them. Peter, Paul, and thousands of the christians fell a prey to his rage, like sheep for the slaughter. This persecution was continued under his successors, with but little interruption, for about two hundred years.

But, under all these pressures, the church bore up her head; yea, the more she was trodden, the more she spread and flourished; and at length she was delivered from oppression by Constantine the Great, about the year 320. But now she had a more dangerous enemy to encounter, I mean prosperity: and this did her much more injury than all the persecutions of her enemies. Now the kingdom of Christ began to be corrupted with heresies: the ministry of the gospel, formerly the most dangerous posts in the world, now became a place of honour and profit, and men began to thrust themselves into it from principles of avarice and ambition; superstition and corruption of morals increased; and at length the Bishop of Rome set up for universal head of the church in the year 606, and gradually the whole monstrous system of popery was formed and established, and continued in force for near a thousand years. The kingdom of Christ was now at a low ebb; and tyranny and superstition reigned under that name over the greatest part of the christian world. Nevertheless our Lord still had his witnesses. The Waldenses and Albigenses, John Hus, and Jerome of Prague, and Wickliffe in England, opposed the torrent of corruption; until at length, Luther, Calvin, Zuinglius, and several others, were made the honoured instruments of introducing the Reformation from popery; when sundry whole kingdoms, which had given their power to the beast, and particularly our mother-country, shook off the papal authority, and admitted the pure light of the gospel. Since that time the kingdom of Christ has struggled hard, and it has lost ground in several countries; particularly in France, Poland, Bohemia, &c. where there once were many Protestant churches; but they are now in ruins. And, alas! those countries that still retain the reformed religion, have too generally reduced it into a mere formality; and it has but little influence upon the hearts and lives even of its professors. Thus we find the case remarkably among us. This gracious kingdom makes but little way in Virginia. The calamities of war and famine cannot, alas! draw subjects to it; but we seem generally determined to perish in our rebellion rather than submit. Thus it has been in this country from its first settlement; and how long it will continue in this situation is unknown to mortals: however, this we may know, it will not be so always. We have the strongest assurances that Jesus will yet take to him his great power, and reign in a more extensive and illustrious manner than he has ever yet done; and that the kingdoms of the earth shall yet become *the kingdoms of our Lord and of his Christ.* There are various parts of the heathen world where the gospel has never yet been; and the Jews have never yet been converted as a nation; but both the calling of the Jews and the fulness of the Gentiles, you will find plainly foretold in the 11th chapter to the Romans; and it is, no doubt, to render the accomplishment of this event the more conspicuous, that the Jews, who are dispersed all over the world, have, by a strange, unprecedented, and singular providence, been kept a distinct people to this day, for 1700 years; though all other nations have been so mixt and blended together, who were not half so much dispersed into different countries, that their distinct original cannot be traced. Posterity shall see this glorious event in some happy future period. How far it is from us, I will not determine: though, upon some grounds, I apprehend it is not very remote. I shall live and die in the unshaken belief that our guilty world shall yet see glorious days. Yes, my brethren, this despised gospel, that has so little effect in our age and country, shall yet shine like lightning, or like the sun, through all the dark regions of the earth. It shall triumph over Heathenism, Mahometism, Judaism, Popery, and all those dangerous errors that have infected the christian church. This gospel, poor negroes, shall yet reach your countryman, whom you left behind you in Africa, in darkness and the shadow of death, and bless your eyes with the light of salvation: and the Indian savages, that are now ravaging our country, shall yet be transformed into lambs and doves by the gospel of peace. The scheme of Providence is not yet completed, and much remains to be accomplished of what God has spoken by his prophets, to ripen the world for the universal judgement; but when all these things are finished, then proclamation shall be made through all nature, "That Time shall be no more:" then the Supreme Judge, the same Jesus that ascended the cross, will ascend the throne, and review the affairs of time: then will he put an end to the present course of nature, and the present form of administration. Then shall heaven and hell be filled with their respective inhabitants: then will time close, and eternity run on in one uniform tenor, without end. But the kingdom of Christ, though altered in its situation and form of government, will not then come to a conclusion. His kingdom is strictly the kingdom of heaven; and at the end of this world, his subjects will only be removed from these lower regions into a more glorious country, where they and their King shall live together for ever in the most endearing intimacy; where the noise and commotions of this restless world, the revolutions and perturbations of kingdoms, the terrors of war and persecution, shall no more reach them; but all will be perfect peace, love, and happiness, through immeasurable duration. This is the last and most illustrious state of the kingdom of Christ, now so small and weak in appearance: this is the final grand result of his administration: and it will appear to admiring worlds wisely planned, gloriously executed, and perfectly finished.

What conqueror ever erected such a kingdom! What subjects so completely, so lastingly happy, as those of the blessed Jesus!

SERMON XI.

Things unseen to be preferred to Things seen.

2 COR. iv. 18. *While we look not at the Things which are seen, but at the Things which are not seen; for the Things which are seen are temporal: but the Things which are not seen are eternal.*

AMONG all the causes of the stupid unconcernedness of sinners about religion, and the feeble endeavours of saints to improve in it, there is none more common or more effectual, than their not forming a due estimate of the things of time in comparison of those of eternity. Our present affairs engross all our thoughts, and exhaust all our activity, though they are but transitory trifles; while the awful realities of the future world are hid from our eyes by the veil of flesh and the clouds of ignorance. Did these break in upon our minds in all their almighty evidence and tremendous importance, they would annihilate the most majestic vanities of the present state, obscure the glare of earthly glory, render all its pleasures insipid, and give us a noble insensibility under all its sorrows. A realizing view of these would shock the libertine in his thoughtless career, tear off the hypocrite's mask, and inflame the devotion of languishing saints. The concern of mankind would then be how they might make a safe *exit* out of this world, and not how they may live happy in it. Present pleasure and pain would be swallowed up in the prospect of everlasting happiness or misery hereafter. Eternity, awful eternity, would then be our serious contemplation. The pleasures of sin would strike us with horror, if they issue in eternal pain, and our present afflictions, however tedious and severe, would appear but light and momentary, if they work out for us *a far more exceeding and eternal weight of glory*.

These were the views the apostle had of things, and these their effects upon him. He informs us in this chapter of his unwearied zeal to propagate the gospel amidst all the hardships and dangers that attended the painful discharge of his ministry. Though he bore about in his body the dying of the Lord Jesus, though he was always delivered unto death for Jesus' sake, yet he fainted not; and this was the prospect that animated him, that his *light afflictions, which was but for a moment, would work for him a far more exceeding and eternal weight of glory*. When we view his sufferings absolutely, without any reference to eternity, they were very heavy and of many years continuance; and when he represents them in this view, how moving is the relation! see 2. Cor. xi. 23—29. But when he views them in the light of eternity, and compared with their glorious issues, they sink into nothing: then scourging, stoning, imprisonment, and all the various deaths to which he was daily exposed, are but light, trifling afflictions, hardly worth naming; then a series of uninterrupted sufferings for many years are but afflictions that endure for a moment. And when he views a glorious futurity, human language cannot express the ideas he has of the happiness reserved for him; it is *a far more exceeding and eternal weight of glory*; a noble sentiment! and exprest in the sublimest manner the language of mortals can admit of.

It is glory, in opposition to affliction; a weight of glory, in opposition to light affliction; a massy oppressive blessedness, which it requires all the powers in the soul, in their full exertion, to support: and in opposition to affliction for a moment, it is eternal glory: to finish all, it is a *far more exceeding glory**. What greater idea can be grasped by the human mind, or expressed in the feeble language of mortality! Nothing but feeling that weight of glory could enlarge his conception; and nothing but the dialect of heaven could better express it. No wonder that, with this view of things, *he should reckon that the sufferings of the present life are not worthy to be compared with the glory that shall be revealed*. Rom. viii. 18.

The apostle observes, that he formed this estimate of things, while he looked not at the "things which are seen, but at those which are not seen." By the things that are seen, are meant the present life, and all the things of time; all the pleasures and pains,

---

* The original far surpasses the best translation. The adjective absolute (τὸ ἐλαφρὸν τῆς θλίψεως) is very significant; and καθ᾽ ὑπερβολὴν εἰς ὑπερβολὴν is inimitable in our language.

Serm. 11. *preferred to Things seen.*

all the labours, pursuits, and amusements of the present state. By the things that are not seen, are intended all the invisible realities of the eternal world; all the beings, the enjoyments and sufferings that lie beyond the reach of human sight; as the great Father of spirits, the joys of paradise, and the punishments of hell. We look on these invisible things, and not on those that are seen. This seems like a contradiction; but it is easily solved by understanding this act, described by looking, to be the act not of the bodily eye, but of faith and enlightened reason. Faith is defined by this apostle to be *the substance of things hoped for, and the evidence of things not seen.* Heb. xi. 1. And it is the apostle's chief design in that chapter, to give instances of the surprising efficacy of such a realizing belief of eternal invisible things; see particularly ver. 10, 13, 14, 16, 25, 26, 27. Hence to look not at visible, but invisible things, signifies that the apostle made the latter the chief objects of his contemplations, that he was governed in the whole of his conduct by the impression of eternal things, and not by the present; that he formed his maxims and schemes from a comprehensive survey of futurities, and not from a partial view of things present; and, in short, that he acted as an expectant of eternity, and not as an everlasting inhabitant of this wretched world. This he elsewhere expresses in equivalent terms, *We walk by faith, and not by sight.* 2 Cor. v. 7.

Further, he assigns a reason why he had a greater regard to invisible things than visible in the regulating of his conduct; *for the things which are seen are temporal; but the things which are not seen,* says he, *are eternal.* An important reason indeed! Eternity annexed to a trifle would advance it into infinite importance, but when it is the attribute of the most perfect happiness, or of the most exquisite misery, then it transcends all comparison: then all temporal happiness and misery, however great and long continued, shrink into nothing, is drowned and lost, like the small drop of a bucket in the boundless ocean.

My present design, and the contents of the text, prescribe to me the following method:

I. I shall give you a comparative view of visible and invisible things, that you may see the trifling nature of the one, and the importance of the other. This I choose to do under one head, because by placing these two classes of things in an immediate opposition, we may the more easily compare them, and see their infinite disparity. And,

II. I shall shew you the great and happy influence a suitable impression of the superior importance of invisible to visible things would have upon us.

I. I shall give you a comparative view of visible and invisible things; and we may compare visible and invisible things, as to their intrinsic value, and as to their duration.

1. As to their intrinsic value; and in this respect the disparity is inconceivable.

This I shall illustrate in the two comprehensive instances of pleasure and pain. To shun the one, and obtain the other, is the natural effort of the human mind. This is its aim in all its endeavours and pursuits. The innate desire of happiness and aversion to misery are the two great springs of all human activity; and, were these springs relaxed or broken, all business would cease, all activity would stagnate, and universal torpor would seize the world. And these principles are co-existent with the soul itself, and will continue in full vigour in a future state. Nay, as the soul will then be matured, and all its powers arrived to their complete perfection, this eagerness after happiness, and aversion to misery, will be also more quick and vigorous. The soul in its present state of infancy, like a young child, or a man enfeebled and stupified by sickness, is incapable of very deep sensations of pleasure and pain; and hence an excess of joy, as well as sorrow, has sometimes dissolved its feeble union with the body. On this account we are incapable of such degrees of happiness or misery from the things of this world as beings of more lively sensations might receive from them: and much more are we incapable of the happiness or misery of the future world, until we have put on immortality. We cannot see God and live. Should the glory of heaven blaze upon us in all its insuperable splendour, it would overwhelm our feeble nature; we could not support such a weight of glory. And one twinge of the agonies of hell would dislodge the soul from its earthly mansion: one pang would convulse and stupify it, were not its powers strengthened by the separation from the body. But in the future world all the powers of the soul will be mature and strong, and the body will be clothed with immortality; the union between them after the resurrection will be inseparable, and able to support the most oppressive weight of glory, or the most intolerable load of torment. Hence it follows that pleasure and pain include all that we can desire or fear in the present or future world; and therefore a comparative view of present and future pleasure and pain is sufficient to enable us to form a due estimate of visible and invisible things. By present pleasure, I mean all the happiness we can receive from present things, as from riches, honours, sensual gratifications, learning, and intellectual improvements, and all the amusements and exercises of this life. And by future pleasure, or the pleasure which results from invisible things, I mean all the fruitions and enjoyments in which heavenly happiness consists. By present pain, I intend all the uneasiness which we can receive from the things of the present life; as poverty, losses, disappointments, bereavements, sickness, and bodily pains. And by future pain, I mean all the punishments of hell; as banishment from God, and a privation of all created blessings, the agonizing reflections of a guilty conscience, the horrid company and exprobations of infernal ghosts, and the torture of infernal flames.

Now let us put these in the balance, and the one will sink into nothing, and the other rise into infinite importance.

Temporal things are of a contracted nature, and not adequate to the capacities of the human soul; but eternal things are great, and capable of communicating all the happiness and misery which it can receive. The soul in its present state is not capable of such degrees of happiness and misery as it will be in the future, when it dwells among invisible realities. All that pleasure and pain which we receive from things that are seen, is intermingled with some ingredients of a contrary nature; but those proceeding from things that are not seen, are pure and unmingled.

1. Visible things are not equal to the capacities of the human soul. This little spark of being, the soul, which lies obscured in this prison of flesh, gives frequent discoveries of surprising powers: its desires in particular have a kind of infinity. But all temporary objects are mean and contracted; they cannot afford it a happiness equal to its capacity, nor render it as miserable as its capacity of suffering will bear. Hence, in the greatest affluence of temporal enjoyments, in the midst of honours, pleasures, riches, friends, &c. it still feels a painful void within, and finds an unknown something wanting to complete its happiness. Kings have been unhappy upon their thrones, and all their grandeur have been but majestic misery. So Solomon found it, who had opportunity and curiosity to make the experiment; and this is his verdict upon all earthly enjoyments, after the most impartial trial, " Vanity of vanities," saith the preacher, " Vanity of vanities; all is vanity and vexation of spirit." On the other hand, the soul may possess some degree of happiness, under all the miseries it is capable of suffering from external and temporal things. Guilt indeed denies it this support; but if there be no intestine broils, no anguish resulting from its own reflections, not all the visible things can render it perfectly miserable; its capacity of suffering is not put to its utmost stretch. This has been attested by the experience of multitudes who have suffered for righteousness sake. But, O, when we take a survey of invisible things, we find them all great and majestic, not only equal but infinitely superior to the most enlarged powers the human and even of the angelic nature. In the eternal world the great Invisible dwells, and there he acts with his own immediate hand. It is he that immediately communicates happiness through the heavenly regions; and it is his immediate breath that, like a stream of brimstone, kindles the flames of hell: whereas in the present world he rarely communicates happiness,

and inflicts punishment, but by the instrumentality of creatures; and it is impossible the extremes of either should be communicated through this channel. This the infinite God alone can do, and, though in the future world he will use his creatures to heighten the happiness or misery of each other, yet he will have a more immediate agency in them himself. He will communicate happiness immediately from himself, the infinite fountain of it, into the vessels of mercy: and he will immediately shew his wrath, and make his power known upon the vessels of wrath. I may add, that those creatures, angels and devils, which will be the instruments of happiness or misery to the human soul in the invisible world, are incomparably more powerful than any in this; and consequently capable of contributing more to our pleasure or pain. And let me also observe, that all the objects about which our faculties will be employed then, will be great and majestic; whereas, at present, we grovel among little sordid things. The objects of our contemplation will then be either the unveiled glories of the divine nature, and the naked wonders of creation, providence, and redemption; or the terrors of divine justice, the dreadful nature and aggravations of our sin, the horrors of everlasting punishment, &c. And since this is the case, how little should we regard the things that are seen, in comparison of them that are not seen? But though visible things were adequate to our present capacities, yet they are not to be compared with the things that are not seen, because,

2. The soul is at present in a state of infancy, and incapable of such degrees of pleasure or pain as it can bear in the future world. The enjoyments of this life are like the play-things of children; and none but childish souls would trifle with them, or fret and vex themselves or one another about them; but the invisible realities before us are manly and great, and such as an adult soul ought to concern itself with. The soul in another world can no more be happy or miserable from such toys, than men can be happy or wretched in the possession or loss of the baubles of children; it will then demand great things to give it pleasure or pain. The apostle illustrates this matter in this manner. 1. Cor. xiii. 9, 10, 11. How foolish is it then to be chiefly governed by these puerilities, while we neglect the manly concern of eternity, that can make our souls perfectly happy or miserable, when their powers are come to perfection!

3. And lastly, All the happiness and misery of the present state, resulting from things that are seen, are intermingled with contrary ingredients. We are never so happy in this world, as to have no uneasiness; in the greatest affluence we languish for want of some absent good, or grieve under some incumbent evil. On the other hand, we are never so miserable as to have no ingredient of hap-

piness. When we labour under a thousand calamities, we may still see ourselves surrounded with, perhaps, an equal number of blessings. And where is there a wretch so miserable as to endure simple unmingled misery without one comfortable ingredient? But in the invisible world there is an eternal separation made between good and evil, pleasure and pain: and they shall never mingle more. In heaven the rivers of pleasures flow untroubled with a drop of sorrow; in hell, there is not a drop of water to mitigate the fury of the flame. And who then would not prefer the things that are not seen to those that are seen? Especially, if we consider,

2. The infinite disparity between them as to duration. This is the difference particularly intended in the text; *the things that are seen are temporal; but the things that are not seen are eternal.*

The transitoriness of visible things, implies, both that the things themselves are perishable, and they may soon leave us; and that our residence among them is temporary, and we must soon leave them.

And the eternity of invisible things implies the quite contrary, that the things themselves are of endless duration; and that we shall always exist to receive happiness or misery from them.

Before we illustrate these instances of disparity, let us take a view of Time and Eternity in themselves, and as compared to one another.

Time is the duration of creatures in the present state. It commenced at the creation, and near 6000 years of it are since elapsed; and how much of it yet remains we know not. But this we know, that the duration of the world itself is as nothing in comparison of eternity. But what is our duration compared with the duration even of this world? It is but a span, an hair's breadth; sixty, seventy, or eighty years, is generally the highest standard of human life, and it is by far the smallest number of mankind that arrives to these periods. The most of them die like a flower blasted in the morning, or at noon; and we have more reason to expect it will be our fate than to hope the contrary. Now the span of time we enjoy in life is all our time; we have no more property in the rest of it than in the years before the flood. All beside is eternity. "Eternity!" We are alarmed at the sound! Lost in the prospect! Eternity with respect to God, is a duration without beginning as well as without end: Eternity, as it is the attribute of human nature, is a duration that had a beginning but shall never have an end. This is inalienably entailed upon us poor dying worms: and let us survey our inheritance. Eternity! it is a duration that excludes all number and computation; days, and months, and years, yea, and ages are lost in it, like drops in the ocean. Millions of millions of years, as many years as there are sands on the sea shore, or particles of dust in the globe of the earth, and these multiplied to the highest reach of number, all these are nothing to eternity. They do not bear the least imaginable proportion to it; for these will come to an end, as certain as day; but eternity will never, never come to an end. It is a line without end; it is an ocean without a shore. Alas! what shall I say of it! It is an infinite unknown something, that neither human thought can grasp, nor human language describe.

Now place time in comparison with eternity, and what is it? It shrinks into nothing, and less than nothing. What then is that little span of time in which we have any property? Alas! it is too diminutive a point to be conceived. Indeed, properly speaking, we can call no part of time our own but the present moment, this fleeting *now:* future time is uncertain, and we may never enjoy it; the breath we now respire may be our last; and as to our past time, it is gone, and will never be ours again. Our past days are dead and buried, though perhaps guilt, their ghost, may haunt us still. And what is a moment to eternity? The disparity is too great to admit of comparison.

Let me now resume the former particulars, implied in the transitoriness of visible and eternity of invisible things.

Visible things are perishable, and may soon leave us. When we think they are ours, they often fly from our embrace. Riches may vanish into smoke and ashes by an accidental fire. We may be thrown down from the pinnacle of honour, and sink the lower into disgrace. Sensual pleasures often end in satiety and disgust, or in sickness and death. Our friends are tore from our bleeding hearts by the inexorable hand of death. Our liberty and property may be wrested from us by the hand of tyranny, oppression, or fraud. In a word, what do we enjoy but we may lose? On the other hand, our miseries here are temporary; the heart receives many a wound, but it heals again. Poverty may end in riches; a clouded character may clear up, and from disgrace we may rise to honour; we may recover from sickness; and if we lose one comfort, we may obtain another. But in eternity every thing is everlasting and unchangeable. Happiness and misery are both of them without end; and the subjects of both well know that this is the case. It is this perpetuity that finishes that happiness of the inhabitants of heaven; the least suspicion of an end would intermingle itself with all their enjoyments, and embitter them; and the greater the happiness, the greater the anxiety at the expectation of losing it. But, O how transporting for the saints on high to look forward through the succession of eternal ages, with an assurance that they shall be happy through them all, and that they shall feel no change but from glory to glory! On the other hand, this is the bitterest ingredient in the cup of divine displeasure in the future state, that the misery is eternal. O with what horror does that despairing cry, Forever, forever, forever! echo through the vaults of hell! Eternity is such an important attribute, that it gives infinite weight to things that would be infignificant, were they temporary. A small degree of happiness, if it be eternal, exceeds the greatest degree that is transitory; and a small degree of misery that is everlasting, of greater importance than the greatest degree that soon comes to an end. Would you rather endure the most painful tortures that nature can bear for a moment, than an eternal tooth-ach or head-ach? Again, should we consider, all the ingredients and causes of future happiness and misery, we should find them all everlasting. The blessed God is an inexhaustible perennial fountain of bliss; his image can never be erased from the hearts of glorified spirits; the great contemplation will always lie obvious to them; and they will always exist as the partakers and promoters of mutual bliss. On the other hand, in hell the worm of conscience dieth not, and the fire is not quenched; divine justice is immortal; malignant spirits will always exist as mutual tormentors, and their wicked habits will never be extirpated.

And now, need I offer any thing farther to convince you of the superior importance of invisible and eternal to visible and temporary things? Can a rational creature be at a loss to choose in so plain a case? Can you need any arguments to convince you that an eternity of the most perfect happiness is rather to be chosen than a few years of sordid unsatisfying delight? Or that the former should not be forfeited for the sake of the latter? Have you any remaining scruples, whether the little anxieties and mortifications of a pious life are more intolerable than everlasting punishment? O! it is a plain case: what then mean an infatuated world, who lay out all their concern on temporal things, and neglect the important affairs of eternity; Let us illustrate this matter by a supposition. Suppose a bird were to pick up and carry away a grain of sand or dust from the globe of the earth once in a thousand years, till it should be at length wholly carried away; the duration which this would take up appears a kind of eternity to us. Now suppose it were put to our choice, either to be happy during this time, and miserable ever after, or to be miserable during this time, and happy ever after, which would you choose? Why, though this duration seems endless, yet he would be a fool that would not make the latter choice; for, O! behind this vast duration, there lies an eternity, which exceeds it infinitely more than this duration exceeds a moment. But we have no such seemingly puzzling choice as this; the matter with us stands thus— Will you choose the little sordid pleasures of sin that may perhaps not last an hour, at most not many years, rather than everlasting pleasure of the sublimest kind? Will you rather endure intolerable torment forever, than painfully endeavour to be holy! What does your conduct, my brethren, answer to these questions? If your tongues reply, they will perhaps for your credit give a right answer; but what say your prevailing disposition and common practice? Are you not more thoughtful for time than eternity? more concerned about visible vanities than invisible realities? If so, you make a fool's choice indeed.

But let it be further considered, that the transitoriness of invisible things may imply that we must ere long be removed from them. Though they were immortal it would be nothing to us, since we are not so in our present state. Within a few years, at most, we shall be beyond the reach of all happiness and misery from temporal things.

But when we pass out of this transitory state, we enter upon an everlasting state. Our souls will always exist; exist in a state of unchangeable, boundless happiness or misery. It is but a little while since we came in to being out of a state of eternal non-existence; but we shall never relapse into that state again. These little sparks of being shall never be extinguished; they will survive the ruins of the world, and kindle into immortality. When millions of millions of ages are past, we shall still be in existence; and O! in what unknown region? In that of endless bliss, or of interminable misery!—Be this the most anxious inquiry of our lives!

Seeing then we must soon leave this world, and all its joys and sorrows, and seeing we must enter on an unchangeable everlasting state of happiness or misery, be it our chief concern to end our present pilgrimage well. It matters but little whether we lie easy or not during this night of existence, if so be we awake in eternal day. It is but a trifle, hardly worth a thought, whether we be happy or miserable here, if we be happy for ever hereafter. What then mean the bustle and noise of mankind about the things of time? O, sirs! eternity, awful all-important eternity, is the only thing that deserves a thought. I come,

II. To shew the great and happy influence a suitable impression of the superior importance of invisible to visible things would have upon us. This I might exemplify in a variety of instances with respect to saints and sinners.

When we are tempted to any unlawful pleasures, how would we shrink away with horror from the pursuit, had we a due sense of the misery incurred, and the happiness forfeited by it!

When we find our hearts excessively eager after things below, had we a suitable view of eternal things, all these things would shrink into trifles hardly worth a thought, much less our principal concern.

When the sinner, for the sake of a little present ease, and to avoid a little present uneasiness, stifles his conscience, refuses to examine his condition, cafts the thoughts of eternity out of his mind, and thinks it too hard to attend painfully on all the means of grace, has he then a due eftimate of eternal things? Alas! no; he only looks at the things that are feen. Were the mouth of hell open before him, that he might behold its torments, and had he a fight of the joys of paradife, they would harden him into a generous infenfibility of all the forrows and anxieties of this life, and his inquiry would not be, Whether thefe things required of him are eafy? but, Whether they are neceffary to obtain eternal happinefs, and avoid everlafting mifery?

When we fuffer any reproach or contempt on a religious account, how would a due eftimate of eternal things fortify us with undaunted courage, and makes us willing to climb to heaven through difgrace, rather than fink to hell with general applaufe!

How would a realizing view of eternal things animate us in our devotions? Were this thought impreffed on our hearts when in the fecret or focial duties of religion, " I am now acting for eternity," do you think we fhould pray, read, or hear with fo much indifferency and languor? O no; it would roufe us out of our dead frames, and call forth all the vigour of our fouls. With what unwearied importunity fhould we cry to God! with what eagernefs hear the word of falvation!

How powerful an influence would a view of futurity have to alarm the fecure finner that has thought little of eternity all his life, though it be the only thing worth thinking of!

How would it haften the determination of the lingering, wavering finner, and fhock him at the thought of living one day unprepared on the very brink of eternity!

In a word, a fuitable impreffion of this would quite alter the afpect of things in the world, and would turn the concern and activity of the world into another channel. Eternity then would be the principal concern. Our inquiries would not be, Who will fhew us any temporal good? What fhall we eat, or what fhall we drink? But, What fhall we do to be faved? How fhall we efcape the wrath to come? Let us then endeavour to imprefs our hearts with invifible things, and for that purpofe confider, that

We fhall, ere long, be ingulphed in this awful eternity, whether we think of it or not. A few days or years will lanuch us there; and O, the furprifing fcenes that will then open to us!—

Without deep impreffions of eternity on our hearts, and frequent thoughtfulnefs about it, we cannot be prepared for it.

And if we are not prepared for it, O, how inconceivably miferable our cafe! But if prepared, how inconceivably happy!

Look not then at the things which are feen, but at the things which are not feen; for the things which are feen are temporal: but the things which are not feen are eternal.

SERMON XII.

The Sacred Import of the Chriſtian Name.

Acts xi. 26. *The Diſciples were called Chriſtians firſt at Antioch.*

MERE names are empty ſounds, and but of little conſe‑quence: and yet it muſt be owned there are names of ho‑nour and ſignificancy; and, when they are attended with the things ſignified by them, they are of great and ſacred importance. Such is the Chriſtian name; a name about ſeventeen hundred years old. And now, when the name is almoſt loſt in party-diſ‑tinctions, and the thing is almoſt loſt in ignorance, error, vice, hypocriſy, and formality, it may be worth our while to conſider the original import of that ſacred name, as a proper expedient to recover both name and thing.

The name of Chriſtian was not the firſt by which the follow‑ers of Chriſt were diſtinguiſhed. Their enemies called them Ga‑lileans, Nazarenes, and other names of contempt: and among themſelves they were called Saints, from their holineſs; Diſci‑ples, from their learning their religion from Chriſt as their teach‑er; Believers, from their believing in him as the Meſſiah; and Brethren, from their mutual love and their relation to God and each other. But after ſome time they were diſtinguiſhed by the name of Chriſtians. This they firſt received in Antioch, an hea‑then city, a city infamous for all manner of vice and debauchery; a city that had its name from Antiochus Epiphanes, the bittereſt enemy the church of the Jews ever had. A city very rich and powerful, from whence the chriſtian name would have an exten‑five circulation; but it is long ſince laid in ruin, unprotected by that ſacred name: in ſuch a city was Chriſt pleaſed to confer his name upon his followers: and you cannot but ſee that the very choice of the place diſcovers his wiſdom, grace, and juſtice.

The original word, which is here rendered *called*, ſeems to in‑timate, that they were called chriſtians by divine appointment, for it generally ſignifies an oracular nomination, or a declaration from God; and to this purpoſe it is generally tranſlated.* Hence

---

* It is this word that is uſed, Matt. ii. 12. Καὶ χρηματιϑέντες, being warned of God, and the like in Matt. ii. 22. So in Rom. xi. 4. χρηματισμος, is render-

Serm. 12.   *the Christian Name.*   227

it follows, that the very name christian, as well as the thing, was a divine original; assumed not by a private agreement of the disciples among themselves, but by the appointment of God. And in this view it is a remarkable accomplishment of an old prophecy of Isaiah, chapter lxii. 2. *The Gentiles shall see thy righteousness, and all kings thy glory, and thou shalt be called by a new name, which the mouth of the Lord shall name.* So *Isaiah* lxv. 15. *The Lord shall call his servants by another name.*

This name was at first confined to few; but it soon had a surprisingly extensive propagation thro' the world. In many countries, indeed, it was lost, and miserably exchanged for that of Heathen, Mahometan, or Musselman. Yet the European nations still retain the honor of wearing it. A few scattered christians are also still to be found here and there in Asia and Africa, though crushed under the oppressions of Mahometans and Pagans. This name has likewise crossed the wide ocean to the wilderness of America, and is worn by the sundry European colonies on this continent. We, in particular, call ourselves christians, and should take it ill to be denied the honour of that distinction. But do we not know the meaning and sacred import of that name? Do we not know what it is to be christans indeed? That is, to be in reality what we are in name: certainly it is time for us to consider the matter; and it is my present design that we should do so.

Now we may consider this name in various views: particularly as a name of distinction from the rest of the world, who know not the Lord Jesus, or reject him as an impostor;—as a patronymic name, pointing out the Father and Founder of our holy religion and the christain church;—as a badge of our relation to Christ as his servants, his children, his bride;—as intimating our unction by the holy spirit, or our being the subjects of his influences; as Christ was anointed by the holy spirit, or replenished with his gifts above measure (for you are to observe that *anointed* is the English of the Greek name *Christ* and of the Hebrew, *Messiah**): and as a name of appropriation, signifying that we are the property of Christ, and his peculiar people. Each of these parti-

ed the answer of God. Rom. vii. 3. χρηματισει, she shall be called, (viz. by the divine law) an adultress. Luke ii. 26, χρηματισμον, it was revealed to him by the Holy Ghost. Acts x. 22. εχρηματισθι, was warned from God. Heb. viii. 5, Κεχρηματισαι Μωσης, Moses was admonished of God. Heb. xi. 7. Noah being warned of God, χρηματισθεις. Heb. xii. 25. If they escaped not, who refused Him that spake on earth; viz. by divine inspiration. These are all the places perhaps in which the word is used in the New Testament; and in all these it seems to mean a revelation from God, or something oracular. And this is a strong presumption that the word is to be so understood in the text.

* Psalm cv. 15. Touch not my Christs; that is, my anointed people.—So the *Seventy*.

culars might be profitably illustrated.* But my present design confines me to consider the Christian name only in two views; namely, as a catholic name, intended to bury all party denominations; and as a name of obligation upon all that wear it to be christians indeed, or to form their temper and practice upon the sacred model of christianity.

I. Let us consider the christian name as a catholic name, intended to bury all party denominations.

The name Gentile was odious to the Jews, and the name Jew was odious to the Gentiles. The name christian swallows up both in one common and agreeable appellation. He that hath taken down the partition-wall, has taken away partition-names, and united all his followers in his own name, as a common denomination. For now, says Paul, *there is neither Greek nor Jew, circumcision nor uncircumcision, barbarian, Scythian, bond nor free; but Christ is all and in all.* Col. iii. 11. And *ye are all one in Christ Jesus.* Gal. iii. 28. According to a prophecy of Zechariah *The Lord shall be king over all the earth; and in that day there shall be one Lord, and his name one.* Zech. xiv. 9.

It is but a due honour to Jesus Christ, the founder of christianity, that all who profess his religion should wear his name; and they pay an extravagant and even idolatrous compliment to his subordinate officers and ministers, when they take their denomination from them. Had this humour prevailed in the primitive church, instead of the common name christians, there would have been as many party-names as there were apostles or eminent ministers. There would have been Paulites from Paul; Peterites from Peter; Johnites from John; Barnabites from Barnabas, &c. Paul took pains to crush the first risings of this party-spirit in those churhes which he planted; particularly in Corinth, where it most prevailed. While they where saying, *I am of Paul; and I of Apollos; and I of Cephas; and I of Christ,* he puts this pungent question to them: " Is Christ divided ? Are his servants the ringleaders of so many parties? Was Paul crucified for you ? or were ye baptized in or into the name of Paul, that ye should be so fond to take your name from him? He counted it a happiness that providence had directed him to such a conduct as gave no umbrage of encouragement to such a humour. *I thank God,* says he *that I baptized none of you, but Crispus and Gaius: lest any should take occasion to say, I baptized into my own name, and was gathering a party for myself.* 1 Cor. i. 12—15.

But alas! how little has this convictive reasoning of the apostle been regarded in the future ages of the church? What an endless

* See a fine illustration of them in Dr. Grosvenor's excellent Essay on the Christian Name; from whom I am not ashamed to borrow several amiable sentiments.

variety of denominations taken from some men of character, or from some little peculiarities, has prevailed in the christian world, and crumbled it to pieces, while the christian name is hardly regarded? Not to take notice of Jesuits, Jansenists, Dominicans, Franciscans, and other denominations and orders in the popish church, where, having corrupted the thing, they act very consistently to lay aside the name, what party-names have been adopted by the protestant churches, whose religion is substantially the same common christianity, and who agree in much more important articles than in those they differ; and who therefore might peaceably unite under the common name of Christians? We have Lutherans, Calvinists, Arminians, Zuinglians, Churchmen, Presbyterians, Independents, Baptists, and a long list of names which I cannot now enumerate. To be a christian is not enough now-a-days, but a man must also be something more and better; that is, he must be a strenuous bigot to this or that particular church. But where is the reason or propriety of this? I may indeed believe the same things which Luther or Calvin believed; but I do not believe them on the authority of Luther or Calvin, but upon the sole authority of Jesus Christ, and therefore I should not call myself by their name, as one of their disciples, but by the name of Christ, whom alone I acknowledge as the Author of my religion, and my only master and Lord. If I learn my religion from one of these great men, it is indeed proper I should assume their name. If I learn it from a parliament or convocation, and make their acts and canons the rule and ground of my faith, then it is enough for me to be of the established religion, be that what it will: I may with propriety be called a mere conformist; that is my highest character: but I cannot be properly called a christian; for a christian learns his religion, not from acts of parliament or from the determinations of councils, but from Jesus Christ and his gospel.

To guard against mistakes on this head, I would observe that every man has a natural and legal right to judge and choose for himself in matters of religion; and that is a mean supple soul indeed, and utterly careless about all religion, that makes a compliment of this right to any man, or body of men upon earth, whether pope, king, parliament, convocation, or synod. In the exercise of this right, and searching for himself, he will find that he agrees more fully in lesser as well as more important articles with some particular church than others; and thereupon it is his duty to join in stated communion with that church; and he may, if he pleases, assume the name which that church wears, by way of distinction from others: this is not what I condemn. But for me to glory in the denomination of any particular church, as my highest character; to lay more stress upon the name of a presbyterian or a churchman, than on the sacred name of christian; to make a punctilious agreement with my sentiments in the little peculiarities of a party the test of all religion; to make it the object of my zeal to gain proselytes to some other than the christian name; to connive at the faults of those of my own party, and to be blind to the good qualities of others, or invidiously to misrepresent or diminish them; these are the things which deserve universal condemnation from God and man; these proceed from a spirit of bigotry and faction, directly opposite to the generous catholic spirit of christianity, and subversive of it. And yet how common is this spirit among all denominations! And what mischief has it done in the world! Hence proceed contentions and animosities, uncharitable suspicions and censures, slander and detraction, partiality and unreasonable prejudices, and a hideous group of evils, which I cannot now describe. This spirit also hinders the progress of serious practical religion, by turning the attention of men from the great concerns of eternity, and the essentials of christianity, to vain jangling and contest about circumstances and trifles. Thus the christian is swallowed up in the partisan, and fundamentals lost in extra-essentials.

My brethren, I would now warn you against this wretched mischievous spirit of party. I would not have you entirely sceptical and undetermined even about the smaller points of religion, the modes and forms, which are the matters of contention between different churches; nor would I have you quite indifferent what particular church to join with in stated communion. Endeavour to find out the truth, even in these circumstantials, at least so far as is necessary for the direction of your own conduct. But do not make these the whole or the principal part of your religion: do not be excessively zealous about them, nor break the peace of the church by magisterially imposing them upon others. 'Hast thou faith in these little disputables,' It is well; 'but have it to thyself before God,' and do not disturb others with it. You may, if you please, call yourselves presbyterians and dissenters, and you shall bear without shame or resentment all the names of reproach and contempt which the world may brand you with. But as you should not be mortified on the one side, so neither should you glory on the other. A christian! a christian! let that be your highest distinction; let that be the name which you labour to deserve. God forbid that my ministry should be the occasion of diverting your attention to any thing else. But I am so happy that I can appeal to yourselves, whether I have during several years of my ministry among you, laboured to instil into you the principles of bigotry, and make you warm proselytes to a party: or whether it has not been the great object of my zeal to inculcate upon you the grand essentials of our holy religion, and make you sincere practical chriſtians. Alas! my dear people, unleſs I ſucceed in this, I labour to very little purpoſe, though I ſhould preſbyterianize the whole colony.

Calumny and ſlander it is hoped, have by this time talked themſelves out of breath; and the lying ſpirit may be at a loſs for materials to form a popular plauſible falſehood, which is likely to be credited where the diſſenters are known. But you have heard formerly, and ſome of you may ſtill hear ſtrange and uncommon ſurmiſes, wild conjectures, and moſt diſmal inſinuations. But if you would know the truth at once, if you would be fully informed by one that beſt knows what religion I am of, I will tell you (with Mr. Baxter) 'I am a chriſtian, a mere chriſtian; of no other religion: my church is the chriſtian church.' The Bible! the Bible! is my religion; and if I am a diſſenter, I diſſent only from modes and forms of religion which I cannot find in my Bible; and which therefore I conclude have nothing to do with religion, much leſs ſhould they be made terms of chriſtian communion, ſince Chriſt, the only lawgiver of his church, has not made them ſuch. Let this congregation be that of a chriſtian ſociety, and I little care what other name it wears. Let it be a little Antioch, where the followers of Chriſt ſhall be diſtinguiſhed by their old catholic name, Chriſtians. To bear and deſerve this character, let this be our ambition, this our labour. Let popes pronounce, and councils decree what they pleaſe; let ſtateſmen aud eccleſiaſtics preſcribe what to believe: as for us, let us ſtudy our Bibles: let us learn of Chriſt; and if we are not dignified with the ſmiles, or enriched with the emoluments of an eſtabliſhment, we ſhall have his approbation, who is the only Lord and Sovereign of the realm of conſcience, and by whoſe judgment we muſt ſtand or fall for ever.

But it is time for me to proceed to conſider the other view of the chriſtian name, on which I intend principally to inſiſt; and that is,

II. As a name of obligation upon all that wear it to be chriſtians indeed, or to form their temper and practice upon the ſacred model of chriſtianity. The proſecution of this ſubject will lead me to anſwer this important inquiry, What is it to be a Chriſtian?

To be a chriſtian, in the popular and faſhionable ſenſe, is no difficult or excellent thing. It is to be baptized, to profeſs the chriſtian religion, to believe, like our neighbours, that Chriſt is the Meſſiah, and to attend upon public worſhip once a week, in ſome church or other that bears only the chriſtian name. In this ſenſe a man may be a chriſtian, and yet be habitually careleſs about eternal things; a chriſtian, and yet fall ſhort of the morality of many of the heathens; a chriſtian, and yet a drunkard, a ſwearer, or a ſlave to ſome vice or other; a chriſtian, and yet a wilful impenitent offender againſt God and man. To be a chriſtian in this sense is no high character ; and, if this be the whole of christianity, it is very little matter whether the world be christianized or not. But is this to be a christian in the original and proper sense of the word? No; that is something of a very different and superior kind. To be a christian indeed, is the highest character and dignity of which the human nature is capable : it is the most excellent thing that ever adorned our world : it is a thing that Heaven itself beholds with approbation and delight.

To be a christian is to be like to Christ, from whom the name is taken : it is to be a follower and imitator of him ; to be possessed of his spirit and temper ; and to live as he lived in the world : it is to have those just, exalted, and divine notions of God and divine things, and that just and full view of our duty to God and man, which Christ taught : in short, it is to have our sentiments, our temper, and practice formed upon the sacred model of the gospel. Let me expatiate a little upon this amiable character.

1. To be a christian, is to depart from iniquity. To this the name obliges us; and without this we have no title to the name; —*Let every one that nameth the name of Christ, depart from iniquity*, 2 Tim. ii. 19. ; that is, let him depart from iniquity, or not dare to touch that sacred name. Christ was perfectly free from sin ; he was *holy, harmless, undefiled, and separate from sinners*. His followers also shall be perfectly free from sin in a little time ; ere long they will enter into the pure regions of perfect holiness, and will drop all their sins, with their mortal bodies, into the grave. But this, alas! is not their character in the present state, but the remains of sin still cleave to them. Yet, even in the present state, they are labouring after perfection in holiness. Nothing can satisfy them until they are conformed to the image of God's dear Son. They are hourly conflicting with every temptation, and vigorously resisting every iniquity in its most alluring forms. And, though sin is perpetually struggling for the mastery, and sometimes in an inadvertent hour, gets an advantage over them, yet, as they are not under the law, but under grace, they are assisted with recruits of grace, so that no sin has any habitual dominion over them. Rom. vi. 14. Hence they are free from the gross vices of the age, and are men of good morals. This is their habitual universal character ; and to pretend to be christians without this requisite, is the greatest absurdity.

What then shall we think of the drunken, swearing, debauched, defrauding, rakish, profligate, profane christians, that have over-run the Christian world? can there be a greater contradiction? A loyal subject in arms against his sovereign, an ignorant scholar, a sober drunkard, a charitable miser, an honest thief, is not a greater absurdity, or a more direct contradiction. To depart from iniquity is effential to chriftianity, and without it, there can be no fuch thing. There was nothing that Chrift was fo remote from as fin; and therefore for thofe that indulge themfelves in it to wear his name, is juft as abfurd and ridiculous as for a coward to denominate himfelf from Alexander the Great, or an illiterate dunce to call himfelf a Newtonian philofopher. Therefore, if you will not renounce iniquity, renounce the chriftian name; for you cannot confiftently retain both. Alexander had a fellow in his army that was of his own name, but a mere coward. " Either be like me," fays Alexander, " or lay afide my name." Ye fervants of fin, it is in vain for you to wear the name of Chrift, it renders you the more ridiculous, and aggravates your guilt: you may with as much propriety call yourfelves lords, or dukes, or kings, as chriftians, while you are fo unlike to Chrift. His name is a farcafm, a reproach to you, and you are a fcandal to his name. His name is blafphemed among the Gentiles through you.

2. To be a chriftian is to deny yourfelves and take up the crofs, and follow Chrift. Thefe are the terms of difciplefhip fixt by Chrift himfelf. *He faid to them all, If any man will come after me, let him deny himfelf and take up his crofs daily, and follow me.* Luke ix. 23. To deny ourfelves is to abftain from the pleafures of fin, to moderate our fenfual appetites, to deny our own intereft for the fake of Chrift, and in fhort to facrifice every thing inconfiftent with our duty to him, when thefe come in competition. To take up our crofs, is to bear fufferings, to encounter difficulties, and break through them all in imitation of Jefus Chrift, and for his fake. To follow him, is to trace his fteps, and imitate his example, whatever it coft us. But this obfervation will coincide with the next head, and therefore I now difmifs it. Thefe, Sirs, and thefe only are the terms, if you would be chriftians, or the difciples of Chrift. Thefe he honeftly warned mankind of when he firft called them to be his difciples. He did not take an advantage of them, but let them know beforehand upon what terms they were admitted. He makes this declaration in the midft of a great crowd, in Luke xiv. 25, &c. *There went a great multitude with him,* fond of becoming his followers: *but he turned, and faid unto them, if any man come to me and hate not his father, and mother, and wife and children, and fifters, yea, and his own life alfo, he cannot be my difciple.* By hating is here meant a fmaller degree of love, or a comparative hatred; that is, if we would be Chrift's difciples, we muft be willing to part with our deareft relations, and even our lives, when we cannot retain them confiftently with our duty to him. He goes on: *Whofoever does not bear his crofs,* and encounter the greateft fufferings after my example, *cannot be my difciple.* The love of Chrift is the ruling paffion of every true

christian, and for his sake he is ready to give up all, and to suffer all that earth or hell can inflict. He must run all risks, and cleave to his cause at all adventures. This is the essential character of every true christian.

What then shall we think of those crowds among us who retain the christian name, and yet will not deny themselves of their sensual pleasures, nor part with their temporal interest for the sake of Christ? Who are so far from being willing to lay down their lives that they cannot stand the force of a laugh or a sneer in the cause of religion, but immediately stumble and fall away? or, are they christians, whom the commands of Christ cannot restrain from what their depraved hearts desire? No; a christian, without self-denial, mortification, and a supreme love to Jesus Christ, is as great a contradiction as fire without heat, or a sun without light, an hero without courage, or a friend without love. And does not this strip some of you of the christian name, and prove that you have no title at all to it?

3. I have repeatedly observed, that a true christian must be a follower or imitator of Christ. *Be ye followers of me,* says St. Paul, *as I also am of Christ.* 1 Cor. xi. 1. Christ is the model after whom every christian is formed; for, says St. Peter, *he left us an example that we should follow his steps.* 1 Pet. ii. 21. St. Paul tells us, that *we must be conformed to the image of God's dear Son,* Rom. viii. 29. and that *the same mind must be in us which was also in Christ Jesus,* Phil. ii. 5.; unless we partake of his spirit, and resemble him in practice; unless we be as he was in the world, we have no right to partake of his name.

Here I would observe, that what was miraculous in our Lord's conduct, and peculiar to him as the Son of God and Mediator, is not a pattern for our imitation, but only what was done in obedience to that law of God which was common to him and us. His heart glowed with love to his Father, he delighted in universal obedience to him; it was his meat and his drink to do his will, even in the most painful and self-denying instances; he abounded in devotion, in prayer, meditation, fasting, and every religious duty. He was also full of every grace and virtue towards mankind: meek and lowly, kind and benevolent, just and charitable, merciful and compassionate; a dutiful son, a loyal subject, a faithful friend, a good master, and an active, useful, public-spirited member of society. He was patient and resigned, and yet undaunted and brave under sufferings: he had all his appetites and passions under proper government, he was heavenly-minded, above this world in heart while he dwelt in it. Beneficence to the souls and bodies of men was the business of his life; for *he went about doing good.* Acts x. 38. This is an imperfect sketch of his amiable character; and in these things every one that deserves to be called after his name, does in some measure resemble and imitate him. This is not only his earnest endeavour, but what he actually attains, though in a much inferior degree; and his imperfections are the grief of his heart. This resemblance and imitation of Christ is essential to the very being of a christian, and without it, it is a vain pretence. And does your christianity, my brethren, stand this test? may one know that you belong to Christ by your living like him, and discovering the same temper and spirit? Do the manners of the divine Master spread through all his family; and do you shew that you belong to it by your temper and conduct? Alas! if you must be denominated from hence, would not some of you with more propriety be called Epicureans from Epicurus, the sensual Atheistic philosopher, or Mammonites from Mammon, the imaginary god of riches, or Bacchanals from Bacchus, the god of wine, than Christians from Christ, the most perfect pattern of living holiness and virtue that ever was exhibited to the world?

If you claim the name of Christians, where is that ardent devotion, that affectionate love to God, that zeal for his glory, that alacrity in his service, that resignation to his will, that generous benevolence to mankind, that zeal to promote their best interests, that meekness and forbearance under ill usage, that unwearied activity in doing good to all, that self-denial and heavenly mindedness which shone so conspicuous in Christ, whose holy name you bear? Alas! while you are destitute of those graces, and yet wear his name, you burlesque it, and turn it into a reproach both to him and yourselves.

I might add, that the christian name is not hereditary to you by your natural birth, but you must be born anew of the spirit to entitle you to this new name; that a Christian is a Believer, believing in Him after whom he is called as his only Saviour and Lord, and that he is a true penitent. Repentance was incompatible with Christ's character, who was perfectly righteous, and had no sin of which to repent; but it is a proper virtue in a sinner, without which he cannot be a christian. On these and several other particulars I might enlarge, but my time will not allow; I shall therefore conclude with a few reflections.

First, You may hence see that the christian character is the highest, the most excellent and sublime in all the world: it includes every thing truly great and amiable. The christian has exalted sentiments of the supreme Being, just notions of duty, and a proper temper and conduct towards God and man. A christian is a devout worshipper of the God of heaven, a cheerful observer of his whole law, and a broken hearted penitent of his imperfections. A christian is a complication of all the amiable and useful graces and virtues; temperate and sober, just, liberal, compassionate and benevolent, humble, meek, gentle, peaceable, and in all things conscientious. A christian is a good parent, a good child, a good master, a good servant, a good husband, a good wife, a faithful friend, an obliging neighbour, a dutiful subject, a good ruler, a zealous patriot, and an honest statesman; and as far as he is such, so far, and no farther, he is a christian. And can there be a more amiable and excellent character exhibited to your view? It is an angelic, a divine character. Let it be your glory and your ambition to wear it with a good grace, to wear it so as to adorn it.

To acquire the title of kings and lords is not in your power; to spread your fame as scholars, philosophers, or heroes, may be beyond your reach; but here is a character more excellent, more amiable, more honourable than all these, which it is your business to deserve and maintain. And blessed be God, this is a dignity which the meanest among you, which beggars and slaves may attain. Let this therefore be an object of universal ambition and pursuit, and let every other name and title be despised in comparison of it. This is the way to rise to true honour in the estimate of God, angels, and good men. What though the antichristian christians of our age and country ridicule you? let them consider their own absurd conduct and be ashamed. They think it an honour to wear the christian name, and yet persist in unchristian practices; and who but a fool, with such palpable contradiction, would think so? A begger that fancies himself a king, and trails his rags with the gait of majesty, as though they were royal robes, is not so ridiculous as one that will usurp the christian name without a christian practice; and yet such christians are the favourites of the world. To renounce the profession of christianity is barbarous and prophane; to live according to that profession, and practise christianity, is preciseness and fanaticism. Can any thing be more preposterous? This is as if one should ridicule learning, and yet glory in the character of a scholar; or laugh at bravery, and yet celebrate the praises of heroes. And are they fit to judge of the wisdom and propriety, or their censures to be regarded, who fall into such an absurdity themselves?

Secondly, Hence you may see that, if all the professors of christianity should behave in character, the religion of Christ would soon appear divine to all mankind, and spread through all nations of the earth. Were christianity exhibited to the life in all its native and inherent glories, it would be as needless to offer arguments to prove it divine, as to prove that the sun is full of light: the conviction would flash upon all mankind by its own intrinsic evidence. Did christians exemplify the religion they profess, all the world would immediately see that *that* religion which rendered them so different a people from all the rest of mankind, is indeed divine, and every way worthy of universal acceptance. Then we should have no such monsters as Atheists, Deists, and Infidels in christian countries. Then would Heathenism, Mahometism, and all the false religions in the world, fall before the heaven-born religion of Jesus Christ. Then it would be sufficient to convince an infidel just to bring him into a christian county, and let him observe the different face of things there from all the world beside. But alas!

Thirdly, How different is the christian world from the christian religion? Who would imagine that they who take their name from Christ have any relation to him, if we observe their spirit and practice? Should a stranger learn christianity from what he sees in popish countries, he would conclude it principally consisted in bodily austerities, in worshipping saints, images, relics, and a thousand trifles, in theatrical fopperies and insignificant ceremonies, in believing implicitly all the determinations of a fallible man infallibly true, and in persecuting all that differ from them, and shewing their love to their souls by burning their bodies. In protestant countries, alas! the face of things is but little better as to good morals and practical religion. Let us take our own country for a sample. Suppose an Heathen or Mahometan should take a tour through Virginia to learn the religion of the inhabitants from their general conduct, what would he conclude? would he not conclude that all the religion of the generality consisted in a few Sunday formalities, and that the rest of the week they had nothing to do with God, or any religion, but were at liberty to live as they please; And were he told these were the followers of one Christ, and were of his religion, would he not conclude that he was certainly an impostor, and the minister of sin? But when he came to find that, notwithstanding all this licentiousness, they professed the pure and holy religion of the Bible, how would he be astonished, and pronounce them the most inconsistent bare-faced hypocrites! My brethren, 'great and heavy is the guilt that lies upon our country upon this account. It is a scandel to the christian name: it is guilty of confirming the neighbouring Heathen in their prejudices, and hinders the propagation of christianity through the world. O let not us be accessary to this dreadful guilt, but do all we can to recommend our religion to universal acceptance!—I add,

Fourthly, and lastly, Let us examine whether we have any just title to the christian name; that is, whether we are christians indeed; for if we have not the thing, to retain the name is the most inconsistent folly and hypocrisy, and will answer no end but to aggravate our condemnation. A lost christian is the most shocking character in hell; and, unless you be such christians as I have described, it will ere long be your character. Therefore, be followers of Chrift, imbibe his fpirit, practife his precepts, and depart from iniquity, otherwife he will fentence you from him at laft as workers of iniquity. *And then will I profefs unto them* (they are Chrift's own words) *I never knew you; depart from me, ye that work iniquity.* Matthew vii. 23.

SERMON XIII.

The Divine Mercy to mourning Penitents.

JEREMIAH xxxi. 18, 19, 20. *I have furely heard Ephraim bemoaning himfelf thus, Thou haft chaftifed me, and I was chaftifed, as a bullock unaccuftomed to the yoke: turn thou me, and I fhall be turned; for thou art the Lord my God. Surely after that I was turned, I repented; and after that I was inftructed, I fmote upon my thigh: I was afhamed, yea, even confounded, becaufe I did bear the reproach of my youth. Is Ephraim my dear fon? is he a pleafant child? for fince I fpake againft him, I do earneftly remember him ftill: therefore my bowels are troubled for him: I will furely have mercy upon him, faith the Lord.*

IN thefe words the mourning language of a penitent child, fenfible of ingratitude, and at once defirous and afhamed to return, and the tender language of a compaffionate father, at once chaftifing, pitying and pardoning, are fweetly blended: and the images are fo lively and moving, that, if they were regarded only as poetical defcriptions founded upon fiction, they would be irrefiftibly ftriking. But when we confider them as the moft important realities, as defcriptive of that ingenuous repentance which we muft all feel, and of that gracious acceptance we muft all obtain from God before we can be happy, what almighty energy fhould they have upon us! how may our hearts diffolve within us at the found of fuch pathetic complaints, and fuch gracious encouragements! Hard indeed is that heart that can hear thefe penitential ftrains without being melted into the like tender relentings: and inveterate is that melancholy, incurable is that defpondency, that can liften to fuch expreffions of fatherly compaffion and love, without being cheered and animated.

This whole chapter had a primary reference to the Jews, and fuch of the Ifraelites as might mingle with them in their return from the Babylonian captivity. As they were enflaved to foreigners, and removed from their native land for their sin, so they could not be restored but upon their repentance. Upon this condition only a restoration was promised them. *Lev.* xxvi. 40—43. *Deut.* xxx. 1—16.

In this chapter we have a prediction of their repentance under the heavy chastisement of seventy years captivity, and of their return thereupon to their own land. In the text the whole body of penitents among them is called by the name of a single person, Ephraim. In the prophetic writings, the kingdom of the ten tribes, as distinguished from that of Judah, is frequently denominated by this name, because the Ephraimites were a principal family among them. And sometimes, as here, the name is given to the Jews, probably, on account of the great number of Ephraimites mingled with them, especially on their return from captivity. All the penitent Jews are included under this single name, to intimate their unanimity in their repentance; their hearts consented, like the heart of one man, to turn to the Lord, from whom with horrid unanimity they had revolted. This single name Ephraim also renders this passage more easily applicable to particular penitents in all ages. Every one of such may insert his own name, instead of that of Ephraim, and claim the encouragement originally given to them. And indeed this whole passage is applicable to all true penitents. Repenting Ephraim did but speak the language of every one of you, my brethren, who is made sensible of the plague of his own heart, and turned to the Lord; and the tender language of forgiving grace to mourning Ephraim is addressed to each of you; and it is with a view to you that I intend to consider this scripture.

The text naturally resolves itself into three parts, as it consists of three verses. In the first verse we find the careless, resolute impenitent, reduced by chastisement to a sense of his danger, and the necessity of turning to God; and yet sensible of his utter inability, and therefore crying for the attractive influences of divine grace. You hear Ephraim bemoaning his wretched case, and pouring out importunate groans for relief, thus: *Thou hast chastised me, and I was chastised, like a bullock unaccustomed to the yoke,* that struggles and wearies himself in vain to get free from it, and must be broken and tamed with severe usage.—
" Thus stubborn and unmanageable have I been; and now when
" I am convinced of the necessity of a return to thee, I feel my
" obstinate heart reluctate, like a wild ox, and I cannot come.
" I therefore cry to thee for the attractive influence of thy grace;"
Turn thou me, and I shall be turned; draw me, and I shall run after thee. " To whom but to thee should I return? and to whom
" but to thee should I apply for strength to return? For thou
" only art the Lord my God, who can help me, and whom I am

"under infinite obligations to ferve."—Thus the awakened finner prayed; and mercy liftened to his cries. The attractive influences of divine grace are granted, and he is enabled to return; which introduces the fecond branch of the text in the 19th verfe, in which the new convert is reprefented as reflecting upon the efficacy of converting grace, and the glorious change wrought in him by it.: *Surely after that I was turned, I repented; and after that I was inftructed, I fmote upon my thigh: I was afhamed, yea, even confounded, becaufe I did bear the reproach of my youth.*

While the returning prodigal is venting himfelf in thefe plantive ftrains in fome folitary corner, his heavenly Father's bowels are moving over him. The third part of the text reprefents the bleffed God liftening to the cries of his mourning child. *I have furely heard;* or, according to the emphafis of the original, hearing I have heard *Ephraim bemoaning himfelf:* and while Ephraim is going on in his paffionate complaints, God as it were interrupts him, and furprifes him with the foothing voice of mercy. *Is Ephraim my dear fon? is he a pleafaut child?** furely he is. Or we may underftand the words thus, as if God fhould fay, "Whofe "mourning voice is this I hear? Is this Ephraim my dear fon? "Is this my pleafant child, that bemoans himfelf as a helplefs or- "phan, or one abandoned by his father? And can I bear to hear "his complaints without mingling divine confolations with them, "and affuring him of pardon? No; for fince I fpake againft him "in my threatenings, I do earneftly remember him ftill:" *therefore my bowels are troubled for him; I will furely have mercy upon him, faith the Lord.*

I fhall endeavour to illuftrate each of thefe parts of the text, and thus fhall be led to defcribe the preparative exercifes, the nature and concomitants of true repentance; and the tender compaffions of heaven towards mourning penitents.

I. Let us view the returning finner under his firft fpiritual concern, which is generally preparatory to evangelical repentance.

And where fhall we find him? And what is he doing? We fhall not find him, as ufual, in a thoughtlefs hurry about earthly things, confining all his attention to thefe trifles, and unmindful of the important concerns of eternity. We fhall not find him merry, inconfiderate, and vain, in a circle of jovial, carelefs companions; much lefs fhall we find him intrepid and fecure in a courfe of fin, gratifying his flefh, and indulging his lufts. In this enchanted road the crowd of hardy impenitents pafs fecure and cheerful down to the chambers of death, but the awakened finner flies from it with horror; or, if his depraved heart would tempt him to walk in it, he cannot take many fteps before he is

---

* Though affirmative interrogations are generally to be underftood as ftrong negations, yet fometimes they are to be underftood affirmatively. See 1. *Sam*. ii. 27, 28. *Job* xx. 4.

shocked with the horrid apparition of impending danger. He finds the flattering paths of sin haunted with the terrible spectres of guilt, and the sword of divine vengeance gleams bright and dreadful before him, and seems lifted to give the fatal blow. You will therefore find the awakened sinner solitary and solemn in some retired corner, not deceiving himself with vain hopes of safety in his present state, but alarmed with apprehensions of danger; not planning schemes for his secular advantage, nor asking with sordid anxiety, " Who will shew me any temporal good?" but solicitous about his perishing soul, and anxiously enquiring, *what shall I do to be saved?* He is not congratulating himself upon the imaginary goodness of his heart or life, or priding himself with secret wonder in a rich conceit of his excellencies, but you will hear him in his sorrowful retirement bemoaning, or (as the original signifies) condoling himself. He sees his case to be really awful and sad, and he, as it were, takes up a lamentation over himself. He is no more senseless, hard-hearted, and self-applauding, as he was wont to be; but like a mourning turtle he bewails himself in such tragical strains as these: " Unhappy creature that I am! into what a deplorable state have I brought myself! and how long have I continued in it with the insensibility of a rock, and the stupidity of a brute? Now I may mourn over my past neglected, and unimproved days, as so many deceased friends, sent indeed from heaven to do me good, but cruelly killed by my ungrateful neglect and continued delays as to a return to God and holiness. Fly back, ye abused months and years; arise from the dead; restore me your precious moments again, that I may unravel the web of life, and form it anew; and that I may improve the opportunities I have squandered away. Vain and desperate wish! the wheels of time will not return, and what shall I do? Here I am a guilty obnoxious creature, uncertain of life, and unfit to die; alienated from God, and incapable (alas! I may add unwilling) to return a slave to sin, and too feeble to break the fetters of inveterate habits; liable to the arrest of divine justice, and unable to deliver myself; exposed to the vengeance of heaven, yet can make no atonement; destitute of an interest in Christ, and uncertain, awfully uncertain, whether I shall ever obtain it. Unhappy creature! How justly may I take up a lamentation over myself! Pity me, ye brute creation, that know not to sin, and therefore cannot know the misery of my case; and have pity upon me, have pity upon me, O ye my friends! and if these guilty lips may dare to pronounce thy injured name, O thou God of grace have pity upon me! But alas! I deserve no pity, for how long have I denied to myself! Ah! infatuated wretch! why did not I sooner begin to secure my unhappy soul, that has lain all this time neglected, and unpitied upon the brink of ruin! Why did I not sooner lay my condition to heart? Alas, I should have gone on thoughtless still, had I not been awakened by the kind feverity, the gracious chaltifements of my difhonoured Father.

Thou haft chaftifed me. This, as fpoken by Ephraim, had a particular reference to the Babylonifh captivity ; but we may naturally take occafion from it to fpeak of thofe calamities in general, whether outward or inward, that are made the means of alarming the fecure finner.

There are many ways which our heavenly Father takes to correct his undutiful children until they return to him. Sometimes he kindly takes away their health, the abufed occafion of their wantonnefs and fecurity, and reftrains them from their lufts with fetters of afflidtion. This is beautifully defcribed by Elihu : *He is chaftened with pain upon his bed, and the multitude of his bones with ftrong pain ; fo that his life abhorreth bread, and his foul dainty meat. His flesh is confumed away, that it cannot be feen, and his bones, that were not feen, ftick out ; yea, his foul draweth near unto the grave, and his life unto the deftroyers. If there be a meffenger with him, a peculiarly fkilful interpreter, one among a thoufand, to shew unto man his uprightnefs, then he is gracious unto him, and faith, Deliver him from going down to the pit ;—I have found a ranfom.* Job xxxiii. 19, &c. Sometimes God awakens the finner to bethink himfelf, by ftripping him of his earthly fupports and comforts, his eftate, or his relatives, which drew away his heart from eternal things, and thus brings him to fee the neceffity of turning to God, the fountain of blifs, upon the failure of the ftreams. Thus he dealt with profligate Manaffeh. 2 Chron. xxxiii. 11, 12. He was taken in *thorns, and bound in fetters, and carried to Babylon ; and when he was in affliction he befought the Lord, and humbled himfelf greatly before him, and prayed unto him,* &c. Thus alfo God promifes to do with his chofen ; *I will caufe you to pafs under my rod, and bring you into the bond of my covenant.* Ezek. xx. 37. Pfal. lxxxix. 32. Prov. xxii. 15. xxix. 15.

But the principal means of correction which God ufes for the end of return to him is that of confcience ; and indeed without this, all the reft are in vain. Outward afflictions are of fervice only as they tend to awaken the confcience from its lethargy to a faithful difcharge of its truft. It is confcience that makes the finner fenfible of his mifery, and fcourges him till he return to his duty. This is a chaftifement the moft fevere that human nature can endure. The lafhes of a guilty confcience are intolerable ; and fome under them have chofen ftrangling and death rather than life. The fpirit of a man may bear him up under outward infirmities ; but when the fpirit itfelf is wounded, *who can bear it?* Prov. xviii. 14. Confcience is a ferpent in its breaft, which bites and gnaws his heart ; and he can no more avoid it than he can fly from himfelf. Its force is fo great and univerfal that even the heathen poet Juvenal, not famous for the delicacy of his morals, taught by experience, could fpeak feelingly of its fecret blows, and of agonizing fweats under its tortures*.

Let not fuch of you as have never been tortured with its remorfe, congratulate yourfelves upon your happinefs, for you are not innocents; and therefore confcience will not always fleep; it will not always lie torpid and inactive, like a fnake benumbed with cold, in your breaft. It will awaken you either to your converfion or condemnation. Either the fire of God's wrath flaming from his law will enliven it in this world to fting you with midicinal anguifh; or the unquenfhable fire of his vengence in the lake of fire and brimftone will thaw it into life, and then it will horribly rage in your breaft, and diffufe its tormenting poifon through your whole frame : and then it will become a never-dying worm, and prey upon your hearts for ever. But if you now fuffer it to pain you with falutary remorfe, and awaken you to a tender fenfibility of your danger, this inteftine enemy will in the end become your bofom friend, will fupport you under every calamity, and be your faithful companion and guardian through the moft dangerous paths of life. Therefore now fubmit to its wholefome feverities, now yield to its chaftifements. Such of you as have fubmitted to its authority, and obeyed its faithful admonitions, find it your beft friend ; and you may blefs the day in which you complied with its demands though before divine grace renewed your heart, your wills were ftubborn and reluctant ; and you might fay with Ephraim,

I was chaftifed as a bullock unaccuftomed to the yoke; that is, " As a wild young ox, unbroken from the herd, is unmanageable, refufes the yoke, becomes outrageous at the whip or goad, and wearies himfelf in effectual ftruggles to throw off the burden clapt upon him, and regain his favage liberty, and never will fubmit untill wearied out, and unable to refift any longer ; fo has my ftubborn heart unaccuftomed to obey, refufed the yoke of thy law, O my God, and ftruggled with fullen obftinacy under thy chaftifements. Inftead of calmly fubmitting to thy rod, and immediately reforming under correction, inftead of turning to thee, and flying to thy arms to avoid the falling blow, I was unyielding and outrageous, like *a wild bull in a net.* Ifaiah li. 20. I wearied myfelf in defperate ftruggles to free myfelf from thy chaftifing hand; or vainly tried to harden myfelf to bear it with obdurate

---
* ——— Frigida mens eft
Criminibus, tacita fudant præcordia culpa.
JUVEN. Sat. I.

——— Cur tamen hos tu
Erafiffe putes, quos diri confcia facti
Mens habet attonitos, & furdo verbere cædit,
Occultum quatiente animo tortore flagellum?
Id. Sat. XIII.

insensibility. I tried to break the rod of conscience that I might no more groan under its lashes, and my heart reluctated and rebelled against the gracious design of thy correction, which was to bring me back to thee my heavenly Father. But now I am wearied out, now I am sensible I must submit, or perish, and that my conscience is too strong for me, and must prevail."

You see, my brethren, the obstinate reluctance of an awakened sinner to return to God. Like a wild young bullock, he would range at large, and is impatient of the yoke of the law, and the restraints of conscience. He loves his sin and cannot bear to part with it. He has no relish for the exercises of devotion and ascetic mortification; and therefore will not submit to them. The way of holiness is disagreeable to his depraved heart, and he will not turn his feet to it. He loves to be stupidly easy and serene in mind, and cannot bear to be checked in his pursuit of business or pleasure by anxieties of heart, and therefore he is impatient of the honest warnings of his conscience, and uses a variety of wretched expedients to silence its clamorous remonstrances. In short, he will do any thing, he will turn to any thing rather than turn to God. If his conscience will be but satisfied, he will forsake many of his sins? he will, like Herod, Mark vi. 20. do many things, and walk in the whole round of outward duties. All this he will do, if his conscience will be but bribed by it. But if conscience enlarges its demands, and, after he has reformed his life, requires him to make him a new heart, requires him to turn not only from the outward practice of gross vices, but from the love of all sin; not only to turn to the observance of religious duties, but to turn to the Lord with all his heart, and surrender himself entirely to him, and make it the main business of life to serve him; if conscience, I say, carries its demands thus far, he cannot bear it, he struggles to throw off the yoke. And some are cursed with horrid success in the attempt: they are permitted to rest content in a partial reformation, or external religion, as sufficient, and so go down to the grave *with a lie in their right hand*. But the happy soul, on whom divine grace is determined to finish its work in spite of all opposition, is suffered to weary itself out in a vain resistance of the chastisements of conscience, till it is obliged to yield, and submit to the yoke. And then with Ephraim it will cry,

Turn thou me, and I shall be turned. This is the mourning sinner's language, when convinced that he must submit and turn to God, and in the mean time finds himself utterly unable to turn. Many essays he makes to give himself to the Lord; but O! his heart starts back, and shrinks away, as though he were rushing into flames, when he is but flying to the gracious embraces of his Father. He strives, and strives to drag it along, but all in vain. And what shall he do in this extremity, but cry, " *Lord, turn thou me,* and I shall be turned; draw me, and I shall run after thee. Work in me to will and to do, and then I shall work out my own salvation! Lord, though I am sensible of the necessity of turning to thee, though I exert my feeble strength in many a languid effort to come, yet I cannot; I cannot so much as creep towards thee, though I should die on the spot. Not only thy word, but my own experience now convinces me that I cannot come unto thee, unless thou draw me. John vi. 44. Others vainly boast of their imaginary power, as though, when they set themselves about it they could perform some great achievements. Thus I once flattered myself, but now, when I am most capable of judging, that is, when I come to the trial, all my boasts are humbled. Here I lie, an helpless creature, unable to go to the physician, unable to accept of pardon and life on the easy terms of the gospel, and unable to free myself from the bondage of sin: and thus I must lie for ever, unless that God from whom I have revolted, draws me back to himself. Turn me, O thou that hast the hearts of all men in thy hands, and canst turn them whithersoever thou pleasest, turn me; and then, weak and reluctant as I am, I shall be turned; this backward heart will yield to the almighty attraction of thy grace.

"Here am I as passive clay in the hand of the potter; incapable to fashion myself into a vessel fit for thy house; but thou canst form me as thou pleasest. This hard and stubborn heart will be ductile and pliable to thine irresistible power." Thus you see the awakened sinner is driven to earnest prayer in his exigence. Never did a drowning man call for help, or a condemned malefactor plead for pardon with more sincerity and ardour. If the sinner had neglected prayer all his life before now he flies to it as the only expedient left, or if he formerly ran it over in a careless unthinking manner, as an insignificant form, now he exerts all the importunity of his soul; now he prays as for his life, and cannot rest till his desires are answered.

The sinner ventures to enforce his petition by pleading his relation to God; *Turn me,—for thou art the Lord my God.* There is a sense in which a sinner in his unregenerate state cannot call God his God; that is, he cannot claim a special interest in him as his portion, nor cry "Abba, Father," with the spirit of adoption, as reconciled to God. But even an unregenerate sinner may call him my God in other senses, he is his God by right, that is, though he has idolatrously yielded himself to other gods, yet by right he should have acknowledged him only. He is his God, as that name denotes authority and power, to which all should be subject: his God, as he would now choose him to be his God, his portion, and his all, which is implied in turning to him; he is his God by anticipation and hope, as upon his turning to him he will become his reconciled God in covenant; and he is his

God by outward profeſſion and viſible relation. The force of this argument to urge his petition for converting grace, may be viewed in various lights.

It may be underſtood thus: "Turn thou me, for thou only, who art the Lord of the univerſe, and haſt all the creation at thy controul; thou only, who art my God and ruler, and in whoſe hand my heart is, art able to turn ſo obſtinate a creature. In vain do I ſeek for help elſewhere. Not all the means upon earth, not all the perſuaſions, exortations, invitations, and terrors that can be uſed with me, can turn this heart; it is a work becoming the Lord God Almighty, and it is thou alone canſt effect it."

Or we may underſtand the plea thus: "Turn thou me, and I ſhall turn to thee; to thee who art the Lord my God, and to whom I am under the moſt ſacred obligations to return. I would reſign thine own right to thee; I would ſubmit to thee who alone haſt a juſt claim to me as thy ſervant."

Or the words may be underſtood as an abjuration of all the idol-luſts to which the ſinner was enſlaved before. "I will turn to thee; for to whom ſhould I turn but to the Lord my God; *What have I to do any more with idols?* Hoſea xiv. 8. Why ſhould I any longer ſubmit to other Lords, who have no right to me? I would renounce them all; I would throw off all ſubjection to them, and avouch thee alone for the Lord my God." Thus the Jews renounced their falſe gods upon their return from Babylon.

Or we may underſtand the words as an encouragement to hope for converting grace, ſince it is aſked from a God of infinite power and goodneſs. "Though I have moſt grievouſly offended, and had I done the thouſandth part ſo much againſt my fellow creatures, I could never expect a favourable admiſſion into their preſence; yet I dare aſk ſo great a favour of thee, for thou art God, and not man: thy power and thy grace are all divine, ſuch as become a God. I therefore dare to hope for that from thy hands, which I might deſpair of from all the univerſe of beings beſides."

Or finally, the paſſage may be looked upon as a plea drawn from the ſinner's external relation to God, as a member of his viſible church, and as dedicated to him. "Turn me, and I will turn to thee, whoſe name I bear, and to whom I have been early devoted. I would now of my own choice acknowledge the God of my fathers, and return to the guide of my youth. And, ſince thou haſt honoured me with a place in thy viſible church, I humbly hope thou wilt not reject me now, when I would ſincerely conſecrate myſelf to thee, and become thy ſervant in reality, as well as in appearance." In this ſenſe the plea might be uſed with peculiar propriety by the Jews, who had been nationally adopted as the peculiar people of God.

In whatever fenfe we underftand the words, they convey to us this important truth, that the awakened finner is obliged to take all his encouragement from God, and not from himfelf. All his truft is in the divine mercy, and he is brought to an happy felf-defpair.

Having viewed Ephraim under the preparatory work of legal ·conviction, and the dawn of evangelical repentance, let us view him,

II. As reflecting upon the furprifing efficacy of grace he had fought, and which was beftowed upon him in anfwer to his prayer.

We left him juft now crying, *Turn thou me, and I shall be turned;* here we find him actually turned. *Surely after that I was turned, I repented.* When the Lord exerts his power to fubdue the ftubbornnefs of the finner, and fweetly to allure him to himfelf, then the finner repents; then his heart diffolves in ingenuous difinterefted relentings. His forrow and concern before converfion are forced and mercenary; they are occafioned only by a felfifh fear of punifhment, and he would willingly get rid of them, but now his grief is free and fpontaneous; it flows from his heart as freely as ftreams from a fountain; and he takes pleafure in tender relentings before the Lord for his fin; he delights to be humble, and to feel his heart diffolve within him. An heart of flefh, foft and fufceptive of impreffions, is his choice, and a ftony infenfible heart his greateft burden; the more penitent the more happy, and the more fenfelefs, the more miferable he finds himfelf. Now alfo his heart is actuated with a generous concern for the glory of God; and he fees the horrid evil of fin as contrary to the holinefs of God, and an ungrateful requital of his uninterrupted beneficence.

We learn from this paffage, that the true penitent is fenfible of a mighty turn in his temper and inclinations. *Surely after that I was turned, I repented.* His whole foul is turned from what he formerly delighted in, and turned to what he had no relifh for before. Particularly his thoughts, his will, and affections are turned to God; there is an heavenly bias communicated to them which draws them to holinefs, like the law of gravitation in the material world. There is indeed a new turn given to his outward practice; the world may in fome meafure fee that he is a new man; but this is not all; the firft fpring that turns all the wheels of the foul and actions of life is the heart, and this is firft fet right. The change within is as evident as that without, could our eyes penetrate the heart. In fhort, *If any man be in Chrift, he is throughout a new creature; old thing are paffed away, and behold, all things are become new.*

Apply this touchstone to your hearts, my brethren, and see if they will stand the test.

The penitent proceeds, *After that I was instructed, I smote upon my thigh.* The same grace that turns him does also instruct him; nay, it is by discovering to him the beauty of holiness, and the glory of God in the face of Jesus Christ, that it draws him. He is brought out of darkness into marvellous and astonishing light, that surprises him with new discoveries of things: he is instructed particularly, as to the necessity of turning to God, as to the horrid ingratitude, vileness, and deformity of sin, and as to his folly and wickedness in continuing so long alienated from God. By the way, have you ever been let into these secrets, my hearers? And when instructed in these,

" He smites upon his thigh." This gesture denotes consternation and amazement; and nature directs us thus to express these passions. Ezekiel is enjoined to use this gesture as a prophetic action signifying the horror and astonishment of his mind. *Ezekiel* xxi. 12. This action, therefore, of the penitent, intimates what consternation and amazement he is cast into, when these new discoveries flash upon his soul. He stands amazed at himself. He is struck with horror to think what an ungrateful, ignorant, stupid wretch he has been all his life till this happy moment. " Alas! what have I been doing? abusing all my days in ruining my own soul, and dishonouring the God of all my mercies! contentedly estranged from him, and not seeking to return! Where were my eyes, that I never before saw the horrid evil of my conduct, and the shocking deformity of sin, which now opens to me in all its hideous colours! Amazing! that divine vengeance has not broken out upon me before now! Can it be that I am yet alive! in the land of hope too! yea, alive, an humble pardoned penitent! Let heaven and earth wonder at this, for surely the sun never shone upon a wretch so undeserving! so great a monument of mercy!"

The pardoned penitent proceeds,—*I was ashamed, yea, even confounded, because I did bear the reproach of my youth.* We are ashamed when we are caught in a mean, base and scandalous action; we blush, and are confounded, and know not where to look, or what to say, Thus the penitent is heartily ashamed of himself, when he reflects upon the sordid dispositions he has indulged, and the base and scandalous actions he has committed. He blushes at his own inspection; he is confounded at his own tribunal. He appears to himself, a mean, base, contemptible wretch; and, though the world may honour him, he loaths himself, as viler than the earth he treads on; and is secretly ashamed to see the face of man. And how then shall he appear before God? how shall he hold up his face in the presence of his injured

Father? He comes to him ashamed, and covering his head. He knows not what to say to him; he knows not how to look him in the face, but he falls down abashed and confounded at his feet. Thus was penitent Ezra ashamed before God. He fell upon his knees, and lifted up his hands (his eyes, like the publican, he durst not lift up) unto the heavens, and he says, *O my God, I am ashamed, and blush to lift up my face to thee, my God; for our iniquities are increased over our heads, and our trespasses are grown up unto the heavens.—And now, O our God, what shall we say after this? for we have broken thy commandments.* Ezra ix. 5—10. Thus it was foretold concerning the repenting Jews. *Then thou shalt remember thy evil ways and be ashamed. Thou shalt be confounded, and never open thy mouth any more, because of thy shame.* Ezek. xvi. 61, 63. There is good reason for this conscious shame, and therefore it is enjoined as a duty: *Not for your sakes do I this unto you, saith the Lord God, be it known unto you: be ashamed and confounded for your own ways, O house of Israel.* Ezek. xxxvi. 32.

And what is the cause of this shame in the mourning penitent? " O (says he) it is *because I bear the reproach of my youth.*" " I carry upon me (as the original word signifies) the brand of infamy. My youth, alas! was spent in a thoughtless neglect of God and the duties I owed him; my vigorous days were wasted in sensual extravagances, and gratifying my criminal inclinations. My prime of life, which should have been sacred to the Author of my existence, was spent in rebellion against him. Alas! my first thoughts, my virgin-love, did not aspire to him; nor did my young desires, as soon as fledged, wing their flight to heaven. In short, the temper of my heart, and my course of life, from the first exercises of reason to this happy hour of my conversion, were a disgrace to my rational nature; I have degraded myself beneath the beasts that perish." *Behold, I am vile! I loath and abhor myself for all my filthiness and abominations.* Ezek. xxxvi. 31. " And how amazing the grace of God, to honour so base a wretch with a place among the children of his love!"

Thus I have delineated the heart of penitent Ephraim; and let me ask you my brethren, is this your picture? Have you ever felt such ingenuous relentings, such just consternation, such holy shame and confusion? There can be no transition from nature to grace without previous concern &c. You all bear the reproach of that youth, you have all spent some unhappy days in the scandalous ways of sin, and your consciences still bear the brand of infamy. And have you ever been made deeply sensible of it? Has God ever heard you bemoaning yourselves thus in some mournful solitude, " Thou hast chastised me, and I was chastised, as a bullock unaccustomed to the yoke." Is there any such mourner here this day?

then listen to the gracious voice of your heavenly Father, while,

III. I am illustrating the last, the sweetest part of the text, which expresses the tender compassion of God towards mourning penitents.

While they are bemoaning their case, and conscious that they do not deserve one look of love from God, he is represented as attentively listening to catch the first penitential groan that breaks from their hearts. Ephraim, in the depth of his despondency, probably did hardly hope that God took any notice of his secret sorrows, which he suppressed as much as possible from the public view: but God heard him, God was watching to hear the first mournful cry; and he repeats all his complaints, to let him know (after the manner of men) what particular notice he had taken of them. " *I have surely heard*, or hearing I have heard;" that is, " I have attentively heard Ephraim bemoaning himself thus."

What strong consolation may this give to desponding mourners, who think themselves neglected by that God to whom they are pouring out their weeping supplications! He hears your secret groans, he courts your sighs, and puts your tears into his bottle. His eyes penetrate all the secrets of your heart, and he observes all their feeble struggles to turn to himself; and he beholds you not as an unconcerned spectator, but with all the tender emotions of fatherly compassion : for,

While he is listening to Ephraim's mournful complaints, he abruptly breaks in upon him, and sweetly surprises him with the warmest declarations of pity and grace. " Is this Ephraim, my dear son, whose mourning voice I hear ? Is this my pleasant child, or (as it might be rendered) the child of my delights, who thus wounds my ear with his heart-rending groans?" What strange language this to an ungrateful, unyielding rebel, that continued obstinate till he was wearied out ; that would not turn till drawn ; that deserved to fall a victim to justice! This is the language of compassion all divine, of grace that becomes a God.

This passage contains a most encouraging truth, that, however vile and abandoned a sinner has been, yet, upon his repentance, he becomes God's dear son, his favourite child. He will, from that moment regard him, provide for him, protect him, and bring him to his heavenly inheritance, as his son and heir ; for *Neither death, nor life, nor angels, nor principalities, nor powers, nor things present, nor things to come*, &c. Rom. viii. 38, &c. *shall separate him from his Father's love ; but he shall inherit all things*. Rev. xxi. 7. Yea, all things are his already in title, and he shall be made *greater than the kings of the earth ;* he shall be made such as becomes so dignified a relation as that of a Son to the King of kings, and Lord of lords.

And is not this magnet sufficient to attract all this assembly to their Father's house? Can you resist the almighty energy of such compassion? Return, ye perishing prodigals! Return; though you have *sinned against Heaven, and before your father, and are no more worthy to be called his sons,* yet return, and you shall be made his dear sons, his pleasant children.

Are none of you in need of such strong consolation as this? Do you want encouragement to return, and are you ready to spring up and run to your father's arms, upon the first assurance of acceptance? If this be what you want, you have an abundance for your supply. Are all your souls then in motion to return? Does that eye which darts through the whole creation at once, now behold your hearts moving towards God? Or am I wasting these gracious encouragements upon stupid creatures, void of sensation, that do not care for them, or that are so conceited of their own worth, as not to need them? If so, I retract these consolations, with respect to you, and shall presently tell you your doom. But let us farther pursue these melting strains of paternal pity.

" For since I spake against him, I do earnestly remember him still." Many and dreadful were the threatenings denounced against the sinner, while impenitent; and, had he continued impenitent, they would certainly have been executed upon him.—But the primary and immediate design of the threatenings are to make men happy, and not to make them miserable; they are designed to deter them from disobedience, which is naturally productive of misery, or to reclaim them from it, which is but to restrain them in their career to ruin. And consequently these threatenings proceed from love as well as the promises of our God, from love to the person, though from hatred to sin. So the same love which prompts a parent to promise a reward to his son for obedience, will prompt him also to threaten him, if he takes some dangerous weapon to play with: or, to choose a more pertinent illustration, for God is the moral ruler as well as father of the rational world; the same regard to the public weal, which induces a lawgiver to annex a reward to obedience, will also prompt him to add penalties to his law to deter from disobedience; and his immediate design is not to make any of his subjects miserable, but to keep them from making themselves and others miserable by disobedience; though, when the threatening is once denounced, it is necessary it should be executed, to vindicate the veracity of the lawgiver, and secure his government from insult and contempt. Thus when the primary end of the divine threatenings, namely, the deterring and reclaiming men from disobedience is not obtained, then it becomes necessary that they should be executed upon the impenitent in all their dreadful extent; but when the sinner is brought to repentance, and to submit to the divine government, then all these threatenings are repealed, and they shall not hurt one hair of his head. And the sinner himself will acknowledge that these threatenings proved necessary mercies to him, and that the denunciation of everlasting punishment was one means of bringing him to everlasting happiness, and that divine vengeance in this sense conspired with divine grace to save him.

Consider this, ye desponding penitents, and allay your terrors. That God, who has written such bitter things against you in his word, earnestly and affectionately remembers you still, and it was with a kind intent to you that he thundered out these terrors at which you tremble. These acids, this bitter physic, were necessary for your recovery. These coals of fire were necessary to awaken you out of your lethargy. Therefore read the love of your Father, even in these solemn warnings. He affectionately remembers you still; he cannot put you out of his thoughts.

Therefore my bowels (adds the all-gracious Jehovah) *are troubled for him.* Astonishing beyond conception! How can we bear up under such words as these? Surely they must break our hearts, and overwhelm our spirit! Here is the great God, who has millions of superior beings to serve him, and who is absolutely independent upon them all, troubled, his very bowels troubled, for a rebellious, useless, trifling worm! Be astonished at this, ye angels of light, who are the witnesses of such amazing, such unbounded compassion! and wonder at it, O ye sons of men, who are more intimately concerned in it, stand and adore, as it were, in statues of admiration! It is true these words are not to be taken literally, as though the Deity were capable of sorrow, or any of the human passions; but he here condescends to adapt himself to the language of mortals, and to borrow such images as will convey to us the most lively ideas of his grace and tenderness to mourning penitents; and no image can answer this end better than that of a Father, whose bowels are yearning over his mourning child, prostrate at his feet, and who, with eager embraces, raises him up, assuring him of pardon and acceptance. If any of you now know what it is to receive a penitent child in this manner, while all the father is tenderly working within you, you may form some affecting ideas of the readiness of our heavenly Father to receive returning sinners from this tender illustration.

The Lord concludes this moving speech with a promise that includes in it more than we can ask or think, sealed with his own sacred name. *I will surely have mercy*, or (according to the more emphatical original) with Mercy, *I will have mercy upon him, saith the Lord:* that is, I will shew abundant mercy to him, I will give him all the blessings that infinite mercy can bestow; and what can be needed more? This promise includes pardon, acceptance, sanctification, joy in the Holy Ghost, peace of conscience, and immortal life and glory in the future world. O firs! what a God, what a Father is this! *Who is a God like unto thee, that pardoneth iniquity,* &c. Micah vii. 18.

And can you, ye mourners in Zion, can you fear a rejection from such a tender Father? Can you dread to venture upon such abundant mercies? Is there a mourning Ephraim in this assembly? I may call you, as God did Adam, *Ephraim, where art thou?* Let the word of God find you out, and force a little encouragement upon you: your heavenly Father, whose angry hand you fear, is listening to your groans, and will measure you out a mercy for every groan, a blessing for every sigh, a drop, a draught of consolation, for every tear. His bowels are moving over you, and he addresses you in such language as this, " Is this my dear son? is this my pleasant child?" &c.

And as to you, ye hardy impenitents, ye abandoned profligates, ye careless formalists, ye almost christians, can you hear these things, and not begin now to relent? Do you not find your frozen hearts begin to thaw within you? Can you resist such alluring grace? Can you bear the thoughts of continuing enemies to so good, so forgiving a Father? Does not Ephraim's petition now rise in your hearts, *Turn thou me, and I shall be turned?* then I congratulate you upon this happy day; you are this day become God's dear sons, the children of his delights, &c.

Is there a wretch so senseless, so wicked, so abandoned, as to refuse to return? Where art thou, hardy rebel? Stand forth, and meet the terrors of thy doom. To thee I must change my voice, and, instead of representing the tender compassions of a father, must denounce the terrors of an angry judge. Thy doom is declared and fixt by the same lips that speak to penitents in such encouraging strains; by those gracious lips that never uttered an harsh censure. *God is angry with thee every day.* Psalm vii. 11. *Except thou repentest, thou shalt surely perish.* Luke xiii. 3. The example of Christ authorises me to repeat it again; *Except thou repentest, thou shalt surely perish,* ver. 5. *The God that made thee will destroy thee; and he that formed thee will shew thee no favour.* Isa. xxvi. 11. *Thou art treasuring up wrath* in horrid affluence *against the day of wrath.* Rom ii. 5. *God is jealous, and revengeth; the Lord revengeth, and is furious; the Lord will take vengeance on his adversaries; and he reserveth wrath for his enemies. The mountains quake at him: the hills melt; the earth is burnt at his presence: yea, the world, and they that dwell therein. Who can stand before his indignation? Who can endure in the fierceness of his anger? His fury is poured out like fire, and the rocks are thrown down by him.* Nahum i. 2—6. These flaming thunder-bolts, sinner, are aimed at thy heart, and, if thou canst harden thyself against their terror, let me read thee thy doom before we part. You have it pronounced by God himself in Deuteronomy, the twenty-ninth chapter, at the nineteenth and following verses, *If it come to pass that when he heareth the words of this course, that he bless himself in his heart, saying, I shall have peace, though I walk in the imagination of my heart—The Lord will not spare him; but then the anger of the Lord and his jealousy shall smoke against that man, and all the curses that are written in this book shall lie upon him, and the Lord shall blot out his name from under heaven; and the Lord shall separate him unto evil out of all the tribes of Israel, according to all the curses of the covenant that are written in this book of the law.* And now sinner, if thou canst return home careless and senseless with this heavy curse upon thee, expect not a word of comfort, expect no blessing till thou art made truly penitent; for " how shall I bless whom God has not blessed?" The ministerial blessing falls upon one on thy right hand, and one on thy left, but it lights not upon thee. The curse is thy lot, and this must thou have at the hand of God, if thou continuest hardened and insolent in sin. *Thou must lie down in sorrow.* Isai. l. 11. *Consider this, all ye that forget God, lest he tear you in pieces, and there be none to deliver.* Psalm l. 22.

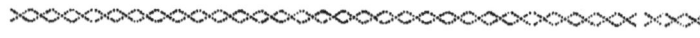

SERMON XIV.

Christ precious to all true Believers.

1 PETER ii. 7. *Unto you therefore which believe, He is precious.**

YES; blessed be God! though a great part of the creation is disaffected to Jesus Christ; though fallen spirits, both in flesh and without flesh, both upon earth and in hell, neglect him, or profess themselves open enemies to him, yet he is precious; precious, not only in himself, not only to his Father, not only to the choirs of Heaven, who beheld his full glory without a veil, but precious to some even in our guilty world; precious to a sort of persons of our sinful race, who make no great figure in mortal eyes, who have no idea of their own goodness, who are mean unworthy creatures in their own view, and who are generally despicable in the view of others; I mean he is precious to all true believers. And though they are but few comparatively in our world; though there are, I am afraid, but few additions made to them from

---

* Or *preciousness* in the abstract, τιμη.

among us; yet, bleffed be God, there are fome believers even upon our guilty globe; and, I doubt not, but I am now fpeaking to fome fuch.

My believing brethren (if I may venture to claim kindred with you) I am now entering upon a defign, which I know you have much at heart; and that is, to make the bleffed Jefus more precious to you, and if poffible, to recommend him to the affections of the crowd that neglect him. You know, alas! you love him but little; but very little, compared to his infinite excellency and your obligations to him; and you know that multitudes love him not at all. Whatever they profefs, their practice fhews that their carnal minds is enmity againft him. This you often fee, and the fight affects your hearts. It deeply affects you to think fo much excellency fhould be neglected and defpifed, and fo much love meet with fuch bafe returns of ingratitude. And you cannot but pity your poor fellow-finners, that they are fo blind to the brighteft glory and their own higheft intereft, and that they fhould perifh, through wilful neglect of their deliverer; perifh, as it were, within reach of the hand ftretched out to fave them. This is indeed a very affecting, very lamentable, and alas! a very common fight. And will you not then bid me God fpeed this day in my attempt to recommend this precious, though neglected, Jefus? Will you not contribute your fhare towards my fuccefs in fo pious and benevolent a defign by your earneft prayers? Now, fhall not the interceding figh rife to Heaven from every heart, and every foul be caft into a praying pofture? I fhall hope to difcharge my duty with more comfort and advantage, if you afford me this affiftance. And furely fuch of you cannot deny me this aid, who defire that Jefus may become ftill more precious to your own hearts. and that he may be the object of univerfal love from all the fons of men, who are now difaffected to him!

To you that believe, he is precious—He?—Who? Is it Mammon, the God of the world? Is it pleafure, or honour? No; none of thefe is the darling of the believing heart. But it is he who is the uppermoft in every pious heart; he, who is firft in the thoughts and affections; he whom every friend of his muft know, even without a name; if it be but faid of him, he is precious, this is enough to diftinguifh him from all others. "If it be he the apof-
"tle means, may every believer fay, who is moft precious to my
"foul, then I can eafily point him out, though without a name.
"It muft be Jefus, for O! it is he that is moft precious to me."
The connection alfo of the text directs us to the fame perfon. It is he the apoftle means, whom he had juft defcribed as a living ftone, chofen of God, and the precious; the chief corner-ftone, the great foundation of the church, that fpiritual temple of God, fo ftately and glorious, and reaching from earth to heaven; it is

this precious stone, this heavenly jewel, that is precious to believers.

" To you that *believe, he is precious* ;" i. e. He is highly valued by you. You esteem him one of infinite worth, and he has the highest place in your affections. He is dearer to your hearts than all other persons and things. The word τιμη requires a still stronger translation : " To you that believe, he is *preciousness* ;" preciousness in the abstract ; all preciousness, and nothing but preciousness ; a precious stone without one blemish. Or it may be translated with a little variation, " To you that believe, he is honour." It confers the highest honour upon you to be related to him ; and you esteem it your highest honour to sustain that relation. Though Jesus and his cross are names of reproach in the unbelieving world, you glory in them, and they reflect a real glory upon you. Or, " To you that believe there is honour."* Honour is now conferred upon you in your being built as living stones in the temple of God upon this precious foundation ; and honour is reserved for you in heaven, where the crown of righteousness awaits you.

" To you which believe, he is precious ;" that is to say, the value of this precious stone is, alas ! unknown to the crowd. It is so far from being precious, that it is a stone of stumbling, and a rock of offence ; a stone disallowed of men (v. 4.) rejected even by the builders (v. 7.) ; but you believers, ye happy few, have another estimate of it. Faith enables you to see the glories of the blessed Jesus ; and, when you know him through this medium, you cannot but love him. The blind world neglect the Lord of Glory, because they know him not : but you believers know him, and therefore to you he is precious. Faith presents him to your view in a just light, and directs you to form a proper estimate of him. It is truly lamentable that such real excellency should be despised ; but so it will be with the world till they believe. The mere speculative recommendation of their reason, the prepossessions of education, in his favour, and the best human means, are not sufficient to render Jesus precious to them. Nothing but saving faith can effect this.

To you therefore which believe, he is precious. The illative particle therefore shews this passage is an inference from what went before ; and the reasoning seems to be this : " This stone is precious to God, therefore it is precious to you that believe. You have the same estimate of Jesus Christ which God the Father has ; and for that very reason he is precious to you, because he is precious to him." That this is the connection, will appear if you look back to the 4th and 6th verses ; where you find Jesus described as " a

---

* The pronoun he, is not in the original ; but the passage reads thus : To you who believe, honour.

chief corner ftone, laid in Zion, elect or chofen, and precious—difallowed indeed of men, but chofen of God, and precious."* Men wickedly difapprove this ftone, and even many of the profeffed builders of his church reject him. This, fays the apoftle, muft be granted. But this is no objection to his real worth. He is precious to God, who knows him beft, and who is a perfect judge of real excellency; and for that very reafon he is precious to you that believe. Faith teaches you to look upon perfons and things in the fame light in which God views them; it makes your fentiments conformed to his. Chrift is the Father's beloved Son, in whom he is well pleafed; and he is your beloved Saviour, in whom you are well pleafed.

Is it any wonder that Jefus fhould be precious to believers, when he is fo precious in himfelf and in his offices, fo precious to the angelic armies, and fo precious to his Father?

1. He is precious in himfelf. He is Immanuel, God-man; and confequently, whatever excellencies belong either to the divine or human nature, center in him. If wifdom, power, and goodnefs, divine or human, created or uncreated, can render him worthy of the higheft affection, he has a juft claim to it.—Whatever excellencies, natural or moral, appear in any part of the vaft univerfe, they are but faint fhadows of his beauty and glory. *All things were created by him and for him; and through him all things confift.* Col. i. 16, 17. and whatever excellencies are in the effect muft be eminently in the caufe. You do not wonder nor cenfure, when you fee men delighted with the glories of the fun, and the various luminaries of the fky; you do not wonder nor blame when they take pleafure in the beautiful profpects of nature, or in that rich variety of good things, which earth and fea, and every element furnifhes for the fupport of man, or the gratification of his fenfes: you do not wonder and blame, when they are ftruck with moral beauty, when you fee them admire and approve wifdom, benevolence, juftice, veracity, meeknefs, and mercy: you never think it ftrange much lefs cenfurable, that men fhould love thefe things, and count them precious; and can you be aftonifhed, can you ridicule or find fault that Jefus is precious to poor believers? If the copy be fo fair and lovely, who would not love the original, that has eyes to behold it? Believers fee fo much of the worth of Chrift as is fufficient to captivate their hearts, and convince them of their guilt in loving him no more; and the clearer their views are of him, the more are they mortified at the criminal defects of their love; for O! they fee he deferves infinitely more!

2. The Lord Jefus is precious in his offices. His mediatorial

---

* The word ufed in ver. 4 and 6, is a compound, rendered precious in the text. And this is an intimation that the text is an inference from the above verfes.

office is generally subdivided into three parts; namely, that of a prophet, of a priest, and of a king: and how precious is Christ in each of these!

As a prophet, how sweet are his instructions to a bewildered soul! How precious the words of his lips, which are the words of eternal life! How delightful to sit and hear him teach the way of duty and happiness, revealing the father, and the wonders of the invisible state! How transporting to hear him declare upon what terms an offended God may be reconciled! a discovery beyond the searches of all the sages and philosophers of the heathen world! How reviving is it to listen to his gracious promises and invitations! promises and invitations to the poor, the weary, and heavy laden, the broken-hearted, and even to the chief of sinners! The word of Christ has been the treasure, the support, and joy of believers in all ages. *I have esteemed the words of his mouth*, says Job, *more than my necessary food.* Job. xxiii. 12. It is this precious word the Psalmist, so often and so highly celebrates. He celebrates it as *more to be desired than gold; yea, than much fine gold: sweeter also than honey, and the honey-comb.* Psalm. xix. 10. *O how I love thy law!* says he; *it is my meditation all the day.* Ps. cxix. 97. *How sweet are thy words unto my taste! yea, sweeter than honey to my mouth.* ver. 103. *The law of thy mouth is better than thousands of gold and silver.* ver. 72. *Behold, I have longed after thy precepts.* ver. 40. *Thy statutes had been my song in the house of my pilgrimage.* ver. 54. *In my affliction thy word hath quickened me.* ver. 50. *Unless thy law hath been my delight, I should then have perished in my affliction.* ver. 92. This is the language of David, in honour of this divine Prophet, near three thousand years ago, when Christ had not revealed the full gospel to the world, but only some rays of it shone through the veil of the Mosaic dispensation. And must not believers now, who live under the more complete and clear instructions of this great Prophet, entertain the same sentiments of him? Yes, to such of you as believe, even in this age, he is most precious.

But this external objective instruction is not all that Christ as a prophet communicates; and indeed, did he do no more than this, it would answer no valuable end. The mind of man, in his present fallen state, like a disordered eye, is incapable of perceiving divine things in a proper light, however clearly they are revealed; and therefore, till the perceiving faculty be rectified, all external revelation is in vain, and is only like opening a fair prospect to a blind eye. Hence this great Prophet carries his instructions farther, not only by proposing divine things in a clear objective light by his word, but inwardly enlightening the mind, and enabling it to perceive what is revealed by his Spirit. And how precious are these internal subjective instructions! How sweet to feel a disordered dark mind opening to admit the shinings of heavenly day; to perceive the glory of God in the face of Jesus Christ, the beauties of holiness, and the majestic wonders of the eternal world! Speak, ye that know by happy experience, and tell how precious Jesus appears to you, when by his own blessed Spirit he scatters the cloud that benighted your understandings, and lets in the rays of his glory upon your admiring souls; when he opens your eyes to see the wonders contained in his law, and the glorious mysteries of his gospel. What a divine glory does then spread upon every page of the sacred volume! Then it indeed appears the Book of God, God-like, and worthy its Author. O precious Jesus! let us all this day feel thine enlightening influences, that experience may teach us how sweet they are! Come, great Prophet! come, and make thine own spirit our teacher, and then shall we be divinely wise!

Again, the Lord Jesus is precious to believers as a great High Priest. As an high priest, he made a complete atonement for sin by his propitiatory sacrifice on the cross? and he still makes intercession for the transgressors on his throne in heaven. It was his sacrifice that satisfied the demands of the law, and justice of God, and rendered him reconcileable to the guilty, upon terms consistent with his honour and the rights of his government. It was by virtue of this sacrifice that he procured pardon of sin, the favour of God, freedom from hell, and eternal life for condemned obnoxious rebels. And such of you who have ever felt the pangs of a guilty conscience, and obtained relief from Jesus Christ, you can tell how precious his atoning sacrifice. How did it ease your self-tormenting consciences, and heal your broken hearts! How did it change the frowns of an angry God into smiles of love, and your trembling apprehensions of vengeance into delightful hopes of mercy! How precious did Jesus appear, with a pardon in his hand, with atoning blood gushing from his opened veins, and making his cross, as it were, the key to open the gates of heaven for your admission! Blessed Saviour! our great High Priest, thus appear to us in all thy pontifical robes dyed in thine own blood, and cause us all to feel the efficacy of thy propitiation!

Let us next turn our eyes upwards, and view this great High Priest as our intercessor in the presence of God. There he appears as a lamb that was slain, bearing the memorials of his sacrifice, and putting the Father in remembrance of the blessings purchased for his people. There he urges it as his pleasure, as his authoritative will, that these blessings should in due time be conferred upon those for whom they were purchased. In this authoritative manner he could intercede even in the days of his humiliation upon earth, because of the Father's covenant-engagements with him, the accomplishment of which he has a right to demand, as well as humbly to petition: *Father, I will, I will that those whom thou haſt given to me, may be with me,* &c. John xvii. 24. Now how precious muſt Chriſt appear in the character of Interceſſor! That the friendleſs ſinner ſhould have an all-prevailing advocate in the court of heaven to undertake his cauſe! that the great High Prieſt ſhould offer up the grateful incenſe of his own merit, with the prayers of the ſaints! that he ſhould add the ſanction of his authoritative will to the humble petitions of faith! that he ſhould urge the claims of his people, as his own claims, founded upon an unchangeable covenant with his Father, of which he has fully performed the conditions required! that he ſhould not intercede occaſionally, but always appear in the holy of holies as the conſtant ever-living Interceſſor, and maintain the ſame intereſt, the ſame importunity at all times, even when the petitions of his people languiſh upon their lips! What delightful reflections are theſe! and how warmly may they recommend the Lord Jeſus to the hearts of believers! How juſt is the apoſtle's inference, *Having an High Prieſt over the houſe of God, let us draw near with a true heart, in full aſſurance of faith; and let us hold faſt the profeſſion of our faith without wavering.* Heb. x. 21—23. *He is able to ſave to the uttermoſt all that come unto God by him;* for this reaſon, becauſe *he ever liveth to make interceſſion for them.* Heb. vii. 25. May each of us intruſt his cauſe to this all-prevailing Advocate, and we ſhall certainly gain it! The unchangeable promiſe has paſſed his lips, *that whatſoever we aſk the Father in faith and in his name, he will give it us.* John xvi. 23.

Let me add, the kingly office of Chriſt is precious to believers. As King he gives laws, laws perfectly wiſe and good, and enforced with the moſt important ſanctions, everlaſting rewards and puniſhments. And how delightful, how advantageous, to live under ſuch a government! to have our duty diſcovered with ſo much clearneſs and certainty, which frees us from ſo many painful anxieties, and to have ſuch powerful motives to obedience, which have a tendency to infuſe vigour and ſpirit into our endeavours! As King, he appoints ordinances of worſhip. And how ſweet to converſe with him in theſe ordinances, and to be freed from perplexity about that manner of worſhip which God will accept, without being expoſed to that queſtion, ſo confounding to will-worſhippers, *Who hath required this at your hands?* As King, he is head over all things to his church, and manages the whole creation, as is moſt ſubſervient to her good. The various ranks of creatures in heaven, earth, and hell, are ſubject to his direction and controul; and they muſt all co-operate for the good of his people. He reclaims, confounds, ſubdues, or deſtroys their enemies, according to his pleaſure. And how precious muſt he be in this auguſt character to the feeble helpleſs believer! To have an almighty friend sitting at the helm of the universe, with the supreme management of all things in his hands; to be assured that even the most injurious enemy can do the believer no real or lasting injury, but shall at length concur to work his greatest good; and that, come what will, it shall go well with him, and he shall at last be made triumphant over all difficulty and opposition. O! what transporting considerations are here! But this is not the whole exercise of the royal power of Christ. He not only makes laws and ordinances, and restrains the enemies of his people, but he exercises his power inwardly upon their hearts. He is the King of souls; he reigns in the hearts of his subjects; and how infinitely dear and precious is he in this view! To feel him subdue the rebellion within, sweetly bending the stubborn heart into willing obedience, and reducing every thought into a cheerful captivity to himself, writing his law upon the heart, making the dispositions of his subjects a transcript of his will, corresponding to it, like wax to the seal, how delightful is all this! O the pleasures of humble submission! How pleasant to lie as subjects at the feet of this mediatorial King without arrogating the sovereignty ourselves, for which we are utterly insufficient! Blessed Jesus! thus reign in our hearts! thus subdue the nations to the obedience of faith! *Gird thy sword upon thy thigh, O most mighty! and ride prosperously, attended with majesty, truth, meekness, and righteousness.* Psalm xlv. 3, 4. *Send the rod of thy strength out of Sion: rule thou in the midst of thine enemies,* Psalm cx. 2. rule us, and subdue the rebel in our hearts.

Thus you see the Lord Jesus is precious to believers in all the views of his mediatorial office. But he is not precious to them alone; he is beloved as far as known, and the more known the more beloved: which leads me to add,

3. He is precious to all the angels of heaven.

St. Peter tells us that the things now reported to us by the gospel are *things which the angels desire to look into.* 1 Pet. i. 12. Jesus is the wonder of angels now in heaven; and he was so even when he appeared in the form of a servant upon earth. St. Paul mentions it as one part of the great mystry of godliness, that *God manifested in the flesh was seen of angels.* 1 Tim. iii. 16. Angels saw him and admired and loved him in the various stages of his life, from his birth to his return to his native heaven. Hear the manner in which angels celebrated his entrance into our world. One of them spread his wings, and flew with joyful haste to a company of poor shepherds that kept their midnight watches in the field, and abruptly tells the news, of which his heart was full: *Behold, I bring you good tidings of great joy, which shall be to all people: for to you is born this day, in the city of David, a Saviour, which is Christ the Lord: and suddenly there was with the angel a multitude of the heavenly host.* Crowds of angels left their stations in the celestial court in that memorable hour, and hovered over the place where their incarnate God lay in a manger: Jesus, their darling, was gone down to earth, and they must follow him; for who would not be where Jesus is? Men, ungrateful men, were silent upon that occasion, but angels tuned their song of praise. The astonished shepherds heard them sing, *Glory to God in the highest; on earth peace; good-will to men.* Luke ii. 10—14. When he bringeth his first born into the world, the Father saith, *Let all the angels of God worship him.* Heb. i. 6. This seems to intimate that all the angels crowded round the manger, where the infant God lay, and paid him their humble worship. We are told, that when the Devil had finished his long process of temptations, after forty days, and had left him, the *angels came and ministered unto him.* Matt. iv. 11. When this disagreeable companion had left him, his old attendants were fond of renewing their service to him. In every hour of difficulty they were ready to fly to his aid. He was seen of angels, in his hard conflict, in the garden of Gethsemane; and one of them *appeared unto him from heaven, strengthening him.* Luke xxii. 43. With what wonder, sympathy, and readiness did this angelic assistant raise his prostrate Lord from the cold ground, wipe off his bloody sweat, and support his sinking spirit with divine encouragements! But, O! ye blessed angels, ye usual spectators, and adorers of the divine glories of our Redeemer, with what astonishment and horror were you struck, when you saw him expire on the cross!

> " Around the bloody tree
> " Ye press'd with strong desire,
> " That wondrous sight to see,
> " The Lord of life expire!
> " And, could your eyes
> " Have known a tear,
> " Had dropt it there
> " In sad surprize."*

Ye also hovered round his tomb, while he lay in the prison of the grave. The weeping women and his other friends found you stationed there in their early impatient visits to the sepulchre. O what wonders, then appeared to your astonished minds! Could you, that pry so deep into the secrets of heaven, you that know so well what divine love can do, could you have thought that even divine love could have gone so far? could have laid the Lord of Glory a pale, mangled, senseless corpse in the mansions of the dead? Was not this a strange surprize even to you? And, when the appointed day began to draw, with what eager and joyful haste did ye roll away the stone, and set open the prison doors, that the rising conqueror might march forth!

* Doddridge.

> " And when array'd in light,
> " The shining conqueror rode,
> " Ye hail'd his rapt'rous flight
> " Up to the throne of God;
> " And wav'd around
> " Your golden wings.
> " And struck your strings
> " Of sweetest sound."†

When he ascended on high, he was attended *with the chariots of God, which are twenty thousand, even thousands of angels.* Psalm lxviii. 17, 18. And now, when he is returned to dwell among them, Jesus is still the darling of angels. His name sounds from all their harps, and his love is the subject of their everlasting song. St. John once heard them, and I hope we shall ere long hear them, saying with a loud voice, *Worthy is the Lamb that was slain, to receive power, and riches, and wisdom, and strength, and honour, and glory, and blessing.* Rev. v. 11, 12.—This is the song of angels, as well as of the redeemed from among men:

> " Jesus, the Lord, their harps employs;
> " Jesus, my love, they sing;
> " Jesus, the name of both our joys,
> " Sounds sweet from ev'ry string."*

O my brethren, could we see what is doing in heaven at this instant, how would it surprize, astonish, and confound us! Do you think the name of Jesus is of as little importance there as in our world? Do you think there is one lukewarm or disaffected heart there among ten thousand times ten thousand, of thousands of thousands? O no! there his love is the ruling passion of every heart, and the favourite theme of every song. And is he so precious to angels? to angels, who are less interested in him, and less indebted to him? And must he not be precious to poor believers bought with his blood, and entitled to life by his death? Yes, you that believe have an angelic spirit in this respect; you love Jesus, though unseen, as well as they who see him as he is, though, alas! in a far less degree. But to bring his worth to the highest standard of all, I add,

4. He is infinitely precious to his Father, who thoroughly knows him, and is an infallible Judge of real worth. He proclaimed more than once from the excellent glory, *This is my beloved Son, in whom I am pleased; hear ye him. Behold,* says he, *my servant whom I uphold; mine elect, in whom my soul delighteth.* Isa. xlii. 1. He is called by the names of the tenderest endearment; his Son, his own Son, his dear Son, the Son of his love.

† An excellent hymn of Dr. Doddridge's on 1 Tim. iii. 16.—Seen of Angels.
* Watt's Hor. Lyric.

He is a stone, disallowed indeed of men; if their approbation were the true standard of merit, he must be looked upon as a very worthless, insignificant being, unworthy of their thoughts and affections. But let men form what estimate of him they please, he is *chosen of God, and precious*. And shall not the love of the omniscient God have weight with believers to love him too? Yes, the apostle expressly draws the consequence; he is precious to God, therefore to you that believe, he is precious. It is the characteristic of even the meanest believer, that he is God-like. He is a partaker of the divine nature, and therefore views things, in some measure, as God does; and is affected towards them as God is, though there be an infinite difference as to the degree. He prevailingly loves what God loves, and that because God loves it.

And now, my hearers, what think you of Christ? Will you not think of him as believers do? If so, he will be precious to your hearts above all things for the future. Or if you disregard this standard of excellence, as being but the estimate of fallible creatures, will you not think of him as angels do; angels, those bright intelligences, to whom he reveals his unveiled glories, who are more capable of perceiving and judging of him, and who therefore must know him better than you; angels, who have had a long acquaintance with him at home, if I may so speak, for near six thousand years, as God, *i. e.* ever since their creation, and for near two thousand years as God-man? Since angels then, who know him so thoroughly, love him so highly, certainly you may safely venture to love him; you might safely venture to love him implicitly, upon their word. He died for you, which is more than ever he did for them, and will you not love him after all this love? It is not the mode to think much of him in our world, but it is the mode in heaven. Yes, blessed be God, if he be despised and rejected of men, he is not despised and rejected of angels. Angels, that know him best, love him above all, and, as far as their capacity will allow, do justice to his merit: and this is a very comfortable thought to a heart broken with a sense of the neglect and contempt he meets with among men. — Blessed Jesus! may not one congregation be got together, even upon our guilty earth, that shall in this respect be like the angels, all lovers of thee? O! why should this be impossible, while they are all so much in need of thee, all so much obliged to thee, and thou art so lovely in thyself! Why, my brethren, should not this congregation be made up of such, and such only as are lovers of Jesus? Why should he not be precious to every one of you, rich and poor, old and young, white and black? What reason can any one of you give why you in particular should neglect him? I am sure you can give none. And will you, without any reason, dissent from all the angels in heaven, in point of which they must be the most competent judges? Will you differ from them, and agree in your sentiments of Christ with the ghosts of hell, his implacable, but conquered and miserable enemies?

If all this has no weight with you, let me ask you farther, Will you not agree to that estimate of Jesus which his Father has of him? Will you run counter to the supreme reason? Will you set up yourselves as wiser than omniscience? How must Jehovah resent it to see a worm at his foot-stool daring to despise him, whom he loves so highly? O let him be precious to you, because he is so to God, who knows him best.

But I am shocked at my own attempt.—O precious Jesus! are matters come to that pass in our world, that creatures bought with thy blood, creatures that owe all their hopes to thee, should stand in need of persuasions to love thee? What horrors attend the thought! However, blessed be God, there are some, even among men, to whom he is precious. This world is not entirely peopled with the despisers of Christ. To as many of you as believe, he is precious, though to none else.

Would you know the reason of this; I will tell you; none but believers have eyes to see his glory, none but they are sensible of their need of him, and none but they have learned from experience how precious he is.

1. None but believers have eyes to see the glory of Christ. As the knowledge of Christ is entirely from revelation, an avowed unbeliever, who rejects that revelation, can have no right knowledge of him, and therefore must be entirely indifferent towards him, as one unknown, or must despise and abhor him as an enthusiast or impostor. But one, who is not an unbeliever in profession or speculation, may yet be destitute of that faith which constitutes a true believer, and which renders Jesus precious to the soul. Even devils are very orthodox in speculation: Devils believe, and tremble; and they could cry out, *What have we to do with thee, Jesus of Nazareth? We know thee, who thou art; even the Holy One of God.* Mark i. 24. And there are crowds among us who believe, after a fashion, that Christ is the true Messiah, who yet shew by their practices that they neglect him in their hearts, and are not believers in the full import of the character. True faith includes not only a speculative knowledge and belief, but a clear, affecting, realizing view, and an hearty approbation of the things known and believed concerning Jesus Christ; and such a view, such an approbation, cannot be produced by any human means, but only by the enlightening influence of the holy Spirit shining into the heart.—Without such a faith as this, the mind is all dark and blind as to the glory of Jesus Christ; it can see no beauty in him, that he should be desired. Honourable and sublime speculations concerning him may hover in the under-

standing, and the tongue may pronounce many pompous panegyrics in his praise, but the understanding has no realizing, affecting views of his excellency; nor does the heart delight in him and love him as infinitely precious and lovely. The God of this world, the prince of darkness, has blinded the minds of them that believe not, lest the light of the glorious gospel of Christ should shine into them. But as to the enlightened believer, God, who first commanded light to shine out of darkness, has shined into his heart, to give him the light of the knowledge of the glory of God in the face of Jesus Christ. This divine illumination pierces the cloud that obscured his understanding, and enables him to view the Lord Jesus in a strong and striking light; a light entirely different from that of the crowd around him; a light, in which it is impossible to view this glorious object without loving him. A believer and an unbeliever may be equally orthodox in speculation, and have the same notions in theory concerning Jesus Christ, and yet it is certainly true, that their views of him are vastly different. Believers! do you think that, if the Christ-despising multitude around you had the same views of his worth and preciousness which you have, they could neglect him as they do? It is impossible. You could once neglect him, as others do now; you were no more charmed with his beauty than they. But O! when you were brought out of darkness into God's marvellous light, when the glories of the neglected Saviour broke in upon your astonished minds, then was it possible for you to withhold your love from him? Were not your hearts captivated with delightful violence? You could no more resist. Did not your hearts then as naturally and freely love him, whom they had once disgusted, as ever they loved a dear child or a friend, or the sweetest created enjoyment? The improving your reason into faith is setting the disordered eye of the mind right, that it may be able to see this object; and when once you viewed it with this eye of reason restored and improved, how did the precious stone sparkle before you, and charm you with its brilliancy and excellence? Christ is one of those things unseen and hoped for, of which St. Paul says, *Faith is the substance and evidence*. Heb. xi. 1. Faith gives Christ a present subsistence in the mind, not as a majestic phantom, but as the most glorious and important reality; and this faith is a clear affecting demonstration, or conviction, of his existence, and of his being in reality what his word represents him. It is by such a faith, that is, under its habitual influence, that the believer lives; and hence, while he lives, Jesus is still precious to him.

2. None but believers are properly sensible of their need of Christ. They are deeply sensible of their ignorance and the disorder of their understanding, and therefore they are sensible of

their want of both the external and internal instructions of this divine Prophet. But as to others, they are puffed up with intellectual pride, and apprehend themselves in very little need of religious instructions; and therefore they think but very slightly of him. Believers feel themselves guilty, destitute of all righteousness, and incapable of making attonement for their sins, or recommending themselves to God, and therefore the satisfaction and righteousness of Jesus Christ are most precious to them, and they rejoice in him as their all-prevailing Intercessor. But as to the unbelieving crowd, they have no such mortifying thoughts of themselves: they have so many excuses to make for their sins, that they bring down their guilt to a very trifling thing, hardly worthy of divine resentment; and they magnify their good works to such an height, that they imagine they will nearly balance their bad, and procure them some favour at least from God, and therefore they must look upon this High Priest as needless. They also love to be free from the restraints of religion, and to have the command of themselves. They would usurp the power of self-government, and make their own pleasure their rule; and therefore the Lord Jesus Christ, as a King, is so far from being precious, that he is very unacceptable to such obstinate, head-strong rebels. They choose to have no lawgiver, but their own wills; and therefore they trample upon his laws, and, as it were, form insurrections against his government. But the poor believer, sensible of his incapacity for self-government, loves to be under direction, and delights to feel the dependent, submissive, pliant spirit of a subject. He counts it a mercy not to have the management of himself, and feels his need of this mediatoral King to rule him. He hates the rebel within, hates every insurrection of sin, and longs to have it entirely subdued, and every thought, every motion of his soul, brought into captivity to the obedience of Christ; and therefore he feels the need of his royal power to make an entire conquest of his hostile spirit. His commands are not uneasy impositions, but most acceptable and friendly directions to him; and the prohibitions of his law are not painful restraints, but a kind of privileges in his esteem. The language of his heart is, " Precious Jesus! be thou my King. I love to live in humble subjection to thee. I would voluntarily submit myself to thy controul and direction. Thy will, not mine, be done! O subdue every rebellious principle within, and make me all resignation and cheerful obedience to thee!" To such a soul it is no wonder Jesus should be exceeding precious: but O how different is this spirit from that which generally prevails in the world? Let me add but one reason more why Jesus is precious to believers, and them only; namely,

3. None but believers have known by experience how precious he is. They, and only they, can reflect upon the glorious views

of him, which themselves have had, to captivate their hearts forever to him. They, and only they, have known what it is to feel a bleeding heart healed by his gentle hand; and a clamourous languishing conscience pacified by his atoning blood. They, and only they, know by experience how sweet it is to feel his love shed abroad in their hearts, to feel an heart, ravished with his glory, pant, and long, and breathe after him, and exerting the various acts of faith, desire, joy, and hope towards him. They, and only they, know by experience how pleasant it is to converse, with him in his ordinances, and to spend an hour of devotion in some retirement, as it were, in his company. They, and only they have experienced the exertions of his royal power, conquering their mightiest sins, and sweetly subduing them to himself. These are, in some measure, matters of experience with every true believer, and therefore it is no wonder Jesus should be precious to them. But as to the unbelieving multitude, poor creatures! they are entire strangers to these things. They may have some superficial notions of them floating in their heads, but they have never felt them in their hearts, and therefore the infinitely precious Lord Jesus is a worthless, insignificant Being to them: and thus alas! it will be with the unhappy creatures, until experience becomes their teacher; until they taste for themselves *that the Lord is gracious.* 1 Peter ii. 3.

There is an interesting question, which, I doubt not, has risen in the minds of such of you as have heard what has been said with a particular application to yourselves, and keeps you in a painful suspence: with an answer to which I shall conclude: " Am I indeed a true believer? may some of you say; and is Christ precious to me? My satisfaction in this sweet subject is vastly abated, till this question is solved. Sometimes, I humbly think, the evidence is in my favour, and I begin to hope that he is indeed precious to my soul; but alas my love for him soon languishes, and then my doubts and fears return, and I know not what to do, nor what to think of myself." Do not some of you, my brethren, long to have this perplexing case cleared up? O what would you not give, if you might return home this evening fully satisfied in this point? Well, I would willingly help you, for experience has taught me to sympathize with you under this difficulty. O my heart! how often haft thou been suspicious of thyself in this respect? The readiest way I can now take to clear up the matter is to answer another question, naturally resulting from my subject; and that is, " How does that high esteem which a believer has for Jesus Christ discover itself? For how does he shew that Christ is indeed precious to him?" I answer, he shews it in various ways, particularly by his affectionate thoughts of him, which often rise in his mind, and always find welcome there. He discovers that Jesus is precious to him by hating and refisting whatever is displeasing to him, and by parting with every thing that comes in competition with him. He will let all go rather than part with Christ. Honour, reputation, ease, riches, pleasure, and even life itself, are nothing to him in comparison of Christ, and he will run the risque of all; nay, will actually lose all, if he may but win Christ. He discovers this high esteem for him by the pleasure he takes in feeling his heart suitably affected towards him, and by his uneasiness when it is otherwise. O! when he can love Jesus, when his thoughts affectionately clasp around him, and whem he has an heart to serve him, then he is happy, his soul is well, and he is lively and cheerful. But alas! when it is otherwise with him, when his love languishes, when his heart hardens, when it becomes out of order for his service, then he grows uneasy and discontented, and cannot be at rest. When Jesus favours him with his gracious presence, and revives him with his influence, how does he rejoice! But when his beloved withdraws himself and is gone, how does he lament his absence, and long for his return! He weeps and cries like a bereaved, deserted orphan, and moans like a loving turtle in the absence of its mate. Because Christ is so precious to him, he cannot bear the thought of parting with him, and the least jealousy of his love pierces his very heart. Because he loves him he longs for the full enjoyment of him, and is ravished with the prospect of it. Because Christ is precious to him, his interests are so too, and he longs to see his kingdom flourish, and all men flourish, and all men fired with his love. Because he loves him, he loves his ordinances; loves to here, because it is the word of Jesus? loves to pray, because it is maintaining intercourse with Jesus; loves to sit at his table, because it is a memorial of Jesus; and loves his people, because they love Jesus. Whatever has a relation to his precious Saviour is for that reason precious to him; and when he feels any thing of a contrary disposition, alas! it grieves him, and makes him abhor himself. These things are sufficient to shew that the Lord Jesus has his heart, and is indeed precious to him; and is not this the very picture of some trembling doubting souls among you? If it be, take courage. After so many vain searches, you have at length discovered the welcome secret, that Christ is indeed precious to you: and if so, you may be sure that you are precious to him. *You shall be mine, saith the Lord, in the day that I make up my jewels.* Mal. iii. 17. If you are now satisfied, after thorough trial of the case, retain your hope, and let not every discouraging appearance renew your jealousies again: labour to be steady and firm Christians and do not stagger through unbelief.

But alas! I fear that many of you know nothing experimentally of the exercises of a believing heart, which I have been describing, and confequently that Chrift is not precious to you. If this is the cafe, you may be fure indeed you are hateful to him. He is angry with the wicked every day. "Thofe that honour him he will honour; but they that defpife him fhall be lightly efteemed." 1 Sam. ii. 30. And what will you do if Chrift fhould become your enemy and fight againft you? If this precious ftone fhould become a ftone of ftumbling and a rock of offence to you, over which you will fall into ruin, O how dreadful muft the fall be! What muft you expect but to lie down in unutterable and everlafting forrow!

SERMON XV.

The Danger of Lukewarmnefs in Religion.

REVELATION iii. 15, 16. *I know thy works, that thou art neither cold nor hot: I would thou wert cold or hot. So then, becaufe thou art lukewarm, and neither cold nor hot, I will fpue thee out of my mouth.*

THE foul of man is endowed with fuch active powers, that it cannot be idle; and, if we look round the world, we fee it all alive and bufy in fome purfuit or other. What vigorous action, what labour and toil, what hurry, noife, and commotion about the neceffaries of life, about riches and honours! Here men are in earneft: here there is no diffimulation, no indifferency about the event. They fincerely defire, and eagerly ftrive for thefe tranfient delights, or vain embellifhments of a moral life.

And may we infer farther, that creatures, thus formed for action, and thus laborious and unwearied in thefe inferior purfuits, are proportionably vigorous and in earneft in matters of infinitely greater importance? May we conclude, that they proportion their labour and activity to the nature of things, and that they are moft in earneft where they are moft concerned? A ftranger to our world, that could conclude nothing concerning the conduct of mankind but from the generous prefumptions of his own charitable heart, might perfuade himfelf that this is the cafe. But one that has been but a little while converfant with them, and taken the leaft notice of their temper and practice with regard to that moft interefting thing, Religion, muft know it is quite otherwife. For look round you, and what do you fee? Here and there indeed you may see a few unfashionable creatures, who act as if they looked upon religion to be the most interesting concern; and who seem determined, let others do as they will, to make sure of salvation, whatever becomes of them in other respects: but as to the generality, they are very indifferent about it. They will not indeed renounce all religion entirely; they will make some little profession of the religion that happens to be most modish and reputable in their country, and they will conform to some of its institutions; but it is a matter of indifferency with them, and they are but little concerned about it; or, in the language of my text, they are *lukewarm, and neither cold nor hot*.

This threatening, *I will spue thee out of my mouth*, has been long ago executed with a dreadful severity upon the Laodicean church; and it is now succeeded by a mongrel race of Pagans and Mahometans; and the name of Christ is not heard among them. But, though this church has been demolished for so many hundreds of years, that lukewarmness of spirit in religion which brought this judgment upon them, still lives, and possesses the christians of our age: it may therefore be expedient for us to consider Christ's friendly warning to them, that we may escape their doom.

The epistles to the seven churches in Asia are introduced with this solemn and striking preface, " I know thy works:" that is to say, your character is drawn by one that thoroughly knows you; one who inspects all your conduct, and takes notice of you when you take no notice of yourselves; one that cannot be imposed upon by an empty profession and artifice, but searches the heart and the reins. O that this truth were deeply impressed upon our hearts: for surely we could not trifle and offend while sensible that we are under the eye of our Judge!

I know thy works, says he to the Laodicean church, *that thou art neither cold nor hot*. This church was in a very bad condition, and Christ reproves her with the greatest severity;* and yet we do not find her charged with the practice or toleration of any gross immoralities, as some of the other churches were. She is not censured for indulging fornication among her members, or communicating with idolaters in eating things sacrificed to idols, like some of the rest. She was free from the infection of the Nicolaitans, which had spread among them. What then is her charge? It is a subtle, latent wickedness, that has no shocking appearance, that makes no gross blemish in the outward character of a professor in the view of others, and may escape his own notice; it is, *Thou art lukewarm, and neither cold nor hot:* as if our Lord had said,

---
* She was as loathsome to him as lukewarm water to the stomach, and he characterises her as " wretched, and miserable, and poor, and blind, and naked." What condition can be more deplorable and dangerous?

Thou doft not entirely renounce and openly difregard the chriftian religion, and thou doft not make it a ferious bufinefs, and mind it as thy grand concern. Thou haft a form of godlinefs, but denieft the power. All thy religion is a dull, languid thing, a mere indifferency; thine heart is not in it; it is not animated with the fervour of thy fpirit. Thou haft neither the coldnefs of the profligate finner, nor the facred fire and life of the true chriftian; but thou keepeft in a fort of medium between them. In fome things thou refembleft the one, in other things the other; as lukewarmnefs partakes of the nature both of heat and cold.

Now fuch a lukewarmnefs is an eternal folecifm in religion; it is the moft abfurd and inconfiftent thing imaginable; more fo than avowed impiety, or a profeffed rejection of all religion: therefore, fays Chrift, *I would thou wert cold or hot,*—i. e. "You might be any thing more confiftently than what you are. If you looked upon religion as a cheat, and openly rejected the profeffion of it, it would not be ftrange that you fhould be carelefs about it, and difregard it in practice. But to own it true, and make a profeffion of it, and yet be lukewarm and indifferent about it, this is the moft abfurd conduct that can be conceived; for, if it be true, it is certainly the moft important and interefting truth in all the world, and requires the utmoft exertion of all your powers."

When Chrift expreffes his abhorrence of lukewarmnefs in the form of a wifh, *I would thou wert cold or hot,* we are not to fuppofe his meaning to be, that coldnefs or fervour in religion are equally acceptable, or that coldnefs is at all acceptable to him; for reafon and revelation concur to affure us, that the open rejection and avowed contempt of religion is an aggravated wickednefs, as well as an hypocritical profeffion. But our Lord's defign is to exprefs in the ftrongeft manner poffible, how odious and abominable their lukewarmnefs was to him; as if he fhould fay, "Your ftate is fo bad, that you cannot change for the worfe; I would rather you were any thing than what you are." You are ready to obferve, that the lukewarm profeffor is in reality wicked and corrupt at heart, a flave to fin, and an enemy to God, as well as the avowed finner; and therefore they are both hateful in the fight of God, and both in a ftate of condemnation. But there are fome aggravations peculiar to the lukewarm profeffor that render him peculiarly odious; as, 1. He adds the fin of an hypocritical profeffion to his other fins. The wickednefs of real irreligion, and the wickednefs of falfely pretending to be religious, meet and center in him at once. 2. To all this he adds the guilt of prefumption, pride, and felf-flattery, imagining he is in a fafe ftate and in favour with God; whereas he that makes no pretenfions to religion, has no fuch umbrage for this conceit and delufion. Thus the miferable Laodiceans "thought themfelves rich, and increafed in goods, and in need of nothing." 3. Hence it follows, that the lukewarm profeſſor is in the moſt dangerous condition, as he is not liable to conviction, nor ſo likely to be brought to repentance. Thus publicans and harlots received the goſpel more readily than the ſelf-righteous Phariſees. 4. The honour of God and religion is more injured by the negligent, unconſcientious behaviour of theſe Laodiceans, than by the vices of thoſe who make no pretenſions to religion; with whom therefore its honour has no connection. On theſe accounts you ſee lukewarmneſs is more aggravatedly ſinful and dangerous than entire coldneſs about religion.

So then, ſays Chriſt, *Becauſe thou art lukewarm, and neither cold nor hot, I will ſpue thee out of my mouth:* this is their doom; as if he ſhould ſay, "As lukewarm water is more diſagreeable to the ſtomach than either cold or hot, ſo you, of all others, are the moſt abominable to me. I am quite ſick of ſuch profeſſors, and I will caſt them out of my church, and reject them for ever."

My preſent deſign is to expoſe the peculiar abſurdity and wickedneſs of lukewarmneſs or indifference in religion; a diſeaſe that has ſpread its deadly contagion far and wide among us, and calls for a ſpeedy cure. And let me previouſly obſerve to you, that, if I do not offer you ſufficient arguments to convince your own reaſon of the abſurdity and wickedneſs of ſuch a temper, then you may ſtill indulge it; but that if my arguments are ſufficient, then ſhake off your ſloth, and be fervent in ſpirit; and if you neglect your duty, be it at your peril.

In illuſtrating this point I ſhall proceed upon this plain principle, *That religion is, of all things, the moſt important in itſelf, and the moſt intereſting to us.* This we cannot deny, without openly pronouncing it an impoſture. If there be a God, as religion teaches us, he is the moſt glorious, the moſt venerable, and the moſt lovely Being; and nothing can be ſo important to us as his favour, and nothing ſo terrible as his diſpleaſure. If he be our Maker, our Benefactor, our Lawgiver and Judge, it muſt be our greateſt concern to ſerve him with all our might. If Jeſus Chriſt be ſuch a Saviour as our religion repreſents, and we profeſs to believe, he demands our warmeſt love and moſt lively ſervices. If eternity, if heaven and hell, and the final judgment, are realities, they are certainly the moſt auguſt, the moſt awful, important, and intereſting realities; and, in compariſon of them, the moſt weighty concerns of the preſent life are but trifles, dreams, and ſhadows. If prayer and other religious exerciſes are our duty, certainly they require all the vigour of our ſouls; and nothing can be more abſurd or incongruous than to perform them in a languid, ſpiritleſs manner, as if we knew not what we were about. If there be any life within us, theſe are proper objects to call it forth: if our ſouls are endowed with active powers, here are objects that demand their utmoſt exertion. Here we can never be ſo much in earneſt as the caſe requires. Trifle about any thing, but O do not trifle here! Be careless and indifferent about crowns and kingdoms, about health, life, and all the world, but O be not careless and indifferent about such immense concerns as these!

But to be more particular: let us take a view of a lukewarm temper in various attitudes, or with respect to several objects, particularly towards God—towards Jesus Christ—a future state of happiness or misery—and in the duties of religion; and in each of these views we cannot but be shocked at so monstrous a temper, especially if we consider our difficulties and dangers in a religious life, and the eagerness and activity of mankind in inferior pursuits.

1. Consider who and what God is. He is the original uncreated beauty, the sum total of all natural and moral perfections, the origin of all the excellencies that are scattered through this glorious universe; he is the supreme good, and the only proper portion for our immortal spirits. He also sustains the most majestic and endearing relations to us; our Father, our Preserver and Benefactor, our Lawgiver, and our Judge. And is such a Being to be put off with heartless, lukewarm services? What can be more absurd or impious then to dishonour supreme excellency and beauty with a languid love and esteem; to trifle in the presence of the most venerable Majesty; treat the best of Beings with indifferency; to be careless about our duty to such a Father; to return such a Benefactor only insipid complimental expressions of gratitude; to be dull and spiritless in obedience to such a Lawgiver; and to be indifferent about the favour or displeasure of such a Judge! I appeal to Heaven and earth, if this be not the most shocking conduct imaginable. Does not your reason pronounce it horrid and most daringly wicked? And yet thus is the great and blessed God treated by the generality of mankind. It is most astonishing that he should bear with such treatment so long, and that mankind themselves are not shocked at it: but such the case really is. And are there not some lukewarm Laodiceans in this assembly? Jesus knows your works, that you are neither cold not hot; and it is fit you should also know them. May you not be convinced, upon a little inquiry, that your hearts are habitually indifferent towards God? You may indeed entertain a speculative esteem or a good opinion of him, but are your souls alive towards him? Do they burn with his love? And are you fervent in spirit when you are serving him? Some of you, I hope, amid all your infirmities, can give comfortable answers to these inquiries. But alas! how few! But yet as to such of you as are lukewarm, and neither cold nor hot, you are the most abominable creatures upon earth to an holy God.—*Be zealous*, be warm, *therefore, and repent.* (ver. 19.)

2. Is lukewarmness a proper temper towards Jesus Christ? Is this a suitable return for that love which brought him down from his native paradise into our wretched world? That love which kept his mind for thirty-three painful and tedious years intent upon this one object, the salvation of sinners? That love which rendered him cheerfully patient of the shame, the curse, the tortures of crucifixion, and all the agonies of the most painful death? That love which makes him the sinner's friend still in the courts of Heaven, where he appears as our prevailing Advocate and Intercessor? Blessed Jesus! is lukewarmness a proper return to thee for all this kindness? No; methinks devils cannot treat thee worse. My fellow-mortals, my fellow-sinners, who are the objects of all this love, can you put him off with languid devotions and faint services? Then every grateful and generous passion is extinct in your souls, and you are qualified to venture upon every form of ingratitude and baseness. O was Christ indifferent about your salvation? Was his love lukewarm towards you? No; your salvation was the object of his most intense application night and day through the whole course of his life, and it lay nearest his heart in the agonies of death. For this he had *a baptism to be baptized with*, a baptism, an immersion in tears and blood; *and how am I straitened*, says he, *till it be accomplished!* For this, *with desire he desired to eat his last passover,* because it introduced the last scene of his sufferings. His love! what shall I say of it? What language can describe its strength and ardor? *His love was strong as death; the coals thereof were coals of fire, which had a most vehement flame: many waters could not quench it, nor the floods drown it.* Cant. viii. 6, 7. Never did a tender mother love her sucking child with a love equal to his. Never was a father more earnest to rescue an only son from the hands of a murderer, or to pluck him out of the fire, than Jesus was to save perishing sinners. Now to neglect him after all; to forget him; or to think of him with indifferency, as though he were a being of but little importance, and we but little obliged to him, what is all this but the most unnatural, barbarous ingratitude, and the most shocking wickedness? Do you not expect everlasting happiness from him purchased at the expence of his blood? And can you hope for such an immense blessing from him without feeling yourselves most sensibly obliged to him? Can you hope he will do so much for you, and can you be content to do nothing for him, or to go through his service with lukewarmness and langour, as if you cared not how you hurried through it, or how little you had to do with it? Can any thing be more absurd or impious than this? Methinks you may defy hell to shew a worse temper. May not Christ justly wish you were either cold or hot; wish you were any thing, rather than thus lukewarm towards him under a profession of friendship? Alas! my brethren, if this be your habitual temper, instead of being

saved by him you may expect he will reject you with the most nauseating disgust and abhorrence. But,

3. Is lukewarmness and indifferency a suitable temper with respect to a future state of happiness or misery? Is it a suitable temper with respect to an happiness far exceeding the utmost bounds of our present thoughts and wishes; an happiness equal to the largest capacites of our souls in their most improved and perfected state; an happiness beyond the grave, when all the enjoyments of this transitory life have taken an eternal flight from us, and leave us hungry and famishing for ever, if these be our only portion; an happiness that will last aslong as our immortal spirits, and never fade or fly from us? Or are lukewarmness and indifferency a suitable temper with respect to a misery beyond expression, beyond conception dreadful; a misery inflicted by a God of almighty power and inexorable justice upon a number of obstinate, incorrigible rebels for numberless, wilful, and daring provocations, inflicted on purpose to shew his wrath and make his power known; a misery proceeding from the united fury of divine indignation, of turbulent passions, of a guilty conscience, of malicious, tormenting devils; a misery (who can bear up under the horror of the thought!) that shall last as long as the eternal God shall live to inflict it; as long as sin shall continue evil to deserve it; as long as an immortal spirit shall endure to bear it; a misery that shall never be mitigated, never intermitted, never, never, never see an end? And remember, that a state of happiness or misery is not far remote from us, but near us, just before us; the next year, the next hour, or the next moment, we may enter into it; is a state for which we are now candidates, now upon trial; now our eternal all lies at stake: and, O sirs, does an inactive, careless posture become us in such a situation? Is a state of such happiness, or such misery; is such a state just—just before us, a matter of indifferency to us? O can you be lukewarm about such matters? Was ever such prodigious stupidity seen under the canopy of heaven, or even in the regions of hell, which abound with monstrous and horrid dispositions? No; the hardest ghost below cannot make light of these things. Mortals! can you trifle about them? Well trifle a little longer, and your trifling will be over for ever. You may be indifferent about the improving of your time; but time is not indifferent whether to pass by or not; it is determined to continue its rapid course, and hurry you into the ocean of eternity, though you should continue sleeping and dreaming through all the passage. Therefore awake, arise; exert yourselves before your doom be unchangeably fixed. If you have any fire within you, here let it burn; if you have any active powers, here let them be exerted; here or no where, and on no occasion. Be active, be in earnest where you should be; or debase and sink yourselves into stocks and stones, and escape the curse of being reasonable and active

Serm. 15. *Lukewarmness in Religion.* 277

creatures. Let the criminal condemned to die to-morrow, be indifferent about a reprieve or a pardon; let a drowning man be careless about catching at the only plank that can save him; but O do not be careless and indifferent about eternity, and such amazing realities as heaven and hell. If you disbelieve these things, you are infidels; if you believe these things, and yet are unaffected with them, you are worse than infidels: you are a sort of shocking singularities, and prodigies in nature. Not hell itself can find a precedent of such a conduct. The devils believe, and tremble; you believe, and trifle with things whose very name strike solemnity and awe through heaven and hell. But,

4. Let us see how this lukewarm temper agrees with the duties of religion. And as I cannot particularize them all, I shall only mention an instance or two. View a lukewarm professor in prayer; he pays to an omniscient God the compliment of a bended knee, as though he could impose upon him with such an empty pretence. When he is addressing the Supreme Majesty of Heaven and earth he hardly ever recollects in whose presence he is, or whom he is speaking to, but seems as if he were worshipping without an object, or pouring out empty words into the air: perhaps through the whole prayer he had not so much as one solemn, affecting thought of that God whose name he so often invoked. Here is a criminal petitioning for pardon so carelessly, that he scarcely knows what he is about. Here is a needy famishing beggar pleading for such immense blessings as everlasting salvation, and all the joys of heaven, so lukewarmly and thoughtlessly as if he cared not whether his requests were granted or not. He is an obnoxious offender confessing his sins with an heart untouched with sorrow; worshipping the living God with a dead heart; making great requests, but he forgets them as soon as he rises from his knees, and is not at all inquisitive what become of them, and whether they were accepted or not. And can there be a more shocking, impious, and daring conduct than this? To trifle in the royal presence would not be such an audacious affront. For a criminal to catch flies or sport with a feather when pleading with his judge for his pardon, would be but a faint shadow of such religious trifling! What are such prayers but solemn mockeries and disguised insults? And yet, is not this the usual method in which many of you address the great God! The words proceed no further than from your tongue: you do not pour them out from the bottom of your hearts; they have no life or spirit in them, and you hardly ever reflect upon their meaning. And when you have talked away to God in this manner, you will have it to pass for a prayer. But surely such prayers must bring down a curse upon you instead of a blessing: such sacrifices must be *an abomination to the Lord*, Prov. xv. 8. and it is astonishing that he has not mingled your blood with your sacrifices, and sent you from your knees to hell.

from thoughtless, unmeaning prayer to real blasphemy and torture.

The next instance I shall mention is with regard to the word of God. You own it divine you profess it the standard of your religion, and the most excellent book in the world. Now, if this be the case, it is God that speaks to you; it is God that sends you an epistle when you are reading or hearing his word. How impious and provoking then must it be to neglect it, to let it lie by you as an antiquated, useless book, or to read it in a careless, superficial manner, and hear it with an inattentive, wandering mind? How would you take it, if, when you spoke to your servant about his own interest, he should turn away from you, and not regard you? Or if you should write a letter to your son, and he should not so much as carefully read it, or labour to understand it? And do not some of you treat the sacred oracles in this manner? You make but little use of your Bible, but to teach your children to read: Or if you read or hear its contents yourselves, are you not unaffected with them? One would think you would be all attention and reverence to every word; you would drink it in, and thirst for it as new-born babes for their mother's milk; you would feel its energy, and acquire the character of that happy man to whom the God of heaven vouchsafes to look; you would tremble at his word. It reveals the only method of your salvation: it contains the only character of all your blessings. In short, you have the nearest personal interest in it, and can you be unconcerned hearers of it? I am sure your reason and conscience must condemn such stupidity and indifferency as incongruous, and outrageously wicked.

And now let me remind you of the observation I made upon entering upon this subject, that if I should not offer sufficient matter of conviction, you might go on in your lukewarmness; but if your own reason should be fully convinced that such a temper is most wicked and unreasonable, then you might indulge it at your peril. What do you say now in the issue? Ye modern Laodiceans, are you not yet struck with horror at the thought of that insipid, formal, spiritless religion you have hitherto been contented with? And do you not see the necessity of following the advice of Christ to the Laodicean church, *be zealous*, be fervent for the future, *and repent*, bitterly repent of what is past? To urge this the more, I have two considerations in reserve, of no small weight. 1. Consider the difficulties and dangers in your way. O sirs, if you knew the difficulty of the work of your salvation, and the great danger of miscarrying in it, you could not be so indifferent about it, nor could you flatter yourselves such languid endeavours will ever succeed. It is a labour, a striving, a race, a warfare; so it is called in the sacred writings: but would there be any propriety in these expressions if it were a course of sloth and inactivity? Consider, you have strong lusts to be subdued, an hard heart to be broken, a variety of graces which you are entirely destitute of to be implanted and cherished, and that in an unnatural soil where they will not grow without careful cultivation, and that you have many temptations to be encountered and resisted. In short, you must be made new men, quite other creatures than you now are. And O! can this work be successfully performed while you make such faint and feeble efforts? Indeed God is the Agent, and all your best endeavours can never effect the blessed revolution without him. But his assistance is not to be expected in the neglect, or careless use of means, nor is it intended to encourage idleness, but activity and labour; and when he comes to work, he will soon inflame your hearts, and put an end to your lukewarmness. Again, your dangers are also great and numerous; you are in danger from presumption and from despondency; from coldness, from lukewarmness, and from false fires and enthusiastic heats; in danger from self-righteousness, and then open wickedness, from your own corrupt hearts, from this ensnaring world, and from the temptations of the devil: you are in great danger of sleeping on in security without ever being thoroughly awakened; or, if you should be awakened, you are in danger of resting short of vital religion; and in either of these cases you are undone for ever. In a word, dangers crowd thick around you on every hand, from every quarter; dangers, into which thousands, millions of your fellow-men have fallen and never recovered. Indeed, all things considered, it is very doubtful whether ever you will be saved who are now lukewarm and secure: I do not mean that your success is uncertain if you be brought to use means with proper earnestness; but alas! it is awfully uncertain whether ever you will be brought to use them in this manner. And, O sirs, can you continue secure and inactive when you have such difficulties to encounter with in a work of absolute necessity, and when you are surrounded with so many and so great dangers? Alas! are you capable of such destructive madness? O that you knew the true state of the case! Such a knowledge would soon fire you with the greatest ardor, and make you all life and vigour in this important work.

2. Consider how earnest and active men are in other pursuits. Should we form a judgment of the faculties of human nature by the conduct of the generality in religion, we should be apt to conclude that men are mere snails, and that they have no active powers belonging to them. But view them about other affairs, and you find they are all life, fire, and hurry. What labour and toil! what schemes and contrivances! what solicitude about success! what fears of disappointment! hands, heads, hearts, all busy.

And all this to procure those enjoyments which at best they cannot long retain, and which the next hour may tear from them. To acquire a name or a diadem, to obtain riches or honours, what hardships are undergone! what dangers dared! what rivers of blood shed! how many millions of lives have been lost! and how many more endangered! In short, the world is all alive, all in motion with business. On sea and land, at home and abroad, you will find men eagerly pursuing some temporal good. They grow grey-headed, and die in the attempt without reaching their end; but this disappointment does not discourage the survivors and successors; still they will continue, or renew the endeavour. Now here men act like themselves; and they shew they are alive, and endowed with powers of great activity. And shall they be thus zealous and laborious in the pursuit of earthly vanities, and be quite indifferent and sluggish in the infinitely more important concerns of eternity? What, solicitous about a mortal body, but careless about an immortal soul! Eager in pursuit of joys of a few years, but careless and remiss in seeking an immortality of perfect happiness! Anxious to avoid poverty, shame, sickness, pain, and all the evils, real or imaginary, of the present life; but indifferent about an whole eternity of the most intolerable misery! O the destructive folly, the daring wickedness of such a conduct! My brethern, is religion the only thing which demands the utmost exertion of all your powers, and alas! is that the only thing in which you will be dull and inactive? Is everlasting happiness the only thing about which you will be remiss? Is eternal punishment the only misery which you are indifferent whether you escape or not? Is God the only good which you pursue with faint and lazy desires? How preposterous! how absurd is this! You can love the world; you can love a father, a child, or a friend; nay, you can love that abominable, hateful thing, sin: these you can love with ardor, serve with pleasure, pursue with eagerness, and with all your might; but the ever-blessed God, and the Lord Jesus, your best friend, you put off with a lukewarm heart and spiritless services. O inexpressibly monstrous! Lord, what is this that has befallen thine own offspring, that they are so disaffected towards thee? Blessed Jesus, what hast thou done that thou shouldest be treated thus? O sinners! what will be the consequence of such a conduct? Will that God take you into the bosom of his love? will that Jesus save you by his blood, whom you make so light of? No, you may go and seek a heaven where you can find it; for God will give you none. Go, shift for yourselves, or look out for a Saviour where you will; Jesus will have nothing to do with you, except to take care to inflict proper punishment upon you if you retain this lukewarm temper towards him. Hence, by way of improvement, learn,

1. The vanity and wickedness of a lukewarm religion. Though you should profess the best religion that ever came from heaven, it will not save you; nay, it will condemn you with peculiar aggravations if you are lukewarm in it. This spirit of indifferency diffused through it, turns it all into deadly poison. Your religious duties are all abominable to God while the vigour of your spirits is not exerted in them. Your prayers are insults, and he will answer them as such by terrible things in righteousness. And do any of you hope to be saved by such a religion? I tell you from the God of truth, it will be so far from saving you, that it will certainly ruin you for ever : continue as you are till the last, and you will be as certainly damned to all eternity as Judas, or Beelzebub, or any ghost in hell. But alas!

2. How common, how fashionable is this lukewarm religion! This is the prevailing, epidemical sin of our age and country; and it is well if it has not the same fatal effect upon us as it had upon Laodicea : Laodicea lost its liberty, its religion, and its all. Therefore let Virginia hear and fear, and do no more so wickedly. We have thousands of christians, such as they are ; as many christians as white men ; but alas! they are generally of the Laodicean stamp; they are neither cold nor hot. But it is our first concern to know how it is with ourselves; therefore let this inquiry go round this congregation : Are you not such lukewarm christians? Is there any fire and life in your devotions? Or are not all your active powers engrossed by other pursuits?—Impartially make the inquiry, for infinitely more depends upon it than upon your temporal life.

3. If you have hitherto been possessed with this Laodicean spirit, I beseech you indulge it no longer. You have seen that it mars all your religion, and will end in your eternal ruin : and I hope you are not so hardened as to be proof against the energy of this consideration. Why halt you so long between two opinions? *I would you were cold or hot.* Either make thorough work of religion, or do not pretend to it. Why should you profess a religion which is but an insipid indifferency with you ? Such a religion is good for nothing. Therefore awake, arise, exert yourselves. Strive to enter in at the strait gate ; strive earnestly, or you are shut out for ever. Infuse heart and spirit into your religion. " Whatever your hand findeth to do, do it with your might." Now, this moment, while my voice sounds in your ears, now begin the vigorous enterprize. Now collect all the vigour of your souls, and breathe it out in such a prayer as this, " Lord, fire this heart with thy love." Prayer is a proper introduction : for let me remind you of what I should never forget, that God is the only Author of this sacred fire ; it is only he that can quicken you ; therefore, ye poor careless creatures, fly to him in an agony of importunity, and never desist, never grow weary till you prevail.

4. And lastly, Let the best of us lament our lukewarmness, and earnestly seek more fervour of spirit. Some of you have a little life; you enjoy some warm and vigorous moments; O! they are divinely sweet. But reflect how soon your spirits flag, your devotion cools, and your zeal languishes. Think of this, and be humble,: think of this, and apply for more life. You know where to apply. Christ is your life: therefore cry to him for the communications of it. "Lord Jesus! a little more life, a little more vital heat to a languishing soul." Take this method, and *you shall run, and not be weary; you shall walk and not faint.* Isaiah xl. 31.

SERMON XVI.

The Divine Government the Joy of our World.

PSALM xcvii. 1. *The Lord reigneth, let the earth rejoice; let the multitude of the isles be glad thereof.*

WISE and good rulers are justly accounted an extensive blessing to their subjects. In a government where wisdom sits at the helm; and justice, tempered with clemency, holds the ballance of retribution, liberty and property are secured, encroaching ambition is checked, helpless innocence is protected, and universal order is established, and consequently peace and happiness diffuse their streams through the land. In such a situation every heart must rejoice, every countenance look cheerful, and every bosom glow with gratitude to the happy instruments of such extended beneficence.

But, on the other hand, *Wo to thee, O land, when thy king is a child.* Ecclef. x. 16. weak, injudicious, humoursome, and peevish. This is the denunciation of Solomon, a sage philosopher, and an opulent king, whose station, capacity, and inclination, conspired to give him the deepest skill in politics: and this denunciation has been accomplished in every age. Empires have fallen, liberty has been fettered, property has been invaded, the lives of men have been arbitrarily taken away, and misery and desolation have broken in like a flood, when the government has been intrusted in the hands of tyranny, of luxury, or rashness; and the advantages of climate and soil, and all others which nature could bestow, have not been able to make the subjects happy under the baleful influence of such an administration.

It has frequently been the unhappy fate of nations to be enflaved to fuch rulers ; but fuch is the unavoidable imperfection of all human governments, that when, like our own, they are managed by the beft hands, they are attended with many calamities, and cannot anfwer feveral valuable ends ; and from both thefe confiderations we may infer the neceflity of a divine government over the whole univerfe, and particularly over the earth, in which we are more efpecially concerned. Without this fupreme univerfal Monarch, the affairs of this world would fall into confufion ; and the concerns of the next could not be managed at all. The capacities of the wifeft of men are fcanty, and not equal to all the purpofes of government ; and hence many affairs of importance will be unavoidably mifconducted ; and dangerous plots and aggravated crimes may be undifcovered for want of knowledge, or pafs unpunifhed for want of power. A wife and good ruler may be diffufing among his fubjects all that happinefs which can refult from the imperfect adminiftration of mortals, but he may be tumbled from his throne, and his government thrown into the greateft diforder by a more powerful invader ; fo that the beft ruler could not make his fubjects laftingly happy, unlefs he were univerfal monarch of the globe (a province too great for any mortal) and above the reach of the ambitious power of others. Further, Human dominion cannot extend to the fouls and confciences of men : civil rulers can neither know nor govern them ; and yet thefe muft be governed and brought into fubjection to the eternal laws of reafon, otherwife tranquility cannot fubfift on earth ; and efpecially the great purpofes of religion, which regard a future ftate, cannot be anfwered.

Men are placed here to be formed by a proper education for another world, for another clafs, and other employments ; but civil rulers cannot form them for thefe important ends, and therefore they muft be under the government of one who has axcefs to their fpirits, and can manage them as he pleafes.

Deeply impreft with thefe and other confiderations, which fhall be prefently mentioned, the Pfalmift is tranfported into this reflection, *The Lord reigneth, let the earth rejoice ; let the multitude of the ifles be glad thereof.*

The Pfalmift feems to have the mediatorial empire of grace erected by Immanuel more immediately in view ; and this indeed deferves our fpecial notice ; but no doubt he included the divine government in general, which is a juft ground of univerfal joy : and in this latitude I fhall confider the text.

Perfons in a tranfport are apt to fpeak abruptly, and omit the particles of connection and inference ufual in calm reafoning. Thus the Pfalmift cries out, *The Lord reigneth, let the earth rejoice ; let the multitude of the ifles be glad thereof!* but if we reduce the paſſage into an argumentative form, it will ſtand thus, " The Lord reigneth, therefore let the earth rejoice; and let the multitude of the iſles be glad upon this account."

The earth may here ſignify, by an uſual metonymy, the rational inhabitants of the earth, who are eſpecially concerned in the divine government; or, by a beautiful poetical proſopopœia, it may ſignify the inanimate globe of the earth; and then it intimates that the divine government is ſo important a bleſſing, that even the inanimate and ſenſeleſs creation would rejoice in it, were it capable of ſuch paſſions*. The iſles may likewiſe be taken figuratively for their inhabitants, particularly the Gentiles, who reſided in them; or literally for tracts of land ſurrounded with water.

My preſent deſign is,

To illuſtrate this glorious truth, that Jehovah's ſupreme government is a juſt cauſe of univerſal joy.

For that end I ſhall conſider the divine government in various views, as legiſlative, providential, mediatorial, and judicial; and ſhew that in each of theſe views the divine government is matter of univerſal joy.

I. The Lord reigneth upon a throne of legiſlation, *let the earth rejoice; let the multitude of the iſles be glad thereof.*

He is the one ſupreme Lawgiver, *Jam.* iv. 12. and is perfectly qualified for that important truſt. Nothing tends more to the advantage of civil ſociety than to have good laws eſtabliſhed, according to which mankind are to conduct themſelves, and according to which their rulers will deal with them. Now the ſupreme and univerſal King has erected and publiſhed the beſt laws for the government of the moral world, and of the human race in particular.

Let the earth then rejoice that God has clearly revealed his will to us, and not left us in inextricable perplexities about our duty to him and mankind. Human reaſon, or the light of nature, gives us ſome intimations of the duties of morality, even in our degenerate ſtate, and for this information we ſhould bleſs God; but alas! theſe diſcoveries are very imperfect, and we need ſupernatural revelation to make known to us the way of life. Accordingly, the Lord has favoured us with the ſacred oracles as a ſupplement to the feeble light of nature; and in them we are fully " taught what is good, and what the Lord requireth of us." And what cauſe of joy is this! How painful are the anxieties that attend uncertainty about matters of duty! How diſtreſſing a doubtful, fluctuating mind in an affair of ſuch tremendous importance!

---

* By the ſame figure the inanimate parts of the creation are called upon to praiſe the Lord, *Pſalm* cxlviii. and are ſaid to travel and groan under the ſin of man. *Rom.* viii. 22.

This, no doubt, some of you that are conscientious have had the experience of, in particular cases, when you were at a loss to apply to them the general directions in sacred scripture.

Again, *Let the earth rejoice ; let the multitude of the isles be glad* that these laws are suitably enforced with proper sanctions. The sanctions are such as become a God of infinite wisdom, almighty power, inexorable justice, untainted holiness, and unbounded goodness and grace, and such as are agreeable to the nature of reasonable creatures formed for an immortal duration. The rewards of obedience in the divine legislation are not such toys as posts of honour and profit, crowns and empires, which are the highest rewards that civil rulers can promise or bestow ; but rational peace and serenity of mind, undaunted bravery under the frowns of adversity, a cheerful confidence in the divine guardianship under all the calamities of life, and in the future world an entire exemption from all sorrow, and from sin, the fruitful source of all our affections ; the possession of every good, the enjoyment of the divine presence, of the society of angels and the spirits of just men made perfect ; in short, the fruition of an happiness above our present wishes, and equal to our then mature faculties, and all this for ever : these are the rewards of evangelical obedience, not indeed for its own sake, but upon account of righteousness of the blessed Jesus ; and if these fail to allure men to obedience, what can prevail? And how happy is it to live under a government, where virtue and religion, which in their own nature tend to our happiness, are enforced with such resistless arguments! On the other hand, the penalty annext by the divine Lawgiver to disobedience is proportionably dreadful. To pine and languish under the secret curse of angry Heaven, which, like a contagious poison, diffuses itself through all the enjoyments of the wicked, *Mal.* ii. 2. to sweat under the agonies of a guilty conscience in this world, and in the future world to be banished from the beatific presence of God and all the joys of heaven ; to feel the anguish and remorse of guilty reflections ; to burn in unquenchable fire, to consume a miserable eternity in the horrid society of malignant ghosts ; and all this without the least rational expectation ; nay, without so much as a deluded hope of deliverance, or the mitigation of torture, through the revolutions of endless ages, all this is a faint representation of the penalty annext to disobedience ; and it is a penalty worthy a God to inflict, and equal to the infinite malignity of sin. And *let the earth rejoice ; let the multitude of the isles be glad*, on account not only of the promissory sanction of the law, but also of this tremendous penalty ; for it flows not only from justice, but from goodness, as well as its promise. The penalty is not annext to the law, nor will it be executed from a malignant pleasure in the misery of the creature, but it is annext from a regard to the happiness of mankind, and will be executed upon individuals for the extensive good of the whole as well as for the honourable display of the divine purity and justice. A penalty is primarily intended to deter men from disobedience. Now disobedience tends in its own nature to make us miserable ; it renders it impossible, in the nature of things, that we should be happy in the enjoyment of God and the employments of heaven, which are eternally and immutably contrary to sinful depositions ; and it fills us with those malignant and unruly passions which cannot but make us uneasy. Hence it follows, that, since the penalty tends to deter us from sin, and since sin naturally tends to make us miserable, therefore the penalty is a kind of gracious inclosure round the pit of misery, to keep us from falling into it : it is a friendly admonition not to drink poison ; it is, in a word, a kind of restraint upon us in our career to ruin ; and indeed it is a blessing we could not spare ; for we find, that, notwithstanding the terror of the threatening, men will run on in sin ; and with how much more horrid alacrity and infernal zeal would they continue their course if there were no divine threatening to check and withhold them ? The earth may also rejoice for the execution of the penalty of the divine law against sin ; for the conspicuous punishment of the disobedient may serve as a loud warning to all rational beings that now exist, or that may hereafter be created, not to offend against God ; and thus it may be the means of preserving them in obedience, and so promote the general good ; and it may be that the number of those that shall be punished of the human and angelic natures, when compared to the number of reasonable beings that shall be confirmed in holiness and happiness by observing their doom, may bear no more proportion than the number of criminals executed in a government as public examples, does to all the subjects of it ; and consequently such punishment may be vindicated on the same principles. Farther, Justice is an amiable attribute in itself, and it appears so to all rational beings but criminals, whose interest it is, that it should not be displayed ; and therefore the infliction of just punishment should be matter of general joy, since it is amiable in itself. So it is in human governments ; while we are innocent, we approve of the conduct of our magistrates in inflicting capital punishment upon notorious malefactors, though the malefactors themselves view it with horror. But to proceed :

Let the earth rejoice ; let the multitude of the isles be glad, that the divine laws reach the inner man, and have power upon the hearts and consciences of men. Human laws can only smooth our external conduct at best, but the heart in the mean time may be disloyal and wicked. Now this defect is supplied by the laws of the King of heaven, which are spiritual. They require a complete uniformity, and self-consistency in us, that heart and life may agree ; and therefore they are wifely framed to make us entirely good. They have alfo an inimitable power upon the confciences of men. Should all the world acquit us, yet we cannot acquit ourfelves when we violate them. The confcioufnefs of a crime has made many an hardy offender fweat and agonize with remorfe, though no human eye could witnefs to his offence. Now what caufe of joy is it that thefe laws are quick and powerful, and that they are attended with almighty energy, which in fome meafure intimidates and reftrains the moft audacious, and infpires the confcientious with a pious fear of offending!

II. " The Lord reigneth by his Providence, let the earth therefore rejoice ; and the multitude of the ifles be glad thereof."

The Providence of God is well defcribed in our Shorter Cathechifm : " It is his moft holy, wife, and powerful preferving and governing all his creatures, and all their actions." To particularize all the inftances of providential government which may be matter of joy to the earth would be endlefs, therefore I fhall only mention the following :

Let the earth rejoice; and the multitude of the ifles be glad, that the Lord reigneth over the kingdoms of the earth, and manages all their affairs according to his fovereign and wife pleafure. We fometimes hear of wars, and rumours of wars, of thrones tottering, and kingdoms falling, of the nations tumultuoufly raging and dafhing in angry conflict, like the waves of the boifterous ocean. In fuch a juncture we may fay, *The floods have lifted up, O Lord, the floods have lifted up their voice. The floods lift up their waves. But the Lord reigneth, therefore the world fhall be eftablifhed that it cannot be moved.—The Lord on high is mightier than the noife of many waters; yea, than the mighty waves of the fea.* Pfalm xciii. Sometimes the ambition of foreign power, or the encroachments of domeftic tyranny, may threaten our liberties, and perfecution may feem ready to difcharge its artillery againft the church of God, while every pious heart trembles for the ark, left it fhould be carried into the land of its enemies. But the Lord reigneth ! let the earth, let the church rejoice ; *the eternal God is her refuge, and underneath her are the everlafting arms.* Deut. xxxiii. 27. He will over-rule the various revolutions of the world for her good ; he will give kings for her ranfom, Æthiopia and Seba for her ; and the united powers of earth and hell fhall not prevail againft her. Though the frame of Nature fhould be unhinged, we may find refuge in our God. Yet it muft be owned, that the Lord for the chaftifement of his people may fuffer their enemies to break in upon them, and may caft them into the furnace of affliction. But let the earth rejoice, let the church be glad that the Lord reigneth over her moft powerful enemies, and that they are but executing his will even when they have no regard to it, but are gratifying their own ambition. They are but a rod in the hand of a tender father, who corrects only to amend: and when he has ufed the rod for this gracious purpofe, he will then lay it afide. In this language the Almighty fpeaks of the haughty Affyrian monarch who had pufhed his conquefts fo far and wide. Ifaiah x. 5, 6, 7. *O Affyrian, the rod of mine anger,* &c. *I will give him my commiffion, and fend him againft the Jews, my favourite people; becaufe they are degenerated into an hypocritical nation, and he fhall execute my orders.—* " Howbeit, he meaneth not fo; it is far from his heart to obey my will in this expedition; but his only defign is to aggrandize himfelf, and to deftroy and cut off nations not a few." And when this inftrument of the divine vengeance arrogates to himfelf the honour of his own fucceffes, with what juft infult and difdain does the King of kings fpeak of him! ver. 12—15. *Shall the ax boaft itfelf againft him that heweth therewith? As if the rod fhould fhake itfelf againft him that lifteth it up,* &c. The defign of God in thefe chaftifements is to purge away the iniquity of his people; and this is all the fruit of them to take away their fin; and when this gracious defign is anfwered, they fhall be removed; *and the rod of the wicked fhall not always lie upon the lot of the righteous.* Pfalm cxxv. 3. Now what caufe of univerfal joy is this, that One infinitely wife fits at the helm, and can fteer the feeble veffel of his church through all the outrageous ftorms of this unfriendly climate and tempeftuous ocean! He may feem at times to lie afleep, but in the article of extreme danger he will awake and ftill the winds and the fea with his fovereign mandate, *Peace, be ftill.* Men may form deep and politic fchemes, and purpofe their accomplifhment in defiance of Heaven, *but God difappointeth the devices of the crafty, fo that their hands cannot perform their enterprife. He taketh the wife in their own craftinefs, and the counfel of the froward is carried headlong.* Job v. 12, 13. This was exemplified in the cafe of Ahithophel, 1 Sam. xvii. 14. The hearts of men, yea of kings, *are in the hand of the Lord, and he turneth them whitherfoever he will.* Prov. xxi. 1, (fee alfo chap. xvi. 1, 9. and xix. 21.) And how joyful a thought this, that we are not at the arbitrary difpofal of our fellow-mortals, and that affairs are not managed according to their capricious pleafure, but that our God is in the heaven, and doth whatfoever he pleafeth! Pfalm cxv. 3.

Again, the church may be endangered by inteftine divifions and offences. The profeffors of religion may ftumble and fall, and fo wound the hearts of the friends of Zion, and give matter of triumph and infult to its enemies. Some may apoftatize, and return like the dog to his vomit. A general lukewarmnefs may diffufe itfelf through the church, and even thofe who retain their integrity in the main feel the contagion. Divifions and animofities may be inflamed, mutual love may be extinguifhed, and a fpirit of difcord succeed in its place. A most melancholy case this, and too much like our own; and our hearts sink at times beneath the burden. But *the Lord reigneth; let the earth be glad.* He can reduce this confusion into order, and make the wrath of man to praise him, and restrain the remainder of it. Psalm lxxvi. 10. It is the peculiarity of divine wisdom to educe good out of evil, and let us rejoice in it. God is supreme, and therefore can controul all the wicked passions of the mind. He has the residue of the spirit, and can rekindle the languishing flame of devotion. And O let us apply to him with the most vigorous and unwearied importunity for so necessary a blessing!

Again, we are exposed to numberless accidental and unforeseen dangers, which we cannot prevent nor encounter. Sickness and death may proceed from a thousand unsuspected causes. Our friends, our estates, and, in short, all our earthly enjoyments, may be torn from us by a variety of accidents. We walk, as it were, in the dark, and may tread on remediless dangers ere we are aware. *But the Lord reigneth; let the earth be glad!* Contingent events are at his disposal, and necessity at his controul. The smallest things are not beneath the notice of his providence, and the greatest are not above it. Diseases and misfortunes that seem to happen by chance, are commissioned by the Lord of all; and they that result evidently from natural causes are sent by his almighty will. He says to one, go, and it goeth; and to another come, and it cometh: he orders the devastations that are made by the most outrageous elements. If flames lay our houses in ashes, they are kindled by his breath. If hurricanes sweep through our land, and carry desolation along with them, they perform his will, and can do nothing beyond it: his hand hurls the thunder, and directs it where to strike. An arrow or a bullet shot at a venture in the heat of battle, is carried to its mark by divine direction. How wretched a world would this be were it not under the wise management of divine Providence! If chance or blind fate were its rulers, what desolations would croud upon us every moment! we should soon be crushed in the ruins of a fallen world. Every wind that blows might blast us with death, and fire and water would mingle in a blended chaos, and bury us in their destruction. But so extensive is the care of Providence, that even the sparrows may find safety in it; and we cannot lose so much as an hair of our heads without its permission. *Matt.* x. 29, 30, 31. And how much more then are our persons and our affairs of importance under its guardianship and direction!

Again, we are in perpetual danger from the malignant agency of infernal spirits, who watch all opportunities to ruin the souls, bodies, and estates of men. These subtile spirits can inject insnaring thoughts into our minds, and present such images to the fancy as may allure the foul to fin. This is repeatedly afferted in fcripture, and attefted by the melancholy experience of multitudes in all ages. That they have power alfo in the material world to raife ftorms and tempefts, and to ruin men's eftates, and inflict difeafes on their bodies, is plain from the cafe of Job, and many in our Saviour's time, and from Satan's being called *the prince of the power of the air*; and his affociates *spiritual wickedneffes in high places*. And what horrid devaftations would thefe powerful and malicious beings fpread through the world if they were not under the controul of divine Providence! They would perpetually haunt our minds with infnaring or terrifying images, would meet us with temptations at every turn, and lead us willing captives to hell. They would alfo ftrip us entirely of all temporal enjoyments, torture our bodies with grievous pains, or moulder them into duft with confuming and loathfome difeafes. *But the Lord reigneth ; let the earth be glad.* He keeps the infernal lions in chains, and reftrains their rage. He fees all their fubtle plots and machinations againft his feeble fheep, and baffles them all, "He will not fuffer his people to be tempted above what they are able to bear; but with the temptation will alfo make a way to efcape. 1 *Cor.* x. 13. And when he fuffers them to be buffetted, his grace fhall be fufficient for them, &c. 2 *Cor.* xii. 7, 9. He hath alfo (as Satan himfelf confeffed with regard to Job)made an hedge about us about our houfes, and about all that we have on every fide, *Job.* i. 10. and hence we live and enjoy the bleffings of life. What caufe of greatful joy is this! Who would not rather die than live in a world ungoverned by divine Providence! This earth would foon be turned into a hell, if the infernal armies were let loofe upon it.

III. The Lord reigneth upon a throne of grace! "let the earth rejoice, and the multitude of the ifles be glad."

It is the mediatoral government of the Meffiah which the Pfalmift had more immediately in view ; and this is the principal, caufe of joy to the earth and its guilty inhabitants. This is a kind of government peculiar to the human race : the upright angels do not need it, and the fallen angles are not favoured with it. This is invefted in the perfon of Immanuel, "who is made head over all things to his church," *Ephef.* i. 22. "to whom all power in heaven and earth is given." *Matt.* xi. 27. and xxviii. 18. This is the kingdom defcribed in fuch auguft language in *Dan.* ii ver. 44, 45. and vii. 14. *Luke* i. 32, 33. Hence that Jefus who was mocked with a crown of thorns, and condemned as a criminal at Pilate's bar, wears on his vefture and on his thigh this majeftic infcription, *King of kings, and Lord of lords.* Rev. xix. 16. And behold I bring you glad tidings; this kingdom of God is come unto you, and you are called to become its fubjects, and fhare in its bleffings. Wherever the gofpel is preached, there Jehovah fits upon a mercy-feat in majefty tempered with condefcending grace. From thence he invites rebels that had rejected his government to return to their allegiance, and paffes an act of grace upon all that comply with the invitation. To his throne of grace he invites all to come, and offers them the richeft bleffings. From thence he publifhes peace on earth, and good will towards men. From thence he offers pardon to all that will fubmit to his government, and renounce their fins, thofe weapons of rebellion. From thence he diftributes the influences of his Spirit to fubdue obftinate hearts into cheerful fubmiffion, to fupport his fubjects under every burden and furnifh them with ftrength for the fpiritual warfare. He fubdues their rebellious corruptions, animates their languifhing graces, and protects them from their fpiritual enemies.* He enacts laws for the regulation of his church, appoints ordinances for her edification, and qualifies minifters to difpence them. He hath *afcended up on high*; he hath received gifts for men; and thefe he hath diftributed, and given *fome prophets; and fome, apoftles; and fome, evangelifts; and fome, paftors and teachers; for the perfection of the faints, for the work of the miniftry, for the edifying of the body of Chrift.* Ephef. iv. 8, 11, 12. And it is by virtue of authority derived from him that his minifters now officiate, and you receive his ordinances at their hands. Now how happy are we, that we live under the mediatorial adminiftration! under the empire of grace !—*Let the earth rejoice: let the multitude of the ifles be glad* upon this account. And let us pray that all nations may become the willing fubjects of our gracious fovereign. If this adminiftration of grace had not yet been erected, in what a miferable fituation fhould we have been! guilty, miferable, and hopelefs! Let us rejoice that the King of heaven, from whom we had revolted, has not fuffered us to perifh without remedy in our unnatural rebellion, but holds out the fceptre of his grace to us, that we may touch it and live.

IV. And laftly, the Lord will reign ere long upon a throne of univerfal judgment confpicuous to the affembled univerfe, *let the earth* therefore *rejoice*, and *the multitude of the ifles be glad.*

Here I may borrow the inimitable language of the Pfalmift, Pfalm xcvi. 10, 13, *The Lord fhall judge the people righteoufly. Let the heavens rejoice, and let the earth be glad: let the fea roar, and the fulnefs thereof: let the fields be joyful, and all that is therein; then fhall all the trees of the wood rejoice before the Lord, for he cometh! for he cometh to judge the earth.* "He fhall judge the world with righteoufnefs and the people with his truth." This will indeed be a day of infupportable terror to his enemies, Rev. vi. 15, 16. but, on many accounts, it will prove a day of joy and triumph.

* See his reign moft beautifully defcribed under the type of *Solomon.* Pfalm lxxii.

This day will unfold all the myſteries of divine Providence, which are now unſearchable. There are many diſpenſations now for which we cannot account. Many bleſſings are beſtowed, many calamities fall, and many events happen, of which mortals cannot ſee the reaſon. Proſperity is the lot of ſome who ſeem the peculiar objects of divine vengeance; and many groan under afflictions who ſeem more proper objects of providential beneficence. We are often led into ways, the end of which we cannot ſee, and are bewildered in various perplexities about the deſigns of divine Providence towards us. Hence alſo impiety takes occaſion to cavil at the ways of God as not equal, and to cenſure his government as weakly adminiſtered. But in that day all his ways will appear to be judgment. The clouds and darkneſs that now ſurround them will vaniſh, and the beams of wiſdom, goodneſs, and juſtice, will ſhine illuſtrious before the whole univerſe, and every creature ſhall join the plaudit, *He hath done all things well!* Now we can at beſt but ſee a few links in the chain of providence, but then we ſhall ſee it all entire and complete; then the whole ſyſtem will be expoſed to view at once, which will diſcover the ſtrange ſymmetry, connections, dependencies, and references of all the parts, without which we can no more judge of the excellency of the procedure than a ruſtic could tell the uſe of the ſeveral parts of a watch, if he ſaw them ſcattered in various places. Let the earth therefore be glad in expectation of this glorious diſcovery.

Again, let the earth rejoice that in that day the preſent unequal diſtributions of Providence will be for ever adjuſted, and regulated according to the ſtricteſt juſtice. This is not the place or ſeaſon for retribution, and therefore we need not be ſurpriſed that the bleſſings and calamities of this life are not diſpoſed according to men's real characters; but then man ſhall be dealt with according to his works. Oppreſſed innocence will be redreſſed, and inſolence for ever mortified: calumny will be confuted, and flattery expoſed: Lazarus ſhall be comforted, and Dives tormented: impious kings ſhall be driven into the infernal pit, while pious beggars ſhall be advanced to the heights of happineſs. In ſhort, all matters will then be ſet right, and therefore let the earth rejoice.

Again, let the earth rejoice that in that day the righteous ſhall be completely delivered from all ſin and ſorrow, and advanced to the perfection of heavenly happineſs. Then they ſhall enter upon the full fruition of that bliſs, which is now the object of all their anxious hopes and earneſt labours.

But we muſt change the ſcene into tragedy, and take a view of trembling criminals hearing their dreadful doom, and ſinking to hell with horrible anguiſh. And muſt the earth rejoice in this too? Yes, but with a ſolemn tremendous joy. Even the condemnation and everlaſting miſery of theſe is right and juſt, is amiable and glorious ; and God, angels, and faints, will at the great day rejoice in it. The awful grandeur of juſtice will be illuſtrated in it; and this is matter of joy. The puniſhment of irreclaimable impenitents will be an effectual warning to all reaſonable beings, and to all future creations, as has been obſerved ; and by it they will be deterred from diſobedience ; and this is the cauſe of joy. Theſe criminals will then be beyond repentance and reformation, and therefore it is impoſſible in the nature of things they ſhould be happy ; and why then ſhould Heaven be encumbered with then ? Is it not cauſe of joy that they ſhould be confined in priſon who have made themſelves unfit for ſociety ? In the preſent ſtate ſinners are objects of our compaſſion and ſorrow, and the whole creation mourns for them. Rom. viii. 22. But God will then rejoice in their ruin, and laugh at their calamity, Prov. i. 26. and all dutiful creatures will join in his joy.

Thus you ſee that the Lord reigneth. And who, poor feeble ſaints, who is this that ſuſtains this univerſal government, and rules the whole creation according to his pleaſure ? It is your Father, your Saviour, your Friend ! It is he that entertains a tenderer regard for you than ever glowed in an human breaſt. And can you be ſo fooliſh as to regard the ſurmiſes of unbelief? Can you force yourſelves to fear that he will ever leave or forſake you ? Can you ſuſpect that he will ſuffer you to fall an helpleſs prey to your enemies ? No, your Lord reigneth, therefore rejoice. *Rejoice in the Lord always ; and again I ſay rejoice.* While he keeps the throne of the univerſe, you ſhall be ſafe and happy. Your Father is greater than all, and none can pluck you out of his hands. Remember he ſits upon a throne of grace, therefore come to him with boldneſs. You may ſmile at calamity and confuſion, and rejoice amid the ruins of the world : you may borrow the language of David, Pſalm xlvi. or of Habbakuk, ch. iii. ver. 17, 18. Remember alſo, that as he is a king he demands your cheerful obedience, and therefore make his ſervice the buſineſs of your life.

And, unhappy ſinners ! let me aſk you, Who is this that reigns King of the univerſe ? Why, it is he whom you have rejected from being King over you ; it is he againſt whom you have rebelled, and who is therefore your juſt enemy. And are you able to make good your cauſe againſt him who has univerſal nature at his nod ? How dreadful is your ſituation ! That which may make the earth rejoice, may make you fear and tremble. The Lord reigneth, let ſinners tremble. You muſt fall before him, if you will not cheerfully ſubmit to his government. Let me therefore renew the uſual neglected declaration, " He ſits upon a throne of grace." Let me once more in his name proclaim reconciliation ! reconciliation ! in your ears, and invite you to return to your allegiance. Lay down your arms, forſake your ſins. Haſten, haſten to him. The fword of his juſtice now hangs over your heads while I am managing the treaty with you ; and therefore delay not. Yield ! yield, or die ; ſurrender, or periſh ; for you have no other alternative. Submit, and you may join the general joy at his government. You upon earth, and devils and damned ghoſts in hell, are the only beings that are ſorry for it ; but upon your ſubmiſſion your ſorrow ſhall be turned into joy, and you ſhall exult *when the Lord of all comes to judge the world with righteouſneſs, and the people with his truth.* Pſalm xcvi. 13.

SERMON XVII.

The Name of God proclaimed by himſelf.

EXOD. xxxiii. 18, 19. *And he ſaid, I beſeech thee, ſhew me thy glory. And he ſaid, I will make all my goodneſs paſs before thee, and I will proclaim the name of the Lord before thee—*

WITH

CHAP. xxxiv. 6, 7. *And the Lord paſſed by before him, and proclaimed, The Lord, The Lord God, merciful and gracious, long-ſuffering, and abundant in goodneſs and truth ; keeping mercy for thouſands, forgiving iniquity and tranſgreſſion and ſin, and that will by no means clear the guilty.*

IT is a very natural and proper inquiry for a creature, "Where is God my Maker ?" And an heart that loves him muſt long to know more of him, and is ever ready to join with Moſes in his petition, *Shew me, I pray thee, thy glory ;* or, "Reveal thyſelf to me." That thou *art*, I infer from my own exiſtence, and from thy numerous works all around me ; and that thou art *glorious*, I learn from the diſplay of thy perfections in thy vaſt creation, and in the government of the world thou haſt made. But, alas ! how ſmall a portion of God is known in the earth ? How faintly does thy glory ſhine in the feeble eyes of mortals ? My knowledge of things in the preſent ſtate of fleſh and blood depends in a great meaſure upon the ſenſes ; but God is a ſpirit inviſible to eyes of fleſh, and imperceptible through the groſs medium of ſenſation. How and when ſhall I know thee as thou art, thou great, thou dear unknown ? In what a ſtrange ſituation am I ! I am ſurrounded with thy omnipreſence, yet I cannot perceive thee : thou art as near me as I am to myſelf; "thou knoweſt my riſing up and my ſitting down; thou underſtandeſt my thoughts afar off; thou penetrateſt my very eſſence, and knoweſt me altogether. Pſalm cxxxix. 2, &c." But to me thou dwelleſt in impervious darkneſs, or, which is the ſame, in light inacceſſible. *O that I knew where I might find him! Behold I go forward, but he is not there; and backward, but I cannot perceive him: on the left hand, where he doth work, but I cannot behold him: he hideth himſelf on the right hand, that I cannot ſee him.* Job xxiii. 3, 8, 9. I ſee his perfections beaming upon me from all his works, and his providence ever-active ruling the vaſt univerſe, and diffuſing life, motion, and vigour through the whole: the virtue of his wiſdom, power, and goodneſs,

> Warms in the ſun, refreſhes in the breeze;
> Glows in the ſtars, and bloſſoms in the trees;
> Lives in all life, extends through all extent;
> Spreads undivided, operates unſpent;
> Inſpires our ſoul, informs our vital part.— POPE.

But where is the great Agent himſelf? Theſe are his works, and they are glorious; "in wiſdom has he made them all," but where is the divine Artificer? From theſe diſplays of his glory, which ſtrike my ſenſes, I derive ſome ideas of him; but O! how faint and glimmering! how unlike to the all-perfect Archetype and Original! I have alſo heard of him by the hearing of the ear: I read his own deſcriptions of himſelf in his word; I contemplate the repreſentations he has given of himſelf in his ordinances; and theſe are truly glorious, but they are adapted to the dark and groveling minds of mortals in this obſcure region, and fall infinitely ſhort of the original glory. I can think of him; I can love him; I can converſe and carry on a ſpiritual intercourſe with him; I feel him working in my heart; I receive ſenſible communications of love and grace from him; I dwell at times with unknown delight in the contemplation of his glory, and am tranſported with the ſurvey: but, alas! I cannot fully know him; I cannot dive deep into this myſtery of glory: my ſenſes cannot perceive him; and my intellectual powers in the preſent ſtate are not qualified to converſe with ſpiritual objects, and form a full acquaintance with them. O! if it would pleaſe my God to ſhew me his glory in its full luſtre! O that he would reveal himſelf to me ſo as that my ſenſes may aſſiſt my mind; if ſuch a manner of revelation be poſſible!

Such thoughts as theſe may naturally riſe in our minds; and probably ſome ſuch thoughts poſſeſſed the mind of Moſes, and were the occaſion of his requeſt, *I beſeech thee ſhew me thy glory.*

Theſe chapters whence we have taken our ſubject of diſcourſe, preſent us with tranſactions that muſt ſeem very ſtrange and incredible to a mind that knows nothing of communion with the Father of Spirits, and that is furnished only with modern ideas.

Here is, not an angel, but a man ; not a creature only but a sinner, a sinner once as depraved as ourselves, in intimate audience with the Deity. Jehovah speaks to him *face to face, as a man speaketh to his friend*. Moses uses his interest in favour of a rebellious people, and it was so great that he prevailed : nay, to shew the force of his intercessions, and to give him an encouragement to use them, God condescends to represent himself as restrained by this importunate petitioner, and unable to punish the ungrateful Israelites, while Moses pleaded for them, *Let me alone*, says he, *that my wrath may wax hot against this people, that I may consume them*. Exod. xxxii. 10. Moses urges petition upon petition ; and he obtains blessing upon blessing, as though God could deny nothing to such a favourite. He first deprecates the divine wrath, that it might not immediately break out upon the Israelites, and cut them off, verses 11—14. When he has gained this point, he advances farther, and pleads that God would be their Conductor through the wilderness, as he had been till that time, and lead them into the promised land. In this article God seems to put him off, and to devolve the work of conducting them upon himself ; but Moses, sensible that he was not equal to it, insists upon the request, and with a sacred dexterity, urges the divine promises to enforce it. Jehovah at length appears, as it were, partly prevailed upon, and promises to send his angel before him as his guide. Chap. xxxii. 34. and xxxiii. 2. But alas ! an angel cannot fill up his place ; and Moses renews his petition to the Lord, and humbly tells him that he had rather stay, or even die where they were in the wilderness, than go up to the promised land without him. *If thy presence go not with me, carry us not up hence*, chap. xxxiii. 15. " alas ! the company of an angel, and the possession of a land flowing with milk and honey will not satisfy us without thyself." His prayers prevail for this blessing also, and Jehovah will not deny him any thing. O the surprising prevalency of faith ! O the efficacy of the fervent prayer of a righteous man !

And now, when his people are restored unto the divine favour, and God has engaged to go with them, has Moses any thing more to ask ? Yes, he found he had indeed great interest with God, and O ! he loved him, and longed, and languished for a clearer knowledge of him : he found that after all his friendly interviews and conferences he knew but little of his glory ; and now, thought he, it is a proper time to put in a petition for this manifestation ; who knows but it may be granted ! Accordingly he prays with a mixture of filial boldness and trembling modesty, *I beseech thee, shew me thy glory :* that is to say, " Now I am in converse with thee, I perceive thou art the most glorious of all beings ; but it is but little of thy glory I as yet know. O! is it possible for a guilty mortal to receive clearer discoveries of it? If so, I pray thee favour me with a more full and bright view." This petition is also granted, and the Lord promises him, *I will make all my goodness pass before thee, and I will proclaim the name of the Lord before thee.*

That you may the better understand this strange history, I would have you observe a few things.

1st, In the earliest ages of the world it was a very common thing for God to assume some visible form, and in it to converse freely with his servants. Of this you frequently read in the history of the patriarchs, particularly of Adam, Abraham, Jacob, &c. It is also a tradition almost universally received in all ages, and among all nations, that God has sometimes appeared in a sensible form to mortals. You can hardly meet with one heathen writer but what you will find in him some traces of this tradition. Upon this, in particular, are founded the many extravagant stories of the poets concerning the appearances of their gods. Had there been no original truth in some appearances of the true God to men, there would have been no colour for such fables; for they would have evidently appeared groundless and unnatural to every reader. This tradition therefore was no doubt originally derived from the appearances of the Deity in a corporeal form in early ages*. Sometimes God assumed an human shape, and appeared as a man. Thus he appeared to Abraham, in company with two angels. Gen. xviii. and that good patriarch entertained them with food as travellers; yet one of them is repeatedly stiled the Lord, or Jehovah, the incommunicable name of God; see verses 13, 20, 22, 26, &c. and speaks in a language proper to him only, verses 14, 21, &c. Sometimes he appeared as a visible brightness, or a body of light, or in some other sensible form of majesty and glory. Thus he was seen by Moses in the bush as a burning fire; thus he attended the Israelites through the wilderness, in the symbol of fire by night, and a cloud by day; and thus he often appeared in the tabernacle, and at the dedication of Solomon's temple, in some sensible form of glorious brightness, which the Jews called the *Schechinah;* and looked upon as a certain symbol of the divine presence.

2ndly, You are to observe that God, who is a spirit, cannot be perceived by the senses; nor were these sensible forms intended

---

* These appearances were probably made in the person of the Son, and might be intended as a prelude or earnest of his assuming human nature, in the fulness of time, and his dwelling among mortals. He was the immediate Agent in the creation of the world; and the Father devolved upon him the whole œconomy of Providence from the beginning; and hence he had frequent occasions to appear on some grand design. It cannot seem incredible that he should thus assume some visible form, to such as believe that God was at length really *manifested in the flesh;* for this temporary apparent incarnation cannot be deemed more strange than his really being *made flesh, and dwelling among us.*

to represent the divine essence, which is wholly immaterial. You can no more see God than you can see your own soul; and a bodily form can no more represent his nature than shape or colour can represent a thought, or the affection of love. Yet,

3dly, It must be allowed that majestic and glorious emblems, or representations of God exhibited to the senses, may help to raise our ideas of him. When the senses and the imagination assist the power of pure understanding, its ideas are more lively and impressive: and though no sensible representations can bear any strict resemblance to the divine nature, yet they may strike our minds deeply, and fill them with images of grandeur and majesty. When I see a magnificent palace, it naturally tends to give me a great idea of the owner or builder. The retinue and pomp of kings, their glittering crowns, sceptres, and other regalia, tend to inspire us with ideas of majesty. In like manner, those sensible representations of Deity, especially when attended with some rational descriptions of the divine nature, may help us to form higher conceptions of the glory of God: and the want of such representations may occasion less reverence and awe. For instance, had the description of the Deity, *the Lord God merciful and gracious*, &c. been only suggested to the mind of Moses as an object of calm contemplation, it would not have struck him with such profound reverence, nor given him such clear or impressive ideas as when it was proclaimed with a loud, majestic voice, and attended with a visible glory too bright for mortal eyes. Human nature is of such a make, that it cannot but be affected with things of this nature.

Consider the matter well in the light which I have set it, and you may see something of the propriety and good tendency of these appearances, and at the same time guard yourselves against mistakes. Let me now give you what I apprehend the true history of this remarkable and illustrious appearance of God to Moses.

Moses had enjoyed frequent interviews with God, and seen many symbols of his presence and representations of his glory; but he still finds his knowledge of him very defective, and apprehends that God might give him some representation of his glory more striking and illustrious than any he had seen. Therefore, finding that now he was in great favour with him, he humbly moves this petition, *I beseech thee shew me thy glory;* "give me some more full and majestic representation of thy glory than I have hitherto seen." The Lord answers him, "I will cause all my goodness," that is, a glorious, visible representation of my goodness, which is, "my glory, to pass before thee," which may strike thy senses, and make them the medium of conveying to thy mind more illustrious and majestic ideas of my glory. And as no sensible forms can fully represent the spiritual essence and perfections of my nature, while I cause a visible representation of my glory to pafs before thee, I will at the fame time proclaim the name of the Lord,* and defcribe fome of the principal perfections which conftitute my glory and goodnefs. But fo bright will be the luftre of that form which I fhall affume, that thou art not able to fee my face, or the moft fplendid part of the reprefentation; the glory is too bright to be beheld by any mortal, ver. 20. But there is a place in a rock where thou mayeft wait, and I will caft darknefs over it till the brighteft part of the form of glory in which I fhall appear is paffed by, and then I will open a medium of light, and thou fhalt fee my back parts; that is, thofe parts of the reprefentation which are lefs illuftrious, and which pafs by laft: the glory of thefe thou fhalt be enabled to bear, but my face fhall not be feen." .Ver. 2—23.

Thus God condefcended to promife; and when matters were duly prepared, he performs his engagement. The Lord affumed a vifible form of glory, *and paffed by before him, and proclaimed his name*, which includes his perfections. Things are known by their names, and God is known by his attributes, therefore his name includes his attributes. The proclamation ran in this auguft ftyle, *The Lord, the Lord God, merciful and gracious, long-fuffering, abundant in goodnefs and truth, keeping mercy for thoufands, forgiving iniquity, tranfgreffion, and fin*. Mofes was ftruck with reverence and admiration, and bowed and worfhipped.

My prefent defign is to explain the feveral names and perfections here afcribed to God, and fhew that they all concur to conftitute his goodnefs. For you muft obferve this is the connection. Mofes prays for a view of God's glory, God promifes him a view of his goodnefs, which intimates that his goodnefs is his glory; and when he defcribes his goodnefs, what is the defcription? It is *the Lord, the Lord God, merciful and gracious, long-fuffering, abundant in goodnefs and truth, keeping* mercy for thoufands, forgiving iniquity, tranfgreffion, and fin†. That thefe attributes belong to his goodnefs we eafily and naturally conceive; but what fhall we think of his punitive juftice, that awful and tremendous attribute, the objects of terror and averfion to finners? Is that a part of his goodnefs too? Yes, when God caufes his goodnefs to pafs before Mofes, he proclaims as one part of it, that *he will by no means clear*

---

* The LXX render the paffage, *I will call by my name, the Lord, before thee*. And this is the moft literal tranflation of the Hebrew: they are rendered, *Inclimabo nominatim Jehova ante faciem tuam*, by Junius and Tremellious. According to this verfion the fenfe feems to be, "When the fymbol of my glory is paffing by, I will give thee notice, and call by my name the Lord, that I may not pafs by unobferved."

† The Hebrews obferve, that the firft letter of the word tranflated *keeping*, is much larger than ufual; which fhews that a particular emphafis is to be laid upon it; as if he fhould fay, "I moft ftrictly and richly keep mercy for thoufands; the treafure is immenfe, and can never be exhaufted."

the guilty; and that he visits the iniquities of the fathers upon the children to the third and fourth generation. This awful attribute is an important part of his goodness, and without it he could not be good, amiable, or glorious.

I am now about to enter upon a subject the most sublime, august, and important, that can come within the compass of human or angelic minds, the name and perfections of the infinite and ever-glorious God. I attempt it with trembling and reverence, and I foresee I shall finish it with shame and confusion: for *who by searching can find out God? who can find out the Almighty unto perfection?* Job xi. 7. The question of Agar mortifies the pride of human knowledge; *What is his name, or what is his son's name, if thou canst tell?* Prov. xxx. 4. *Such knowledge is too wonderful for me; it is high, I cannot attain unto it.* Psalm cxxxix. 6. *It is as high as Heaven, what can I know? deeper than hell, what can I do? the measure thereof is longer than the earth, and broader than the sea.* Job xi. 1, 9. Lend me your skill, ye angels, who have seen his face without intermission from the first moment of your happy existence; or ye saints above, that *see him as he is, and know even as you are known,* inspire me with your exalted ideas, and teach me your celestial language, while I attempt to bring Heaven down to earth, and reveal its glories to the eyes of mortals. In vain I ask; their knowledge is incommunicable to the inhabitants of flesh, and none but immortals can learn the language of immortality. But why do I ask of them? O thou Father of angels and of men, who *canst perfect thy praise even out of the mouths of babes and sucklings,* and who canst open all the avenues of knowledge and pour thy glory upon created minds, do thou shine into my heart, to give the light of the knowledge of thy glory: *I beseech thee shew me thy glory;* cause it to shine upon my understanding, while I try to display it to thy people, that they may behold, adore, and love.

As to you, my brethren, I solicit your most solemn and reverential attention, while I would lead you into the knowledge of the Lord your Maker. One would think a kind of filial curiosity would inspire you with eager desires to be acquainted with your divine Parent and original. You would not be willing to worship you know not what, or, with the Athenians, adore an unknown God. Do you not long to know the greatest and best of beings, the the glimmerings of whose glory shine upon you from heaven and earth? Would you not know him in whose presence you hope to dwell and be happy for ever and ever? Come then, be all awe and attention, while I proclaim to you his name and perfections, *The Lord, The Lord God, merciful and gracious, long-suffering, and abundant in goodness and truth; keeping mercy for thousands, forgiving iniquity, transgression, and sin.*

We may be sure God has assumed to himself such names as are best adapted to describe his nature, as far as mortal language can reach. And every thing belonging to him is so dear and important, that his very name deserves a particular consideration. This is not to make empty criticisms upon an arbitrary, unmeaning sound, but to derive useful knowledge from a word of the greatest emphasis and significancy.

The first name, in the order of the text, and in its own dignity, is, *the Lord*, or Jehovah; a name here twice repeated, to shew its importance, *the Lord, the Lord*, or Jehovah, Jehovah. This is a name peculiar to God, and incommunicable to the most exalted creature. The apostle tells us, *There are Gods many, and Lords many*. 1 Cor. viii. 5. Magistrates in particular are so called, because their authority is some shadow of the divine authority. But the name Jehovah, which is rendered *Lord* in my text, and in all those places in the Bible where it is written in capitals, I say, this name Jehovah is appropriated to the Supreme Being, and never applied to any other. He claims it to himself, as his peculiar glory. Thus in Psalm lxxxiii. ver. 18. *Thou, whose name alone is Jehovah, art the Most High over all the earth.* And in Isaiah, xlii. ver. 8. *I am the Lord*, or (as it is in the original) *Jehovah; that is my name, my proper incommunicable name, and my glory will I not give to another;* that is, I will not allow another to share with me in the glory of wearing this name. Thus also in Amos vi. ver. 13. *Lo, he that formeth the mountains, and createth the wind, that declareth to man what is in his thoughts*, &c. *the Lord, the God of Hosts, is his name*, his distinguishing, appropriated name. There must therefore be something peculiarly sacred and significant in this name, since it is thus incommunicably appropriated to the only one God.

The Jews had such a prodigious veneration for this name as amounted to a superstitious excess. They call it "That name," by way of distinction, "The great name, the glorious name, the appropriated name, the unutterable name, the expounded name*," because they never pronounced it, except in one instance, which I shall mention presently, but always expounded it by some other: thus when the name Jehovah occurred in the Old Testament, they always read it *Adonai*, or *Elohim*, the usual and less sacred names, which we translate *Lord God*. It was never pronounced by the Jews in reading, prayer, or the most solemn act of worship, much less in common conversation, except once a year, on the great day of atonement, and then only by the high priest in the sanctuary, in pronouncing the benediction; but at all other times, places and occasions, and to all other persons, the pronunciation was deemed

---

* They also distinguish it by the name of the four letters that composed it, *jodh, he, vau, he;* and hence the Greeks called it *the four-letter'd Name.* See Buxtorf.

unlawful. The benediction was that which you read in *Numbers* vi. verses 24, 25, 26. where the name Jehovah is thrice repeated in the Hebrew, *Jehovah bless thee, and keep thee : Jehovah make his face to shine upon thee, and be gracious to thee : Jehovah lift up the light of his countenance upon thee, and give thee peace.* When this venerable name was pronounced upon this occasion, we are told by the Jewish rabbies, " that all the vast congregation then present bowed the knee, and fell down in the humblest prostration, crying out, *Blessed be his glorious name for ever and ever.* They supposed this name had a miraculous virtue in it, and that by it Moses and others wrought such wonders : nay, so great was their superstition, that they thought it a kind of charm or magical word, and that he that had it about him, and knew its true pronunciation and virtue, could perform the most surprising things, and even shake heaven and earth.*

I do not mention these things with approbation, but only to shew that there is something peculiarly significant, important, and sacred in this name, from whence the Jews took occasion for such extravagant notions : and this will appear from its etymology. You know it is not my usual method to carry a great quantity of learned disquisition with me into the pulpit, or to spend your time in trifling, pedantic criticisms upon words, which may indeed have a shew of literature, and amuse those who admire what they do not understand, but can answer no valuable end in a popular audience. However, at present I must take the liberty of shewing you the original meaning of the name *Jehovah*, that I may thoroughly explain my text, and that you may know the import of a name that will occur so often to you in reading your bibles ; for, as I told you, wherever you meet with the word *Lord* in large letters, it is always *Jehovah* in the original.

The name Jehovah is derived from the Hebrew verb, *to be ;* and therefore the meaning of the word Jehovah is, *The existent, the being,* or, *He that is.* Thus it seems explained in Exodus iii. ver. 14. *I am that I am,* or, " I am because I am ;" that is, I exist, and have being in and of myself without dependence upon any cause ; and my existence or being is always the same, unchangeable and eternal. St. John well explains this name by the *Who is, who was, and who is to come ;* or, as the passage might be rendered, " The present Being, the past Being, and the future Being ;" or, The Being that is, the Being that was, and the Being that will be ; that is, the perpetual, the eternal, and unchangea-

---

* This name seems not to have been unknown among other nations. Hence probably is derived the name *Jovis, Jove*, the Latin name for the supreme God. And it is probably in allusion to this that Varro says, "Deum Judæorum esse Jovem." The Moors also call God *Jabah*, and the Mahometans *Hou*; which in their language signifies the same with Jehovah, namely, *He who is.* See Univ. Hist. Vol. III. p. 357, note 1.

ble Being. I shall only observe farther, that Jehovah is not a relative, but an absolute name : there is no pronoun or relative word that is ever joined with it : we can say, 'My Lord, our Lord, our God, &c. but the Hebrews never say or write, My Jehovah, our Jehovah, &c. so that this name represents him as he is in himself, without any relation to his creatures, as he would have been if they had never existed. He would still have been the Being, the absolute, independent existent, in which view he has nothing to do with his creatures, and can sustain no relation to them.

From this name, thus explained, we learn the following glorious, incommunicable perfections of God ; that he is self-existent and independent ; that his being is necessary ; that he is eternal ; and that he is unchangeable.

While I am about to enter upon these subjects, I seem to stand upon the brink of an unbounded, fathomless ocean, and tremble to launch into it ; but, under the conduct of scripture and humble reason, let us make the adventure ; for it is an happiness to be lost and swallowed up in such an ocean of perfection.

I. The name Jehovah implies that God is *self-existent* and independent. I do not mean by this that he produced himself, for that would be a direct contradiction, and suppose him to exist, and not to exist at the same time : but I mean that the reason and ground of his existence is in his own nature, and does not at all depend upon any thing besides. Being is essential to him. He contains an infinite fulness of being in himself, and no other being has contributed in the least towards his existence ; and hence with great propriety he assumes that strange name, *I am*. He is Being throughout, perfectly and universally vital ; and the reason of this is entirely within his own nature.

How glorious is he distinguished in this respect from all other beings, even the most illustrious and powerful ! Time was, when they were nothing. Angels and archangels, men and beasts, sun, moon, and stars ; in short, the whole universe besides were once nothing, had no being at all : and what was the reason that they ever came into being ? Certainly it was not in them : when they were nothing there was no reason at all in them why they should ever be something ; for in not being, they can be no reason or ground for being. The mere pleasure of God, the fiat of this self-existing Jehovah, is the only reason and sole cause of their existence. If it had not been for him, they would have continued nothing as they were : their being therefore is entirely precarious, dependent, and wholly proceeds from a cause without themselves. But Jehovah glories in an unborrowed, underived, independent being. Whatever he is, it is his own ; he owes it only to himself. What a glorious Being is this! how infinitely different from and superior to the whole system of creatures! Are you not already constrained to bow the knee before him, and wonder, adore, and love? But,

II. Hence it follows that his existence is necessary; that is, it is impossible for him not *to be*. His being does not depend upon any thing without him, nor does it depend upon his own arbitrary will, but it is essential to his nature. That he should not be is as great an impossibility as that two and two should not make four. It is impossible that any thing should be more closely connected with any thing than being is with his essence, and it is impossible any thing should be more opposite to any thing than he is to nonexistence. Since he received his being from nothing without himself, and since the reason of his existence is not derived from any other, it follows, that unless he exists by the necessity of his own nature, he must exist without any necessity; that is, without any reason at all, which is the same as to say that nothing is the cause or ground of his existence; and what imagination can be more absurd? His being therefore must exist by an absolute, independent necessity.

What a glorious Being is this! how infinitely distant from nothing, or a possibility of not being! What an unbounded fund of existence, what an immense ocean of Being is here! Alas! what are we, what is the whole universe besides in this comparison? They *are nothing, less than nothing, and vanity.* Our being is not only derived but arbitrary, depending entirely upon the mere pleasure of Jehovah. There was no necessity from our nature that we should *be* at all; and now there is no necessity that we should continue to *be.* If we exist, it is not owing to us. " He made us, and not we ourselves;" and if we shall continue to be for ever, it is not owing to a fund of being within ourselves, but to the same God who first formed us. It is but lately since we sprung from nothing, and how near are we still to the confines of nothing! We hang over the dreadful gulph of annihilation by a slender thread of being, sustained by the self-originated Jehovah. Remove him, take away his agency, and universal nature sinks into nothing at once. Take away the root, and the branches wither: dry up the fountain, and the streams cease. If any of you are such fools as to wish in your hearts there were no God, you imprecate annihilation upon the whole universe; you wish total destruction to yourself and every thing else; you wish the extinction of all being. All depend upon God, the uncaused cause, the only necessary Being. Suffer me here to make a digression, Is this the God whom the daring sons of men so much forget, dishonour, and disobey? Are they so entirely dependent upon him, and yet careless how they behave towards him, careless whether they love and please him? Do they owe their being and their all entirely to him? And are they wholly in his hand? What then do they mean by withholding their thoughts and affections from him, breaking his laws and neglecting his gospel? Can you find a name for such a conduct? Would it not be entirely incredible did we not see it with our eyes all around us? Sinners, what mean you by this conduct? Let the infant rend the womb that conceived it, or tear the breasts that cherish it; go, poison or destroy the bread that should feed you; dry up the streams that should allay your thirst; stop the breath that keeps you in life: do these things, or do any thing, but O! do not forget, disobey, and provoke the very Father of your being, to whom you owe it that you are not as much nothing now as you were ten thousand years ago, and on whom you depend, not only for this and that mercy, but for your very being, every moment of your existence, in time and eternity. He can do very well without you, but O what are you without him! a stream without a fountain, a branch without a root, an effect without a cause, a mere blank, a nothing. He indeed is self-sufficient and self-existent. It is nothing to him, as to his existence, whether creation exists or not. Let men and angels and every creature sink to nothing, from whence they came, his being is still secure: he enjoys an unprecarious being of his own, necessarily, unchangeably, and eternally existent. Men and angels bow the knee, fall prostrate and adore before this Being of beings. How mean are you in his presence! what poor, arbitrary, dependent, perishing creatures! what shadows of existence! what mere nothings! And is it not fit you should humbly acknowledge it? Can there be any thing more unnatural, any thing more foolish, any thing more audaciously wicked, than to neglect or contemn such a Being, the Being of beings, the Being that includes all being? I can hardly bear up under the horror of the thought.

III. The name Jehovah implies that God is eternal; that is, he always was, is, and ever will be. *From everlasting to everlasting he is God.* Psalm xc. 2. This is his grand peculiar, *he only hath immortality,* 2 Tim. vi. 16. in a full and absolute sense. Men and angels indeed are immortal, but it is but a kind of half-eternity they enjoy. They once were nothing, and continued in that state through an eternal duration. But as Jehovah never will have an end, so he never had a beginning. This follows from his necessary self-existence. If the reason of his existence be in himself, then unless he always existed he never could exist, for nothing without himself could cause him to exist. And if he exists by absolute necessity, he must always exist, for absolute necessity is always the same, without any relation to time or place. Therefore he always was and ever will be.

And what a wonderful Being is this! a Being unbegun, and that can never have an end! a Being possessed of a complete, entire eternity. Here, my brethren, let your thoughts take wing, and fly backward and forward, and see if you can trace his existence. Fly back in thought about six thousand years, and all nature, as far as appears to us, was a mere blank; no heaven nor earth no men nor angels. But still the great Eternal lived, lived alone, self-sufficient and self-happy. Fly forward in thought as far as the conflagration, and you will see *the heavens dissolving, and the earth and the things that are therein burnt up:* but still Jehovah lives unchangeable, and absolutely independent. Exert all the powers of number, add centuries to centuries, thousands to thousands, millions to millions, fly back, back, back as far as thought can possibly carry you, still Jehovah exists; nay, you are even then as far from the first moment of his existence as you are now, or ever can be. Take the same prospect before you, and you will find the King eternal and immortal still the same: he is then no nearer an end than at the creation, or millions of ages before it.

What a glorious Being is this! Here again, let men and angels, and all the offspring of time bow the knee and adore. Let them lose themselves in this ocean, and spend their eternity in extatic admiration and love of this eternal Jehovah.

O! what a glorious portion is he to his people! Your earthly enjoyments may pass away like a shadow; your friends die, yourselves must die, and heaven and earth may vanish like a dream, but your God lives! he lives for ever, to give you an happiness equal to your immortal duration. Therefore, *blessed, blessed is the people whose God is the Lord!*

But O! let sinners, let wicked men and devils tremble before him, for how dreadful an enemy is an eternal God! He lives for ever to punish you. He lives for ever to hate your sin, to resent your rebellion, and to display his justice; and while he lives you must be miserable. What a dismal situation are you in, when the eternal existence of Jehovah is an inexhaustible fund of terror to you! O how have you inverted the order of things, when you have made it your interest that the Fountain of being should cease to be, and that with him yourselves and all other creatures should vanish into nothing! What a malignant thing is sin, that makes existence a curse, and universal annihilation a blessing! What a strange region is hell, where being, so sweet in itself, and the capacity of all enjoyments, is become the most intolerable burden, and every wish is an imprecation of universal annihilation! Sinners, you have now time to consider these miseries and avoid them, and will you be so senseless and fool-hardy as to rush headlong into them? O! if you were but sensible what will be the consequences of your conduct in a few years, you would not need persuasions to reform it: but O the fatal blindness and stupidity of mortals, who will not be convinced of these things till the conviction be too late!

IV. The name Jehovah implies that God is unchangeable, or always the same. If he exists necessarily, he must always necessarily be what he is, and cannot be any thing else. He is dependent upon none, and therefore he can be subject to no change from another; and he is infinitely perfect, and therefore cannot desire to change himself. So that he must be always the same through all duration, from eternity to eternity: the same not only as to his being, but as to his perfections; the same in power, wisdom, goodness, justice, and happiness. Thus he represents himself in his word, as *the Father of lights, with whom there is no variableness, nor shadow of turning,* James. i. 17. *the same yesterday, to-day, and for ever.* Heb. xiii. 8.—What a distinguishing perfection is this! and indeed it is in Jehovah only that immutability can be a perfection. The most excellent creature is capable of progressive improvements, and seems intended for it; and to fix such a creature at first in an immutable state, would be to limit and restrain it from higher degrees of perfection, and keep it always in a state of infancy. But Jehovah is absolutely, completly, and infinitely perfect, at the highest summit of all possible excellency, infinitely beyond any addition to his perfection, and absolutely incapable of improvement; and consequently as there is no room for, so there is no need of a change in him; and his immutability is a perpetual, invariable continuance in the highest degree of excellency, and therefore the highest perfection. He is the cause and the spectator of an endless variety of changes in the universe, without the least change in himself. He sees worlds springing into being, existing a while, and then dissolving. He sees kingdoms and empires forming, rising, and rushing headlong to ruin. He change the times and the seasons; *removeth kings, and he setteth up kings,* Dan. ii. 21. and he sees the fickleness and vicissitudes of mortals; he sees generations upon generations vanishing like successive shadows; he sees them now wise, now foolish; now in pursuit of one thing, now of another; now happy, now miserable, and in a thousand different forms. He sees the revolutions in nature, the successions of the seasons, and of night and day. These and a thousand other alterations he beholds, and they are all produced or permitted by his all-ruling Providence; but all these make no change in him; his being, his perfections, his counsels, and his happiness are invariably and eternally the same. He is not wise, good, just, or happy only at times, but he is equally, steadily, and immutably so through the whole of his infinite duration. O how unlike the fleeting offspring of time, and especially the changing race of man!

Since Jehovah is thus constant and unchangeable, how worthy is he to be chosen as our best friend! You that love him need fear no change in him. They are not small matters that will turn his heart from you : his love is fixed with judgment, and he never will fee reafon to reverfe it : it is not a tranfient fit of fondnefs, but it is deliberate, calm, and fteady. You may fafely truft your all in his hands, for he cannot deceive you ; and whatever or whoever fail you, he will not. You live in a fickle, uncertain world ; your beft friends may prove treacherous or cool towards you ; all your earthly comforts may wither and die around you ; yea, heaven and earth may pafs away ; but your God is ftill the fame. He has affured you of it with his own mouth, and pointed out to you the happy confequence of it, *I am the Lord Jehovah*, fays he, *I change not ; therefore ye fons of Jacob are not confumed*. Mal. iii. 6.

What a complete happinefs is this Jehovah to thofe who have chofen him for their portion ! If an infinite God is now fufficient to fatisfy your utmoft defires, he will be fo to all eternity. He is an ocean of communicative happinefs that never ebbs or flows, and therefore completely bleffed will you ever be who have an intereft in him.

But O ! how miferable are they who are the enemies of this Jehovah ! Sinners, he is unchangeable, and can never lay afide his refentments againft fin, or abate in the leaft degree in his love of virtue and holinefs. He will never recede from his purpofe to punifh impenitent rebels, nor loofe his power to accomplifh it. His hatred of all moral evil is not a tranfient paffion, but a fixed, invariable, deep-rooted hatred. Therefore, if ever you be happy, there muft be a change in you. As you are fo oppofite to him, there muft be an alteration in the one or the other : you fee it cannot be in him, and therefore it muft be in you ; and this you ought to labour for above all other things. Let us then have grace, *whereby we may ferve God acceptably with reverence and godly fear, for our God is a confuming fire* (Heb. xii. 28, 29.) to his impenitent and implacable enemies.*

---

* Our author has evidently not finifhed his fubject, and I do not find it profecuted in any of the difcourfes that are come to my hands ; but yet I determined to publifh the Sermon, not only for its own (if I miftake not) fubftantial worth, but the rather as the Sermon that next follows in order, may be confidered as a profecution, if not a completion of the great and glorious fubject he has undertaken, particularly of his profeffed defign in this Sermon, " of explaining the feveral perfections here afcribed to God, and fhewing that they all concur to conftitute his goodnefs." *The Editor.*

SERMON XVIII.

God is Love.

1 JOHN iv. 8. *God is Love.*

LOVE is a gentle, pleasing theme, the noblest passion of the human breast, and the fairest ornament of the rational nature. Love is the cement of society, and the source of social happiness; and without it the great community of the rational universe would dissolve, and men and angels would turn savages, and roam apart in barbarous solitude. Love is the spring of every pleasure; for who could take pleasure in the possession of what he does not love! Love is the foundation of religion and morality; for what is more monstrous than religion without love to that God who is the object of it! Or who can perform social duties without feeling the endearments of those relations to which they belong! Love is the softener and polisher of human minds, and transforms barbarians into men; its pleasures are refined and delicate, and even its pains and anxieties have something in them soothing and pleasing. In a word, love is the brightest beam of divinity that has ever irradiated the creation? the nearest resemblance to the ever-blessed God; for *God is Love.*

God is love. There is an unfathomable depth in this concise laconic sentence, which even the penetration of an angel's mind cannot reach; an ineffable excellence, which even celestial eloquence cannot fully represent. *God is love;* not only lovely and loving, but love itself; pure, unmixed love, nothing but love; love in his nature and in his operations; the object, source, and quintessence of all love.

My present design is to recommend the Deity to your affections under the amiable idea of Love, and for that end to shew that his other perfections are but various modifications of love.

I. Love comprehends the various forms of divine nature beneficence. Goodness, that extends its bounties to innumerable ranks of creatures, and diffuses happiness through the various regions of the universe, except that which is set apart for the dreadful, but salutary and benevolent purpose of confining and punishing incorrigible malefactors; Grace, which so richly showers its blessings upon the undeserving, without past merit of the prospect of future compensation; Mercy, that commiserates and relieves the miserable as well as the undeserving; Patience and Long-suffering, which so long tolerate insolent and provoking offenders; what is all this beneficence in all these its different forms towards different objects, what but Love under various names? It is gracious, merciful, patient and long suffering love! love variegated, overflowing, and unbounded! what but love was the Creator of such a world as this, so well accommodated, so richly furnished for the sustenance and comfort of its inhabitants? and what but love has planted it so thick with an endless variety of beings, all capable of receiving some stream of happiness from that immense fountain of it, the divine goodness? Is it not love that preserves such an huge unwieldy world as this in order and harmony from age to age, and supplies all its numerous inhabitants with every good? and O! was it not love, free, rich, unmerited love, that provided a Saviour for the guilty children of men? It was because *God loved the world, that he gave his only begotten Son, that whosoever believeth in him should not perish, but have everlasting life.'* John iii. 16. O love! what hast thou done! what wonders hast thou wrought! It was thou, almighty love, that broughtest down the Lord of glory from his celestial throne to die upon a cross an atoning sacrifice for the sins of the world. And what but love is it that peoples the heavenly world with colonies transplanted from this rebellious province of Jehovah's dominions; that forms such miracles of glory and happiness out of the dust, and the shattered polluted fragments of human nature! and what but eternal love perpetuates their bliss through an eternal duration? but it is so evident, that these instances of divine goodness are only the effects of love, that it is needless to attempt any farther illustration.

II. What is divine wisdom but a modification of divine love, planning the best adapted schemes for communicating itself in the most advantageous beneficent, and honourable manner, so as to promote the good of the great whole or collective system of creatures by the happiness of individuals; or to render the punishment and misery of individuals, which for important reasons of state may be sometimes necessary in a good government, subservient to the same benevolent end? Whatever traces of divine wisdom we see in creation; as the order and harmony of the great system of nature, its rich and various furniture, and the conspiracy of all its parts to produce the good of each other and the whole; whatever divine wisdom appears in conducting the great scheme of providence through the various ages of time; or in the more astonishing and godlike work of redemption: in a word, whatever displays of divine wisdom appear in any part of the universe, they are only the signatures of divine love. Why was yonder sun fixed where he is, and enriched with such extensive vital influences, but because divine love saw it was best and from conducive to the good of the system? Why were our bodies so wonderfully and fearfully made, and all their parts so well fitted for action and enjoyment, but because divine love drew the plan, and stamped its own amiable image upon them? Why was the manifold wisdom of God displayed, not only to mortals, but also to angelic *principalities and powers*, Ephes. iii. 10. in the scheme of redemption, which advances at once the honours of the divine perfections and government, and the happiness of rebellious and ruined creatures, by an expedient which nothing but infinite wisdom could ever devise the incarnation, the obedience, and passion of the co-equal son of God? Why, I say, but because divine love would otherwise be under restraint, and incapable of giving full scope to its kind propensions in a manner honourable to itself and conducive to the public good? In short, divine wisdom appears to be nothing else but the sagacity of love, to discover ways and means to exercise itself to the greatest advantage; or, which is the same, divine wisdom always acts under the benign determination and conduct of love: it is the counsellor of love to project schemes subservient to its gracious purposes; and in all its councils love presides.

III. What is divine power but the omnipotence of love! Why did omnipotence exert itself in the production of this vast amazing world out of nothing? It was to open a channel in which the overflowing ocean of love might extend itself, and diffuse its streams from creature to creature, upwards as high as the most exalted archangel, and downwards as low as the meanest vital particle of being, and extensive as the remotest limits of the universe, and all the innumerable intermediate ranks of existences in the endless chain of nature. And why does divine power still support this prodigious frame, but to keep the channel of love open from age to age? and for this purpose it will be exerted to all eternity. Perhaps I should assist your ideas of Divine Power, if I should call it the acting hand, the instrument, the servant of love, to perform its orders, and execute its gracious designs.

IV. What is the holiness of God but love? Pure, refined, and honourable love. What is it but the love of excellence, rectitude, and moral goodness? Holiness, in its own nature, has a tendency to promote the happiness of the universe: it is the health, the good constitution of a reasonable being; without which it has no capacity of relishing those enjoyments which are suitable to its nature. It is no arbitrary mandate of heaven that has established the inseparable connection between holiness and happiness, between vice and misery. The connection is as necessary, as immutable, and as much founded in the nature of things, as that between health of body and a capacity of animal enjoyments, or between sickness and a disrelish for the most agreeable food. Every creature in the universe, as far as he is holy is happy; and as far as he is unholy he is miserable. Therefore, by how much the more holy Jehovah is, by so much the more fit he is to communicate happiness to all that enjoy him; and consequently he is an infinite happiness, for he is infinitely holy. His taking so much care to promote holiness is but taking care of the public good. The strict exactions of his law, which contains every ingredient of the most perfect holiness, and admits of no dispensation, are but strict injunctions to his subjects to pursue that course which infallibly leads them to the most consummate happiness; and every abatement in his demands of obedience would be a licence to them to deduct so much from their happiness, and render themselves so far miserable with his consent. That mitigation of the rigor of his law, which some imagine he has made to bring it down to a level with the abilities of degenerate creatures, disabled by their voluntary wickedness, would no more contribute to their felicity than the allowing a sick man to gratify his vitiated taste by mixing a little deadly poison in his food would contribute to the recovery of his health, or the preservation of his life. The penal sanctions of the divine law are but friendly warnings against danger and misery, and honest admonitions of the destructive consequences of sin, according to the unchangeable nature of things; they are threatnings which discover no malignity or ill-nature, as sinners are apt to imagine, but the infinite benevolence of the heart of God: threatenings which are not primarily and unconditionally intended to be executed, but to prevent all occasion of their being executed, by preventing sin, the natural source, as well as the meritorious cause of every misery: threatenings which are not executed, but as the only expedient left in a desperate case, when all other means have been used in vain, and no other method can secure the public good, or render a worthless criminal *a vessel of wrath fitted for destruction*, and fit for nothing else; of no other service to the great community of rational beings. These are some of the ingredients and displays of the holiness of God: and what are these but so many exertions of pure love and benevolence? It is because he loves his creatures so much that he requires them to be so holy; and that very thing, against which there are so many cavils and objections, as too severe and oppressive, and a rigid restraint from the pursuit of pleasure, is the highest instance of the love of God for them, and his regard for their happiness.

Let me therefore commence advocate for God with my fellow-men, though it strikes me with horror to think there should be any occasion for it. Ye children of the most tender Father, ye subjects of the most gracious and righteous Sovereign, ye beneficiaries of divine love, why do you harbour hard thoughts of him? Is it becaufe his laws are fo ftrict, and tolerate you in no guilty pleafure? This appointment is the kind reftraint of love: the love of fo good a being will not allow him to difpenfe with your obfervance of any thing that may contribute to your improvement and advantage, nor indulge you in any thing that is in its own nature deadly and deftructive, no more than a father will fuffer a favourite child to play with a viper, or a good government permit a madman to run at large armed with weapons to deftroy himfelf and others. Do you think hard of God becaufe he hates all moral evil to fuch a degree, that he has annexed to it everlafting mifery of the moft exquifite kind? But what is this but an expreffion of his infinite hatred to every thing that is hurtful to his creatures, and his infinite regard to whatever tends to their benefit? Or has he been too rigid in exacting holinefs as a neceffary prerequifite to the happinefs of heaven? You may as well complain of the conftitution of nature, that renders abftinence from poifon neceffary to the prefervation of health, or that does not allow you to quench your thirft in a fever with cold water. Let me remind you once more, that holinefs is effential to the happinefs of heaven, and that without it you labour under a moral incapacity of enjoyment; and a moral incapacity will as inevitably deprive you of the pleafures of enjoyment as if it were natural. While unholy, you can no more be happy even in the region of happinefs than a ftone can enjoy the pleafures of animal life, or a mere animal thofe of reafon. " But why," you will perhaps murmur and object, " why has God formed fuch an heaven as cannot be univerfally enjoyed? Why has he not provided an happinefs for every tafte?" You may as well afk why he has not created a light that would be equally agreeable to every eye; to the mole and the owl, as well as to man and the eagle? Or why has he not formed light with all the properties of darknefs; that is, why has he not performed contradictions? You may as well query, why has he not given us equal capacities of enjoyment in ficknefs and in health, and furnifhed us with equal pleafures in both? I tell you that, in the nature of things, the low and impure pleafures which would fuit the depraved tafte of the wicked, would be naufeous and painful to pure minds refined and fanctified; and they cannot mingle, they cannot approach each other without being deftroyed. The element of water may as well be converted into a fit refidence for the inhabitants of dry land, and yet retain all its properties that are fuitable to its prefent natives; or the folid earth become a fit receptacle for fifhes, and yet both it and the fifhes retain their ufual qualities. In fhort, men, beafts, birds, fifhes, infects, angles, devils, the inhabitants of every zone and climate, of every planet, or any other region of the univerfe, may as well form one fociety in one and the same place, and mingle their respective food and pleasures, as an heaven of happiness be prepared that would suit every taste. God has prepared the only kind of heaven that is in its own nature possible; the only one that would be an expression of love, or afford real and extensive happiness to such of his creatures as are capable of it. The heaven of sinners would be a nuisance to all other beings in the universe; a private good only to malefactors, at the expence of the public; an open reward of wickedness, and a public discountenancing of all moral goodness. This would be the case upon the supposition that the heaven of sinners were possible. But the supposition is infinitely absurd; it is as impossible as the pleasures of sickness, the sensibility of a stone, or the meridian splendors of midnight.

Therefore acknowledge, admire, and love the beauty of the Lord, his holiness. *Give thanks*, says the Psalmist, *at the remembrance of his holiness*, Psalm xcvii. 12. of his holiness, as well as of his goodness and love; for it is the brightest modification of his love and goodness. An unholy being, in the character of supreme magistrate of the universe, cannot be all love, or communicate nothing but what is pleasing to all; nay, as far as he is unholy he must have a malignant disposition towards the public happiness, and be essentially deficient in benevolence.

V. What is the justice, even the punitive justice of God, but a modification of love and goodness!

As there is no divine perfection which appears so terrible to offenders as this, which therefore they toil and sweat to disapprove or explain away, I shall dwell the longer upon it. And I hope to convince you that justice is not that grim, stern, tremendous attribute which is delineated by the guilty partial imagination of sinners, who have made it their interest that there should be no such attribute in Deity, but that it is infinite, amiable and lovely, as well as awful and majestic; nay, that it is love and benevolence itself.

By the punitive justice of God, I mean that perfection of his nature which executes the sentence of his law upon offenders, or inflicts upon them the punishment he had threatened to disobedience, exactly according to his own denunciation. The present world, which is a state of trial and discipline, and not of final rewards and punishments, is not the proper theatre of vindictive justice, but of a promiscuous providence; *All things come alike to all,* and no man can know the love or hatred of the Ruler of the world towards him, *by all that is before him*. Ecclef. ix. 1, 2. Yet sometimes, even in this life, justice arrests the guilty, and displays its illustrious terrors upon them, especially upon guilty nations that have no existence in a national capacity in the eternal world, and therefore can be punished in that capacity in this only. It was vindictive justice that deluged the whole world in a flood of vengeance ! that kindled the flames of Sodom and Gomorrah ; and that cut off the nations of Canaan when they *had filled up the meafure of their iniquities*. It is juftice that arms kingdoms from age to age, and makes them the executioners of divine wrath upon one another, while they are gratifying their own ambition, avarice, or revenge. The devaftations of earthquakes, inundations, plagues, epidemical ficknefles, famines, and the various calamities in which mankind have been involved, are fo many difplays of divine juftice ; and their being brought on the world according to the courfe of nature, and by means of fecondary caufes, will by no means prove that they are not fo, but only that the very make and conftitution of this world are fo planned and formed by divine wifdom as to admit of the execution of juftice at proper periods, and that all its parts are the inftruments of juftice to accomplifh its defigns. But thefe and all the other judgments of Heaven upon our world are only preludes and fpecimens of the moft perfect adminiftration of it in a future ftate. There the penalty of the law will be executed upon impenitent offenders with the utmoft impartiality. And Revelation affures us that the punifhment will be endlefs in duration, and of as exquifite a kind and high degree as the utmoft capacity of the fubjects will admit ; and confequently that it will not, like fatherly chaftifements, have any tendency to their reformation or advantage, but to their entire and everlafting deftruction. Now it is this difplay of punitive juftice that appears fo terrible and cruel to the guilty children of men ; and therefore this is what I fhall principally endeavour to vindicate and to clothe with all the gentle and amiable glories of Love and public Benevolence.

For this end I beg you would confider, that whatever has a tendency to prevent fin tends to prevent mifery alfo, and to promote the happinefs of the world and of all the individuals in it ; that good laws are abfolutely neceffary for the prevention of fin ; that penal fanctions are effential to good laws ; and that the execution of the penal fanctions upon offenders is abfolutely neceffary to their efficacy and good tendency; and confequently the execution of them is a difplay of love and benevolence.

Confider alfo, that many are excited to feek everlafting happinefs, and deterred from the ways that lead down to deftruction, by means of the threatenings of the law ; that even thofe on whom they are finally executed were once in a capacity of receiving immortal advantage from them, but defeated their good influence and tendency by their own wilful obftinacy : and that the righteous execution of thefe threatenings upon the incorrigible, may promote the common good of the univerfe.

Confider farther, that criminals are incompetent judges of vindictive juftice, becaufe they are parties ; and therefore we fhould not form an estimate of it by their prejudices, but from the judgment of the disinterested and impartial part of the creation.

Finally consider, that proceedings similar to those of the divine government, are not only approved of as just in all human governments, but also loved and admired as amiable and praise-worthy, and essential to the goodness and benevolence of a ruler.

Let us briefly illustrate these several classes of propositions.

I. " Whatever has a tendency to prevent sin, tends to prevent misery also, and to promote the happiness of the universe and of all the individuals in it : good laws are absolutely necessary for the prevention of sin : penal sanctions are essential to good laws ; and the seasonable executions of those sanctions is absolutely necessary to their efficacy and good tendency ; and consequently the execution of them is a display of love and benevolence."

" Whatever has a tendency to prevent sin, tends to prevent misery also," and that for this reason, because sin is necessarily productive of misery, and destructive of happiness. Can a rational creature be happy that is disaffected to the supreme good, the only source of that kind of happiness which is adapted to a rational nature? This is as impossible as that you should enjoy animal pleasures while you abhor all animal enjoyments. Can a social creature be happy in eternal solitude, or in a state of society, while ill-affected towards the other members of society, or while they are ill-affected towards him and he to them, *hateful, and hating one another?* Can a creature, formed capable of felicity superior to what any good can communicate, be happy in the eager pursuit of bubbles ; that is, of its highest happiness in inferior enjoyments? All those dispositions of heart, and the practices resulting from them, in which sin consists, enmity to God, uneasy murmurings and insurrections against his perfections, and the government of his law and Providence ; a churlish, malignant, envious temper towards mankind ; an anxious, excessive eagerness of desire after vain, unsatisfactory enjoyments ; a disrelish for the exalted pleasures of holiness and benevolence ; what are these and the like dispositions, but so many ingredients of misery, and so many abatements of happiness? and consequently all measures that are taken for the prevention of sin are so many benevolent expedients for the prevention of misery and the increase of happiness.

I add, " Good laws are absolutely necessary for the prevention of sin." Indeed those dispositions and actions which are sinful and forbidden by the divine law would be of a deadly nature to the soul even if they were not forbidden, as a stab to the heart would prove mortal to the body, although there were no laws against it, and for that very reason laws have been made against it. Therefore the laws of God do not properly constitute the destructive nature of sin, but only point out and warn us against what is destructive in its own nature previous to all explicit law. And is it not absolutely necessary, and an act of the highest benevolence, that the supreme Lawgiver should warn us against this pernicious evil, and plainly inform us what it is? This is the design of his laws both natural and revealed. And without them, what sure instructor, what unerring guide, or what strong inducements to a proper conduct could we have in this most important case? Is it not necessary, is it not kind, that the supreme Legislator should interpose his authority, and lay us under the strongest obligation to avoid our own ruin? And if good laws are necessary, so are penal sanctions; for, "penal sanctions are essential to good laws." Laws without penalties would be only the advices of an equal or an inferior, and not the obligatory commands of authority. They might be observed or not, according to pleasure, and consequently would answer no valuable purpose. They would also be infinitely absurd in their own nature; for if what the law enjoins be reasonable, necessary, and of good tendency, is it not necessary and fit that they who do not deserve it should feel the bad effects of their omission? And what is this but a penalty? But on a point so plain I need not multiply words; I appeal to the common sense of mankind, I appeal to the universal practice of all governments. Have there ever been, or can there possibly be any laws without penal sanctions: would not such laws be exposed to perpetual insult and contempt, and be destitute of all force and energy? The common sense and universal practice of all the world, in all ages, remonstrate against such an absurdity. But if penal sanctions are essential to good laws, then so is their execution; for,

" The seasonable execution of penal sanctions is absolutely necessary to their efficacy and good tendency." Penalties denounced can have no efficacy upon the subjects of the law; that is, they cannot excite fear, and by that means deter them from disobedience, unless they are believed, and their execution expected. But they could soon cease to be believed, and their execution would no longer be expected, if in several instances they should be dispensed with, and a succession of sinners should pass with impunity. Other sinners, judging of future events by past facts, would expect the same indulgence, and therefore venture upon disobence without any restraint from the penalty of the law. Here again I shall bring the matter to a quick decision, by appealing to the common reason and universal practice of mankind. Would human laws have any force if the penalty was hung up as an empty terror and never executed? Would not such laws be liable to perpetual violation and insult, and become the sport of daring offenders? Would not the escapes of former offenders encourage all future generations to give themselves a-loose, in hopes of the same exemption? Is it not necessary in all governments that public justice should make examples of some, to warn and deter others? Have not all nations, especially the more civilized, made such examples? And have not all the impartial world commended their proceedings as necessary to the safety and happiness of society, and expressive of their regard to the public good?

View all these things together, and methinks I may bid defiance to common sense to draw any other conclusion than that the justice of God in executing the penalties of his law upon impenitent offenders, is the height of goodness and love. If love requires that all proper expedients be used for the prevention of sin; if good laws are necessary for this end; if penalties are essential to good laws; and if the seasonable execution of penalties be absolutely necessary to give them their benevolent force and good tendency, does it not unavoidably follow, that love itself requires both the enacting of penal sanctions to the law of God, and the execution of them upon proper subjects? Without this wholesome severity, the divine laws would be less secure from contempt, and the divine government would be the less favourable to the peace and happiness of the subjects than the laws and governments of mortals in all civilized nations.

"But why does the penalty rise so high? Why is the execution lengthened out through everlasting ages? Why might not a gentler punishment suffice?" This is the grand objection; and in such language as this the enmity of the rebellious heart against the justice of God generally expresses itself. But if the original design and natural tendency of the threatened penalty be to prevent sin, then by how much severer the penalty, by so much the more effectual tendency has it to answer this kind of design? No punishments can rise higher than those which a righteous God has annexed to disobedience, the natural source of every misery; and what is this but to say that no methods more effectual can be taken to prevent it than what he has actually taken? We may therefore infer the ardor of the love of God from the terror of his threatenings. He has denounced the greatest misery against sin, in order to restrain his creatures from running into that very misery; and threatens the loss of heaven, in order to prevent his creatures from losing it.

I must also here repeat the common argument, which appears to me as valid as common; "that as the essence of sin consists in the breach of an obligation, the evil of sin must be exactly proportioned to the strength of the obligation;" that as we are undoubtedly under infinite obligations to a God of infinite excellency, our Maker, Ruler, and Benefactor, the evil of sin, which violates those obligations, must be infinite also; and that no punishment short of what is infinite can be adequate to the demerit of an infinite evil and consequently sinners ought to suffer a finite punishment through an infinite duration, becaufe that is the only way in which they are able to bear an infinite punifhment. But on this common topic a few hints may fuffice.

I proceed to the next fet of propofitions.

II. "That many are excited to the purfuit of everlafting happinefs, and deterred from the ways of deftruction, by means of threatenings of the divine law; that even thofe unhappy creatures on whom they are finally executed were once in a capacity of receiving immortal advantage from them, but defeated their good influence and tendency by their own wilful obftinacy; and that the righteous execution of thefe threatenings upon the incorrigible may promote the common good of the univerfe."

"Many are excited to the purfuit of everlafting happinefs, and deterred from the ways of deftruction, by means of the threatenings of the divine law." I appeal to experience and obfervation, whether the terrors of the Lord are not the very firft thing that gives a check to finners in their headlong career to ruin? It is *the law* that *worketh wrath*, Rom. iv. 15. that is, an alarming apprehenfion of the wrath of God againft fin, and conftrains them to ufe the inftituted means of deliverance. Thus even the terrors of the law are made fubfervient to divine law, in *turning finners from the error of their way, and faving fouls from death*. And could we confult the glorious affembly of the fpirits of juft men made perfect, they would all own that if their heavenly Father had not threatened them fo feverely, they would always have continued undutiful, and confequently rendered themfelves miferable; and that they were faved from hell by being honeftly warned of the danger of falling into it. It is true there are multitudes who do not receive this advantage by the penal fanctions of the divine law, but are made miferable for ever by the execution of them; yet it may be added,

"That even thofe unhappy creatures on whom they are executed, were once in a capacity of receiving infinite advantage from them, but defeated their good influence and tendency in their own wilful obftinacy." The threatenings of the divine law had the fame good tendency in their own nature with refpect to them, to deter them from difobedience, and urge their purfuit of happinefs, as with refpect to others; and thefe were fome of the means God appointed for their falvation. But they hardened themfelves againft them, and thus defeated their good tendency, and obftinately ruined themfelves in defiance of warning: they even forced a paffage into the infernal pit through the ftrongeft enclofures. But if they had not been thus warned, they only would not have been faved in the event, but they would not have enjoyed the means of falvation. Now their enjoying thefe means was in itfelf an inexpreffible bleffing, though in the iffue it only aggravates their misery; and consequently the enacting those penalties to the divine law was really an act of kindness even to them; and their abuse of the blessing does not alter its nature. The primary and direct end of a penalty is not the punishment of the subjects, but to restrain them from things injurious to themselves and others, and urge them to pursue their own interest. But when this good end is not answered, by reason of their wilful folly and disobedience, then, and not till then, the execution is necessary for the good of others;* which leads me to add,

"That the righteous execution of the threatened penalty upon the incorrigible may promote the common good of the universe." This world is a public theatre, surrounded with numerous spectators, who are interested in its affairs. Angels in particular, are witnesses of the proceedings of Providence towards mankind, and thence learn the perfections of God, and the maxims of his government. Hell is also a region dreadfully conspicuous to them; and there, no doubt, the offended Judge intends to shew his wrath, and make his power known to them as well as to mankind. Now they are held in obedience by rational motives, and not by mechanical compulsion. And, among other motives of a gentler kind, no doubt this is one of no small weight; namely, their observing the destructive consequences of sin upon men and angels, and the terrible displeasure of God against it. It is not at all inconsistent with their dignity and purity to suppose them swayed by this motive in a proper connection with others of a more disinterested and generous nature. Therefore the confirmation of the elect angels in holiness, and their everlasting happiness, is no doubt not a little secured and promoted by the execution of righteous punishment upon some notorious hardened malefactors, both of their own order and of the human race.

The same thing may be said of *the spirits of just men made perfect;* they are happily incapable of sinning, and consequently of becoming miserable; but their incapacity arises from the clear conviction of their understanding, which has the conduct of their will; and, while sin appears to them so deadly and destructive an evil, it is impossible, according to the make of a rational nature, that they should choose it. But the consequences of sin upon the

---

* Penalties operate, like final causes, by a kind of retrospective influence; that is, whilst they are only threatened, and the subject expects they will be executed, should he turn disobedient, they have a powerful tendency to deter him from disobedience. But they could not have this benevolent tendency, unless they be executed upon those, on whom their primary and chief design is not obtained; namely, the restraining of them from sin. It is enough that the offenders themselves once had an opportunity of taking warning, and reaping the advantage of the threatened penalty, while they were in a state of trial, and candidates for eternity. But it is absurd that they should receive any benefit from it, when, after sufficient trial, it appears they will take no warning, but are resolved to persist in sin, in defiance of the most tremendous penalties.

Serm. 18.   *God is Love.*   321

wretched creatures on whom the penalty denounced againſt it is executed, is no doubt one thing that affords them this conviction; and ſo it contributes to their perſeverance in obedience and happineſs. Thus the joys of heaven are ſecured by the pains of hell, and even the moſt noxious criminals, the enemies of God and his creatures, are not uſeleſs in the univerſe, but anſwer the terrible but benevolent end of warning all other creatures againſt diſobedience; which would involve them in the ſame miſery, juſt as the execution of a few malefactors in human governments is of extenſive ſervice to the reſt of the ſubjects.

But as the greater part of mankind periſh, it may be queried, "How is it conſiſtent with love and goodneſs, that the majority ſhould be puniſhed and made monuments of juſtice, for the benefit of the ſmaller number?" To this I reply, that though it be equally evident from ſcripture and obſervation, that the greater part of mankind go down to deſtruction in the ſmooth, broad, deſcending road of ſin, in the ordinary ages of the world; and though revelation aſſures us that the number of the apoſtate angels is very great, yet I think we have no reaſon to conclude that the greater part of the rational creation ſhall be miſerable; nay, it is poſſible the number of thoſe on whom the penalty of the divine law is inflicted, may bear no more proportion to that of the innumerable ranks of creatures that may be retained in obedience and happineſs by means of their conſpicuous and exemplary puniſhment, than the number of criminals executed in our government for the warning of others bears to the reſt of the ſubjects. If we conſider that thoſe who have been *redeemed from the earth*, even in the ordinary ages of the world, though comparatively but few, yet abſolutely are a *multitude which no man can number, out of every kindred, and people, and language*, Rev. viii. 9. and that the elect angels are *an innumerable company*,* Heb. xii. 29. perhaps much greater than the legions of hell; if to theſe we add the prodigious numbers that ſhall be converted in that long and bleſſed ſeaſon when Satan ſhall be bound, when the Prince of peace ſhall reign, and when *the kingdom and dominion, and the greatneſs of the kingdom under the whole heaven ſhall be given to the people of the ſaints of the moſt high*, Dan. vii. 27. in which not only the greater number of the generations that ſhall live in that glorious millennium ſhall be ſaved, but perhaps a greater number than all that periſhed in former generations, which is very probable if we conſider the long continuance of that time, and that the world will then be under the peculiar bleſſing of Heaven, and conſequently mankind will multiply faſter, and not be diminiſhed as they now

---

* I do not forget that the original is *myriads of angels*. But the word is often, I think, generally uſed in the Greek claſſes, not for any definite number, but for a great and innumerable multitude. And ſo it is uſed here.

are by the calamities of war, plagues, epidemical sickneſses, and the other judgements of God upon thoſe times of rebellion; if we also borrow a little light from the hypotheſis of philoſophy, and ſuppoſe that the other planets of our ſyſtem are peopled like our earth with proper inhabitants, and particularly with reaſonable creatures (for he that made thoſe vaſt bodies *made them not in vain, he made them to be inhabited;*) if we further ſuppoſe that each of the innumerable fixed ſtars is a ſun, the centre of habitable worlds, and that all theſe worlds, like our own, ſwarm with life, and particularly with various claſſes of reaſonable beings (which is not at all unlikely if we argue from parity of caſes, from things well known to things leſs known, or from the immenſe over-flowing goodneſs, wiſdom and power of the great Creator, who can repleniſh the infinite voids of ſpace with being, life, and reaſon, and with equal eaſe produce and ſupport ten thouſand worlds as ten thouſand grains;) if we ſuppoſe that his creative perfections will not lie inactive for ever, contented with one exertion for ſix days, but that he ſtill employs and will employ them for ever in cauſing new worlds, repleniſhed with moral agents, to ſtart into exiſtence here and there in the endleſs vacancies of ſpace; and finally, if we ſuppoſe that the flames of hell will blaze dreadfully bright and conſpicuous in the view of all preſent and future creations, or that the deſtructive nature of ſin will be ſome way or another made known to the rational inhabitants of all worlds by the puniſhment inflicted upon a number of men and angels, and that by this means they are effectually deterred from ſin, and preſerved from the miſery inſeperable from it; I ſay, if we admit theſe ſuppoſitions, ſome of which are undoubtedly true, and the reſt I think not improbable, then it will follow that the number of holy and happy creatures in the univerſe will be incomparably greater than that of miſerable criminals; and that the puniſhment of the latter is one principle mean of preſerving this infinite number in obedience and happineſs; and conſequently is highly conducive to the public happineſs, and expreſſive of the love and goodneſs of the univerſal Ruler to the immenſe community of his ſubjects. And thus *God is love,* even in the moſt terrible diſplays of his vindictive juſtice.

To illuſtrate this ſubject, conſider farther.

III. "That criminals are incompetent judges of vindictive juſtice." They are parties, and it is their intereſt there ſhould be no ſuch attribute as juſtice in the Deity. It is natural for them to flatter themſelves that their crimes are ſmall; that their Judge will ſuffer them to eſcape with impunity, or with a gentle puniſhment; and that if he ſhould do otherwiſe he would be unmerciful, unjuſt, and cruel. The exceſs of ſelf-love ſuggeſts to them a thouſand excuſes and extenuations of their guilt, and flatters them

Serm. 18.   *God is Love.*   323

with a thousand favourable presumptions. An impenitent criminal is always an ungenerous, mean-spirited, selfish creature, and has nothing of that noble disinterested self-denial and impartiality which would generously condemn himself and approve of that sentence by which he dies. A little acquaintance with the conduct of mankind will soon make us sensible of their partiality and wrong judgments in matters where self is concerned; and particularly how unfit they are to form an estimate of justice when themselves are to stand as criminals at its bar. Now this is the case of all mankind in the affair now under consideration. They are criminals at the bar of divine justice; they are the parties to be tried; they are under the dominion of a selfish spirit; it is natural to them to palliate their own crimes, and to form flattering expectations from the clemency of their Judge. And are they fit persons to prescribe to their Judge how he should deal with them, or what measure of punishment he ought to inflict upon them? Sinners! dare you usurp this high province? Dare you

" Snatch from his hand the balance and the rod,
" Rejudge his justice, be the god of God?"*

Rather stand at the bar, ye criminals! that is your place. Do not dare to ascend the throne; that is the place of your Judge. Stand silent, and await his righteous sentence, which is always just, always best: or, if creatures must judge of the justice of their Sovereign, I appeal to the saints; I appeal to angels, those competent, disinterested judges; I appeal to every upright impartial being in the universe. They approve, they celebrate, they admire, and love all the displays of punitive justice as necessary to the public good; and their judgment may be depended on: it is not misled by ignorance nor perverted by self-interest. To whom would you appeal as judges of the proceedings of courts of justice among men? To malefactors in a dungeon, who have made justice their enemy, and who are therefore enemies to it? No; but you would appeal to obedient subjects, who are not obnoxious to justice themselves, but enjoy protection under its guardianship, and are sensible of its beauty and public utility? They all approve it with one voice, and would look upon a supreme magistrate without it as a very contemptible and odious character, and essentially deficient in goodness. Hence it follows that even the punitive justice of God not only is in reality, but to all impartial judges appears to be a most amiable, engaging, and beneficent perfection; majestic indeed, but not forbidding; awful, but not sullen and hateful; terrible, but only to criminals; and destruc-

* Pope's Essay on Man.

tive only to what destroys the public good. I have so far anticipated myself that I need hardly add,

IV. "That proceedings similar to those of the divine government are not only approved of as just in all human governments, but also loved and admired as amiable and praise-worthy, and highly essential to the goodness and benevolence of a Ruler."

Does the supreme Lawgiver annex severe penalties to his laws which render the disobedient miserable for ever? So do human governments with the unanimous approbation of their subjects; they inflict punishments that affect life, and cut off the offender from civil society for ever; and this is the only kind of everlasting punishment that can be endured or executed by mortals. Does Jehovah maintain good order in his immense empire, protect his subjects, and deter them from offending by making examples of the guilty? and does he secure and advance the good of the whole by the conspicuous punishment of obnoxious individuals? This is done every day for the same ends in human governments, and that with universal approbation. Does he inflict punishments that are not at all intended for the reformation and advantage of the guilty sufferer, but only for the admonition and benefit of others? This is always the case in human governments when the punishment reaches to the life, for then the offender himself is put out of all capacity of reformation or personal advantage by it, but he suffers entirely for the good of others. Even criminals must be made useful to society; and this is the only use they are fit to answer. Would it not be inexpedient and greatly injurious for a magistrate in his public character to forgive crimes and suffer criminals to escape, though to do so in a private character might be a virtue? Just so God, who is the supreme Magistrate of the universe, and not at all to be considered in this case as a private person acting only in a private character, the great God I say is obliged by his regard for his own honour and the benefit of his subjects, to inflict proper punishments and distribute his pardoning mercy to individuals consistently with the general good of the whole. What would be revenge in a private person, which is the ruling passion of devils, is justice, honour and benevolence itself in the supreme Ruler of the world; and a failure in this would render him not only less glorious and majestic, but less amiable, less beneficent to his creatures.

I know hardly any thing of so much importance to give us just sentiments of the proceedings of God with his creatures, as that we should conceive of him as a moral Ruler or the supreme Magistrate of the world. And it is owing to their not considering him in this character that sinners indulge such mistaken dangerous presumptions concerning him. They choose to conceive of him under some fond and tender name, as a Being of infinite grace, the indulgent Father of his creatures, &c. All this is true; but it is equally true that he is their moral Ruler as well as their Father. His creatures are his subjects as well as his children; and he must act the wise and righteous Magistrate as well as the tender Father towards them. His goodness is that of a Ruler, and not of a private person; and his pardoning of sin and receiving offenders into favour, are not private kindnesses but acts of government, and therefore they must be conducted with the utmost wisdom; for a wrong step in his infinite administration, which effects such innumerable multitudes of subjects, would be an infinite evil, and might admit of no reparation.

Though I have thus enlarged upon this subject, yet I am far from exhausting my materials. But these things I hope are sufficient to convince your understandings that divine justice is not that unkind, cruel, and savage thing sinners are wont to imagine it; but that God is just, because *God is love:* and that he punishes not because he is the enemy, but because he is the friend of his creatures, and because he loves the whole too well to let particular offenders do mischief with impunity*.

I shall only add, that this is the view Jehovah has given of himself in the clearest manifestation of his perfections that he ever made to mortals. He promises his favourite Moses, that he would *make all his goodness pass before him.* Observe, it is his goodness he intends to exhibit; and the proclamation runs thus; *The Lord, the Lord God, merciful and gracious, long-suffering, forgiving iniquity,* &c. That these are acts or modifications of goodness, will be easily granted. But observe, it is added even in this proclamation of his goodness, *That he will by no means clear the guilty;* intimating, that to be just and punish sin is an act of goodness, as well as to be merciful and to forgive it.

And now when we have this copious subject in review, does it not suggest to us such conclusions as these:

I. May we not conclude that the case of impenitent sinners is desperate indeed when it is not excessive rigour, not a malignity of temper, nor tyranny, or a savage delight in torture that condemns

---

* It may perhaps be objected, "That to represent justice under the notion of love, is to affect singularity in language, to destroy the distinction of the divine attributes, and the essential differences of things."—To which I answer, 1. That a catachresis may be beautiful and emphatical, though it be always a seeming impropriety in language. Such is this representation, "Divine Justice, divine love." 2. I do not deny that God's executing righteous punishment upon the guilty may be called justice; but then it is his love to the public that excites him to do this; and therefore his doing it may be properly denominated love, as well as justice, or love under the name of justice, which is love still. 3. I do not mean that the usual names of things should be changed, but that we should affix suitable ideas to them. We may retain the name of justice still, but let us not affix ideas to it that are inconsistent with divine love. Let us not look upon it as the attribute of a tyrant, but of a wise and good ruler.

them, but goodness itself, love itself? Even the gentler perfections of the Deity, those from which they derive their presumptuous hopes, are conspired against them, and unite their forces to render them miserable, in order to prevent greater misery from spreading through the universe. Impenitent sinners! even the unbounded love of God to his creatures is your enemy. Love, under the name and form of justice, which is equally love still demands your execution; and to suffer you to escape would not only be an act of injustice, but an act of malignity and hostility against the whole system of rational beings. Therefore repent and be holy, otherwise divine love will not suffer you to be happy. *God is love;* therefore will he confine you in the infernal prison, as a regard to the public welfare in human governments shuts up criminals in a dungeon, and madmen in Bedlam.

II. May we not hence conclude that all the acts of the Deity may be resolved into the benevolent principle of love? *God is love;* therefore he made this vast universe, and planted it so thick with variegated life. *God is love;* therefore he still rules the world he has made, and inflicts chastisements and judgments upon it from every age. *God is love;* therefore he spared not his own Son, but made him the victim of his justice. *God is love;* therefore he requires perfect holiness, perfect obedience from all his subjects. *God is love;* therefore he has enacted such tremendous sanctions to his law, and executes them in their full extent upon offenders. *God is love;* therefore he has made the prison of hell, and there confines in chains of everlasting darkness those malevolent creatures that would be nuisances to society, and public mischiefs if suffered to run at large. In short, whatever he does, he does it because he is love. How amiable a view of him this! Therefore,

III. We may certainly conclude that if God be love, then all his creatures ought to love him. Love him, O all ye inhabitants of Heaven! But they need not my exhortation; they know him, and therefore cannot but love him. Love him, all ye inhabitants of the planetary worlds! if such there be. These also I hope need no exhortation, for we would willingly persuade ourselves that other territories of his immense empire have not rebelled against him as this earth has done. Love him, O ye children of men! To you I call: but O! I fear I shall call in vain. To love him who is all love is the most hopeless proposal one can make to the world. But whatever others do, love the Lord, all ye his saints! You I know cannot resist the motion. Surely your love even now is all on fire. *Love the Lord, O my soul!* Amen.

SERMON XIX.

The General Resurrection.

—⋙⋘—

John v. 28, 29. *The hour is coming in the which all that are in the grave shall hear his voice, and shall come forth; they that have done good, unto the resurrection of life; and they that have done evil, to the resurrection of damnation.*

EVER since sin entered into the world, and death by sin, this earth has been a vast grave-yard, or burying-place for her children. In every age, and in every country, that sentence has been executing, *Dust thou art, and unto dust thou shalt return.* The earth has been arched with graves, the last lodgings of mortals, and the bottom of the ocean paved with the bones of men*. Human nature was at first confined to one pair, but how soon and how wide did it spread! How inconceivably numerous are the sons of Adam! How many different nations on our globe contain many millions of men, even in one generation! And how many generations have succeeded one another in the long run of near six thousand years! Let imagination call up this vast army; children that just light upon our globe and then wing their flight into an unknown world; the grey-headed that have had a long journey through life; the blooming youth and the middle-aged, let them pass in review before us from all countries and from all ages; and how vast and astonishing the multitude! If the posterity of one man (Abraham) by one son was, according to the divine promise, as the stars of Heaven, or as the sand by the sea-shore, innumerable, what numbers can compute the multitudes that have sprung from all the Patriarchs, the sons of Adam and Noah! But what is become of them all? Alas! they are turned into earth, their original element; they are all imprisoned in the grave except the present generation, and we are dropping one after another in a quick succession into that *place appointed for all living.* There has not been perhaps a moment of time for five thousand years, but what some one or other has sunk into the mansions of the dead; and in some fatal hours, by the sword of war or the devouring jaws of earthquakes, thousands have been cut off and

---

* No spot on earth but has supply'd a grave;
And human sculls the spacious ocean pave. YOUNG.

swept away at once, and left in one huge promiscuous carnage. The greatest number of mankind beyond comparison are sleeping under ground. There lies beauty mouldering into dust, rotting into stench and loathsomeness, and feeding the vilest worms. There lies the head that once wore a crown, as low and contemptible as the meanest beggar. There lie the mighty giants, the heroes and conquerors, the Samsons, the Ajax's, the Alexanders, and the Cæsars of the world; there they lie stupid, senseless, and inactive, and unable to drive off the worms that riot on their marrow, and make their houses in those sockets where the eyes sparkled with living lustre. There lie the wife and the learned, as rotten, as helpless as the fool. There lie some that we once conversed with, some that were our friends our companions; and there lie our fathers and mothers, our brothers and sisters.

And shall they lie there always? Shall this body, this curious workmanship of Heaven, so wonderfully and fearfully made, always lie in ruins, and never be repaired? Shall the wide-extended valleys of dry bones never more live? This we know, that *it is not a thing impossible with God to raise the dead.* He that could first form our bodies out of nothing, is certainly able to form them anew, and repair the wastes of time and death. But what is his declared will in this case? On this the matter turns; and this is fully revealed in my text. *The hour is coming, when all that are in the graves,* all that are dead, without exception, *shall hear the voice of the Son of God, and shall come forth.*

And for what end shall they come forth? O! for very different purposes; *some to the resurrection of life; and some to the resurrection of damnation.*

And what is the ground of this vast distinction? Or what is the difference in character between those that shall receive so different a doom? It is this, *They that have done good shall rise to life, and they that have done evil, to damnation.* It is this, and this only, that will then be the rule of distinction.

I would avoid all art in my method of handling this subject, and intend only to illustrate the several parts of the text. *All that are in the graves shall hear his voice, and shall come forth; they that have done well, to the resurrection of life; and they that have done evil, to the resurrection of damnation!*

I. They that are in the graves shall hear his voice. The voice of the Son of God here probably means the sound of the archangel's trumpet, which is called his voice, because sounded by his orders and attended with his all-quickening power. This all-awakening call to the tenants of the grave we frequently find foretold in scripture. I shall refer you to two plain passages. *Behold,* says St. Paul, *I shew you a mystery,* an important and astonishing secret, *we shall not all sleep;* that is, mankind will not all be sleeping in death when that day comes, there will be a generation then alive upon earth ; and though they cannot have a proper refurrection, yet they fhall pafs through a change equivalent to it. *We fhall all be changed,* fays he, *in a moment, in the twinkling of an eye, at the laft trump, for the trumpet fhall found,* it fhall give the alarm ; and no fooner is the awful clangour heard than all the living fhall be transformed into immortals ; *and the dead fhall be raifed incorruptible; and we, who are then alive, fhall be changed,* 1 Cor. xv. 51, 52. this is all the difference, *they fhall be raifed, and we fhall be changed.* This awful prelude of the trumpet is alfo mentioned in 1 Theff. iv. 15, 16. *We which are alive, and remain unto the coming of the Lord, fhall not prevent them which are afleep ;* that is, we fhall not be beforehand with them in meeting our defcending Lord, *for the Lord himfelf fhall defcend from heaven with a fhout, with the voice of the archangel, and with the trump of God ;* that is, with a godlike trump, fuch as it becomes his majefty to found, *and the dead in Chrift fhall rife firft ;* that is, before the living fhall be caught up in the clouds to meet the Lord in the air ; and when they are rifen, and the living transformed, they fhall afcend together to the place of judgment.

My brethren, realize the majefty and terror of this univerfal alarm. When the dead are fleeping in the filent grave · when the living are thoughtlefs and unapprehenfive of the grand event, or intent on other purfuits ; fome of them afleep in the dead of night; fome of them diffolved in fenfual pleafures, eating and drinking, marrying and giving in marriage ; fome of them planning or executing fchemes for riches or honours ; fome in the very act of fin ; the generality ftupid and carelefs about the concerns of eternity, and the dreadful day juft at hand ; and a few here and there converfing with their God, and *looking for the glorious appearance of their Lord and Saviour;* when the courfe of nature runs on uniform and regular as ufual, and infidel fcoffers are taking umbrage from thence to afk, *Where is the promife of his coming ? for fince the fathers fell afleep, all things continue as they were from the beginning of the creation.* 2 Pet. iii. 4. In fhort, when there are no more vifible appearances of this approaching day, than of the deftruction of Sodom on that fine clear morning in which Lot fled away ; or of the deluge, when Noah entered into the ark : then in that hour of unapprehenfive fecurity, then fuddenly fhall the heavens open over the aftonifhed world; then fhall the all-alarming clangour break over their heads like a clap of thunder in a clear fky. Immediately the living turn their gazing eyes upon the amazing phænomenon : a few hear the long-expected found with rapture, and lift up their heads with joy, affured that *the day of their redemption is come,* while the thoughtlefs world are ftruck with the wildeft horror and confternation. In the fame inftant the found reaches all the manſions of the dead, and in a moment, in the twinkling of an eye, they are raiſed, and the living are changed. This call will be as animating to all the ſons of men as that call to a ſingle perſon, *Lazarus, come forth*. O what a ſurpriſe will this be to the thoughtleſs world! Should this alarm burſt over our heads this moment, into what a terror would it ſtrike many in this aſſembly? Such will be the terror, ſuch the conſternation, when it actually comes to paſs. Sinners will be the ſame timorous, ſelf-condemned creatures then as they are now. And then they will not be able to ſtop their ears, who are deaf to all the gentler calls of the goſpel now. Then the trump of God will conſtrain them to hear and fear, to whom the miniſters of Chriſt now preach in vain. Then they muſt all hear, for,

II. My text tells you, *all that are in the graves*, all without exception, *ſhall hear his voice*. Now the voice of mercy calls, reaſon pleads, conſcience warns, but multitudes will not hear. But this is a voice which ſhall, which muſt reach every one of the millions of mankind, and not one of them will be able to ſtop his ears. Infants and giants, kings and ſubjects, all ranks, all ages of mankind ſhall hear the call. The living ſhall ſtart and be changed, and the dead riſe at the ſound. The duſt that was once alive and formed a human body, whether it flies in the air, floats in the ocean, or vegetates on earth, ſhall hear the new-creating fiat. Wherever the fragments of the human frame are ſcattered, this all-penetrating call ſhall reach and ſpeak them into life. We may conſider this voice as a ſummons not only to dead bodies to riſe, but to the ſouls that once animated them, to appear and be re-united to them, whether in heaven or hell. To the grave the call will be, *Ariſe, ye dead, and come to judgment;* to heaven, ye *ſpirits of juſt men made perfect;* "deſcend to the world whence you originally came; and aſſume your new-formed bodies;" to hell, "Come forth and appear, ye damned ghoſts, ye priſoners of darkneſs, and be again united to the bodies in which you once ſinned, that in them ye may now ſuffer." Thus will this ſummons ſpread through every corner of the univerſe; and Heaven, Earth and Hell, and all their inhabitants, ſhall hear and obey. Devils, as well as the ſinners of our race, will tremble at the ſound; for now they know they can plead no more as they once did, *Torment us not before the time;* for the time is come, and they muſt mingle with the priſoners at the bar. And now when all that are in the graves hear this all-quickening voice,

III. *They ſhall come forth*. Now methinks I ſee, I hear the earth heaving, charnel-houſes rattling, tombs burſting, graves opening. Now the nations under ground begin to ſtir. There is a noiſe and a ſhaking among the dry bones. The duſt is all alive, and in motion, and the globe breaks and trembles, as with an earthquake, while this vast army is working its way through and bursting into life. The ruins of human bodies are scattered far and wide, and have passed through many and surprising transformations. A limb in one country, and another in another; here the head and there the trunk, and the ocean rolling between*. Multitudes have sunk in a watery grave, been swallowed up by the monsters of the deep, and transformed into a part of their flesh. Multitudes have been eaten by beasts and birds of prey, and incorporated with them; and some have been devoured by their fellow-men in the rage of a desperate hunger, or of unnatural cannibal appetite, and digested into a part of them. Multitudes have mouldered into dust, and this dust has been blown about by winds, and washed away with water, or it has petrified into stone, or been burnt into brick to form dwellings for their posterity; or it has grown up in grain, trees, plants, and other vegetables, which are the support of man and beast, and are transformed into their flesh and blood. But through all these various transformations and changes, not a particle that was essential to one human body has been lost, or incorporated with another human body, so as to become an essential part of it. And as to those particles that were not essential, they are not necessary to the identity of the body or of the person; and therefore we need not think they will be raised again. The omniscient God knows how to collect, distinguish, and compound all those scattered and mingled seeds of our mortal bodies. And now, at the sound of the trumpet, they shall all be collected, wherever they were scattered; all properly sorted and united, however they were confused; atom to its fellow-atom, bone to its fellow-bone. Now methinks you may see the air darkened with fragments of bodies flying from country to country, to meet and join their proper parts:

> ——— " Scatter'd limbs, and all
> The various bones obsequious to the call,
> Self-mov'd, advance; the neck perhaps to meet
> The distant head, the distant legs, the feet.
> Dreadful to view, see through the dusky sky
> Fragments of bodies in confusion fly,
> To distant regions journeying, there to claim
> Deserted members, and complete the frame—
> The fever'd head and trunk shall join once more,
> Tho' realms now rise between, and oceans roar.
> The trumpet's sound each vagrant mote shall hear,
> Or fixt in earth, or if afloat in air,

* This was the fate of Pompey, who was slain on the African shore. His body was left there, and his head carried over the Mediterranean to Julius Cæsar.

Obey the fignal, wafted in the wind,
And not one fleeping atom lag behind."—*
All hear; and now, in fairer profpect fhewn,
Limb clings to limb, and bone rejoins its bone.—†

Then, my brethren, your duft and mine fhall be re-animated and organized; *and though after our fkin worms deftroy thefe bodies, yet in our flefh fhall we fee God.* Job xix. 16.

And what a vaft improvement will the frail nature of man then receive? Our bodies will then be fubftantially the fame; but how different in qualities, in ftrength, in agility, in capacities for pleafure or pain, in beauty or deformity, in glory or terror, according to the moral character of the perfons to whom they belong? Matter, we know, is capable of prodigious alterations and refinements; and there it will appear in the higheft perfection. The bodies of the faints will be formed glorious, incorruptible, without the feeds of ficknefs and death. The glorified body of Chrift, which is undoubtedly carried to the higheft perfection that matter is capable of, will be the pattern after which they fhall be formed. *He will change our vile body,* fays St. Paul, *that it may be fashioned like unto his glorious body.* Phil. iii. 21. *Flesh and blood,* in their prefent ftate of groffnefs and frailty, *cannot inherit the kingdom of God; neither doth corruption inherit incorruption. But this corruptible body muft put on incorruption; aud this mortal muft put on immortality.* Cor. xv. 50, 53. And how vaft the change, how high the improvement from its prefent ftate! *It was fown in corruption, it shall be raifed in incorruption; it was fown in dishonour, it shall be raifed in glory; it was fown in weaknefs, it shall be raifed in power,* verfe 42, 43, &c. Then will the body be able to bear up under the exceeding great and eternal weight of glory: it will no longer be a clog or an incumbrance to the foul, but a proper inftrument and affiftant in all the exalted fervices and enjoyments of the heavenly ftate.

* Young's Laft Day, Book II.
† Thefe two laft lines are taken from a poem, which is a lively imitation of Dr. Young, entitled, *The Day of Judgment,* afcribed to Mr. Ogilvie, a promifing young genius of Aberdeen, in Scotland, not above nineteen years of age, as I was informed, when he compofed this poem. The lines preceding thefe quoted are as follow:

> O'er boiling waves the fevered members fwim,
> Each breeze is loaded with a broken limb:
> The living atoms, with peculiar care,
> 'Drawn from their cells, come flying thro' the air.
> Where'er they lurk'd, thro' ages undecay'd,
> Deep in the rock, or cloth'd fome fmiling mead;
> Or in the lily's fnowy bofom grew,
> Or ting'd the faphire with its lovely blue;

The bodies of the wicked will alſo be improved, but their improvements will all be terrible and vindictive. Their capacities will be thoroughly enlarged, but then it will be that they may be made capable of greater miſery: they will be ſtrengthened, but it will be that they may bear the heavier load of torment. Their ſenſations will be more quick and ſtrong, but it will be that they may feel the more exquiſite pain. They will be raiſed immortal, that they may not be conſumed by everlaſting fire, or eſcape puniſhment by diſſolution or annihilation. In ſhort, their augmented ſtrength, their enlarged capacities, and their immortality will be their eternal curſe; and they would willingly exchange them for the fleeting duration of a fading flower, or the faint ſenſations of an infant. The only power they would rejoice in is, that of ſelf-annihilation.

And now when the bodies are completely formed and fit to be inhabited, the ſouls that once animated them, being collected from Heaven and Hell, re-enter and take poſſeſſion of their old manſions. They are united in bonds which ſhall never more be diſſolved; and the mouldering tabernacles are now become everlaſting habitations.

And with what joy will the ſpirits of the righteous welcome their old companions from their long ſleep in the duſt, and congratulate their glorious reſurrection! How will they rejoice to re-enter their old habitations, now ſo completely repaired and highly improved? to find thoſe bodies which were once their incumbrance, once frail and mortal, in which they were impriſoned and languiſhed, once their temptation, tainted with the ſeeds of ſin, now their aſſiſtants and co-partners in the buſineſs of Heaven, now vigorous, incorruptible, and immortal, now free from all corrupt mixtures, and ſhining in all the beauties of perfect holineſs? In theſe bodies they once ſerved their God with honeſt though feeble efforts, conflicted with ſin and temptation, and paſſed through all the united trials and hardſhips of mortality and the chriſtian life.

> Or in ſome purling ſtream refreſh'd the plains;
> Or form'd the mountain's adamantine veins;
> Or gaily ſporting in the breathing ſpring,
> Perfum'd the whiſp'ring Zephyr's balmy wing.
> All hear, &c.

The thought ſeems to be borrowed from Mr. Addiſon's fine Latin poem on the Reſurrection, in which are the following beautiful lines:

> Jam pulvis varias terræ diſperſa per oras,
> Sive inter venas teneri concreti metalli,
> Senſim diriguit, ſeu ſeſe immiſcuit herbis,
> Explicita eſt; molem rurſus coaleſcit in unam
> Diviſum Funus, ſparſos prior all'gat artus
> Junctura, aptanturq; iterum coeuntia membra.

But now they are united to them for more exalted and blifsful purpofes. The lungs that were want to heave with penitential fighs and groans, fhall now fhout forth their joys and the praifes of their God and Saviour. The heart that was once broken with forrows fhall now be bound up for ever, and overflow with immortal pleafures. Thofe very eyes, that were wont to run down with tears and to behold many a tragical fight, fhall now *behold the King in his beauty*, fhall behold the Saviour whom, though unfeen, they loved, and all the glories of heaven; and *God fhall wipe away all their tears*. All the fenfes, which were once avenues of pain, fhall now be inlets of the moft exalted pleafure. In fhort, every organ, every member fhall be employed in the moft noble fervices and enjoyments, inftead of the fordid and laborious drudgery, and the painful fufferings of the prefent ftate. Blefled change indeed! Rejoice, ye children of God, in the profpect of it.

But how fhall I glance a thought upon the dreadful cafe of the wicked in that tremendous day! While their bodies burft from their graves, the miferable fpectacles of horror and deformity, fee the millions of gloomy ghofts that once animated them, rife like pillars of fmoke from the bottomlefs pit! and with what reluctance and anguifh do they re-enter their old habitations! O what a dreadful meeting! what fhocking falutations! "And muft I be chained to thee again (may the guilty foul fay) O thou accurfed, polluted body, thou fyftem of deformity and terror! In thee I once finned, by thee I was once enfnared, debafed, and ruined: to gratify thy vile lufts and appetites I neglected my own immortal interefts, degraded my native dignity, and made myfelf miferable for ever. And haft thou now met me to torment me for ever? O that thou hadft ftill flept in the duft, and never been repaired again! Let me rather be condemned to animate a toad or ferpent than that odious body once defiled with fin, and the inftrument of my guilty pleafures, now made ftrong and immortal to torment me with ftrong and immortal pains. Once indeed I received fenfations of pleafure from thee, but now thou art transformed into an engine of torture. No more fhall I through thine eyes behold the cheerful light of the day and the beautiful profpects of nature, but the thick glooms of hell, grim and ghaftly ghofts, heaven at an impaffible diftance, and all the horrid fights of woe in the infernal regions. No more fhall thine ears charm me with the harmony of founds, but terrify and diftrefs me with the echo of eternal groans, and the thunder of almighty vengeance! No more fhall the gratification of thine appetites afford me pleafures, but thine appetites, for ever hungry, for ever unfatisfied, fhall eternally torment me with their eagar importunate cravings. No more fhall thy tongue be employed in mirth, and jeft, and fong, but complain and groan, and blaspheme, and roar for ever. Thy feet, that once walked in the flowery enchanted paths of sin, must now walk on the dismal burning soil of hell. O my wretched companion! I parted with thee with pain and reluctance in the struggles of death, but now I meet thee with greater terror and agony. Return to thy bed in the dust; there sleep and rot, and let me never see thy shocking visage more.'' In vain the petition! the reluctant soul must enter its prison, from whence it shall never more be dismissed. And if we might indulge imagination so far, we might suppose the body begins to recriminate in such language as this: "Come, guilty soul, enter thy old mansion; if it be horrible and shocking, it is owing to thyself. Was not the animal frame, the brutal nature, subjected to thy government, who art a rational principal? Instead of being debased by me, it became thee to have not only retained the dignity of thy nature, but to have exalted mine, by noble employments and gratifications worthy an earthly body united to an immortal spirit. Thou mightest have restrained my members from being the instruments of sin, and made them the instruments of righteousness. My knees would have bowed at the throne of grace, but thou didst not affect that posture. Mine eyes would have read, and mine ears heard the word of life; but thou wouldest not set them to that employ, or wouldest not attend to it. And now it is but just the body thou didst prostitute to sin should be the instrument of thy punishment. Indeed, fain would I relapse into senseless earth as I was, and continue in that insensibility for ever :—but didst thou not hear the all-rousing trumpet just now? did it not even shake the foundations of thy infernal prison? It was that call that awakened me, and summoned me to meet thee, and I could not resist it. Therefore come, miserable soul, take possession of this frame, and let us prepare for everlasting burning. O that it were now possible to die! O that we could be again seperated, and never be united more! Vain wish; the weight of mountains, the pangs of hell, the flames of unquenchable fire, can never dissolve these chains which now bind us together!''*

* The Rev. Mr. John Reynolds, in his poem entitled *Death's Vision*, introduces the soul speaking against the body, and afterwards checking its censures, and turning them upon itself, in a vein of thought not unlike that of Mr. Davies.

> Go, tempter, go, as thou hast been
> A quick extinguisher of heav'nly fires!
> A source of black enormity and sin,
> Thou cramp of sacred motions and desires?
>   How brave and bless'd am I,
>   Unfetter'd from the company,
> Thou enemy of my joys and me?
>   But pardon that I thus

O! Sirs, what a shocking interview is this! O the glorious, dreadful morning of the resurrection! What scenes of unknown joy and terror will then open? Methinks we must always have it in prospect; it must even now engage our thoughts, and fill us with trembling solicitude, and make it the great object of our labour and pursuit to share in the resurrection of the just.

But for what ends do these sleeping multitudes rise? For what purposes do they come forth? My text will tell you.

IV. They shall come forth, *some to the resurrection of life, and some to the resurrection of damnation.* They are summoned from their graves to stand at the bar, and brought out of prison by angelic guards to pass their last trial. And as in this impartial trial they will be found to be persons of very different characters, the righteous Judge of the earth will accordingly pronounce their different doom.

See a glorious *multitude, which none can number,* openly acquitted, pronounced blessed, and welcomed *into the kingdom prepared for them from the foundation of the world.* Now they enter upon a state which deserves the name of life. They are all vital, all active, all glorious, all happy. They *shine brighter than the stars in the firmament; like the sun for ever and ever.* All their faculties overflow with happiness. They mingle with the glorious company of angels; they behold that Saviour whom unseen they loved; they dwell in eternal intimacy with the Father of their spirits; they are employed with ever-new and growing delight in the exalted services of the heavenly sanctuary. They shall never more fear nor feel the least touch of sorrow, pain, or any kind of misery, but shall be as happy as their natures can admit through an immortal duration. What a glorious new creation is here! what illustrious creatures formed of the dust! And shall any of us join in this happy company, O shall any of us, feeble, dying, sinful creatures, shine in their glory and happiness? This is a most interesting enquiry, and I would have you think of it with trembling anxiety; and I shall presently answer it in its place.

The prospect would be delightful, if our charity could hope that this will be the happy end of all the sons of men. But, alas! multitudes, and we have reason to fear the far greater number shall come forth, not to the resurrection of life, but to the resurrection of damnation! what terror is in the sound. If audacious sinners in our world make light of it, and pray for it on every trifling occasion, their infernal brethren that feel its tremendous import are not so hardy, but tremble and groan, and can trifle with it no more.

> Unconsciously accuse!
> How much more cruel have I been to thee!
> " 'Twas cruel I oblig'd thee to obey
> " The wilful dictates of my guilty sway."

Let us realize the miferable doom of this clafs of mankind. See them burfting into life from their fubterranean dungeons, hideous fhapes of deformity and terror, expreffive of the vindictive defign for which their bodies are repaired, and of the boifterous and malignant paffions that ravage their fouls. Horror throbs through every vein, and glares wild and furious in their eyes. Every joint trembles, and every countenance looks down-caft and gloomy. Now they fee that tremendous day of which they were warned in vain, and fhudder at thofe terrors of which they once made light. They immediately know the grand bufinefs of the day, and the dreadful purpofe for which they are roufed from their flumbers in the grave; to be tried, to be convicted, to be condemned, and to be dragged away to execution. Confcience has been anticipating the trial in a feperate ftate; and no fooner is the foul united to the body than immediately confcience afcends its throne in the breaft, and begins to accufe, to convict, to pafs fentence, to upbraid, and to torment. The finner is condemned, condemned at his own tribunal, before he arrives at the bar of his Judge. The firft act of confcioufnefs in his own ftate of exiftence is a conviction that he is condemned, an irrevocably condemned creature. He enters the court, knowing beforehand how it will go with him. When he finds himfelf ordered to the left hand of his Judge, when he hears the dreadful fentence thundered out againft him, *depart from me accurfed*, it was but what he expected. Now he can flatter himfelf with vain hopes, and fhut his eyes againft the light of conviction, but then he will not be able to hope better; then he muft know the worft of his cafe. The formality of the judicial trial is neceffary for the conviction of the world, but not for his; his own confcience has already determined his condition. However, to convince others of the juftice of his doom, he is dragged and guarded from his grave to the judgment-feat by fierce unrelenting devils, now his tempters, but then his tormentors. With what horror does he view the burning throne and the frowning face of his Judge, that Jefus whom he once difregarded, in fpite of all his dying love and the falvation he offered! How does he wifh for a covering of rocks and mountains to conceal him from his angry eye! but all in vain. Appear he muft. He is ordered to the left among the trembling criminals; and now the trial comes on. All his evil deeds, and all his omiffions of duty, are now produced againft him. All the mercies he abufed, all the chaftifements he defpifed, all the means of grace he neglected or mifimproved, every finful, and even every idle word, nay, his moft fecret thoughts and difpofitions are all expofed, and brought into judgment againft him. And when the Judge puts it to him, " Is it not fo finner? Are not thefe charges true?" confcience obliges him to confefs and cry out, Guilty! guilty!

And now the trembling criminal being plainly convicted, and left without all plea and all excuse, the supreme Judge, in stern majesty and inexorable justice, thunders out the dreadful sentence, *Depart from me ye curfed, into everlafting fire, prepared for the devil and his angels.* Matt. xxv. 41. O tremendous doom! every word is big with terror, and shoots a thunder-bolt through the heart. "Depart: away from my presence; I cannot bear so loathsome a sight. I once invited thee to come to me, that thou mightest have life, but thou wouldest not regard the invitation; and now thou shalt never hear that inviting voice more. Depart from me; from me, the only Fountain of happiness, the only proper Good for an immortal mind." 'But, Lord,' (we may suppose the criminal to say) 'if I must depart; bless me before I go.' "No," says the angry Judge, "depart accursed; depart with my eternal and heavy curse upon thee; the curse of that power that made thee; a curse dreadfully efficacious, that blasts whatever it falls upon like flashes of consuming, irresistible lightning." 'But if I must go away under thy curse (the criminal may be supposed to say) let that be all my punishment; let me depart to some agreeable, or at least tolerable recess, where I may meet with something to mitigate the curse.' "No, depart into fire; there burn in all the excruciating tortures of that outrageous element." 'But, Lord, if I must make my bed in fire, O let it be a transient blaze, that will soon burn itself out, and put an end to my torment.' "No, depart into everlafting fire; there burn without consuming, and be tormented without end." 'But, Lord, grant me (cries the poor wretch) at least the mitigation of friendly, entertaining, and sympathifing company; or, if this cannot be granted, grant me this small, this almost no request, to be doomed to some solitary corner in Hell, where I shall be punished only by my own conscience and thine immediate hand; but O deliver me from these malicious, tormenting devils; banish me into some apartment in the infernal pit far from their society.' "No, depart into everlafting fire prepared for the devil and his angels: thou must make one of their wretched crew for ever: thou didst join with them in sinning, and now must share in their punishment: thou didst submit to them as thy tempters, and now thou must submit to them as thy tormentors."

Sentence being pronounced, it is immediately executed. *These shall go away into everlafting punishment.* Matt. xxv. 46. Devils drag them away to the pit, and push them down headlong. There they are confined in chains of darkness, and in a lake burning with fire and brimstone, for ever, for ever! In that dreadful word lies the emphasis of torment: it is an hell in hell. If they might be but released from pain, though it were by annihilation, after they have wept away ten thousand millions of ages in extremity of pain, it would be some mitigation, some encouragement; but, alas! when as many millions of ages are passed as the stars of heaven, or the sand on the sea-shore, or the atoms of dust in this huge globe of earth, their punishment is as far from an end as when the sentence was pronounced upon them. For ever! there is no exhausting of that word; and when it is affixed to the highest degree of misery, the terror of the sound is utterly insupportable. See, Sirs, what depends upon time, that span of time we enjoy in this fleeting life. Eternity! awful, all-important eternity depends upon it.

All this while conscience tears the sinner's heart with the most tormenting reflections. " O what a fair opportunity I once had for salvation, had I improved it! I was warned of the consequences of a life of sin and carelessness: I was told of the necessity of faith, repentance, and universal holiness of heart and life; I enjoyed a sufficient space for repentance, and all the necessary means of salvation, but, fool that I was, I neglected all, I abused all; I refused to part with my sins; I refused to engage seriously in religion, and to seek God in earnest; and now I am lost for ever without hope. O! for one of those months, one of those weeks, or even so much as one of those days or hours I once trifled away! with what earnestness, with what solicitude would I improve it! But all my opportunities are past, beyond recovery, and not a moment shall be given me for this purpose any more. O what a fool was I to sell my soul for such trifles! to set so light by heaven, and fall into hell through mere neglect and carelessness! Ye impenitent, unthinking sinners, though you may now be able to silence or drown the clamours of your consciences, yet the time, or rather the dread eternity is coming, when they will speak in spite of you; when they will speak home, and be felt by the most hardened and remorseless heart. Therefore now regard their warnings while they may be the means of your recovery.

You and I, my brethren, are concerned in the solemn transaction of the day I have been describing. You and I shall either be changed in a moment, in the twinkling of an eye, or while mouldering *in the grave, we shall hear the voice of the Son of God, and come forth, either to the resurrection of life, or to the resurrection of damnation.* And which, my brethren, shall be our doom? Can we foreknow it at this distance of time? I proposed it to your enquiry already, whether you have any good reason to hope you shall be of that happy number who shall rise to life? and now I propose it again with this counterpart, Have you any evidences to hope you shall not be of that wretched numerous multitude who shall rise to damnation? If there be an enquiry within the compass of human knowledge that demands your solicitous thoughts, certainly it is this. Methinks you cannot enjoy one moment's ease or security while this is undetermined. And is it an anfwerable enquiry? Can we now know what are the prefent diftinguifhing characters of thofe who fhall then receive fo different a doom? Yes, my text determines the point; for,

V. *They that have done good fhall come forth to the refurrection of life, and they that have done evil to the refurrection of damnation.* Thefe are the grounds of the diftinction that fhall then be made in the final ftates of men, doing good and doing evil. And certainly this diftinction is perceivable now; to do good and to do evil are not fo much alike as that it fhould be impoffible to diftinguifh between them. Let us then fee what is implied in thefe characters, and to whom of us they refpectively belong.

1. What is it to do good? This implies, 1ft, An honeft endeavour to keep all God's commandments; I fay, all his commandments, with regard to God, our neighbour, and ourfelves, whether eafy or difficult, whether fafhionable or not, whether agreeable to our natural conftitution or not, whether enjoining the performance of duty or forbidding the commiffion of fin, whether regarding the heart or the outward practice. I fay an uniform, impartial regard to all God's commandments, of whatever kind, in all circumftances, and at all times, is implied in doing good; for if we do any thing becaufe God commands it, we will endeavour to do every thing that he commands, becaufe where the reafon of our conduct is the fame, our conduct itfelf will be the fame. I do not mean that good men in the prefent ftate perfectly keep the commandments of God in every thing, or indeed in any thing; but I mean that univerfal obedience is their honeft endeavour. Their character is in fome meafure uniform and all of a piece; that is, they do not place all their religion in obedience to fome commands which may be agreeable to them, as though that would make atonement for their neglect of others; but, like David, they are for having a refpect, and indeed *have a refpect to all God's commandments.* Pfalm cxix. 6. My brethren, try yourfelves by this teft.

2. To do good in an acceptable manner pre-fuppofes a change of nature and a new principle. Our nature is fo corrupted that nothing really and formally good can be performed by us till it be renewed. To confirm this I fhall only refer you to Eph. ii. 10. and Ezek. xxxvi. 26, 27. where being created in Chrift Jefus to good works, and recceiving a new heart of flefh, are mentioned as pre-requifites to our walking in God's ftatutes. As for the principle of obedience, *it is the love of God,* 1 John v. 3. that is, we muft obey God becaufe we love him; we muft do good becaufe we delight to do good; otherwife it is all hypocrify, conftraint, or felfifhnefs, and cannot be acceptable to God. Here again, my brethren, look into your hearts and examine what is the principle of your obedience, and whether ever you have been made new creatures.

3. I must add, especially as we live under the gospel, that your dependence for life must not be upon the good you do, but entirely upon the righteousness of Jesus Christ. After you have done all, you must acknowledge you are but unprofitable servants, and renounce all your works in point of merit, while you abound in them in point of practice. Phil. iii. 7, 8. This is an essential characteristic of evangelical obedience, and without it you cannot expect to have a resurrection to eternal life and blessedness.

I might enlarge upon this head, but time will not permit; and I hope these three characters may suffice to shew you what is implied in doing good. Let us now proceed to the opposite character.

2. What is it to do evil? This implies such things as these: The habitual neglect of well-doing, or the performance of duties in a languid, formal manner, or without a right principle, and the wilful indulgence of any one sin; the secret love of sin, though not suffered to break forth into the outward practice. Here it is evident at first sight that profane sinners, drunkards, swearers, defrauders, avowed neglecters of religion, &c. have this dismal brand upon them, that they are such as do evil. Nay, all such who are in their natural state, without regeneration, whatever their outside be, must be ranked in this class: *for that which is born of the flesh is flesh*, John iii. 6. *and they that are in the flesh cannot please God, nor be rightly subject to his law:* Rom. viii. 7, 8.

And now who is for life, and who for damnation among you? These characters are intended to make the distinction among you, and I pray you apply them for that purpose.

As for such of you, who, amidst all your lamented infirmities, are endeavouring honestly to do good, and grieved at heart that you can do no more, you also must die; you must die, and feed the worms in the dust. But you shall rise gloriously improved, rise to an immortal life, and in all the terrors and consternation of that last day, you will be secure, serene, and undisturbed. The almighty Judge will be your friend, and that is enough. Let this thought disarm the king of terrors, and give you courage to look down into the grave, and forward to the great rising day. O what an happy immortality opens its glorious prospects beyond the ken of sight before you! and after a few struggles more in this state of warfare, and resting awhile in the bed of death, at the regions of eternal blessedness you will arrive, and take up your residence there for ever.

But are there not some here who are conscious that these favourable characters do not belong to them? that know that well-doing is not the business of their life, but that they are workers of iniquity? I tell you plainly, and with all the authority the word of God can give, that if you continue such, you shall rise to damnation. That will undoubtedly be your doom, unless you are greatly changed and reformed in heart and life. And will this be no excitement to vigorous endeavours? Are you proof against the energy of such a consideration? Ye careless sinners, awake out of your security, and prepare for death and judgment! this fleeting life is all the time you have for preparation, and can you trifle it away? Your all, your eternal all is set upon the single cast of life, and you must stand the hazard of the dye. You can make but one experiment, and if that fail, through your sloth or mismanagement, you are irrecoverably undone for ever. Therefore, by the dread authority of the great God, by the terrors of death, and the great rising day, by the joys of heaven, and the torments of hell, and by the value of your immortal souls, I intreat, I charge, I adjure you to awake out of your security, and improve the precious moments of life. The world is dying all around you. And can you rest easy in such a world, while unprepared for eternity? Awake to righteousness now, at the gentle call of the gospel, before the last trumpet give you an alarm of another kind.

SERMON XX.

The Universal Judgment.

ACTS xvii. 30, 31. *And the times of this ignorance God winked at; but now commandeth all men every where to repent, because he hath appointed a day in the which he will judge the world in righteousness by that Man whom he hath ordained; whereof he hath given assurance unto all men, in that he hath raised him from the dead.*

THE present state is the infancy of human nature; and all the events of time, even those that make such noise, and determine the fate of kingdoms, are but the little affairs of children. But if we look forwards and trace human nature to maturity, we meet with events vast, interesting and majestic; and such as nothing but divine authority can render credible to us who are so apt to judge of things by what we see. To one of those scenes I would direct your attention this day; I mean the solemn, tremendous, and glorious scene of the universal judgment.

Serm. 20. *The Univerfal Judgment.*

You have fometimes feen a ftately building in ruins; come now and view the ruins of a demolifhed world. You have often feen a feeble mortal ftruggling in the agonies of death, and his fhattered frame diffolved; come now and view univerfal nature feverely labouring and agonizing in her laft convulfions, and her well-compacted fyftem diffolved. You have heard of earthquakes here and there that have laid Lifbon, Palermo, and a few other cities in ruins; come now and feel the tremors and convulfions of the whole globe, that blend cities and countries, oceans and continents, mountains, plains and vallies, in one promifcuous heap. You have a thoufand times beheld the moon walking in brightnefs, and the fun fhining in his ftrength; now look and fee the fun turned into darknefs, and the moon into blood.

It is our lot to live in an age of confufion, blood, and flaughter; an age in which our attention is engaged by the clafh of arms, the clangor of trumpets, the roar of artillery, and the dubious fate of kingdoms; but draw off your thoughts from thefe objects for an hour, and fix them on objects more folemn and interefting: come view

> " A fcene that yields
> A louder trumpet, and more dreadful fields;
> The World alarm'd, both Earth and Heav'n o'erthrown,
> And gafping Nature's laft tremendous groan;
> Death's ancient fceptre broke, the teeming Tomb,
> The righteous Judge, and man's eternal Doom." YOUNG.

Such a fcene there certainly is before us; for St. Paul tells us that *God hath given affurance to all men he will judge the world in righteoufnefs by that Man whom he hath ordained;* and that his refurrection, the refurrection of him who is God and man, is a demonftrative proof of it.

My text is the conclufion of St. Paul's defence or fermon before the famous court of Areopagus, in the learned and philofophical city of Athens. In this auguft and polite affembly he fpeaks with the boldnefs, and in the evangelical ftrain, of an apoftle of Chrift. He firft inculcates upon them the great truths of natural religion, and labours faithfully, though in a very gentle and inoffenfive manner, to reform them from that ftupid idolatry and fuperftition into which even this learned and philofophical city was funk, though a Socrates, a Plato, and the moft celebrated fages and moralifts of pagan antiquity had lived and taught in it. Afterwards, in the clofe of his difcourfe, he introduces the glorious peculiarities of Chriftianity, particularly the great duty of repentance, from evangelical motives, the resurrection of the dead, and the final judgment. But no sooner has he entered upon this subject than he is interrupted, and seems to have broken off abruptly; for when he had just hinted at the then unpopular doctrine of the resurrection of the dead, we are told, *some mocked*, and others put it off to another hearing: *We will hear thee again of this matter.*

In these dark times of ignorance which preceded the publication of the gospel, God seemed to wink or connive at the idolatry and various forms of wickedness that had overspread the world; that is, he seemed to overlook* or take no notice of them, so as either to punish them, or to give the nations explicit calls to repentance. But now, says St. Paul, the case is altered. Now the gospel is published through the world, and therefore God will no longer seem to connive at the wickedness and impenitence of mankind, but publishes his great mandate to a rebel world, explicitly and loudly, *commanding all men every where to repent;* and he now gives them particular motives and encouragements to this duty.

One motive of the greatest weight, which was never so clearly or extensively published before, is the doctrine of the universal judgment. This the connection implies: *He now commandeth all men to repent, because he hath appointed a day for judging all men.* And surely the prospect of a judgment must be a strong motive to sinners to repent:—this, if any thing, will rouse them from their thoughtless security, and bring them to repentance. Repentance should, and one would think must, be as extensive as this reason for it. This St. Paul intimates. *He now commandeth all men to repent, because he hath given assurance to all men* that he has *appointed a day to judge the world.* Wherever the gospel publishes the doctrine of a future judgment, there it requires all men to repent; and wherever it requires repentance, there it enforces the command of this alarming doctrine.

God has *given assurance to all men;* that is, to all that hear the gospel, that he has appointed a day for this great purpose, and that Jesus Christ, God-man, is to preside in person in this majestic solemnity. He has given assurance of this; that is, sufficient ground of faith; and the assurance consists in this, that *he hath raised him from the dead.*

The resurrection of Christ gives assurance of this in several respects. It is a specimen and a pledge of a general resurrection, that grand preparative for the judgment: it is an incontestible proof of his divine mission; for God will never work so unprecedented a miracle in favour of an impostor: it is also an authentic attestation of all our Lord's claims; and he expressly claimed

---

* *yperidon.*

the authority of fupreme Judge as delegated to him by the Father : *the Father judgeth no man, but hath committed all judgment to the Son.* John v. 22.

There is a peculiar fitnefs and propriety in this conftitution. It is fit that a world placed under the adminiftration of a Mediator fhould have a mediatorial Judge. It is fit this high office fhould be conferred upon him as an honorary reward for his important fervices and extreme abafement. *Becaufe he humbled himfelf, therefore God hath highly exalted him.* Phil. ii. 8, 9. It is fit that creatures cloathed with bodies fhould be judged by a man cloathed in a body like themfelves. Hence it is faid that *all judgment is given to the Son, becaufe he is the Son of Man.* John v. 27. This would feem a ftrange reafon, did we not underftand it in this light. Indeed, was Jefus Chrift man only, he would be infinitely unequal to the office of univerfal Judge; but he is God and Man, *Immanuel, God with us;* and is the fitteft perfon in the univerfe for the work. It is alfo fit that Chrift fhould be the fupreme Judge, as it will be a great encouragement to his people for their Mediator to execute this office; and it may be added, that hereby the condemnation of the wicked will be rendered more confpicuoufly juft; for, if a Mediator, a Saviour, the Friend of Sinners, condemns them, they muft be worthy of condemnation indeed.

Let us now enter upon the majeftic fcene. But, alas! what images fhall I ufe to reprefent it? Nothing that we have feen, nothing that we have heard, nothing that has ever happened on the ftage of time, can furnifh us with proper illuftrations. All is low and grovelling, all is faint and obfcure that ever the fun fhone upon, when compared with the grand phenomena of that day; and we are fo accuftomed to low and little objects, that it is impoffible we fhould ever raife our thoughts to a fuitable pitch of elevation. Ere long we fhall be amazed fpectators of thefe majeftic wonders, and our eyes and our ears will be our inftructors. But now it is neceffary we fhould have fuch ideas of them as may affect our hearts, and prepare us for them. Let us therefore prefent to our view thofe reprefentations which divine revelation, our only guide in this cafe, gives us of the perfon of the Judge, and the manner of his appearance; of the refurrection of the dead, and the transformation of the living; of the univerfel convention of all the fons of men before the fupreme tribunal; of their feparation to the right and left hand of the Judge, according to their characters; of the judicial procefs itfelf: of the decifive fentence; of its execution, and of the conflagration of the world.

As to the perfon of the Judge, the pfalmift tells you, *God is Judge himfelf.* Pfalm 1. 6. Yet Chrift tells us, *the Father judg-*

eth no man, but hath committed all judgment to the Son; and that he hath given him authority to execute judgment, because he is the Son of man. John v. 22, 27. It is therefore Christ Jesus, God-man, as I observed, who shall sustain this high character; and for the reasons already alledged, it is most fit it should be devolved upon him. Being God and man, all the advantages of divinity and humanity center in him, and render him more fit for this office than if he were God only, or man only. This is the august Judge before whom we must stand; and the prospect may inspire us with reverence, joy and terror.

As for the manner of his appearance, it will be such as becomes the dignity of his person and office. He will shine in all the uncreated glories of the Godhead, and in all the gentler glories of a perfect man. His attendants will add a dignity to the grand appearance, and the sympathy of nature will increase the solemnity and terror of the day. Let his own word describe him. *The Son of man shall come in his glory, and in the glory of his Father, and all the holy angels with him; and then shall he sit upon the throne of his glory.* Matt. xxv. 31. xvi. 27. *The Lord Jesus shall be revealed from heaven with his mighty angels in flaming fire, taking vengeance on them that know not God, and that obey not the gospel of our Lord Jesus Christ.* 2 Thess. i. 7, 8. And not only with the angels, those illustrious ministers of the court of Heaven, attend upon that solemn occasion, but also all the saints who left the world from Adam to that day; for *those that sleep in Jesus*, says St. Paul, *will God bring with him.* 1 Thess. iv. 14. The grand imagery in Daniel's vision is applicable to this day: and perhaps to this it primarily refers: *I beheld till the thrones were cast down*, or rather set up,* *and the Ancient of Days did sit, whose garment was white as snow, and the hair of his head like the pure wool. His throne was like the fiery flame, and his wheels as burning fire. A fiery stream issued, and came forth from before him: thousands thousands ministered unto him, and ten thousand times ten thousand stood before him.* Dan. vii. 9, 10. Perhaps our Lord may exhibit himself to the whole world upon this grand occasion, in the same glorious form in which he was seen by his favourite John, *cloathed with a garment down to the foot, and girt about the breasts with a golden girdle: his head and his hairs white like wool, as white as snow: his eyes as a flame of fire: his feet like unto fine brass, as if they burned in a furnace: his voice as the sound of many waters, and his countenance as the sun shining in his strength.* Rev. i. 13, &c. Another image of inimitable majesty and terror

---

* This sense is most agreeable to the connection, and the original word will bear it; which signifies *to pitch down*, or *place*, as well as *to throw down*, or *demolish*. And the LXX translate it, *the thrones were put up*, or *fixed*.

Serm. 20. *The Univerfal Judgment.* 347

the fame writer gives us, when he fays, *I faw a great white throne, and him that fat on it, from whofe face the earth and the heaven fled away, and there was found no place for them.* Aftonifhing! what an image is this! the ftable earth and heaven cannot bear the majefty and terror of his look :- they fly away affrighted, and feek a place to hide themfelves, but no place is found to fhelter them; every region through the immenfity of fpace lies open before him.* Rev. xx. 11.

This is the Judge before whom we muft ftand; and this is the manner of his appearance. But is this the babe of Bethlehem that lay and wept in the manger? Is this the fuppofed fon of the carpenter, the defpifed Galilean? Is this the man of forrows? Is this he that was arrefted, was condemned, was buffetted, was fpit upon, was crowned with thorns, was executed as a flave and a criminal upon the crofs? Yes, it is he; the very fame Jefus of Nazareth. But O how changed! how defervedly exalted! Let heaven and earth congratulate his advancement. Now let his enemies appear, and fhew their ufual contempt and malignity. Now, Pilate, condemn the King of the Jews as an ufurper. Now ye Jews, raife the clamour, *crucify him, crucify him.*

" Now bow the knee in fcorn, prefent the reed;
" Now tell the fcourg'd Impoftor he muft bleed." YOUNG.

Now, ye Deifts and Infidels, difpute his divinity and the truth of his religion if you can. Now, ye hypocritical chriftians, try to impofe upon him with your idle pretences. Now defpife his grace; laugh at his threatenings, and make light of his difpleafure if you are able. Ah! now their courage fails, and terror furround them like armed men. Now *they hide themfelves in the dens, and in the rocks of the mountains ; and fay to the mountains and rocks, fall on us,*

---
* This is the picture drawn by the pencil of infpiration. We may now contemplate the imagery of a fine human pen.

——— From his great abode
Full on a whirlwind rides the dreadful God :
The tempeft's rattling winds, the fiery car,
Ten thoufand hofts his minifters of war,
The flaming Cherubim, attend his flight,
And Heaven's foundations groan beneath the weight.
Thro' all the fkies the forky lightnings play,
And radiant fplendors round his head difplay.
From his bright eyes affrighted worlds retire :
He fpeaks in thunder and he breathes in fire.
Garment of heavenly light array the God;
His throne a bright confolidated cloud—
Support me, Heaven, I fhudder with affright;
I quake, I fink with terror at the fight!

*The Day of Judgment, a Poem,
a little varied.*

and hide us from the face of him that sitteth on the throne, and from the wrath of the Lamb; for the lamb that once bled as a sacrifice for sin now appears in all the terrors of a lion; and *the great day of his wrath is come, and who shall be able to stand?* Rev. vi. 15. O! could they hide themselves in the bottom of the ocean, or in some rock that bears the weight of the mountains, how happy would they think themselves. But, alas!

> " Seas cast the monsters forth to meet their doom,
> " And rocks but prison up for wrath to come." YOUNG.

While the Judge is descending, the parties to be judged will be summoned to appear. But where are they? They are all asleep in their dusty beds, except the then generation. And how shall they be roused from their long sleep of thousands of years? *Why the Lord himself shall descend from heaven with a shout, with the voice of the archangel and with the trump of God.* 1 Thess. iv. 16. *The trumpet shall sound,* and they that are then alive shall not pass into eternity through the beaten road of death, but *at the last trumpet they shall be changed,* changed into immortals *in a moment, in the twinkling of an eye.* 1 Cor. xv. 51, 52. Now all the millions of mankind, of whatever country and nation, whether they expect this tremendous day or not, all feel a shock through their whole frames, while they are instantaneously metamorphosed in every limb, and the pulse of immortality begins to beat strong in every part. Now also the slumberers under ground begin to stir, to rouse and spring to life. Now see graves opening, tombs bursting, charnel houses rattling, the earth heaving, and all alive, while these subterranean armies are bursting their way through. See clouds of human dust and broken bones darkening the air, and flying from country to country over intervening continents and oceans to meet their kindred fragments, and repair the shattered frame with pieces collected from a thousand different quarters, whither they were blown away by winds, or washed by waters. See what millions start up in company in the spots where Nineveh, Babylon, Jerusalem, Rome, and London, once stood! Whole armies spring to life in fields where they once lost their lives in battle, and were left unburied; in fields which fattened with their blood, produced a thousand harvests, and now produce a crop of men. See a succession of thousands of years rising in crowds from grave-yards round the places where they once attended, in order to prepare for this decisive day. Nay, graves yawn, and swarms burst into life under palaces and buildings of pride and pleasure, in fields and forests, in thousands of places where graves were never suspected. How are the living surprised to find men starting into life under their feet, or just beside them; some beginning to stir, and heave the ground; others half-rifen, and others quite difengaged from the incumbrance of earth, and ftanding upright before them! What vaft multitudes that had flept in a watery grave, now emerge from rivers, and feas, and oceans, and throw them into a tumult! Now appear to the view of all the world the Goliaths, the Anakims, and the other giants of ancient times; and now the millions of infants, thofe little particles of life, ftart up at once, perhaps in full maturity, or perhaps in the loweft clafs of mankind, dwarfs of immortality. *The dead, fmall and great, will arife to ftand before God; and the fea shall give up the dead which were in it.* Rev. xx, 12, 13. Now the *many that fleep in the duft shall awake and come forth; fome to everlafting life, and fome to shame and everlafting contempt.* Dan. xii. 2. *Now the hour is come when all that are in the grave shall hear the voice of the Son of God, and shall come forth; they that have done good, to the refurrection of life; and they that have done evil, to the refurrection of damnation.* John v. 28. *Though after our skin worms deftroy this body, yet in our flesh shall we fee God, whom we shall fee for ourfelves; and thefe eyes shall behold him, and not another.* Job xix. 26, 27. Then *this corruptible* [body] *shall put on incorruption, and this mortal shall put on immortality.* 1 Cor. xv. 53.

As the characters, and confequently the doom of mankind will be very different, fo we may reafonably fuppofe they will rife in very different forms of glory or difhonour, of beauty or deformity. Their bodies indeed will all be improved to the higheft degree, and all made vigorous, capacious and immortal. But here lies the difference: the bodies of the righteous will be ftrengthened to bear *an exceeding great and eternal weight of glory,* but thofe of the wicked will be ftrengthened to fuftain an heavier load of mifery; their ftrength will be but mere ftrength to fuffer an horrid capacity of greater pain. The immortality of the righteous will be the duration of their happinefs, but that of the wicked of their mifery: their immortality, the higheft privilege of their nature, will be their heavieft curfe; and they would willingly exchange their duration with an infect of a day, or a fading flower. The bodies of the righteous will *shine as the fun, and as the ftars in the firmament for ever and ever;* but thofe of the wicked will be grim and shocking, and ugly, and hateful as hell. The bodies of the righteous will be fit manfions for their heavenly fpirits to inhabit, and every feature will fpeak the delightful paffions that agreeably work within; but the wicked will be but fpirits of hell clothed in the material bodies; and malice, rage, defpair, and all the infernal paffions will lower in their countenances, and caft a difmal gloom around them. O! they will then be nothing elfe but shapes of deformity and terror! they will look like the natives of hell, and spread horror around them with every look*.

With what reluctance may we suppose will the souls of the wicked enter again into a state of union with these shocking forms, that will be everlasting engines of torture to them, as they once were instruments of sin! But O! with what joy will the souls of the righteous return to their old habitations, in which they once served their God with honest, though feeble endeavours, now so gloriously repaired and improved! How will they congratulate the resurrection of their old companions from their long sleep in death, now made fit to share with them in the sublime employments and fruitions of heaven! Every organ will be an instrument of service and an inlet of pleasure, and the soul shall no longer be encumbered but assisted by this union to the body. O what surprising creatures can Omnipotence raise from the dust! To what an high degree of beauty can the Almighty refine the offspring of the earth! and into what miracles of glory and blessedness can he form them!†

Now the Judge is come, the judgment seat is erected, the dead are raised. And what follows? Why the universal convention of all the sons of men before the judgment-seat. The place of judgment will probably be the extensive region of the air, the most capacious for the reception of such a multitude; for St. Paul tells us, the saints shall *be caught up together in the clouds to meet the Lord in the air.* 1 Thess. iv. 17. And that the air will be the place of judicature, perhaps, may be intimated when our Lord is represented as coming in the clouds, and sitting upon a cloudy throne. These expressions can hardly be understood literally, for clouds which consist of vapours and rarified particles of water, seem very improper materials for a chariot of state, or a throne of judgment; but they may very properly intimate that Christ will make his appearance, and hold his court in the region of the clouds; that is, in the air; and perhaps that the rays of light and majestic darkness shall

---

* How weak, how pale, how haggard, how obscene,
What more than death in every face and mien!
With what distress, and glarings of affright
They shock the heart, and turn away the sight!
In gloomy orbs their trembling eye-balls roll,
And tell the horrid secrets of the soul.
Each gesture mourns, each look is black with care:
And every groan is loaden with despair.   YOUNG.

† Mark, on the right, how amiable a grace!
Their Maker's image fresh in every face!
What purple bloom my ravish'd soul admires,
And their eyes sparkling with immortal fires!
Triumphant beauty! charms that rise above
This world, and in blest angels kindle love!——
O! the transcendent glories of the Just!   YOUNG.

be so blended around him as to form the appearance of a cloud to the view of the wondering and gazing world.

To this upper region, from whence our globe will lie open to view far and wide, will all the sons of men be convened. And they will be gathered together by the ministry of angels, the officers of this grand court. *The Son of man, when he comes in the clouds of heaven with power and great glory, shall send forth his angels with a great sound of the trumpet ; and they shall gather together his elect from the four winds, and from one end of heaven to the other.* Matt. xxiv. 30, 31. Their ministry also extends to the wicked, whom they will drag away to judgment and execution, and separate from the righteous. For *in the end of the world,* says Christ, *the Son of man shall send forth his angels, and they shall gather out of his kingdom all things that offend, and them that work iniquity, and shall cast them into a furnace of fire: there shall be wailing and gnashing of teeth.* Matt. xiii. 40, 41, 42.

What an august convocation, what a vast assembly is this! See flights of angels darting round the globe from east to west, from pole to pole, gathering up here and there the scattered saints, choosing them out from among the crowd of the ungodly, and bearing them aloft on their wings *to meet their Lord in the air!* while the wretched crowd look and gaze, and stretch their hands, and would mount up along with them ; but, alas ! they must be left behind, and wait for another kind of convoy ; a convoy of cruel, unrelenting devils, who shall snatch them up as their prey with malignant joy, and place them before the flaming tribunal. Now all the sons of men meet in one immense assembly. Adam beholds the long line of his posterity, and they behold their common father. Now Europeans and Asiatics, the swarthy sons of Africa and the savages of America, mingle together. Christians, Jews, Mahometans, and Pagans, the learned and the ignorant, kings and subjects, rich and poor, free and bond, form one promiscuous crowd. Now all the vast armies that conquered or fell under Xerxes, Darius, Alexander, Cæsar, Scipio, Tamerlane, Marlborough, and other illustrious warriors, unite in one vast army. There, in short, all the successive inhabitants of the earth for thousands of years appear in one assembly. And how inconceivably great must the number be! When the inhabitants of but one country are met together, you are struck with the survey. Were all the inhabitants of a kingdom convened in one place, how much more striking would be the sight ! Were all the inhabitants of all the kingdoms of the earth convened in one general rendezvous, how astonishing and vast would be the multitude ! But what is even this vast multitude compared with the long succession of generations that have peopled the globe, in all ages, and in all countries, from the first commencement of time to the last day ! Here numbers fail, and our thoughts are loft in the immenfe furvey. The extenfive region of the air is very properly chofen as the place of judgment; for this globe would not be fufficient for fuch a multitude to ftand upon. In that prodigious affembly, my brethren, you and I muft mingle. And we fhall not be loft in the crowd, nor efcape the notice of our Judge; but his eye will be as particularly fixed upon every one as though there were but one before him.

To increafe the number, and add a majefty and terror to the affembly, the fallen angels alfo make their appearance at the bar. This they have long expected with horror, as the period when their confummate mifery is to commence. When Chrift, in the form of a fervant, exercifed a God-like power over them in the days of his refidence upon earth, they almoft miftook his firft coming as a Saviour for his fecond coming as their Judge; and therefore they expoftulated, *Art thou come to torment us before the time?* Matt. viii. 29. That is to fay, We expect thou wilt at laft appear to torment us, but we did not expect thy coming fo foon. Agreeable to this, St. Peter tells us, *God fpared not the angels that finned, but caft them down to hell, and delivered them as prifoners into chains of darknefs, to be referved unto judgment.* 2 Peter ii. 4. To the fame purpofe St. Jude fpeaks: *The angels which kept not their firft eftate, but left their own habitation, he hath referved in everlafting chains under darknefs, unto the judgment of the great day.* Jude 6. What horribly majeftic figures will thefe be! and what a dreadful appearance will they make at the bar! angels and archangels, thrones, and dominions, and principalities, and powers blafted, ftripped of their primæval glories, and lying in ruins; yet majeftic even in ruins, gigantic forms of terror and deformity; great though degraded, horribly illuftrious, angels fallen, gods undefied and depofed.*

Now the Judge is feated, and anxious millions ftand before him waiting for their doom. As yet there is no feperation made between them; but men and devils, faints and finners, are promifcuoufly blended together. But fee! at the order of the Judge, the crowd is all in motion; they part, they fort together according to their character, and divide to the right and left. *When all nations are gathered before the Son of man,* himfelf has told us, *he shall feperate them one from another, as a shepherd divideth his sheep*

---

* —————— the foe of God and man,
From his dark den, blafpheming, drags his chain,
And rears his brazen front, with thunder fcarr'd;
Receives his fentence, and begins his hell.
All vengeance paft, now feems abundant grace!
Like meteors in a ftormy fky, how roll
His baleful eyes! he curfes whom he dreads,
And deems it the firft moment of his fall.   Young.

Serm. 20. *The Univerfal Judgment.*

from the goats; and he shall set the sheep on his right hand, but the goats on the left. Matt. xxv. 32, 33. And, O ! what ftrange feperations are now made ! what multitudes that once ranked themfelves among the faints, and were highly efteemed for their piety by others as well as themfelves, are now banifhed from among them, and placed with the trembling criminals on the left hand ! and how many poor, honeft-hearted, doubting, defponding fouls, whofe foreboding fears had often placed them there, now find themfelves, to their agreeable furprife, ftationed on the right hand of their Judge, who fmiles upon them ! What connections are now broken ! what hearts torn afunder ! what intimate companions, what dear relations, parted forever ! neighbour from neighbour, mafters from fervants, friend from friend, parents from children, hufband from wife ; thofe who were but one flefh, and who lay in one another's bofoms, muft part for ever. Thofe that lived in the fame country, who fuftained the fame denomination, who worfhipped in the fame place, who lived under one roof, who lay in the fame womb, and fucked the fame breafts, muft now part for ever. And is there no feperation likely to be made then in our families or in our congregation ? Is it likely we fhall all be placed in a body upon the right hand ? Are all the members of our families prepared for that glorious ftation ? Alas ! are there not fome families among us who, it is to be feared, fhall all be fent off to the left hand, without fo much as one exception ? for who are thofe miferable multitudes on the left hand ? There, through the medium of revelation, I fee the drunkard, the fwearer, the whoremonger, the liar, the defrauder, and the various claffes of profane, profligate finners. There I fee the unbeliever, the impenitent the lukewarm formalift, and the various claffes of hypocrites and half-chriftians. There I fee the *families that call not upon God's name*, and whole nations that forget him. And, O ! what vaft multitudes, what millions of millions of millions do all thefe make ! And do not fome, alas ! do not many of you belong to one or other of thefe claffes of finners whom God, and Chrift, and fcripture, and confcience confpire to condemn ? If fo, to the left hand you muft depart among devils and trembling criminals, whofe guilty minds forbode their doom before the judicial procefs begins. But who are thofe glorious immortals upon the right hand ? They are thofe who now mourn over their fins, refift and forfake them ; they are thofe who have furrendered themfelves entirely to God, through Jefus Chrift, who have heartily complied with the method of falvation revealed in the gofpel ; who have been formed new creatures by the almighty power of God ; who make it the moft earneft perfevering endeavour of their lives to work out their own falvation, and to live righteoufly, foberly, and godly in the world. Thefe are fome of the principal lines.

ments of their character who shall have their safe and honourable station at the right hand of the sovereign Judge. And is not this the prevailing character of some of you? I hope and believe it is. Through the medium of scripture-revelation then I see you in that blessed station. And, O! I would make an appointment with you this day to meet you there. Yes, let us this day appoint the time and place where we shall meet after the seperation and dispersion that death will make among us: and let it be at the right hand of the Judge at the last day. If I be so happy as to obtain some humble place there, I shall look out for you, my dear people. There I shall expect your company, that we may ascend together to join in the more exalted services and enjoyments of heaven, as we have frequently in the humbler forms of worship in the church on earth. But, O! when I think what unexpected seperations will then be made, I tremble lest I should miss some of you there. And are you not afraid lest you should miss some of your friends, or some of your families there? or that you should then see them move off to the left hand, and looking back with eagerness upon you as if they would say, " This is my doom through your carelessness; had you but acted a faithful part towards me, while conversant with you or under your care, I might now have had my place among the saints." O! how could you bear such significant piercing looks from a child, a servant, or a friend? Therefore now do all in your power to *convert sinners from the error of their way, and to save their souls from death.*

When we entered upon this practical digression, we left all things ready for the judicial process. And now the trials begins. Now *God judges the secrets of men by Jesus Christ.* Rom. ii. 16. All the works of all the sons of men will then be tried; *for,* says St. Paul, *we must all appear before the judgment-seat of Christ, that every man may receive the things done in the body according to what he hath done, whether it be good, or whether it be evil.* 2 Cor. v. 10. St. John in his vision *saw the dead judged according to their works.* Rev. xx. 12, 13. These works immediately refer to the actions of the life, but they may also include the inward temper, and thoughts of the soul, and the words of the lips; for all these shall be brought into judgment. *God,* says Solomon, *will bring every work into judgment, and every secret thing, whether it be good, or whether it be evil.* Eccl. xii. xii. 14. And though we are too apt to think our words are free, he that is to be our Judge has told us that *for every idle word which men shall speak, they shall give an account in the day of judgment; for by thy words,* as well as thy actions, *thou shalt be justified; and by thy words thou shalt be condemned.* Matt. xii. 36, 37.

What strange discoveries will this trial make! what noble dispositions that never shone in full beauty to mortal eyes; what generous purposes crushed in embryo for want of power to execute them; what pious and noble actions concealed under the veil of modesty, or misconstrued by ignorance and prejudice; what affectionate aspirations, what devout exercises of heart, which lay open only to the eyes of Omniscience, are now brought to full light, and receive the approbation of the supreme Judge before the assembled universe? But on the other hand, what works of shame and darkness, what hidden things of dishonesty, what dire secrets of treachery, hypocrisy, lewdness, and various forms of wickedness artfully and industriously concealed from human sight, what horrid exploits of sin now burst to light in all their hellish colours, to the confusion of the guilty, and the astonishment and horror of the universe? Sure, the history of mankind must then appear like the annals of hell, or the biography of devils! Then the mask of dissimulation will be torn off. Clouded characters will clear up, and men as well as things will appear in their true light. Their hearts will be as it were turned outwards, and all their secrets exposed to full view. The design of the judicial inquiry will not be to inform the omniscient Judge, but to convince all worlds of the justice of his proceedings; and this design renders it necessary that all these things should be laid open to their sight, that they may see the grounds upon which he passes sentence. And may not the prospect of such a discovery fill some of you with horror? for many of your actions, and especially of your thoughts, will not bear the light. How would it confound you, if they were now all published, even in the small circle of your acquaintance? How then can you bear to have them all fully exposed before God, angels, and men! Will it not confound you with shame, and make you objects of everlasting contempt to all worlds?

These are the facts to be tried. But by what rule shall they be tried? From the goodness and justice of God we may conclude that men will be judged by some rule known to them, or which at least it was in their power to know. Now the light of reason, the law of nature, or conscience, is an universal rule, and universally known, or at least knowable by all the sons of men, Heathens and Mahometans as well as Jews and Christians: and therefore all mankind shall be judged by this rule. This the conscience of all now forebodes; *for when the Gentiles, which have not the law, do by nature the things contained in the law, these, not having the law, are a law unto themselves, which shew the works of the law written in their hearts, their conscience also bearing witness, and their thoughts, the mean while, accusing or else excusing one another.* Rom. ii. 14, 15. By this rule their consciences now acquit or condemn them, becaufe they know that by this rule they fhall then be judged: this feems to be a kind of innate prefentment of human nature. As the heathens were invincibly ignorant of every rule but this, they fhall be judged by this only. But as to thofe parts of the world that enjoyed or might enjoy the advantages of revelation, whether by tradition with the Ante-Mofaic world, or in the writings of Mofes and the prophets with the Jews, or in the clearer difpenfation of the gofpel with the Chriftian world, they fhall be judged by this revealed law. And by how much the more perfect the rule, by fo much the ftricter will their account be. That which would be an excufable infirmity in an African or an American Indian, may be an aggravated crime in us who enjoy fuch fuperior advantages. This is evident from the repeated declarations of facred writ. *As many as have finned without the law,* (that is, without the written law) *shall alfo perish without the law;* and as many as have finned in the law fhall be judged by the law, in the day when God fhall judge the fecrets of men according to my gofpel. Rom. ii. 12, 16. *If I had not come and fpoken unto them,* fays the bleffed Jefus, *they would not have had fin;* that is, they would not have had fin fo aggravated, or they would not have had the particular fin of unbelief in rejecting the Meffiah: *but now they have no cloak for their fin,* John xv. 22. that is, now when they have had fuch abundant conviction, they are utterly inexcufable. *This,* fays he, *is the condemnation;* that is, this is the occafion of the moft aggravated condemnation, *that light is come into the world, and men love darknefs rather than light, becaufe their deeds are evil.* John iii. 19. *That fervant which knew his Lord's will, and prepared not himfelf, neither did according to his will, shall be beaten with many ftripes; but he that knew not, and did commit things worthy of ftripes* (obferve, ignorance is no fufficient excufe, except when invincible) *shall be beaten with few ftripes; for unto whomfoever much is given, of him shall be much required.* Luke xii. 47, 48. Upon thefe maxims of eternal righteoufnefs, the Judge will proceed in pronouncing the doom of the world; and it was upon thefe principles he declared, in the days of his flefh, *that it should be more tolerable in the day of judgment for Sodom and Gomorrah, for Tyre and Sidon,* than for thofe places that enjoyed the advantages of his miniftry, and mifimproved it. Matt. xi. 21, 24. Whether upon thefe principles finners among us have not reafon to expect they will obtain an horrid precedence among the millions of finners in that day, I leave you to judge, and to tremble at the thought.

There is another reprefentation of this proceeding, which we often meet with in the facred writings, in allufion to the forms of proceedings in human courts. In courts of law law-books are referred to, opened, and read for the direction of the judges, and sentence is passed according to them. In allusion to this custom, Daniel, in vision, saw *the judgment seat, and the books were opened*. Dan. vii. 10. And St. John had the same representation made to him: *I saw the dead*, says he, *small and great, stand before God, and the books were opened; and another book was opened, which is the book of life; and the dead were judged out of the things which were written in the books, according to their works*. Rev. xx. 12.

Should we pursue this significant allusion, we may say, then will be opened the book of the law of nature; and mankind will be tried according to its precepts, and doomed according to its sentence.—This is a plain and vast volume, open and legible now to all that can read their own hearts; that have eyes to look round upon the works of God, which shew his glory and their duty; and who have ears to hear the lectures which the sun and moon, and all the works of creation, read to them night and day. Then too will be opened the book of scripture-revelation, in all its parts, both the law of Moses and the gospel of Christ; and according to it will those be judged who lived under one or other of these dispensations. Then it will appear that *that* neglected, old-fashioned book called the Bible, is not a romance, or a system of trifling truths, but the standard of life and death to all who had access to it. Then will also be opened the book of God's remembrance. In that are recorded all the thoughts, words, actions, both good and bad, of all the sons of men; and now the immense account shall be publicly read before the assembled universe. Then likewise, as a counterpart to this, will be opened the book of conscience; conscience which, though unnoticed, writes our whole history as with an iron pen, and the point of a diamond.* Then also, we are expressly told, will be opened the book of life, Rev. xx. 12. in which are contained

---

* O treacherous Conscience! while she seems to sleep
On rose and myrtle, lull'd with Syren song;
While she seems, nodding o'er her charge, to drop
On headlong appetite the flackened rein,
And give us up to licence unrecall'd,
Unmark'd—as from behind her secret stand
The sly informer minutes ev'ry fault,
And her dread diary with horror fills—
Unnoted notes each moment misapply'd,
In leaves more durable than leaves of brass,
Writes our whole history; which Death shall read
In every pale offender's private ear;
And Judgment publish, publish to more worlds
Than this; and endless age in groans refound.
Such, sinner, is that sleeper in thy breast:
Such is her slumber; and her vengeance such
For slighted counsel ——————

Young.

all the names of all the heirs of Heaven. This seems to be an allusion to those registers which are kept in cities or corporations, of the names of all the citizens or members who have a right to all the privileges of the society. And I know not what we can understand by it so properly as the perfect knowledge which the omniscient God has, and always had from eternity, of those on whom he purposed to bestow eternal life, and whom he has from eternity, as it were, registered as members of the general assembly and church of the first-born, who are written in Heaven, or as denizens of that blessed city. These, having been all prepared by his grace in time, shall be admitted into the New Jerusalem in that day of the Lord.

Farther, the representation which the scripture gives us of the proceedings of that day, leads us to conceive of witnesses being produced to prove the facts. The omniscient Judge will be a witness against the guilty. *I will come near to you to judgment, and I will be a swift witness against the sorcerers, and against the swearers, and against the adulterers, and against those that oppress, and against those that fear not me, saith the Lord of Hosts.* Mal. iii. 5. And he will, no doubt, be a witness for his people, and attest their sincere piety, their interest in Christ, and those good dispositions or actions which were known only to him.

Angels also, that ministered to the heirs of salvation, and no doubt inspected the affairs of mankind, will be witnesses. Devils too, who once tempted, will now become accusers. Conscience within will also be a witness! it shall acquit the righteous of many unjust imputations, and attest the sincerity of their hearts and their many good actions. But, O! it will be the most terrible witness against the ungodly!—They will be witnesses against themselves (Josh. xxiv. 22.) and this will render them self-tormentors. Conscience will re-echo to the voice of the Judge, and cry Guilty, guilty, to all his accusations. And who can make the wicked happy, when they torment themselves? Who can acquit them, when they are self-condemned? Conscience, whose evidence is now so often suppressed, will then have full scope, and shall be regarded. Whom conscience condemns, the righteous Judge will also condemn: *for if our hearts condemn us, God is greater than our hearts, and knoweth all things.* 1 John iii. 20. knoweth many more grounds for condemning us than we, and therefore much more will he condemn us. In short, so full will be evidence against the sinner, that the scripture, which is full of striking imagery to affect human nature, gives life to inanimated things upon this occasion, and represents them as speaking. Stones and dust shall witness against the ungodly. The dust under the feet of their ministers shall witness against them. Matt. x. 14. *The stone shall cry out of the wall, and the beam out of the timber shall answer it.* Hab. ii. 11. The rust of their gold and silver shall be a witness against them, and shall eat their flesh as it were fire. James v. 3. Nay, the heavens shall reveal their iniquity, and the earth shall rise up against them. Job xx. 27. Heaven and earth were called to witness that life and death were set before them. Deut. xxx. 19. and now they will give in their evidence that they chuse death. Thus God and all his creatures, heaven, earth and hell, rise up against them, accuse and condemn them. And will not sinners accuse and witness against one another? Undoubtedly they will. They who lived or conversed together upon earth, and were spectators of each other's conduct, will then turn mutual witnesses against each other. O, tremendous thought! that friend should inform and witness against friend; parents against children, and children against parents; ministers against their people, and people against their ministers! Alas! what a confounding testimony against each other must those give in who are now sinning together!

Thus the way is prepared for the passing sentence. The case was always clear to the omniscient Judge, but now it is so fully discussed and attested by so many evidences, that it is quite plain to the whole world of creatures, who can judge only by such evidence, and for whose conviction the formality of a judicial process is appointed. How long a time this grand court will sit, we cannot determine, nor has God thought fit to inform us; but when we consider how particular the trial will be, and the innumerable multitude to be tried, it seems reasonable to suppose it will be a long session. It is indeed often called a day; but it is evident a day in such cases, does not signify a natural day, but the space of time allotted for transacting a business, though it be an hundred, or even a thousand years. . Creatures are incapable of viewing all things at once, and therefore, since the trial, as I observed, is intended to convince them of the equity of the divine proceedings, it is proper the proceedings should be particular and leisurely, that they may have time to observe them.

We are now come to the grand crisis, upon which the eternal states of all mankind turn; I mean the passing the great decisive sentence. Heaven and earth are all silence and attention, while the Judge, with smiles in his face, and a voice sweeter than heavenly music, turns to the glorious company on his right hand, and pours all the joys of heaven into their souls, in that transporting sentence, of which he has graciously left us a copy: *Come, ye blessed of my Father; inherit the kingdom prepared for you from the foundation of the world.* Every word is full of emphasis, full of heaven, and exactly agreeable to the desires of those to whom it is addressed. They desired, and longed, and languished to be near their Lord; and now their Lord invites them, Come near me, and dwell with me for ever. There was nothing they desired so much as the blessing of God, nothing they feared so much as his curse, and now their fears are entirely removed, and their designs fully accomplished, for the supreme Judge pronounces them blessed of his Father. They were all poor in spirit, most of them poor in this world, and all sensible of their unworthiness. How agreeable then are they surprised to hear themselves invited to a kingdom, invited to inherit a kingdom, as princes of the blood-royal, born to thrones and crowns! How will they be lost in wonder, joy, and praise, to find that the great God entertained thoughts of love towards them, before they had a being, or the world in which they dwelt had its foundation laid, and that he was preparing a kingdom for them, while they were nothing, unknown even in idea, except to himself? O! brethren, dare any of us expect this sentence will be passed upon us? Methinks the very thought overwhelms us. Methinks our feeble frames must be unable to bear up under the extatic hope of so sweetly oppressive a blessedness. O! if this be our sentence in that day, it is no matter what we suffer in the intermediate space; that sentence would compensate for all, and annihilate the sufferings of ten thousand years.

But hark! another sentence breaks from the mouth of the angry Judge, like vengeful thunder. Nature gives a deep tremendous groan; the heavens lower and gather blackness, the earth trembles, and guilty millions sink with horror at the sound! And see! he whose words are works, whose fiat produced worlds out of nothing; he who could remand ten thousand worlds into nothing at a frown; he whose thunder quelled the insurrection of rebel-angels in heaven, and hurled them headlong down, down, down to the dungeon of hell; see, he turns to the guilty croud on his left hand; his angry countenance discovers the righteous indignation that glows in his breast:—His countenance bespeaks him inexorable, and that there is now no room for prayers and tears. Now the sweet, mild, mediatorial hour is past, and nothing appears but the majesty and terror of the Judge. Horror and darkness frown upon his brows, and vindictive lightnings flash from his eyes. And now (O! who can bear the sound!) he speaks, *Depart from me, ye cursed, into everlasting fire, prepared for the devil and his angels*. O! the cutting emphasis of every word! Depart! depart from Me; from Me, the Author of all good, the Fountain of all good, the Fountain of all happiness. Depart, with all my heavy all-consuming curse upon you. Depart into fire, into everlasting, into everlasting fire, prepared, furnished with fuel, and blown up into rage, prepared for the

Serm. 20. *The Universal Judgment.*

devil and his angels; once your companions in sin, and now the companions and executioners of your punishment.

Now the grand period is arrived in which the final everlasting states of mankind are unchangeably settled. From this all-important æra their happiness or misery runs on in one uniform, uninterrupted tenor; no change, no gradation, but from glory to glory, in the scale of perfection, or from gulph to gulph in hell. This is the day in which all the schemes of Providence, carried on for thousands of years, terminate.

> " Great day! for which all other days were made:
> For which earth rose from chaos; man from earth;
> And an eternity, the date of gods,
> Descended on poor earth-created man!"—   YOUNG.

Time was; but is no more! Now all the sons of men enter upon a duration not to be measured by the revolutions of the sun, nor by days, and months, and years. Now eternity dawns, a day that shall never see an evening. And this terribly illustrious morning is solemnized with the execution of the sentence. No sooner is it passed than immediately the wicked *go away into everlasting punishment, but the righteous into life eternal.* Matt. xxv. 46. See the astonished thunder-struck multitude on the left hand, with sullen horror, and grief, and despair in their looks, writhing with agony, crying and wringing their hands, and glancing a wishful eye towards that heaven which they lost: dragged away by devils to the place of execution! See hell expands her voracious jaws, and swallows them up! and now an eternal farewell to earth and all its enjoyments! Farewell to the chearful light of Heaven! Farewell to hope, that sweet relief of affliction!

> ———" Farewell happy fields,
> Where joy for ever dwells! Hail horrors! hail
> Infernal world! and thou profoundest hell,
> Receive thy new possessors!"   MILTON.

Heaven frowns upon them from above, the horrors of hell spread far and wide around them, and conscience within preys upon their hearts. Conscience! O thou abused, exasperated power, that now sleepest in so many breasts, what severe, ample revenge wilt thou then take upon those that now dare to do thee violence! O the dire reflections which memory will then suggest! the remembrance of mercies abused! of a Saviour slighted! of means and opportunities of salvation neglected and lost! this remembrance will sting the heart like a scorpion. But O eternity! eternity! with what horror will thy name circulate through the vaults of hell! eternity in misery! no end to pain! no hope of an end! O this is the hell of Hell! this is the parent of despair! despair the direct ingredient of mifery, the moft tormenting paffion which devils feel.—But let us view a more delightful and illuftrious fcene.

See the bright and triumphant army marching up to their eternal home, under the conduct of the Captain of their falvation, where they *shall ever be with the Lord.* 1 Theff. iv. 17. as happy as their nature in its higheft improvements is capable of being made. With what fhouts of joy and triumph do they afcend! with what fublime hallelujahs do they crown their Deliverer! with what wonder and joy, with what pleafing horror, like one that has narrowly efcaped fome tremendous precipice, do they look back upon what they once were! once mean, guilty, depraved, condemned finners! afterward imperfect, broken-hearted, fighing, weeping faints! but now innocent, holy, happy, glorious immortals!

"Are thefe the forms that moulder'd in the duft?
O the tranfcendant glories of the juft!"   YOUNG.

Now with what pleafure and rapture do they look forward through the long, long profpect of immortality, and call it their own! the duration not only of their exiftence, but of their happinefs and glory! O fhall any of us fhare in this immenfely valuable privilege! how immenfely tranfporting the thought!

Shall we, who fome few years ago were lefs
Than worm, or mite, or fhadow can exprefs;
Were nothing; fhall we live, when every fire
Of every ftar fhall languifh or expire?
When earth's no more, fhall we furvive above,
And through the fhining ranks of angels move?
Or, as before the throne of God we ftand,
See new worlds rolling from his mighty hand?—
All that has being in full concert join,
And celebrate the depths of love divine!   YOUNG.

O what exploits, what miracles of power and grace, are thefe! But why do I darken fuch fplendors with words without knowledge? the language of mortals was formed for lower defcriptions? *Eye hath not feen, ear has not heard, nor have entered into the heart of man the things that God hath laid up for them that love him.* 1 Cor. ii. 9.

And now when the inhabitants of our world, for whofe fake it was formed, are all removed to other regions, and it is left a wide extended defert, what remains, but that it alfo meet its fate? It is fit fo guilty a globe, that had been the ftage of fin for fo many thoufands of years, and which even fupported the crofs on which its maker expired, fhould be made a monument of the divine difpleafure, and either be laid in ruins, or refined by fire. And fee! the univerfal blaze begins! *the heavens pafs away with a great noife;*

Serm 20.   *The Univerfal Judgment.*   363

the elements melt with fervent heat ; the earth and the works that are therein are burnt up. 2 Pet. iii. 10. Now ftars rufh from their orbits ; comets glare ; the earth trembles with convulfions ; the Alps, the Andes, and all the lofty peaks or long extended ridges of mountains burft out into fo many burning Ætnas, or thunder, and lighten, and fmoke, and flame, and quake like Sinai, when God defcended upon it to publifh his fiery law ! Rocks melt and run down in torrents of flame ; rivers, lakes, and oceans boil and evaporate. Sheets of fire and pillars of fmoke, outrageous and infufferable thunders and lightnings burft, and bellow, and blaze, and involve the atmofphere from pole to pole.* The whole globe is now diffolved into a fhorelefs ocean of liquid fire. And where now fhall we find the places where cities ftood, where armies fought, where mountains ftretched their ridges, and reared their heads on high ? Alas ! they are all loft, and have left no trace behind them where they once ftood. Where art thou, O my country ? Sunk with the reft, as a drop into the burning ocean. Where now are your houfes, your lands, and thofe earthly poffeffions you were once fo fond of ? They are no where to be found. How forry a portion for an immortal mind is fuch a dying world as this ! And, O !

<blockquote>
" How rich that God who can fuch charge defray,
" And bear to fling ten thoufand worlds away !"   Young.
</blockquote>

Thus, my brethren, I have given you a view of the folemnities of the laft day which our world fhall fee. The view has indeed been but very faint and obfcure : and fuch will be all our views and defcriptions of it, till our eyes and our ears teach us better. Through thefe avenues you will at length receive your inftructions. Yes, brethren, thofe ears that now hear my voice fhall hear the all-alarming clangour of the laft trumpet, the decifive fentence from the mouth of the univerfal Judge, and the horrid crafh of falling worlds. Thefe very eyes with which you now fee one another, fhall yet fee the defcending Judge, the affembled multitudes, and all the majeftic phenomena of that day. And we fhall not fee them as indifferent fpectators ; no, we are as much concerned in this great tranfaction as any of the children of men. We muft all appear before the judgment-feat, and receive our fentence according to the deeds done in the body. And if fo, what are we doing that we are not more diligently preparing ? Why does not the

---

* See all the formidable fons of Fire,
Eruptions, Earthquakes, Comets, Lightnings play
Their various engines ; all at once difcharge
Their blazing magazines ; and take by ftorm
This poor terreftrial citadel of man.   Young.

prospect affect us more? Why does it not transport the righteous with *joy unspeakable, and full of glory.* 1 Peter i. 8. And why are not the *sinners in Zion afraid? Why does not fearfulness surprise the hypocrites?* Isa. xxxiii. 14. Can one of you be careless from this hour till you are in readiness for that tremendous day?

What do the sinners among you now think of repentance? Repentance is the grand preparative for this awful day; and the apostle, as I observed, mentions the final judgment in my text as a powerful motive to repentance. And what will criminals think of repentance when they see the Judge ascend his throne? Come, sinners, look forward and see the flaming tribunal erected, your crimes exposed, your doom pronounced, and your hell begun; see a whole world demolished, and ravaged by boundless conflagration for your sins! With these objects before you, I call you to repent?—I call you! I retract the words: God, the great God whom heaven and earth obey, commands you to repent. Whatever be your characters, whether rich or poor, old or young, white or black, wherever you sit or stand, this command reaches you; *for God now commandeth all men every where to repent.* You are this day firmly bound to this duty by his authority. And dare you disobey with the prospect of all the awful solemnities of judgment before you in so near a view? O! methinks I have now brought you into such a situation, that the often repeated but hitherto neglected call to repentance will be regarded by you. Repent you must, either upon earth or in hell. You must either spend your time or your eternity in repentance. It is absolutely unavoidable. Putting it off now does not remove the necessity, but will only render it the more bitter and severe hereafter. Which then do you choose? the tolerable, hopeful, medicinal repentance of the present life, or the intolerable, unprofitable, despairing repentance of hell? Will you choose to spend time or eternity in this melancholy exercise? O! make the choice which God, which reason, which self-interest, which common sense recommend to you. Now repent at the command of God, *because he hath appointed a day in which he will judge the world in righteousness, by that Man whom he hath ordained; of which he hath given you all full assurance in that he hath raised him from the dead.* Amen.

SERMON XXI.

The one Thing needful.

LUKE x. 41, 42. *And Jesus answered and said unto her, Martha, Martha, thou art careful and troubled about many things; but one thing is needful: and Mary hath chosen that good part, which shall not be taken away from her.*

FOR what are we placed in this world? Is it to dwell here always? You cannot think so, when the millions of mankind that have appeared upon the stage of time are so many instances of the contrary. The true notion therefore of the present state is, that it is a state of preparation and trial for the eternal world; a state of education for our adult age. As children are sent to school, and youth bound out to trades, to prepare them for business, and qualify them to live in the world, so we are placed here to prepare us for the grand business of immortality, the state of our maturity, and to qualify us to live for ever. And is there an heaven of the most perfect happiness, and an hell of the most exquisite misery, just before us, perhaps not a year or even a day distant from us? And is it the great design, the business and duty of the present state, to obtain the one and escape the other? Then what are we doing? What is the world doing all around us? Are they acting as it becomes candidates for eternity? Are they indeed making that the principal object of their most zealous endeavours, which is the grand design, business and duty of the present state? Are they minding this at all adventures whatever else they neglect? This is what we might expect from them as reasonable creatures, as creatures that love themselves, and have a strong innate desire of happiness. This a stranger to our world might charitably presume concerning them. But, alas! look upon the conduct of the world around you, or look nearer home, and where you are more nearly interested, upon your own conduct, and you will see this is not generally the case. No; instead of pursuing the one thing needful, the world is all in motion, all bustle and hurry, like ants upon a mole-hill, about other affairs. They are in a still higher degree than officious Martha, *careful and troubled about many things*. Now to recall you from this endless variety of vain pursuits, and direct your endeavours to the proper object, I can think of no better expedient than to explain and inculcate upon you the admonition of Chrift to Martha, and his commendation of Mary upon this head.

Martha was the head of a little family, probably a widow, in a village near Jerufalem, called Bethany. Her brother and fifter, Lazarus and Mary, lived along with her. And what is remarkable concerning this little family is, that they were all lovers of Jefus: and their love was not without returns on his fide; for we are exprefsly told that *Jefus loved Martha, and her fifter, and Lazarus.*—What an happy family is this! but O how rare in the world! This was a convenient place of retirement to Jefus, af'er the labours and fatigues of his miniftry in the city: and here we often find him. Though fpent and exhaufted with his public fervices, yet when he gets into the circle of a few friends in a private houfe, he cannot be idle: he ftill inftructs them with his heavenly difcourfe; and his converfation is a conftant fermon. Mary, who 'was paffionately devout and eager for inftruction, would not let fuch a rare opportunity flip, but fits down at the feet of this great Teacher, which was the pofture of the Jewifh pupils before their mafters,* and eagerly catches every word from his lips; from which dropt knowledge fweeter than honey from the honeycomb. Though fhe is folicitous for the comfort of her heavenly gueft, yet fhe makes no great ftir to provide for him an elegant or fumptuous entertainment; for fhe knew his happinefs did not confift in luxurious eating and drinking: it was his *meat and his drink to do the will of his Father;* and as for the fuftenance of his body, plain food was moft acceptable to him. He was not willing that any fhould lofe their fouls by lofing opportunities of inftruction, while they were making fumptuous provifion for him. Mary was alfo fo deeply engaged about her falvation, that fhe was nobly carelefs about the little decencies of entertainments. The body and all its fupports and gratifications appeared of very fmall importance to her when compared with the immortal foul. O! if that be but fed with the words of eternal life, it is enough. All this fhe did with Chrift's warm approbation, and therefore her conduct is an example worthy of our imitation: and if it were imitated it would happily reform the pride, luxury, exceffive delicacy, and multiform extravagance which have crept in upon us under the ingratiating names of politenefs, decency, hofpitality, good œconomy, and I know not what. Thefe guilty fuperfluities and refinements render the life of fome a courfe of idolatry to fo fordid a god as their bellies, and that of others a courfe of bufy, laborious, and expenfive trifling.—But to return:

---

* Hence St. Paul's expreffion, that he was brought up at the feet of Gamaliel.

Martha, though a pious moman, yet like too many among us, was too folicitous about thefe things. She feemed more concerned to maintain her reputation for good œconomy and hofpitality than to improve in divine knowledge at every opportunity; and to entertain her gueft rather as a gentleman than as a divine teacher and the Saviour of fouls. Hence, inftead of fitting at his feet with her fifter in the pofture of a humble difciple, fhe was bufy in making preparations; and her mind was diftracted with the cares of her family. As moderate labour and care about earthly things is lawful, and even a duty, perfons are not readily fufpicious or eafily convinced of their guilty exceffes in thefe labours and cares. Hence Martha is fo far from condemning herfelf in this account, that fhe blames her devout fifter for not following her example. Nay, fhe has the confidence to complain to Chrift himfelf of her neglect, and that in language too that founds fomewhat rude and irreverent. "Careft thou not that my fifter hath left me to ferve alone?" Art thou fo partial as to fuffer her to devolve all the trouble upon me while fhe fits idle at thy feet?

Jefus turns upon her with juft feverity, and throws the blame where it fhould lie. *Martha, Martha !* There is a vehemence and pungency in the repetition, *Martha, Martha, thou art careful and troubled about many things.* "Thy worldly mind has many objects, and many objects excite many cares and troubles, fruitlefs troubles and ufelefs cares. Thy reftlefs mind is fcattered among a thoufand things, and toffed from one to another with an endlefs variety of anxieties. But let me collect my thoughts and cares to one point, a point where they fhould all terminate : *one thing is needful;* and therefore dropping thy exceffive care about many things, make this one thing the great object of thy purfuit. This one thing is what thy fifter is now attending to, while thou art vainly careful about many things; and therefore, inftead of blaming her conduct, I muft approve it. She has made the beft choice, for fhe *hath chofen that good part, which fhall not be taken away from her.* After all thy care and labour, the things of this vain world muft be given up at laft, and loft for ever. But Mary hath made a wifer choice, the portion fhe hath chofen fhall be hers for ever ; it fhall never be taken away from her."

But what does Chrift mean by this one thing which alone is needful?

I anfwer, We may learn what he meant by the occafion and circumftances of his fpeaking. He mentions this one thing in an admonition to Martha for exceffive worldly cares and the neglect of an opportunity for promoting her falvation ; and he exprefsly oppofes this one thing to the many things which engroffed her care ; and therefore it muft mean fomething different from and superior to all the pursuits of time. This one thing is that which Mary was so much concerned about while attentively listening to his instructions. And what can that be but salvation as the end, and holiness as the means, or a proper care of the soul? This is that which is opposite and superior to the many cares of life:—this is that which Mary was attending to and pursuing: and I may add, this is that good part which Mary had chosen, which should never be taken away from her; for that good part which Mary had chosen seems intended by Christ to explain what he meant by the one thing needful. Therefore the one thing needful must mean the salvation of the soul, and an earnest application to the means necessary to obtain this end above all other things in the world. To be holy in order to be happy; to pray, to hear, to meditate, and use all the means of grace appointed to produce or cherish holiness in us; to use these means which constancy, frequency, earnestness, and zeal; to use them diligently whatever else be neglected, or to make all other things give way in comparison of this; this I apprehend is the one thing needful which Christ here intends: this is that which is absolutely necessary, necessary above all other things, and necessary for ever. The end, namely, salvation, will be granted by all to be necessary, and the necessity of the end renders the means also necessary. If it be necessary you should be for ever happy, and escape everlasting misery, it is necessary you should be holy; for you can no more be saved without holiness than you can be healthy without health, see without light, or live without food. And if holiness be necessary, then the earnest use of the means appointed for the production and improvement of holiness in us must be necessary too; for you can no more expect to become holy without the use of these means, than to reap without sowing, or become truly virtuous and good by chance or fatality. To be holy in order to be happy, and to use all the means of grace in order to be holy, is therefore the one thing needful.

But why is this concern which is so complex called One Thing?

I answer: Though salvation and holiness include various ingredients, and though the means of grace are various, yet they may be all taken collectively and called one thing; that is, one great business, one important object of pursuit, in which all our endeavours and aims should center and terminate. It is also said to be one, in opposition to the many things that are the objects of a worldly mind. This world owes its variety in a great measure to contradiction and inconsistency. There is no harmony or unity in the earthly objects of mens pursuits, nor in the means they use to secure them. Riches, honours, and pleasures generally clash.

If a man will be rich he muſt reſtrain himſelf in the pleaſures of gratifying his eagar appetites, and perhaps uſe ſome mean artifices that may ſtain his honour. If he would be honourable, he muſt often be prodigal of his riches, and abſtain from ſome ſordid pleaſures. If he would have the full enjoyment of ſenſual pleaſures, he muſt often ſquander away his riches, and injure his honour to procure them. The luſts of men as well as their objects, are alſo various and contradictory. Covetouſneſs and ſenſuality, pride and tranquility, envy and the love of eaſe, and a thouſand jarring paſſions, maintain a conſtant fight in the ſinner's breaſt. The means for gratifying theſe luſts are likewiſe contrary; ſometimes truth, ſometimes falſhood, ſometimes indolence, ſometimes action and labour are neceſſary. In theſe things there is no unity of deſign, nor conſiſtency of means; but the ſinner is properly diſtracted, drawn this way and that, toſſed from wave to wave; and there is no ſteadineſs or uniformity in his purſuits. But the work of ſalvation is one, the means and the end correſpond, and the means are conſiſtent one with another; and therefore the whole, though conſiſting of many parts, may be ſaid to be one.

It may alſo be called the one thing needful, to intimate that this is needful above all other things. It is a common form of ſpeech to ſay of that which is neceſſary above all other things, that it is the one or only thing neceſſary: ſo we may underſtand this paſſage. There are what we call the real neceſſaries of life; ſuch as food and raiment: there are alſo neceſſary callings and neceſſary labours. All theſe are neceſſary in a lower ſenſe; neceſſary in their proper place. But in compariſon of the great work of our ſalvation, they are all unneceſſary; if we be but ſaved, we may do very well without them all. This is ſo neceſſary, that nothing elſe deſerves to be called neceſſary in compariſon of it.

This ſhews you alſo, not only why this is called one thing, but why or in what ſenſe it is ſaid to be neceſſary. It is of abſolute and incomparable neceſſity. There is no abſolute neceſſity to our happineſs that we ſhould be rich or honourable; nay, there is no abſolute neceſſity to our happineſs that we ſhould live in this world at all, for we may live infinitely more happy in another. And if life itſelf be not abſolutely neceſſary, then much leſs are food, or raiment, or health, or any of thoſe things which in a lower ſenſe we call the neceſſaries of life. In compariſon of this, they are all, needleſs. I add farther, this one thing may be ſaid to be neceſſary, becauſe it is neceſſary always, or for ever. The neceſſaris of this life we cannot want long, for we muſt ſoon remove into a world where there is no room for them; but holineſs and ſalvation we ſhall find needful always: needful under the calamities of life; needful in the agonies of death; needful in the world of spirits; needful millions of ages hence; needful to all eternity; and without it we are eternally undone. This is a neceſſity indeed! a neceſſity, in compariſon of which all other neceſſaries are but ſuperfluities.

I hope by this ſhort explication I have cleared the way through your underſtandings to your hearts, and to your hearts I would now addreſs myſelf. However ſolemnly I may ſpeak upon this intereſting ſubject, you will have more reaſon to blame me for the deficiency than for the exceſs of my zeal and ſolemnity. I hope I have entered this ſacred place to-day with a ſincere deſire to do ſome ſervice to your immortal ſouls before I leave it. And may I not hope you have come here with a deſire to receive ſome advantage? If not, you may number this ſeeming act of religion among the ſins of your life; you have come here to-day to ſin away theſe ſacred hours in hypocriſy, and a profane mockery of the great God. But if you are willing to receive any benefit, hear attentively: hear, that your ſouls may live.

My firſt requeſt to you is,* that you would make this paſſage the teſt of your characters, and ſeriouſly inquire whether you have lived in the world as thoſe that really and practically believe that this is the one thing of abſolute neceſſity? Are not all the joys of heaven and your immortal ſouls worth the little pains of ſeriouſly putting this ſhort queſtion to your conſciences? Review your life, look into your hearts, and inquire, has this one thing lain more upon your hearts than all other things together? Has this been, above all other things, the object of your moſt vehement deſire, your moſt earneſt endeavours, and eager purſuit? I do not aſk whether you have heard or read that this one thing is neceſſary, or whether you have ſometimes talked about it. I do not aſk whether you have paid to God the compliment of appearing in his houſe once a week, or of performing him a little lip-ſervice morning and evening in your families, or in your cloſets, after you have ſerved yourſelves and the world all the reſt of your time, without one affectionate thought of God. Nor do I inquire whether in a pang of horror after the commiſſion of ſome groſs ſin you have tried to make your conſcience eaſy by a few prayers and tears, of which you form an opiate to caſt you again into a dead ſleep in ſin, I do not aſk whether you have performed many actions that are materially good, and abſtained from many ſins. All this you may have done, and yet have neglected the one thing needful all your lives.

---

* Many of the following ſentiments, as to the ſubſtance of them, are borrowed from Mr. Baxter's excellent diſcourſe, intitled, A SAINT OR A BRUTE: and I know no better pattern for a miniſter to follow in his addreſs to ſinners, than that flaming and ſucceſsful preacher.

But I afk you, whether this one thing needful has been habitually uppermoſt in your hearts, the favourite object of your defires, the prize of your moſt vigorous endeavours, the fupreme happinefs of your fouls, and the principal object of your concern above all things in the world? Sirs, you may now hear this queſtion with ſtupid unconcern and indifferency; but I muſt tell you, you will find, another day, how much depends upon it. In that day it will be found, that the main difference between true Chriſtians and the various claſſes of ſinners is this :—God, Chriſt, holinefs, and the concerns of eternity, are habitually uppermoſt in the hearts of the former; but, to the latter, they are generally but things by the by; and the world engroſſes the vigour of their fouls, and is the principal concern of their lives. To ferve God, to obtain his favour, and to be happy for ever in his love, is the main buſineſs of the faint, to which all the concerns of the world and the fleſh muſt give way; but to live in eafe, in reputation, in pleafure, or riches, or to gratify himfelf in the purfuit and enjoyment of fome created good, this is the main concern of the ſinner. The one has made an hearty reſignation of himſelf, and all that he is and has, to God, through Jefus Chriſt: he ferves him with the beſt, and thinks nothing too good for him. But the other has his exceptions and referves: he will ferve God willingly, provided it may confiſt with his eafe, and pleafure, and temporal intereſt; he will ferve God with a bended knee, and the external forms of devotion; but, with the vigour of his ſpirit, he ſerves the world and his fleſh. This is the grand difference between a true Chriſtian and the various forms of half-chriſtians and hypocrites. And certainly this is a difference that may be difcerned. The tenor of a man's practice, and the object of his love, efpecially of his higheſt love and practical eſteem, muſt certainly be very diſtinguiſhable from a thing by the by, and from the object of a languid paſſion, or mere fpeculation. Therefore, if you make but an impartial trial, you have reafon to hope you will make a juſt difcovery of your true character: or if you cannot make the difcovery yourfelves, call in the affiſtance of others. Aſk not your worldly and fenfual neighbours, for they are but poor judges, and they will flatter you in felf-defence; but aſk your pious friends whether you have fpoke and acted like perfons that practically made this the one thing needful. They can tell you what ſubject you talked moſt ſeriouſly about, what purfuit feemed to lie moſt upon your heart, and chiefly to exhauſt your activity. Brethren, I befeech you, by one means or other, to bring this matter to an iſſue, and let it hang in fufpence no longer. Why are you fo indifferent how this matter ſtands with you? Is it becaufe you imagine you may be true Chriſtians, and obtain falvation, however this matter be with you? But be not deceived : no man can ferve two mafters, whofe commands are contrary ; and *ye cannot ferve God and Mammon*, with a fervice equally devoted to both. *If any man love the world with fupreme affections, the love of the Father is not in him.* 1 John ii. 15. *Be not deceived, God is not mocked; whatfoever a man foweth that fhall he reap ; if you fow to the flefh, of the flefh you fhall reap corruption :* A miferable harveft indeed! *But if you fow to the fpirit, you fhall of the fpirit reap everlafting life.* Gal. vi. 7, 8. Therefore you may be fure that *if you live after the flefh, you fhall die ;* and that you can never enjoy the one thing needful unlefs you mind and purfue it above all other things.

But I fhall not urge you any farther to try yourfelves by this teft. I take it for granted the confciences of fome of you have determined the matter, and that you are plainly convicted of having hitherto neglected the one thing needful. Allow me then honeftly to expofe your conduct in its proper colours, and tell you what you have been doing while you were bufy about other things, and neglecting this one thing needful.

1. However well you have improved your time for other purpofes, you have loft it all, unlefs you have improved it in fecuring the one thing needful. The proper notion of time is, that it is a fpace for repentance. Time is given us to prepare for eternity. If this is done we have lived long enough, and the great end of time and life is anfwered, whatever elfe be undone. But if this be undone, you have lived in vain, and all your time is loft, however bufily and fuccefsfully you have purfued other things. Though you have ftudied yourfelves pale, to furnifh your minds with knowledge ; though you have fpent the night and the day in heaping up riches, or climbing up to the pinnacle of honour, and not loft an hour that might be turned to your advantage, yet you have been moft wretchedly fooling away your time, and loft it all, if you have not laid it out in fecuring the one thing needful. And, believe me, time is a precious thing. So it will appear in a dying hour, or in the eternal world, to the greateft fpendthrift among you. Then, O for a year, or even a week, or a day, to fecure that one thing which you are now neglecting! And will you now wafte your time, while you enjoy it? Shall fo precious a bleffing be loft? By this calculation, how many days, how many years, have you loft for ever? For is not that loft which is fpent in croffing the end for which it was given you? Time was given you to fecure an eternity of happinefs, but you have fpent it in adding fin to fin, and confequently in treafuring up wrath againft the day of wrath. And is not your time then a thoufand times worfe than loft? Let me tell you, if you continue in this courfe to the end, you will wifh a thoufand times, either that you had never had one

Serm. 21. *The one Thing needful.*

hour's time given you, or that you had made a better use of it.

2. Whatever elfe you have been doing, you have loft your labour with your time, if you have not laboured above all things for this one thing needful. No doubt you have been bufy about fomething all your life; but you might as well have been idle: you have been bufy in doing nothing. You have perhaps toiled through many anxious and laborious days, and your nights have fhared in the anxieties and labours of your days. But if you have not laboured for the one thing neceffary, all your labour and all the fruits of it are loft. Indeed God may have made ufe of you for the good of his church, or of your country, as we make ufe of thorns and briars to ftop a breach, or of ufelefs wood for firing to warm our families; but as to any lafting and folid advantage to yourfelves, all your labour has been loft.

But this is not all. Not only your fecular labour is loft, but all your toil and pains, if you have ufed any in the duties of religion, they are loft likewife. Your reading, hearing, praying, and communicating; all your ferious thoughts of death and eternity, all your ftruggles with particular lufts and temptations, all the kind offices you have done to mankind, all are loft, fince you have performed them by halves with a lukewarm heart, and have not made the one thing needful your great bufinefs and purfuit. All thefe things will not fave you; and what is that religion good for which will not fave your fouls? What do thofe religious endeavours avail which will fuffer you to fall into hell after all? Certainly fuch religion is vain.

And now, my hearers, do you believe this, or do you not? If you do, will you, dare you ftill go on in the fame courfe? If you do not believe it, let me reafon the matter with you a little. You will not believe that all the labour and pains you have taken all your life have been quite loft: no, you now enjoy the fruits of them. But fhew me, now if you can, what you have gotten by all that ftir you have made that will follow one ftep beyond the grave, or that you can call your own to-morrow? Where is that fure immortal acquifition that you can carry with you into the eternal world? Were you to die this hour, would it afford you any pleafure to reflect that you have lived a merry life, and had a fatiety of fenfual pleafures, or that you have laboured for riches and honours, and perhaps acquired them? will this reflection afford you pleafure or pain? will this abate the agony of eternal pain, or make up for the lofs of heaven, which you wilfully incurred by an over-eager purfuit of thefe perifhing vanities?

Do you not fee the extravagant folly, the diftracted phrenfy of fuch a conduct? Alas! while you are neglecting the one thing needful, what are you doing but fpending your time and labour in laborious idleness, honourably debasing yourselves, delightfully tormenting yourselves, wisely befooling yourselves, and frugally impoverishing and ruining yourselves for ever? A child or an idiot riding upon a staff, building their mimic houses, or playing with a feather, are not so foolish as you in your conduct, while you are so seriously pursuing the affairs of time, and neglecting those of eternity. But,

3. This is not all: All your labour and pains have not only been lost while you have neglected this one thing, but you have taken pains to ruin yourselves, and laboured hard all your lives for your own destruction. To this you will immediately answer, "God forbid we should do any thing to hurt ourselves! we were far from having any such design." But the question is not what was your design? but, what is the unavoidable consequence of your conduct, according to the nature of things, and the unchangeable constitution of heaven? Whatever you design in going on in sin, *the wages of sin is death*, eternal death. You may indulge the carnal mind, and walk after the flesh, and yet hope no bad consequence will follow; but God has told you that *to be carnally minded is death*, and that if you live after the flesh you shall die. The robber on the highway has no design to be hanged; but this does not render him a jot safer. Therefore, design what you will, it is certain you are positively destroying yourselves while your labours about other things hinder you from pursuing the one thing needful.—And does not this thought shock you, that you should be acting the part of enemies against yourselves, the most pernicious and deadly enemies to yourselves in the whole universe? No enemy in the whole universe could do you that injury without your consent which you are doing to yourselves. To tempt you to sin is all the devil can do; but the temptation alone can do you no injury; it is consenting to it that ruins you; and this consent is your own voluntary act. All the devils in hell could not force you to sin without your consent, and therefore all the devils in hell do not injure you as you do yourselves. God has not given them so much power over you as he has given you over yourselves: and this power you abuse to your own destruction.

O! in what a distracted state is the world of the ungodly! If any other men be their enemy, how do they resent it! But they are their own worst enemies, and yet never fall out with themselves. If another occasion them a disappointment in their pursuits, defraud them of an expected good, or lay schemes to make them miserable, what sullen grudge, what keen revenge, what flaming resentments immediately rise in their breasts against him? And yet they are all their lives disinheriting themselves of the heavenly inheritance, laying a train to blow up all their own hopes, and heaping a mountain of guilt upon themselves to sink them into the bottomlefs pit; and all this while they think they are the beft friends to themfelves, and confulting their own intereft. As for the devil, the common enemy of mankind, they abhor him, and blefs themfelves from him; but they are worfe to themfelves than devils, and yet never fall out with themfelves for it.

This, finners, may feem an harfh reprefentation of your conduct, but, alas! it is true. And if it be fo fhocking to you to hear it, what muft it be to be guilty of it! And, O! think what muft be the confequences of fuch a conduct, fuch unnatural fuicide!

4. If you have hitherto neglected the one thing needful, you have unmanned yourfelves, acted beneath and contrary to your own reafon, and in plain terms behaved as if you had been out of your fenfes. If you have the ufe of your reafon, it muft certainly tell you for what it was given to you. And I befeech you tell me what was it given to you for but to ferve the God that made you, to fecure his favour, to prepare for your eternal ftate, and to enjoy the fupreme good as your portion? Can you once think your reafon, that *divinæ particula auræ*, was given you for fuch low purpofes as the contrivances, labour and purfuits of this vain life, and to make you a more ingenious fort of brutes? He was mafter of an unufual fhare of reafon who faid, " There is very little difference between having reafon and having none, if we had nothing to do with it but cunningly to lay up for our food, and make provifion for this corruptible flefh, and had not another life to mind." Therefore I may fafely affirm that you have caft away your reafon, and acted as if you were out of your wits, if you have not employed your rational powers in the purfuit of the one thing needful. Where was your reafon when your dying flefh was preferred to your immortal fpirits? was reafon your guide when you chofe the trafh of this perifhing world, and fought it more than the favour of God and all the joys of heaven? Can you pretend to common fenfe, when you might have had the pardon of fin, fanctifying grace, and a title to heaven fecured to you ere now? But you have neglected all, and inftead of having a fure title to heaven, or being prepared for it, you are fitted for deftruction, and nothing elfe; and are only waiting for a fever or a flux, or fome other executioner of divine vengeance, to cut the thread of life and let you fink to hell by your own weight. Thither you gravitate under the load of fin as naturally as a ftone to the center; and you need no other weight to fink you down. What have you done all your life to make a wife man think you truly reafonable? Is that your reafon, to be wife to do evil, while to do good you have no knowledge; or to be ingenious and active about the trifles of time, while you neglect that great work for which you were created and redeemed? Can you be wife and yet not confider your latter end? Nay, can you pretend to fo much as common fenfe, while

you sell your eternal salvation for the sordid pleasures of a few flying years? Have you common sense, when you will not keep yourselves out of everlasting fire? What can a madman do worse than wilfully destroy himself? And this you are doing every day.

And yet these very persons are proud of their madness, and are apt to fling the charge of folly upon others, especially if they observe some poor weak creatures, though it be but one in five hundred, fall into melancholy, or lose their reason for a time, while they are groaning under a sense of sin, and anxious about their eternal state; then what a clamour against religion and preciseness, as the ready way to make people run mad! then they even dare to publish their resolution that they will not read and pore so much upon these things, left it should drive them out of their senses. O miserable mortals! is it possible they should be more dangerously mad than they are already! Do you lay out your reason, your strength, and time in pursuing vain shadows, and in feeding a mortal body for the grave, while the important real ties of the eternal world, and the salvation of your immortal souls are forgotten or neglected! Do you sell your Saviour with Judas for a little money, and change your part in God and heaven for the sordid pleasures of sin, which are but for a season! and are you afraid of seriously reflecting upon this course that you may reform it for fear such thoughts should make you mad? What greater madness than this can you fear? Will you run from God, from Christ, from mercy, from the saints, from heaven itself, for fear of being mad? Alas! you are mad in the worst sense already. Will you run to hell to prove yourselves in your senses? He was a wise and good man who said, "Though the loss of a man's understanding is a grievous affliction, and such as I hope God will never lay upon me, yet I had a thousand times rather go distracted to Bedlam with the excessive care about my salvation, than to be one of you that cast away the care of your salvation for fear of being distracted, and will go among the infernal Bedlams into hell for fear of being mad." Distraction in itself is not a moral evil, but a physical, like those disorders of the body from which it often proceeds, and therefore is no object for punishment, and had you no capacity of understanding you would have a cloak for your sin; but your madness is your crime, because it is voluntary, and therefore you must give an account for it to the Supreme Judge.

It would be easy to offer many more considerations to expose the absurdity and danger of your conduct in neglecting the one thing necessary; but these must suffice for the present hour. And I only desire you to consider farther, if this be a just view of the conduct of such as are guilty of this neglect, in what a miserable, pitiable condition is the world in general! I have so often tried the utmost energy of my own words upon you with so little succefs as to many, that I am grown quite weary of them. Allow me therefore for once to borrow the more ftriking and pungent words of one now in heaven ; of one who had more fuccefs than almoft any of his cotemporaries or fucceffors in the important work of *converting finners from the error of their way, and faving fouls from death;* I mean that incomparable preacher, Mr. Baxter, who fowed an immortal feed in his parifh of Kidderminfter, which grows and brings forth fruit to this day. His words have, through the divine blefliag, been irrefiftible to thoufands ; and O that fuch of you, my dear hearers, whofe hearts may have been proof againft mine, may not be fo againft his alfo !

" Look upon this text of fcripture, fays he, and look alfo upon the courfe of the earth, and confider of the difagreement ; and whether it be not ftill as before the flood, that *all the imaginations of man's heart are evil continually ?* Gen. vi. 5. Were it poffible for a man to fee the affections and motions of all the world at once, as God feeth them, what a pitiful fight it would be ! What a ftir do they make, alas, poor fouls ! for they know not what ! while they forget, or flight, or hate the one thing needful. What an heap of gadding ants fhould we fee that do nothing but gather fticks and ftraws ! Look among perfons of every rank, in city and country, and look into families about you, and fee what trade it is they are moft bufily driving on, whether it be for heaven or earth ? And whether you can difcern by their care and labours that they underftand what is the one-thing neceffary ? Thefe are as bufy as bees ; but not for honey, but in fpinning'fuch a fpider's web as the befom of death will prefently fweep down. Job viii. 14. They labour hard ; but for what ? *For the food that perifheth,* but not for that *which endureth to everlafting life.* John. vi. 27. They are diligent feekers ; but for what ? Not firft for God, his kingdom and righteoufnefs, but for that which they might have had as an addition to their bleffednefs. Matt. vi. 33. They are ftill doing ; what are they doing ? Even undoing themfelves by running away from God, to hunt after the perifhing pleafures of the world. Inftead of providing for the life to come, they are making *provifion for the flefh to fulfil its lufts.* Rom. xiii. 14. Some of them hear the word of God, but they prefently choke it *by the deceitfulnefs of riches and the cares of this life.* Luke viii. 14. They *are careful and troubled about many things ;* but the one thing that fhould be all to them is caft by as if it were nothing. Providing for the flefh and minding the world is the employment of their lives. They labour with a canine appetite for their trafh ; but to holinefs they have no appetite, and are worfe than indifferent to the things that are indeed defirable. They have no covetoufnefs for the things which they are commanded *earneftly to covet.* 1 Cor. xii. 31. They have fo little hunger and thirft after righteoufnefs, that a very little or none will satisfy them. Here they are pleading always for moderation, and against too much, and too earnest, and too long; and all is too much with them that is above stark nought, or dead hypocrisy; and all is too earnest and too long that would make religion seem a business, or engage them to seem serious in their own profession, or put them past jest in the worship of God and the matters of their salvation. Let but their children or servants neglect their worldly business (which I confess they should not do) and they shall hear of it with both their ears; but if they sin against God, or neglect his word or worship, they shall meet with more patience than Eli's son did: a cold reproof is usually the most; and it is well if they be not encouraged in their sin: it is well if a child or servant that begins to be serious for salvation be not rebuked, derided and hindered by them. If on their days of labour they oversleep themselves, they shall be sure to be called up to work (and good reason) but when do they call them up to prayer? when do they urge them to consider or converse upon the things that concern their everlasting life. The Lord's own day, which is appointed to be set apart for matters of this nature, is wasted in idleness or worldly talk. Come at any time into their company and you may talk enough, and too much of news, or other mens matters, of their worldly business, sports and pleasures, but about God and their salvation they have so little to say, and that so heartlesly and on the by, as if they were things that belonged not to their care and duty, and no whit concerned them. Talk with them about the renovation of the soul, the nature of holiness, and the life to come, and you will find them almost as dumb as a fish. The most understand not matters of this nature, nor much desire or care to understand them. If one would teach them personally, they are too old to be catechised or to learn, though not too old to be ignorant of the matters they were made for and preserved for in the world. They are too wise to learn to be wise, and too good to be taught how to be good, though not too wise to follow the seducements of the devil and the world, nor too good to be the slaves of Satan and the despisers and enemies of goodness. If they do any thing which they call serving God, it is some cold and heartless use of words to make themselves believe that for all their sins they shall be saved; so that God will call that a serving their sins and abominations, which they call a serving of God. Some of them will confess that holiness is good, but they hope God will be merciful to them without it; and some do so hate it, that it is a displeasing, irksome thing to them to hear any serious discourse of holiness; and they detest and deride those as fanatical, troublesome precisians that diligently seek the one thing necessary: so that if the belief of the most may be judged by their practices, we may confidently say, that they do not practically believe that ever they should be brought to judgment, or that there is any heaven or hell to be expected; and that their confeſſion of the truth of the ſcriptures and the articles of the chriſtian faith are no proofs that they heartily take them to be true. Who can be ſuch a ſtranger to the world as not to ſee that this is the caſe of the greateſt part of men. And, which is worſt of all, they go on in this courſe againſt all that can be ſaid to them, and will give no impartial, conſiderate hearing to the truth, which would recover them to their wits, but live as if it would be a felicity to them in hell to think that they came thither by wilful reſolution, and in deſpite of the remedy."

This, ſinners, is a true repreſentation of your caſe, drawn by one that well knew it and lamented it. And what do you now think of it yourſelves? What do you think will be the conſequence of ſuch a courſe? Is it ſafe to perſiſt in it? or ſhall I be ſo happy as to bring you to a ſtand? Will you ſtill go on, troubling yourſelves with many things? or will you reſolve for the future to mind the one thing needful above all? I beſeech you to come to ſome reſolution. Time is on the wing, and does not allow you to heſitate in ſo plain and important an affair. Do you need any farther excitements? Then I ſhall try the force of one conſideration more contained in my text, and that is Neceſſity.

Remember neceſſity, the moſt preſſing, abſolute neceſſity, enforces this care upon you. One thing is needful, abſolutely needful, and needful above all other things. This, one would think, is ſuch an argument as cannot but prevail. What exploits has neceſſity performed in the world! What arts has it diſcovered as the mother of invention! what labours, what fatigues, what ſufferings has it undergone! What dangers has it encountered! What difficulties has it overcome? Neceſſity is a plea which you think will warrant you to do any thing and excuſe any thing. Reaſoning againſt neceſſity is but reaſoning againſt a hurricane; it bears all before it. To obtain the neceſſaries of life, as they are called, how much will men do and ſuffer! Nay, with what hardſhips and perils will they not conflict for things that they imagine neceſſary, not to their life but to their eaſe, their honour, or pleaſure! But what is this neceſſity when compared to that which I am now urging upon you? In compariſon of this, the moſt neceſſary of thoſe things are but ſuperfluities; for if your eaſe, or honour, or pleaſure, or even your life in this world be not abſolutely neceſſary, as they cannot be to the heirs of immortality, then certainly thoſe things which you imagine neceſſary to your eaſe, your honour, your pleaſure, or mortal life, are ſtill leſs neceſſary. But O! to eſcape everlaſting miſery, and to ſecure everlaſting ſalvation, this is the grand neceſſity! This will appear neceſſary in every point of your immortal duration; neceſfary when you have done with this world for ever, and muſt leave all its cares, enjoyments, and purſuits behind you. And ſhall not this grand neceſſity prevail upon you to work out your ſalvation, and make that your great buſineſs, when a far leſs neceſſity, a neceſſity that will laſt but a few years at moſt, ſets you and the world around you upon ſuch hard labours and eager purſuits for periſhing vanities? All the neceſſity in the world is nothing in compariſon of that which lies upon you to work out your ſalvation; and ſhall this have no weight? If you do not labour or contrive for *the bread that periſheth*, you muſt beg or ſtarve? but if you will not labour for the bread that endureth unto everlaſting life, you muſt burn in hell for ever. You muſt lie in priſon if your debts with men be not paid; but, O! what is it to the priſon of hell, where you muſt be confined for ever if your debts to the juſtice of God be not remitted, and you do not obtain an intereſt in the righteouſneſs of Chriſt, which alone can make ſatisfaction for them! You muſt ſuffer hunger and nakedneſs unleſs you take care to provide food and raiment; but you muſt ſuffer eternal baniſhment from God and all the joys of his preſence if you do not labour to ſecure the one thing needful. Without the riches of this world you may be rich in faith and heirs of the heavenly inheritance. Without earthly pleaſures you may have joy unſpeakable, and full of glory in the love of God, and the expectation of the kingdom reſerved in heaven for you. Without health of body you may have happineſs of ſpirit; and even without this mortal life you may enjoy eternal life. Without the things of the world you may live in want for a little while, but then you will ſoon be upon an equality with the greateſt princes. But without this one thing needful you are undone, abſolutely undone. Though you were as rich as Crœſus, you *are wretched, and miſerable, and poor, and blind, and naked.* Your very being becomes a curſe to you. It is your curſe that you are a man, a reaſonable creature. It had been infinitely better for you if you had been a toad or a ſnake, and ſo incapable of ſin and of immortality, and conſequently of puniſhment. O then let this grand neceſſity prevail with you!

I know you have other wants, which you ſhould moderately labour to provide for, but O how ſmall and of how ſhort continuance! If life and all ſhould be loſt, you may more than find all in heaven. But if you miſs at this one thing, all the world cannot make up the loſs.

Therefore, to conclude with the awakening and reſiſtleſs words of the author I before quoted, "Awake, you ſluggiſh, careleſs ſouls! your houſe over your head is in a flame! the hand of God is lifted up! If you love yourſelves, prevent the ſtroke. Vengeance is at your backs, the wrath of God purſues your ſin, and wo to you if he find it upon you when he overtaketh you. Away with it fpeedily! up and begone; return to God! make Chrift and mercy your friends in time, if you love your lives! the Judge is coming! for all that you have heard of it fo long, yet ftill you believe it not. You fhall fhortly fee the majefty of his appearance and the dreadful glory of his face; and yet do you not begin to look about you, and make ready for fuch a day? Yea, before that day, your feparated fouls fhall begin to reap as you have fowed here. Though now the partition that ftands between you and the world to come do keep unbelievers ftrangers to the things that moft concern them, yet death will quickly find a portal to let you in: and then, finners, you will find fuch doings there as you little thought of, or did not fenfibly regard upon earth.—Before your friends will have time enough to wrap up your pale corps in your winding-fheet, you will fee and feel that which will tell you to the quick, that one thing was neceffary. If you die without this one thing neceffary, before your friends can have finifhed your funerals, your fouls will have taken up their places among devils in endlefs torments and defpair, and all the wealth, and honour, and pleafure that the world afforded you will not eafe you. This is fad, but it is true, firs; for God hath fpoken it. Up therefore and beftir you for the life of your fouls. Neceffity will awake even the fluggard. Neceffity, we fay, will break through ftone walls. The proudeft will ftoop to neceffity: the moft flothful will beftir themfelves in neceffity: the moft carelefs will be induftrious in neceffity: neceffity will make men do any thing that is poffible to be done. And is not neceffity, the higheft neceffity, your own neceffity, able to make you caft away your fins, and take up an holy and heavenly life? O poor fouls! is there a greater neceffity of your fin than of your falvation, and of pleafing your flefh for a little time than of pleafing the Lord and efcaping everlafting mifery?" O that you would confider what I fay! and the Lord give you underftanding in all things Amen.

SERMON XXII.

Saints saved with difficulty, and the certain perdition of sinners.

1 Pet. iv. 18. *And if the righteous scarcely be saved, where shall the ungodly and the sinner appear.*

THIS text may sound in your ears like a message from the dead; for it is at the request of our deceased friend * that I now insist upon it. He knew so much from the trials he made in life, that if he should be saved at all, it would be with great difficulty, and if he should escape destruction at all, it would be a very narrow escape; and he also knew so much of this stupid, careless world, that they stood in need of a solemn warning on this head; and therefore desired that his death should give occasion to a sermon on this alarming subject. But now the unknown wonders of the invisible world lie open to his eyes; and now also he can take a full review of his passage through this mortal life; now he sees the many unsuspected dangers he narrowly escaped, and the many fiery darts of the devil which the shield of faith repelled; now, like a ship arrived in port, he reviews the rocks and shoals he passed through, many of which lay under water and out of sight; and therefore now he is more fully acquainted with the difficulty of salvation than ever. And should he now rise and make his appearance in this assembly in the solemn and dread attire of an inhabitant of the world of spirits, and again direct me to a more proper subject, methinks he would still stand to his choice, and propose it to your serious thoughts, that *if the righteous scarcely be saved, where shall the ungodly and the sinner appear?*

The apostle's principal design in the context seems to be to prepare the Christians for those sufferings which he saw coming upon them, on account of their religion. *Beloved,* says he, *think it not strange concerning the fiery trial which is to try you, as though some strange thing happened unto you,* verse 12. *but rejoice inasmuch as ye are partakers of Christ's sufferings*: it is no strange thing that you should suffer on account of your religion in such a

---

* The person was Mr. James Hooper; and the Sermon is dated August 21, 1756.

Serm. 22. *Saints saved with Difficulty, &c*

wicked world as this, for Christ the founder of your religion met with the same treatment; and it is enough that the servant be as his master, ver. 13. only he advises them, that if they must suffer, that they did not suffer as malefactors, but only for the name of Christ, ver. 14, 15. *But*, says he, *if any man suffer as a Christian, let him not be ashamed*, ver. 16. *for the time is come that judgment must begin at the house of God*. He seems to have a particular view to the cruel persecution that a little after this was raised against the christians by the tyrant Nero, and more directly to that which was raised against them every where by the seditious Jews, who were the most inveterate enemies of christianity. The dreadful destruction of Jerusalem, which was plainly foretold by Christ in the hearing of St. Peter, was now at hand. And from the sufferings which christians, the favourites of heaven, endured, he infers how much more dreadful the vengeance would be which should fall upon their enemies the infidel Jews. If judgment begin at the house of God, his church, what shall be the doom of the camp of rebels? If it begin at us christians who obey the gospel, what shall be the end of them that obey it not? Alas! what shall become of them? *Them that obey not the gospel of God*, is a description of the unbelieving Jews, to whom it was peculiarly applicable; and the apostle may have a primary reference to the dreadful destruction of their city and nation which was much more severe than all the sufferings the persecuted christians had then endured. But I see no reason for confining the apostle's view entirely to this temporal destruction of the Jews: he seems to refer farther to that still more terrible destruction that awaits all that obey not the gospel in the eternal world; that is to say, if the children are so severely chastised in this world, what shall become of rebels in the world to come, the proper state of retribution? How much more tremendous must be their fate!

In the text he carries on the same reflection. *If the righteous scarcely be saved, where shall the ungodly and the sinner appear?* The righteous is the common character of all good men or true christians; and the ungodly and sinner are characters which may include the wicked of all nations and ages. Now, says he, " if the righteous be but scarcely saved, saved with great difficulty, just saved, and no more, where shall idolaters and vicious sinners appear, whose characters are so opposite?"

The abrupt and pungent form of expression is very emphatical. *Where shall the ungodly and the sinner appear!* I need not tell you, your own reason will inform you: I appeal to yourselves for an answer, for you are all capable of determining upon so plain a case. *Where shall the ungodly and the sinner appear?* Alas! it strikes me dumb with horror to think of it: it is so shocking and terrible that

I cannot bear to describe it. Now they are gay, merry, and rich; but when I look a little forward, I see them appear in very different circumstances, and the horror of the prospect is hardly supportable."

St. Peter here supposes that there is something in the condition and character of a righteous man that renders his salvation comparatively easy; something from whence we might expect that he will certainly be saved, and that without much difficulty: and, on the other hand, that there is something in the opposite character and condition of the ungodly and the sinner, that gives us reason to conclude that there is no probability at all of their salvation while they continue such. But he asserts that even the righteous, whose salvation seems so likely and comparatively easy, is not saved without great difficulty; he is just saved, and that is all: what then shall we conclude of the ungodly and the sinner, whose character gives no ground for favourable expectations at all? If our hopes are but just accomplished, with regard to the most promising, what shall become of those whose case is evidently hopeless? Alas! where shall they appear?

The method in which I intend to prosecute our subject is this:

I. I shall point out the principal difficulties, which even the righteous meet with in the way to salvation.

II. I shall mention those things in the condition and character of the righteous, which render his salvation so promising and seemingly easy, and then show you that, if with all these favourable and hopeful circumstances he is not saved but with great difficulty and danger, those who are of an opposite character, and whose condition is so evidently and apparently desperate, cannot be saved at all.

I. I am to point out the principal difficulties which even the righteous meet with in the way to salvation.

Here I would premise, that such who have become truly religious, and persevered in the way of holiness and virtue to the last, will meet with no difficulty at all to be admitted into the kingdom of heaven. The difficulty does not lie here, for the same apostle Peter assures us, that if we give all diligence *to make our calling and election sure,* we shall never fall; but *so an entrance shall be administered unto us abundantly into the everlasting kingdom of our Lord and Saviour Jesus Christ.* 2 Peter, i. 10, 11. But the difficulty lies in this, that, all things considered, it is a very difficult thing to obtain, and persevere in real religion in the present corrupt state of things, where we meet with so many temptations and such powerful opposition. Or, in other words, it is difficult in such a world as this to prepare for salvation; and this renders it difficult to be saved, because we cannot be saved without preparation.

It must also be observed, that a religious life is attended with the most pure and solid pleasures even in this world; and they who choose it act the wifest part with respect to the present state: they are really the happiest people upon our globe. Yet, were it otherwise, the blessed consequences of a religious life in the eternal world would make amends for all, and recommend such a course, notwithstanding the greatest difficulties and the severest sufferings that might attend it.

But notwithstanding this concession, the christian course is full of hardships, oppositions, trials, and discouragements. This we may learn from the metaphorical representations of it in the sacred writings, which strongly imply that it is attended with difficulties which require the utmost exertion of all our power to surmount. It is called a warfare, 1 Tim. i. 18. fighting, 2 Tim. iv. 7. The graces of the christian, and the means of begetting and cherishing them, are called weapons of war: there is the shield of faith; the hope of salvation, which is the helmet; the sword of the spirit, which is the word of God. 2 Cor. x. 4. Eph. vi. 13—17. The end of the Christian's course is victory after conflict. Rev. ii. 7. And christians are soldiers; and as such must endure hardships. 2 Tim. ii. 3. Now a military life you know is a scene of labour, hardships, and dangers; and therefore so is the christian life, which is compared to it in these respects. It is compared to a race, Heb. xii. 1, 2. to wrestling and the other vigorous exercises of the Olympic games, Eph. vi. 12. Luke xiii. 24. to walking in a narrow way, Matt. vii. 14. and entering at the strait gate. Luke xiii. 24. This, my brethren, and this only, is the way to salvation. And is this the way in which you are walking? Or is it the smooth, easy, downward road to destruction? You may slide along that without exertion or difficulty, like a dead fish swimming with the stream; but, O! look before you, and see whither it leads!

The enemies that oppose our religious progress are the devil, the world, and the flesh. These form a powerful alliance against our salvation, and leave no artifice untried to obstruct it.

The things of the world, though good in themselves, are temptations to such depraved hearts as ours. Riches, honours, and pleasure spread their charms, and tempt us to the pursuit of flying shadows, to the neglect of the one thing needful. These engross the thoughts, and concern the affections and labours of multitudes. They engage with such eagerness in an excessive hurry of business and anxious care, or so debauch and stupify themselves with sensual pleasures, that the voice of God is not heard, the clamours of conscience are drowned, the state of their souls is not enquired into, the interest of eternity are forgotten, the eternal God, the joys of heaven, and the pains of hell are cast out of mind, and disregarded; and they care not for any or all of these important realities, if they can but gratify the lust of avarice, ambition, and sensuality. And are such likely to perform the arduous work of salvation? No;

they do not so much as seriously attempt it. Now these things which are fatal to multitudes throw great difficulties in the way even of the righteous man. He finds it hard to keep his mind intent upon his great concern in the midst of such labours and cares as he is obliged to engage in; and frequently he feels his heart estranged from God and ensnared into the ways of sin, his devotion cooled, and his whole soul disordered by these allurements. In short, he finds it one of the hardest things in the world to maintain an heavenly mind in such an earthly region, a spiritual temper among so many carnal objects.

The men of this world also increase his difficulties. Their vain, trifling, or wicked conversation, their ensnaring examples, their persuasions, false reasonings, reproaches, menaces, and all their arts of flattery and terror, have sometimes a very sensible effect upon him. These would draw him into some guilty compliances, damp his courage, and tempt him to apostatize, were he not always upon his guard; and sometimes in an inadvertent hour he feels their fatal influence upon him. As for the generality, they yield themselves up to these temptations, and make little or no resistance; and thus are carried down the stream into the infernal pit. Alas! how many ruin themselves through a base, unmanly complaisance, and a servile conformity to the mode! Believe it, Sirs, to be fashionably religious and no more, is to be really irreligious in the sight of God. The way of the multitude may seem easy, pleasant and sociable; but, alas! my brethren, see where it ends! it leadeth down into destruction. Matt. vii. 14.

But, in the next place, the greatest difficulty in our way arises from the corruption and wickedness of our own hearts. This is an enemy within; and it is this that betrays us into the hands of our enemies without. When we turn our eyes to this quarter, what vast difficulties rise in our way! difficulties which are impossibilities to us, unless the almighty power enables us to surmount them. Such are a blind mind, ignorant of divine things, or that can speculate only upon them, but does not see their reality and dread importance; a mind empty of God and full of the lumber and vanities of this world. Such are a hard heart, insensible of sin, insensible of the glory of God, and the beauties of holiness, and the infinite moment of eternal things. Such are an heart disaffected to God and his service, bent upon sin, and impatient of restraint. Such are wild, unruly passions thrown into a ferment by every trifle, raised by vanities, erroneous in the choice of objects, irregular in their motions, and extravagant in the degree of attachment. Such difficulties are strong ungovernable lusts and appetites in animal nature, eager for gratification, and turbulent under restraint. And how strangely does this inward corruption indispose men for religion! Hence their ignorance, their security, carelessness, presumptuous hopes, and impenitence. Hence their unwillingness to admit conviction, their resistance to the holy spirit and their own consciences, their love of ease and impatience of sorrow for sin, and of solicitude about their eternal state. Hence their contempt of the gospel, their disregard to all religious instructions, their neglect of the means of grace, and the ordinances of Christ, or their careless, formal, lukewarm attendance upon them. Hence their earthly-mindedness, their sensuality, and excessive love of animal pleasures. Hence it is so difficult to awaken them to a just sense of their spiritual condition, and to suitable earnestness in their religious endeavours: and hence their fickleness and inconstancy, their relapses and backslidings, when they have been a little alarmed. Hence it is so difficult to bring their religious impressions to a right issue, and to lead them to Jesus Christ as the only Saviour. In short, hence it is that so many thousands perish amidst the means of salvation. These difficulties prove eventually insuperable to the generality; and they never surmount them. But even the righteous, who is daily conquering them by the aid of divine grace, and will at last be more than a conqueror, he still finds many hinderances and discouragements from this quarter. The remains of these innate corruptions still cleave to him in the present state, and these render his progress heavenward so slow and heavy. These render his life a constant warfare, and he is obliged to fight his way through. These frequently check the aspirations of his soul to God, cool his devotion, damp his courage, ensnare his thoughts and affections to things below, and expose him to the successful attacks of temptation. Alas! it is his innate corruption that involves him in darkness and jealousies, in tears and terrors, after hours of spiritual light, joy and confidence. It is this that banishes him from the comfortable presence of his God, and causes him to go mourning without the light of his countenance. Were it not for this, he would glide along through life easy and unmolested; he would find the ways of religion to be ways of pleasantness, and all her paths peace. In short, it is this that lies upon his heart as the heaviest burden, and renders his course so rugged and dangerous. And such of you as do not know this by experience, know nothing at all of true experimental christianity.

Finally, the devil and his angels are active, powerful and artful enemies to our salvation: their agency is often unperceived, but it is insinuating, unsuspected, and therefore the more dangerous and successful. These malignant spirits present ensnaring images to the imagination, and no doubt blow the flame of passion and appetite. They labour to banish serious thoughts from the mind, and entertain it with trifles. They give force to the attacks of temptation from the world, and raise and foment insurrections of sin within. And if they cannot hinder the righteous man from entering upon a religious course, or divert him from it, they will at least render it as difficult, laborious, and uncomfortable to him as possible.

See, my brethren, see the way in which you must walk if you would enter into the kingdom of heaven. In this rugged road they have all walked who are now safe arrived at their journey's end, the land of rest. They were saved, but it was with great difficulty: they escaped the fatal rocks and shoals, but it was a very narrow escape: and methinks it is with a kind of pleasing horror they now review the numerous dangers through which they passed, many of which they did not perhaps suspect till they were over.* And is this the way in which you are walking? Is your religion a course of watchfulness, labour, conflict, and vigorous exertion? Are you indeed in earnest in it above all things in this world? Or are not many of you lukewarm Laodiceans and indifferent Gallios about these things? If your religion (if it may be so called) is a course of security, carelessness, sloth, and formality. Alas! if all the vigour and exertion of the righteous man be but just sufficient for his salvation, where, O where shall you appear? Which leads me,

II. To mention those things in the character and condition of the righteous, which render his salvation so promising and seemingly easy, and then shew that if with all those hopeful circumstances he shall not be saved but with great difficulty, that they whose character is directly opposite, and has nothing encouraging in it, cannot possibly be saved at all. And this head I shall cast into such a form as to exemplify the text.

1. If those that abstain from immorality and vice be but scarcely saved, where shall the vicious, profligate sinner appear?

It is the habitual character of a righteous man to be temperate and sober, chaste, just, and charitable; to revere the name of God, and every thing sacred, and religiously observe the holy hours devoted to the service of God. This is always an essential part of his character, though not the whole of it. Now such a man looks promising; he evidently appears so far prepared for the heavenly state, because he is so far conformed to the law of God, and free from those enormities which are never found in the region of happiness. And if such shall scarcely be saved, where shall those

---

    * There, on a green and flow'ry mount,
      Their weary souls now sit;
      And with transporting joys recount
      The labours of their feet.
      Eternal glories to the King
      That brought them safely thro';
      Their lips shall never cease to sing,
      And endless praise renew.

Serm. 22.   *the certain Perdition of Sinners.*   389

of the oppofite character appear? Where fhall the brute of a drunkard, the audacious fwearer, the fcoffer at religion, the unclean, lecherous wretch, the liar, the defrauder, the thief, the extortioner, the Sabbath-breaker, the reveller, where fhall thefe appear? Are thefe likely to ſtand in the congregation of the righteous, or to appear in the prefence of God with joy? Is there the leaſt likelihood that fuch fhall be faved? If you will regard the authority of an infpired apoſtle in the cafe, I can direct you to thofe places where you may find his exprefs determination. 1 Cor. vi. 9, 10. *Know ye not that the unrighteous fhall not inherit the kingdom of God? Be not deceived; neither fornicators, nor adulterers, nor abufers of themfelves with mankind, nor thieves, nor covetous, nor drunkards, nor revilers, nor extortioners, fhall inherit the kingdom of God.* So Gal. v. 19—21. *The works of the flefh are manifeft, which are thefe, adultery, fornication, uncleannefs, lafcivioufnefs, hatred, variance, emulations, wrath, ſtrife, herefies, feditions, envyings, revellings, and fuch like; of the which I tell you before;* that is, I honeſtly forewarn you, as I have alfo told you in time paſt, that they who do fuch things, fhall not inherit the kingdom of God. Rev. xxi. 8. *The fearful* (that is, the cowardly in the caufe of religion) *the unbelieving and the abominable, and murderers, and whoremongers, and all liars, fhall have their part in the lake that burneth with fire and brimſtone.* You fee, my brethren, the declarations of the fcripture are exprefs enough and repeated on this point. And are there not fome of you here who indulge yourfelves in one or other of thefe vices, and yet hope to be faved in that courfe? that is, you hope your Bible and your religion too are falfe; for it is only on that fuppofition that your hope of falvation can be accomplifhed. Alas! will you venture your eternal All upon the truth of fuch a blafphemous fuppofition as this? But,

2. If thofe that confcientioufly perform the duties of religion be fcarcely faved, where fhall the neglecters of them appear?

The righteous are characterized as perfons that honeſtly endeavour to perform all the duties they owe to God. They devoutly read and hear his word, and make divine things their ſtudy; they are no ſtrangers to the throne of grace; they live a life of prayer in their retirements, and in a focial capacity. They make their families little churches, in which divine worſhip is folemnly performed. Let others do as they will; as for them and their houfes, like Joſhua, *they will ſerve the Lord.* Joſh. xxiv. 15. They gratefully commemorate the fufferings of Chriſt, and give themfelves up to him at his table; and ferioufly improve all the ordinances of the gofpel. In ſhort, like Zecharias and Elizabeth, they *walk in all the ſtatutes and ordinances of God blamelefs.* Luke i. 6. This is their prevailing habitual character. And there is fomething in this character that gives reafon to prefume they will be faved; for they now have a relish for the service of God, in which the happiness of heaven consists: they are training up in the humble forms of devotion in the church below, for the more exalted employments of the church triumphant on high. Now if persons of this character are but *scarcely saved, where shall the ungodly appear,* who persist in the wilful neglect of these known duties of religion? Can they be saved, who do not so much as use the means of salvation? Can those that do not study their Bible, the only directory to eternal life, expect to find the way thither! Can prayerless souls receive answers to prayer? Will all the bliss of heaven be thrown away upon such as do not think it worth their while importunately to ask it? Are they likely to be admitted into the general assembly and church of the first-born in heaven, who do not endeavour to make their families little circles of religion here upon earth? In a word, are they likely to join for ever in the devotions of the heavenly state, who do not accustom themselves to these sacred exercises in this preparatory state? Will you venture your souls upon it that you shall be saved, notwithstanding these improbabilities, or rather impossibilities? Alas! are they any of you that have no better hopes of heaven than these? Where then will you appear?

3. If they that are more than externally moral and religious in their conduct; that have been born again, created in Christ Jesus to good works, as every man that is truly righteous has been: if such, I say, be but scarcely saved, where shall they appear who rest in their mere outward morality, their proud self-righteous virtue, and their religious formalities, and have never been made new creatures, never had the inward principle of action changed by the power of God, and the inbred disorders of the heart rectified? Where shall they appear who have nothing but a self-sprung religion, the genuine offspring of degenerate nature, and never had a supernatural principle of grace implanted in their souls? Has that solemn asseveration of the Amen, the faithful and true witness, lost all its force, and become falsehood in our age and country? *Verily, verily I say unto thee, except a man be born again, he cannot see the kingdom of heaven.* John iii. 3. Is there no weight in such apostolic declarations as these? *If any man be in Christ, he is a new creature; old things are passed away, and behold all things are become new:* and all these new things are of God. 2 Cor. v. 17. *Neither circumcision availeth any thing, nor uncircumcision,* Gal. vi. 15. that is to say, a conformity to the rituals of the Jewish or Christian religion availeth nothing, but the new creature. Can men flatter themselves they shall be saved by the Christian religion, in opposition to these plain, strong and repeated declarations of the Christian revelation? And yet are there not many here who are entirely ignorant of this renovation of the temper of their mind, of this inward heaven-born religion?

4. If they that are striving to enter in at the strait gate, and pressing into the kingdom of heaven, do but just obtain admission; if they who forget the things that are behind, and reach after these that are before them, and press with all their might towards the goal, do scarcely obtain the prize, what shall become of those lukewarm, careless, formal, presumptuous professors of christianity who are so numerous among us? Where shall they appear who have *but a form of godliness without the power*, 2 Tim. iii. 5. and have no spiritual life in their religion, *but only a name to live?* Rev. iii. 1. If those whose hearts are habitually solicitous about their eternal state, who labour in earnest for the immortal bread, who pray with unutterable groans, Rom. viii. 26. who in short make the care of their souls the principal business of their life, and in some measure proportion their industry and earnestness to the importance and difficulty of the work; if such are but scarcely saved with all their labour and pains, where shall they appear who are at ease in Zion, Amos vi. 1. whose religion is but a mere indifferency, a thing by the by with them? If we cannot enter into the kingdom of heaven unless our righteousness exceed that of the Scribes and the Pharisees, Matt. v. 20. where shall they appear whose righteousness is far short of theirs? And are there not many such in this assembly? Alas! my brethren, where do you expect to appear?

5. If they that have believed in Jesus Christ, which is the grand condition of salvation, be but scarcely saved, where shall the unbeliever appear?

Faith in Christ is an essential ingredient in the character of a righteous man: and faith cannot be implanted in our hearts till we have been made deeply sensible of our sins, of our condemnation by the law of God, and our utter inability to procure pardon and salvation by the merit of our repentance, reformation, or any thing we can do. And when we are reduced to this extremity, then we shall listen with eager ears to the proposal of a Saviour. And when we see his glory and sufficiency, and cast our guilty souls upon him, when we submit to his commands, depend entirely upon his atonement, and give up ourselves to God through him, then we believe. Now if they who thus believe, to whom salvation is so often ensured, be not saved but with great difficulty, where shall those appear who never have experienced those exercises which are the antecedents or constituents of saving faith? who have never seen their own guilt and helplessness in an affecting light; who have never seen the glory of God in the face of Jesus Christ; who have never submitted to him as their Prophet, Priest, and King, and who do not live in the flesh by faith in the Son of God? Alas! are they likely to be saved who are destitute of the grand pre-requisite of salvation? And yet is not this the

E e e

melancholy case of some of you? You may not be avowed unbelievers; you may believe there is one God, and that Jesus is the true Messiah: in this you do well, but still it is no mighty attainment, for the devils also believe and tremble, and you may have this speculative faith, and yet be wholly destitute of the faith of the operation of God, the precious faith of God's elect; that faith which purifies the heart, produces good works, and unites the soul to Jesus Christ. Certainly the having or not having of such a faith must make a great difference in a man's character, and must be followed by a proportionally different doom. And if they that have it be but scarcely saved, I appeal to yourselves, can they be saved at all who have it not?

6. If true penitents be scarcely saved, where shall the impenitent appear?

It is the character of the righteous that he is deeply affected with sorrow for his sins in heart and practice; that he hates them without exception with an implacable enmity; that he strives against them, and would resist them even unto blood; that his repentance is attended with reformation, and that he forsakes those things for the commission of which his heart is broken with sorrows. Now repentance appears evidently to the common reason of mankind an hopeful preparative for acceptance with God and eternal happiness: and therefore if they who repent are saved with great difficulty, where shall they appear who persist impenitent in sin? Where shall they appear who have hard unbroken hearts in their breasts, who are insensible of the evil of sin, who indulge themselves in it, and cannot be persuaded to forsake it? Can you be at any loss to know the doom of such, after Christ has told us with his own lips, which never pronounced an harsh censure, *Except ye repent, ye shall all likewise perish.* Luke xiii. 3, 5. And are there not some of this character in this assembly? Alas! there is not the least likelihood, or even possibility of your salvation in such a condition.

7. The righteous man has the love of God shed abroad in his heart, and it produces the usual sentiments and conduct of love towards him. God is dearer to him than all other things in heaven and earth; the *strength of his heart, and* his *portion for ever.* Psalm lxxiii. 25, 26. His affectionate thoughts fix upon him, Psalm lxiii. 6. he rejoices in the light of his countenance, Psalm iv. 7. and longs and languishes for him in his absence. Psalm xlii. 1, 2. and lxiii. 1. Cant. iii. 1. His love is a powerful principle of willing obedience, and carries him to keep his commandments. 1 John v. 3. He delights in the law and service of God, and in communion with him in his ordinances. Now such a principle of love is a very hopeful preparative for heaven, the region of love, and for the enjoyment of God. Such an one would take pleasure in

him and in his fervice, and therefore he certainly fhall never be excluded. But if even fuch are but fcarcely faved, where fhall they appear who are deftitute of the love of God? There are few indeed but pretend to be lovers of God, but their love has not the infeparable properties of that facred paffion. Their pretence to it is an abfurdity, and if put into language, would be fuch jargon as this, ' Lord, I love thee above all things, though I hardly ever affectionately think of thee ; I love thee above all, though I am not careful to pleafe thee ; I love thee above all, though my conduct towards thee is quite the reverfe of what it is towards one I love.' Will fuch an inconfiftency as this pafs for genuine fupreme love to God, when it will not pafs for common friendfhip among men? No, fuch have not the leaft fpark of that heavenly fire in their breafts, for their carnal mind is enmity againft God. And are thefe likely to be faved? likely to be admitted into the region of love, where there is not one cold or difloyal heart? likely to be happy in the prefence and fervice of that God to whom they are difaffected? Alas! no. Where then fhall they appear? O! in what forlorn, remote region of eternal exile from the bleffed God!

I fhall now conclude with a few reflections. 1. You may hence fee the work of falvation is not that eafy, trifling thing which many take it to be. They feem mighty cautious of laying out too much pains upon it ; and they cannot bear that people fhould make fuch ado, and keep fuch a ftir and noife about it*. For their part, they hope to go to heaven as well as the beft of them, without all this precifenefs : and upon thefe principles they act. They think they can never be too much in earneft, or too laborious in the purfuit of earthly things ; but religion is a matter by the by with them ; only the bufinefs of an hour once a week. But have thefe learned their religion from Chrift the founder of it, or from his apoftles, whom he appointed teachers of it? No,'they have formed fome eafy fyftem from their own imaginations fuited to their depraved tafte, indulgent to their floth and carnality, and favourable to their lufts ; and this they call chriftianity. But you have feen this is not the religion of the Bible : this is not the way to life laid out by God, but it is the fmooth downward road to deftruction. Therefore,

2. Examine yourfelves to which clafs you belong, whether to that of the righteous, who fhall be faved, though with difficulty, or to that of the ungodly and the finner, who muft appear in a very different fituation. To determine this important inquiry, recollect the fundry parts of the righteous man's character which I have briefly defcribed, and fee whether they belong to you. Do you carefully abftain from vice and immorality ? Do you make

* I here affect this low ftile on purpofe, to reprefent more exactly the fentiments of fuch carelefs finners in their own ufual language.

conscience of every duty of religion? Have you ever been born again of God, and made more than externally religious? Are you sensible of the difficulties in your way from Satan, the world, and the flesh? And do you exert yourselves as in a field of battle or in a race? Do you work out your salvation with fear and trembling, and press into the kingdom of God? Are you true believers, penitents, and lovers of God? Are these or the contrary the constituents of your habitual character? I pray you make an impartial trial, for much depends upon it.

3. If this be your habitual character, be of good cheer for you shall be saved, though with difficulty. Be not discouraged when you fall into fiery trials, for they are no strange things in the present state. All that have walked in the same narrow road before you have met with them, but now they are safe arrived in their eternal home. Let your dependence be upon the aids of divine grace to bear you through, and you will overcome at last. But,

4. If your character be that of the ungodly and the sinner, pause and think, where shall you appear at last? When, like our deceased friend, you leave this mortal state, and launch into regions unknown, where will you then appear? Must it not be in the region of sin, which is your element now? in the society of the devils, whom you resemble in temper, and imitate in conduct? among the trembling criminals at the left hand of the Judge, where the ungodly and sinners shall all be crowded? If you continue such as you now are, have you any reason at all to hope for a more favourable doom?

I shall conclude with a reflection to exemplify the context in another view, and that is, "If judgment begin at the house of God, what shall be the end of them that obey not the gospel? If the righteous, the favourites of heaven, suffer so much in this world, what shall sinners, with whom God is angry every day, and who are vessels of wrath fitted for destruction, what shall they suffer in the eternal world, the proper place for rewards and punishments, and where an equitable Providence deals with every man according to his works? If the children are chastised with various calamities, and even die in common with the rest of mankind, what shall be the doom of enemies and rebels? If those meet with so many difficulties in the pursuit of salvation, what shall these suffer in enduring damnation? If the infernal powers are permitted to worry Christ's sheep, how will they rend and tear the wicked as their proper prey? O that you may in *this your day know the things that belong to your peace, before they are for ever hid from your eyes.* Luke xix. 42.

SERMON XXIII.

Indifference to Life urged, from its Shortness and Vanity*.

—⋄⋄⋄⋄⋄⋄—

1 COR. vii. 29, 30, 31. *But this, I say, brethren, that the time is short: it remaineth that both they that have wives be as though they had none; and they that weep, as though they wept not; and they that rejoice, as though they rejoiced not; and they that buy, as though they possessed not; and they that use this world, as not abusing it: for the fashion of this world passeth away.*

A CREATURE treading every moment upon the slippery brink of the grave, and ready every moment to shoot the gulph of eternity, and launch away to some unknown coast, ought to stand always in the posture of serious expectation; ought every day to be in his own mind taking leave of this world, breaking off the connections of his heart from it, and preparing for his last remove into that world in which he must reside, not for a few months or years as in this, but through a boundless everlasting duration. Such a situation requires habitual constant thoughtfulness, abstraction from the world, and serious preparation for death and eternity. But when we are called, as we frequently are, to perform the last sad offices to our friends and neighbours who have taken their flight a little before us; when the solemn pomp and horrors of death strike our senses, then certainly it becomes us to be unusually thoughtful and serious. Dying beds, the last struggles and groans of dissolving nature, pale, cold, ghastly corpses,

"The knell, the shroud, the mattock, and the grave;
"The deep damp vault, the darkness, and the worm;"

these are very alarming monitors of our own mortality: these outpreach the loudest preacher; and they must be deep and senseless rocks, and not men, who do not hear and feel their voice. Among the numberless instances of the divine skill in bringing good out of evil this is one, that past generations have sickened and died to warn their successors. One here and there also is singled

* This sermon is dated, at Mr. Thompson's funeral, February 16, 1759.

out of our neighbourhood or families, and made an example, a *memento mori*, to us that survive, to rouse us out of our stupid sleep, to give us the signal of the approach of the last enemy, Death, to constrain us to let go our eager grasp of this vain world, and set us upon looking out and preparing for another. And may I hope my hearers are come here to-day determined to make this improvement of this melancholy occasion, and to gain this great advantage from our loss? To this I call you as with a voice from the grave; and therefore *he that hath ears let him hear*.

One great reason of mens excessive attachment to the present state, and their stupid neglect to the concerns of eternity, is their forming too high an estimate of the affairs of time in comparison with those of eternity. While the important realities of the eternal world are out of view, unthought of, and disregarded, as, alas! they generally are by the most of mankind, what mighty things in their esteem are the relations, the joys and sorrows, the possessions and bereavements, the acquisitions and pursuits of this life? What airs of importance do they put on in their view? How do they engross their anxious thoughts and cares, and exhaust their strength and spirits? To be happy, to be rich, to be great and honourable, to enjoy your fill of pleasure in this world, is not this a great matter, the main interest with many of you? is not this the object of your ambition, your eager desire and laborious pursuit? But to consume away your life in sickness and pain, in poverty and disgrace, in abortive schemes and disappointed pursuits, what a serious calamity, what an huge affliction is this in your esteem? What is there in the compass of the universe that you are so much afraid of, and so cautiously shunning? Whether large profits or losses in trade be not a mighty matter, ask the busy, anxious merchant. Whether poverty be not a most miserable state, ask the poor that feel it, and the rich that fear it. Whether riches be not a very important happiness, ask the possessors; or rather ask the restless pursuers of them, who expect still greater happiness from them than those that are taught by experience can flatter themselves with. Whether the pleasures of the conjugal state are not great and delicate, consult the few happy pairs here and there who enjoy them. Whether the loss of an affectionate husband and a tender father be not a most afflictive bereavement, a torturing separation of heart from heart, or rather a tearing of one's heart in pieces, ask the mourning, weeping widow, and fatherless children, when hovering round his dying bed, or conducting his dear remains to the cold grave. In short, it is evident from a thousand instances, that the enjoyments, pursuits, and sorrows of this life are mighty matters! nay, are all in all in the esteem of the generality of mankind. These are the things they most deeply feel, the things about which they are chiefly concerned, and which are the objects of their strongest passions.

Serm. 23. *from its Shortness and Vanity.*

But this is a juſt eſtimate of things? Are the affairs of this world then indeed ſo intereſting and all important? Yes, if eternity be a dream, and heaven and hell but majeſtic chimeras or fairy lands; if we are always to live in this world, and had no concern with any thing beyond it; if the joys of earth were the higheſt we could hope for, or its miſeries the moſt terrible we could fear, then indeed we might take this world for our all, and regard its affairs as the moſt important that our nature is capable of. *But this I ſay, brethren* (and I pronounce it as the echo of an inſpired apoſtle's voice) this I ſay, *the time is ſhort;* the time of life in which we have any thing to do with theſe affairs is a ſhort contracted ſpan. Therefore *it remaineth,* that is, this is the inference we ſhould draw from the ſhortneſs of time, *they that have wives, be as though they had none; and they that weep, as though they wept not; and they that rejoice, as though they rejoiced not; and they that buy, as though they poſſeſſed not; and they that uſe this world, as not abuſing it, or uſing it to exceſs; for the faſhion of this world,* theſe tender relations, this weeping and rejoicing, this buying and poſſeſſing, and uſing this world, *paſſeth away.* The phantom will ſoon vaniſh, the ſhadow will ſoon fly off: and they that have wives or huſbands in this tranſitory life, will in reality be as though they had none; and they that weep now, as though they wept not: and they that now rejoice, as though they rejoiced not; and they that now buy, poſſeſs and uſe this world, as though they never had the leaſt property in it. This is the ſolemn mortifying doctrine I am now to inculcate upon you in the further illuſtration of the ſeveral parts of my text; a doctrine juſtly alarming to the lovers of this world, and the neglecters of that life which is to come.

When St. Paul pronounces any thing with an unuſual air of ſolemnity and authority; and after the formality of an introduction to gain attention, it muſt be a matter of uncommon weight, and worthy of the moſt ſerious regard. In this manner he introduces the funeral ſentiments in my text. *This I ſay brethren;* this I ſolemnly pronounce as the mouth of God: this I declare as a great truth but little regarded; and which therefore there is much need I ſhould repeatedly declare: this I ſay with all the authority of an apoſtle, a meſſenger from heaven: and I demand your ſerious attention to what I am going to ſay.

And what is it he is introducing with all this ſolemn formality? Why, it is an old, plain, familiar truth univerſally known and confeſſed, namely, That the time of our continuance in this world is ſhort. But why ſo much formality in introducing ſuch a common plain truth as this? Becauſe, however generally it be known and confeſſed, it is very rarely regarded; and it requires more than even the moſt ſolemn addreſs of an apoſtle to turn the attention of a thoughtleſs world to it. How many of you, my brethren, are convinced againſt your wills of this melancholy truth, and yet turn every way to avoid the mortifying thought, are always uneaſy when it forces itſelf upon your minds, and do not ſuffer it to have a proper influence upon your temper and practice, but live as if you believed the time of life were long, and even everlaſting? O! when will the happy hour come when you will think and act like thoſe that believe that common uncontroverted truth, that the time of life is ſhort? Then you would no longer think of delays, nor contrive artifices to put off the work of your ſalvation; then you could not bear the thought of ſuch negligent, or languid, feeble endeavours in a work that muſt be done, and that in ſo ſhort a time.

This, I ſay, my brethren, *the time is ſhort;* the time of life is abſolutely ſhort; a ſpan, an inch, a hair's breadth. How near the neighbourhood between the cradle and the grave! How ſhort the journey from infancy to old age, through all the intermediate ſtages! Let the few among you who bear the marks of old age upon you in grey hairs, wrinkles, weakneſs, and pains, look back upon your tireſome pilgrimage through life, and does it not appear to you, as though you commenced men but yeſterday? And how little a way can you trace it back till you are loſt in the forgotten unconſcious days of infancy, or in that eternal non-exiſtence in which you lay before your creation! But they are but a very few that drag on their lives through ſeventy or eighty years. Old men can hardly find contemporaries: a new race has ſtarted up, and they are become almoſt ſtrangers in their own neighbourhoods. By the beſt calculations that have been made, at leaſt one half of mankind die under ſeven years old. They are little particles of life, ſparks of being juſt kindled and then quenched, or rather diſmiſſed from their ſuffocating confinement in clay, that they may aſpire, blaze out, and mingle with their kindred flames in the eternal world, the proper region, the native element of ſpirits.

And how ſtrongly does the ſhortneſs of this life prove the certainty of another? Would it be worth while, would it be conſiſtent with the wiſdom and goodneſs of the Deity, to ſend ſo many infant millions of reaſonable creatures into this world, to live the low life of a vegetable or an animal for a few moments or days, or years, if there were no other world for theſe young immortals to remove to, in which their powers might open, enlarge, and ripen? Certainly men are not ſuch inſects of a day: certainly this is not th laſt ſtage of human nature: certainly there is an eternity; there is a heaven and a hell:—otherwiſe we might expoſtulate with our Maker, as David once did upon that ſuppoſition *Wherefore haſt thou made all men in vain?* Pſalm lxxxix. 47.

Serm. 23.   *from its Shortness and Vanity.*

In that awful eternity we must all be in a short time. Yes, my brethren, I may venture to prophecy that, in less than seventy or eighty years, the most, if not all this assembly, must be in some apartment of that strange untried world. The merry, unthinking, irreligious multitude in that doleful mansion which I must mention, grating as the sound is to their ears, and that is hell!* and the pious, penitent, believing few in the blissful seats of heaven. There we shall reside a long, long time indeed; or rather through a long, endless eternity. Which leads me to add,

That as the time of life is short absolutely in itself, so especially it is short comparatively; that is, in comparison with eternity. In this comparison, even the long life of Methusalah and the antediluvians shrink into a mere point, a nothing. Indeed no duration of time, however long, will bear the comparison. Millions of millions of years? as many years as the sand upon the sea shore! as many years as the particles of dust in this huge globe of earth; as many years as the particles of matter in the vaster heavenly bodies that roll above us, and even in the whole material universe, all these years do not bear so much proportion to eternity as a moment, a pulse, or the twinkling of an eye, to ten thousand ages! not so much as a hair's breadth to the distance from the spot where we stand to the farthest star, or the remotest corner of the creation. In short, they do not bear the least imaginable proportion at all; for all this length of years, though beyond the power of distinct enumeration to us, will as certainly come to an end as an hour or a moment; and when it comes to an end, it is entirely and irrecoverable past: but eternity (O the solemn tremendous sound!) eternity will never, never, never come to an end! eternity will never, never, never be past!

And is this eternity, this awful all-important eternity, entailed upon us? upon us the offspring of the dust! the creatures of yesterday! upon us who a little while ago were less than a gnat, less than a mote, were nothing! upon us who are every moment liable to the arrest of death, sinking into the grave, and mouldering into dust one after another in a thick succession! upon us whose thoughts, and cares, and pursuits, are so confined to time and earth, as if we had nothing to do with any thing beyond! O! is this immense inheritance unalienably ours! Yes, brethren, it is; reason and revelation prove our title beyond all dispute. It is an inheritance entailed upon us, whether we will or not; whether we have made it our interest it should be ours or not. To command our-

---

* Regions of sorrow! doleful shades! where Peace
And Rest can never dwell! Hope never comes,
That comes to all: but torture without end
Still urges, and a fiery deluge fed
With ever-burning sulphur unconsum'd   MILTON.

selves into nothing is as much above our power as to bring ourselves into being. Sin may make our souls miserable, but it cannot make them mortal. Sin may forfeit an happy eternity, and render our immortality a curse; so that it would be better for us if we never had been born: but sin cannot put an end to our being, as it can to our happiness, nor procure for us the shocking relief of rest in the hideous gulph of annihilation.

And is a little time, a few months or years, a great matter to us? to us who are heirs of an eternal duration? How insignificant is a moment in seventy or eighty years! but how much more insignificant is even the longest life upon earth, when compared with eternity! How trifling are all the concerns of time to those of immortality! What is it to us who are to live for ever, whether we live happy or miserable for an hour? whether we have wives, or whether we have none; whether we rejoice, or whether we weep; whether we buy, possess, and use this world, or whether we consume away our life in hunger, and nakedness, and the want of all things, it will be all one in a little, little time. Eternity will level all; and eternity is at the door.

And how shall we spend this eternal duration that is thus entailed upon us? Shall we sleep it away in a stupid insensibility or in a state of indifferency, neither happy nor miserable? No, no, my brethren; we must spend it in the heighth of happiness or in the depth of misery. The happiness and misery of the world to come will not consist in such childish toys as those that give us pleasure and pain in this infant state of our existence, but in the most substantial realities suitable to an immortal spirit, capable of vast improvements and arrived at its adult age. Now, as the apostle illustrates it, we are children, and we speak like children, we understand like children; but then we shall become men, and put away childish things. 1 Cor. xiii. 11. Then we shall be beyond receiving pleasure or pain from such trifles as excite them in this puerile state. This is not the place of rewards or punishments, and therefore the great Ruler of the world does not exert his perfections in the distribution of either; but eternity is allotted for that very purpose, and therefore he will then distribute rewards and punishments worthy himself, such as will proclaim him God in acts of grace and vengeance, as he has appeared in all his other works. Then he will *shew his wrath,* and *make* his power *known on the vessels of wrath who have made themselves fit for destruction* and nothing else; *and he will shew the riches of the glory of his grace upon the vessels of mercy whom he prepared beforehand for glory.* Rom. ix. 22, 23. Thus heaven and hell will proclaim the God, will shew him to be the Author of their respective joys and pains, by their agreeable or terrible magnificence and grandeur. O eternity! with what majestic wonders art thou replenished, where Jehovah

Serm. 23. *from its Shortness and Vanity.*

acts with his own immediate hand, and displays himself God-like and unrivalled, in his exploits both of vengeance and of grace! In this present state, our good and evil are blended; our happiness has some bitter ingredients, and our miseries has some agreeable mitigations: but in the eternal world good and evil shall be entirely and for ever separated; all will be pure, unmingled happiness, or pure, unmingled misery, In the present state the best have not uninterrupted peace within; conscience has frequent cause to make them uneasy: some mote or other falls into its tender eye, and sets it a weeping: and the worst also have their arts to keep conscience sometimes easy, and silence its clamours. But then conscience will have its full scope. It will never more pass a censure upon the righteous, and it will never more be a friend, or even an inactive enemy to the wicked for so much as one moment. And O what a perennial fountain of bliss or pain will conscience then be! Society contributes much to our happiness or misery. But what misery can be felt or feared in the immediate presence and fellowship of the blessed God and Jesus (the friend of man;) of angels and saints, and all the glorious natives of heaven? But, on the other hand, what happiness can be enjoyed or hoped for, what misery can be escaped in the horrid society of lost abandoned ghosts of the angelic and human nature; dreadfully mighty and malignant, and rejoicing only in each other's misery; mutual enemies, and mutual tormentors bound together inseparably in everlasting chains of darkness! O the horror of the thought! In short, even an heathen * could say,

" Had I an hundred tongues, an hundred mouths,
An iron voice, I could not comprehend
The various forms and punishments of vice."

The most terrible images which even the pencil of divine inspiration can draw, such as *a lake of fire and brimstone, utter darkness, the blackness of darkness, a never-dying worm, unquenchable, everlasting fire*, and all the most dreadful figures that can be drawn from all parts of the universe, are not sufficient to represent the punishments of the eternal world. And, on the other hand, *the eye, which has ranged through so many objects, has not seen; the ear, which has had still more extensive intelligence, has not heard; nor has the heart*, which is even unbounded in its conceptions, *conceived the things that God hath laid up for them that love him.* The enjoyments of time fall as much short of those of eternity, as time itself falls short of eternity itself.

* Non, mihi si linguæ centum sint, oraque centum,
Ferrea vox, omnes scelerum comprendere formas,
Omnia pœnarum percurrere nomina possum.
VIRG. Æn. VI. 1. 625.

But what gives infinite importance to thefe joys and forrows is, that as they are enjoyed or fuffered in the eternal world, they are themfelves eternal. Eternal joys! eternal pains! joys and pains that will laft as long as the King eternal and immortal will live to diftribute them! as long as our immortal fpirits will live to feel them! O what joys and pains are thefe!

And thefe, my brethren, are awaiting every one of us. Thefe pleafures, or thefe pains, are felt this moment by fuch of our friends and acquaintance as have fhot the gulph before us; and in a little, little while, you and I muft feel them.

And what then have we to do with time and earth? Are the pleafures and pains of this world worthy to be compared with thefe? *Vanity of vanities, all is vanity;* the enjoyments and fufferings, the labours and purfuits, the laughter and tears of the prefent ftate, are all nothing in this comparifon. What is the lofs of an eftate or of a dear relative to the lofs of an happy immortality? But if our heavenly inheritance be fecure, what though we fhould be reduced into Job's forlorn fituation, we have enough left more than to fill up all deficiencies. What though we are poor, fickly, melancholy, racked with pains, and involved in every human mifery, heaven will more than make amends for all. But if we have no evidences of our title to that, the fenfe of thefe tranfitory diftreffes may be fwallowed up in the juft fear of the miferies of eternity. Alas! what avails it that we play away a few years in mirth and gaiety, in grandeur and pleafure, if when thefe few years are fled, we lift up our eyes in hell, tormented in flames! O what are all thefe things to a candidate for eternity! an heir of everlafting happinefs, or everlafting mifery!

It is from fuch convictive premifes as thefe that St. Paul draws his inference in my text; *It remaineth therefore that they that have wives be as though they had none; and they that weep, as though they wept not; and they that rejoice, as though they rejoiced not; and they that buy, as though they poffeffed not; and they that ufe this world, as not abufing it.*

The firft branch of the inference refers to the dear and tender relations that we fuftain in this life. *It remaineth that thofe that have wives,* and by a parity of reafon, thofe that have hufbands, parents, children, or friends dear as their own fouls, *be as though they had none.* St. Paul is far from recommending a ftoical neglect of thefe dear relations. That he tenderly felt the fenfations, and warmly recommended the mutual duties of fuch relations, appears in the ftrongeft light in other parts of his writings, where he is addreffing himfelf to hufbands and wives, parents and children. But his defign here is to reprefent the infignificancy even of thefe dear relations, confidering how fhort and vanifhing they are, and comparing them with the infinite concerns of eternity.

These dear creatures we shall be able to call our own for so short a time, that it is hardly worth while to esteem them ours now. The concerns of eternity are of so much greater moment, that it is very little matter whether we enjoy these comforts or not. In a few years at most, it will be all one. The dear ties that now unite the hearts of husband and wife, parent and child, friend and friend, will be broken for ever. In that world where we must all be in a little, little time, they neither marry nor are given in marriage; but are in this respect like the angels. And of how small consequence is it to creatures that are to exist for ever in the most perfect happiness or misery, and that must so soon break off all their tender connections with the dear creatures that were united to their hearts in the present transitory state! of how small consequence is it to such, whether they spend a few years of their existence in all the delights of the conjugal state and the social life, or are forlorn, bereaved, destitute, widowed, childless, fatherless, friendless! The grave and eternity will level all these little inequalities. The dust of Job has no more sense of his past calamities, than that of Solomon who felt so few; and their immortal parts are equally happy in heaven, if they were equally holy upon earth. And of how small consequence is it to Judas now, after he has been above seventeen hundred years in his own place, whether he died single or married, a parent or childless? This makes no distinction in heaven or hell, unless that, as relations increase, the duties belonging to them are multiplied, and the trust becomes the heavier; the discharge of which meets with a more glorious reward in heaven, and the neglect of which suffers a severer punishment in hell.

Farther, the apostle, in saying that *they who have wives should be as though they had none*, intends that we should not excessively set our hearts upon any of our dearest relatives so as to tempt us to neglect the superior concerns of the world to come, or draw off our affections from God. We should always remember who it was that said, *He that loveth father, or mother, or wife, or children, more than me, is not worthy of me*. He that is married, says St. Paul in the context, *careth for the things of the world, how he may please his wife*. verse 33. But we should beware lest this care should run to excess, and render us careless of the interests of our souls, and the concerns of immortality. To moderate excessive care and anxiety about the things of this world is the design the apostle has immediately in view in my text; for having taught *those that have wives to be as though they had none*, &c. he immediately adds, *I would have you without carefulness;* and this is the reason why I would have you form such an estimate of all the conditions of life, and count them as on a level. Those that have the agreeable weights of these relations ought no more to abandon themselves to the over-eager pursuit of this world, or place their happiness in it; ought no more to neglect the concerns of religion and eternity, than if they did not bear these relations. The busy head of a numerous family is as much concerned to secure his everlasting interest as a single man. Whatever becomes of him and his in this vanishing world, he must by no means neglect to provide for his subsistence in the eternal world; and nothing in this world can at all excuse that neglect.

O that these thoughts may deeply affect the hearts of such of us as are agreeably connected in such relations! and may they inspire us with a proper insensibility and indifference towards them when compared with the affairs of religion and eternity! May this consideration moderate the sorrows of the mourners on this melancholy occasion, and teach them to esteem the gain or loss of an happy eternity as that which should swallow up every other concern!

The next branch of the inference refers to the sorrows of life. *It remaineth that they that weep be as if they wept not.* Whatever afflictions may befal us here, they will not last long, but will soon be swallowed up in the greater joys or sorrows of the eternal world. These tears will not always flow; these sighs will not always heave our breasts. We can sigh no longer than the vital breath inspires our lungs; and we can weep no longer than till death stops all the fountains of our tears; and that will be in a very little time. And when we enter into the eternal world, if we have been the dutiful children of God here, his own gentle hand shall wipe away every tear from our faces, and he will comfort the mourners. Then all the sorrows of life will cease for ever, and no more painful remembrance of them will remain than of the pains and sickness of our unconscious infancy. But if all the discipline of our heavenly Father fails to reduce us to our duty, if we still continue rebellious and incorrigible under his rod, and consequently the miseries of this life convey us to those of the future, the smaller will be swallowed up and lost in the greater as a drop in the ocean. Some desperate sinners have hardened themselves in sin with this cold comfort, ' That since they must be miserable hereafter, they will at least take their fill of pleasures here, and take a merry journey to hell.' But, alas! what a sorry mitigation will this be! how entirely will all this career of pleasure be forgotten at the first pang of infernal anguish! O! what poor relief to a soul lost for ever, to reflect that this eternity of pain followed upon and was procured by a few months or years of sordid guilty pleasure! Was that a relief or an aggravation which Abraham mentions to his lost son, when he puts him in mind, *Son, remember that thou in thy life-time receivedst thy good things.* Luke xvi. 25. Thou hadst then all the share of good which thou ever shalt enjoy; thou hadst thy portion in that world where thou didst choose to have it, and therefore stand to the consequences of thine own choice, and look for no other portion. O! who can bear to be thus reminded and upbraided in the midst of remediless misery!

Upon the whole, whatever afflictions or bereavements we suffer in this world, let us moderate our sorrows and keep them within bounds. Let them not work up and ferment into murmurings and insurrections against God, who gives and takes away, and blessed be his name! Let them not sink us into a sullen dislike of the mercies still left in our possession. How unreasonable and ungrateful, that God's retaking one of his mercies should tempt us to despise all the rest! Take a view of the rich inventory of blessings still remaining, and you will find them much more numerous and important than those you have lost. Do not mistake me, as if I recommended or expected an utter insensibility under the calamities of life. I allow nature its moderate tears; but let them not rise to floods of inconsolable sorrows; I allow you to feel your afflictions like men and christians, but then you must bear them like men and christians too. May God grant that we may all exemplify this direction when we are put to the trial!

The third branch of the inference refers to the joys and pleasures of life. *The time is short, it remaineth therefore that they that rejoice be as if they rejoiced not;* that is, the joys of this life, from whatever earthly cause they spring, are so short and transitory, that they are as of no account to a creature that is to exist for ever; to exist for ever in joys or pains of an infinitely higher and more important kind. To such a creature it is an indifferency whether he laughs or weeps, whether he be joyful or sad, for only a few fleeting moments. These vanishing, uncertain joys, should not engross our hearts as our chief happiness, nor cause us to neglect and forfeit the divine and everlasting joys above the skies. The pleasure we receive from any created enjoyment should not ensnare us to make it our idol, to forget that we must part with it, or to fret and murmur, and repine when the parting hour comes. When we are rejoicing in the abundance of earthly blessings, we should be as careful and laborious in securing the favour of God and everlasting happiness as if we rejoiced not. If our eternal All is secure it is enough; and it will not at all be heightened or diminished by the reflection that we lived a joyful or a sad life in this pilgrimage. But if we spend our immortality in misery, what sorry comfort will it be that we laughed, and played, and frolicked away a few years upon earth? years that were given us for a serious purpose, as a space for repentance, and preparation for eternity. Therefore *&c.* "*they that rejoice be as though they rejoiced not;*" that is, he nobly indifferent to all the little amusements and pleasures of so short a life.

And let those that buy be as if they possessed not.—This is the fourth particular in the inference from the shortness of time, and it refers to the trade and business of life. It refers not only to the busy merchant, whose life is a vicissitude of buying and selling, but also to the planter, the tradesman, and indeed to every man among us; for we are all carrying on a commerce, more or less, for the purposes of this life.—You all buy, and sell, and exchange, in some form or other; and the things of this world are perpetually passing from hand to hand. Sometimes you have good bargains, and make large acquisitions. But set not your hearts upon them; but in the midst of all your possessions, live as if you possessed them not. Alas! of what small account are all the things you call your own upon earth, to you who are to stay here so short a time; to you who must so soon bid an eternal farewell to them all, and go as naked out of the world as you came into it; to you who must spend an everlasting duration far beyond the reach of all these enjoyments? It is not worth your while to call them your own, since you must so soon resign them to other hands. The melancholy occasion of this day may convince you that success in trade, and a plentiful estate, procured and kept by industry and good management, is neither a security against death, nor a comfort in it. Alas! what service can these houses, and lands, and numerous domestics perform to the old clay that moulders in yonder grave, or to the immortal spirit that is fled we know not where! Therefore buy, sensible that you can buy nothing upon a sure and lasting title; nothing that you can certainly call yours to-morrow. Buy, but do not sell your hearts to the trifles you buy, and let them not tempt you to act as if this were your final home, or to neglect to lay up for yourselves treasures in heaven; treasures which you can call your own when this world is laid in ashes, and which you can enjoy and live upon in what I may call an angelic state, when these bodies have nothing but a coffin, a shroud, and a few feet of earth.

Finally, let "those that use this world, use it as not abusing it." This is the fifth branch of the inference from the shortness of time; and it seems to have a particular reference to such as have had such success in their pursuit of the world, that they have now retired from business, and appear to themselves to have nothing to do but enjoy the world, for which they so long toiled. Or it may refer to those who are born heirs to plentiful estates, and therefore are not concerned to acquire the world, but to use and enjoy it. To such I say, "Use this world as not abusing it;" that is, use it, enjoy it, take moderate pleasure in it, but do not abuse it by prostituting it to sinful purposes, making provision for the flesh to fulfil the lusts thereof, indulging yourselves in debauchery and extravagance, placing your confidence in it, and singing a *requiem* to your

Serm. 23.   *from its Shortness and Vanity.*   407

souls. "Soul, take thine ease; eat, drink, and be merry; for thou hast much goods laid up in store for many years." O! presumptuous "fool, this night thy soul may be required of thee." Luke xii. 19, 20. Do not use this world to excess* (so the word may be translated) by placing your hearts excessively upon it as your favourite portion and principal happiness, and by suffering it to draw off your thoughts and affections from the superior blessedness of the world to come. Use the world, but let it not tempt you to excess in eating, drinking, dress, equipage, or in any article of the parade of riches. Religion by no means enjoins a sordid, niggardly, churlish manner of living; it allows you to enjoy the blessings of life, but then it forbids all excess, and requires you to keep within the bounds of moderation in your enjoyments. Thus *use this world as not abusing it.*

The apostle's inference is not only drawn from strong premises, but also enforced with a very weighty reason; *for the fashion of this world passeth away.* The whole scheme and system of worldly affairs, all this marrying, and rejoicing, and weeping, and buying, and enjoying *passeth away,* passeth away this moment; it not only will pass away, but it is even now passing away. The stream of time, with all the trifles that float on it, and all the eager pursuers of these bubbles, is in motion, in swift incessant motion, to empty itself and all that sail upon it, into the shoreless ocean of eternity, where all will be absorbed and lost for ever. And shall we excessively doat upon things that are perpetually flying from us, and in a little time will be no more our property than the riches of the world before the flood? *O ye sons of men, how long will you follow after vanity? why do you spend your money for that which is not bread, and your labour for that which profiteth not?*

Some critics apprehend this sentence, *the fashion of this world passeth away,* contains a fine striking allusion to the stage, and that it might be rendered, "the scene of this world passeth away." 'You know,' says a fine writer † upon this text, 'that upon the stage the actors assume imaginary characters, and appear in borrowed forms. One mimics the courage and triumphs of the hero; another appears with a crown and a sceptre, and struts about with all the solemnity and majesty of a prince; a third puts on the fawning smile of a courtier, or the haughtiness of a successful favourite; and the fourth is represented in the dress of a scholar or a divine. An hour or two they act their several parts on the stage, and amuse the spectators; but the scenes are constantly shifting: and when the play is concluded, the feigned characters are laid aside, and the imaginary kings and emperors are immediately di-

* *katachrēmenoi.* So it is rendered by Doddridge, and others.
† Dunlop's Sermons, Vol. I. p. 212, 213, 214.

vested of their pretended authority and ensigns of royalty, and appear in their native meanness.

'Just so this world is a great stage that presents as variable scenes, and as fantastical characters; princes, politicians, and warriors, the rich, the learned, and the wise: and, on the other hand, the poor weak and despised part of mankind possess their several places on the theatre; some lurk obscurely in a corner, seldom come from behind the scenes, or creep along unnoticed; others make a splendid show and a loud noise, are adorned with the honours of a crown, or possessed of large estates and great powers; fill the world with the glory of their names and actions; conquer in the field, or are laboriously employed in the cabinet. Well, in a little time the scene is shifted, and all these vain phantoms disappear. The king of terrors clears the stage of the busy actors, strips them of all their fictitious ornaments, and ends the vain farce of life: and, being brought all upon a level, they go down to the grave in their original nakedness, are jumbled together undistinguished, and pass away as a tale that is told.

Farther: 'Upon the Greek or Roman theatres, to which the apostle alludes, the actors, if I mistake not, frequently, if not always, came upon the stage in a disguise, with a false face, which was adapted to the different person or character they designed to assume; so that no man was to be seen with his real face, but all put on borrowed visages. And in allusion to this, the text might be rendered, "The masquerade of the world passeth away," pointing out the fraud and disguises which mankind put on, and the flattering forms in which they generally appear, which will all pass away when the grave shall pull off the mask; and they go down to the other world naked and open,' and appear at the supreme tribunal in their due characters, 'and can no more be varnished over with fraudulent colouring.' *

Others apprehend, the apostle here alludes to some grand procession, in which pageants or emblematical figures pass along the crowded streets. The staring crowd wait their appearance with eager eyes, and place themselves in the most convenient posture of observation; they gape at the passing show; they follow it with a wondering gaze;—and now it is past; and now it begins to look dim to the sight; and now it disappears. Just such is this transitory world. Thus it begins to attract the eager gaze of mankind; thus it marches by in swift procession from our eyes to meet the eyes of others; and thus it soon vanishes and disappears.†

---

* Dunlop's Sermons, Vol. I. p. 215.

† Thus Dr. Doddridge understands the text, FAMILY EXPOSITOR, in loc. and thus he beautifully describes it in his Hymns:

'The empty pageant rolls along;
'The giddy inexperienc'd throng

And shall we always be stupidly staring upon this empty parade, and forget that world of substantial realities to which we are hastening? No; let us live and act as the expectants of that world, and as having nothing to do with this world, but only as a school, a state of discipline, to educate and prepare us for another.

O! that I could succesfully impress this exhortation upon all your hearts! O! that I could prevail upon you all this day to break off your over-fond attachment to earth, and to make ready for immortality! Could I carry this point, it would be a greater advantage than all the dead could receive by any funeral panegyrics from me. I speak for the advantage of the living upon such occasions, and not to celebrate the virtues of those who have passed the trial, and received their sentence from the Supreme Judge. And I am well satisfied the mourning relatives of our deceased friend, who best knew and esteemed his worth, would be rather offended than pleased, if I should prostitute the present hour to so mean a purpose. Indeed, many a character less worthy of praise, often makes a shining figure in funeral sermons. Many that have not been such tender husbands, such affectionate fathers, such kind masters, such sincere upright friends, so honest and punctual in trade, such zealous lovers of religion and good men, have had their putrifying remains perfumed with public praise from a place so solemn as the pulpit; but you can witness for me, it is not my usual foible to run to this extreme. My business is with you, who are as yet alive, to hear me. To you I call, as with the voice of your deceased friend and neighbour,—Prepare! prepare for eternity! O! if the spirits that you once knew, while clothed in flesh, should take my place, would not this be their united voice, ' Prepare, prepare for eternity! ye frail short-lived mortals! ye near neighbours to the world of spirits! ye borderers upon heaven or hell; make ready, loosen your hearts from earth, and all that it contains: weigh anchor, and prepare to launch away into the boundless ocean of eternity, which methinks is now within your ken, and roars within hearing.' And remember, ' this I say, brethren,' with great confidence, *the time is short: it remaineth therefore*, for the future,—*that they that have wives, be as if they had none; and they that weep, as if they wept not; and they that rejoice, as if they rejoiced not; and they that buy, as if they possessed not; and they that use this world, as not abusing it: for the fashion of this world,* all its scheme of affairs, all the vain parade, all the idle farce of life, *passeth away.*

' Pursue it with enchanted eyes;
' It passeth in swift march away,
' Still more and more its charms decay,
' Till the last gaudy colours dies.   See HYMN 268.

Lucian has the best illustration of this passage, in this view, that I have seen. Dialogue XXXII. Murphy's Edit.——

And away let it pafs, if we may at laft obtain a better country; that is, an heavenly: which may God grant for Jefus' fake! Amen.

SERMON XXIV.

The Preaching of Chrift crucified the Mean of Salvation.

1 COR. i. 22—24. *For the Jews required a fign, and the Greeks feek after wifdom; but we preach Chrift crucified unto the Jews a ftumbling-block, and unto the Greeks foolifhnefs; but unto them which are called both Jews and Greeks, Chrift the power of God, and the wifdom of God.*

IF we fhould confider Chriftianity only as an improvement of natural religion, containing a complete fyftem of morality, and prefcribing a pure plan of worfhip, it is a matter of the utmoft importance, and worthy of univerfal acceptance. In the one view, it is neceffary to inform the world in matters of fin and duty, and reform their vicious practices; and in the other, to put an end to that foolifh and barbarous fuperftition which had over-run the earth, under the notion of religious worfhip. And thefe ends the Chriftian religion fully anfwers. Never was there fuch a finifhed fyftem of morality, or fuch a fpiritual and divine model of worfhip invented or revealed, as by the defpifed Galilean, and the twelve fifhermen that received their inftruments from him.

But this is not the principal excellency of the gofpel! and did it carry its difcoveries no farther, alas! it would be far from revealing a fuitable religion for finners. A religion for finners muft reveal a method of falvation for the loft; of pardon for the guilty, and of fanctifying grace for the weak and wicked. And, bleffed be God, the gofpel anfwers this end? and it is its peculiar excellency that it does fo. It is its peculiar excellency that it publifhes a crucified Chrift as an all-fufficient Saviour to a guilty, perifhing world. It is its glorious peculiarity that it reveals a method of falvation every way honourable to God and his government, and every way fuitable to our neceffities; and that is, by the fufferings of Chrift, the Founder of this religion. This is the ground, the fubftance, and marrow of the gofpel; and it is this, above all other things, that its minifters ought to preach and inculcate. It fhould have the same place in their sermons which it has in that gospel which it is their business to preach ; that is, it should be the foundation, the substance, the center, and draft of all.

This was the practice of the most successful preacher of the gospel that ever bore that commission : I mean St. Paul. And in this he was not singular ? his fellow-apostles heartily concurred with him, *We preach Christ crucified*. The sufferings of Christ, which had a dreadful consummation in his crucifixion, their necessity, design, and consequences, and the way of salvation thereby opened for a guilty world, these are the principal materials of our preaching ; to instruct mankind in these is the great object of our ministry, and the unwearied labour of our lives. We might easily choose subjects more pleasing and popular, more fit to display our learning and abilities, and set off the strong reasoner, or the fine orator : but our commission, as ministers of a crucified Jesus, binds us to the subject ; and the necessity of the world peculiarly requires it. Further, this was not the apostle's occasional practice, or an hasty wavering purpose ; but he was determined upon it. *I determined*, says he, *not to know any thing among you, save Jesus Christ, and him crucified.** 1 Cor. ii. 2. This theme, as it were, engrossed all his thoughts ; he dwelt so much upon it, as if he had known nothing else : and as if nothing else had been worth knowing. Indeed he openly avows such a neglect and contempt of all other knowledge, in comparison of this : *I count all things but loss, for the excellency of the knowledge of Jesus Christ my Lord.* Phil. iii. 8. The crucifixion of Christ, which was the most ignominious circumstance in the whole course of his abasement, was an object in which he gloried ; and he is struck with horror at the thought of glorying in any thing else. *God forbid*, says he, *that I should glory, save in the cross of our Lord Jesus Christ!* Gal. vi. 14. In short, he looked upon it as the perfection of his character as a christian and an apostle, to be a constant student, and a zealous indefatigable preacher of the cross of Christ.

But though a crucified Jesus was of so much importance in a religion for sinners ; though his doctrine was the substance of the gospel, and the principal object of the apostle's ministry ; yet, as it was not the invention of human reason, so neither was it agreeable to the proud reasoning, or corrupt taste of the world. *The preaching of the cross is to them that perish, foolishness.* However, there were some that had the same sentiment of it with St. Paul ; even as many as were in the way of salvation. *Unto us that are saved, it is the power of God.* ver. 18. To such, that weak and contemptible thing, the cross, was the brightest display of divine power to be found in the universe.

---

* Which Dr. Doddridge renders *Christ Jesus, even that crucified one*. Christ Jesus, and that under the most ignominious circumstances possible, viz. as crucified, was the principal object of his study, and the substance of his preaching.

Mankind had had time enough to try what expedients their reason could find out for the reformation and salvation of a degenerate and perishing world. The sages and philosophers of the heathen world had had a clear stage for many hundreds of years; and they might have done their utmost without controul. But, alas! did any of them, amid all their boasted improvements, succeed in the experiment? Or could they so much as find out a method in which sinners might be reconciled to their God? No; in this most interesting point, they were either stupidly thoughtless, or all their searches issued in perplexity, or in the most absurd and impious contrivances. *Where is the wise? where is the scribe? where is the disputer of this world?* Let them appear, and produce their schemes upon this head. But *hath not God made foolish the wisdom of this world?* (ver. 20.) Yes, indeed he has, by proposing a method most perfectly adapted for this end, which they not only never would have once thought of, but which, when revealed, their wisdom cannot relish. Their wisdom appears but folly, in that when they had the world to themselves about four thousand years they could not in all that time find out any successful expedient to amend and save it. And now, if any thing be done at all, it is time for God to do it; and how strange, how unexpected, how mysterious was his expedient! and yet how glorious and effectual! *For after that, in the wisdom of God, the world by wisdom knew not God, it pleased God, by the foolishness of preaching, to save them that believe.* ver. 21. This was the contrivance for effecting what all the wisdom and learning of the world could never effect; the plain unadorned preaching of Christ crucified; which, both for the matter and manner of it, was counted foolishness.

But how did the world bear this mortification of their intellectual pride? And what reception did this bounteous divine scheme meet with when revealed? Alas! I am sorry to tell you: The prejudices of their education were different; but they were unitedly set against the gospel. The Jews had been educated in a religion established by a series of miracles; and therefore they were extravagant in their demands of this sort of evidence. Notwithstanding all the miracles Christ was working daily before their eyes, they were perpetually asking him, *What sign shewest thou?*—Those that are resolved not to be convinced, will be always complaining of the want of proof, and demanding more to vindicate their infidelity. As for the Greeks, their prejudices were of another kind; it was even a proverb among them, that " miracles were for fools;" * and therefore they did not desire that sort of evidence. But *they seek after wisdom.* They had been accustomed to fine orations, strong reasoning, and a parade of learning; and these were

* Thaumata morois.

the evidences they defired to recommend a doctrine to them. And, finding the doctrine of Chrift crucified had none of thefe embellifh-ments, they defpifed and rejected it as foolifhnefs and nonfenfe.

The method of falvation by the crucifixion of a fuppofed male-factor, was fo extremely oppofite to the reafoning, pride, and pre-judices of Jews and Gentiles, that they could not bear it. The Jews expected the Meffiah would appear as a victorious temporal prince, who, inftead of falling a prey to his enemies, would fubdue them all with an irrefiftible power, and advance the family of Da-vid to univerfal empire. And of all other deaths, that of crucifix-ion was the moft odious and abominable to them, becaufe, accord-ing to the cuftom of the Romans, it was the punifhment only of flaves; and by their own law it was pronounced accurfed; *for it is written, curfed is every one that hangeth on a tree.* Gal. iii. 13. Deut. xxi. 23. Hence, by way of contempt, the Jews called the bleffed Jefus, *the Hanged Man.*—Nay, this was a fhock to the faith of the apoftles themfelves, until their Jewifh prejudices were re-moved by better information. Finding that, inftead of fetting up a glorious kingdom, their Mafter was apprehended by his enemies, and hung upon a crofs, they had nothing to fay, but, *We trufted this was he that fhould have delivered Ifrael:* we fimply thought fo; but, alas! now we fee our miftake. Luke xxiv. 21. No wonder the crofs of Chrift fhould be a ftumbling-block to fuch as had im-bibed fuch notions of the Meffiah. When, inftead of the power of figns and miracles, which they were extravagantly demanding, they faw him crucified in weaknefs, they could not admit the thought that this was that illuftrious character of an univerfal king. They were fo dazzled with worldly glory, and fo infenfible of their fpiritual wants, that they had no notions of a fpiritual Savi-our, and a kingdom of grace; nor could they fee how fuch pro-phecies were accomplifhed in one that only profeffed to deliver from the flavery of fin and Satan, and the wrath to come. Hence they ftumbled at the crofs, as an obftacle which they could not get over. When Chrift called Lazarus from the dead, he had crowds of followers, who attended his triumphant proceffion into Jerufa-lem as a mighty conqueror: and when he had fed fo many with a few loaves, they were about forcibly to make him king; for they knew that one who could raife his foldiers to life after they had been killed, and fupport an army with fo little provifions, could eafily conquer the world, and refcue them from the power of the Romans. But when they faw him feized by his enemies without making refiftance, or working a miracle for his own defence, they immediately abandoned him; and the hofannas of the multitude were turned into another kind of cry, *Crucify him, crucify him.* And when they faw him hanging helplefs and dying upon the crofs, it was demonftration to them that he was an impoftor. It was this that rendered the preaching of Chrift by his apoftles fo unpopular among the Jews: It feemed to them like a panegyric upon an infamous malefactor: and they thought it an infult to their nation to have fuch a one propofed to them as their Meffiah. Thus Chrift crucified was to the Jews a ftumbling-block.

As to the Greeks, who were a learned philofophical people, it feemed to them the wildeft folly to worfhip one as a God who had been crucified as a malefactor; and to truft in one for falvation who had not faved himfelf. Their Jupiter had his thunder, and according to their tradition, had crufhed the formidable rebellion of the giants againft heaven: their Bacchus had avenged himfelf upon the defpifers of his worfhip; and the whole rabble of their deities had done fome god-like exploit, if the fables of their poets were true: and would they abandon fuch gods, and receive in their ftead a defpifed Nazarene, who had been executed as the vileft criminal by his own nation? Would they give up all their boafted wifdom and learning, and become the humbleft difciples of the crofs, and receive for their teachers a company of illiterate fifhermen, and a tent-maker from the defpifed nation of the Jews, whom they held in the utmoft contempt for their ignorance, bigotry, and fuperftition? No, the pride of their underftandings could not bear fuch a mortification. If their curiofity led them to be St. Paul's hearers, they expected to be entertained with a flourifh of words, and fine philofophic reafoning; and when they found themfelves difappointed, they pronounced him a babbler (Acts xvii. 28.) and his preaching foolifhnefs.—Corinth, to which this epiftle was fent by St. Paul, was a noted city among the Greeks; and therefore, what he fays upon this head was peculiarly pertinent and well applied.

The prejudices of the Jews and Greeks in this refpect outlived the apoftolic age, as we learn from the writings of the primitive fathers of the chriftian church, who lived among them, and were converfant with them. Trypho the Jew, in a dialogue with Juftin Martyr, about an hundred years after St. Paul wrote this epiftle, charges it upon the chriftians as the greateft abfurdity and impiety, that they placed their hopes in a crucified man. Juftin, after long reafoning, couftrains him at length to make fundry conceffions, as, that the prophecies which he had mentioned did really refer to the Meffiah; and that, according to thefe prophecies, the Meffiah was to fuffer. 'But (fays the Jew) that Chrift fhould be fo ignominioufly crucified; that he fhould die a death which the law pronounces accurfed, this we cannot but doubt; this I yet find a very hard thing to believe: and therefore if you have any further evidence upon this head, would willingly hear it.' Here you fee the crofs was a ftumbling-block, which the Jews could not get over in a hundred years; nay, they have not got over it to this day. Lactantius, about three hundred years after Chrift's birth, obferves, that the fufferings of Chrift were wont to be caft upon chriftians as a reproach: it was thought a ftrange and fcandalous thing that they fhould worfhip a man; a man that had been crucified, and put to the moft infamous and tormenting death by men.* An heathen, in Minutius Fœlix, is introduced as faying, 'He who reprefents a man punifhed for his crimes with the fevereft punifhment, and the favage wood of the crofs, as the object of their worfhip, and a ceremony of their religion, afcribes a very proper altar to fuch abandoned and wicked creatures, that they may worfhip that which they deferve to hang upon.'† And referring to the many barbarous perfecutions they then groaned under, he jeers them; 'See here,' fays he, 'are threatenings for you, punifhments, torture and croffes, not to be adored, but endured.'‡ 'The calumniating Greeks,' fays Athanafius, 'ridicule us, and fet up a broad laugh at us, becaufe we regard nothing fo much as the crofs of Chrift.'

Thus, you fee, the doctrine of the crofs was, of all other things, the moft unpopular among Jews and Gentiles, and the moft difagreeable to their tafte. A man could not expect to fhine, or cut a figure as a man of fenfe and learning, by making this the fubject of his difcourfes. But will Paul give it up, and difplay his talents upon fome more acceptable theme? This, as a fine fcholar, he was very capable of; but he abhors the thought.

'Let the Jews and Greeks defire what they pleafe; we,' fays he, 'will not humour them, nor gratify their tafte: however they take it, we will preach Chrift crucified; though to the Jews he fhould prove a ftumbling-block, and to the Greeks foolifhnefs.' And there are fome that relifh this humble doctrine. To them that believe, both Jews and Greeks, whether learned or unlearned, whether educated in the Jewifh or Pagan religion, however different their prejudices, or their natural taftes, to all that believe, notwithftanding thefe differences, Chrift, that is, *Chrift crucified, is the power of God and the wifdom of God*. The wifdom and power of God are not the only perfections that fhine in this method of falvation by the crofs; but the apoftle particularly mentions thefe, as directly anfwering to the refpective demands of Jews and Greeks. If the Jew defires the fign of power in working miracles, the be-

*— Paffionem quæ velut opprobrium nobis objectari folet: quod & hominem, & ab hominibus infigni fupplicio affectum & excruciatum colamus.—De ver. Sap. L. IV. c. 16.

† Qui hominem fummo fupplicio pro facinore punitum, & crucis ligna feralia eorum Ceremonias fabulatur, congruentia perditis fceleratifque tribuit altaria, ut id celant quod merentur. P. 9.

‡ Ecce vobis minae, fupplicia, tormenta, etiam, non adorandae, fed fubeundae cruces. P. 11.

liever fees in Chrift crucified a power fuperior to all the powers of miracles. If the Greek feeks after wifdom, here, in a crucified Chrift, the wifdom of God fhines in the higheft perfection. Whatever fign or wifdom the Jew or Greek defires and feeks after, the believer finds more than an equivalent in the crofs. This is the greateft miracle of power, the greateft myftery of wifdom in all the world.

The prejudices of the Jews and Gentiles were not only confined to the early ages of Chriftianity; the fame depraved tafte, the fame contempt of the humble doctrines of the crofs may be found among us, though profeffed Chriftians: fome refemble the Jews, who were perpetually demanding figns: they affect vifions and impulfes, and all the reveries of enthufiafm, inftead of the preaching of Chrift crucified. Others like the Greeks, through an affectation of florid harangues, moral difcourfes, and a parade of learning and philofophy, naufeate this fort of preaching, and count it foolifhnefs. It is therefore high time for the minifters of the gofpel to ftand up as advocates for the crofs, and with a pious obftinacy to adhere to this fubject, whatever contempt and ridicule it may expofe them to. For my part, I know not what I have to do, as a minifter of the gofpel, but to preach Chrift crucified. I would make him the fubftance, the center, the end of all my miniftrations. *And if we*, or an angel from heaven, *preach unto you any other gofpel*—you know his doom—*let him be accurfed*. Gal. i. 9.

We are to confider the apoftles as fent out into the world to reform and fave the corrupt and perifhing fons of men, and the preaching of Chrift crucified as the mean they ufed for this important end. This is the formal view the apoftle had of preaching Chrift in this place, viz. as a mean found out by the wifdom of God to fave them that believe, after that all the wifdom of the world had tried in vain to find out a method for this end. This is evident from ver. 21. *After that the world by all its wifdom knew not God, it pleafed God, by the foolifhnefs of preaching;* that is, by the preaching a crucified Saviour, which the world counts foolifhnefs, *to fave them that believe.* This is the excellency of this preaching, this is the reafon why the apoftle could not be prevailed upon by any motive to defert it, that it is the only mean to falvation : and it is in this view I now intend to confider it. And if your everlafting falvation be of any importance to you, certainly this fubject demands your moft ferious attention.

I have been the longer in explaining the context, becaufe it is fo clofely connected with the fubject I have in view, and reflects light upon it. And I fhall only add, that preaching Chrift crucified is the fame thing as preaching falvation through the fufferings of Chrift. His fufferings were of long continuance, even from his conception to his refurrection; and they were of various kinds, poverty, weariness and labour, hunger and thirst, contempt and reproach, buffetting, scourging and a thorny crown. But there are two words, which by a synecdoche are often used in scripture to signify all his sufferings of every kind, from first to last; viz. his blood and his cross. And the reason is, the shedding of his blood, and the death of the cross, were the worst kind and highest degree of his sufferings. In his crucifixion all his other sufferings were united and centered: this was a complete summary and consummation of them all; and therefore, they are frequently included under this. In this latitude I shall use the word in this discourse; which I hope you will take notice of, that no part of the meaning may escape you.

Our inquiry shall be,

What are the reasons that the preaching of Christ crucified is, above all others, the best, and the only effectual mean for the salvation of sinners?

These reasons may be reduced under two general heads; namely, That through the crucifixion of Christ, and through that only, a way is really opened for the salvation of sinners; and that the preaching of Christ crucified makes such a discovery of things, as has the most direct tendency to bring them to repentance, and produce in them that temper which is necessary to salvation. Or, in other words, in this way salvation is provided, and sinners are made fit to enjoy it; both which are absolutely necessary. Our world is deeply and universally sunk in sin. Men have cast contempt upon the divine government, broken the divine law, and so incurred its penalty; they have forfeited the favour of God, and rendered themselves liable to his displeasure. Had mankind continued innocent, there would have been no difficulty in their case. It would be very plain what would be fit for the divine government to do with dutiful subjects. But, alas! rebellion against God has made its entrance into our world, and all its inhabitants are up in arms against Heaven. This has thrown all into confusion, and rendered it a perplexing case what to do with them. In one view, indeed, the case is plain, viz. that proper punishments should be executed upon them. This would appear evidently just to the whole universe, and no objection could be made against it, though the criminals themselves, who are parties, and therefore not fit judges, might murmur against it as unmerciful and severe. But the difficulty is, how such rebels may not only be delivered from the punishments they deserve, but made happy for ever? If they cannot be saved in a way that displays the perfections of God, and does honour to his government; a way in which sin will meet with no encouragement, but, on the other hand, an effectual warning will be given against it; a way in which depraved creatures may be sanctified, and made fit for the pure blifs of Heaven; I fay, if they cannot be faved in fuch a way as this, they cannot be faved at all : their falvation is quite impoffible; for each of thefe particulars is of fuch importance, that it cannot be difpenfed with. God is the beft and moft glorious Being in himfelf; and it is fit he fhould do juftice to his own perfections, and exhibit them in the moft God-like and glorious manner to his creatures; to do otherwife would be to wrong himfelf, to obfcure the brighteft glory, and difhonor the higheft excellency. This therefore cannot be done : men and angels muft be happy, in a way confiftent with his glory, otherwife they muft perifh; for the difplay of his glory is a greater good, and a matter of more importance, than the happinefs of the whole creation. God is alfo the moral Governor of the world. And his government over our world is a government over a country of rebels: and that is a tender point, and requires a judicious management. An error in government, in fuch a cafe, may have the moft fatal confequences, both as to the ruler and his fubjects in all parts of his dominions. A private perfon may, if he pleafes, give up his rights, may pardon offenders, and conceal his juftice, and other qualities for government; but a ruler is not at liberty in this cafe. He muft maintain his character, make known his capacity for government, and fupport the dignity of the law : otherwife, all might rufh into confufion and lawlefs violence. If the ruler of a fmall kingdom on our little globe fhould fail to difcover his juftice; if he fhould pardon criminals, and admit them into favour, and into pofts of honour and profit, without giving proper expreffions of his difpleafure againft their conduct, and a ftriking warning againft all difobedience, how fatal would be the confequences? how foon would fuch a ruler fall into contempt, and his government be unhinged? and how foon would his kingdom become a fcene of confufion and violence? Criminals might like fuch an adminiftration : but, I appeal to yourfelves, would you choofe to live under it? Now, how much more terrible and extenfively mifchievous would be the confequences, if the univerfal Ruler of men and angels, and of more worlds than we have heard the fame of, fhould exercife fuch a government over our rebellious world? It would be reproachful to himfelf; and it would be moft injurious to his fubjects : in fhort, it might throw heaven and earth, and unknown regions of the univerfe, into confufion.* He muft therefore difplay his own rectoral virtues ; he muft maintain the honour of his government, he muft fhew his difpleafure againft difobedience, and deter his fubjects from it; I fay,

---

* Pardoning fin, receiving into favour, and beftowing happinefs, are not to be confidered, in this cafe, as private favours; but they are acts of government.

Serm. 24. *the Mean of Salvation.* 419

he muſt do theſe things in ſaving the ſinners of Adam's race, or he cannot ſave them at all. Should he ſave them upon other terms, it would reflect diſhonour upon himſelf and adminiſtration; and it would be injurious to the good of the whole, which is always the end of a wiſe ruler; for the favour thus injudiciouſly ſhewn to a part of the creation in our world, might occaſion a more extenſive miſchief in other more important worlds; and ſo it would be promoting a private intereſt to the detriment of the public, which is always the character of a weak or wicked ruler. Again, ſinners cannot be ſaved, until their diſpoſitions be changed, ſo that they can reliſh and delight in the fruition and employments of the heavenly ſtate. Proviſion therefore muſt be made for this; otherwiſe, their ſalvation is impoſſible.

Now, the way of ſalvation, through Chriſt crucified, moſt completely anſwers theſe ends in the moſt illuſtrious manner.

1. The ſalvation of ſinners, in this way, gives the brighteſt diſplay of the perfections of God, and particularly of thoſe that belong to him, as the ſupreme Ruler of the rational world, and maintains the honour of his government.

Juſtice and clemency, duly tempered, and exerciſed with wiſdom, is a ſummary of thoſe virtues that belong to a good ruler. Now theſe are moſt illuſtriouſly diſplayed in a happy conjunction in Chriſt crucified. Juſtice ſhines brighter than if every ſin had been puniſhed upon offenders, without any mercy; and mercy and clemency ſhine brighter than if every ſin had been pardoned, and every ſinner made happy, without any execution of juſtice. Mercy appears in turning the divine mind with ſuch a ſtrong propenſity upon the ſalvation of ſinners; and juſtice appears, in that when the heart of God was ſo much ſet upon it, yet he would not ſave them without a complete ſatisfaction to his juſtice. Mercy appears in providing ſuch a Saviour; and juſtice, in inflicting the puniſhment due to ſin upon him, without abatement, though he loved him more than the whole univerſe of creatures. Mercy, in transferring the guilt from the ſinner upon the ſurety, and accepting a vicarious ſatisfaction: juſtice, in exacting the ſatisfaction, and not paſſing by ſin, when it was but imputed to the darling Son of God. Mercy, in pardoning and ſaving guilty ſinners: juſtice, in puniſhing their ſin. Mercy, in juſtifying them, though deſtitute of all perſonal merit and righteouſneſs: juſtice, in juſtifying them only and entirely on account of the merit and righteouſneſs of Chriſt. Thus the righteouſneſs or juſtice of God is declared not only in the puniſhment, but in the remiſſion of ſins, Rom. iii. 26. and we are juſtified freely through his grace, and in the mean time by the redemption that is in Jeſus Chriſt, (ver. 24.). Mercy appears in providing a Saviour of such infinite dignity : justice, in refusing satisfaction from an inferior person. Mercy, in forgiving sin : justice, in not forgiving not so much as one sin without a sufficient atonement. Mercy, rich free mercy towards the sinner : justice, strict inexorable justice towards the surety. In short, mercy and justice, as it were, walk hand in hand through every step of this amazing scheme. They are not only glorious each of them apart, but they mingle their beams, and reflect a glory upon each other. By this scheme of salvation by the cross of Christ, also the honour of the divine government is secured and advanced. The clemency and compassion of God towards his rebellious subjects, are most illustriously displayed; but, in the mean time, he takes care to secure the sacred rights of his government. Though innumerable multitudes of rebels are pardoned, yet not one of them is pardoned until their rebellion is punished according to its demerit in the person of the surety. The precept of the law, which they had broken, was perfectly obeyed; the penalty which they had incurred, was fully endured, not by themselves indeed, but by one that presented himself in their place: and it is only on this footing they are received into favour. So that the law is magnified, and made honourable, and the rights of government are preserved sacred and inviolable, and yet the prisoners of justice are set free, and advanced to the highest honours and blessedness.

2. In this way of salvation, God's hatred to sin is discovered in the most striking light; the evil of sin is exposed in the most dreadful colours; and so an effectual warning is given to all worlds to deter them from it. Now it appears, that such is the divine hatred against all sin, that God can, by no means, connive at it, or suffer it to pass without punishment; and that all the infinite benevolence of his nature towards his creatures, cannot prevail upon him to pardon the least sin without an adequate satisfaction. Nay, now it appears, that when so malignant and abominable a thing is but imputed to his dear Son, his co-equal, his darling, his favourite, even he could not escape unpunished, but was made a monument of vindictive justice to all worlds. And what can more strongly expose the evil of sin ? It is such an intolerably malignant and abominable thing, that even a God of infinite mercy and grace cannot let the least instance of it pass unpunished. It was not a small thing that could arm his justice against the son of his love. But when he was but made sin for us, and was perfectly innocent in himself, God spared not his own Son, but delivered him up unto death, the shameful, tormenting, and accursed death of the cross. Go, ye fools, that make a mock at sin, go and learn its malignity and demerit at the cross of Jesus. Who is it that hangs there writhing in the ago-

nies of death, his hands and feet pierced with nails, his fide with a fpear, his face bruifed with blows, and drenched with tears and blood, his heart melting like wax, his whole frame racked and disjointed; forfaken by his friends, and even by his Father; tempted by devils, and infulted by men? Who is this amazing fpectacle of woe and torture? It is Jefus, the eternal word of God; the man that is his fellow; his elect, in whom his foul delighteth! his beloved Son, in whom he is well pleafed. And what has he done? He did no wickednefs; he knew no fin; but was holy, harmlefs, undefiled, and feparate from finners. And whence then all thefe dreadful fufferings from heaven, earth, and hell? Why, he only ftood in the law-place of finners; he only received their fin by imputation. And you fee what it has brought upon him! you fee how low it has reduced him! and what an horrid evil muft that be, which has fuch tremendous confequences, even upon the darling of Heaven! O! what ftill more dreadful havock would it have made, if it had been punifhed upon the finner himfelf in his own perfon? Surely, all the various miferies which have been inflicted upon our guilty world in all ages, and even all the punifhments of hell, do not fo loudly proclaim the terrible defert and malignity of fin as the crofs of Chrift! and hence it follows, that in this way of falvation, the moft effectual warning is given to the whole univerfe, to deter them from difobedience. Rebels are pardoned, and made happy, without making a bad precedent, or giving any encouragement to others to repeat the tranfgreffion. And this was the tender and critical point. If rebels can be pardoned, without reflecting difhonour upon the government and doing injury to the fociety, it is well; but how this fhall be done, is the difficulty. But by the ftrange expedient of a crucified Saviour, all the difficulty is removed. Sinners can no more prefume upon fin, with a pretence that the fupreme Ruler has no great indignation againft it, or that there is no great evil in it; for, as I obferved, his hatred to fin, and the infinite malignity of it, appears no where in fo ftriking and awful a light as in the crofs of Chrift. Let a reafonable creature take but one ferious view of that, and fure he muft ever after tremble at the thought of the leaft fin. Again, though finners are pardoned in this way, yet no encouragement is given to the various territories of the divine dominions to flatter themfelves that they alfo will be forgiven in cafe they fhould imitate the race of man in their rebellion. There is but one inftance that we know of in the whole univerfe of the forgivenefs of fin, and the reftoration of rebels into favour, and we are fo happy as to find that only inftance in our guilty world. But what a ftrange revolution has been brought about! what amazing miracles have been wrought in order to prepare the way for it! The eternal Son of God muſt become a man, and die the death of a criminal and a ſlave upon the croſs. The very firſt effort of pardoning grace went thus far; and is it poſſible it ſhould go any farther? or is there reaſon to hope that ſuch a miracle ſhould often be repeated? That the Son of God ſhould hang upon a croſs as often as any race of creatures may fall into ſin? Such hopes receive a damp from the caſe of the apoſtate angels, for whom he refuſed to die and aſſume the office of a Saviour. Or is there any other being that can perform that taſk for ſome other kingdom of rebels which Chriſt has diſcharged for the ſons of men? No; he only is equal to it; and none elſe has ſufficient dignity, power, or love. This therefore muſt ſtrike a terror into all worlds at the thought of ſin, and leave them no umbrage to preſume they ſhall eſcape puniſhment, when they obſerve that the redeemed from among men could not be ſaved but at ſo prodigious an expence, and that the fallen angels are ſuffered to periſh without any ſalvation provided for them at all.

3. In this way proviſion is made for the ſanctification of ſinners, that they may be fit for the fruitions and employments of the heavenly ſtate. Their taſte is ſo vitiated, that they have no reliſh for that pure bliſs, and therefore can no more be happy there than a ſick man can reliſh the entertainments of a feaſt. And they are ſo far gone with the deadly diſeaſe of ſin, that they are not able to recover themſelves; nay, they are not ſo much as diſpoſed to uſe means for that end. They are eſtranged from God, and engaged in rebellion againſt him; and they love to continue ſo. They will not ſubmit, nor return to their duty and allegiance. Hence, there is need of a ſuperior power to ſubdue their ſtubborn hearts, and ſweetly conſtrain them to ſubjection; to inſpire them with the love of God, and an implacable deteſtation of all ſin. And for this purpoſe, the holy ſpirit of God is ſent into the world: for this purpoſe he is at work, from age to age, upon the hearts of men. And though he be moſt ungratefully reſiſted, grieved, and deſpitefully treated, and he gives up many to the luſts of their own hearts, yet, numerous and glorious are the conqueſts he has gained over rebellious ſinners. Many a ſtubborn will has he ſweetly ſubdued: many an heart of ſtone has he ſoftened, and diſſolved into ingenuous repentance, like ſnow before the ſun: many a depraved ſoul has he purified, and at length brought to the heavenly ſtate in all the beauties of perfect holineſs. And hence it is, that there is any ſuch thing as true religion to be found upon earth, and that any of the ſons of men are recovered to obedience and happineſs. But for this ineſtimable bleſſing we are indebted to a crucified Chriſt. It is the dear purchaſe of his blood, and had it not been ſo purchaſed, it would never have been communicated to our guilty world;

and consequently never would one rebel have submitted, never would one heart have felt the love of God, among all the sons of men.

Thus, my brethren, you see a way is really opened for the salvation of sinners through the crucifixion of Christ. And O! what an amazing, unexpected, mysterious way! how far beyond the reach of human wisdom! and how brilliant a display of the divine! To display the perfection of God by occasion of sin more illustriously than if sin had never entered into the world, and thus bring the greatest good out of the greatest evil—to pardon and save the sinner, and yet condemn and punish his sin—to give the brightest display of justice in the freest exercise of mercy; and the richest discovery of mercy in the most rigorous execution of justice—to dismiss rebels from punishment, and advance them to the highest honours, and yet secure and even advance the honour of the government against which they had rebelled—to give the most effectual warning against sin, even in rewarding the sinner; and to let it pass unpunished, without making a bad precedent, or giving any encouragement to it—to magnify the law in justifying those that had broken it—to discover the utmost hatred against sin, in showing the highest love to the sinner—what an astonishing God-like scheme is this! What a stupendous display of the infinite wisdom of God! Could the Socrateses, the Platos, and other oracles of the heathen world ever have found out an expedient to answer this end, and reconcile these seeming contradictions! No; this would have nonpulsed men and angels; for in what a strange unthought-of way is it brought about! that the Son of God should become the Son of man; the head of the universe appear in the form of a servant; the Author of life died upon a cross; the Lawgiver became the subject of his own law, and suffer its penalty though perfectly innocent! who would ever have thought of such strange events as these! This is to accomplish astonishing things in an astonishing way. You may as well set an human understanding to draw the plan of a world, as to form such a scheme as this. O! it is all divine; it is the wonder of angels; and the greatest miracle in the universe.

Thus, you see, there are very good reasons, reducible to this head, why the cross of Christ should be the grand weapon to destroy the kingdom of darkness, and rescue sinners and bring them into a state of liberty and glory.

And there are reasons, equally important, that fall under the other head, viz. That the preaching of Christ crucified makes such a discovery of things, as has the most direct tendency to bring sinners to repentance, and produce in them that temper which is necessary to their salvation.

If a representation of the most moving, the most alluring, and most alarming matters, can effect the mind of man, certainly the preaching of the cross cannot be without effect; for,

1. The preaching of a crucified Saviour gives the strongest assurance to the guilty sons of men, that their offended God is reconcilable to them, and willing to receive them into favour again, upon their penitent return to him. The provision he has made for this end, and particularly his appointing his Son to be their Saviour, and delivering him up to the death of the cross for them, leaves no room for doubt upon this head. It is full demonstration that he is not only willing, but that his heart is earnestly set upon reconciliation; otherwise he would not have been at such infinite pains and expence to remove obstructions, and clear the way for it. Now this is an assurance that the light of nature could never give. It leaves us dreadfully in the dark. And indeed, nothing but an express declaration from God himself can inform us what he intends to do with criminals that lie entirely at mercy, and that he may do what he pleases with. The heathen world were either stupidly thoughtless about this point, or full of anxiety; and their philosophers, amid all their boasted knowledge, could only offer plausible conjectures. And yet this assurance is necessary to keep up religion in the world, and encourage rebellious sinners to return to obedience; for with what heart can they serve that God, as to whom they fear he will accept of no service at their hands, or to return to him, when they have no encouragement that he will receive them! The hope of acceptance is the spring of repentance and all attempts for reformation; and when once the sinner concludes there is no hope, he lies down inactive and sullen in despair, or confirms himself in hardened impenitence, and gives the full reign to his lusts. This the psalmist observed long ago: *There is forgiveness with thee, O Lord, that thou mayest be feared.* Psal. cxxx. 4. The fear of God is often used in scripture for the whole of religion; and so it seems taken here. As much as to say, " There is forgiveness with thee; and thou hast assured us of it, that religion might be preserved in the world, that mankind may not abandon thy service as wholly in vain; or give up themselves to sin, as despairing of acceptance upon their repentance." O! what an acceptable assurance must this be to a guilty trembling sinner! And how suitable a remedy to such sinners is the preaching of the cross of Christ, which alone gives them this welcome assurance.

2. The preaching of a crucified Saviour gives the most moving display of the love of God; and love is a strong attractive to repentance and obedience.—There cannot be so strong an expression of love as the sufferings of Christ. For God to give us life, and breath, and all things, what is this, in comparison of the gift of his Son, and those immortal blessings which he has purchased with his

blood? To create such a world as this for our residence, to furnish it with such a rich variety of blessings for our accommodation, and to exercise a tender providence over us every moment of our lives, this is amazing love and goodness. But what is this in comparison of his dying love! To speak an all-creating word, and to hang, and agonize, and expire upon a cross; to give us the blessings of the earth, and to give the blood of his heart; these are very different things; they will not hold comparison.

My brethren, let me make an experiment upon you with the cross of Christ, and try with what weapon to slay your sins, and break your hearts. Can you view such agonies and question the love that endured them? Or can you place yourselves under the warm beams of that love, and yet feel no love kindled in your hearts in return? What! not the love of a worm for the dying love of a God! The apostle John reasons very naturally, when he says, *We love him, because he first loved us.* 1 John, iv. 19. Love for love is but a reasonable retaliation; especially the love of a redeemed sinner for the love of a crucified Saviour. St. Paul felt the energy of this love irresistible: *The love of Christ constraineth us,* 2 Cor. v. 14. or according to the emphasis of the original word,* it carries us away, like a resistless torrent. And it appeared to him so shocking, that he could not mention it without weeping, that any should be enemies to the cross of Christ. Phil. iii. 18. Hear what expectations he had from the energy of his cross who himself hung upon it. *I,* says he, *if I be lifted up from the earth, will draw all men unto me.* Phil. iii. 18. This the evangelist teaches us to understand of the manner of his death, viz. his being raised up from the earth, and suspended on the cross. There, sinners, he hung to attract your love; and can you resist the force of this attraction, this almighty magnet? Jesus, if I may so speak, expects that this will carry all before it: that every sinner who sees him hanging there will immediately melt into repentance, and be drawn to him by the cords of love. And, O! can you find in your hearts to resist? Where then is the gratitude? Is that generous principle quite dead within you? I must honestly tell you, if the love of a crucified Saviour does not attract your love, nothing else will: you will continue his enemies, and perish as such. This is the most powerful inducement that can be proposed to you: all the reasonings of the ablest philosophers, all the persuasions of the ministers of the gospel, all the goodness of God in creation and providence, will never prevail upon you, if your hearts are proof against the attraction of the cross. But, blessed be his name who died upon it, many an obstinate and reluctant heart has this cross allured and subdued: and O! that we may all feel its sweet constraints!

Synechei. So Dr. Doddridge translates it.

3. The preaching of Chriſt crucified gives ſuch a repreſentation of the evil of ſin, and the dreadful puniſhment due to it, as naturally tends to turn ſinners from it, and bring them to repentance. In the croſs of Chriſt the ſinner may ſee what malignity there is in ſin, when it brought ſuch heavy vengeance on the head of the ſurety. There the ſinner may ſee how God hates it, when he puniſhed it ſo ſeverely in his beloved Son. If the almighty Redeemer ſunk under the load, how ſhall the feeble ſinner bear up under it? If God ſpared not his own Son, who was but a ſurety, how can the ſinner eſcape, who is the original debtor? O ſinners, never call it cruel that God ſhould puniſh you for your ſins: ſo he dealt with Jeſus, his favourite; and how can you hope for more favour! Read the nature of ſin as written in characters of blood on the croſs of Chriſt, and ſurely you can make light of it no more. You muſt tremble at the very thought of it; and immediately reform and repent of it. All the harangues of moraliſts upon the intrinſic deformity, the unreaſonableneſs, the incongruity of vice, never can repreſent it in ſuch a ſhocking light as you view it in the ſufferings of Chriſt. And can you look upon your ſins piercing him, ſtretching him upon the croſs, and ſlaughtering him, and yet not mourn over them! O! can you indulge the murderous things that ſhed his blood! Then you practically pronounce him an impoſtor, and join the cry of the Jewiſh rabble, *Crucify him, crucify him.*

4. The preaching of Chriſt crucified preſents us with ſuch a perfect pattern of obedience, as has at once the force of an example, and an inducement to holineſs. We need no longer view the law in theory: we ſee it reduced into an uniform practice, and preſented to the life, in the whole of our Lord's conduct towards God and man. We ſee one in our nature, upon our guilty globe in our circumſtances, behaving exactly agreeable to the divine law, and leaving us an example that we might follow his ſteps. And ſhall we not delight to imitate our beſt friend, and the moſt perfect pattern that ever was exhibited! O! how ſweet to walk as he walked in the world, and to trace the ſteps of his lovely feet! Until the doctrine of the croſs was introduced, the world was ſadly at a loſs about a rule of duty. All the admired writings of pagan antiquity cannot furniſh out one compleat ſyſtem even of morality; but here we have a perfect law, and a perfect example, which has the force of a law. Therefore, let us be followers of this incarnate God as dear children.

For an application:

1. Hence we may learn our great happineſs in enjoying the preaching of Chriſt crucified. It is but a very ſmall part of the world that has heard this joyful ſound; and the time has been, when none of the ſons of men enjoyed it in that full evidence which we are favoured with. Now ſince it pleaſes God, by this

foolishness of preaching, to save them that believe, since this is the most effectual mean for our recovery from sin and ruin—how great, how distinguishing, how peculiar is our privilege ! It becomes us, my brethren, to know our happiness that we may be thankful. How few among the sons of men enjoy this privilege ! How does the whole world lie in wickedness ! Alas ! they are fatally unconcerned, or fruitlessly anxious about a way of reconciliation with God. Their priests and philosophers can afford them no relief in this case ; but either mislead them or increase their perplexity. But we have the strongest assurance that God is reconcileable to us ; and the clearest discovery of the way. We have the most powerful inducements to repentance, and the most effectual restraints from sin. And what gratitude does this call for from us, to our divine Benefactor ! and how solicitous should we be to make a proper improvement of our peculiar advantages !

2. Hence we may learn the shocking guilt and danger of our modern infidels, the Deists, who, like the Greeks, count the preaching of Christ crucified foolishness, and deny the Lord that bought them. This is to reject the best, the last, the only remedy. Now let them consult their feeble reason ; let them go to the oracles of wisdom in the heathen world, and ask of them how guilty offenders may be restored into favour, in consistency with the honour of the divine perfections and government ! Alas they can find no satisfactory answer. Now also they have lost the strongest motive to love and obedience, when they have turned away their eyes from the cross. They have lost the most full and amiable view of the divine nature and perfections that ever was exhibited to the world. Should they shut their eyes against the light of the sun, and abhor all the beauties of nature, it would not be such an astonishing instance of infatuation. St. Paul represents it as the most amazing folly, nay, a kind of witchcraft and incantation, that any should desert the truth, that had ever had the least view of Christ crucified. *O foolish Galatians ! who hath bewitched you, that you should not obey the truth, before whose eyes Jesus Christ had been evidently set forth, crucified among you ?* Gal. iii. 1. What wickedness, what madness, what an unnatural conspiracy against their own lives must it be for men to reject the only expedient found out by infinite wisdom and goodness for their salvation ! What base ingratitude thus to requite the dying love of Jesus ! Can such monsters expect salvation from his hands ? No ; they willfully cut themselves off from all hope, and bring upon themselves swift destruction. If the cross of Christ does not break their hearts, it is impossible to bring them to repentance : the last and most powerful remedy has proved ineffectual : the last and strongest effort of divine grace has been used with them in vain. Since

they obstinately reject the sacrifice of Christ, there remains no other sacrifice for their sin, and nothing awaits them but a fearful expectation of wrath and fiery indignation, which shall devour them as adversaries.

3. Hence we should inquire what effect the preaching of Christ crucified has been upon us. Since this is the grand mean Divine Wisdom has found out for the recovery of our wicked world, when all other means had been in vain, it is of the utmost importance to us, that we should inquire, whether it is likely to answer this end upon us. *It pleases God by this foolishness of preaching, to save them that believe.* Observe the limitation—*them that believe.* They, and only they, can be saved by it. As for unbelievers, they cannot be saved in this or any other way. Let us then abandon every other concern for a while, and seriously examine ourselves in this point. Faith comes by hearing; and have we been brought to believe by hearing the preaching of the cross? Do we relish this humble despised doctrine with peculiar pleasure? Is it the life and nourishment of our souls, and the ground of all our hopes? Or do we secretly wonder what there can be in it, that some should be so much affected with it? *To them that perish*, says the apostle, and to them only, *the preaching of the cross is foolishness.* And is that our dreadful characteristic? Or does a crucified Christ appear to us as the wisdom of God, and the power of God, as he does to all them that believe, however different their natural tastes and the prejudices of their education, and their outward circumstances? Do we suspend all our hopes upon the cross of Christ? Do we glory in it above all other things, whatever contempt the world may pour upon it? Do we feel our necessity of a Mediator in all our transactions with God, and depend entirely upon the merit of his death for acceptance, sensible that we have no merit of our own to procure one smile from God? Have we ever had our hearts enlightened to behold the glory of God in the face of Jesus Christ? Have we admired the scheme of salvation through a crucified Jesus, as illustrating the perfections of God, and securing the honour of the divine government, while it secures our salvation? And do we delight in it upon that account? Or are we quite indifferent about the glory of God, if we may be but saved? Alas! hereby we show we are entirely under the government of selfish principles, and have no regard for God at all. Do our thoughts frequently hover and cluster about the cross with the tenderest affections? And has the view of it melted our hearts into the most ingenuous relentings for sin, and given us such a hatred against it, that we can never indulge it more? My brethren, put such questions as these home to your hearts, and then endeavour to come to some just conclu-

sion with regard to yourselves.—And if the conclusion be against you, then,

4. Consider your guilt and danger—consider your ingratitude, in rejecting all the love of God, and a crucified Saviour—your hardness of heart, that has not been broken by such a moving representation—the aversion of your souls to God, that have not been allured to him by the powerful attraction of the cross—and O! consider your danger: the last remedy has been tried upon you in vain: Christ's grand expedient for the salvation of sinners has had no effect upon you. Had the religion of the Jews or of the heathen world failed to bring you to repentance, there might be still some hope that the preaching of Christ crucified might prevail. But, alas! when that fails, how discouraging is your case! Therefore, I pray you, take the alarm, and labour to get your hearts affected with this representation. O yield to the attraction of the cross: let him draw you to himself, whom you see lifted up on it; and do not attempt such an exploit of wickedness as to resist the allurements of such love. And O! cry to God for his enlightening spirit. Alas! it is your blindness that renders you unaffected with this moving object. Did you but know the Lord of glory, who was crucified; did you but see the glory of the plan of salvation through his sufferings, you would immediately become the captives of his cross, conquered by the power of his love. And such, believe me, such you must be, before you can be saved.—But if the result of your examination turns out in your favour, then,

5. You may entertain the joyful hope of salvation; of salvation through one that was insulted as not able to save himself; of crowns of glory through him that wore the crown of thorns; of fulness of joy through the man of sorrows; of immortal life through one that died upon a cross; I say, you may entertain a joyful hope of all this; for in this way of salvation there is no hindrance, no objection. God will be glorified in glorifying you, the law magnified in justifying you. In short, the honour of God and his government concurs with your interest; and therefore if you heartily embrace this plan of salvation, you may be as sure that God will save you, as that he will take care of his own glory, for they are inseparably connected. And do not your hearts, dead as they are, spring within you at the thought? Do you not long to see your Saviour on the throne, to whose cross you are indebted for all your hopes? And O! will you not praise his name while you live, and continue the song through all eternity? Are you not ready to anticipate the anthem of heaven, *Worthy is the Lamb that was slain, to receive power, and riches, and wisdom, and strength, and honour, and glory, and blessing: for thou hast redeemed us unto God by thy blood.* Rev. v. 9, 12.

Finally, let me congratulate * my reverend brethren on their being made minifters of the New Teftament, which reveals that glorious and delightful fubject, *Chrift crucified*, in full light, and diffufes it through all their ftudies and difcourfes. The Lamb that was flain is the theme that animates the fongs of angels and faints above, and even our unhallowed lips are allowed to touch it without profanation. Let us therefore, my dear brethren, delight to dwell upon it. Let us do juftice to the refined morality of the gofpel: let us often explain and enforce the precepts, the graces, and the virtues of chriftianity; and teach men to live righteoufly, foberly, and godly, in the world. But let us do this in an evangelical ftrain, as minifters of the crucified Jefus, and not as the fcholars of Epictetus or Seneca. Let us labour to bring men to an hearty compliance with the method of falvation through Chrift; and then we fhall find it comparatively an eafy matter, a thing of courfe, to make them good moralifts. Then a fhort hint of their duty to God and man will be more forcible than whole volumes of ethics, while their fpirits are not caft in the gofpel-mould. Thus may we be enabled to go on, till our great Mafter fhall take our charge off our hands, and call us to give an account of our ftewardfhip!

* The author, towards the end of the difcourfe, writes, "At a Prefbytery in Augufta, April 25, 1759;" which accounts for this particular addrefs to minifters.

END OF THE FIRST VOLUME.